STELLENBOSCH HANDBOOKS IN AFRICAN CONSTITUTIONAL LAW

The Stellenbosch Handbooks in African Constitutional Law series engages with contemporary issues of constitutionalism in Africa. The first experiments in democratic and constitutional governance in Africa that started after independence were soon overtaken by dictatorships, and arbitrary and repressive rule. The pulling down of the Berlin Wall followed by the collapse of the Soviet Union unleashed new forces of democratization and new hopes for the establishment and entrenchment of constitutional governance and constitutionalism in Africa. This series is designed to identify, analyse, and promote serious discussion of the critical issues that can shape, refine, and deepen the consolidation of constitutionalism in Africa.

Although comparative constitutional law has become a major field of legal scholarship, most of the extensive research that has been carried out has focused on long- established democracies. The only African country that has attracted sustained research interest from a comparative law perspective is South Africa. The few books that present perspectives on African comparative constitutional law focus narrowly and exclusively on developments in either anglophone, francophone, or arabophone Africa without cutting across these divides. Yet, since 1990, Africa has been at the centre of profound and far- reaching constitutional developments. Little comparative research has been carried out to understand the nature of these constitutional changes, to review their impact on the ethos of constitutionalism on the continent, and to explore prospects for the future.

The objectives of the Stellenbosch Handbooks in African Constitutional Law series are, first, to stimulate interest in comparative constitutional research and the different constitutional traditions operating in Africa by presenting a comprehensive analysis of the latest thinking, research, and practice. In this way, the series intends to fill the huge gap in the existing literature on comparative African constitutional law as well as point to directions for future research. Second, each volume will bring together high quality innovative and original material from diverse perspectives written by scholars and legal practitioners drawn from the different constitutional traditions operating on the continent. In this respect, each volume will strive to cover anglophone, arabophone, francophone, hispanophone, and lusophone Africa. In many respects, this will ensure that African voices are heard in the global constitutional debates. Third, because most African countries share many common features, such as the colonial legacy, geographical proximity, and social, economic, political, and cultural conditions, the volumes in the series adopt a comparative approach that highlights gaps and good practices in a manner that will provide a rich source of authoritative information for promoting an inter- African legal dialogue and the cross- fertilization of ideas between different constitutional traditions. Finally, the volumes in the series are intended to act as a repository for the accumulation of knowledge, experience, and expertise on the continent. Each handbook stands alone and is intended to provide an invaluable source of authoritative reference material for academics, researchers, students at all levels, as well as legal practitioners and policymakers.

STELLENBOSCH HANDBOOKS IN AFRICAN CONSTITUTIONAL LAW

Constitutional Change and Constitutionalism in Africa

Edited by

CHARLES M. FOMBAD

Director, Institute for International and Comparative Law in Africa, Faculty of Law, University of Pretoria, South Africa

NICO STEYTLER

Professor Emeritus, Dullah Omar Institute of Constitutional Law, Governance and Human Rights, University of the Western Cape, South Africa

OXFORD
UNIVERSITY PRESS

OXFORD
UNIVERSITY PRESS

Great Clarendon Street, Oxford, OX2 6DP,
United Kingdom

Oxford University Press is a department of the University of Oxford.
It furthers the University's objective of excellence in research, scholarship,
and education by publishing worldwide. Oxford is a registered trade mark of
Oxford University Press in the UK and in certain other countries

Published in the United States of America by Oxford University Press
198 Madison Avenue, New York, NY 10016, United States of America

British Library Cataloguing in Publication Data
Data available

Library of Congress Control Number: 2025931258

ISBN 9780198957003

DOI: 10.1093/9780198957034.001.0001

Printed and bound by
CPI Group (UK) Ltd., Croydon, CR0 4YY

MIX
Paper | Supporting responsible forestry
FSC® C013604

The manufacturer's authorised representative in the EU for product safety is Oxford University Press España S.A. of El Parque Empresarial San Fernando de Henares, Avenida de Castilla, 2 – 28830 Madrid (www.oup.es/en or product.safety@oup.com). OUP España S.A. also acts as importer into Spain of products made by the manufacturer.

Preface

Like the preceding books published in this Stellenbosch Handbooks in African Constitutional Law series, this eighth book is based on the Ninth Stellenbosch Annual Seminar on Constitutionalism in Africa that took take place in Stellenbosch (South Africa) from Tuesday 13 to Friday 16 September 2022. The stated aim of the series has continued to be that of publishing works of high quality and originality dealing with topical issues of constitutional law in Africa.

The theme for the SASCA 2022 seminar was 'constitutional change and constitutionalism in Africa'. Moves to craft a new generation of African constitutions that began in the 1990s promised a new dawn of radical transformation of the continent's governance landscape, and a concerted attempt to eliminate the risks of coups, political instability, and other social and economic problems that had plagued the continent since decolonization and the granting of independence to countries from 1957 onwards. The reality, however, is that the post-1990 wave of constitutional reforms appears to have provoked a contagious fever of making, unmaking, and remaking of African constitutions. The nature of these changes, their frequency, and the fact that they have affected most countries in the region raises many questions of a practical and theoretical nature. It is, however, the resultant instability that threatens to undermine the few strides made to entrench a culture of constitutionalism, good governance, and respect for the rule of law that is increasingly becoming a matter of great concern. It is, therefore, no surprise that there is now almost universal agreement that Africa is presently going through a severe and profound crisis of democracy and constitutionalism.

The 2022 seminar interrogated the nature and extent of the changes that have been taking place on a rather more frequent—and sometimes arbitrary—basis than was expected. Amongst the main questions that were investigated were the nature of the constitution-making process, and the role of diverse actors such as the legislature, the executive, and the judiciary, as well as external actors such as the African Union (AU) and Regional Economic Communities (RECs), in the different processes of constitutional change taking place. There were also case studies to identify distinct patterns of change. Ultimately, the discussions tried to see how the processes of constitutional change, where inevitable and unavoidable, or where contrived, can be undertaken in a manner that does not undermine or threaten the efforts made to entrench constitutionalism, good governance, and respect for the rule of law on the continent.

The chapters in this book span a broad array of themes that were discussed. One volume cannot adequately capture the often complex issues that frequent changes in constitutions provoke in Africa. Nevertheless, taken as a whole, the essays collectively offer valuable insights on what is happening. The essays provide food for thought, and it is our hope that they will provoke serious debate and discussions on how to deal with the issue of frequent and arbitrary changes of constitutions, which is one of the root causes of political instability in Africa.

We are profoundly indebted to the director of the Stellenbosch Institute for Advanced Study (STIAS), Professor Edward Kirumira, and his team led by Professor Johann Groenewald, the coordinator of strategic initiatives, and Mrs Nel-Mari Loock and Mrs Gina Humphreys, for providing logistical assistance. We are also grateful to Dr Lukman Abdulrauf of the Faculty of Law, Ilorin University, Nigeria and Dr Henry Gichana, post-doctoral fellow at South African Research Chair in Multilevel Government, Law and Development (SARChI) at the Dullah Omar Institute, University of the Western Cape, for their assistance with organization. We appreciate and acknowledge the financial support of the Swedish Riksbankens Jubileumsfornd to STIAS to fund the SASCA programme and the financial support also from the Konrad Adenauer Stiftung (KAS) Rule of Law Programme Sub-Saharan Africa (Anglophone Countries), based in Nairobi, and the South African Research Chair in Multilevel Government, Law and Development (SARChI) at the Dullah Omar Institute, University of the Western Cape. Finally, we thank all the peer reviewers who helped to ensure the quality of the end product, our copy-editor Andre Wiesner, and the OUP staff, especially Mr Brian Stone, Ms Paulina dos Santos, and Mr Reyman Joseph.

Charles M. Fombad and Nico Steytler
Pretoria and Cape Town
November 2024

Contents

Table of Cases

AFRICAN COMMISSION ON HUMAN AND PEOPLES' RIGHTS

ANGOLA

BENIN

BURKINA FASO

BURUNDI

CABO VERDE

CENTRAL AFRICAN REPUBLIC

CANADA

CHAD

CONGO, REPUBLIC OF

CÔTE D'IVOIRE

ETHIOPIA

FRANCE

GERMANY

GHANA

INDIA

KENYA

MALAWI

MALI

NAMIBIA

NIGER

NIGERIA

SENEGAL

SEYCHELLES

SOUTH AFRICA

TANZANIA

UNITED STATES OF AMERICA

ZAMBIA

Table of Legislation, Statutes, and International Instruments

CÔTE D'IVOIRE

CYPRUS

DEMOCRATIC REPUBLIC OF CONGO

DJIBOUTI

EGYPT

EQUATORIAL GUINEA

ERITREA

ESWATINI

ETHIOPIA

GABON

GAMBIA

GERMANY

GHANA

GUINEA-BISSAU

JAMAICA

KENYA

LESOTHO

LIBYA

MADAGASCAR

MALAWI

Abbreviations

ACDEG	African Charter on Democracy, Elections and Governance
ACLED	Armed Conflict Location and Event Data Project
CAN	Action Christian National
ADP	Amhara Democratic Party
AFORD	Alliance for Democracy
AFP	Agence-France Presse
AIC	African Independent Congress
ANC	African National Congress
AU	African Union
BBI	Building Bridges Initiative
CC	Constitutional Commission
CCI	Council of Constitutional Inquiry
CEMAC	Communauté Economiques des États de l'Afrique Centrale/Central African Economic and Monetary Community
CEO	chief executive officer
CHRAJ	Commission on Human and Administrative Justice
CIPEV	Commission of Inquiry on Post-Election Violence
CJ	Chief Justice
CKAB	Constitution of Kenya (Amendment) Bill of 2020
CKRA	Constitution of Kenya Review Act
CKRC	Constitution of Kenya Review Commission
CODESA	Convention for a Democratic South Africa
CoE	Committee of Experts
COPAC	Select Committee of Parliament on the New Constitution
CoR	Council of Representatives
CPs	Constitutional Principles
CP VI	Constitutional Principle VI
CRC	Constitutional Review Commission
CRIC	Constitutional Review Implementation Committee
CSOs	civil society organizations
DCJ	Deputy Chief Justice
DP	Democratic Party
DPCI	Directorate of Priority Crime Investigation
DPP	Democratic Progressive Party
DRC	Democratic Republic of the Congo
DSO	Directorate of Special Operations
DTA	Democratic Turnhalle Alliance
EAC	East African Community
ECOWAS	Economic Community of West African States
EMB	Election Management Body
EPLF	Eritrean People's Liberation Front

EPRDF	Ethiopian People's Revolutionary Democratic Front
EPRP	Ethiopian People's Revolutionary Party
ESM	Ethiopian Student Movement
FIRS	Federal Inland Revenue Service
FRELIMO	Frente de Libertação Moçambique
GNC	General National Congress
GPA	Global Political Agreement
HCDTF	Host Community Development Trust Fund
HoF	House of Federation
HPR	House of Peoples' Representatives
ICD	Interim Constitutional Declaration
IEBC	Independent Electoral and Boundaries Commission
IFES	International Foundation for Electoral Systems
IFP	Inkatha Freedom Party
INEC	Independent National Electoral Commission
International IDEA	International Institute for Democracy and Electoral Assistance
IPPG	Inter-Parties Parliamentary Group
IREC	Independent Review Commission
JA	Judge of Appeal
JICS	Judicial Inspectorate of Correctional Services
JJSC	Justices of the Supreme Court
JSC	Judicial Services Commission
KADU	Kenya African Democratic Union
KANU	Kenya African National Union
KAS	Konrad Adenauer Stiftung
KHRC	Kenya Human Rights Commission
KNDR	Kenya National Dialogue and Reconciliation
KZN	KwaZulu-Natal
LCDAs	local council development areas
LGAs	local government areas
MCP	Malawi Congress Party
MDC	Movement for Democratic Change
MOPA	modern purposive approach
MoU	memorandum of understanding
MP	Member of Parliament
MPLA	Movimento Popular de Libertação de Angola
MSCA	Malawi Supreme Court of Appeal
NARC	National Rainbow Coalition
NCA	National Constitutional Assembly
NCC	National Constitutional Conference
NCD	National Commission for Democracy
NCEC	National Convention Executive Council
NCOP	National Council of Provinces
NDA	National Democratic Alliance
NDPP	National Director of Public Prosecutions
NEBE	National Electoral Board of Ethiopia
NEC	National Executive Committee
NGOs	non-governmental organizations

NMC	National Media Commission
NP	National Party
NPA	National Prosecuting Authority
NPF	Nigeria Police Force
NRM	National Resistance Movement
NTC	National Transitional Council
NULGE	National Union of Local Government Employees
NWRRC	Nigeria Water Resources Regulatory Commission
OAU	Organisation of African Unity
ODP	Oromo Democratic Party
OFC	Oromo Federalist Congress
OLF	Oromo Liberation Front
OPDO	Oromo People's Democratic Organization
PAIGC	Partido Africano de Independência da Guine e Cabo Verde
PIA	Petroleum Industry Act of 2021
PNDC	Provisional National Defence Council
PP	Prosperity Party
PRC	Provisional Ruling Council
PRECCA	Prevention and Combatting of Corrupt Activities Act 12 of 2004
PSC	Peace and Security Council
PWDs	persons with disabilities
RECs	Regional Economic Communities
SADC	Southern African Development Community
SAPS	South African Police Services
SARChI	South African Research Chair in Multilevel Government, Law and Development
SASCA	Stellenbosch Annual Seminar on Constitutionalism in Africa
SCJ	Supreme Court Justice
SIEC	State Independent Electoral Commission
SMC	Supreme Military Council
SMS	Short Message Service
SNC	Sovereign National Conference
SNNPR	Southern Nations, Nationalities and Peoples' Regional State
STIAS	Stellenbosch Institute for Advanced Study
SWAPO	South West African People's Organisation
TANU	Tanganyika African National Union
TGE	Transitional Government of Ethiopia
TJRC	Truth, Justice and Reconciliation Commission
TPC	Transitional Period Charter
TPLF	Tigray People's Liberation Front
UCA	unconstitutional constitutional amendments
UDA	United Democratic Alliance
UDF	United Democratic Front
UN	United Nations
UNDP	United Nations Development Programme
UNIP	United National Independence Party
UNITA	National Union for the Total Independence of Angola
UNSC	United Nations Security Council
UNSMIL	United Nations Support Mission in Libya

US	United States of America
USSR	Union of Soviet Socialist Republics
VAT	value added tax
WPE	Workers' Party of Ethiopia
ZANU(PF)	Zimbabwean African National Union (Patriotic Front)
ZBC	Zimbabwe Broadcast Corporation

List of Contributors

Adem Kassie Abebe, LLD, is Senior Advisor, Constitution Building Processes, International Institute for Democracy and Electoral Assistance (IDEA), The Hague, Netherlands; Faculty of Law, University of Pretoria, Pretoria, South Africa, https://orcid.org/0009-0002-4833-4344

Migai Akech, JSD, is Professor of Law, Faculty of Law, University of Nairobi, Nairobi, Kenya

Zemelak Ayitenew Ayele, PhD, is Associate Professor, Centre for Federalism and Governance Studies, College of Law, Addis Ababa University, Addis Ababa, Ethiopia; Extraordinary Associate Professor Dullah Omar Institute, University of the Western Cape, Cape Town

Abdou Khadre Diop, PhD, is Associate Professor in Public Law, Université Numérique Cheikh Hamidou Kane (Senegal), Dakar, Senegal

Assefa Fiseha, PhD, is Professor, Director of the Centre of Excellence Center for Federalism and Governance Studies, Addis Ababa University, Addis Ababa, Ethiopia

Charles M. Fombad is Director, Institute for International and Comparative Law in Africa, Faculty of Law, University of Pretoria, South Africa, https://orcid.org/0000-0002-7794-1496

Henry Paul Gichana, LLD, is Devolution and Research Lead, Katiba Institute, Nairobi, Kenya, https://orcid.org/0000-0002-7554-5350

Babacar Kanté is Emeritus Professor of Law, University of Gaston Berger, Saint Louis, Senegal

Rania Hussein Khafaga, PhD, is Associate Professor of African Politics, Cairo University, Cairo, Egypt, https://orcid.org/0000-0001-7947-5655

Heinz Klug is John and Rylla Bosshard Professor of Law, University of Wisconsin Law School, University of Wisconsin, Madison, United States; University of Witwatersrand School of Law, Johannesburg, South Africa; University of Ghana School of Law, Accra, Ghana, https://orcid.org/0000-0002-1706-3230

Lauren Kohn is the Founder and Director of the Law And Governance Academy of Southern Africa (LAGASA), former Senior Lecturer, University of Cape Town, Visiting Research Fellow of Leiden Law School, the Netherlands; and an Advocate of the High Court of SA (Practicing Roll), Cape Town, South Africa, https://orcid.org/0000-0002-8453-4952

Trésor Muhindo Makunya is Associate Professor, University of Goma, Democratic Republic of Congo; Extraordinary Lecturer, Centre for Human Rights, University of Pretoria, South Africa, https://orcid.org/0000-0002-5645-1391

Maame A.S. Mensa-Bonsu, DPhil, is Associate Professor of Law, Ashesi University, Ghana

Mwiza Jo Nkhata, LLD, is Honorary Professor, University of South Africa, Pretoria, South Africa, https://orcid.org/0000-0002-7695-5503

Marystella Simiyu is Africa Senior Legal Advocacy Officer, International Press Institute, Vienna, Austria

Nico Steytler is Professor Emeritus, Dullah Omar Institute of Constitutional Law, Governance and Human Rights, University of the Western Cape, South Africa, https://orcid.org/0000-0003-2918-8484

Rotimi T. Suberu, PhD, is Professor, Society, Culture, and Thought (SCT), Bennington College, Bennington, United States

André Thomashausen, Dr jur, Attorney (Germany), is Professor Emeritus of Comparative and International Law, University of South Africa, Pretoria, South Africa, https://orcid.org/0009-0006-4162-5199

Introductory Remarks

30 Years of Constitutionalism in Africa: Between Myth and Reality

Babacar Kanté

1. Introduction

When African heads of state met in Addis Ababa to create the Organisation of African Unity on 25 May 1963, the first problem they faced was whether to admit the presence of the Togolese government, since it had come to power as the result of a coup. It is therefore important to remember that the problems of constitutional changes and of the unconstitutional accession to power are unfortunately not new on the African continent. They do not date from today. We have been living with them since the accession of our states to independence and even before that (with the first *coup d'état* on the continent having taken place in Sudan in 1958).

Everything has already been tried from a legal point of view to ensure the stability of constitutions on the continent. But political power, which is supposed to be limited by the constitution, has always found ways to circumvent the legal barriers imposed on it, resulting in chronic constitutional instability on the continent.

In a somewhat caricatural way, one could say that African countries have gone through three main phases in terms of constitutionalism. The first, from 1960 to 1990, corresponded to a negation of constitutionalism in the material sense: constitutionalism was merely formal. According to Okoth Ogendo's famous formula, we were living in an era of 'constitutions without constitutionalism'. Then, from the beginning of the 1990s to the 2020s, with what was called the opening of the democratic transition, we saw the beginnings of the submission of political authority to the law. But the hope born in 1990 seems to have been dashed since the start of the 2020s and the recurrence of constitutional changes relating to presidential term limits as well as the various *coups d'état*. Indeed, in the current period, we seem to be witnessing a challenge to all the democratic gains. The recent *coups d'état* in West and Central Africa, Mali, Chad, Burkina Faso, and Guinea are a perfect illustration.

This is also true for some North African countries, which, after the so-called 'Arab Spring', have fallen back into instability too. After the momentum created by the 2011 revolts in Tunisia, these countries are now experiencing either a return to the situation before the popular uprisings of a decade ago or even worse conditions. One might wonder, then, whether constitutionalism in Africa does not follow 30-year constitutional cycles, alternating between advances and setbacks.

Babacar Kanté, *Introductory Remarks* In: *Constitutional Change and Constitutionalism in Africa*. Edited by: Charles M. Fombad and Nico Steytler, Oxford University Press. © Babacar Kanté 2025. DOI: 10.1093/9780198957034.003.0001

Legal scholars have extensively analysed the phenomenon, the procedures for amending constitutions, and their consequences for the legal and political lives of the countries concerned. But it seems to me that the fundamental question is how and why this has happened. Why are African countries subject to this constitutional instability? This is, in my opinion, a fundamental question because, before even trying to find solutions to the problem, we must try to identify the causes. The proposed solutions will only be effective if they are based on an etiological approach that identifies and treats the causes and not the symptoms.

Such an approach requires going beyond the law. Indeed, in order to answer the question of why we have seen the relative failure of constitutionalism in Africa, it is necessary to place the problem in its context. For example, the situation in the West African countries that interests me here may throw some light on the problem.

These countries are trying to resist as best they can two major constraints that are imposed on almost all contemporary political regimes. The first is the tendency for models to converge towards a global constitutionalism through adherence to common democratic values. Curiously, it does not seem to have any hold on our states, which are setting up regimes that are sometimes hybrid. The second is the ever-increasing demands of citizens for more democracy and more social justice. This constraint also seems to leave indifferent the de facto African political regimes that have neither legality nor legitimacy, and which develop erratic public policies.

The importance of the political, social, economic, security, and humanitarian contexts of these countries leads one, from a methodological point of view, to consider not only constitutional law as it is taught (the law in the books) but, above all, constitutional law as it is practiced (the law in action).

I have come to this conclusion after a little practical experience with politicians, and after visiting a number of countries, such as Mali, Chad, Burkina Faso, and Guinea, following the recent *coups d'état* there. What I retain from these experiences, drawn, on the one hand, from my practice as a former constitutional judge, and, on the other, from observing political regimes in transition, is that the sociopolitical context of the countries that interest us remains best characterized as one still dominated by anomie; that is to say, a legal disorganization and an absence of accepted social norms. Indeed, some authors, such as Donald Kaberuka, have no hesitation in speaking of the 'fragile state syndrome' as a way of characterizing African political systems.[1]

However, it remains difficult to determine exactly whether it is the *coups d'états* that lead to this fragility or whether, conversely, it is the *coups d'états* themselves that are a result of this form of chronic vulnerability in our states. In a general context of alternating periods of democratic consolidation and retreat, and consequently a loss of reference points, constitutionalism seems to be more of a fiction than a reality. In this case, the basic principles of constitutionalism, such as the separation of powers, the independence of the judiciary, and political accountability, may have more of a mythical function than anything else. That is to say, they are more a matter of imagination and incantation, and play a role of external use. In the end, then, would constitutionalism in West Africa be nothing more than a legal myth in the sense envisaged by Mathieu Touzeil-Divina in his book *Dix Myths du Droit Public*,

[1] Donald Kaberuka, 'High-level Panel on Fragile States' https://www.afdb.org/en/topics-and-sectors/initiatives-partnerships/high-level-panel-on-fragile-states accessed 1 August 2023.

meaning 'a construction of the mind intended to put forward selected symbols, events or ideas'?[2]

If such a hypothesis is correct, would not one of the explanations for this be that the legal rules to which political power should in principle be subject, in a regime respectful of the rule of law, have proved to be insignificant with regard to guaranteeing this submission? In order to overcome this inadequacy, and to guarantee a real constitutionalism, should we not then turn to another approach, one which consists in having recourse to extra-legal factors? It is to these two questions that I would like to try to give a modest answer in putting a few hypotheses across.

2. How does the insignificance of the rule of law make constitutionalism a myth?

Whether there is a reality to constitutionalism in the West African subregion is debatable. Constitutional law has no influence on the exercise of political power. Constitutionalism would fall into the category of legal myths that Touzeil-Divina would no doubt consider 'modern' and 'utilitarian'. This mythical character of its founding principles manifests itself in at least three forms.

2.1 The ineffectiveness of power's submission to the law

One of the basic principles of the rule of law *(etat de droit)* and constitutionalism consists in respect for the rule of law *(règle de droit)* by the administration and by the political power. However, in reality, the rule of law only exists in practice when it works as a stable reference standard that is imposed on everyone, starting above all with the political power. It is the existence of such a reference standard that guarantees the stability of the legal system and the security of citizens.

In fact, it is rather the great mutability of West African constitutions and their real instability which are most in evidence. To give just two examples, the Senegalese Constitution of 2001 has been amended some fifteen times in fifteen years by the government in power. The same is true of Benin's 1990 Constitution, which, after some 30 years of resistance, was amended in 2018 at the initiative of the current president.

Constitutional amendments in West Africa very often concern electoral rules. This is despite the 2001 Protocol A/SP1/12/01 on Democracy and Good Governance Supplementary to the Protocol Relating to the Mechanism for Conflict Prevention, Management, Resolution, Peacekeeping and Security of the Economic Community of West African States (ECOWAS). This prohibits the modification of provisions relating to elections six months prior to an election, without a consensus.

Instability has been aggravated in recent years by the recurrent practice of *coups d'état*. In such cases, it is almost always the number and length of presidential terms that are challenged. Studies conducted by American universities in Kentucky and Florida reveal that,

[2] Mathieu Touzeil-Divina, *Dix Myths du Droit Public* (LGDJ 2019), author's translation.

from 1960 to 1999, the African continent experienced 158 attempted coups, with no fewer than 76 of them succeeding. Burkina Faso alone has now had nine, including one in 2022 (as was also the case in Mali in 2020 and 2021).[3]

However, it remains all the more important to understand the reasons for these. Beyond the fact of their multiplicity and diversity, the circumstances provoking *coups d'état* are better understood today. To stay only within the constitutional domain, it is the suspension of the constitution and the adoption, often in haste and through improvisation, of a new transitional charter that create many problems. Through such constitutional changes, we are no longer changing *the* constitution but constitutions in general. The main consequence of these constitutional upheavals is to create uncertainty about the existence of a reference standard. Can we talk about the effectiveness of constitutionalism when the reference norm is itself so unstable and uncertain? Under these conditions, constitutionalism becomes, if not downright impossible, at least very difficult to achieve.

2.2 The inefficacy of the submission of government power to law

The practice of constitutionalism by West African countries has consisted, for the most part, of incorporating in their basic texts the major principles and mechanisms that underlie the submission of governmental power to law. It so happens that these mechanisms are more theoretical than practical. When this is so they can be said to enjoy no more than a mythical character. Take, for instance, the principle of the separation of powers. Initially conceived not to directly promote democracy per se but to limit power and protect the ordinary citizen, it is something which has been adopted by all African constitutions. One wonders whether this is done simply to avoid being labelled negatively from the start, since article 16 of the 1789 Declaration of the Rights of Man and of the Citizen in France states: 'Any society in which the guarantee of rights is not assured, nor the separation of powers determined, has no constitution.'

However, in reality, as is indeed widespread in the so-called democratic countries, the principle of the separation of powers is not fully respected. In the United States of America, the vice president is also president of the Senate and enjoys a casting vote in the event of a tie; in France, the prime minister is president of the Council of State, which is responsible for controlling the administration; while in Great Britain, the leader of the majority is automatically designated prime minister.

Given this background, was it reasonable to suppose that the principle would find a firmer footing on the African continent? Not surprisingly, its application and effectiveness are even more in question in West Africa. Also, in order to subject power to the authority of the constitution and the law, could African countries not give priority to the principle of separation of functions? Would it not be conceivable to consider the state power *(le pouvoir d'Etat)*, or the power of the state *(le pouvoir de l'Etat)*, or power in the state *(le pouvoir dans l'Etat)*, as being unique, and that it is indeed in the exercise of their different functions that public authorities commit excesses of power? Indeed, African constituent powers would do well to implement mechanisms to regulate political offices by subjecting them to somewhat

[3] See Megan Duzor and Brian Williamson, 'Coups in Africa' https://projects.voanews.com/african-coups/ accessed 1 August 2023.

stricter rules of eligibility for office and personal accountability, as is increasingly the case in some of the advanced democratic countries.

2.3 The inefficiency of the submission of power to the law

If the submission of political power to the law is not sanctioned, the principle remains meaningless. Experience unfortunately reveals that the sanctioning of the violation of the rules governing the action of the political authorities concerned is either absent or, when it does occur, remains weak. The checks and balances that normally play a role in a democratic system are inoperative here.

In the past, the main reason for this was to be found in the prevalence of the one-party system. Today, despite the predominance of the multiparty system, the weak intervention of institutional checks and balances persists. Parliamentary oversight is ineffective, in part because the results of legislative elections do not always reflect the reality of political power relations.

Judicial institutions, especially constitutional courts, suffer from at least two shortcomings. First of all, in civil law systems such as ours (Senegal's), citizens generally lack direct access to the judge. The result is that they cannot, under these conditions, demand that the state respect the law by asserting their rights. So it is that, in Senegal, most cases before the Constitutional Council concern electoral disputes; there have been fewer than ten cases relating to exceptions of unconstitutionality since the creation of the Constitutional Council in 1992.

The second shortcoming of the judicial institutions is related to judges and the conceptions they have of their role. Comparison of the book by Judge Albie Sachs, former member of the Constitutional Court of South Africa, entitled *L'étrange Alchimie de la Vie et de la Loi*,[4] with the answers to the questionnaire of the ninth Congress of French-speaking constitutional courts, is edifying in this respect. The theme of the Congress was 'the constitutional judge and human rights'. While the former emphasizes the protection of the economic and social rights of citizens, the latter, at least in African countries, give priority to civil and political rights such as the right to vote and the resolution of electoral disputes. In West Africa, the characteristics of the judicial system and the learning process of democracy are explanatory factors. The system seems to be running on empty because the institutional and jurisdictional mechanisms for limiting and sanctioning power are not working.

There are currently four African countries under sanction by the African Union; but, curiously, these suspensions seem to have no practical effect on the countries concerned.[5] Take, for instance, the sanctions imposed by the Economic Community of West African States. These seem to have had only counterproductive effects. They are supported neither by public opinion in general nor by the organs of civil society. On the contrary, they have served only to increase levels of support for the military juntas.

[4] Albie Sachs, *L'étrange Alchimie de la Vie et de la Loi* https://www.pulp.up.ac.za/monographs/l-etrange-alchimie-de-la-vie-et-de-la-loi accessed 1 August 2023.

[5] 'African Union Reaffirms Suspension of Burkina Faso, Mali, Guinea and Sudan' (*AfricaNews*, 20 February 2023) https://www.africanews.com/2023/02/20/african-union-reaffirms-suspension-of-burkina-faso-mali-guinea-and-sudan// accessed 1 August 2023.

3. Recourse to extra-legal factors to foster a real constitutionalism?

In these conditions, if we are to hope to see the development of real constitutionalism in Africa, we must, perhaps paradoxically, reach beyond the law. It seems that several preconditions are not met in West Africa for an efficient and effective implementation of the mechanisms of constitutionalism. Let us now examine some hypotheses for remedying the weak influence that the law seems to have on African political regimes; these hypotheses may perhaps best be understood under the rubric of legal realism. Three avenues in particular might be explored.

3.1 A process of appropriation of the constitution

In the process of adopting constitutions in our subregion, the substance—meaning the allegedly substantive innovations and the legal regime of certain provisions—seems to have primacy. It is important to remember that amendments often take place in a context of crisis. The consequence is that new constitutions, which follow on from transitional charters, generally respond to both the urgent need to provide a legal basis for transitional bodies (that may already be in place) and also to organize the elections necessary to bring the crisis to an end. Disadvantages do follow from this approach. First, it is often the case that incoherent provisions are adopted under the pressure of the moment. Secondly, the focus on solving immediate electoral problems entails a frequent absence of a long-term vision.

Against this, and for the constitution to have a good chance of success, it would be best for it to give primary importance to the process of its adoption, even prior to any debate on its actual content: form should come before substance. Unfortunately, this has rarely been the case, and it is noticeable that the new constitutions were often adopted in haste and have generally not been the subject of consultation in the various national languages so as to obtain the explicit support of the citizens around the values of the founding constitution.

From this point of view, I believe that the process followed in the development of the Constitution of the Republic of South Africa is a useful example for West Africa to consider. The first great idea that made the constitution-making process in that country so special was the adoption of an interim constitution. The thinking around the constitution had time to mature before its actual drafting, in a process that was open to a wide variety of external inputs but also, and above all, to a series of in-depth consultations.

Such consultations, if conducted seriously in West Africa, could result in a strong sense of ownership by the new citizens and a powerful aura of legitimacy. Instead, with the current military regimes, we are witnessing a craze for meetings called 'political dialogues' or 'national assemblies', with no one really understanding the difference between the two. The question of legitimacy is crucial; without it, the constitution remains entirely a matter between elites and one dealing essentially with the gaining or preservation of power.

3.2 The culture of political ethics

If certain principles are better applied in some countries than in others, the explanation certainly relies, in part at least, on the political ethics demonstrated by the men and women responsible for applying the principles. Otherwise, how can we understand, out of context, that the same principles could produce such different effects in different places? So it is that the vice president of the United States does not generally abuse his position as president of the Senate; the French prime minister never actually chairs the Council of State; and, in Great Britain, the prime minister is often removed by his or her own political party.

These examples suggest that politicians should impose a code of conduct on themselves for the exercise of their responsibilities. This ethic, which is a variant of humility, is a virtue of democracy. Politicians should impose self-limitations in certain cases. The accountability that is now required of all institutions is not only legal; it is also—and, in many cases today, purely—ethical. This is evident in the fact that a form of moral code of conduct is increasingly being imposed on elected officials and members of the executive branch across the world.

Unfortunately, any such approach is very much lacking among the politicians in our subregion. Greed for gaining power or preserving it is the main driver of their actions, and especially so when it comes to the question of amending or adopting a constitution. The belief in the rule of law (or at the very least, the fear of punishment) should be their credo, as it is for all citizens. The fear of punishment should not be stronger for the citizen than it is for the political authority. If this is indeed the case, it means the law is no longer the same for everyone, and is then no longer the rule of law. In any case, we may note that this fear is more real in countries with advanced democracies than it is in West African countries that have not experienced it.

3.3 Enhancing the role of the judge

Constitutionalism cannot be a system in which political power submits to the law only voluntarily. This would be a naive and idealistic view. The keystone of the rule of law is the possibility of the courts to impose sanctions when political power violates any of the obligations placed upon it by the constitution.

The role of the judge in guaranteeing the submission of power to the law is therefore decisive. The stronger the court whose responsibility it is to keep the government under control, the more chance there is that constitutionalism will flourish. In all major democracies, the constitutional court stands as the pillar of constitutionalism. But, in West Africa, as has already been said, the status of the constitutional court does not necessarily allow it to act as a guarantor of constitutionalism. In this case, strong political will is necessary to see to the buttressing of the judge's role.

Ideally, our regimes should be built on a judicial system that empowers judges. The judge's role is to ensure that the constitution is given a soul that respects the rights of citizens by limiting the power of the political authority. If the judge's role is supported, then it will be possible to build a jurisprudence that distinguishes between times when the authorities must intervene to facilitate the enjoyment of rights by their beneficiaries and times when they should abstain from intervention in order to allow the free exercise of citizens' rights.

4. Conclusion

In conclusion, I can only observe that, for the past 60 years or so, African countries have sought to put in place and implement the necessary mechanisms for constitutionalism.

These efforts have not always been successful (although real attempts have been made). Constitutional lawyers have also tried as best they can to watch over and analyse this development. But, once again, is it the case that we only tend to take a purely normative perspective on the problem?

Thus, I wonder if it is not time to change direction and go to other disciplines—such as history, sociology, and philosophy—to answer the question of how did we get here. The report published by the Citizen's Coalition for the Sahel in June 2022, entitled *Sahel: What Has Changed*, can help lead us to such introspection. The humanitarian problems revealed by the statistics in this report on the number of victims of terrorism, the number of displaced persons, the number of women raped, and the number of children who no longer go to school cannot leave us indifferent as we reflect on the ways and means of anchoring constitutionalism in Africa.[6]

It is, therefore, with this invitation and a wish that I would like to conclude. I wish that jurists would turn a little more to other disciplines to help them understand why our countries do not manage to produce a constitutional law adapted to their context, why the constitution is not always respected by the political power, and why the sanctions provided for are not operational. Otherwise, my fear is that we risk reaching our limits and ending up in an intellectual cul-de-sac.

But now let me end on a more positive note by renewing my warm congratulations to the organizers of the Stellenbosch seminar for the increasingly remarkable quality of the organization, as well as for the regularity of their work. I would like to thank them warmly for their invitation to participate, and wish them every success in this endeavour.

Bibliography

'African Union Reaffirms Suspension of Burkina Faso, Mali, Guinea and Sudan' *AfricaNews* (20 February 2023) https://www.africanews.com/2023/02/20/african-union-reaffirms-suspension-of-burkina-faso-mali-guinea-and-sudan// accessed 1 August 2023

Coalition citoyenne pour le Sahel, 'Sahel: Ce qui a changé – Rapport de suivi de la Coalition citoyenne pour le Sahel' (2022) https://reliefweb.int/report/burkina-faso/sahel-ce-qui-change-rapport-de-suivi-de-la-coalition-citoyenne-pour-le-sahel-juin-2022 accessed 1 August 2023

Duzor M. and Williamson B., 'Coups in Africa' https://projects.voanews.com/african-coups/ accessed 1 August 2023

Kaberuka D., 'High-level Panel on Fragile States' https://www.afdb.org/en/topics-and-sectors/initiatives-partnerships/high-level-panel-on-fragile-states accessed 1 August 2023

Sachs A., *L'étrange Alchimie de la Vie et de la Loi* (PULP, 2021) https://www.pulp.up.ac.za/monographs/l-etrange-alchimie-de-la-vie-et-de-la-loiaccessed 1 August 2023

Touzeil-Divina M., *Dix Myths du Droit Public* (LGDJ 2019)

[6] Coalition citoyenne pour le Sahel, 'Sahel: Ce qui a changé – Rapport de suivi de la Coalition citoyenne pour le Sahel' (2022) https://reliefweb.int/report/burkina-faso/sahel-ce-qui-change-rapport-de-suivi-de-la-coalition-citoyenne-pour-le-sahel-juin-2022 accessed 1 August 2023.

General Introduction

Constitutional Change and Constitutionalism in Africa

Nico Steytler and Charles M. Fombad

1. Introduction

The new generation of African constitutions that were crafted in the 1990s began a trend that promised a new dawn of radical transformation of the continent's governance landscape and a concerted attempt to eliminate the risks of coups, political instability, and other social and economic problems that had plagued the continent since decolonization and the granting of independence to countries from 1957 onwards. It provided an opportunity for African constitution-builders and politicians to design constitutions which, for the first time, were supposed not only to reflect and take into account the social, economic, and other contextual realities of the continent, but also draw from the considerable experience of past decades of blunders and failures. If pre-independence constitution-making was a staged, ad hoc event that took place in secret and behind closed doors, this was supposed to have changed with the advent of the new generation of so-called 'made in Africa' constitutions.

However, the reality is that the post-1990 wave of constitutional reforms appears to have provoked a contagious fever of making, unmaking, and remaking constitutions. The nature of these changes, their frequency, and the fact that most countries in the region have engaged in them raises many questions of both a practical and theoretical nature. What is, however, increasingly a matter of concern is the resultant instability, which threatens to undermine the few strides made to entrench a culture of constitutionalism, good governance, and respect for the rule of law. The new constitutional dispensation that had seen the introduction of new constitutions or the profound revision of earlier ones does not appear to have provided a reliable and effective framework for managing constitutional change and ensuring political stability. It is, therefore, no surprise that there is almost universal agreement that Africa is now facing a profound crisis of democracy and constitutionalism.[1]

Revising a constitution never attracts as much attention as writing a new one. Yet such revision has the potential to undo much of what the new constitution promised. Modern African constitutions usually spell out the manner in which the constitution can be changed and the role that the different actors involved in the process can play. These role-players

[1] See generally Charles M Fombad and Nico Steytler (eds.), *Democracy, Elections and Constitutionalism in Africa* (OUP 2021).

Nico Steytler and Charles M. Fombad, *General Introduction* In: *Constitutional Change and Constitutionalism in Africa*.
Edited by: Charles M. Fombad and Nico Steytler, Oxford University Press.
DOI: 10.1093/9780198957034.003.0002

usually consist of politicians (with the process being initiated by the executive and then approved by parliament), ordinary citizens (usually where a referendum or plebiscite is provided for), and judges (who deal with disputes regarding procedural or substantive compliance with the relevant constitutional provisions).

In spite of the fact that the new constitutions contained many progressive ideas, the reality is that these are being steadily and stealthily diluted by the diverse forms of constitutional change which are now taking place. This book interrogates the nature and extent of such changes: changes that have been taking place on a rather more frequent—and sometimes arbitrary—basis than was ever anticipated. Amongst the main questions that are investigated is the nature of the constitution-making process, as well as the role of diverse internal actors, such as the legislature, the executive, and the judiciary, and of external actors, such as the African Union (AU) and Regional Economic Communities (RECs), in the different processes of constitutional change. There are also case studies that identify distinct patterns of change. Ultimately, the discussions strive to see how the processes of constitutional change, whether inevitable and unavoidable or contrived, can be undertaken in a manner that does not undermine or threaten the efforts made to entrench democracy, constitutionalism, good governance, and respect for the rule of law on the African continent.

Constitution-making and change take place against the backdrop of constitutionalism, one of the hallmarks of the new constitutions of the 1990s. In his introductory remarks, '30 Years of Constitutionalism in Africa: Between Myth and Reality', Babacar Kanté points out that African countries have gone through three main phases with regard to constitutionalism. The first (from 1960 to 1990) involved a negation of constitutionalism through *coups d'état* and the adoption of various modes of one-party rule, which functioned with no regard for the rule of law. The next 30 years (1990 to 2020) saw a wave of democratization and the ostensible entrenchment of constitutionalism. The third phase (from 2020 onwards) is witnessing the decline of constitutionalism in a fresh spate of *coups d'état* and constitutional amendments.

Kanté thus asks why there is such constitutional instability in African countries. He argues that only once the causes are identified and understood can there be a chance of finding solutions to the problem. With reference to West African countries, he remarks that they are trying to resist two major constraints: first, the demands of a global constitutionalism through adherence to common democratic values; and second, the ever-increasing demands of citizens for more democracy and social justice. Underlying this resistance is legal disorganization and an absence of accepted social norms. In this context, he concludes, constitutionalism seems to be more of a fiction than a reality. How, then, can real constitutionalism be guaranteed?

Kanté argues that the answer is not so much a legal one: instead, it lies in a recourse to extra-legal factors. First, constitution-making processes should be inclusive, allowing citizens to have a sense of ownership and placing process before substance. Second, politicians should impose a code of conduct on themselves in the exercise of their responsibilities. Third, given the crucial role that the courts play in guaranteeing the submission of the state to law (the rule of law), strong political will is needed to strengthen the role of the judge. In conclusion, he encourages jurists to pay attention to other disciplines so as to help them understand why constitutions do not always suit their context, why they are not always respected by the political power, and why judicial guarantees are not effective.

2. Overview

Constitution-building is not a 'once-off' process that starts and ends with the drafting of a constitution; neither is the legitimacy of the process, once earned, a carte blanche for frequent and arbitrary alterations to the constitution. The question that arises here is whether today's fever of unmaking and remaking constitutions reflects the way these constitutions were made and/or the mechanisms provided within them for subsequent changes. This raises the question of what it is that triggers the process of constitutional change.

There are different schools of thought with regard to the legitimacy of certain forms or methods as well as the extent of change (important distinctions are being made between constitutional amendment versus constitutional replacement, or constitutional revision versus constitutional dismemberment). In addition, there are practical and theoretical issues concerning who participated in the constitution-making processes, whether there were any normative or procedural limits on the processes, and what were the outcomes of such processes. Do the present challenges have to do with whether the processes were inclusive and participatory in nature? Ultimately, the question is whether there are any new and emerging trends in constitution-making that offer the prospect of constitutional stability.

In Chapter 1, 'An Overview of the Legal Framework for Amending Modern African Constitutions', Charles Fombad sets out the various patterns of constitutional amendment procedures and the protections they provide. He observes that, since 1990, diverse measures have been adopted to regulate the manner in which African constitutions can be amended and thereby prevent the frequent and abusive changes to constitutions that had been a regular feature of pre-1990 African constitutional practice.

The chapter begins with an account of the way in which constitutional amendment is conceptualized. Although different terms are used for constitutional change (amendment, revision, or replacement), what is most important is whether the envisioned change is legitimate. Legitimacy is defined along three axes: first, changes are legitimate if adopted in accordance with the existing constitutional and other legal rules, principles, and norms (legal legitimacy); second, they are legitimate if they reflect the general will through national ownership (political legitimacy); and third, changes are legitimate when reflecting the shared values, desires, and hopes of the people (moral legitimacy).

The chapter proceeds to examine different methods of amendment and the limitations provided for them. Formal amendments are made in terms of the constitution itself and should balance two imperatives: flexibility and rigidity. Fombad distinguishes between four types of amendment procedures: the first applies to the entire constitution and usually requires a supermajority; the second consist in special procedures for amending certain provisions; the third involves time-specified amendments; and the fourth are extraordinary amendment procedures (which are to be found only in a few constitutions). Constitutional change may also occur informally, including through judicial interpretation, unwritten understandings and conventions, and inaction or neglect by executive or legislative actors.

Given the continent's history of abusive and arbitrary constitutional amendments, Fombad describes how a number of African constitutions impose limitations on the manner and/or scope of the exercise of amendment powers, including explicit or implicit prohibitions against amending certain provisions, as well as circumstantial or temporal limitations. In addition, the judiciary has invented a limitation in the form of the 'basic structure' doctrine.

Who are the main actors whose participation is essential for legitimizing the process? Fombad notes that, although key stakeholders go beyond officials from the three branches of government and include civil society organizations (CSOs), non-governmental organizations (NGOs), lobbyists, and academics, in practice only a limited role is provided for public participation.

However well-drafted protective measures may be, compliance is what counts. A key mechanism in this regard, Fombad argues, is judicial review. Its effectiveness depends, in turn, on the scope of judicial review powers and, of course, on the existence of real judicial independence. Some constitutions explicitly or implicitly purport to exclude judicial review, while others contemplate various forms of non-judicial review of compliance.

In conclusion, Fombad contends that, although the measures nowadays entrenched in constitutions to limit abusive amendments are much better than those in the pre-1990 era, weaknesses remain that are open to exploitation by unscrupulous politicians. He suggests that, in seeking to strengthen protective measures, the possibility of exerting external pressure on domestic constitution-makers should be explored, and notes in particular the opportunities provided by the African Commission and African Court for putting pressure on African governments to comply not only with their constitutional obligations but also with the duties imposed on them by the numerous AU and REC instruments. At a domestic level, he suggests that one possible way to contain abusive and arbitrary amendments is to entrench a permanent constitutional review commission akin to the permanent law revision commissions that are common in anglophone African countries.

3. Constitution-building, constitution-making, constitutional change, and constitutionalism

In a number of countries, dedicated constitution-making processes were initiated after a revolution, a constitutional crisis, or a deliberate renewal. These processes are always major occasions, signifying a new beginning and, among other things, calling for civic participation and negotiation between key political forces. Different forms of constitution-making are possible. For instance, instead of a parliament adopting a new constitution, a distinct constitutional body may be established for that purpose, such as a constitutional assembly; then, to secure popular legitimacy, a referendum may follow the adoption of the constitution. The process of constitution-making itself may vary. Sometimes a constitutional commission or committee is charged with the drafting of a constitution for adoption by a political body; at other times, it is the political body itself that does the drafting and adoption after negotiations have taken place.

In Chapter 2, 'Changing Modes of Constitution-making in Africa: Do the Means Guarantee the Ends?', Heinz Klug notes that Africa has experienced several waves of constitution-making, with the most recent being the post-Cold War wave. The chapter examines the different forms of constitution-making within these waves. Each wave, from the colonial era through to independence and into the post-colonial era, has been characterized by certain forms of constitution-making, such that a particular form is seen to be dominant during a particular wave.

While imposed constitutions were predominant during the colonial era, the post-Cold War wave presents a number of constitution-making forms that seem to promise more sustainable constitutionalism in those countries that have embraced greater democratic involvement in their constitution-making processes. Klug hypothesizes that greater degrees of public participation and democratic process in each of these constitution-making waves have brought greater legitimacy to both the process and product of constitution-making across Africa. If this is the case, he argues, then there should be increasing resilience in the lives of these constitutions, and thus a strengthening of constitutionalism across the continent. However, the resurgence of military coups and extra-constitutional means of resolving intra-elite conflict in several countries points in the opposite direction.

Can this latter trend be curtailed? In Chapter 3, 'Reimagining Constitutional Change and Democracy in Africa: Emerging Supranational Standards for Constitutional Change', Adem K Abebe examines how, at both continental (AU) and regional (REC) levels, substantive and procedural standards have been put in place to avoid regressive constitutional amendments. He argues that, in addition to compliance with fundamental democratic principles, the principle of 'national consensus' has emerged as the emblem of the continental attempt to establish and sustain legitimate constitutional frameworks.

Abebe contends that the continental standards require four cumulative conditions: (1) legality, namely compliance with the letter and spirit of domestic constitutional requirements for amendment, as well as with continental normative standards; (2) a consultative and participatory process (which may in certain cases involve referenda); (3) a free and stable political environment; and (4) inclusive majoritarianism.

With regard to the last-mentioned condition, Abebe's argument is that constitutional amendments to core aspects of the democratic framework must be supported by groups beyond the ruling party or coalition, regardless of the incumbent's representative dominance. Inclusive majoritarianism calls for the reimagination of the traditional reliance on legislative supermajorities, referenda, unamendable provisions, and judicial review as the means of protecting constitutional frameworks—precisely the issues that historically have attracted scholarly and political attention. The chapter suggests that, seen in this light, the emerging continental standards for constitutional change could play an important role in simultaneously inspiring and constraining domestic reform processes.

Nevertheless, Abebe points out that the AU would need to engage proactively by elaborating on, popularizing, and securing buy-in for the standards, as well as monitoring and identifying constitutional reform processes and providing technical support and capacity enhancement to reform processes as they happen at the domestic level—rather than simply reactively criticizing reforms or subsequently challenging them in African courts.

Amending constitutions in federal or hybrid-federal countries invokes a further dimension of discussion and analysis. According to federal theory, one of the characteristics of a federation is that its constitution cannot be changed unilaterally by either its federal or subnational governments. Thus, the constituent units must participate in any proposed amendment to the constitution, or at least insofar as the federal aspects are concerned. Specific rules have developed which prescribe how such participation should take place. These amendment rules may have a strong bearing on the ways in which a federal constitution was initially drafted and adopted.

Accordingly, in Chapter 4, 'Making and Amending Federal Constitutions in Africa', Nico Steytler, Zemelak, Ayitenew Ayele, and Henry Paul Gichana pose the following question: has the manner in which African federations or hybrid federations have been formed (whether by integration or disaggregation) had any influence on the mode of protection relating to the amendment of the constitution in general and/or of the federal arrangements in particular? A federation is formed by integration when two or more independent states merge to found a new state: this is the so-called 'coming-together' federation exemplified by the old federations of the United States, Canada, and Australia. Federation-forming by disaggregation, on the other hand, occurs when a once unitary state decentralizes in order to secure peace and the integrity of a state: the so-called 'holding-together' federation.

The chapter addresses this question with reference to Africa's four main federations or hybrid federations—South Africa, Ethiopia, Nigeria, and Kenya—all of which have been formed by disaggregation and are thus 'holding-together' federal systems. The authors argue, however, that within the broad category of 'holding-together' federations, there is a continuum between 'integration' on the one end and 'disaggregation' on the other, and federations can be plotted across this. A unitary state which has experienced severe conflict on a territorial basis shows elements of 'integration' or a 'coming together' of the warring factions in a federation. It is thus postulated that federations leaning towards the integration side of the continuum may have stronger protective amendment procedures to secure the federal compact than others found on the disaggregation side. The four cases discussed bear some evidence of this. In one way or another, subnational governments have an important role in constitutional amendments; however, while there is some variation in the constitutional amendment rules among the African federations, what is also apparent is their similarity to the rules of old 'coming-together' federations. It is thus suggested that such amendment rules, although not born of African soil, have become standard features in the federal toolbox.

4. Eternity clauses and constitutional unamendability

Constitutional change may trigger questions of 'eternity clauses', either explicitly or implicitly. This raises the question of whether there are any parts of a constitution that are not amendable. Almost all civil law jurisdictions in Africa have eternity and/or unamendable provisions which purport to prohibit any changes to those provisions. In some common law systems, there are similar provisions. For example, the Namibian Constitution of 1990 stipulates that the Bill of Rights may not be amended. The aim of this is to ensure stability and prevent the undermining of constitutionalism. Even where such constitutional provisions are absent, courts might discover deep structural features that may not be amended. The crucial issue is how such provisions (either through use or abuse) have impacted on constitutionalism in practice.

In Chapter 5, 'Eternalized Core Provisions in the Constitutions of the Lusophone Countries in Africa and their Uncertain Destinies', André Thomashausen examines the use of eternity clauses in these countries, which form part of the civil law family. He notes that clauses to exclude certain fundamental principles from constitutional amendment are found in all five lusophone constitutions in Africa: Angola (2010), Cabo Verde (2010), Guinea-Bissau (1996), Mozambique (2018), and São Tomé and Principe (2003). These 'eternity clauses' all took the eternity clause in the Portuguese constitutions of 1976 and 1989 as their model. A broad range of constitutional tenets are protected. Almost uniformly, they include the independence, sovereignty, and unity of the state; the republican form of government; the separation between religious denominations and the state; fundamental human rights; universal, direct, secret, personal, equal, and regular elections; pluralism of expression and political organization, including recognition of political parties and the right of democratic opposition; the separation of powers; and the independence of the judiciary.

However, across all five African lusophone jurisdictions, the judicial view prevails that the eternity clauses may be subject to amendment. The logic here is that there is the possibility of amendment where such amendment is not explicitly prohibited. In the case of Mozambique, amendment is explicitly allowed, albeit subject to a popular referendum, in that the electorate is deemed the origin of all political power. In Angola, the Constitutional Court twice considered the application of constitutional amendments to eternity clauses and only to a very limited extent invalidated an aspect of one amendment. In Cabo Verde, the Constitutional Court used the eternity clauses not directly relating to constitutional amendments but as indicators that some parts of the constitution have a higher value when assessing the constitutionality of ordinary legislation.

The efficacy of eternity clauses, Thomashausen suggests, lies in their serving 'as a powerful tool of constitutional interpretation if they are considered to establish a normative hierarchy of fundamental constitutional values'. However, he notes, this efficacy '[is] compromised when the eternity clause is verbose and all-embracing, instead of remaining limited to the truly most important and fundamental norms'.

In francophone Africa, a similar scenario is evident. In Chapter 6, 'Eternity Clauses in African Constitutionalism: A Case Study of CEMAC Countries', Abdou Khadre Diop focuses on the member states of the Central African Economic and Monetary Community (CEMAC)—Cameroon, the Central African Republic, Chad, Congo, Gabon, and Equatorial Guinea. They all have francophone civil law systems (with the exception of Equatorial Guinea, which is lusophone), and their constitutions reflect the Gaullist model of the Fifth Republic of France. All of these constitutions include provisions that declare as immutable certain fundamental characteristics of the state, human rights commitments, and/or of executive term limits. Diop argues that such clauses were included because they serve as indicators of what constitutional designers considered as 'the public good of constitutionalism'. That there may be a need for such protection is clear: these countries have been characterized by a high level of constitutional instability due to the frequency of constitutional changes and *coups d'etat*. In this context, Diop critically examines the concept of unamendability (touted as a legal tool to entrench constitutional values and principles) by placing it in the context of practical realities in the CEMAC countries.

The scope of the eternity clauses in the CEMAC countries is similar to that of the eternity clauses in Africa's lusophone countries: the republican and secular form of the state; territorial integrity or national unity; and democratic values. Diop points out that the unamendability clauses are formulated as principles and, as such, regarded as general guidelines rather than clear, enforceable rules. He thus contends that, in adopting such an approach, 'the constitutional drafters seem to provide them with just an aspirational or declarative function'.

Diop goes on to question the utility of the eternity clauses and finds they were no protection against either unconstitutional constitutional changes or unconstitutional changes in government *(coups d'état)*. In Congo, the entire 2002 Constitution was replaced in 2015 with a new one conveniently omitting the unamendable term-limit clause, thereby allowing the incumbent president continued tenure. Diop shows how political leaders are able to undermine or circumvent eternity clauses, in the process opening up a huge gap between the text providing for eternity clauses and how these clauses actually function in practice. In the light of all this, he concludes that eternity clauses are merely 'illusory'.

This raises the question of the role of the judiciary in giving effect to such clauses. Is it that the courts are capable of enforcing them but fail to do so or that they are simply powerless to do so at all? Diop is of the opinion that the CEMAC courts generally lack the explicit authority to pronounce on constitutional amendments. Even on the few occasions when the courts were asked to intervene in the constitutional amendment process, their interpretation of those clauses resulted only in a weakening of them. For Diop, a part of the problem is that the French model of constitutional review does not empower courts to undertake a proper constitutional review of constitutional amendments.

In conclusion, Diop finds that eternity clauses in the CEMAC countries are 'largely irrelevant in theory and in practice to ensure the entrenchment of constitutional values'. Such a conclusion justifies the exploration of other options to better secure constitutional stability.

5. The judiciary, constitutional change, and constitutionalism

The judiciary, as the guardian of the constitution, is mandated to stand as the bulwark against any attempt to make abusive changes to the constitution. It is tasked instead to ensure that such changes as do occur are made in conformity with the constitution. However, in serving their function as interpreters of the constitution, courts themselves, directly or indirectly, may be responsible for 'judge-made constitutional change'. In most cases, such changes are likely to advance constitutionalism, but in some, they achieve the opposite. Sometimes judicial activism results in judicial populism, or even adventurism, as in the cases where judges adopt an interpretation of the constitution which is swayed by public opinion, the media, or a populist government, and disregards constitutional principles and rules in a way that alters a particular aspect of the constitution.

What has been the record in regard to judge-made constitutional change? More specifically, to what extent has the judiciary in African countries indulged in it in a manner that impacts negatively on its duty to defend constitutionalism and respect for the rule of law? This volume presents three case studies of such questions, drawing on experiences in Ghana, South Africa, and Kenya.

In Chapter 7, 'The Trouble with Judicial Amendments: Lessons from Ghana', Maame AS Mensa-Bonsu discusses cases where an amendment purports to improve the outcomes or operation of the constitution, as well as ones where amendment either exacerbates preexisting problems or creates new ones. She begins with the premise that the Ghanaian Supreme Court is appointed to 'interpret and enforce' the Constitution of 1992 in relation to legislation and executive actions and then asks what happens when the Court goes beyond this mandate and actually changes the Constitution.

Mensa-Bonsu defines a 'judicial constitutional amendment' as a judicial decision that effectually adds to, removes from, or modifies the meaning of a constitution in a manner which is inconsistent with the text in its original or modern meaning, with the intent of the relevant provision, and/or with the expectations of the broader political community. In the main, the Ghanaian Supreme Court has done much to expand the Constitution's reach through its interpretation of the Bill of Rights, but, Mensa-Bonsu argues, it has overstepped the boundaries of its power in three cases since 1992. In these instances, the Court 'let itself be lured into the trap of believing it is entitled to "do the right thing"'.

In *Agyei-Twum v AG*,[2] the Court required that, before the President could set up a committee to investigate a petition for the removal of the Chief Justice, he had to be 'satisfied that there is a *prima facie* case', even though the text of article 146(6) of the Constitution does not anywhere mention this as a requirement for the committee's appointment. In *Ransford France (No 3)*,[3] the Court changed a mandatory obligation under section 47 of Constitution into a discretionary one. In *Occupy Ghana v Auditor-General*,[4] it did the reverse: it interpreted a discretionary power as mandatory, finding the original meaning 'impracticable' and insisting that a crucial 'may' should rather be read as 'shall' and treated as mandatory. As Mensa-Bonsu points out, the Court admitted what the plain meaning of the Constitution was, 'but then boldly declared that it knew better and was going to overrule it on this occasion'. Such cases were, on the whole, rare, and Mensa-Bonsu shows how in general the Supreme Court has resisted the temptation to rewrite the Constitution.
She concludes that: 'The borders of judicial authority need to be patrolled vigilantly lest, under the guise of "constitutional interpretation", courts engage in judicial adventurism and in the process make a mockery of the constitutional supremacy without which efforts to advance constitutionalism will yield little reward'.
As a consequence, she argues, academics have a public duty to scrutinize judgments and ring the alarm whenever courts exceed their role in interpreting the constitution.

Similar arguments are raised with regard to several judgments by the South African Constitutional Court. In Chapter 8, 'Time to Reduce Judicial Adventurism: Reflections on *Glenister II* and *Sonke Gender Justice* through the Lens of the Separation of Powers and Proposals for Reform', Lauren Kohn sketches out how, in responding to an overwhelming wave of corruption, the Constitutional Court sought to 'do the right thing'. *Glenister v President of the Republic of South Africa*[5] challenged legislation that disbanded the corruption-busting unit, the Scorpions (then housed within the semi-independent National Prosecuting Authority), and replaced it with the Hawks (located inside the South African Police Service). Despite the lack of any specific provision in the 1996 Constitution for there to be an 'independent' investigative unit focusing on corruption, the Court adduced the existence of an obligation for such a unit from a blend of background rights, a principle of accountability, and international law in general. It therefore ruled that the Act of Parliament which did away with the Scorpions was unconstitutional and gave Parliament a two-year period in which to fix the Act.

Building on this judgment, the next challenge to emerge concerned the Judicial Inspectorate for Correctional Service's lack of independence. Again, although correctional services are not even mentioned in the Constitution, the Court—in *Sonke Gender Justice NPC v President of the Republic of South Africa*[6]—invalidated sections of the Correctional Services Act, 1998, for failing to ensure an adequate level of independence for the Inspectorate. It based the reading-in of this constitutional principle with reference

[2] *Frank Agyei-Twum v Attorney-General* (2006) JELR 68390 (SC).
[3] *Ransford France (No 3) v Electoral Commission & Attorney-General* [2012] 1 SCGLR 705.
[4] *Occupy Ghana v Auditor-General* (J1 19 of 2016) [2017] GHASC 24.
[5] 2011 (3) SA 347 (CC).
[6] 2021 (3) BCLR 269 (CC).

to prisoners' rights as provided in the Constitution. The majority in both judgments found that the statutory structure in question offended an implied obligation in section 7(2) of Constitution: the state's duty to respect, protect, promote, and fulfil the listed rights, and therefore to create independent oversight entities to tackle corruption and protect the rights of incarcerated persons.

While these outcomes were widely welcomed by the public, Kohn argues that the judgments fundamentally undermined the very basis of the Constitution in the separation of powers and, therefore, constitutionalism itself. She concludes the chapter by arguing that, rather than continuing the practice of judicial tinkering with the Constitution, it would be better to create and insert an express provision for combating corruption. She hence proposes that section 10 (containing the right to dignity) be amended to give expression to a right of freedom from fear that the state does not serve its citizens, coupled with an assurance of a state free of state capture and corruption and committed to the tenets of integrity and accountability.

In Kenya, the charge of judicial adventurism was levelled against the High Court and Court of Appeal for their decisions in reviewing the constitutionality of the Constitution of Kenya Amendment Bill of 2020. At issue was the question of whether the courts could apply 'the basic structure doctrine' in their reading of the Constitution of 2010. In Chapter 9, 'The Basic Structure Doctrine and the Politics of Constitutional Change in Kenya: A Case of Judicial Adventurism?', Migai Akech evaluates the application of this doctrine by the two courts and also by the Supreme Court in its response to them. The basic structure doctrine posits that a constitution contains core principles that are either stated explicitly or are inferable by a court. In the latter case, the court asserts the power to read in implied limitations on Parliament's amendment power. These limitations are thus, in effect, judicially created eternity clauses (discussed in Chapters 5 and 6), as first developed by the Supreme Court of India with respect to the federal nature of that country. The power to read in such limitations is controversial, as it raises the question of the proper role of courts in a constitutional democracy.

In Kenya, to give effect to the Building Bridges Initiative (BBI), the central government introduced the Amendment Bill of 2020. This would result in far-reaching changes to the executive (including the introduction of the office of a prime minister). The Constitution prescribes different ways in which amendments can be adopted (among other things, these concern instances when voters can propose an amendment, and when a referendum is necessary). The High Court and the Court of Appeal held that the basic structure doctrine was part of Kenyan law, and they thus invalidated the Amendment Bill. This was not on the grounds that the bill was adopted contrary to the prescribed amendment procedures, but that it violated the basic structure doctrine, which, in Kenya, required that the people's voice should be heard through a referendum. The Supreme Court, in *Attorney-General & 2 others v David Ndii & others*,[7] adopted a restrained approach. This appreciated that courts should limit their role to applying the Constitution and invalidate constitutional amendments only when they are enacted through processes that do not adhere to the Constitution's provisions. In the specific case, the Court invalidated the Amendment Bill because the government initiated the amendment procedure which was open only to the

[7] *Attorney General & 2 others v Ndii & others*, Supreme Court Petition No 12 of 2021 as consolidated with Petitions Nos 11 and 13 of 2021.

voters to use, securing one million voter signatures; the amendment process was thus fundamentally flawed.

Akech also analyses how the three courts dealt with the question of public participation in constitutional amendment initiatives. He criticizes the Kenyan Supreme Court's test of the adequacy of public participation for being unclear, and argues that it could be used 'to frustrate participatory constitutional amendment processes or approve amendment processes that are not sufficiently participatory, depending on the inclination of the judges'. In either event, it would allow courts to inappropriately approve or decline amendments to the Constitution.

6. Case studies: Profiles of constitutional change

The case studies look at the different formal and informal modes of constitutional changes in particular countries, and seek to understand how these changes may impact on the promotion of constitutionalism, good governance, and respect for the rule of law.

Nigeria is a country with many sectional fault lines. The main one is that between the predominantly Muslim north and the predominantly Christian south, but this is itself complicated by the existence of three major ethnic groups (Muslim Hausa-Fulani, Christian Igbo, and the religiously bi-communal Yoruba). In addition, there are hundreds of smaller ethnic communities. In Chapter 10, 'A Divided Quest for a More Perfect Union: Ethno-regionalism, Recurrent Constitutional Alterations, and the Failure of Institutional Change in Nigeria's Fourth Republic', Rotimi T Suberu explores how these divisions can be addressed within the current constitutional framework for constitutional change. The key constitutional reform issues involve fiscal decentralization, subnational policing, local government, the very idea of political restructuring, and the procedures for constitutional amendment.

Suberu points out that the Fourth Republic (from 1999 to the present) has seen successive cycles of constitutional amendment, but none of these have dealt with the deep cleavages bedevilling Nigeria because of the absence of a broad-based national consensus on the need for comprehensive political change. The 'alterations' (or constitutional amendments) focused largely on a narrower set of exigent or emerging administrative, political, and electoral concerns. The fourth cycle of alterations, in 2017, were broader in scope and included setting two-term limits for chief political executives at national and state levels. A fifth cycle of changes, in 2023, included amendments that transferred railways, correctional services (prisons), and national grid electricity generation, transmission, and distribution away from the exclusive list of federal legislative powers to the concurrent list of powers shared by the federal and state governments. These amendments were criticized for not addressing the fundamental issues above, and for continuing to centralize powers at the federal level.

North–south cleavages and ethno-regional contestations are evident in many ways. There are, in the first place, the fiscal federalism issues of oil revenue allocation, the control of value added tax (VAT), and the proposal for a National Water Resources Bill, which would have a centralizing effect. Second, calls are being made for devolving policing powers to states in the face of a single national police force and its failure to curb crime. Third, north–south tensions also play out with regard to the questions of whether local governments should be organized uniformly across the federation; whether they should be funded primarily by federally collected oil and other revenues from the Federation Account; whether they should have their boundaries and names listed in the federal constitution; and whether they should be designated and recognized as the third order of Nigeria's federal system. Fourth, at a fundamental level, there remains the question of the redesign of the basic structure and foundations of Nigeria's federal constitutional architecture, with calls from the south urging a more decentralized federation.

Suberu makes the point that the official procedures for altering the Constitution (which require supermajorities in the National Assembly, ratification by two-thirds of state assemblies, and the assent of the President) make fundamental change very difficult, as any such change goes against the vested interests of those elected to the relevant legislative bodies. Moreover, given the solid majorities the north enjoys in national and subnational legislatures, 'current constitutional amendment rules seem inherently skewed towards preserving northern primacy and prerogatives'. However, Suberu remains convinced that it is possible to reach a national consensus on the need for the fundamental changes that could stabilize the country.

Ethiopia is, like Nigeria, a federation in need of change if it is to address its underlying political, economic, and social fragility. Unlike Nigeria, though, Ethiopia has not formally amended its Constitution since its adoption in 1995. However, federal governance has not followed the letter of the law, given that changes to the Constitution have been achieved through various devices and stratagems. In Chapter 11, 'Constitutional Adaptation and Change in Ethiopia', Assefa Fiseha examines how, although the Constitution has never been formally amended, significant changes to it have been made through policy design, the decisions of political organs, and interpretation.

Fiseha points out that the Ethiopian Constitution has a rigid procedure for constitutional amendment. The provisions prescribing the procedure for amendment, as well as those governing fundamental rights and freedoms, may be amended only if approved by a majority vote in all the states and by a two-thirds majority vote in each of the federal houses. Other provisions, including those governing the relationship between the federal and state governments, can be amended only if approved by a two-thirds majority vote in a joint session of both federal houses and also by a simple majority vote of the legislative councils of two-thirds of the states. Although this appears to set the bar high for any amendment, in reality the complete dominance of the ruling party—the Ethiopian People's Revolutionary Democratic Front (EPRDF), which morphed into the Prosperity Party in 2019—at federal and state levels has made amendment more than possible.

Two amendments have been made—one related to a concurrent taxing power, and the other to the number of constituent units in the Ethiopian federation—but they were incomplete, as they were never formally proclaimed or published in the government gazette; nevertheless, the government has regarded them as binding. Thus, despite the formation of two new states, the Constitution counts only nine: no formal attempt has been made to add the two to the 'official' list of states.

This refusal to follow the rules, Fiseha argues, has set the tone for ignoring the letter of the Constitution in other matters as well. When the federal government sought to postpone the federal and state elections scheduled for October 2020 and extend the terms of the legislatures in view of the Covid-19 pandemic, the House of Federation, the second chamber of the federal parliament and final interpreter of the Constitution, endorsed the decision despite the clear time limit of five years set in the Constitution. As the House of

Federation is, too, controlled by the ruling party, the political bias was evident to all, and this event was one of the triggers for the outbreak of civil war with Tigray. Over time, state self-government has been hollowed out by central party rule and, following the ascension of Abiy Ahmed as prime minister in 2018, centralization has been driven more by the needs of authoritarian leadership than the party apparatus itself.

Fiseha thus concludes that, in Ethiopia, ideology, party structure, and personal rule have effectually displaced the provisions of the Constitution. While constitutional review is one avenue for checking the validity of amendments, this has not applied in Ethiopia, as the interpreter—the House of Federation—is aligned with the power-holders.

While the two previous chapters focus on the institutional difficulties and constraints involved in amending constitutions—the role of legislatures and political parties—Chapter 12, 'Citizens' Collective Action, Constitutional Changes, and Constitutionalism: Lessons from the Building Bridges Initiative in Kenya', is concerned with how voters can act as a brake on retrogressive constitutional initiatives by institutional actors. Marystella A Simiyu and Trésor Muhindo Makunya discuss the attempts to amend the 2010 Constitution of Kenya and the impact of collective (voter) action on opportunistic constitutional changes. This chapter also examines the Amendment Bill of 2019, which sought to change executive structures so as to give effect to the BBI, previously discussed by Migai Akech in Chapter 9. However, whereas Akech's analysis focuses on the 'basic structure doctrine', Chapter 12 is concerned with the role that civil society groups, citizens, and social movements played in opposing the bill.

Popular referenda have played a key role in the adoption of constitutions in Kenya. Voters rejected the mangled version of the Bomas Draft (the Wako Draft) in 2005, while confirming the harmonized draft of the 2010 Constitution. Overall, as Simiyu and Makunya observe, '[t]he 2010 Constitution was the product of a nearly two-decades-long pro-democracy and constitutional reform movement, one spearheaded by civil society, including non-governmental organizations (NGOs), lawyers, religious groups, and various politicians.'

The chapter examines the historical events that characterized Kenya's constitution-making process and shaped the Kenyan culture of resistance to opportunistic constitutional amendments. It further analyses the potential force of extra-institutional mobilization and collective action through institutional channels. The chapter concludes by noting that, while amending a constitution is a natural democratic process, the will of the people must be given primary consideration to ensure that amendments do not undermine the principles of constitutionalism.

The Malawian Constitution of 1994 has also undergone several amendments which followed prescribed amendment procedures. In Chapter 13, 'Craving Stability, Flirting with Change: Understanding Constitutional Amendment in Malawi Since 1994', Mwiza Jo Nkhata analyses both these amendments as well as those effected informally by the courts. The amendments have ranged from the technical to the substantive, and Nkhata examines their impact on democracy, constitutionalism, and the rule of law in Malawi.

The Constitution of the Republic of Malawi (1994) reintroduced multiparty democracy and sought to entrench the basic principles of constitutionalism after years of one-party rule. It prescribes two procedures for amendment. The first deals with so-called 'unscheduled' provisions, allowing the National Assembly to amend these by a two-thirds majority. For listed previsions (so-called 'scheduled' provisions), two possibilities exist: the first requires the support of the voters in a referendum before the National Assembly may pass the amendment with a simple majority. With the second, the amendment may be adopted without a referendum, but the procedure then requires a two-thirds majority in the National Assembly and includes the proviso that the Speaker certifies that the amendment 'would not affect the substance or effect of the Constitution'. The scheduled provisions cover human rights and the fundamentals of the organization of the state, including the legislature, the executive, and the judiciary. As Nkhata notes, there is 'no hard and fast delineation of provisions whose amendment may affect the substance and effect of the Constitution'.

In the past 29 years, fifteen amendment Acts have been passed, affecting at least 139 provisions. Nkhata points out that a substantial number of these were made necessary by the need to correct textual error and prevent ambiguity, as well as to improve the text. However, he argues, political expedience and opportunism have been key factors in the push for substantive amendments of a kind which did not advance democracy or constitutionalism: calls for the abolition of the Senate, the deletion of the recall provision, and the failed attempt to delete the two-term limit on the presidency.

Outside of Parliament, Nkhata contends, several main actors are also engaged in pushing for constitutional amendments. One significant force is the Malawi Supreme Court of Appeal, whose interpretations of the constitutional text amount to informal amendments to it. Civil society organizations likewise play an important role in the debate on proposed amendments, perhaps most notably with the abortive amendment to rescind presidential term limits. The Malawi Law Commission, too, has had an active engagement with constitutional change processes. Then, overall, political parties play a crucial role through their participation in Parliament. Whether or not their influence is beneficial for democracy and constitutionalism depends above all, argues Nkhata, on their commitment to intra-party democracy.

The final case study examines the important issue of constitution-building in conflict situations. Rania Hussein Khafaga, in Chapter 14, 'The Complex Path of Constitution-making in Conflict-ridden States: A Case Study of Libya', examines how the Libyan experience contributes to the growing literature on how, in unstable environments, constitution-building is related to broader political processes. This is of particular significance because constitution-building in conflict-ridden countries is aimed at addressing the very issues that gave rise to the conflicts in the first place.

Since the popular uprising that ousted Muammar Qaddafi in 2011, the country has been in a prolonged transitional stage. There is, as yet, no constitution in place that could work to unite the three warring factions (the eastern region of Cyrenaica, the western region of Tripoli, and the south-western region of Fezzan) under a single form of government. After the fall of Qaddafi, the self-proclaimed National Transitional Council (NTC) issued an Interim Constitutional Declaration (ICD). This was intended to set the scene for the entire transitional and constitution-making process. According to the Declaration, an elected interim transitional legislature, the General National Congress (GNC), would choose a constitution-drafting body (Constituent Assembly) to prepare a draft of the constitution within 60 days for approval by the GNC. This would then be put before a popular referendum.

This road map was amended in 2013 to make the Constituent Assembly a body elected by direct popular vote, giving equal weight to the three regions regardless of the size of their respective populations. By 2017, a draft was eventually approved by the Constituent

Assembly with the required two-thirds majority. It was then referred to the House of Representatives to be subjected to a referendum; six years later, this has yet to occur.

Khafaga attributes this failure to several factors. First, citizens' participation in the drafting was limited despite the Constituent Assembly's attempts to promote public engagement, and this has meant very low levels of public awareness and concern. Second, the ICD, as the steering document for the constitution-making, was bitterly contested and could not provide a firm foundation for the constitution-making process. Its many amendments (thirteen to date) and unrealistic time frames (none of which have been adhered to) have undermined the legitimacy of the whole process. Third, the role of international actors in Libya's constitutional process has not always been helpful. Most of the technical support for the process came from the United Nations (UN) and its agencies, as part of the UN Support Mission in Libya (UNSMIL). However, UN support for the ICD constitutional process declined when, following the Libyan National Dialogue Forum, support for 'alternative constitutional frameworks' emerged. Finally, the biggest challenge to the constitutional process was its isolation from the broader political settlement.

Khafaga contends that the Constituent Assembly was, in the end, reduced to a mere technical body, which deprived the draft constitution of much-needed political support. At the heart of the nexus between the political processes and constitution-making, she argues, is the sequence of elections and constitution-making. In Libya, the two main political factions are yet to agree on which comes first.

In Chapter 15, Charles M. Fombad observes that, after some respite (due to the surge of constitutional reforms since the 1990s), Africa is again experiencing a wave of frequent and capricious constitutional tampering. This is enabling the re-emergence of the kind of repressive and autocratic regimes that dominated the continent in the 1960s. He points out that the chapters in this volume seek to provide insight, from the perspective of comparative constitutional change, into what has been happening in Africa since the introduction of provisions to regulate and prevent arbitrary constitutional changes. Together, the chapters aim to promote serious rethinking and creative ways to avert this scourge.

In the light of the experiences of the last three decades (and as discussed in the different chapters), Fombad suggests that changing constitutions in a manner that promotes and sustains constitutionalism, democracy, and good governance will require at least two crucial measures.

The first is a more consensual approach to changing constitutions, and the second is that the AU and RECs take a proactive stance with regard to the changing of constitutions by African governments. According to Fombad, it is high time to go beyond constraints on constitutional change that rely solely on checks such as: supermajority approvals in parliament; referenda; the unamendability of certain provisions, concepts, or principles; and judicial oversight. Individually or in combination, these measures have not proved successful in stopping determined political opportunists from altering constitutions in ways that are not necessarily for the good of the country affected.

How might a more consensual approach to changing constitutions work? One important factor would be promoting the role of ordinary citizens in the process; another would be to adopt the emerging idea of setting national consensus as the standard for constitutional change.

Given that abusive changes to post-1990 African constitutions have created the potential for the revival of government by military coup, Fombad argues, too, that the AU and RECs need to intervene more proactively and decisively. There is a growing need to develop uniform standards for amending or writing new constitutions (as mandated by the African Charter on Democracy, Elections and Governance); to popularize these; and to encourage states not only to adopt them, but also to put in place effective monitoring and enforcement mechanisms.

All in all, the main lesson that can be drawn from the studies in this volume is that, while ordinary citizens should do more to guard against abusive constitutional changes, they need unequivocal support from all the promoters of supranational constitutionalism, particularly the AU and its RECs.

PART 1
GENERAL OVERVIEW

1

An Overview of the Legal Framework for Amending Modern African Constitutions

Charles M. Fombad

1. Introduction

The question of constitutional amendment lies at the very heart of constitutional theory and practice. In fact, modern constitutionalism entails, as one of its core elements, the need to regulate and control the manner in which constitutions are amended.[1] Constitutions are bound to obsolesce and need to be regularly updated. An effective and efficient mechanism for regulating constitutional amendments is imperative in order to avoid the twin dangers of extra-legal or revolutionary methods of change, on the one hand, and frequent, hasty, abusive, and opportunistic changes, on the other.[2] Frequent constitutional amendments not only lead to political instability but also often cast doubt on the commitment to constitutionalism, democracy, and respect for the rule of law.

In the last three decades, diverse measures have been adopted to regulate the manner in which African constitutions can be amended and thereby prevent the frequent and abusive changes to constitutions that had been a regular feature of pre-1990 African constitutional practice. The approach adopted by the different countries has been influenced substantially by the two dominant constitutional traditions inherited from the colonial period. The common law approach, based on the British Westminster system, with elements of the US system, and adjusted to the realities of a unitary or federal system, was adopted in almost all anglophone African countries. By contrast, the civilian system, based largely on the French Fifth Republic model, was adopted in most of francophone Africa, with a slight variation of it being adopted in lusophone and hispanophone Africa.

The purpose of this chapter is to provide a general overview of the legal framework laid down by the different African countries for checking against reckless and abusive constitutional changes. Although the focus of the analysis is on the constitutional text,[3] references are also made to case law. The critical question is whether these amendment procedures provide a credible framework for ensuring that the inevitable changes that constitutions

[1] It is a fundamental principle of constitutionalism that a constitution should not be vulnerable to arbitrary changes at the whim of transient majorities and/or unscrupulous politicians. For a discussion of constitutionalism and its core elements, see Charles M Fombad, 'Challenges to Constitutionalism and Constitutional Rights in Africa and the Enabling Role of Political Parties: Lessons Perspectives from Southern Africa' (2007) 55(1) American Journal of Comparative Law 1–46.

[2] See Charles M Fombad, 'Limits on the Power to Amend Constitutions: Recent Trends in Africa and their Potential Impact on Constitutionalism' (2007) 6 University of Botswana Law Journal 27.

[3] Each constitution that is cited will have two dates: the first one is the year that the constitution was adopted, while the second indicates the year of the last amended text used.

Charles M. Fombad, *An Overview of the Legal Framework for Amending Modern African Constitutions* In: *Constitutional Change and Constitutionalism in Africa*. Edited by: Charles M. Fombad and Nico Steytler, Oxford University Press. © Charles M. Fombad 2025.
DOI: 10.1093/9780198957034.003.0003

undergo are made in a manner that ensures orderly change and political stability and act as a legitimate foundation for promoting constitutionalism. Do they ensure that amendments are based on, influenced by, and are reflective of the sovereign will of the people—that they are an expression of their fears, common desires, hopes, and aspirations, rather than self-serving changes that promote and protect the interests of opportunistic elites?

The discussion proceeds in section 2 with a brief examination of the way that constitutional amendment is conceptualized. At issue here is whether the authority to amend a constitution includes the authority to enact a new one. Section 3 examines the different methods of amendment, both formal and informal. The limitations that African constitutions provide for amending their provisions are discussed in section 4. Section 5 examines the main actors in constitutional amendment: actors whose participation is essential for legitimizing the process. Section 6 reviews the ways in which compliance with the constitutional amendment requirements is ensured. The chapter ends with concluding remarks in section 7.

2. Conceptualizing constitutional amendment

African constitutions regulating changes to their provisions use a variety of terms, such as 'amendment', 'alteration', 'revision', 'modification', and in many cases, especially in anglophone Africa, a combination of these.[4] Some even use terms such as 'repeal'[5] and 'review and reform'.[6] There is no consensus in the literature about the use of these terms.[7] For example, Albert Sturm makes a distinction between major and minor constitutional changes, calling the former 'revisions' and the latter 'amendments'.[8] Lutz, for his part, uses 'amendment' to refer to the formal process of constitutional modification, and reserves the use of 'alteration' for those amendment processes done through the legislature or judiciary.[9] Others, such as Walter Murphy, have argued that amending a constitution means correcting or improving it, not deconstructing, reconstructing, or replacing and abandoning the fundamental principles of the constitution.[10] Similar views had been expressed much earlier by the German

[4] Most constitutions in the francophone countries use the term 'revision': eg art 264 of the Constitution of Burundi (2005/2018); art 151 of the Constitution of Central African Republic (2004/2016); art 226 of the Constitution of Chad (1996/2018); art 177 of the Constitution of Côte d'Ivoire (2000/2016); and art 116 of the Constitution of Gabon (1991/2018). Most of the constitutions of anglophone countries contain provisions which, in the interpretation section, define constitutional amendment to include all or some of the terms, such as 'alteration', 'modification', and 'revision'. Examples of these are s 89 of the Constitution of Botswana (1966/2021); s 250 of the Constitution of Eswatini (2005); s 226(9) of the Constitution of the Gambia (1997/2018); s 47(5) of the Constitution of Mauritius (1968/2016); s 108(6) of the Constitution of Sierra Leone (1991/2013); s 98(2) of the Constitution of Tanzania (1977/2005); and s 79(5) of the Constitution of Zambia (1991/2016).

[5] See Constitution of Namibia (1990/2014) art 132.

[6] See Constitution of Equatorial Guinea (1991/2012), art 133.

[7] For a discussion of some of the intricate issues this has given rise to, see Yaniv Roznai, 'Neocracy or Democracy? Assessing Objections to Constitutional Unamendability: Unamendability in Constitutional Democracies' in Richard Albert and Bertil Emrah Oder (eds.), *An Unamendable Constitution? Unamendability in Constitutional Democracies* (Springer 2018) 51–53.

[8] Albert Sturm, *Thirty Years of State Constitution-Making: 1938–1968* (National Municipal League 1970) 29–31. See also Richard Albert, 'How Unwritten Constitutional Norms Change Written Constitutions' (2015) 38(2) Dublin University Law Journal 387–417, where he points out that some constitutional states expressly distinguish between small-scale changes and larger-scale ones, with the former referred to as amendments and the latter as revisions.

[9] Donald Lutz, 'Toward a Theory of Constitutional Amendment' (1994) 88(2) American Political Science Association 355–70.

[10] Walter Murphy, 'Merlin's Memory: The Past and Future Imperfect of Once and Future Polity' in Sanford Levinson (ed.), *Responding to Imperfection: The Theory and Practice of Constitutional Amendment* (Princeton University Press 1995) 163, 177.

constitutional scholar Carl Schmitt, who argued that a distinction must be made between constitutional amendment, constitutional annihilation, and constitutional elimination.[11]

Another leading expert in this area, Richard Albert, has tried to make the distinction between constitutional amendment and what he refers to as constitutional dismemberment.[12] His argument carried the day in the Kenyan Court of Appeal but was rejected, at least in the context of the 2010 Constitution of Kenya, by the Supreme Court in the famous *Attorney General & 2 Others v David Ndi & others* case,[13] popularly referred to as the *Building Bridges Initiative (BBI)* case. In the light of the above, what can we say is the position under the current African constitutions and the practice so far?

First, although most francophone constitutions use the term 'revision' and most anglophone constitutions use a combination of the other terms, the trend, context, and practice appear to suggest that these terms are used interchangeably with no clear intention to suggest that the use of one or the other, or using them in different combinations, indicates the extent and scope of the changes contemplated. Secondly, very few constitutions appear to indicate the extent of the changes contemplated or even explicitly suggest the possibility of a wholesale revision of the whole constitution. The only example of this appears to be in the 2012 Constitution of Somalia. Its article 79(1) states that, 'in accordance with this Constitution, draft legislation consists of the proposal of a draft law, including: (a) Reviewing, *replacing*, and proposing amendments to the Constitution' (emphasis added).[14]

In at least one case, decided by the Constitutional Court of Niger in 2009, the Court was of the view that authorities cannot use the provisions provided for amending the constitution to change the whole constitution completely.[15] The main reason for this conclusion was that the constitution contained an unamendable provision (article 136), which meant that the principles covered by this provision could not be changed.[16] Be that as it may, while it may be difficult to base any of the replacements or substantial changes to most African constitutions that took place after the 1990s on the amendment provisions, it is clear that the manner in which these provisions were formulated did not necessarily exclude the possibility of wholesale revision of the constitutions.[17] After all, as Yaniv Roznai rightly points

[11] For further discussion, see Ulrich Preuss, 'The Implications of "Eternity Clauses": The German Experience' (2011) 44(3) Israel Law Review 438–39.

[12] Richard Albert, 'Constitutional Amendment and Dismemberment' 2018 43(1) Yale Journal of International Law 1–84.

[13] *The Attorney General & 2 Others v David Ndii & 79 Others* (2021) Petition No 12 of 2021 (Consolidated with Petitions Nos 11 & 13 of 2021). For the Court of Appeal decision, see *Independent Electoral Boundaries Commission (IEBC) v David Ndii and 82 Others* (2020) (Constitution Petition No E282 of 2020 as Consolidated with Constitutional Petition Nos 397 of 2020, E400 of 2020, E401 of 2020, E402 of 2020, E416 of 2020, E426 of 2020 & E2 of 2021).

[14] The Constitution of Namibia (1990/2014), in art 132, deals with 'repeal and amendment of the constitution'. Any impression that the drafters intended 'repeal' to be interpreted as meaning wholesale change as opposed to 'amendments' is dispelled by the fact that the several clauses that follow this refer to 'repeal and/or amendment' of provisions in the constitution and not of the constitution itself. See also the Constitution of Uganda (1995/2017), which in art 258 refers to amendments 'by way of addition, variation or repeal'.

[15] See Avis No 02/CC of 25 May 2009.

[16] The question whether an unamendable provision can ever be replaced raises other issues which are dealt with later; however, for a fuller discussion see eg Yaniv Roznai, 'Towards a Theory of Unamendability' (24 February 2015) NYU School of Law, Public Law Research Paper No 15–12 http://dx.doi.org/10.2139/ssrn.2569292 accessed 20 July 2022.

[17] In fact, Hanna Lerner and David Landau, 'Introduction to Comparative Constitution Making' in David Landau and Hanna Lerner (eds.), *Comparative Constitution Making* (Edward Elgar 2019) 2, have argued that the complete changing of an existing constitutional order by a new one happens, by and large, outside of the existing legal order, as few constitutions contain provisions that allow for their replacement.

out, an amendment of a single provision can be considered revolutionary, while revising an entire constitution could still maintain its basic principles.[18] It can be argued, thus, that the present wording of the amendment provisions in African constitutions should be no obstacle to rewriting the constitutions. What is certainly germane is the legitimacy of the changes made.

It can therefore be postulated that, when examining the process and substance of changes to a constitution, regardless of whether these were substantial or slight, the crux of the matter and their validity turns on their legitimacy. From this perspective, the process and outcome of a constitutional amendment exercise must be legitimate in at least three fundamental senses; that is, they must have legal legitimacy, political legitimacy, and moral legitimacy.[19] Legal legitimacy requires that the changes adopted must be in accordance with the existing constitutional and other legal rules, principles, and norms. Political legitimacy requires that they must reflect the general will through the national ownership of the people and be adopted through their sovereign act. Moral legitimacy means that they must reflect the shared values, desires, and hopes of the people and deal with any problems of societal reconciliation and forgiveness necessitated by prolonged conflict, victimization, and social exclusion within the society. The discussion that follows looks at the extent to which the present framework for changing African constitutions provides scope for the manifestation of these three crucial elements of constitutional legitimacy.

3. Methods of amending African constitutions

There are basically two ways in which a constitution can be amended: formally or informally. This section examines the nature and scope of both forms in African constitutional practice.

3.1 Formal methods of constitutional amendment

Formal constitutional amendments refer to those changes that are carried out in accordance with the text of the constitution. Written constitutions usually entrench rules that clearly indicate which political actors will be involved in the amendment process, the formal rules that must be complied with, and such other details that are needed to ensure that both the process and the outcome are legitimate. The method chosen always reflects the degree of commitment to popular sovereignty. For instance, an amendment process through a legislature dominated by a single party with no involvement by citizens carries less legitimacy than one conducted through a parliament with strong opposition parties and involving the full participation of the people in a referendum.

The design of the formal amendment provisions has to balance two important imperatives: flexibility and rigidity. This requires balancing, on the one hand, the need for

[18] Roznai (n 7) 53.

[19] See Winluck Wahiu, 'A Practical Guide to Constitution Building: An Introduction' in Markus Böckenförde, Nora Hedling, and Winluck Wahiu (eds.), *A Practical Guide to Constitution Building* (International IDEA 2011) 2.6.

a process that is not too complicated and protracted and thus capable of ensuring that any changes necessary to improve the governance system in place and adjust it to contemporary political, economic, and social imperatives can be effected timeously, and, on the other, a process that is not too easy and has sufficient safeguards to prevent it from being abused by politicians to advance their self-interested political agendas in disregard of the interests of the people. This entails not just putting into place the different institutions and bodies that will be involved in the process but also building in checks against abuse, such as the nature of qualified majorities required to approve decisions, multiple levels of decision-making, time delays, referendums, and combinations of these and other factors. It is a balance that must facilitate the adoption of necessary reforms while ensuring constitutional certainty and predictability.

A review of the approaches entrenched in African constitutions indicates that there are at least four such approaches. The first are normal amendment procedures provided for in every constitution; the second are special amendment procedures provided for amending certain provisions; the third are time-specified amendments provisions provided for in certain constitutions; and the fourth consist of extraordinary amendment procedures that are also provided for only in certain constitutions.

3.1.1 Normal constitutional amendment procedures

Almost all constitutions, especially in the civilian jurisdictions, provide a standard procedure for amending the constitution. As a result of the special status of the constitution as the supreme law of the land, the procedures are often more rigorous than those provided for enacting or amending ordinary legislation. The normal constitutional amendment procedures in all constitutions specify the main political actors and institutions that will be involved in the process, the timelines for processing the changes, and the special legislative majorities needed to approve the constitution. In most francophone and other civil law jurisdictions, the legislative majority required to approve the amendments to the constitutions ranges from a two-thirds to a three- or four-fifths majority in one or both houses of parliament.[20] In some cases it is provided that, in addition to this, or where this supermajority is not attained, the amendments may be put to the people for approval in a referendum.[21] In federal or quasi-federal states such as Ethiopia, Nigeria, and South Africa, there is an additional requirement that there should be an affirmative vote of a two-thirds or three-fifths majority from all the component parts of the state.[22] Referendums are used with the goal of ensuring that the people are involved in the process, but for the most part this aim is hardly ever achieved because, like elections, they are frequently manipulated to obtain the outcome the government favours, and in many cases voter apathy ensures a low turnout. Two comments will suffice here.[23]

[20] For example, in the Constitution of Algeria (2010/2021), art 230 requires a three-quarters majority in both chambers of Parliament; under art 233 of the Constitution of Angola (2010/2021), a two-thirds majority is required. Other examples include art 286 of the Constitution of Burundi (2005/2018); art 63 of the Constitution of Cameroon (1996/2008); and art 151–53 of the Constitution of Central African Republic (2004/2016).

[21] For example, in the Constitution of Benin (1990/2019), art 155 provides that where the two-thirds majority is not attained, the amendment will need to be approved in a referendum. Similar provisions appear in art 226 of the Constitution of Chad (1996/2018), art 218 of Constitution of DR Congo (2005/2011), art 133 of the Constitution of Equatorial Guinea (1991/2012), and art 303 of the Constitution of Mozambique (2004/2018).

[22] See Constitution of Ethiopia (1994), art 105; Constitution of Nigeria (1999/2017), s 9; Constitution of South Africa (1996/2013), s 74.

[23] For instances where the referendum has turned into a farce, see Fombad (n 2) 55–56.

First, as explained above, referendums have become ineffective in facilitating an inclusive and participatory process. Although many countries in anglophone Africa have, with limited success, constitutionally entrenched certain measures to ensure that the people's will is actually reflected in referendum outcomes, hardly any such measures have been undertaken in francophone Africa.[24] Second, the laudable objective of supermajority rules is to serve as proxies for cross-party approval and preclude fleeting political majorities from easily altering the constitutional framework to suit their convenience. However, at times these supermajority rules have proven ineffective, the most common example being where incumbent presidents use their dominance to amend or replace constitutions to extend their terms.[25] Apart from a few reasonably democratic countries such as Botswana and South Africa, where the opposition has resisted being co-opted or bribed into approving changes to the constitution, the situation in most states in Africa is that their parliaments have been induced into approving opportunistic constitutional changes by self-seeking politicians.[26]

3.1.2 Special constitutional amendment procedures

For purposes of constitutional amendment, a number of constitutions, almost all in anglophone countries, divide the provisions in the constitution into two categories in following what may be referred to as a dualist approach. They make a distinction between ordinary constitutional amendment procedures, which are reserved for certain specified provisions, and special amendment procedures, which are also reserved for another series of specified provisions. Amendment of this second category of provisions entails more stringent procedural requirements than those specified for the former category of provisions—this underscores the importance of these latter provisions for sustaining the integrity of the constitutional order. Some of the constitutions make the difference clear. For example, in the Constitution of Eswatini (2005), the former are referred to as entrenched provisions and the latter as specially entrenched provisions.[27] Similarly, the Constitution of Ghana (1992/2013) distinguishes between non-entrenched and specially entrenched provisions.[28]

Other constitutions only distinguish between the two categories by specifying which provisions will be amended by one or the other amendment procedure.[29] The problem this could raise is the question of what would happen if the proposed amendments were to cut across the two categories; that is, which amendment procedure would be adopted—the less

[24] A rare example in francophone Africa appears in the Constitution of the Seychelles (1993/1996), where an article provides that approval of an amendment bill is achieved only when 60 per cent of the votes cast are in favour of the change. By contrast, in the Constitution of The Gambia (1997/2018), s 226 requires at least a 50% turnout of registered voters and a 75% approval. Under art 289 of the Constitution of Ghana (1992/1996), the voter turnout must be at least 40% of registered voters and there must be at least a 75% majority vote.

[25] See Julia Grauvogel and Charlotte Heyl, 'The Study of Term Limits in Sub-Saharan Africa: Lessons on Democratisation and Autocratisation' (2021) 55(3) Africa Spectrum 215–27.

[26] For example, in Uganda, President Yoweri Museveni 'openly bribed members of parliament, [and] blackmailed and intimidated others to amend the constitution and remove term limits'. See National Intelligence Council (NIC), *Democratization in Africa: What Progress Toward Institutionalization?* (NIC 2008).

[27] See s 247 for the former and s 246 for the latter.

[28] See arts 291 and 290, respectively.

[29] See the Constitution of Botswana (1996/2021), which distinguishes between the procedure for provisions spelt out in s 89(3) and those in s 89(4); in the Constitution of Malawi (1994/2017), it is between those in s 197 and those in s 196; for the Constitution of Mauritius (1968/2016), it is between those in s 47(2) and in s 47(3); for the Constitution of Tanzania (1977/2005), it is between those in art 98(1)(b) and in art 98(1)(b); for the Constitution of Uganda (1995/2017), it is for those in arts 258 and 259; and finally, for the Constitution of Zambia (1991/2016), it is between the provisions in art 79(2) and those in art 79(3) and (4).

or more stringent procedure? This might pose a real challenge where extensive amendments are contemplated but only a few of them involve provisions covered by the more rigorous amendment procedure. Perhaps one of the most advanced forms of this dualist approach is provided for in the Constitution of Kenya (2010), which actually provides three distinct amendment procedures for amending three specified sets of provisions.[30]

On the whole, the special constitutional amendment procedures appear to cover certain constitutional principles and values that the constitutional drafters feel deserve special protection. In all these cases, unlike in the previous category, a protracted process with strict timelines is specified. This provides for broad consultation designed to prevent hasty changes and ensure that the people are aware of the proposed changes and can contribute meaningfully to the process.

3.1.3 Time-specified constitutional amendments

While most constitutional amendments are undertaken as the need arises to adjust and adapt the constitution to contemporary realities, some constitutions state that their provisions may be reviewed after a specified period. This is usually in addition to the ordinary authority to amend the constitution. For example, under the Constitution of Angola (2010/2021), Parliament may, according to article 235(1), review the constitution five years after it came into force or five years after the last ordinary revision. Similar powers are given to Parliament under articles 151(2) of the Constitution of Sao Tomé and Príncipé (1975/2003).

By contrast, the Constitution of Mozambique (2004/2018), in article 301, prohibits any amendment to be undertaken within five years after it came into force unless Parliament decides to invoke its extraordinary amendment powers to do so. A more specific aspect of the constitution is covered by the time-specified amendment procedure in the Constitution of Nigeria (1999/2017). Although the latter allows the Independent National Electoral Commission (INEC) to review, and if necessary alter, the division of states and of the federation into senatorial districts and federal constituencies as the need arises, it is, however, mandatory for it to do so at intervals of not less than ten years.

In spite of the differences in wording, the idea behind these temporal limits on constitutional changes is to ensure some degree of certainty and predictability.

3.1.4 Extraordinary constitutional amendment procedures

Some constitutions provide for extraordinary amendment intervention in certain circumstances. For example, in the case of the Constitution of Mozambique (2004/2018), as noted earlier, the special amendment procedure can be used only five years after the constitution came into force. Nevertheless, article 301 allows Parliament to invoke its extraordinary amending powers through a majority of three-quarters of votes in favour, in cases of amendments to be undertaken during the first five years after the constitution came into force. Similarly, article 235(2) of the Constitution of Angola (2010/2021) authorizes Parliament to invoke its extraordinary revision powers to overcome the temporal limits on constitutional

[30] These are provided for in arts 255–57. The three distinct processes cover: (i) an amendment by Parliament with a special majority; (ii) an amendment by Parliament subject to approval at a national referendum; and (iii) an amendment by popular initiative subject to approval at a national referendum. See further Migai Akech, in Chapter 9 of this volume.

amendments with a two-thirds majority vote in favour of this. Under the Constitution of Cabo Verde (1992/2010), article 286(2) allows Parliament to assume extraordinary revision powers at any time if four-fifths of its members vote in favour of it.

As in the case of temporal limitations, extraordinary amendment procedures are designed to provide a degree of flexibility and overcome any constraints that may have been imposed by reliance on the ordinary or special amendment procedures.

3.2 Informal methods of constitutional amendments

The formal constitutional amendment rules and processes discussed above offer, at best, an incomplete picture of all the rules that regulate constitutional amendments.[31] Besides these formal rules, there are a variety of informal constitutional changes that may take place during the operation of the constitution as a result of the activities of the different political actors and institutional bodies. However, the critical point to note is that the resulting changes generally leave the constitutional text unchanged and still politically valid.

Such informal amendments occur for a variety of reasons. For example, it may be that the processes provided for formal amendments are too cumbersome and lead to a search for faster and more convenient alternative means of introducing desirable changes. It may also be that this is the best way to achieve a much-needed compromise. Regardless of the reasons for such informal non-textual constitutional amendments, the main forms that are discussed in this overview are the following:

- Informal amendments resulting from judicial interpretation of the constitution.
- Informal amendments resulting from unwritten understandings and conventions.
- Informal amendments resulting from inaction and neglect.
- informal amendments resulting from executive or legislative action.

It is important to note that the different types of informal amendments, depending on the country and its constitutional context, do not always have the same impact and effect.

3.2.1 Informal amendment through judicial interpretation

Constitutions never really contain any provisions that empower courts to formally amend their provisions when interpreting the constitution in their inherent role as defenders of constitutionalism and the rule of law. Nevertheless, the decisions of courts, specifically apex courts or courts with exclusive and final decisions on constitutional matters, may result in an indirect amendment of the constitution. This is because, unlike lower courts, only the apex courts or those with exclusive authority to interpret the constitution can make final and binding decisions when interpreting the constitution.

The judicial role is particularly important because many provisions in constitutions are couched in vague language, given the need to accommodate the demands of as many diverse interest groups as possible during the constitution-making process. As a result, where the court has to choose between two actual or potentially conflicting positions, the choice

[31] See Richard Albert, 'Constitutional Amendment by Constitutional Desuetude' (2014) 62 American Journal of Comparative Law 641–43.

of one or the other may result in an interpretation that expands or restricts the meaning of a doctrine, principle, or concept and, in this indirect manner, amends the constitution. Constitutional designers are mindful of this, and in many jurisdictions, especially in anglophone Africa, courts are usually given broader, more flexible powers when interpreting the constitution than when interpreting ordinary legislation. This may form the basis either for a liberal, progressive, and activist approach to constitutional interpretation, which may lead to judicial tinkering with, and hence amendment of, the constitution, or for a conservative approach that involves a literal interpretation of the constitution.

The broad formulation of judicial powers, as indicated above, is commonplace in the constitutions of anglophone countries.[32] For example, the cue for what one commentator describes as the basis for 'judicial activism of a special type' under the Constitution of South African (1996/2013) is found in section 39.[33] It appears to do no more than require the South African judge, 'when interpreting' the Constitution, to do what judges should normally do when interpreting a constitution; that is, give effect to its values. This is not necessarily synonymous with judicial activism; nevertheless, it does make it easier than not for a judge to adopt an activist stance. In a number of cases decided since 1996 where the judges can be said to have adopted an activist approach, they invoked expressions, such as 'constitutional values' and 'the spirit, purport and objects of the Bill of Rights', which appear in section 39 of the Constitution.

This has, however, served only as a starting point, for as most of these cases show, the judges often try to adapt the law in a manner that will reflect the changing mores of society. The activist approach has been more pronounced in certain areas of the law than others.[34] The best South African example of judicial amendment occurred early in the life of the Constitutional Court, in the case of *S v Makwanyane*,[35] dealing with the highly sensitive issue of the death penalty, which the apartheid regime had used in seeking to destroy resistance to its inhumane system. The sensitivity of the matter was only compounded by the fact that, while the African National Congress party had long adopted an abolitionist stance on the matter, it came at a time of rising crime. The Constituent Assembly that negotiated the Constitution and the South African Law Commission had been unable to agree on the matter and had agreed to leave it, in the words of the latter, to the 'Solomonic' wisdom of the courts.[36]

The Court, after reviewing the legislative history of the drafting of the Constitution and relying primarily on the prohibition of cruel, inhuman, and degrading treatment and punishment, as well as on the rights to human dignity and equality, concluded that the death penalty did not have a place in the legal system of a democratic South Africa. Thus, in spite of

[32] For a general discussion, see Charles M Fombad, 'An Overview of Contemporary Models of Constitutional Review in Africa' in Charles M Fombad (ed.), *Constitutional Adjudication in Africa* (OUP 2017) 17–50; Charles M Fombad, 'The Struggle to Defend the Independence of the Judiciary in Africa' in Shimon Shetreet, Hiram Chodosh, and Eric Helland (eds.), *Challenged Justice: In Pursuit of Judicial Independence* (Brill Nijhoff 2021) 223–48.

[33] See Hugh Corder, 'Judicial Activism of a Special Type: South Africa's Top Courts Since 1994' in Brice Dickson (ed.), *Judicial Activism in Common Law Supreme Courts* (OUP 2007) 323–62.

[34] See generally Craig Scott and Philip Alston, 'Adjudicating Constitutional Priorities in a Transitional Context: A Comment on *Soobramoney*'s Legacy and *Grootboom*'s Promise' (2000) 16 South African Journal on Human Rights 206–268; Dennis Davis, 'Socio-Economic Rights in South Africa: The Record after Ten Years' (2004) 2 New Zealand Journal of Public and International Law 47; and, for perhaps the most comprehensive account of this, Corder (n 33).

[35] 1995 (3) SA 391 (CC).

[36] See Project 58, *Group and Human Rights Interim Report* (1991) 277.

the absence of a provision expressly mandating this, the Constitutional Court outlawed the death penalty. A similarly activist interpretation was adopted by the Benin Constitutional Court in Decision DCC 06-07 of 8 July 2006. In rejecting a proposed amendment to the Constitution, the Court held, inter alia, that it did not reflect national consensus, declaring this to be a principle of constitutional status even though no such principle was expressly or implicitly incorporated into the 1990 Benin Constitution.

On a number of occasions, judicial amendment of the constitution has been indirect and carried out in blatant disregard of the basic principles of constitutionalism and the rule of law, in what is clearly judicial overreach in its extreme form. This has been a common feature of many of the decisions by the constitutional courts in francophone and other civil law jurisdictions, mainly because of the narrow scope of the jurisdiction conferred on these courts and the excessive control exercised over them by the executive.[37] A number of examples will suffice.

A manifestly dubious interpretation of the Burundi Constitution by the Constitutional Court in 2015 enabled President Nkurunziza to run for a third term as president, in spite of the fact that article 97 states clearly that no one 'can serve more than two consecutive terms'.[38] In 2015, the Constitutional Court of the Republic of Congo gave the go-ahead for a referendum to approve a new constitution that removed the unamendable presidential term limit contained in article 185 of the 2002 Constitution.[39] In the Democratic Republic of the Congo, the Constitutional Court agreed to postpone presidential elections, which in effect eventually extended the president's second mandate by two years.[40] This was so in spite of the fact that article 220 of the 2005 Constitution prohibits any amendment to the number and duration of the terms of the President of the Republic. However, perhaps the most egregious abuse of judicial powers is Decision No. 219/CC of 14 November 2018 delivered by the Constitutional Court of Gabon. In it, the Court held that article 13 of the Constitution contained a lacuna that should be filled by adding another subparagraph; it then proceeded to provide the text of the amendment.[41] This was a decision made to resolve the dilemma posed by the protracted hospitalization overseas of President Ali Bongo Ondimba.

The effect of the courts' decisions in these three cases was illegal judicial amendment of the constitution that facilitated removal of provisions containing unamendable presidential term limits, as a result of which the presidential term was extended. An equally dubious decision that borders on judicial adventurism is that of the Constitutional Court of Benin, which in Decision DCC19-504 declared, inter alia, that in case of necessity, it could correct

[37] See generally Fombad (n 32).

[38] See 'Burundi Court Backs President Nkurunziza on Third-term' (*BBC*, 5 May 2015) https://www.bbc.com/news/world-africa-32588658 accessed 27 August 2023.

[39] See 'Congo Court Confirms Results of Referendum on Presidential 3rd Term' (*News24*, 5 May 2015) https://www.news24.com/news24/drc-court-confirms-results-of-referendum-on-presidential-3rd-term-20151107 accessed 20 July 2022.

[40] See Abdur Rahman Alfa Shaban, 'DRC's Constitutional Court Rules that Elections be Postponed' (*Africanews*, 17 October 2016) https://www.africanews.com/2016/10/17/drc-s-constitutional-court-rules-that-elections-be-postponed// accessed 20 July 2022.

[41] This is what the Constitutional Court added to art 13 of the Constitution: 'In case of temporary indisposition of the President of the Republic for any cause that may be, certain functions devolved to the latter, with the exception of those provided for in Articles 18, 19 and 109, first paragraph, may be exercised, according to the case, either by the Vice President of the Republic, or by the Prime Minister, under special authorization of the Constitutional Court referred to [the matter] by the Prime Minister or one-tenth of the members of the Government, each time that [it is] necessary.'

all formal and substantive errors in the Constitution. In other words, the Court claimed that it has the powers to rewrite the Constitution.

Aside from extreme positions such as those taken by the constitutional courts in Benin and Gabon, one can say that, generally, it is common for constitutional change to be brought about through judicial interpretation of provisions on fundamental rights and freedom. This is because, by their nature, these provisions are usually formulated in broad language that needs continuous elucidation and clarification by the courts. However, an important distinction needs to be made between the creation of new rights, which correctly belongs to the democratic amendment processes, and the extension of existing rights in the course of interpretation by the courts, which is legitimate. It is a distinction that may not always be easy to make but which could be seen as the difference between judicial abuse and adventurism to describe the former situation and judicial activism and pragmatism to describe the latter.

3.2.2 Informal amendment through unwritten understandings and conventions

Like informal constitutional amendment through judicial interpretation, informal amendments through unwritten understandings and conventions occur where the enforceable meaning of the constitution changes without any alterations having been made to the text. In his elaborate study of how unwritten constitutional norms change written constitutions, Richard Albert distinguishes between two types of informal constitutional change: one by incorporation and the other by repudiation.[42] According to him, informal constitutional change by incorporation arises where a new constitutional meaning emerges without a new constitutional writing. This may take two forms. The first is incorporation by void filling, which happens when a convention supplements the written constitution in situations where the subject matter of the convention is not already addressed in the constitutional text and thus fills a void in the existing text. The second form, incorporation by refinement, is where the subject matter is already addressed by the text but the convention adds to it or specifies something new about the understanding of the existing wording without creating an inconsistency with the plain meaning of the text.

The second type of informal constitutional change suggested by Richard Albert arises by way of repudiation. This is where the textually entrenched provision is undermined or replaced by a new political practice. This also has two forms. The first is repudiation by void creation, where a textually entrenched provision loses its binding quality as a result of non-use and sustained repudiation by political actors.[43] The second form, repudiation by substitution, arises where a convention creates a conflicting duty, power, obligation, or other rule effectively substituting a written constitutional provision. As some of the chapters in this book will show, not much of what happens in Africa manifests itself in the manner theorized by Richard Albert.

Besides the examples of informal constitutional changes through unwritten understandings and conventions discussed in some of the chapters in this volume, two examples will suffice.[44] The first example of how informal constitutional changes have a significant

[42] Albert (n 8) 387–417.

[43] He distinguishes this from constitutional desuetude, which he discusses in Albert (n 31) 641–86.

[44] See also Nigussie Afesha, 'The Practice of Informal Changes to the Ethiopian Constitution in the Course of Application' (2016) 10(2) Mizan Law Review 366–99.

impact on constitutional practice comes from Nigeria. This is manifested in at least three ways. One is the unwritten understanding under the 1999 Constitution of Nigeria for zoning and a rotational presidency between the north and the south after the constitutional two-term limits.[45] The other is the practice of the top positions in the major political parties being distributed according to the country's six informal geopolitical zones.[46] Although both aspects of the unwritten constitution are regularly contested,[47] especially by the very politicians who developed it, these two informal practices arguably have been crucial to the country's survival, stability, and unity.[48] Perhaps the most significant practice is the emergence of what is referred to as shariacracy, developed through a constitutional practice resulting from a dialogical interaction of societal forces in a manner that has indirectly altered the secular nature of the state. Although Nigeria has the largest Muslim population in Africa (larger than that in any of the Arab countries on the continent), section 38 of the 1999 Constitution provides for a secular state.[49] However, in October 1999, Zamfara State adopted a law introducing a sharia penal and procedure code and eleven other states followed suit. The twelve states justified the implementation of sharia law, which saw the introduction of harsh penalties such as the amputation of the right arms of thieves and the stoning to death for adultery, by citing several provisions in the Constitution itself, such as sections 2(2) and 4(7).[50] The constitutionality of shariacracy in Nigeria, especially its harsh penal sanctions, are difficult to reconcile with the provisions of the Constitution's Bill of Rights, particularly the prohibition of inhuman or degrading treatment. Nevertheless, it remains a reality of Nigeria's social, political, and constitutional life. This constitutional practice, in spite of its doubtful constitutional foundation, is another attempt to resolve and balance the country's complex and delicate intersections of regionalism (north–south), ethnicity (Hausa, Fulani, Igbo, and Yoruba), and religion (Christianity and Islam)—all critical issues that have defined the country's political and constitutional development and evolution since independence.[51]

[45] See Austyn Ogannah, 'Northern Leaders Should Support Power Rotation to South' (*The Will*, 11 August 2022) https://thewillnigeria.com/news/northern-leaders-should-support-power-rotation-to-south/ accessed 20 July 2022.

[46] The Nigerian federation comprises 36 states, including its Federal Capital Territory, Abuja. The states are grouped in six geopolitical zones: the North Central (NC), North East (NE), North West (NW), South West (SW), South East (SE), and South South (SS).

[47] See eg William Clowes, 'Nigerian Governors Clash over North-South Presidency Rotation' (*Bloomberg*, 28 September 2021) https://www.bloomberg.com/news/articles/2021-09-28/nigerian-governors-clash-over-north-south-presidency-rotation accessed 20 July 2022.

[48] Olayemi Oladele, 'An Assessment of Rotational Presidency as a Mechanism for Political Stability in Nigeria's Fourth Republic' (Master's thesis, University of KwaZulu-Natal 2018).

[49] It provides, inter alia, that neither the federal nor the state governments shall establish a state religion, and prohibits discrimination on religious grounds. It provides for freedom of thought, conscience, and religion, including the freedom to change one's religion and to manifest and propagate religion in worship, teaching, practice, and observance, provided these rights are consistent with the interests of defence, public safety, order, morality, or health, and protecting the rights of others. The Constitution also states it shall be the duty of the state to encourage interfaith marriages and to promote the formation of associations that cut across religious lines and promote national integration. It prohibits political parties that limit membership based on religion or have names that have a religious connotation. The Constitution highlights religious tolerance, among other qualities, as a distinct component of the national ethic.

[50] See Izawa Elaigwu and Habu Galadima, 'The Shadow of Sharia over Nigerian Federalism' (2003) 33 Publius: The Journal of Federalism 123; Andrew Iwobi, 'Tiptoeing through a Constitutional Minefield: The Great Sharia Controversy in Nigeria' in Joshua Castellino (ed.), *Global Minority Rights* (Routledge 2011) 54.

[51] See further Rotimi T. Suberu, 'Religion and Institutions: Federalism and the Management of Conflicts over Sharia in Nigeria' (2009) 21 Journal of International Development 547; Vincent O Nmehielle, 'Sharia Law in Northern States of Nigeria: To Implement or Not to Implement, the Constitutionality is the Question' (2004) 26 Human Rights Quarterly 730.

The other example of the unwritten understandings and conventions that operate in most African countries are those that define the relationship between the constitutionally established authorities that exercise the power of government and the traditional authorities and institutions that coexist alongside them.[52] Owing to the challenges of developing a clear and satisfactorily comprehensive constitutional framework that defines the relationship between the two—and, in particular, the powers and functions of the traditional authorities and their role in modern democratic governance—most constitutions are either silent on this or use obscure language in dealing with the matter.[53] As a result, in most African countries, traditional authorities and institutions continue to exist and operate under informal constitutional arrangements. Even where aspects of traditional institutions, such as customary law, are formally recognized in constitutions, as is the case under section 39(3) of the Constitution of South Africa (1996/2013), the full implementation of this and its alignment with modern human rights principles remain a challenge.[54]

Generally, the major problems with unwritten understandings and conventions, which are manifested in the application of Nigeria's zoning and rotational presidency conventions, are their unpredictability and the fact that, as well as engendering adverse public reaction, they are not legally enforceable obligations. By contrast, the ambivalence about, or silence on, the nature and scope of traditional institutions and traditional law does not mean that they cease to exist, but rather that they continue to operate with a degree of detachment from the supreme law of the land.

3.2.3 Informal amendment through inaction and neglect

An under-researched form of informal constitutional amendment results from executive and legislative inaction and neglect. Perhaps one of the most blatant examples of this occurred under the 1996 Constitution of Cameroon. In the face of intense internal and external pressure, the government introduced a number of key changes, including decentralization through the establishment of regional and local councils, a second chamber of Parliament, and a constitutional council with exclusive jurisdiction in adjudicating constitutional matters. Most of these changes were implemented only after about fifteen years. In other words, executive and legislative inaction and neglect resulted in the implementation of a constitution that differed from the text that was in place. As a result, for many years two constitutions were being enforced in Cameroon—the 1996 Constitution and earlier 1972 Constitution—depending on which of them suited the government's purposes at any given moment. Similar constitutional infidelity resulting in informal 'amendment' of constitutions through executive and legislative inaction and neglect is common in many countries, especially in francophone Africa.[55]

[52] For an elaborate discussion of this, see Heinz Klug, 'Constitutional Identity in the Post-Colony: The Place of Traditional Authority' in Charles M Fombad and Nico Steytler (eds.), *Constitutional Identity and Constitutionalism in Africa* (forthcoming).

[53] See Charles M Fombad, 'Regional and Continental Frameworks for Decentralisation in Africa: The African Charter on Decentralisation' in Charles M Fombad and Nico Steytler (eds.), *Decentralisation and Constitutionalism in Africa* (OUP 2019) 70–97; see also Markus Böckenförde and others, *Judicial Review Systems in West Africa: A Comparative Analysis* (International IDEA 2016) 24.

[54] See Nebo L Morudu and Charles Maimela, 'The Indigenisation of Customary Law: Creating an Indigenous Legal Pluralism within the South African Dispensation: Possible or Not?' (2021) 54(1) De Jure Law Journal 54–69; Christa Rautenbach, 'Some Comments on the Status of Customary Law in Relation to the Bill of Rights' (2003) 14 Stellenbosch Law Review 107–14.

[55] Another extreme example of this is the situation in Angola, where under the 2010 Constitution, the ruling Peoples' Movement for the Liberation of Angola refused to organize the local elections provided for under the

Many instances of informal amendment through inaction and neglect are essentially dictated by the self-centred calculations of political elites who seldom bother about what the ordinary citizens think. This form of informal change must be distinguished from what Richard Albert has described as constitutional amendment by constitutional desuetude.[56] The latter occurs when a constitutional provision loses its binding force upon political actors as a result of its conscious and sustained non-use and public repudiation by political actors.[57] Albert nevertheless makes it clear that non-use alone cannot informally amend an entrenched provision via constitutional desuetude.[58]

What is important to note is that executive and legislative inaction that leads to unconstitutional amendment may be a violation of the constitution. This is particularly so where the constitution, as is the case with section 237 of the Constitution of South Africa (1996/2013), states that 'all constitutional obligations must be performed diligently and without delay'.[59] This effectively creates a legally enforceable obligation to implement the constitution 'without delay' and thus imposes a duty on all stakeholders to enforce it and a duty on the courts to determine whether, in any given circumstances, there was a violation of this duty due to inordinate delay.

3.2.4 Informal amendment through executive and legislative action

Regardless of how elaborate or comprehensive it may seem, a constitution is only meaningful if it is implemented. As noted above, the non-implementation of constitutions is a serious problem.[60] Equally problematical is poor implementation, especially through the adoption of legislation or the taking of action that violates the constitution. Legislation or action taken in violation of the constitution results, if left uncorrected, in indirect and informal constitutional amendment.

The extent to which legislative and executive action can result in informal constitutional amendment has not been studied, but the scope for it in many francophone and other civil law jurisdictions is considerable. The defective system of constitutional adjudication in most of these jurisdictions does not give ordinary citizens the *locus standi* to approach the constitutional courts to challenge the constitutionality of any laws or other action taken by

Constitution for more than twenty years. The credible suspicion is that this is deliberate because it knows that the opposition National Union for the Total Independence of Angola (UNITA) is likely to win. This suspicion has been reinforced by a narrow 51% that the ruling party obtained under very dubious circumstances in the 2022 parliamentary elections. See further Peter Fabricius, 'UNITA Shakes the Foundations of MPLA Rule in Angola' (*ISS*, 2 September 2022) https://issafrica.org/iss-today/unita-shakes-the-foundations-of-mpla-rule-in-angola?utm_source=BenchmarkEmail&utm_campaign=ISS_Today&utm_medium=email accessed 5 September 2022. There are many similar examples in other countries. For example, although arts 157–79 of the Constitution of DR Congo (2005/2011) provide for a Constitutional Court, the members of the Court were appointed only in 2014 and the Court itself only formally inaugurated in March 2015—that is, almost ten years later. This was when it was politically expedient for the then president, Joseph Kabila, to establish the Court and appoint his sympathizers to condone the illegal extension of his mandate that was to occur shortly thereafter. In Togo, the Constitution (1992/2019) was amended in 2002 with a number of provisions that provided for a senate and decentralization, but for a long time these provisions were not implemented. The Cabo Verde Constitutional Court was provided for in art 130 of the Constitutional Act 01/1999 but was established and made operational only in 2015.

[56] Albert (n 31).

[57] See also Peter Suber, *The Paradox of Self-amendment: A Study of Logic, Law, Omnipotence, and Change* (Peter Lang International Academic Publishers 1990).

[58] Albert (n 31) 650.

[59] See also the similarly worded s 324 of the Constitution of Zimbabwe (2013/2017).

[60] See generally Charles M Fombad (ed.), *The Implementation of Modern African Constitutions: Challenges and Prospects* (Pretoria University Press 2016).

the legislature or executive, which may amount directly or indirectly to an amendment of the constitution without any formal change in the text.[61]

4. Limitations on amending African constitutions

To ward against abusive and arbitrary constitutional amendments, a number of African constitutions impose limitations and restrictions on the manner and/or scope of the exercise of amendment powers. This has been done in a variety of ways. In some constitutions, it takes the form of an explicit or implicit prohibition against amending certain provisions or constitutional principles and values, and in others it takes the form of circumstantial or temporal limitations. Some of the limitations are implied by the judiciary in the form of the basic structure doctrine.

4.1 Explicit unamendability

The most serious restrictions to constitutional amendment powers take the form of declarations that certain parts, sections, principles, and/or values of the constitution are unamendable or unalterable. With the exception of the Gambia and Namibia, these so-called eternity or perpetuity provisions appear almost only in the constitutions of francophone and other civil law countries.[62] In fact, 24 of the 55 countries in Africa (44 per cent) have constitutions which, in varying degrees of detail, contain eternity clauses protecting certain provisions or principles.[63] These clauses have generated a great deal of debate in the literature,[64] especially about their practical effectiveness in preventing frequent opportunistic and arbitrary changes to constitutions. It will suffice here to make three general observations about the trend in Africa.

First, the main principles or values usually protected by eternity provisions in these constitutions include the republican nature and form of the state; the integrity of the national territory; the secular nature of the state; the pluralist character of the state; the

[61] For a discussion of the limitations of judicial review in these francophone jurisdictions, see Charles M Fombad, 'An Overview of Contemporary Models of Constitutional Review in Africa' in Charles M Fombad (ed), *Constitutional Adjudication in Africa* (OUP 2017) 17–50.

[62] See s 17 of the Constitution of the Gambia (1997/2018); and arts 131, 132(4), and 132(5)(a) of the Constitution of Namibia (1990/2014).

[63] See art 234, Constitution of Algeria (2010/2021); art 236, Constitution of Angola (2010/2021); art 165, Constitution of Burkina Faso (2015); art 290(1) and (2), Constitution of Cabo Verde (1992/2010); art 153, Constitution of Central African Republic (2004/2016); art 178, Constitution of Côte d'Ivoire (2000/2016); art 220, Constitution of DR Congo (2005/2011); art 92, Constitution of Djibouti (1992/2010); art 130, Constitution of Equatorial Guinea (1991/2012); art 117, Constitution of Gabon (1991/2018); s 17, Constitution of the Gambia (1997/2018); art 153, Constitution of Guinea (2010/2020); art 134, Constitution of Guinea-Bissau (1984/1996); art 163, Constitution of Madagascar (1992/2010); art 118, Constitution of Mali (1992); art 99, Constitution of Mauritania (1991/2017); art 175, Constitution of Morocco (1962/2011); arts 131, 132(4), and 132(5)(a), Constitution of Namibia (1990/2014); art 240, Constitution of Republic of Congo (1992/2015); art 175, Constitution of Rwanda (2003/2015); art 154, Constitution of Sao Tome (1975/2003); art 103, Constitution of Senegal (2001/2019); art 144, Constitution of Togo (1992/2019); arts 1, 2, and 75, Constitution of Tunisia (1959/2014).

[64] See eg Andrew Friedman, 'Dead Hand Constitutionalism: The Danger of Eternity Clauses in New Democracies' (2011) 4(1) Mexican Law Review 77–96 < https://biblioteca.cejamericas.org/bitstream/handle/2015/1696/arc4-11.pdf?sequence=1&isAllowed=y > accessed 20 July 2022; Silva Suteu, *Eternity Clauses in Democratic Constitutionalism* (OUP 2021); Preuss (n 11).

independence of the judiciary; terms limits; and national sovereignty. This is probably a more flexible approach than declaring a provision unamendable, since it allows certain changes to be made as long as they do not affect the core principles or values being protected. However, concepts such as 'sovereignty', 'republicanism', 'fundamental rights', and 'secularism' are not fixed in time but evolve as society develops and reflect changing national and international needs and standards.

Given their broad and inherently dynamic nature, many of the principles and values protected by these unamendable provisions can easily be abused to limit the scope for much-needed amendments. It will thus depend on whether judicial review of constitutional amendments is allowed and, if so, how much freedom judges have to interpret the constitution in the light of changing needs. Ultimately, it must be realized that, unless the constitution provides a double protection for the unamendable provision, there is always scope for the unamendable provision itself to be amended.

One carries out such double amendment first by amending the provision that prohibits amendment and then by amending the content of the previously unamendable provision.[65] For example, article 103 of the Constitution of Senegal (2001/2019) provides a list of unamendable principles in paragraph 7. Paragraph 8 then states that the items listed in paragraph 7 'may not be made the object of a revision'. However, nothing stops article 103 itself from being replaced, which would result in the amendment of paragraph 7.[66] There are, however, a few constitutions that provide a reinforced protection of the eternity provision. An example of this is article 175 of the Constitution of Rwanda (2003/2015), which prohibits any amendment of the provision containing the eternity clause when it states that '[n]o proposal of amendment to this Article [that is, the unamendable article] is permitted.'

Secondly, there are far fewer constitutions with provisions that are declared unamendable.[67] In the case of the Constitution of Namibia, it refers to a wide range of articles but qualifies this by stating the principles that are shielded from amendment. For example, article 131 states that:

> No repeal or amendment of any of the provisions of Chapter 3 hereof, in so far as such repeal or amendment diminishes or detracts from the fundamental rights and freedoms contained and defined in that Chapter, shall be permissible under this Constitution, and no such purported repeal or amendment shall be valid or have any force or effect.

In the absence of reinforced protection through a double-amendment veto, there is nothing that will stop the constitutional provision on unamendability itself from being amended. As noted above, the constitutional courts in the Democratic Republic of Congo and the Republic of Congo did nothing when the presidents of those countries—indirectly in the former case, directly in the latter—effectively amended the eternity clause to extend their tenure, in spite of the term-limit provisions being protected by eternity clauses. Similar term-limit provisions have been ignored in other countries such as Côte d'Ivoire, Guinea, Mali, Rwanda, and Togo.

[65] See further Roznai (n 7).

[66] A similarly weakly formulated unamendable provision is art 153 of the Constitution of the Central African Republic (2004/2016).

[67] See eg arts 1 and 2 of the Constitution of Tunisia (1959/2014).

Finally, constitutional unamendability appears to create the illusion of protection against manipulation of the constitutional amendment powers. Nevertheless, it is a powerful if controversial instrument, given that it has the potential to block democratic avenues for open discussion of reform, and hence it should be used only with great care and in exceptional circumstances. It is better is to provide strict but clear rules on amendments that leave adequate time for open debate and ensure popular participation in the amendment process.

4.2 Implicit unamendability

Unamendability may also be inferred from the wording of provisions in the constitution dealing with constitutional amendment or inferred as a result of judicial interpretation by the courts. The latter is discussed below (4.4); an example of the former appears in article 64 of the Constitution of Cameroon (1996/2008), which states: 'No procedure for the amendment of the Constitution affecting the republican form, unity and territorial integrity of the State and the democratic principles which govern the Republic shall be accepted.' This is clearly a sloppy attempt at an eternity clause. Other constitutions are worded in a similar manner. For example, article 286 of the Constitution of Burundi (2005/2018) refers to 'retaining' a procedure that, inter alia, infringes on national unity and the secularity of the state.[68]

Both of these formulations raise two questions. First, is it possible that the principles that the provisions seek to protect can be violated by the 'procedure' followed during the amendment process or that the drafters meant the outcome of the process? Secondly, who is authorized to accept or not, in the Cameroonian case, or retain or not, in the Burundian situation? Similar questions of interpretation are raised by other constitutions that have such implicit unamendable provisions.[69] What, therefore, look to all intents and purposes like unamendable provisions will ultimately be proven depending on the manner in which they are interpreted by the courts. However, as we will see shortly, this in turn depends on whether the courts have been given the powers to review the constitutionality of any resulting amendments of the constitution. Where this is not the case, the decision of the amending authority on the matter is final. This means that implicit unamendability may, in principle, once again be used by the executive to block much-needed reforms.

4.3 Circumstantial or temporal limitations on amendability

Unlike with the two previous limitations, some constitutions impose circumstantial or temporal limitations that constrain the timing and duration of the constitutional amendment process. Two kinds of circumstantial or temporal limitation appear in some African constitutions. The more common type is one in which the constitution refers to certain temporal situations under which it should not be amended. The situations often referred to are times

[68] In this regard, art 286 of the Constitution of Burundi (2005/2018) states: 'No procedure of revision may be retained if it infringes the national unity, the cohesion of the Burundian People, the secularity of the State, the reconciliation, the democracy or the integrity of the territory of the Republic.'

[69] See art 227 of the Constitution of Chad (1996/2018); art 115 of the Constitution of the Comoros Islands (2001/2018); and art 178 of the Constitution of Côte d'Ivoire (2000/2016).

of war, a state of emergency, martial law, a state of siege, or periods of presidential transition.[70] In BOB No 6/94, the Burundian Constitutional Court declared Law No 1/002 of 13 January 1994, which was introduced to amend article 85(2) of the Constitution, as unconstitutional on the grounds, inter alia, that it violated the constitutional provision which prohibits any such amendment during a period of civil strife when the territorial integrity of the country is under threat. A unique and particularly significant limitation on amendment appears in the 1986 Constitution of Liberia, article 93 of which states: 'The limitation of the Presidential term of office to two terms, each of six years duration, may be subject to amendment; provided that the amendment shall not become effective during the term of office of the incumbent President.' It is surprising that such an important check on abuse of incumbency, which appears in a pre-1990 constitution, was not introduced in the post-1990 constitutions that introduced term limits.

The second form of temporal limitation consists of specific time limits designed to ensure that the constitution cannot be amended too often or too soon after its adoption. Some examples of the latter were discussed earlier with respect to the constitutions of Angola, Cabo Verde, and Mozambique. Another example of such a restriction is found in article 226 of the Constitution of Egypt (2014/2019). It provides that, if a request to amend the Constitution is rejected by the House of Representatives, the same request cannot be resubmitted for consideration before the next legislative term.

Although some of these limitations are desirable, there is the danger that the executive could use, or even declare, a state of emergency in order to block proposed reforms.

4.4 Judicially implied limitations: The 'basic structure' doctrine

Besides the limits to judicial review explicitly or implicitly spelt out in the constitution, the courts in a number of jurisdictions, mainly in anglophone countries, have been confronted with the question of whether a constitutional amendment can be reviewed and invalidated on the grounds that it violates the basic structure of the constitution.

This so-called basic structure doctrine has its origins in the famous Indian Supreme Court decision in *Kesavananda Bharati Sripadagalvaru v State of Kerala*,[71] although the issue had been raised in a number of earlier cases.[72] According to this doctrine, even in the absence of explicit limitations on constitutional amendment powers, Parliament's amendment powers are not unlimited. There are, as a result, implied constitutional limitations that render an amendment unconstitutional if it infringes, negates, or substitutes the basic structure of the constitution, regardless of whether all the formal or procedural requirements of amendment have been met. The Indian Supreme Court, in its various decisions

[70] See art 237, Constitution of Angola (2010/2021); art 165, Constitution of Burundi (2005/2018); art 6(4)(b), Constitution of Cameroon (1996/2008); art 292, Constitution of Cabo Verde (1992/2010); art. 152, Constitution of Central African Republic (2004/2016); art 2019, Constitution of DR Congo (2005/2011); art 131, Constitution of Equatorial Guinea (1991/2012); art 116, Constitution of Gabon (1991/2018); art 153, Constitution of Guinea (2010/2020); art 131, Constitution of Guinea-Bissau (1984/1996); art 163, Constitution of Madagascar (1992/2010); art 302, Constitution of Mozambique (2004/2018); art 104, Constitution of Rwanda (2003/2015); art 155, Constitution of Sao Tome and Príncipe (1975/2003); art 144, Constitution of Togo (1992/2019); art 86, Constitution of Tunisia (1959/2014).

[71] *Kesavananda Bharati Sripadagalvaru v State of Kerala*, AIR 1973 SC 1461 (India)

[72] For an overview of the stages of its evolution, see Prashant Tiwari, 'Doctrine of Basic Structure' (*iPleaders*, 24 October 2018) https://blog.ipleaders.in/doctrine-of-basic structure accessed 20 July 2022.

on the matter, has made it clear that Parliament's power of amendment could not be used to destroy the fundamental characteristics of the Constitution. Thus, the Court's position, as is laid down in a handful of its judgments, is that Parliament can amend the Constitution, but any such amendments that destroy the Constitution's 'basic structure' are invalid.

This doctrine has been invoked in several African courts, most recently in the Kenyan Supreme Court in the *BBI* case. The cases where the doctrine has been invoked in Africa fall into two categories: those where the courts referred to it only *obiter dicta*, and those where it was raised as one of the issues on which the court made a pronouncement. The feature common to both categories is that judicial pronouncements are sometimes lacking in clarity in terms of the basis and scope of the doctrine, and in terms of the consistency of their reasoning.

The only examples in the first category are a series of judgments in South Africa and one in Zambia. In two South African cases, *Premier, KwaZulu Natal v President of the Republic of South Africa*[73] and *Executive Council, Western Cape Legislature v President of the Republic of South Africa*,[74] the courts referred to the doctrine and hinted at the possibility of its application in South Africa. Nevertheless, Mahomed DP's judgment in the former case contains some equivocation in which he hints that the makers of the Constitution expressly applied their minds to which parts of the Constitution could be amended and which could not, and which procedures are to be followed, and that if these procedures were followed, then the amendment is constitutionally unassailable.[75] On the other hand, in *UDM v President of the Republic of South Africa*[76] the Constitutional Court was unwilling to consider the basic structure doctrine, stating that once an amendment has been carried out in accordance with the formal and procedural requirements of the Constitution, it cannot be challenged as an infringement of its basic structure. Cecile van Schalkwyk has argued, and correctly so too, that the Constitutional Assembly included an amendment section that was accepted by the Constitutional Court in the two *Certification*[77] judgments, a fact which indicates that there was never an intention to entrench the basic structure doctrine in South Africa.[78]

The Supreme Court of Zambia was confronted with the application of this doctrine in *Zambia Democratic Congress v Attorney General*.[79] The applicant's contention—namely that the Constitution of Zambia (Amendment) Act 18 of 1996 violated article 79 of the Constitution in that it altered or destroyed the basic structure of the Constitution—was dismissed on a number of technical and procedural grounds. Sakala JS, who delivered the Court's judgment, agreed with the trial court, which, in rejecting the applicant's main contention that the Indian basic structure doctrine applied, had presented the Zambian position on the doctrine as follows:

[73] 1996 (1) SA 769 (CC).
[74] 1995 (4) SA 877 (CC).
[75] See 1996 (1) SA 769 (CC) paras 12, 44.
[76] 2003 (1) SA 495 (CC).
[77] See *Ex parte Chairperson of the Constitutional Assembly of the Republic of South Africa: in Re certification of the Constitution of South Africa, 1996* 1996 (4) SA 744 (CC) (the *First Certification* judgment); and *Certification of the Amended Text of the Constitution of the Republic of South Africa, 1996* 1997 (2) SA 97 (CC) (the *Second Certification* judgment).
[78] See Cecile van Schalkwyk, 'The Basic Structure Doctrine: A Basis for Application in South Africa, or a Violation of the Separation of Powers?'(*LitNet*, 17 June 2015) https://www.litnet.co.za/the-basic-structure-doctrine-a-basis-for-application-in-south-africa-or-a-violation-of-the-separation-of-powers/ accessed 20 July 2022.
[79] SCZ Judgment No 37 of 1999.

> The entrenched provisions can be altered. The theory of basic structure or framework does not exist in Zambia. Until such time that the electorate decides to vote in a party into government that will effect alterations to the constitution that the applicant has in mind, the whole idea cannot be achieved under the present constitution or indeed under the 1991. The answer lies in politics rather than under the law. The court cannot dig into and delve in to that domain. It is a political question.[80]

The second category consists of cases in three countries (Tanzania, Uganda, and, most recently, Kenya) where the courts were invited to apply the doctrine. In Tanzania, the doctrine was invoked in the Court of Appeal case of *Mtikila v Attorney General*.[81] The petitioner argued that a proposed 8th Constitution (Amendment) Act of 1992, amending article 39 of the Tanzanian 1977 Constitution, was a violation of article 21(1), dealing with the citizen's right to participate in governance. The petitioner invited the Court to declare the amendment unconstitutional on the grounds that it meddled with the basic structure of the Constitution. The Court, after describing the doctrine as nebulous with no agreed-upon yardstick to determine what it means, declared that it had no place in the Tanzanian constitutional framework. In the Court's opinion, what the Constitution did was to provide safeguards rather than basic structures, and once the amendment procedure was followed, then the change was valid. In the Ugandan case of *Mabirizi & Others v the Attorney General*,[82] the Supreme Court likewise declared that the doctrine did not apply in the country. Finally, in the *BBI* case,[83] the Supreme Court of Kenya rejected the conclusions arrived at by both the High Court and the Court of Appeal that the doctrine applied under the Kenyan 2010 Constitution.

There are several reasons why one could argue that the courts in various African jurisdictions are correct in their view that importing the basic structure doctrine to Africa is nether desirable nor helpful. First, the sociopolitical context in which the Indian courts intervened to formulate the doctrine is entirely different from the situation in Africa. In the 1970s, the public perception was that the Indian legislature was ineffective, unstable, and corrupt,[84] a situation aggravated by conflicts between the executive and judiciary. As such, the Indian Supreme Court believed that intervening in the way it did was the only way to prevent the dominant Congress Party from abusing its powers to amend the constitution. Unlike the situation in India in 1973, in Africa today the ultimate decision with respect to substantial changes to many a common law constitution rests with the people via referendums, rather than with parliaments.[85]

Second, as we have seen, almost all African constitutions now clearly specify the manner in which the constitution can be amended. What is more, these constitutions already impose important limitations on the amendment of what is considered as supposedly protected by the basic structure doctrine by making them, at least in the constitutions of most

[80] Ibid. 7.
[81] See Misc Civil Cause No 10 of 2005.
[82] Consolidated Constitutional Appeal No 2 of 2018 (on file).
[83] See *IEBC v David Ndii and 82 Others* (n 13).
[84] See NR Madhava Meron, 'Basic Structure: After 30 Years' in Pran Chopra (ed.), *The Supreme Court versus the Constitution: A Challenge to Federalism* (Sage 2006) 61.
[85] These are discussed in Fombad (n 2) 27–60; Charles M Fombad, 'Some Perspectives on Durability and Change under Modern African Constitutions' (2013) 11(2) International Journal of Constitutional Law 382–413.

civil law jurisdictions, unamendable. Nothing stopped constitution-drafters from expressly or implicitly adopting this principle if they thought that it was the best way to check arbitrary constitutional changes. The maxim *expressio unius est exclusio alterius* can therefore be invoked to argue that there is no basis for implicit application of the basic structure doctrine in these modern African constitutions. The inclusion of specific procedures and processes for amending the constitution clearly means that any omissions were intentional. The words of the constitution mean what they say, and the courts invoking the notion of the spirit of the constitution, its values, and its principles, cannot elide the fact that the framers carefully considered and inserted the limitations on constitutional amendments they felt were necessary and appropriate.

One could also argue that the recourse to the basic structure doctrine based on the implicit unamendability of certain portions of the constitution is clearly contradictory and a classic example of approbating and reprobating, as it involves upholding and rejecting the constitution at one and the same time. In one breath, these courts view the constitution as so sacred that interference with its core principles and values is prohibited; in the next, they claim that the constitution's own amendment procedure must be ignored or recognized only to a limited extent. The basic structure doctrine is at best a well-settled convention or precedent and judicial practice in the Indian constitutional system. It cannot be imported and made to prevail over the clear and unambiguous language of Africa's written constitutions.

Third, invoking the basic structure doctrine ignores a number of theoretical problems. One is that each generation has, and should have, its cherished values and political principles that reflect its predicaments and preoccupations; conversely, no generation has the right to impose its own values and political principles on a later generation. Colvin de Silva captures this concern aptly:

> Constitutions are made in terms of the stage of development at which any given society or country has arrived. In terms of that stage of development it looks upon things, and for any generation of people to imagine that it can so completely project itself into infinity of the future so as to be able to decide that its own generation will constrain a future generation or generations forever within the confines of its own postulates is to make the mistake of thinking that any human collectivity is the equivalent of the divinity.[86]

It is unlikely that the framers of the new or revised African constitutions wanted to prevent future generations from repealing these constitutions. A constituent body is omnipotent only to the extent that it has no powers to destroy or limit the omnipotence of a future constituent body. In short, present and future generations should not be ruled by the 'dead hand' of their ancestors.[87]

Fourth, although the Indian doctrine may be working well for India, there is overwhelming evidence that it remains such a controversial and unpredictable legal doctrine

[86] See Fombad (n 2) 27–60, where this is cited from Nihal Jayawickrama, 'The Bill of Rights' in Raymond Wacks (ed.), *Human Rights in Hong Kong* (OUP 1992) 45.

[87] See further Michael W McConnell, 'Textualism and the Dead Hand of the Past' (1998) 60 George Washington Law Review 1127–28; Adam M Samaha, 'Dead Hand Arguments and Constitutional Interpretation' (2008) 108 Columbia Law Review 606.

that it is not rational for any African court to invoke and apply it.[88] This was not surprising because, since the *Kesavananda* case that gave rise to the doctrine, and until today, judges in India themselves have been unable to agree on the precise elements or scope of the doctrine.[89] Writing in 2006, Shankardass argued that 'there was no need to give life to an uncertain and open-ended doctrine of what might be considered the "basic structure" of the Constitution'.[90] It is also worth remembering that Ambedkar, chairman of the Drafting Committee of the Indian 1950 Constitution, maintained that the text of article 368 of the Indian Constitution, dealing with amendments, was sufficiently clear in itself and provided no basis for the basic structure doctrine.[91] Many have seen this undefined and undefinable doctrine as a 'naked usurpation of legislative function under the thin guise of interpretation'.[92] In fact, Shankardass has indicated that 'no majority judgment is available [in India, at least when he wrote in 2006] laying down the features of the Constitution that may be considered "basic"'.[93] The effect of this is that the doctrine needlessly burdens the judiciary with the difficult task of implementing the words and spirit of the constitution while trying to refrain from trespassing in the area of policymaking, which is the preserve of the legislature.

Fifth, the constitutional vagueness of the doctrine could set a precedent which is dangerous for the survival of the constitution, constitutionalism, and the rule of law. By giving unelected judges such sweeping ill-defined powers and tying the hands of the executive and legislative branches, the doctrine creates a real risk of conflict between the branches and could trigger even more serious problems. The manifestly broad and obscure scope indicated for the application of the basic structure doctrine will make it cumbersome, if not impossible, to effect the changes that are inevitably needed for enabling constitutions to address the needs of citizens.

Finally, African judges already face a huge challenge, especially from the other two branches, when acting as the last defenders of the constitution, constitutionalism, and the rule of law. They should not create the impression of being the constitution's violator. While fear of adverse perception should not in the least prevent judges from doing the right thing, the re-energized post-1990 African judiciaries should not rush to render decisions based on imported and dubious legal principles—something which is likely to provoke a backlash against the judiciary.

Given the fragility of Africa's post-authoritarian transition, its courts should focus on strategies to enhance the constitutional amendment procedures provided for in the constitution rather than taking a leap into the unknown world of India's basic structure doctrine and its imponderables. Such judicial adventurism is counterproductive to the positive strides made in many countries, such as Kenya and South Africa, to interpret the constitution in a progressive manner. There is a world of difference between judicial activism, which

[88] See eg NR Madhava Meron (n 84) and RKP Shankardass, 'Anomalies of the Doctrine', both in Pran Chopra (ed) (n 84) 59, 137, and 138. See also David Landau, 'Abusive Constitutionalism' (2013) 47(1) UC Davis Law Review 189.

[89] See the discussion of some of the Supreme Court decisions by Vivek Krishnamurthy, 'Colonial Cousins: Explaining India and Canada's Unwritten Constitutional Principles' (2009) 34 Yale Journal of International Law 228–30.

[90] See Shankardass (n 88) 140.

[91] See Meron (n 84) 61.

[92] Ibid. 63.

[93] See Shankardass (n 88) 142–43.

is necessitated by some of these transformative constitutions, and judicial adventurism, which could lead to chaos and people not knowing which organ of state to look for to stop abuse or misuse of power. Ultimately, the literature on this topic strongly suggests that there are better ways of frustrating attempts to vitiate the letter and spirit of a constitution than by resorting to the basic structure doctrine and unamendable constitutional provisions.[94]

Constitutionalism, democracy, and the rule of law in Africa today will not be advanced or served by a judicially imposed basic structure doctrine. The irony is that the courts that impose the basic structure doctrine in African constitutions fail to realize that this is a momentous change that contradicts the very desire to prevent any fundamental change to the basic structure of the constitution in a manner not provided for by the constitution—unless the courts want to make themselves an exception to this doctrine! Such changes as are necessary should be left to be carried out by the major stakeholders that are envisaged in the constitution itself.

5. Major stakeholders in the constitutional amendment process

The diversity of stakeholders that act as veto players in the constitutional amendment process—and the extent to which this process is an open, transparent one that affords an environment for frank debate and the free exchanges of ideas—is critical to the legitimacy of the outcome. In this era of 'made-in-Africa' constitutions, the key question centres around who initiated the process and to what extent all key stakeholders participated in it. Such key stakeholders must go beyond officials from the three branches of government and include civil society organizations (CSOs), non-governmental organizations (NGOs), lobbyists, and academics.

Two main observations can be made from an analysis of the legal framework for participation in the constitutional amendment process provided under African constitutions. The first is that a limited role is provided for public participation in the amendment process under most constitutions; the second is that, in a few countries, mainly in anglophone Africa, public participation has been constitutionally entrenched.

5.1 Limited public participation in the constitutional amendment process

As mentioned, the process for amending constitutions differs from country to country. In some countries, the initiative may be taken by the president of the republic or the national assembly;[95] the president of the republic and the national assembly;[96] the president of the republic concurrently with the national assembly;[97] or Parliament apparently acting alone,

[94] See Andrew Friedman, 'Dead Hand Constitutionalism' (n 64).

[95] See eg art 63, Constitution of Cameroon (1996/2008); art 226, Constitution of Egypt (2014/2019); art 133, Constitution of Equatorial Guinea (1991/2012); art 59, Constitution of Eritrea (1997); arts 161–62, Constitution of Madagascar (1992/2010); art 299, Constitution of Mozambique (2004/2018); art 175, Constitution of Rwanda (2003/2015); art 143, Constitution of Tunisia (1959/2014); and art 173, Constitution of Morocco (1962/2011).

[96] See arts 230–33, Constitution of Algeria (2010/2021); art 233, Constitution of Angola (2010/2021); and art 154, Constitution of Benin (1990/2019).

[97] See art 284, Constitution of Burundi (2005/2018); art 151, Constitution of Central African Republic (2004/2016); art 226, Constitution of Chad (1996/2018); art 113, Constitution of the Comoros Islands (2001/2018);

which is the approach in most anglophone countries.[98] In almost all these constitutions, the amendments may be adopted only when approved by a supermajority vote of two-thirds, three-fifths, or even four-fifths of Parliament, consisting of a single or two houses sitting separately or in joint session. In the case of federal or quasi-federal jurisdictions such as Ethiopia, Nigeria, and South Africa, there is an additional requirement of an affirmative vote from a qualified majority of two-thirds or three-fifths of all the component parts of the state.[99] Under some of constitutions, especially in francophone Africa, a referendum may be required where the special majority required is not attained, but in other constitutions, especially those in anglophone Africa, a referendum is mandatory for amending certain provisions in the constitution and is an additional requirement over and above the requirement of a special parliamentary majority.

A number of general observations can be made about the overall pattern that has emerged and the extent to which the different measures act as a safeguard against the contagion of hyper-amendment of constitutions.

First, the main arena for constitutional amendments is Parliament. The constitutions of most anglophone countries reserve the initiation of the amendment process almost exclusively to Parliament, unlike the situation in most civil law jurisdictions, where this is often shared with the executive. However, the reality is that, subject to what is discussed in the next section, most constitutional amendments are initiated by the executive. As a result of the dominant-party systems that have more or less replaced the pre-1990s one-party systems, parliamentary approval of amendments, in spite of the special majorities required, has often not been problematic. In some instances where ruling parties did not have the special majority to approve amendments, they did not hesitate to use money and other inducements to ensure they got the required majority.[100] The dominant position of the executive,[101] especially the president, and the subservient role of Parliament in the civil law jurisdictions have made the process of approving constitutional amendments as routine as approving ordinary legislation.[102] By contrast, in most anglophone countries, besides the special parliamentary majorities required, there are other safeguards to enhance broad participation and hence the effectiveness of the process. This includes lengthy lapses

art 177, Constitution of Côte d'Ivoire (2000/2016); art 91, Constitution of Djibouti (1992/2010); art 166, Constitution of Gabon (1991/2018); art 188, Constitution of Mali (1992); art 99, Constitution of Mauritania (1991/2017); art 240, Constitution of Congo Republic (1992/2015); art 103, Constitution of Senegal (2001/2019); and art 144, Constitution of Togo (1992/2019).

[98] See s 89, Constitution of Botswana (1966/2021); s 245, Constitution of Eswatini (2005); s 226, Constitution of the Gambia (1997/2018); s 85, Constitution of Lesotho (1993/2018); art 195, Constitution of Malawi (1994/2017); s 47(1), Constitution of Mauritius (1968/2016); art 132, Constitution of Namibia (1990/2014); art 9, Constitution of Nigeria (1999/2017); ss 108–09, Constitution of Sierra Leone (1991/2013); and s 199, Constitution of South Sudan. A few civilian jurisdictions have also adopted this approach. See eg art 286(2), Constitution of Cabo Verde (1991/2015); art 161, Constitution of Burkina Faso (1991/2015); and art 127, Constitution of Guinea–Bissau (1984/1996).

[99] See art 105, Constitution of Ethiopia (1994); s 9, Constitution of Nigeria (1999/2017); s 74, Constitution of South Africa (1996/2013).

[100] As mentioned, a blatant example of this was President Yoweri Museveni openly bribing, blackmailing, and intimidating Members of Parliament to approve an amendment removing term and age limits in the Ugandan Constitution.

[101] For a discussion of the dominant position of the president in the civilian jurisdictions in Africa, see Charles M Fombad (ed.), *Separation of Powers in African Constitutionalism* (OUP 2016).

[102] For example, the bill amending the Cameroon 1996 Constitution was introduced in Parliament only on the eve of the last day of the session.

of time varying from 30 days to six months between the three readings of bills containing amendments to the constitution and, for changes to certain core provisions, the additional requirement of a referendum.[103]

Second, the use of referendums in addition to, or as an alternative to, parliamentary approval, or even as the sole method of approving an amendment,[104] is potentially an effective means of ensuring that ordinary citizens are actively involved in the process. However, in the absence of the special safeguards that certain constitutions provide to ensure that the referendum is not rigged or that voter apathy does not keep people away, it could end up as merely a piece of theatre serving elite interests.[105] To prevent this, some constitutions impose a minimum voter turnout and approval limit for the results of such a referendum to be legally valid and binding.[106]

Third, in some jurisdictions, a number of other veto players have been added to the process. For example, under article 234(2) of the Constitution of Angola (2010/2021), the President, before assenting to the amendment bill, may request a prior review from the Constitutional Court; or, in other jurisdictions, simply request this court's opinion.[107] A number of other constitutions require that the constitutional amendment bill should be submitted to the president for assent accompanied by a certificate of compliance signed by the leaders of the houses of parliament, or in some cases the chairman of the electoral commission, to confirm compliance with the requirements for amending the constitution.[108]

The Constitution of Sierra Leone (1991/2013), in section 108(6), not only requires a certificate of compliance but goes further, to state that 'every such certificate shall be conclusive for all purposes and shall not be inquired in any court'. In other words, this effectively ousts the jurisdiction of the courts in verifying the accuracy of its content. Although some studies have shown that the likelihood that a constitution will be amended decreases with an increase in the number of veto players involved in the process,[109] it is doubtful whether a prior review from the constitutional court or verification and issuance of a certificate of compliance will add anything to the quality or legitimacy of the process. This is particularly so where this, as the Constitution of Sierra Leone does, replaces a proper judicial review of compliance of the process with the constitutional requirements. Prior review, if strictly

[103] See eg s 89(3) and (4), Constitution of Botswana (1996/2021); arts 290–91 of the Constitution of Ghana (1992/1996); arts 196–97 of the Constitution of Malawi; s 47(2) and (3) of the Constitution of Mauritius (1968/2016); art 98(1)(a) and (b) of the Constitution of Tanzania (1977/2005); and arts 79(2), (3), and (4) of the Constitution of Zambia (1991/2016).

[104] For the use of a referendum as the sole method of approving an amendment, see art 103 of the Constitution of Equatorial Guinea (1991/2012).

[105] For example, see 'Tunisia Approves New Constitution in Vote with Low Turnout' (*France24*, 26 July 2022) https://www.france24.com/en/africa/20220726-tunisian-president-hails-constitutional-referendum-set-to-boost-executive-power accessed 20 August 2022, where Tunisians approved a new constitution granting unchecked powers to the office of President Kais Saied. It was approved with 94.6% of the valid ballots cast but with only a 30.5% registered turnout. Said Benarbia, regional director of the International Commission of Jurists, told Agence-France Presse (AFP) the new constitution would 'give the president almost all powers and dismantle any check on his rule'. He added, '[t]he process was opaque and illegal, the outcome is illegitimate.'

[106] For example, s 226 of the Constitution of the Gambia (1997/2018) requires a minimum of 50% of the registered voter turnout and a 75% vote in favour of the amendment, while under the Constitution of Ghana (1992/1996) there must be a 40% turnout of registered voters and a 75% approval.

[107] See art 95, Constitution of the Central African Republic (2004/2016); art 116, Constitution of Gabon (1991/2018); and art 241, Constitution of the Republic of Congo (1992/2015).

[108] See art 262(2) of the Constitution of Uganda (1995/2017) and s 328(10)(a) and (b) of the Constitution of Zimbabwe (2013/2017).

[109] See Christian B Jensen, Michelle Kuenzi, and Jonathan-Georges Mehanna, 'Changing the Rules: Institutions, Party Systems, and the Frequency of Constitutional Amendments in Africa' (2022) Africa Spectrum 1–22.

followed, might only serve to add rigidity to the process, given that rejection or an adverse opinion by the constitutional court means that the proposal has to go back to Parliament for it to consider the views expressed by the constitutional court before sending it back to this court again for its 'approval'.

Finally, although an overwhelming majority of African constitutions end up using an amendment process very similar to that used in adopting ordinary legislation, this is particularly so in civilian jurisdictions. In contrast, most anglophone constitutions provide for a more elaborate parliamentary process: one which is protracted and ensures there is reasonable time for debate. This is designed to ensure that constitutional amendments cannot be rushed stealthily through Parliament without the people having been made aware of them and participating in the process, especially if a referendum is mandatory. Nevertheless, as we will see, a number of constitutions have set a potentially higher standard that could facilitate more meaningful popular participation.

5.2 Broad public participation in the constitutional amendment process

As noted above, most constitutions directly or indirectly limit the right to initiate constitutional reforms to either or both of the executive and the legislature; the participation of ordinary citizens in the process is often assumed rather than explicitly or implicitly provided for. However, a number of constitutions have made innovations in two important respects: first, by providing ordinary citizens with an opportunity to take the initiative for constitutional reform; and second, by constitutionally entrenching the right of ordinary citizens—and by extension CSOs and NGOs—to participate in the process.

An example of an entrenched provision for bottom-up popular constitutional amendment is article 132(3) of the Constitution of Somalia (2012), which provides that 'a petition signed by at least 40,000 citizens may initiate the amendment process'. The threshold for this is higher in the Constitution of the Democratic Republic of the Congo (2005/2011), which in article 218(4) sets the number of citizens who can initiate the process at 100,000. They can do this by way of a petition addressed to one of the two chambers of Parliament. In article 257 of the Constitution of Kenya (2010), the threshold is at least one million registered voters. Unlike the other two constitutions, the Constitution of Kenya makes it clear that the petitioners must not only be registered voters but also deliver a draft bill and the supporting signatures to the Independent Electoral and Boundaries Commission. Thereafter, the bill goes through the normal but elaborate parliamentary process for amending the constitution. In what must be considered a crucial precedent, the Kenyan Supreme Court in the *BBI* case made it clear that the executive or legislature cannot use the cover of article 257 to initiate a change to the constitution.

In spite of these important openings for enabling ordinary citizens to initiate change to constitutions, the weakness of the provisions is that they do not stipulate that the group taking the initiative should reflect the ethnic and regional diversity of the country. Although this weakness leaves the process open to abuse by either a small or large minority, it is easier for the latter than the former to force through a change that would probably not get popular approval under normal circumstances.

An equally important development is found in three other constitutions. Article 104 of the Constitution of Ethiopia (1994) provides that all proposals for constitutional amendment, when approved by Parliament, must still be 'submitted for discussion and decision to the general public and to those whom the amendment of the Constitution concerns'. It must be assumed that account must be taken of the suggestions and comments made by the general public. The same conclusion may be drawn from section 328(4) of the Constitution of Zimbabwe (2013/2017). It provides that, immediately after the Speaker of Parliament is given notice of a constitutional bill, he or she must 'invite members of the public to express their views on the proposed Bill in public meetings and through written submissions, and must convene meetings and provide facilities to enable the public to do so'.

However, it is the Constitution of South Africa (1996/2013) that contains the most elaborate measures for ensuring public participation in constitutional amendment. Section 74(5) and (6) list a number of things that must be done before a bill amending the Constitution is introduced in Parliament. The bill must comply with several requirements:

- Particulars of the proposed amendment must have been published in the national *Government Gazette* for public comment.
- The bill must be submitted to provincial legislatures for their views.
- It must be submitted to the National Council of Provinces for public debate, if the proposed amendment is not one that is required to be passed by the Council.

When the bill is introduced, the person or committee introducing it must submit written comments received from the public and provincial legislatures. Public participation is a critical aspect of lawmaking, particularly when it concerns bills dealing with the amendment of the Constitution.[110]

It must be pointed out that, in some jurisdictions where there is no explicit or implicit entrenchment of a constitutional amendment process through popular initiative or of the mandatory involvement of ordinary citizens in the process, such a bottom-up approach may well be provided for in ordinary legislation.[111] The disadvantage of such a legislative approach, though, is that it could easily be removed at the convenience of the government by using a simple parliamentary majority. The option of a bottom-up process for initiating constitutional change is crucial to the sustainability, durability, and legitimacy of a constitution. However, this requirement, as well as all the others, is meaningful only if there is an effective process for checking that the changes comply with the stipulations of the constitution.

6. Review of compliance with amendment requirements

Specifying the requirements that must be complied with when amending the constitution will be meaningless if there are no measures to ensure that these are indeed complied with, and to sanction non-compliance with a declaration of unconstitutionality. A key

[110] See Parliamentary Monitoring Group, 'Public Consultations: Constitutional Court Rulings; Constitution Thirteenth Amendment Bill [B24-2007]: briefing' https://pmg.org.za/committee-meeting/8273/ accessed 20 July 2022.

[111] In Decision No 2015 on the verification of compliance with the procedure for revising the constitution by Constitutional Law No 072-2015 of 5 November 2015, the Constitutional Court of Burkina Faso recognized the inclusion of an option of constitutional amendment by popular initiative introduced in an ordinary law.

mechanism in this regard is judicial review. While its effectiveness depends on the scope of judicial review powers allowed, some constitutions explicitly or implicitly purport to exclude judicial review, while others contemplate various forms of non-judicial review of compliance. Generally, judicial review powers will enable courts to decide whether and how the constitution may be amended, and who has the powers to amend the constitution.

6.1 The exclusion of judicial review of compliance

As was pointed out earlier, the Constitution of Sierra Leone (1991/2013) excludes judicial review of compliance with the constitutional amendment requirements once a certificate of compliance has been issued by the Speaker or Deputy Speaker of Parliament. While such exclusion of judicial review is unusual in anglophone jurisdictions, prior to the constitutional reforms of the 1990s it was the norm in most civilian jurisdictions, particularly in francophone Africa.

The trend for such exclusion can be traced back to the French Fifth Republic constitutional heritage. The first case that firmly rejected judicial review of constitutional amendment by the French Constitutional Council is Decision No 1962-20DC of 6 November 1962, where the Council stated: 'Considering that the competence of the Constitutional Council is strictly limited by the constitution ... the Constitutional Council cannot be called upon to rule on matters other than the limited number for which those texts provide.' The same conclusion has been arrived at in later judgments,[112] with the Council arguing that, since the constitutional legislator is sovereign, constitutional amendments cannot be subject to review by other bodies.

The post-1990 revised or new constitutions in francophone states introduced some changes, albeit with the exception of constitutions such as that of Benin, the approach to judicial review has not changed significantly.[113] Hence, the jurisdiction of constitutional courts is often narrowly defined in a manner that excludes matters not explicitly conferred to them. As a result, while some of the courts have followed the approach of the French Constitutional Council, others have adopted a different approach.

In a number of cases where this issue has been raised, the Constitutional Council of Senegal has consistently declared that neither the Constitution nor any organic law gives it the power to review disputes involving the constitutionality of laws amending the Constitution.[114] By contrast, the Mali Constitutional Court, in Decision No 01-128 of 11 and 12 December 2001, declared that it had the jurisdiction to review a law amending the Constitution. It argued that its jurisdiction was based on the 'other categories of law' which it has the power to review in terms of article 88 of the Constitution. The problem with this interpretation is that article 88 deals only with *other categories of laws before their promulgation into law*—in other words, only with bills amending the Constitution.

In Niger, the Constitutional Court, in its Opinion No 02/CC of 25 May 2009, did not indicate the basis on which it accepted to express an opinion. Similarly, a number of decisions

[112] See eg Decision No 92-312 of 2 September 1992 and Decision No 2003-469DC of 26 March 2003.

[113] See Fombad (n 61).

[114] See Decision No 1/C/2003 of 11 June 2003; Decision No 3/C/2005 of 18 January 2006; Decision No 2/C/2009 of 18 June 2009.

dealing with the review of compliance with constitutional requirements have been made by the Benin Constitutional Court, which until recently was probably the most respected such court in francophone Africa. However, the Court has hardly bothered to state the basis on which it accepted jurisdiction in the matters.[115] As a result of this Court's recent politicization, it was able to declare in Decision DCC 19-504 of 6 November 2019 that it had the powers to correct formal and substantive errors in the Constitution, and that on this basis it had 'corrected' the title of a law amending the Constitution. However, in Decision DCC 21-073 of March 2021, the same court declared that it had no jurisdiction to undertake an a priori or a posteriori review of a constitutional amendment law. This is probably correct but nevertheless inconsistent with its previous decisions.

The general position seems to be that, unless the contrary is explicitly or implicitly stated, the constitutional courts in francophone Africa do not have the jurisdiction to review the constitutionality of laws amending the constitution. The relevant provisions of each country's constitution must be studied before drawing any firm conclusions. Similarly, as we will see, the assumption that judicial review is allowed by other constitutions requires careful interpretation of the relevant constitutional provisions.

6.2 Judicial review of compliance with constitutional amendment requirements

Judicial review of constitutional amendments must not be confused with judicial review of ordinary legislation; they are different in principle and practice. As we have seen, in almost all countries, the procedures for amending the constitution are much stricter than those for amending ordinary legislation and typically require a qualified majority in Parliament, time delays between different readings of the constitutional amendment bill, and, sometimes, confirmation through a popular referendum. Nevertheless, the process raises two issues: the first concerns the courts that have competence to undertake such review, and the second the scope of such review.

6.2.1 Courts that have competence

Judicial review of compliance with constitutional amendment requirements can be carried out by ordinary courts, by specialized courts, and sometimes by supranational courts based on a referral or an appeal from national courts.

6.2.1.1 Ordinary courts

Under most constitutions in anglophone Africa, the ordinary courts, starting at the level of the High Court, have the jurisdiction to deal exclusively with issues regarding the interpretation of the constitution. This forms the basis for these courts' dealing with disputes relating to the validity of amendments to the constitution.[116] Nevertheless, with the decentralized

[115] See eg Decision DCC 06-074 of 8 July 2006, which declared Law No 2006-13 amending the Constitution as unconstitutional. Reflecting a similar approach, Decision DCC 19-504 of 6 November 2019 does not explain the basis of the Court's jurisdiction to deal with the matter.

[116] See arts 129–31, Constitution of Ghana (1992/1996); arts 256, 163–65, Constitution of Kenya (2010); ss 128–29, Constitution of Lesotho (1993/2018); ss 103–08, Malawi Constitution (1994/2017); arts 80–81, Constitution of Namibia (1990/2014); and ss 233, 241, and 251, Constitution of Nigeria (1999/2017).

judicial review system in some anglophone countries, the apex or constitutional court sometimes has the final word when dealing with disputes concerning the validity of constitutional amendments. For example, section 167(4)(d) of the Constitution of South Africa (1996/2013) provides that only the Constitutional Court may, inter alia, 'decide on the constitutionality of any amendment to the Constitution'. A similar approach may be inferred from the wording of the constitutions of other anglophone African constitutions.[117]

6.2.1.2 Specialized courts

With the centralized model of judicial review that applies in francophone and other civil law jurisdictions, the approach is different. As noted above, following the precedent set by the French Constitutional Council, these courts, unless explicitly or implicitly authorized to do so, do not have a general power to review the compliance of constitutional amendments with the requirements laid out for undertaking such changes. Their jurisdictional remit is not only often narrowly defined but the language used is obscure. Nevertheless, while a few constitutions limit the power of review to compliance with procedural requirements,[118] others indicate that any amendments that violate certain fundamental principles, such as the infringement of the republican nature of the state, its secular nature, and its sovereignty, are not allowed. The latter determination inevitably requires judicial intervention.[119]

6.2.1.3 Supranational bodies

In the globalized world of today, constitutional amendments are no longer solely a national and domestic issue. It is thus no surprise that the African Union (AU) and its Regional Economic Communities (RECs) have adopted a number of instruments which, in setting standards of democratic governance, sometimes impact on the process of amending national constitutions. The most important of these is the African Charter on Democracy, Elections and Governance (ACDEG) of 2007.

In spite of the weaknesses of the AU's monitoring mechanisms, article 34 of the Protocol to the African Charter on Human and Peoples' Rights on the Establishment of an African Court on Human and Peoples' Rights allows member states, on ratifying the Protocol, to sign a declaration under article 5(3). This declaration gives individuals and NGOs with observer status before the African Commission the right to institute cases directly before it in accordance with article 34(6) of the Protocol. Until recently, twelve countries had signed this declaration but four have since withdrawn.[120] The effect of signing the declaration is that the review of compliance with constitutional amendments requirements laid down in the constitution may be performed at the supranational level by the African Court on Human and Peoples' Rights (the African Court) and the African Commission on Human and Peoples' Rights (the African Commission). Such supranational review is still possible

[117] See eg art 179(1)(a), Constitution of the Gambia (1997/2018); art 137, Constitution of Uganda (1995/2017); and s 128, Constitution of Zambia (1991/2016).

[118] See eg art 154, Constitution of Burkina Faso (1991/2015); art 174, Constitution of Morocco (1962/2011); art 120, Constitution of Tunisia (1959/2014).

[119] See eg art 232, Constitution of Algeria (2010/2021); and art 157, Constitution of the Central African Republic (2004/2016).

[120] The eight countries that have signed are Burkina Faso, Malawi, Mali, Ghana, Tunisia, the Gambia, Niger, and Guinea–Bissau. The four countries that have withdrawn are Benin, Côte d'Ivoire, Tanzania, and Rwanda. See further the official website of the African Court at https://www.african-court.org/wpafc/declarations/ accessed 25 September 2022.

even where review at the national level is not provided for in the constitution or excluded altogether.[121]

Supranational review of the legality of constitutional amendments is justified at the international level. In this respect, article 27 of the 1969 Vienna Convention on the Law of Treaties reaffirms the principle that 'a party may not invoke the provisions of its internal law as justification for its failure to perform a treaty'. A number of cases or complaints raising some of these issues have come before Africa's judicial or quasi-judicial supranational jurisdictions. For example, the African Commission has ruled on the constitutional amendments to presidential eligibility rules[122] and the outlawing of political parties and removal of judicial remedies.[123] It will suffice to cite here two of several African Court cases on unconstitutional constitutional amendments concerning Benin.

In *XYZ v Republic of Benin*,[124] the African Court found that Benin had violated articles 9, 22(1), 23(1), and 26 of the African Charter on Human and Peoples' Rights (the African Charter) and article 10(2) of the ACDEG, due to the Beninese Constitution's having been amended without prior consultation with Beninese society or recourse to referendum. The Court held that, even if the amending law were approved by the Beninese Parliament and the Constitutional Court, in a democratic society all citizens must have access to state-held information in order to encourage governmental transparency and allow civilian participation in debates on the promulgation of national laws. Hence, the Court concluded that the applicant's rights to information; economic, social, and cultural development; and peace and national security under articles 9, 22(1), and 23(1), respectively, had been violated by Benin. In addition, the Court found that Benin had failed to comply with its obligations to guarantee national participation or consensus in enacting laws and the independence of national courts as per article 10(2) of the ACDEG and article 26 of the African Charter.

In the second case, *Houngue Eric Noudenhouenoa v Republic of Benin*,[125] the applicant alleged, inter alia, that a new electoral code and an amendment to the constitution violated several regional and international human rights instruments. The Court declared that the amendment had been adopted in violation of the constitutional obligation to ensure that the procedure for amendment or revision of the constitution is based on national consensus, as enshrined in article 10(2) of the ACDEG. The Court ordered Benin to take all measures to repeal the law revising the 1990 Constitution, along with all subsequent laws relating to the election pursuant to that revision, in order to guarantee that its citizens, including the applicant, could participate freely in forthcoming elections.

Declarations by supranational bodies that constitutional amendments are unconstitutional do not necessarily affect the validity of the amendments in the domestic sphere. Thus, Benin and other countries that lost important cases like these not only ignored the rulings but withdrew their declarations under the African Court's Protocol. Nevertheless, the significance of these and similar cases is that they raise the possibility of bringing peer

[121] For a discussion of the possible role of international bodies in offering some protection against abusive constitutional amendments, see Gabor Halmai, 'Judicial Review of Constitutional Amendments and New Constitutions in Comparative Perspective' (2016) 20 Wake Forest Law Review 101; Suteu (n 64) 186–87.

[122] See *Legal Resources Foundation v Zambia* ACHPR 211/98, 7 May 2001; *Mouvement Ivorien des Droits Humains (MIDH) v Côte d'Ivoire* Communication No 246/02 ACHPR 88, 29 July 2008.

[123] See *Lawyers for Human Rights v Swaziland* ACHPR 251/02, 11 May 2005.

[124] Application No 010/2020, 27 November 2020.

[125] Application No 003/2020, Judgment of 4 December 2020.

pressure to bear against abusive constitutional changes through the negative international publicity which is generated.

6.2.2 Scope of judicial review

Where judicial review of constitutional amendments is explicitly or implicitly permitted, the assumption is that this allows for a review of both the process and its outcome. However, there are constitutions that explicitly or implicitly limit judicial review of amendments either to procedural or substantive matters.[126] Even then, apart from the need for ensuring that eternity or unamendable provisions are not interfered with, it may be argued that it is illogical to undertake a review of substantive compliance without first ensuring that there was procedural compliance.[127]

6.2.2.1 Judicial review limited to procedural compliance

In the absence of an explicit or implicit stipulation to the contrary in the constitution itself, the review of the validity of a constitutional amendment must start with the determination of whether the procedural requirements laid down for the process were fully complied with. A review of challenges related to the failure to comply with procedural requirements is less likely to be controversial because its exercise hardly requires any judicial discretion. However, a number of constitutions limit judicial intervention only to a review of procedural compliance with the constitutional requirements. This may be explicitly stated. For example, article 154 of the Constitution of Burkina Faso (1991/2015) defines and limits the role of the Constitutional Council to assessing 'respect for the procedure of revision of the constitution'.[128] In a series of decisions, the Burkina Faso Constitutional Council has consistently limited its intervention to determining whether or not the procedure for amending the Constitution was followed.[129]

The powers of constitutional courts in most civilian jurisdictions are narrowly defined in a manner that excludes judicial review of the regularity of constitutional amendments, but such courts still have the powers to review any changes for conformity with the constitution in situations where the constitution contains eternity or similar provisions limiting the scope for amending the constitution. It is only through such judicial intervention that it could be conclusively settled that the changes introduced during the amendment process did not violate the restrictions imposed by the constitutions on the scope of amendment powers.

This is the only way the Malian Constitutional Council decision in MLI-2001-A-003-01-128 could be explained. In it, the Council gave two reasons for accepting jurisdiction. It relied on article 88 of the 1997 Constitution: this did not expressly give it powers to review constitutional amendments, but the Council argued that it was covered by the phrase 'other

126 The distinction between substantive (content) and procedural (process) review may not always be very easy to make. See Richard Albert, 'Constructive Unamendability in Canada and the United States' (2014) 67(2) Supreme Court Review 181.

127 See Kemal Gozler, *Judicial Review of Constitutional Amendments: A Comparative Study* (Ekin Press 2008).

128 The same is provided for in art 174 of the Constitution of Morocco (1962/2011) and art 120 of the Constitution of Tunisia (1959/2017).

129 See Decision No 2012-008/CC of 26 April 2012; Decision No 2012-009/CC of 21 May 2012; Decision No 2013-019/CC of 4 December 2013; Decision No 2015-046/CC of 13 November 2015; Decision No 2015-047/CC of 14 November 2015. The last decision raises puzzling questions because it was taken with respect to the revision of a Transitional Charter introduced when the Constitution was suspended after a *coup d'état*.

laws' that appears in the article. As we observed earlier, this strained interpretation ignores the fact that the 'other laws' refer to bills before their promulgation into law. A more convincing reason given by the Council is the argument that it had a duty to ensure that all the relevant procedural rules for amending the Constitution had been complied with. This was not so in this case: the text of the law published as an amendment to the Constitution was different from the one that Parliament had discussed and approved.

A similar approach was adopted by the Constitutional Court of Burundi when, in RCCB/40 of 18 April 1994, it declared, inter alia, that the powers conferred on it to review the constitutionality of laws implicitly also gave it the powers to review the regularity of laws amending the Constitution. This reasoning is not convincing because the special status of constitutional law does not justify its being treated in the same way as ordinary law.

The conclusion that can be drawn here is that, even where the constitution does not expressly or implicitly give the courts the power to review the law amending the constitution, courts, unless prohibited from doing so, have an inherent right to review these laws to ensure that the correct procedures were followed. In civilian jurisdictions, this basically means the constitutional courts, which normally have exclusive jurisdiction over all disputes dealing with the interpretation and application of the constitution, are required to do this. As observed above, this is a better explanation for the Malian Constitutional Council accepting jurisdiction in MLI-2001-A-003-01-127. The reasoning here is that the constitution cannot stipulate that Parliament should approve the bill amending the constitution and confer on the president the power to promulgate this into law, but when he is requested to do so, allow him to stealthily change the text and add other provisions without referring this back for parliamentary approval.

6.2.2.2 Judicial review limited to substantive compliance

Unlike judicial review of procedural regularity, the review of the substantive content of constitutional amendments raises starkly different issues and can only be premised on explicit or implicit authorization by the constitution. As pointed out earlier, while such substantive review can be assumed to be the case under the constitutions of anglophone countries, in civil law jurisdictions, with the exception of the Sierra Leone Constitution alluded to earlier, the scope for substantive review is often narrowly defined in a manner that precludes such review. A few constitutions limit judicial intervention to substantive review only. This can be inferred from a reading of articles 232 and 234 of the Constitution of Algeria (2010/2021).

Perhaps the best examples of implicit powers to review the substantive regularity of laws amending constitutions are provided by those constitutions in civilian jurisdictions that contain eternity or unamendable provisions. Regardless of the jurisdictional remit, there is an implicit power in courts to review any laws amending the constitution in these countries to determine whether these eternity or unamendable provisions have been violated. For example, in the Burkina Faso Decision No 2015-046/CC of 5 November 2015, the issue that the Constitutional Council was called upon to deal with was whether there had been compliance with the procedure for amending the Constitution. Article 154(4) of the Constitution only gave it the powers to review respect for the procedure of revising the Constitution. The Council nevertheless pointed out that it also had a duty to ensure that there had been no violation of the eternity clause contained in the Constitution.[130]

[130] A similar approach was adopted in the earlier case, Decision No 2013-019/CC of 12 November 2013.

A similar approach was adopted by the Burundi Constitutional Court in RCCB/40 of 18 April 1994.[131] In the absence of such unamendable or eternity clauses, the only other possible instance of inherent judicial review for content or substantive compliance is where the proposed amendment violates the basic structure of the constitution. However, as we have seen, this so-called basic structure doctrine has no application in the constitutional revision frameworks provided for under modern African constitutions.

As a result of what Ran Hirschl has described as the 'judicialization of politics', the reliance on courts and judicial means to enforce compliance with the legal framework provided for amending constitutions is likely to increase rather than reduce.[132] Its success will depend on the willingness and ability of these courts to stand up and protect constitutions from the frequent surreptitious assaults they are subjected to by the ruling political elites. It is the only way modern constitutionalism can counter this rising tide of 'autocratic legalism'.[133]

7. Conclusion

It is now accepted that constitutional amendment rules are essential, as they are indispensable for maintaining and sustaining constitutional democracy. In trying to counter the notorious culture of hyper-amendment of constitutions that was commonplace in Africa before the 1990s, one of the things on the minds of constitution-makers was how strike a balance between an amendment process that was rigid and one that was flexible while ensuring, overall, that the process is seen as legitimate by all political actors. Ultimately, whatever legal approach is adopted, the critical issue is whether the process is able, at best, to prevent—or, at worst, to limit—the cancer of frequent, abusive, and opportunistic alteration and manipulation of constitutions to serve the selfish interests of the political elites in a manner that undermines the prospects for constitutionalism, democracy, and good governance.

The preceding discussion has shown that, although two main methods are provided for in amending modern African constitutions, there are significant differences in approach between the two dominant constitutional cultures, namely the common law constitutional tradition in Africa's anglophone countries and the civilian constitutional tradition in its francophone, lusophone, and hispanophone countries. A number of trends are noticeable.

First, it would seem that the procedure for amending the constitution reflects the process that was used in making the constitution. While there was extensive public participation in the making of most anglophone constitutions, in most of the civilian jurisdictions, apart from Benin, the process was controlled by ruling parties and entailed little public participation.[134] It is, therefore, no surprise that the approach to constitution-making in the civilian jurisdictions is replicated in the limited role allowed for public participation in the

131 See BOB No 6/94 6–13.

132 Ran Herschl, 'The Judicialization of Politics' in Robert Goodin (ed.), *The Oxford Handbook of Political Science* (OUP 2011) 253–74.

133 Kim Scheppele, 'Autocratic Legalism' (2018) 85 University of Chicago Law Review 545.

134 See Charles M Fombad, 'Constitutional Reforms and Constitutionalism in Africa: Reflections on Some Current Challenges and Future Prospects' (2011) 59(4) Buffalo Law Review 1007–108; Coel Kirkby and Christina Murray, 'Constitution-Making in Anglophone Africa: "We the People"' in Muna Ndulo and Mamoudou Gazibo (eds.), *Growing Democracy in Africa: Elections, Accountable Governance and Political Economy* (James Currey Publishers 2016) 86–114; Pearl T Robinson, 'The National Conference Phenomenon in Francophone Africa' (1994) 36(3) Comparative Studies in Society and History 575–610.

constitutional amendment processes in most countries in these jurisdictions. An amendment made primarily by the executive and the legislature in these countries, because of the limited involvement of ordinary citizens as the primary constituents, carries less legitimacy than one made with their active involvement. While it is true that under almost all constitutions a special parliamentary majority is required to approve constitutional amendments, this is often easily achieved thanks to the power of dominant parties[135] and, where this is lacking, the use of financial inducements to woo opposition parliamentarians to vote in favour of amendments.

Perhaps the main weakness in many civilian constitutions is that recourse to a referendum is provided as an alternative to parliamentary approval. This often means that the executive can use the referendum to circumvent the parliamentary amendment procedures, especially where it is unable to obtain the requisite special parliamentary majority.[136] Given the fact that a simple majority in the referendum will suffice and, even more significantly, the fact that in many countries executives regularly and easily manipulate elections as well as referendums to ensure the outcomes they desire, procedures that depend only on the executive and legislature in the manner just discussed make it easy for frequent changes to be made to the constitution. At the end of the day, such a top-down approach to constitutional amendment is out of sync with contemporary constitution-building measures, which require continuous active involvement by citizens and civil society throughout the life of the constitution.

Second, the commendable objective of the eternity or unamendable provisions that appear in the constitutions of almost all civilian jurisdictions is to prevent the amendment of certain provisions, principles, or values considered of fundamental importance to the constitution. However, it is doubtful if this serves any useful purpose in curbing abusive constitutional changes because, as noted earlier, African governments have always found a way of ignoring such restrictions and changing the constitution. Besides this, in the struggle to establish a culture of democracy and constitutionalism, the people should be allowed the freedom to discuss and decide on the changes they want to make to the constitution, however fundamental the nature of the changes. The best way to protect fundamental principles or values is not to make them unamendable but rather to set down elaborate procedures for their amendment which ensure that changes cannot be introduced in a hasty, stealthy, and arbitrary manner without the knowledge and active involvement of the people.

Third, although not explicitly provided for in the constitutions of a number of civilian jurisdictions, substantive and procedural review of the exercise of the constitutional amendment powers is an important check against the abuse of these powers. However, courts do not necessarily have the last word on the matter. A judicial decision can still be overridden by the exercise of the primary constituent powers by the people themselves.[137]

[135] For example, in Rwanda, the Upper House of Parliament on 5 November 2015 easily approved the resolution of the Lower House, which, with the complicity of the Supreme Court, paved the way for President Kagame not only to run for a third term but also to stay in office until 2034. See Clement Uwiringiyimana, 'Rwanda's Top Court Clears Way for Kagame Third Term' (*Reuters*, 8 October 2015) https://www.reuters.com/article/us-rwanda-president-idUSKCN0S21AI20151008 accessed 20 July 2022.

[136] For examples of constitutions that provide for this, see art 63, Constitution of Cameroon (1996/2008); art 152, Constitution of Central African Republic (2004/2016); art 177, Constitution of Côte d'Ivoire; and art 116, Constitution of Gabon (1991/2018).

[137] See Max Radin, 'The Judicial Review of Statutes in Continental Europe' (1934–1935) 41(2) West Virginia Law Quarterly 112–30; Roznai (n 7) 29–61.

This will require an alert, active, and engaged civil society that is ready to assert itself, especially where the courts needlessly defer to the executive.[138]

Fourth, because amending a constitution does not usually attract as much national and international attention as writing a new one, the process can easily be used to undermine hard-earned constitutional bargains. Consequently, internal pressure by civil society needs to be reinforced by external pressure. The opportunities provided by the African Commission and African Court open new vistas for putting pressure on African governments to comply not only with their constitutional obligations but also with the duties imposed on them by the numerous AU and RECs instruments they have signed and ratified. The AU also needs to proactively engage member states to sign the declaration under the Protocol to the African Charter on Human and Peoples' Rights on the Establishment of an African Court on Human and Peoples' Rights in order to enable individuals and NGOs to approach the Court. Furthermore, it must put pressure on member states to abide by and implement the decisions and recommendations made by the African Commission and African Court, in conformity with the Constitutive Act.[139] The possibility of supranational referral to the African Commission and the African Court puts pressure on domestic courts to guard against judicial deference and overreach. It also puts peer pressure on states to respect constitutional amendment procedures.

The inevitable adjustments that need to be made to all constitutions to reflect the changing economic, social, political, and other contemporary imperatives of a dynamic modern society require free and open debate, as well as sufficient time for public involvement and engagement. It is a process which, if not carefully designed and managed, is open to abuse by politicians. Ultimately, the ability of constitutional amendment provisions to counter the cancer of high-handed and arbitrary constitutional changes will depend on how well these provisions balance processes that are rigid with those that are flexible. This may entail providing different procedures for dealing with certain categories of provisions, for example by distinguishing between ordinary provisions and entrenched provisions that need special protection. Careful thought must be given to other issues, such as the level of parliamentary majorities required at different stages of approval, the time lapse between different stages of approval, and the extent of public participation by ordinary citizens, CSOs, and NGOs.

Although the measures now entrenched in constitutions to limit abusive amendments are better than those in the pre-1990 constitutional era, they have weaknesses that are still being exploited by unscrupulous politicians. One possible way to strengthen them is to entrench a permanent constitutional review commission akin to the permanent law revision commissions that are common in anglophone African countries. If it is given the relevant powers and shielded from interference in a manner similar to the independent institutions provided for under the Kenyan, South African, and Zimbabwean constitutions, it is likely to make a significant difference.[140] This is probably the best way to enhance the prospects for legitimate constitutional renewal in a manner that is sustainable throughout the life of

[138] As was mentioned, in DR Congo, the Republic of Congo, and Rwanda, illegal changes to the constitutions were aided and abetted by executive-minded and captured apex courts.

[139] See art 23(b) of the Constitutive Act, in terms of which member states undertake to comply with the decisions and the policies of the AU and, by extension, its affiliated institutions.

[140] For a discussion of how these institutions operate, see Charles M Fombad, 'The Diffusion of South African-style Institutions? A Study of Comparative Constitutionalism' in Rosalind Dixon and Theunis Roux (eds.), *Constitutional Triumphs, Constitutional Disappointments: A Critical Assessment of the 1996 South African Constitution's Local and International Influence* (CUP 2018) 359–87.

the constitution and which limits the scope for such renewal being used to distort the constitution for narrow short-term political ends. Ultimately, the role of independent courts in the making, remaking, and unmaking of constitutions remains crucial to political stability, constitutionalism, and the rule of law in Africa.

Bibliography

Afesha N., 'The Practice of Informal Changes to the Ethiopian Constitution in the Course of Application' (2016) 10(2) Mizan Law Review 366–99

Albert R., 'Constitutional Amendment by Constitutional Desuetude' (2014) 62 American Journal of Comparative Law 641–43

Albert R., 'Constructive Unamendability in Canada and the United States' (2014) 67(2) Supreme Court Review 181.

Albert R., 'How Unwritten Constitutional Norms Change Written Constitutions' (2015) 38(2) Dublin University Law Journal 387–417

Albert R., 'Constitutional Amendment and Dismemberment' (2018) 43(1) Yale Journal of International Law 1–84

Böckenförde M. and others, *Judicial Review Systems in West Africa: A Comparative Analysis* (International IDEA 2016)

'Burundi Court Backs President Nkurunziza on Third-term' (*BBC*, 5 May 2015) https://www.bbc.com/news/world-africa-32588658 accessed August 2023

Clowes W., 'Nigerian Governors Clash over North-South Presidency Rotation' (*Bloomberg*, 28 September 2021) https://www.bloomberg.com/news/articles/2021-09-28/nigerian-governors-clash-over-north-south-presidency-rotation accessed July 2022

'Congo Court Confirms Results of Referendum on Presidential 3rd Term' (*BBC*, 5 May 2015) https://www.news24.com/news24/drc-court-confirms-results-of-referendum-on-presidential-3rd-term-20151107 accessed 20 July 2022

Corder H., 'Judicial Activism of a Special Type: South Africa's Top Courts Since 1994' in Dickson B. (ed.), *Judicial Activism in Common Law Supreme Courts* (OUP 2007) 323–62

Davis D, 'Socio-Economic Rights in South Africa: The Record after Ten Years' (2004) 2 New Zealand Journal of Public and International Law 47

Elaigwu I. and Galadima H., 'The Shadow of Sharia over Nigerian Federalism' (2003) 33 Publius: The Journal of Federalism 123

Fabricius P., 'UNITA Shakes the Foundations of MPLA Rule in Angola' (*ISS*, 2 September 2022) https://issafrica.org/iss-today/unita-shakes-the-foundations-of-mpla-rule-in-angola?utm_source=BenchmarkEmail&utm_campaign=ISS_Today&utm_medium=email accessed 5 September 2022.

Fombad C.M., 'Challenges to Constitutionalism and Constitutional Rights in Africa and the Enabling Role of Political Parties: Lessons Perspectives from Southern Africa' (2007) 55(1) American Journal of Comparative Law 1–46

Fombad C.M., 'Limits on the Power to Amend Constitutions: Recent Trends in Africa and their Potential Impact on Constitutionalism' (2007) 6 University of Botswana Law Journal 27–60

Fombad C.M., 'Constitutional Reforms and Constitutionalism in Africa: Reflections on Some Current Challenges and Future Prospects' (2011) 59(4) Buffalo Law Review 1007–108

Fombad C.M., 'Some Perspectives on Durability and Change Under Modern African Constitutions' (2013) 11(2) International Journal of Constitutional Law 382–413

Fombad C.M. (ed.), *The Implementation of Modern African Constitutions: Challenges and Prospects* (Pretoria University Press 2016)

Fombad C.M. (ed.), *Separation of Powers in African Constitutionalism* (OUP 2016)

Fombad C.M., 'An Overview of Contemporary Models of Constitutional Review in Africa' in Fombad C.M. (ed.), *Constitutional Adjudication in Africa* (OUP 2017) 17–50

Fombad C.M., 'The Diffusion of South African-style Institutions? A Study of Comparative Constitutionalism' in Dixon R. and Roux T. (eds.), *Constitutional Triumphs, Constitutional Disappointments: A Critical Assessment of the 1996 South African Constitution's Local and International Influence* (CUP 2018) 359–87

Fombad C.M., 'Regional and Continental Frameworks for Decentralisation in Africa: The African Charter on Decentralisation' in Fombad C.M. and Steytler N. (eds.), *Decentralisation and Constitutionalism in Africa* (OUP 2019) 70–97

Fombad C.M., 'The Struggle to Defend the Independence of the Judiciary in Africa' in Shetreet S., Chodosh H., and Helland E. (eds.), *Challenged Justice: In Pursuit of Judicial Independence* (Brill Nijhoff 2021) 223–48
Fombad C.M. and Steytler N. (eds.), *Constitutional Identity and Constitutionalism in Africa* (forthcoming)
Friedman A., 'Dead Hand Constitutionalism: The Danger of Eternity Clauses in New Democracies' (2011) 4(1) Mexican Law Review 77–96
Gozler K., *Judicial Review of Constitutional Amendments: A Comparative Study* (Ekin Press 2008)
Grauvogel J. and Heyl C., 'The Study of Term Limits in Sub-Saharan Africa: Lessons on Democratisation and Autocratisation' (2021) 55(3) Africa Spectrum 215–27
Halmai G., 'Judicial Review of Constitutional Amendments and New Constitutions in Comparative Perspective' (2016) 20 Wake Forest Law Review 101
Herschl R., 'The Judicialization of Politics' in Goodin R (ed.), *The Oxford Handbook of Political Science* (OUP 2011) 253–74.
Iwobi A., 'Tiptoeing through a Constitutional Minefield: The Great Sharia Controversy in Nigeria' in Castellino J (ed.), *Global Minority Rights* (Routledge 2011) 54
Jayawickrama N., 'The Bill of Rights' in Wacks R (ed.), *Human Rights in Hong Kong* (OUP 1992) 45
Jensen C.B., Kuenzi M., and Mehanna J.G., 'Changing the Rules: Institutions, Party Systems, and the Frequency of Constitutional Amendments in Africa' (2022) Africa Spectrum 1–22
Kirkby C. and Murray C., 'Constitution-Making in Anglophone Africa: "We the People"' in Ndulo M. and Gazibo M. (eds.), *Growing Democracy in Africa: Elections, Accountable Governance and Political Economy* (James Currey Publishers 2016) 86–114
Krishnamurthy V., 'Colonial Cousins: Explaining India and Canada's Unwritten Constitutional Principles' (2009) 34 Yale Journal of International Law 228–30
Landau D., 'Abusive Constitutionalism' (2013) 47(1) UC Davis Law Review 189
Lerner H. and Landau D., 'Introduction to Comparative Constitution Making' in Landau D. and Lerner H. (eds.), *Comparative Constitution Making* (Edward Elgar 2019) 2
Lutz D., 'Toward a Theory of Constitutional Amendment' (1994) 88(2) American Political Science Association 355–70
McConnell M.W., 'Textualism and the Dead Hand of the Past' (1998) 60 George Washington Law Review 1127–28
Meron N.R.M., 'Basic Structure: After 30 Years' in Chopra P. (ed.), *The Supreme Court versus the Constitution: A Challenge to Federalism* (Sage 2006)
Morudu N.L. and Maimela C., 'The Indigenisation of Customary Law: Creating an Indigenous Legal Pluralism within the South African Dispensation: Possible or Not?' (2021) 54(1) De Jure Law Journal 54–69
Murphy W.E., 'Merlin's Memory: The Past and Future Imperfect of Once and Future Polity' in Levinson S. (ed.), *Responding to Imperfection: The Theory and Practice of Constitutional Amendment* (Princeton University Press 1995) 163
National Intelligence Council, *Democratization in Africa: What Progress Toward Institutionalization?* (NIC 2008)
Nmehielle V.O., 'Sharia Law in Northern States of Nigeria to Implement or Not to Implement, the Constitutionality is the Question' (2004) 26 Human Rights Quarterly 730
Ogannah A., 'Northern Leaders Should Support Power Rotation to South' (*The Will*, 11 August 2022) https://thewillnigeria.com/news/northern-leaders-should-support-power-rotation-to-south/ accessed 20 July 2022
Oladele O., 'An Assessment of Rotational Presidency as a Mechanism for Political Stability in Nigeria's Fourth Republic' (Master's thesis, University of KwaZulu-Natal 2018)
Parliamentary Monitoring Group, 'Public Consultations: Constitutional Court Rulings; Constitution Thirteenth Amendment Bill [B24-2007]: briefing' https://pmg.org.za/committee-meeting/8273/ accessed 20 July 2022
Preuss U., 'The Implications of "Eternity Clauses": The German Experience' (2011) 44(3) Israel Law Review 438–39
Radin M., 'The Judicial Review of Statutes in Continental Europe' (1934–1935) 41(2) West Virginia Law Quarterly 112–30
Rahman A.R.A., 'DRC's Constitutional Court Rules that Elections be Postponed' (Africanews, 17 October 2016) https://www.africanews.com/2016/10/17/drc-s-constitutional-court-rules-that-elections-be-postponed// accessed 20 July 2022
Rautenbach C., 'Some Comments on the Status of Customary Law in Relation to the Bill of Rights' (2003) 14 Stellenbosch Law Review 107–14

Robinson P.T., 'The National Conference Phenomenon in Francophone Africa' (1994) 36(3) Comparative Studies in Society and History 575–610
Roznai Y., 'Towards a Theory of Unamendability' (24 February 2015) NYU School of Law, Public Law Research Paper No 15–12 http://dx.doi.org/10.2139/ssrn.2569292 accessed 20 July 2022
Roznai Y., 'Necrocracy or Democracy? Assessing Objections to Constitutional Unamendability: Unamendability in Constitutional Democracies' in Albert R. and Oder B.E. (eds.), *An Unamendable Constitution? Unamendability in Constitutional Democracies* (Springer Link 2018) 29–61
Samaha A.M., 'Dead Hand Arguments and Constitutional Interpretation' (2008) 108 Columbia Law Review 606
Scheppele K., 'Autocratic Legalism' (2018) 85 University of Chicago Law Review 545
Scott C. and Alston P., 'Adjudicating Constitutional Priorities in a Transitional Context: A Comment on *Soobramoney's* Legacy and *Grootboom's* Promise' (2000) 16 South African Journal on Human Rights 206–268
South African Law Commission, 'Project 58: Group and Human Rights Interim Report' (South African Law Commission 1991) 277
Sturm A., *Thirty Years of State Constitution-Making: 1938–1968* (National Municipal League 1970)
Suber P., *The Paradox of Self-amendment: A Study of Logic, Law, Omnipotence, and Change* (Peter Lang International Academic Publishers 1990)
Suberu R.T., 'Religion and Institutions: Federalism and the Management of Conflicts over Sharia in Nigeria' (2009) 21 Journal of International Development 547
Suteu S., *Eternity Clauses in Democratic Constitutionalism* (OUP 2021)
'Tunisia Approves New Constitution in Vote with Low Turnout' (*France24*, 7 July 2022) https://www.france24.com/en/africa/20220726-tunisian-president-hails-constitutional-referendum-set-to-boost-executive-power accessed 20 August 2022
Uwiringiyimana C., 'Rwanda's Top Court Clears Way for Kagame Third Term' (*Reuters*, 8 October 2015) https://www.reuters.com/article/us-rwanda-president-idUSKCN0S21AI20151008 accessed 20 July 2022
Van Schalkwyk C., 'The Basic Structure Doctrine: A Basis for Application in South Africa, or a Violation of the Separation of Powers?' (*LitNet*, 17 June 2015) https://www.litnet.co.za/the-basic-structure-doctrine-a-basis-for-application-in-south-africa-or-a-violation-of-the-separation-of-powers/ accessed 20 July 2022
Wahiu W., 'A Practical Guide to Constitution Building: An Introduction' in Markus, Böckenförde Nora Hedling, and Winluck Wahiu (eds.), *A Practical Guide to Constitution Building* (International IDEA 2011) 2.6

PART 2

CONSTITUTION-BUILDING, CONSTITUTION-MAKING, CONSTITUTIONAL CHANGE, AND CONSTITUTIONALISM

2

Changing Modes of Constitution-making in Africa: Do the Means Guarantee the Ends?

Heinz Klug

1. Introduction

Africa has witnessed several waves of constitution-making.[1] While an Aristotelian exploration of political systems in Africa would identify the constitutional orders of African kingdoms and societies from the pre-colonial era through to the present, the waves of constitution-making that produced the modern state in Africa are more accurately associated with the colonial encounter. If Ethiopia and its Emperor Haile Selassie stand as an example of an African constitutional order that withstood colonial aggression, it was the imposition of indirect rule by Lord Lugard and the 1922 adoption of the Clifford Constitution in Nigeria that began constituting the modern state in the non-settler colonies of Africa.[2] While constitutional developments in the settler colonies produced what Mahmood Mamdani would later identify as bifurcated states,[3] the constitutions imposed on non-settler colonies[4] also reflected the agency of Africans demanding constitutional change in the name of self-determination, led in West Africa in this period by the National Congress of British West Africa.[5] Today, with greater public participation in constitution-making—reflecting increased agency in societies throughout Africa—there is an assumption that new constitutional orders will produce more responsive and resilient forms of governance across the continent. The question, however, is whether changing modes of constitution-making that entail increased popular involvement will indeed guarantee the constitutionalism which is assumed to be the purpose of these processes.

In 2011, Funmi Abioye stated that, in part, 'the continued failure of the rule of law in Africa' can be traced 'to the foundation of the law that is in force in most African countries, the constitution'.[6] Abioye proceeded to focus on the process of constitution-making as the source of this failure, arguing that 'the constitution-making process in many African countries is devoid of popular input; devoid of consent of the society and does

[1] Gedion Timothewos Hessebon, 'The Fourth Constitution-Making Wave of Africa: Constitutions 4.0?' (2014) 28(2) Temple International & Comparative Law Journal 187–214.

[2] Kalu Ezera, *Constitutional Developments in Nigeria* (CUP 1960).

[3] Mahmood Mamdani, *Citizen and Subject: Contemporary Africa and the Legacy of Late Colonialism* (Princeton University Press 1996).

[4] Sir William Dale, 'The Making and Remaking of Commonwealth Constitutions' (1993) 43(1) International and Comparative Law Quarterly 67–83.

[5] Ezera (n 2) 26–27.

[6] Funmi T Abioye, 'Constitution-making, Legitimacy and Rule of Law: A Comparative Analysis' (2011) 44(1) Comparative and International Law Journal of Southern Africa 60.

Heinz Klug, *Changing Modes of Constitution-making in Africa: Do the Means Guarantee the Ends?* In: *Constitutional Change and Constitutionalism in Africa*. Edited by: Charles M. Fombad and Nico Steytler, Oxford University Press. © Heinz Klug 2025.
DOI: 10.1093/9780198957034.003.0004

not reflect the values of the people'.[7] Focusing on 'political and constitutional developments in Francophone Cameroon in 1959 and 1960', Nicodemus Fru Awasom argues that constitution-making 'was an important component in the nation-building project of colonialists in Africa' and that 'African elite involvement by the colonialists in constitution-building was indispensable because Africans had to assume the leadership of their countries on the attainment of independence'.[8]

In a similar vein, Sammy Adelman describes constitution-making in 'many new states of the South' since the Second World War as an 'epidemic of constitution-making' and argues that there is a 'cleavage between [the] social pluralism and rules' that reflect the pluralism of African societies and African constitutions, which 'are increasingly mere variations on a western theme and, as such, appear to encourage pluralism while producing its exact opposite'.[9] Despite Adelman's trenchant critique of external influences on processes of constitution-making and democratization in Africa and his description of faith in constitutions as 'constitutional fetishism',[10] he concludes that democratic participation is a source of state-building, even if 'the context bequeathed to those struggling for democracy in Africa leaves little room for alternatives to a liberal constitutionalism'.[11]

Adopting what Andrew Arato describes as a Kelsenian or normative approach to constitution-making,[12] this chapter will focus on the processes by which the different waves of constitutions were brought into existence in Africa over the previous century. While constitutional orders in the colonial period were usually imposed by the colonial authorities as they sought to contain and govern African communities, there was increasing African agency in the shaping and adoption of constitutions from the end of the Second World War due to decolonization and the emergence of independent African states. Although formally adopted by the British Parliament, local nationalist leaders who participated in self-government, such as Jomo Kenyatte (Kenya), Hastings Banda (Malawi), and Kenneth Kaunda (Zambia), 'had a crucial role in the shaping of the independence constitutions'.[13] Subsequent waves of constitution-making across Africa were shaped by a combination of internal political struggles and global developments, such as the Cold War, which conditioned the environment in which processes of constitution-making and state reconstruction occurred.[14]

While Abioye concludes, in his comparison of the Nigerian and South African cases, that the greater public participation witnessed in South Africa 'induces a "self-binding" commitment to the constitution and other laws of the land in the people',[15] the question which this chapter explores, through a historical overview of constitution-making in Africa, concerns the relationship between different modes of constitution-making and the sustainability of the constitutional orders produced. Is sustainability simply a product of the legitimacy

[7] Ibid.

[8] Nicodemus Fru Awasom, 'Politics and Constitution-making in Francophone Cameroon, 1959–1960' (2002) 49(4) Africa Today 3.

[9] Sammy Adelman, 'Constitutionalism, Pluralism and Democracy in Africa' (1998) 30(42) Journal of Legal Pluralism 73, 73–74.

[10] Ibid. 78.

[11] Ibid. 87.

[12] Andrew Arato, *The Adventures of the Constituent Power: Beyond Revolutions?* (CUP 2017) 3–10. Andrew Arato and Jean L Cohen, 'Civil Society, Populism and Religion' (2017) 24(3) Constellations 233–95.

[13] John Hatchard, Muna Ndulo, and Peter Slinn, *Comparative Constitutionalism and Good Governance in the Commonwealth: An Eastern and Southern African Perspective* (CUP 2004) 18.

[14] Heinz Klug, *Constituting Democracy: Law, Globalism and South Africa's Political Reconstruction* (CUP 2000).

[15] Abioye (n 6) 78.

produced by more democratic or participatory forms of constitution-making or does the resilience of a constitutional order depend on more than the legitimacy of its founding?

Each wave of constitution-making produced different processes through which constitutions were negotiated, drafted, and adopted. This chapter traces these changing forms of constitution-making to explore the factors that produced each of them, as well as the impact, if any, they have had on constitutional legitimacy and resilience. Even though the promise of increasing responsiveness to popular demands and democratic governance has characterized successive waves of constitution-making, it is important to recognize that in many cases new constitutions have failed to bring about significant change. Furthermore, the resurgence of military coups and extra-constitutional means of resolving intra-elite conflict in several countries suggests that the evolving modes of constitution-making might not be advancing the struggle for constitutionalism in Africa to the extent that constitutionalists imagine.

The hypothesis in this chapter is that greater degrees of public participation in each of these waves of constitution-making has brought greater legitimacy to both the process and product of constitution-making across Africa. If this is the case, it might be assumed that we should see increasing resilience in the lives of these constitutions and thus a strengthening of constitutionalism across the continent. While only a thorough empirical study across the more than 48 countries of sub-Saharan Africa could hope to demonstrate the validity of this hypothesis, this chapter aims to make an initial contribution by examining the evolution of forms of constitution-making using examples from several African country cases. This will enable us to explore the question of whether there is any consistent or enduring relationship between modes of constitution-making and efforts to achieve a sustainable African constitutionalism.

In his recent book in which seeks to develop a theory of African constitutionalism, Berihun Gebeye argues for a 'legal syncretic paradigm ... [that] offers us a new perspective for understanding both the past and present of African constitutionalism ... by piercing the veils of legal centralist and legal pluralist paradigms'.[16] By contrast, I argue that a shift in focus from theories of constitutionalism to the history of constitution-making highlights the significance of process and participation as sources of legitimacy. While there have been debates over the causes and nature of the different waves of constitution-making in sub-Saharan Africa, the goal of this chapter is to abstract the different forms of constitution-making in order to explore the relationship between them and any effects on constitutional resilience that they might have. The changing modes of constitution-making identified in my preliminary analysis are not specific to each of the different waves of constitution-making, but, significantly, each wave may be characterized by either the emergence of new forms of constitution-making or the predominance of a particular form within it.

2. Modes of constitution-making

Each wave of constitution-making across Africa may be categorized by the specific modes of constitution-making that predominated in each particular historical moment. At the

[16] Berihun Adugna Gebeye, *A Theory of African Constitutionalism* (OUP 2021) 243.

same time, it is important to acknowledge that both within each wave, and even within each mode of constitution-making, there are significant variations, given the diversity of African experiences. Africa is a vast and diverse continent, and any notion of a singular culture, historical trajectory, or constitutional form would be, on the face of it, a gross and unjustifiable simplification.

Even if it were possible to identify a few broad historical patterns and alternatives etched into the political landscape of Africa by the colonial experience and the nationalist struggles that saw the emergence of independent African states from 1957, these commonalities overlie vast cultural, economic, ethnic, language, and political differences. Furthermore, the emergence of postcolonial independent states spans a period of more than half a century, and while the Cold War was a common element through most of this period, it was the end of the Cold War in 1989 that allowed the decolonization of Namibia and the democratic transition from apartheid, while simultaneously fragmenting the established postcolonial order throughout Africa. The post-Cold War period has, in this context, produced a new, more autochthonous, wave of constitution-making across sub-Saharan Africa.

Reflecting on these different waves of constitution-making and the variation within them, we can identify five broad processes of constitution-making as well as a number of more specific elements within the most recent wave. First, there were the imposed pre-independence constitutions, usually written and adopted by colonial authorities. Second, there were the negotiated Independence Constitutions, which included participation by nationalist movements at the negotiating table. Third, there were the one-party state constitutions adopted by ruling parties in the post-independence and Cold War era. Fourth, in the same era, a succession of military coups across Africa led to a process of constitution-making by military regimes. Fifth, and most recently, there is the post-Cold War era of constitution-making. Within this era, constitution-making has taken a number of forms, including 'national conferences' or round-table negotiations, elected constitutional assemblies, elements of public participation, and, in a context of rising social conflict, a number of hybrid forms of constitution-making. Finally, specific cases of constitution-making often reflect a combination of these different modes.

2.1 Imposed pre-independence constitutions

The first sub-Saharan constitutions, apart from those of the settler colonies of Kenya, Rhodesia, and South Africa, were imposed by colonial authorities and, as was the case in Nigeria, often named after the responsible colonial official. For example, the 1922 Clifford Constitution refers to the then governor of Nigeria, Sir Hugh Clifford. Typical of most Crown Colonies in the British Empire, the making of the Clifford Constitution was dominated by appointed British officials, with only four of the 46-member legislative council having been elected.

In response to growing nationalism and changing conditions caused by the Second World War, a new governor, Sir Arthur Richards, made constitutional proposals in 1944 that introduced the idea of regionalism and integrated the structures of indirect rule by recognized traditional authorities into the constitutional structure of the country.[17] Nigerian

[17] Ezera (n 2).

nationalists articulated their objection to these proposals, submitting a Memorandum on the New Constitution of Nigeria in March 1945, in which they 'not only denounced the constitutional proposals as autocratic in origin but also as designed to create a false impression of providing for an unofficial majority' when in fact the 'unofficial' members of the Legislative Council 'were either chiefs ... appointed by the government, or their nominees'.[18] When a delegation of Nigerian nationalist leaders went to London in June 1947 to protest against certain features of the Richards Constitution, the Secretary of State for the Colonies 'urged the delegation to go home and give the Constitution a trial since it could not be replaced without trial'.[19]

Ignoring calls by the nationalist press for a constituent assembly, a new governor of Nigeria, Sir John Macpherson, told the legislative council in 1948 that there would be constitutional changes but 'that he was determined to avoid the charge of inadequate consultation of public opinion which had been made by his predecessor'.[20] As a result, the colonial administration created a process of consultation involving village and divisional meetings, the representatives of which attended provincial conferences culminating in a general conference that met in Ibadan in January 1950.[21]

While the provincial conferences provided representatives to attend the Ibadan General Conference, they made up only 25 of the 53 delegates. Even though all but three of the delegates were Nigerian, 25 of the non-regional conference delegates were the 'non-official'—that is, appointed—members of the legislative council.[22] As a result, 'the conservative elements and chiefs, many of whom were members of the existing Legislative Council, were able to drown the demands of the nationalist elements',[23] who were demanding 'direct elections, separate municipal constituencies, limitation on the power of the chiefs, ministers with full ministerial powers, and a strong central government'[24]—essentially, the Westminster model of government. The Nigerian nationalist leader Dr Nnamdi Azikiwe refused to participate in the Ibadan General Conference, while the chief organ of his party criticized the outcome 'for its imperialistic ingenuity which stifled the very nationalism the Richards' Constitution had succeeded in stimulating'.[25]

The effect of the 1951 Macpherson Constitution 'was the quick evolution of political party governments' in the three regions defined by the constitution.[26] However, the Constitution's failure to provide for a prime minister or leader of government business at the federal level exacerbated inter-regional friction, producing a series of regional and central constitutional crises that eventuated in another round of constitutional negotiations in London in 1953 and Lagos in 1954. This process led to the revised 1954 Lyttleton Constitution,[27] which provided for the election of a Federal House of Representatives[28] and regional self-government, matters the British insisted on as a transition to full independence.[29]

[18] Ibid. 76.
[19] Ibid. 80.
[20] Ibid. 105.
[21] Ibid. 114.
[22] Ibid. 114–15.
[23] Ibid. 127.
[24] Ibid. 129.
[25] Ibid. 128.
[26] Ibid. 136.
[27] Ibid. 200.
[28] Ibid. 214.
[29] Ibid. 228–29.

The failure of the British to accede to demands for self-government by 1956,[30] as well as continued demands for the creation of a 'federal or quasi-federal state upon a multi-regional basis',[31] produced yet another constitutional conference, in London in May and June 1957.[32] In the shadow of Ghana's independence, this conference saw the Nigerian delegates united in their demand for independence for Nigeria within the Commonwealth,[33] but it was only a year later, at the 1958 conference at Lancaster House in London, that agreement was reached for a date for independence—1 October 1960. Independence came, however, with a constitution first adopted by the British Parliament in London.

2.2 Negotiated Independence Constitutions

A wave of constitution-making came with the post-Second World War process of decolonization. As a consequence of both a changing international context—one that included the establishment of the United Nations—and the struggles of nationalist movements throughout Africa and the colonized world more generally, negotiations between colonial powers and nationalists in the colonies produced constitutions under which new nations emerged. The mode of constitution-making characteristic of these independence constitutions involved negotiations between the colonial authorities and nationalist leaders. In the case of British colonies in Africa, these negotiations most famously took place at Lancaster House in London. However, it has become clear that, while nationalist leaders regularly attempted to influence the framing of their Independence Constitutions, their most pressing concern was for independence itself, and thus they were often impelled to accept the proposals drafted by the British Foreign and Commonwealth Office so as not to delay the transfer of power.

During the process of decolonization, Lancaster House hosted many conferences between the British and the national movements claiming independence, but the most prominent Lancaster House Conferences concerning Africa were in regard to Nigeria in 1957 and 1958; Kenya in 1960, 1962, and 1963; Uganda in September and October 1961; and, finally, Zimbabwe in 1979, with the latter negotiations leading to the Lancaster House Agreement that brought independence to this country. As a mode of constitution-making, this process took the form of intra-elite negotiation based on drafts produced by 'experts' in the Colonial Office. As Basil Davidson notes, 'what the colonial powers thought wise and necessary was the formation and promotion to power of "leading elites" or "middle classes" (those whom the French have so revealingly called *interlocuteurs valuables*—"negotiators worth talking to")'.[34]

By contrast, African nationalists viewed these conferences as a venue to secure decolonization. In the case of Nigeria, the conference, presided over by the British Colonial Secretary, saw the 'Nigerian leaders . . . unanimously demand[ing]' that the 'attainment of independence for Nigeria should be fixed for a date in 1959', but it became clear that the 'British government was not prepared to commit itself'.[35] Instead, Britain insisted that

[30] Ibid. 186–89.
[31] Ibid. 249.
[32] Ibid. 231.
[33] Ibid. 232.
[34] Basil Davidson, *Which Way Africa? The Search for a New Society* (Penguin African Library 1964) 131.
[35] Obafemi Awolowo, *The Autobiography of Chief Obafemi Awolowo* (CUP 1960) 295.

the regional governments created by the imposed colonial constitutions should take self-government as a first, transitional step towards national independence. The formal grant of independence, and the creation of the first Independence Constitution, were, in these cases of negotiated decolonization, conducted under the auspices of the colonial power and justified as necessary for the sake of legal continuity.

The specific form constitution-making took in this process of decolonization in the British colonies was an agreement between the colonial authority and representatives of different groups within the particular colony, most importantly the nationalist organizations demanding independence. Its legal embodiment was a two-part legislative operation of the British Parliament. First, 'the passing of an Act of the United Kingdom Parliament, followed by the making of an Order'.[36] It was usually a schedule of the Order that contained the country's constitution—for example, the Constitution of Zimbabwe was published as a schedule to the Zimbabwe Constitution Order 1979 of the United Kingdom. Each of these Independence Constitutions followed the Westminster model but attempted to limit the power of the legislature by adding bills of rights that were to be judicially enforceable. The limitation on traditional Westminster parliamentary sovereignty was extended to the amendment procedures, which required a two-thirds majority of the new legislature for any change to the constitution.

Even as the sun set on the British Empire, both the officials in the Colonial Office and the advisers to the emerging states assumed that the Westminster model would form the basis of these countries' constitutions. Sir Ivor Jennings, a constitutional scholar, adviser, and drafter of many of the early Independence Constitutions in Asia, 'was convinced that a modified Westminster model would be easy to transplant in Nepal assuming that the Nepali constitutional edifice would revolve around the principles of constitutional monarchy as expounded in the UK'.[37] As Ben Nwabueze noted in his description of the 'Westminster export model', the 'main features of the system are the diffusion of executive power, the partial fusion of the organs of government, and the responsibility of the executive to the legislature'.[38] If the former French colonies all adopted Independence Constitutions that bore a close 'resemblance to the French system', with 'several of their constitutions, especially in the sections dealing with the presidency' following the French Constitution 'almost word for word',[39] a common feature of the Independence Constitutions was the centring of politics and power in the executive branch of government, thereby perpetuating the central administrative dominance of the colonial state.

The tendency to executive dominance was soon reflected in the almost immediate amendment of the Independence Constitutions by the newly elected legislatures. Significantly, some of the earliest amendments addressed the process of constitution-making itself by amending the section of the constitution that dictated that amendments required a higher, two-thirds majority in the legislature. For instance, within its first year of independence, Ghana amended its constitution to remove the two-thirds requirement. In the case of Malawi, far-ranging amendments to the Independence Constitution included a repeal of the proviso that 'gave the Parliament of Malawi power to alter any of these provisions . . . [so

36 Simon Roberts, 'The Constitution of Malawi, 1964' (1964) 8(3) Journal of African Law 178–84, 178.

37 H Kumarasingham (ed.), *Constitution-Maker: Selected Writings of Sir Ivor Jennings* (CUP 2014) 8–9.

38 Benjamin Obi Nwabueze, *Constitutionalism in the Emerging States* (C Hurst & Company 1973) 55.

39 Victor T Le Vine, 'The Fall and Rise of Constitutionalism in West Africa' (1997) 35(2) Journal of Modern African Studies 181–206, 184.

long as the bill] is supported on the second and third readings by the votes of not less than two-thirds of all the members of the Assembly'.[40]

In Nigeria, the Independence Constitution was replaced by the 1963 Republican Constitution that not only removed the British Queen as head of state but also severed the link between the courts and the Privy Council, which had remained the court of final appeal. Most importantly, the new Republican Constitution, adopted by the Federal House of Representatives in September 1963, abolished the dual executive that distinguished the head of state and the head of government and instead created a single executive authority, the president, who was to be elected by a joint session of both houses of the national legislature.[41] While the Constitution continued to provide for a prime minister, executive authority lay with the president, who in turn appointed the prime minister.

2.3 Creating one-party states

A third and more autochthonous form of constitution-making emerged from internal political developments in states where successful liberation movements or dominant ruling parties chose to create one-party states. The French Gaullist model of presidential government and the abandonment of the negotiated Independence Constitutions in Commonwealth Africa saw both the rise of presidentialism and increasing intolerance of opposition parties.[42] While many of the negotiated Independence Constitutions for African Commonwealth states initially retained the British monarch as head of state, the adoption of republican constitutions shortly after independence saw the dual executive transformed into a united executive in which the president served both as titular sovereign or head of state and head of government. Even in cases where a prime minister is invested with the power to implement the law, the fact that they are appointed by the president means there is no question where executive authority ultimately lies.[43]

Soon after gaining independence, Ghana, Nigeria, Tanganyika, and Uganda all adopted new republican constitutions, replacing the British monarch with their own heads of state. Other important changes included withdrawal from the Privy Council, enhancing executive power, and additional powers for emergency rule. Constitution-making in this context took the form of a new constitution being adopted by the existing legislature. In the case of Nigeria, the Constitution of 1963 'was enacted by the parliament established by the Independence (Imperial) Constitution of 1960',[44] while in Ghana, Tanganyika, and Uganda, republican constitutions were enacted by constituent assemblies, which were, however, simply the 'imperially created National Assembly under a different name', as the national assemblies had resolved that they were a constituent assembly, 'and by that name enacted the new republican constitution under the power conferred upon it by an Act of the national assembly itself'.[45] Subsequent processes of negotiated decolonization, such as in Zambia and Malawi, moved directly to republican status. Thus, despite the legacy of Westminster,

[40] Roberts (n 36) 182.
[41] Constitution of Nigeria (1963).
[42] Benjamin Obi Nwabueze, *Presidentialism in Commonwealth Africa* (St Martin's Press 1974).
[43] Ibid. 21.
[44] Ibid. 23.
[45] Ibid. 23–24.

the development of republican constitutions in the immediate post-independence period saw a combination of parliamentarianism and the adoption of an indigenous head of state, producing powerful executives.

Strong executives and dominant parties, usually the nationalist or revolutionary parties that led the struggle against colonialism, deployed a similar legislative or even executive initiative in amending existing constitutions or adopting new ones to create one-party states. Justified as necessary to maintain national unity or achieve economic development, these constitutional changes were usually achieved by legislative or executive fiat. A striking example is that of Prime Minister Milton Obote in Uganda, who abrogated the 1962 Constitution and declared himself president under the interim 'Pigeonhole Constitution', named for the fact that 'Members of Parliament (MPs) were simply told to find a copy of the constitution in their respective pigeon-holes'.[46] While a third constitution for Uganda was adopted by Parliament in 1967, it was 'drawn up by and discussed by MPs, whose term of office had already expired' and who simply adopted a decree that 'turned themselves into a Constituent Assembly and thereafter prolonged their term of office for another five years without holding general elections'.[47]

While many of the one-party states that emerged in the late 1960s came about through the de facto repression of opposition parties rather than constitutional change, in several cases the ruling parties formally declared themselves as the sole political actor and proceeded to amend their constitutions accordingly. In the case of Tanzania, in January 1964 President Nyerere appointed a presidential commission to consider 'the changes in the Constitution of Tanganyika and the Constitution of the Tanganyika African National Union [TANU], and in the practice of Government that might be necessary to bring into effect a democratic One-Party State in Tanganyika'.[48] While TANU had won all but one seat in the 1960 parliamentary elections, the decision of its national executive committee to become a one-party state was 'not open to discussion by the commission or by the people'.[49] In a similar vein, President Kaunda announced at a 1972 press conference that 'Zambia was to become a one-party participatory democracy and that a commission would be set up to advise on the form this should take'.[50] The subsequent constitutional amendment established the ruling UNIP party as the 'one and only political party in Zambia' and prohibited the formation of other political organizations or 'any expression of opinion or other activity in sympathy with such political parties or organisations'.[51]

With the collapse of Portuguese colonialism in 1974, the former colonies were simply abandoned to the liberation movements which had been fighting guerilla wars against the colonial regime. Each of the movements that came to power, whether Frelimo in Mozambique, the MPLA in Angola, or the PAIGC in Guinea–Bissau, adopted one-party state constitutions, reflecting the dominant constitutional form among African states in that era. At its most extreme, dictators such as Idi Amin in Uganda, who took power in 1971, ruled by decree without bothering with the niceties of undertaking constitutional change.

[46] John Waliggo, 'The Main Actors in the Constitution-making Process in Uganda' in Goran Hyden and Denis Venter (eds.), *Constitution-Making and Democratisation in Africa* (Africa Institute of South Africa 2001) 43.
[47] Ibid.
[48] Nwabueze (n 42) 221.
[49] Ibid. 222.
[50] Ibid.
[51] Ibid. 224.

2.4 Constitution-making by military regimes

Another mode of constitution-making in Africa was that adopted by military regimes. Following the many *coups d'état* that swept away the original Independence Constitutions, the military regime in power would seek to legitimate itself by adopting a new constitution. Beginning in January 1963 in Togo, military *coups d'état* toppled constitutional governments across the continent, and military interventions have continued to plague constitutional governance in sub-Saharan Africa ever since. There were 80 successful coups in the 48 states of this region between 1957 and 2001,[52] and while the frequency dropped significantly after the end of the Cold War, there has been a significant increase in recent times. Nwabueze argues that the military intervenes 'not only to keep out the politicians altogether and install themselves, but sometimes also in order to replace one class of politicians or other elite with another'.[53]

While there are a multitude of different reasons as to why militaries intervene in the political process, the significance for constitution-making is that they inevitably seek either to legalize their own exercise of power or to try to facilitate a return to civilian rule by engaging in constitution-making. In the case of Nigeria, the 1966 coup that 'brought the First republic . . . to an abrupt end'[54] saw the Acting President of the Republic announcing in a radio broadcast that the 'Council of Ministers had voluntarily and unanimously decided to hand over the government of the Federation to the armed forces'.[55] However, as Nwabueze argues, even where the military retains portions of the existing constitution, the latter 'is subject to the absolute and supreme power of the military government . . . [which] is the source from which such a constitution derives its authority, and at whose sufferance it must therefore operate'.[56]

Rotimi Suberu argues that, in the case of Nigeria, 'the struggle to stabilize [the country's] fragmented society'[57] saw a 30-year-long period of military rule with a brief five-year 'civilian interregnum' in which a 'relatively decentralized, parliamentary federation of four ethnic regions' was transformed into a 'centrist, presidential, 36-state, federalism'.[58] The form of constitution-making that characterized this constitutional transformation included four elements. First, 'the military set the broad parameters'.[59] Second, it 'entrusted the elaboration of its centrist vision to groups of academics, lawyers and other technocrats, who translated it into constitutional documents'.[60] Third, asserting a formal commitment to democracy, the military 'sought to give broad legitimacy to its constitutional blueprints through directly or indirectly elected constituent assemblies'.[61] These assemblies were, however, given limited powers, were required to debate and ratify blueprints provided by the military's technocrats, and were restricted from venturing outside of these imposed

[52] Patrick J McGowan, 'African Military *Coups d'etat*, 1956–2001: Frequency, Trends and Distribution' 41(3) Journal of Modern African Studies (2003) 340.

[53] Nwabueze (n 38) 226.

[54] Okoi Arikpo, *The Development of Modern Nigeria* (Penguin African Library 1967) 148.

[55] Ibid.

[56] Benjamin Obi Nwabueze, *Military Rule and Constitutionalism in Nigeria* (Spectrum Law Series 1992) 3.

[57] Rotimi Suberu, 'Nigeria's Permanent Constitutional Transition: Military Rule, Civilian Instability and "True Federalism" in a Deeply Divided Society' Forum of Federations, Occasional Paper Series Number 34 (2019) 3.

[58] Ibid.

[59] Ibid. 8.

[60] Ibid.

[61] Ibid.

boundaries. The military also 'reserved to itself final authority to approve, reject, or amend any decisions made by constitutional drafting or debating bodies'.[62] Finally, it attempted to entrench its institutional legacy by instating a 'rigid constitution amending formula' and expanding the issues subject to the entrenched provisions.[63]

While some of the military regimes have argued that their intervention was in the cause of securing democracy, Nwabueze points out that despite Nigeria's military governmentss having 'maintained the conditions of a free society; there are no police state methods, and no regimentation of the individual's life ... civil and political rights have suffered extensive erosions and encroachments';[64] furthermore, the very nature of military government, 'their mental attitude, non-political culture and selfish devotion to their corporate interests',[65] precludes the military from establishing a culture of democratic constitutionalism. The imperative pushing military regimes to look to constitution-making has only burgeoned in the post-Cold War era, during which the international community has increasingly argued that there is a human right to democratic participation and that this should be reflected in the constitutional order of states. Differences over the nature of such participation and the forms democracy might persist; however, the imperative to establish a constitution of some sort seems nearly universal.

2.5 Post-Cold War emergence of multiparty democracies

A fifth form of constitution-making emerged with the end of the Cold War as one-party states and long-time dictators entered into negotiation with their political oppositions. In francophone West Africa, this took the form of 'national conferences' or round-table negotiations, while many other African states either launched processes of constitutional reform or simply abandoned the single-party restrictions and adopted multiparty elections. If constitutions were treated for the first 30 years after independence 'as being of little or no significance',[66] the post-Cold War return to democracy entailed a variety of constitutional forms and processes. On the one hand, there were processes of negotiated constitution-making through national conferences; on the other, there were much more elaborate processes involving popular consultation and even elected constitutional assemblies.

2.6 Elected constitutional assemblies

Since 1989 and the first democratic elections in Namibia, election of constitutional assemblies has emerged as yet another form of constitution-making in Africa. Within a short period, three countries—Namibia, South Africa, and Ethiopia—elected constitutional assemblies. Significantly, all three of these assemblies took the form of constrained constituent bodies in that they were based on prior negotiated agreements that included constitutional principles to guide their work or else, in the case of Ethiopia, were called upon to

[62] Ibid.
[63] Ibid. 9.
[64] Nwabueze (n 56) 18.
[65] Ibid. 327.
[66] Goran Hyden, 'Constitution-making and Democratisation in Africa' in Hyden and Venter (eds.) (n 46) 203.

discuss and adopt a draft constitution which had been produced by a constitutional commission, in this instance one established by the interim government that took control after the defeat of the Derg regime. After being drafted by the constitutional commission, this constitution had to be approved by the Council of Representatives, which served as the interim government's legislature. Only after agreement by the interim government was the draft submitted to the elected Constituent Assembly for ratification.[67]

In both Namibia and South Africa, the elected constitutional assemblies produced and adopted their constitutions. Namibia's first democratic elections were held in terms of United Nations Resolution 435 for the purpose of electing a constituent assembly, the final product of which 'had to be approved by the United Nations Security Council'.[68] At its first meeting, the Constituent Assembly unanimously adopted the 1982 Constitutional Principles that had been put forward by the Western Contact Group on Namibia as the starting point for the new constitution. With the acceptance of these principles, the Constituent Assembly adopted the majority party SWAPO (South West African People's Organisation)'s draft constitution as a working draft around which discussion and debate over the clauses of the new constitution centred.

In South Africa, there was a two-stage constitutional process in which a negotiated Interim Constitution provided for the first democratic elections producing a new government of national unity as well as a Constitutional Assembly made up of the members of both the lower and upper chambers of the newly elected Parliament. The Interim Constitution also set out the process for adopting a final constitution, which included a set of 34 constitutional principles that the parties had agreed would frame the work of the Constitutional Assembly. Finally, the Interim Constitution provided that the newly created Constitutional Court was to certify that the text of the final constitution abided by the constitutional principles.

3. The rise of public participation

Public participation in constitution-making processes emerged as a significant element of the post-1990 era.[69] While varying in form and substance, these processes are distinct from the involvement of the public through elections in the creation of constitution-making bodies. Instead, public participation involves members of the society in different ways in the discussion and debate on constitutional options, and is often combined with other post-conflict processes to increase public confidence and build legitimacy in the constitution-making process. In some cases, public participation has been undertaken by the constitutional assembly and its members, while in others it has involved either a process of education *and* consultation by a constitutional commission, as it works on a draft constitution, and/or a final public referendum to approve or reject a draft constitution.

[67] Kifle Wodajo, 'The Making of the Ethopian Constitution' in Hyden and Venter (eds.) (n 46) 134–41.

[68] Hage G Geingob, *Drafting of Namibia's Constitution* (Trustco 2006) 18. Also available at https://www.kas.de/c/document_library/get_file?uuid=a5fa370c-004f-c92d-0ba3-7b3ca48aab38&groupId=252038 (accessed February 7, 2025).

[69] Coel Kirkby and Christina Murray, 'Constitution-Making in Anglophone Africa: We the People?' in Muna Ndulo and Mamoudou Gazibo (eds.), *Growing Democracy in Africa: Elections, Accountable Governance, and Political Economy* (Cambridge Scholars Publishing 2016).

The Constitutional Assembly in South Africa embarked on an extensive process of public participation, involving the collection of views from the public through telephonic, electronic, and written submissions as well as engagement by members of the Constitutional Assembly in meetings with communities across the country. It also published its own newspaper, *Constitutional Talk*, which reported on the progress of debates in the Assembly, including draft alternative options of particular clauses and a final complete draft that was distributed widely. Yet while this effort raised awareness of the constitution-making process and increased a sense of popular engagement with it, it is less clear whether the nearly two million submissions made any material impact on the debate between the parties who, as elected representatives, had organized party processes for producing and campaigning for particular outcomes.

Two other forms of public participation played out in Uganda and Kenya. In Uganda, the National Resistance Movement (NRM), which gained power in a military victory in 1986, 'committed to establishing a mechanism to enable the people of Uganda to prepare a new Constitution for themselves'.[70] Following its Legal Notice 1 of 1986, the movement's National Resistance Council established a Constitutional Commission to 'gather information from the people as to the form of governance they would like to have' and then draft a constitution 'as the basis for a final Constitution of Uganda'.[71] The Commission argued, however, that only an elected constituent assembly could achieve the legitimacy necessary for the adoption of a new constitution. This led to the election of a Constituent Assembly in March 1994 and the establishment of the Constituent Assembly to review and adopt the draft constitution submitted by the Constitutional Commission in its final report.[72]

While the NRM accepted the Commission's views as well as its constitutional proposals, its dominance of the Constituent Assembly meant that it was able to ignore demands for the return of a multiparty system, in the process failing to resolve tensions over land, language, and the role of traditional authorities.[73] However, the process of public participation through the local resistance councils and the activities of the Constitutional Commission in consulting, educating, and receiving submissions from local councils and committees 'brought the discussion of a new constitution down to the people at grass-roots level and [was] . . . highly successful in generating interest'.[74]

In Kenya, the 1998 Constitution Review Act set in motion a process that 'was to be based on the principles of democracy, accountability, people's participation, human rights and social justice'.[75] The failure of political parties to agree on membership of the commission frustrated these initial efforts, and instead the movement for constitutional change, including religious communities (through the Ufungamano Initiative), opposition parties, and civil society, came together and established the People's Commission of Kenya in June 2000 to 'collect the views of Kenyans and prepare a draft constitution in accordance with the goals of review previously agreed upon by all stakeholders'.[76] The Kenyan Parliament

[70] James Wapakhabulo, 'Managing the Constitution-Making Process in Uganda' in Hyden and Venter (eds.) (n 46) 114–31, 117.

[71] Ibid.

[72] Waliggo (n 46) 57–58.

[73] Wapakhabulo (n 70) 125–28.

[74] Waliggo (n 46) 51.

[75] Constitution of Kenya Review Commission, 'The People's Choice: The Report of the Constitution of Kenya Review Commission, Short Version' (Constitution of Kenya Review Commission, 18 September 2002) 1.

[76] Ibid.

responded by passing the Constitution of Kenya Review Act, which created a parallel process through the establishment of the Constitution of Kenya Review Commission in November 2000.[77] After Professor Yash Ghai was appointed to chair the Commission, he 'initiated negotiations between the parliamentary Select Committee on the Constitution and the *Ufungamano Initiative* ... [to] persuade all the stakeholders to merge the two processes'.[78] As a result, the membership of the Review Commission was expanded in June 2001 to 'include representatives of the People's Commission', and the Commission began its work under a tight deadline imposed by Parliament.

The review process was described in the Commission's report as granting Kenyans 'for the first time ever a chance to decide on the values and rules by which they wish to govern themselves'.[79] Premised on the 'sovereignty of the people', the process, according to the report, had to be 'inclusive, accommodating all the diversities of the Kenyan people', and the people had to be afforded 'ample opportunities to participate in the review'.[80] Accordingly, the Review Commission divided the process of public participation into two parts.

First, it 'conducted and facilitated civic education relating to the process', the existing constitution, and 'constitutional concepts and issues for reform'.[81] This included the creation of a 'national curriculum and teaching materials for civic education' and, '[w]herever possible, papers and documents, originally prepared in English, were translated into Kiswahili'.[82] To 'facilitate meetings and promote debates', the Review Commission set up a 'constituency constitutional forum' in every electoral constituency, 'to mobilise various sectors of society to participate in the review and participate in public hearings'.[83] District coordinators were appointed to mobilize people in districts and constituencies to manage documentation centres, coordinate civic education, and facilitate public participation in Review Commission hearings.[84]

Second, the Review Commission held formal 'Listening to the People' public hearings in the capital, Nairobi, and provincial capitals, in December 2001, and sent 'panels of five to three commissioners' to spend two to three days in every constituency between April and August 2002.[85] This extensive public education and consultation programme by the Review Commission yielded more than 35,000 submissions. Combined with formal hearings, it meant that 'millions of Kenyans, throughout the country and overseas' made their views known to the Commission.[86]

Despite this extensive participation, the proposed draft constitution was rejected in a national referendum in 2005 after Parliament made significant changes to it. It was only after 'the role of Parliament as endorsing body was circumscribed so that it could not easily overturn political agreements'[87] that the revived constitutional reform process could proceed to a successful referendum in 2010, in which the public approved a new constitution. As Kirkby and Murray conclude, there is a tension between 'a highly participatory

[77] Ibid.
[78] Ibid. 2.
[79] Ibid. 3.
[80] Ibid.
[81] Ibid. 4.
[82] Ibid.
[83] Ibid.
[84] Ibid 4–5.
[85] Ibid 5.
[86] Ibid.
[87] Kirkby and Murray (n 69) 17.

process and one that allows political actors the space—and sometimes the secrecy—to compromise'.[88]

4. Social conflict and the rise of hybrid forms of constitution-making

What is most significant about recent processes of constitution-making in Commonwealth Africa is their tendency to combine these different forms—'a highly participatory process' and a process that allows room for reaching compromises—so as to accommodate political elites as well as demands for participation. The two-stage, two-constitution process that marked South Africa's transition from apartheid is one example of this new hybrid form; so too, in their different ways, are the cases of Ghana, Namibia, Kenya, and Zimbabwe. While Andrew Arato considers South Africa an example of what he describes as a 'post-sovereign' or 'post-revolutionary' paradigm of constitution-making,[89] I would argue that it reflects a hybrid form of constitution-making that emerges as a compromise in situations where neither side of a political conflict is able to assert its will. The question this raises is whether these processes hold out more hope than others of affording the final constitutional product greater legitimacy and sustainability. The recent rise in military interventions and the return to appointing commissions to draft new constitutions—a trend evident in some countries on the continent—does raise questions, however, about the broader direction that constitution-making is taking in Africa.

The emergence of a hybrid form of constitution-making which includes elements that may be in tension with one another is, nevertheless, important to explore in its own right. In addition to Namibia and South Africa, examples of such a hybrid form include Kenya and Zimbabwe, while the democratic transition in Ghana provides an earlier example of it. While neither the Kenyan nor Zimbabwean experiences included an 'interim' constitution, they both featured the creation of a first-draft constitution based on greater popular or civil society participation, followed by conflict with the existing political institutions. In both cases, the intervention of politicians in power, whether Parliament in Kenya or President Mugabe and the ruling party in Zimbabwe, led to popular rejection of the drafts in referendums. It was only after a second round of constitution-making by more constrained processes that these constitutions received public approval.

4.1 Ghana

Ghana's transition to a constitutional democracy represents the first example of the emerging hybrid form of constitution-making. Initiated by the Provisional National Defence Council (PNDC), which had come to power in a coup on 31 December 1981, the transition began with the creation of the National Commission for Democracy (NCD), which from 1984 to 1987 solicited input from the public and organized seminars, symposia, and debates to discuss the 'effective realization of a true democracy in Ghana'.[90] The next

[88] Ibid. 20.
[89] Arato (n 12) 233–56.
[90] Joseph RA Ayee, 'Ghana's Return to Constitutional Rule under the Provisional National Defence Council (PNDC)' (1996) 29(4) Verfassung und Recht in Ubersee/Law and Politics in Africa, Asia and Latin America 435.

step in the process saw the creation of District Assemblies, with the Jerry Rawlings regime attempting to use them to 'foist a no-party system of government' on the country.[91] In response, the Movement for Freedom and Justice was formed, calling for 'the release of all political detainees, the granting of an unconditional amnesty to all exiles, the drawing up of a constitutional timetable, and the lifting of the ban on political parties'.[92] Academic institutions also responded, holding seminars and publishing books in the belief that, in so doing, they could 'influence trends towards the building of a constitutional democratic system'.[93] While the District Assemblies called for a 'no-party' system, in March 1991 the NCD reported on the regional fora and 'noted that most Ghanaians were unequivocally in favour of a multi-party system of government'.[94]

After the PNDC adopted the report of the NCD, it created a Committee of Experts to produce constitutional proposals and assist a Consultative Assembly, established under PNDC Law 253 of 1991, to formulate a draft constitution. The Consultative Assembly was made up 'of 117 persons elected by the District Assemblies, 121 persons elected from 62 "identifiable bodies" listed under the Second Schedule of the Law, and not more than 22 persons appointed by the PNDC'.[95] Despite criticism from civil society that the Consultative Assembly was stacked with supporters of the governing regime, and concerns that the popular referendum to decide on the proposed constitution before the lifting of a ban on politics prevented serious contestation over the draft constitution, the constitution was endorsed overwhelmingly by 92 per cent of the 3,680,973 voters who participated.[96]

Significantly, Rawlings defended the use of a referendum on a number of grounds: the need to elicit the 'readiness of Ghanaians to protect it'[the draft constitution]; the need, too, to educate the public on the provisions of the draft constitution; and the idea that referendums were in vogue all over the world. Moreover, he said, 'all our previous constitutions have affirmed the sovereignty of the people as a supreme principle, but none has observed that principle with the actual direct endorsement of the people'.[97]

4.2 Namibia

The Constituent Assembly that produced Namibia's Independence Constitution was the first democratically elected constitution-making body in the history of African constitution-making. However, this body was not unconstrained, since the elections that brought it into being were the result of an international agreement, namely the New York Agreement between South Africa, Angola, and Cuba, which opened the way to the implementation of United Nations Security Council (UNSC) Resolution 435 that provided for the independence of Namibia. Furthermore, it was understood that a new Namibian constitution would

91 Ibid.
92 Ibid. 436.
93 Kwame Ninsen and Francis Drah (eds.), *Ghana's Transition to Constitutional Rule (Proceedings of a Seminar Organised by the Department of Political Science, University of Ghana, Legon)* (Ghana University Press 1991), preface.
94 Ayee (n 90) 436.
95 Ibid. 439.
96 Ibid.
97 Ibid. 442.

be expected to conform to the legal elements governing UNSC Resolution 435. These legal elements, in turn, had been informed by the Constitutional Principles laid down by the Western Contact Group in 1982. According to these Principles, explicitly incorporated into Resolution 435, a new constitution would have to be adopted by 'an absolute two-thirds majority' of the Constituent Assembly, and would include 'a catalogue of substantive principles'.[98]

These substantive criteria included the following: Namibia would be a unitary, sovereign, and democratic state whose constitution would be the supreme law; there would be a tripartite system of government in which the legislature and executive would be constituted by 'periodic and genuine elections which will be held by secret vote'; and there would be 'an independent judicial branch ... responsible for the interpretation of the Constitution and for ensuring its supremacy and the authority of the law'.[99] Finally, the Constitutional Principles required that there would be a declaration of fundamental rights, which would include the rights to life, personal liberty, and freedom of movement; to freedom of conscience; to freedom of expression, including freedom of speech and a free press; to freedom of assembly and association, including political parties and trade unions; to due process and equality before the law; to protection from arbitrary deprivation of private property or deprivation of private property without just compensation; and freedom from racial, ethnic, religious, or sexual discrimination.[100]

Significantly, despite an attempt by the apartheid regime-appointed South West Africa Administrator-General to include these principles in 'legislation he drafted for the establishment and functioning of the Constituent Assembly', this was rejected by the United Nations Special Representative, and the only formal limitation on the Assembly was the requirement that a new constitution be adopted by a two-thirds majority.[101] However, when the Constituent Assembly was formally convened in November 1989, SWAPO, the liberation movement which had struggled for Namibia's independence from South African occupation, immediately proposed a motion that the Assembly approve the Constitutional Principles.

The constitution-writing process itself was first delegated to a 21-member all-party Standing Committee which received completed draft constitutions from three of the four major parties in the Assembly (SWAPO, DTA, and ACN). Once the Standing Committee agreed to accept the SWAPO draft as the basis for the new constitution, there were debates about modifications to the draft; when agreement was reached on the issues, the Standing Committee charged three South African jurists with preparing the final draft.[102] Despite the fact that no final draft was made available to the public, or even to members of the Constituent Assembly, all the members of the Assembly, 'in a somewhat extra-legal but symbolically important act', signed ceremonial copies of the Constitution.[103] Thus, the Constitution was adopted by consensus and went into force five days later.

[98] Paul C Szasz, 'Creating the Namibian Constitution' (1994) 27(3) Verfassung und Recht in Ubersee/Law and Politics in Africa, Asia and Latin America 348.
[99] UN, S/15287, 12 July 1982.
[100] Ibid.
[101] Szasz (n 98) 350.
[102] Ibid. 351.
[103] Ibid.

4.3 South Africa

In the case of South Africa, the two-stage constitution-making process was born out of political necessity. At the height of the anti-apartheid struggle in the mid 1980s, the African National Congress (ANC) released a set of constitutional principles and worked to have the then Organisation of African Unity (OAU) adopt a declaration on the process for a political transition in South Africa that would be acceptable to the international community. The Harare Declaration stated that there should be negotiations to establish an interim government, which would then be in charge of organizing democratic elections for a Constituent Assembly to produce a new constitution for the country. Significantly, the Harare Declaration included a set of constitutional principles, with the result that, even at this stage, the form of constitution-making being proposed assumed a 'constrained' or, in Arato's terms, 'post-revolutionary' form. The principles required the process to conform to internationally acceptable constitutional principles relating to, for instance, multiparty democracy, independent courts, and constitutional rights.

The apartheid regime was thus forced to the negotiating table; however, it refused to hand over power to what would have been an unelected 'interim' government and instead insisted on legal continuity and the transfer of power to a new government that would be bound by an agreed-upon constitution. Given the inability of either the apartheid regime or the liberation movement to impose their will on the process, the compromise was the negotiation of an 'interim' constitution under which Mandela's government was elected. While the apartheid regime had long resisted the idea of a democratically elected constitutional assembly, the 'interim' constitution provided for the creation of a Constitutional Assembly constituted by both houses of the newly elected Parliament, which was required to produce a new constitution within two years. It also included an extensive set of constitutional principles, agreed upon by the parties, which were designed to constrain the Constitutional Assembly. Finally, the 'interim' constitution provided that the newly established Constitutional Court would be required to certify that the new text was in conformity with the constitutional principles. While the Constitutional Court initially refused to certify the text, after the Constitutional Assembly amended the text it was certified and signed into law by President Mandela.

Although the process of constitution-making involved significant degrees of public participation—whether through mass action and public pressure in the early stages of negotiating the 'interim' constitution, or in the formal process of participation organized by the Constitutional Assembly—the process remained under the control of the political parties and, later, the elected members of the Constitutional Assembly. Even the process of legal challenges before the Constitutional Court simply returned the draft text to the Constitutional Assembly for amendment, and the Court accepted the amended text, despite continuing challenges by some political parties which maintained that the amended text was not faithful to the principles.

4.4 Zimbabwe

In Zimbabwe, social tensions unresolved in the first decade of independence, including pressure for land reform, led to increased mobilization against the government and demands 'for a holistic amendment of the constitution'.[104] Responding to the crisis, the Zimbabwe Council of Churches called a number of meetings bringing together trade unions, churches, and civil society. This led, in 1997, to the founding of the National Constitutional Assembly (NCA). The NCA appealed for 'a people driven constitution in which all the people had a right to express their views'.[105]

With the launch of the Movement for Democratic Change (MDC) in 1999, the Mugabe government quickly moved to take the initiative, establishing a Constitutional Commission tasked with writing a new constitution which would be put to a national plebiscite in February 2000. The Commission, chaired by Justice Godfrey Chidyausiku, had 395 members, of whom 150 were Members of Parliament. The remaining members 'included chiefs (presumed to be ZANU(PF), mayors (at the time all ZANU(PF)) as well as a wide range of opposition politicians, church people and NGO representatives'.[106]

The result was continuing tension between the NCA and the Constitutional Commission, leading the NCA to host a 'three-day People's Constitutional Convention, which proposed the launching of an alternative "people driven" constitution-writing process'.[107] The NCA subsequently resolved that its members could not simultaneously serve on the government's Constitutional Commission, resulting in a number of its 'well-respected' members breaking with it and joining the Commission.[108] This, in turn, led to a fracturing of the opposition and even significant organizational divisions in some of Zimbabwe's most important churches and NGOs, including the Anglican and Catholic churches as well as the Zimbabwe Human Rights Association and the Zimbabwe Lawyers for Human Rights.

Despite these divisions, the Constitutional Commission process generated significant public participation and provided fora 'in which ordinary Zimbabwean citizens were able to criticize explicitly the government's policies'.[109] At its three-day plenary meeting in October 1999, which was 'broadcast on ZBC (Zimbabwe Broadcast Corporation) and reported in both the state and independent press', it became clear that there was a divergence between the proposals of the ruling party and those of all the other participants in the Commission, including the 'opposition parties, interest groups and the general public'.[110] When the coordinating committee, which was tasked with producing a draft constitution, presented the draft to the Commission's second plenary meeting in November, the debate went on for three days, after which the chair of the Commission simply 'called a halt to debate and declared the draft adopted'.[111]

With the referendum scheduled for February 2000, the Constitutional Commission and the NCA launched campaigns for and against the draft constitution, respectively. The 'no' campaign argued that the draft's failure to reform, in particular, the structure of the executive presidency meant that the 'people's views were either distorted, ignored or rejected'.[112]

104 Tasar Muguti, Benias Tirivaviri, and Kudakwashe Mapetere, 'A Constitutional "Gamble": Re-visiting the COPAC-driven Constitutional Making Process in Zimbabwe' in Artwell Nhemachena and Munyaradzi Mawere (eds.), *Africa at the Crossroads: Theorising Fundamentalisms in the 21st Century* (Langaa RPCIG 1991) 293.

105 Ibid.

106 Sarah Rich Dorman, 'NGOs and the Constitutional Debate in Zimbabwe: From Inclusion to Exclusion' (2003) 29(4) Journal of Southern African Studies 850.

107 Ibid. 851.

108 Ibid.

109 Ibid. 853.

110 Ibid.

111 Ibid.

112 Ibid.

For example, seven out of ten provinces expressed support for a non-executive head of state and a prime minister as head of government, while the Commission's draft retained the executive president.

Not only was the draft criticized by those who rejected the process, but even more damagingly, many Commissioners themselves questioned 'the undemocratic way in which the draft had been rushed through their final session'.[113] In fact, one of the Commissioners who had left the NCA to join the Commission and served as chair of the latter's subcommittee on the pillars of democracy, Lupi Mushayakarara, 'convinced 24 commissioners to sign a petition against the draft'.[114] In an effort to win votes for the draft constitution, President Mugabe 'gazetted some "corrections and clarifications" to the draft constitution' that would permit the state to take agricultural land and oblige 'the "former colonial power" to compensate farmers'.[115] In the February referendum, the draft constitution was rejected, with 54 per cent of the electorate voting against it and only 44 per cent voting for it.

The response of the ruling party to the rejection of the draft constitution was to close down public debate 'by redefining who and what were legitimate voices within the political spectrum'.[116] The period that followed saw increasing violence against those regarded as opposed to the government and its policies.[117] This culminated in the disputed 2008 presidential election, which was marred by intense violence. In response, the Southern African Development Community (SADC) pressured the divided MDC opposition and ZANU(PF) to agree on a power-sharing agreement that 'left Mugabe very much in control of the security apparatus of the state, but also gave the MDC a share of political power in an envisaged inclusive government'.[118] This Global Political Agreement (GPA) led to the formation of a power-sharing government in 2009 and 'an initial all-stakeholders conference in July 2009 to affirm [the framework]', along with thematic committees of the already established Select Committee of Parliament on the New Constitution (COPAC) to spearhead the process of constitutional reform.[119]

The Select Committee, made up of seventeen men and eight women together representing the three major political parties—ZANU(PF), the two factions of the MDC, and one representative of the traditional authorities—was boycotted by the NCA on the grounds that it was dominated by political elites, yet COPAC managed to produce a draft constitution that was presented to its second all-stakeholders conference in October 2012.[120] After further political negotiations, a final draft was adopted by Parliament in February 2013 and put to a constitutional referendum in March 2013. With more than three million participating in the referendum, the Constitution was approved by a margin of 94.49 per cent.

In July 2013, Zimbabwe held national elections in which ZANU(PF) managed to mobilize nearly one million more voters than had participated in the 2008 election, giving it a

[113] Ibid. 854.

[114] Ibid.

[115] Ibid.

[116] Ibid. 862.

[117] Brian Raftopoulos, 'The Crisis in Zimbabwe, 1998–2008' in Brian Raftopoulos and AS Mlambo (eds.), *Becoming Zimbabwe: A History from the Pre-colonial Period to 2008* (Weaver Press 2009) 215.

[118] Ibid. 230.

[119] International Crisis Group, 'Zimbabwe: The Road to Reform or Another Dead End?' (Africa Report No. 173, 27 April 2011) 12.

[120] Kingston Magaya, 'Constitution by the People or to the People: A Critical Analysis of Zimbabwe's Constitutional Development in View of the Constitution Select Committee (COPAC) Led Process' (1991) 3(2) Political Sciences & Public Affairs 1–10.

significant electoral victory with 61 per cent of the vote. Although the divided opposition parties were sidelined, ZANU(PF)'s return to power was undermined by its own failure to manage its internal succession struggles.[121] The impact on the new Constitution has been a failure to fully implement and fund the independent institutions that are key to its overall scheme, including an independent prosecuting authority, a peace and reconciliation commission, and an anti-corruption commission.

4.5 Kenya

The public's rejection of Kenya's 2005 draft constitution in a referendum was, similar to the case of Zimbabwe in 2008, the result of government intervention at the end of a highly participatory process. The National Constitutional Conference which debated the draft constitution produced by the Constitution of Kenya Review Commission was composed of 629 members, including all 222 Members of Parliament and three members from each district in the country. While the conference reached agreement on a draft, the government persuaded the legislature to make significant changes to the draft before it was submitted to a public referendum. The result was that the draft constitution was rejected, with some voting 'against it because they preferred the earlier draft, some because of general dissatisfaction with the government, and some for tribal reasons'.[122] As a result, the country went to elections in 2008 under the former constitution.

The ensuing post-election violence between supporters of the two major presidential candidates who contested the elections eventually produced an 'internationally brokered agreement' that included a new process for writing a new constitution. The agreement led to the adoption of a law that required a new draft constitution to be produced by an expert committee made up of six Kenyans and three foreign experts. The revised draft constitution was sent to a parliamentary committee before being finalized by the expert committee and sent on to the full Parliament. Parliament, however, could only make changes with a 65 per cent majority and the final adoption of the Constitution would be by public referendum. In order to be adopted, the draft constitution would have to receive a majority of the votes cast in the referendum as well as 'at least 25 percent affirmative votes in at least five of eight provinces'.[123] In August 2010, the Constitution received 67 per cent public support and the required 25 per cent in the provinces. It was promulgated into law a month later by the President of Kenya.

5. Conclusion: The limits of constitution-making

It is clear from this brief survey of forms of constitution-making in Africa that they reflect a significant change in the relationship between constitutions and people in Africa over the last century. While the earliest 'modern' constitutions were imposed by colonial powers in

[121] International Crisis Group, 'Zimbabwe: Stranded in Stasis' (Crisis Group Africa Briefing No 118, 29 February 2014) 3–10.
[122] Michelle Brandt and others, *Constitution-making and Reform: Options for the Process* (Interpeace 2011) 341.
[123] Ibid.

the 1920s, the subsequent ones—from negotiated Independence Constitutions to single-party, military-designed, and contested hybrid forms in the postcolonial period—all reflect an ongoing struggle over governance throughout Africa. Aside from the major substantive issues of governance, democracy, and the role of traditional authorities that seem to dominate most debates about African constitutions, it is the evolving nature of constitution-making processes that provides a lens through which to understand the increasing importance of constitutions and constitution-making across the continent.

Given that the new constitutions in Namibia and South Africa have now outlasted the average life of constitutions around the globe, not to mention most prior African constitutions, it may be fair to argue that the process through which they were produced could have contributed to their legitimacy. If this is the case, then we might conclude that elected constitutional assemblies (even if constrained by agreed-upon principles) and public participation are significant factors in the legitimacy and sustainability of democratic constitutions in Africa. The problem, however, is that despite their longevity, these constitutions have not resolved the social crises that brought them into being. The liberation movements in Namibia and South Africa sought to end colonialism and apartheid, but their victory over those systems of government has not translated into societies that reflect their goals. Indeed, many claim that South Africa's social crisis, while temporarily alleviated during the first years of the ANC's rule, is now as bad as ever, with unemployment, poverty, and inequality on the rise.

Even though they were rejected in the negotiations over the 'interim' Constitution, social and economic rights were made justiciable by the elected constitutional assembly in South Africa, and many hoped they would be a means to address the country's vast inequalities and other legacies of apartheid. Despite this constitution-making effort, the failure of post-apartheid governments to use their constitutional powers to address economic inequality has led to growing disillusionment with both the ANC government and the constitutional order itself. Significantly, however, it has been civil society's ability to rely on constitutional protection—and the ability of political parties, activists, and social movements to use the courts and the Constitution—which until now has averted a full-blown constitutional crisis. Constitutional institutions have withstood repeated attacks, with the state capture inquiry, headed by then Deputy Chief Justice Zondo, exposing extraordinary levels of corruption involving both private and government figures, including the former president of the country.

When seen in the context of the arc of constitution-making in Africa, this recent pattern of hybrid forms of constitution-making reveals both the potential and limits of constitution-making in regard to achieving sustainable governance. Each of these more recent examples of constitution-making exhibits a combination of elite bargaining, public participation, and popular endorsement, either through elected constitutional assemblies or referendums. While the cases are rooted in their own particular social and political histories, it is the combination of negotiation and participation that seems to characterize this emergent form of constitution-making.

In four of the five cases identified here, the constitutional orders that have been built on these constitutions have proven quite resilient despite ongoing social and political conflict. The case of Zimbabwe, however, demonstrates that constitutions, even if the product of negotiation and participation, including very high levels of support in a national referendum, cannot guarantee the promised outcome. This is especially true when dominant political parties are faced with a fractured political opposition, and when the accountability institutions created by a constitution are either under the shadow of the ruling party or simply not fully implemented or given the resources they need in order to function properly.

The arc of constitution-making across sub-Saharan Africa has bent towards greater democratic participation and possibly more resilient legitimacy over the last few decades. Though the challenge of military intervention and autocratic leadership remains, this trend is nonetheless a hopeful sign for the future of constitutionalism across the continent.

Bibliography

Abioye F.T., 'Constitution-making, Legitimacy and Rule of Law: A Comparative Analysis' (2011) 44(1) The Comparative and International Law Journal of Southern Africa 59–79

Adelman S., 'Constitutionalism, Pluralism and Democracy in Africa' (1998) 30(42) Journal of Legal Pluralism 73–88

Arato A., *The Adventures of the Constituent Power: Beyond Revolutions?* (CUP 2017)

Arato A. and Cohen J.L., 'Civil Society, Populism and Religion' (2017) 24(3) Constellations 233–95

Arikpo O., *The Development of Modern Nigeria* (Penguin African Library 1967)

Awasom N.F., 'Politics and Constitution-making in Francophone Cameroon, 1959–1960' (2002) 49(4) Africa Today 3–30

Awolowo O., *The Autobiography of Chief Obafemi Awolowo* (CUP 1960)

Ayee J.R.A., 'Ghana's Return to Constitutional Rule under the Provisional National Defence Council (PNDC)' (1996) 29(4) Verfassung und Recht in Ubersee/Law and Politics in Africa, Asia and Latin America 434–52

Brandt M. and others, *Constitution-making and Reform: Options for the Process* (Interpeace 2011)

Constitution of Kenya Review Commission, 'The People's Choice: The Report of the Constitution of Kenya Review Commission, Short Version' (Constitution of Kenya Review Commission, 18 September 2002)

Dale W., 'The Making and Remaking of Commonwealth Constitutions' (1993) 43(1) International and Comparative Law Quarterly 67–83

Davidson B., *Which Way Africa? The Search for a New Society* (Penguin African Library 1964)

Dorman S.R., 'NGOs and the Constitutional Debate in Zimbabwe: From Inclusion to Exclusion' (2003) 29(4) Journal of Southern African Studies 845–63

Ezera K, *Constitutional Developments in Nigeria* (CUP 1960)

Gebeye B.A., *A Theory of African* Constitutionalism (OUP 2021)

Geingob H.G., *Drafting of Namibia's Constitution* (2004) Available at https://www.kas.de/c/document_library/get_file?uuid=a5fa370c-004f-c92d-0ba3-7b3ca48aab38&groupId=252038

Hatchard J., Ndulo M., and Slinn P., *Comparative Constitutionalism and Good Governance in the Commonwealth: An Eastern and Southern African Perspective* (CUP 2004)

Hessebon G.T., 'The Fourth Constitution-Making Wave of Africa: Constitutions 4.0?' (2014) 28(2) Temple International & Comparative Law Journal 187–214

Hyden G. and Venter D. (eds.), *Constitution-Making and Democratisation in Africa* (Africa Institute of South Africa 2001)

International Crisis Group, 'Zimbabwe: Stranded in Stasis' (Crisis Group Africa Briefing No 118, 29 February 2014)

International Crisis Group, 'Zimbabwe: The Road to Reform or Another Dead End?' (Africa Report No. 173, 27 April 2011)

Kirkby C. and Murray C., 'Constitution-Making in Anglophone Africa: We the People?' in Ndulo M. and Gazibo M. (eds.), *Growing Democracy in Africa: Elections, Accountable Governance, and Political Economy* (Cambridge Scholars Publishing 2016)

Klug H., *Constituting Democracy: Law, Globalism and South Africa's Political* Reconstruction (CUP 2000)

Kumarasingham H. (ed.), *Constitution-Maker: Selected Writings of Sir Ivor Jennings* (CUP 2014)

Le Vine V.T., 'The Fall and Rise of Constitutionalism in West Africa' (1997) 35(2) Journal of Modern African Studies 181–206

Magaya K., 'Constitution by the People or to the People: A Critical Analysis of Zimbabwe's Constitutional Development in View of the Constitution Select Committee (COPAC) Led Process' (1991) 3(2) Political Sciences & Public Affairs 1–10

Mamdani M., *Citizen and Subject: Contemporary Africa and the Legacy of Late Colonialism* (Princeton University Press 1996)
McGowan P.J., 'African Military Coups d'etat, 1956–2001: Frequency, Trends and Distribution' (2003) 41(3) Journal of Modern African Studies 340
Muguti T., Tirivaviri B., and Mapetere K., 'A Constitutional "Gamble": Re-visiting the COPAC-driven Constitutional Making Process in Zimbabwe' in Nhemachena A. and Mawere M. (eds.), *Africa at the Crossroads: Theorising Fundamentalisms in the 21st Century* (Langaa RPCIG 1991)
Ninsen K.A. and Drah F. (eds.), *Ghana's Transition to Constitutional Rule* (Ghana University Press 1991)
Nwabueze B.O., *Constitutionalism in the Emerging States* (C Hurst & Company 1973)
Nwabueze B.O., *Presidentialism in Commonwealth Africa* (St Martin's Press 1974)
Nwabueze B.O., *Military Rule and Constitutionalism in Nigeria* (Spectrum Law Series 1992)
Post K., *The New States of West Africa* (Penguin African Library 1964)
Raftopoulos B., 'The Crisis in Zimbabwe, 1998–2008' in Raftopoulos B. and Mlambo A.S. (eds.), *Becoming Zimbabwe: A History from the Pre-colonial Period to 2008* (Weaver Press 2009)
Roberts S., 'The Constitution of Malawi, 1964' (1964) 8(3) Journal of African Law 178–84
Suberu R., 'Nigeria's Permanent Constitutional Transition: Military Rule, Civilian Instability and "True Federalism" in a Deeply Divided Society' Forum of Federations, Occasional Paper Series Number 34 (2019)
Szasz P.C., 'Creating the Namibian Constitution' (1994) 27(3) Verfassung und Recht in Ubersee/Law and Politics in Africa, Asia and Latin America 346–57
United Nations Security Council, 'Letter Dated 12 July 1982 from the Representatives of Canada, France, Germany, Federal Republic of, the United Kingdom of Great Britain and Northern Ireland and the United States of America addressed to the Secretary-General', s/15287, 12 July 1982
Waliggo J., 'The Main Actors in the Constitution-making Process in Uganda' in Hyden G. and Venter D. (eds.), *Constitution-Making and Democratisation in Africa* (Africa Institute of South Africa 2001)
Wapakhabulo J., 'Managing the Constitution-Making Process in Uganda' in Hyden G. and Venter D. (eds.), *Constitution-Making and Democratisation in Africa* (African Institute of South Africa 2001)
Wodajo K., 'The Making of the Ethopian Constitution' in Hyden G. and Venter D. (eds.), *Constitution-Making and Democratisation in Africa* (African Institute of South Africa 2001)

3

Reimagining Constitutional Change and Democracy in Africa: Emerging Supranational Standards for Constitutional Change

Adem Kassie Abebe

1. Introduction

Africa has not been an exception to the global concern around the phenomenon of democratic erosion and backsliding.[1] Authoritarian regimes, such as in Uganda and Togo, have proven resilient and have even consolidated. Countries such as Benin and Tunisia, long emblematic of democratic progress on the continent, have faced significant erosion of democratic practice. Others, such as Burkina Faso, Chad, Gabon, Guinea, Niger, Mali, and Sudan, saw the return of the spectre of military rule between 2019 and 2023.

The story of crisis of democracy and constitutionalism is, nevertheless, not universal. Only in the last couple of years, countries from the Gambia to Kenya, Malawi to Liberia, and Benin to Sierra Leone and Zambia have reached important heights in consolidating democracy and a tradition of peaceful alternation of power, while Kenya has proven resilient, with the highest courts seeking ways to check the government, including its attempts to fundamentally alter the democratic dispensation through constitutional amendments. Historically democratic countries, such as Botswana, Cabo Verde, Ghana, Mauritius, Senegal, South Africa, and Seychelles remain largely decent democracies, even as challenges persist. Nigeria, the continent's behemoth, representing almost 17 per cent of the population, is still an imperfect (electoral) democracy, but a democracy nonetheless.

To be sure, while Africa has made tremendous progress since 1989, when 91 per cent of the countries were authoritarian, almost two-thirds of the countries on the continent are either hybrid (26 per cent) or authoritarian (38 per cent) regimes, with democracies representing only 36 per cent of the continent as at 2020—an 8 per cent decline from the height of democracy in Africa in 2015, when 44 per cent of countries were categorized as democratic.[2]

One of the key reasons for the stalling and decline in the democratic trajectory, despite consistently high public support for democracy, relates to regressive constitutional changes

[1] International IDEA, *The Global State of Democracy 2021: Building Resilience in a Pandemic Era* (International IDEA 2021) https://www.idea.int/publications/catalogue/global-state-democracy-2021 accessed 14 June 2022.
[2] International IDEA, *The State of Democracy in Africa and the Middle East 2021: Resilient Democratic Aspirations and Opportunities for Consolidation* (International IDEA 2021) https://www.idea.int/publications/catalogue/state-democracy-africa-and-middle-east-2021 accessed 3 June 2022.

Adem Kassie Abebe, *Reimagining Constitutional Change and Democracy in Africa: Emerging Supranational Standards for Constitutional Change* In: *Constitutional Change and Constitutionalism in Africa*. Edited by: Charles M. Fombad and Nico Steytler, Oxford University Press. © Adem Kassie Abebe 2025. DOI: 10.1093/9780198957034.003.0005

that have sought to undermine democratic competition.[3] In addition to pervasive challenges to the practice of constitutionalism and a culture of respect for the rules and spirit of constitutional democracy, 'abusive constitutionalism'[4]—the use of constitutional change and interpretation to reinforce authoritarianism and personalization of power—has also been rampant in Africa.

The ease with which old or new dominant personalities and political groups have sought to reverse key concessions, such as term limits, that were adopted at moments of power balance and incumbent vulnerability[5] reveal the limits of domestic forces to effectively resist constitutional changes undermining constitutional democracy. Recognition of the constraints facing domestic stakeholders has led to calls for, and emergence of, continental and regional standards for the making and changing of constitutions and other fundamental rules governing democratic and electoral processes.

This chapter explores emerging shared continental and regional economic community procedural and normative standards regulating constitution-making and amendments as part of a broader 'Africanization' and harmonization of constitutional law and constitutionalism.[6] It also assesses the propriety, sufficiency, interpretation, and implications of these emerging standards, and proposes ideas to enhance their value and relevance at the domestic level.

In particular, the chapter interrogates the emerging idea of 'national consensus' as a continental standard for constitutional change and discusses what the adoption of the standard means for both the process and legitimacy of amendments—beyond the traditional reliance on supermajorities, referendums, unamendable clauses, and judicial review of amendments. Notably, drawing on the literature on 'the separation of parties, not branches',[7] the chapter argues that constitutional amendment rules should require cross-party support—rather than merely supermajorities, judicial review, or referendums—for the most abused aspects of constitutional and democratic rules. The latter are often agreed upon in pacts at moments of incumbent vulnerability but are then the focus of efforts by old or new incumbents to reverse them during periods of dominance.[8]

While standard amendment procedures, alongside popular protests, have deterred or prevented abusive constitutional changes, dominant leaders have all too often succeeded in passing changes that require high majorities (for example, Uganda); moreover, courts have either been unable to prevent abusive constitutional changes (for example, Senegal and Côte d'Ivoire) or have even enabled them (for example, Burundi and the Democratic Republic of the Congo), while referendums have been used to bypass constitutional rules (for example, Guinea) and institutional resistance (for example, Comoros).

[3] See generally Charles Fombad, 'Some Perspectives on Durability and Change under Modern African Constitutions' (2013) 11(2) International Journal of Constitutional Law 382, 382.

[4] David Landau, 'Abusive Constitutionalism' (2013) 47(1) UC Davis Law Review 189. In the African context, see Fombad (n 3).

[5] See Adem Kassie Abebe, 'The Vulnerability of Constitutional Pacts: Inclusive Majoritarianism as Protection against Democratic Backsliding' in International IDEA, *Annual Review of Constitution-Building 2019* (International IDEA 2020) https://constitutionnet.org/sites/default/files/2021-01/annual-review-of-constitution-building-2019.pdf accessed 10 December 2022.

[6] Micha Wiebusch, 'Africanization of Constitutional Law' in Rosalind Dixon, Tom Ginsburg, and Adem Kassie Abebe (eds), *Comparative Constitutional Law in Africa* (Edward Elgar 2022).

[7] Daryl J Levinson and Richard H Pildes, 'Separation of Parties, Not Powers' (2006) 119(8) Harvard Law Review 2311.

[8] Abebe (n 5).

Quite simply, amendment rules that rely on supermajorities, referendums, unamendable provisions, or even judicial review assume a level of democratic competition and judicial independence that can be hard to find in certain countries. Indeed, some of the constitutional changes seek precisely to undermine competition and judicial independence, both of which are necessary for the effectiveness of traditional amendment rules.

Against this backdrop, section 2 of this chapter provides examples of the nature and manifestations of abusive constitutional reform (including both new constitution-making and amendment) from across the continent. Section 3 explores emerging continental and regional normative and procedural standards on constitutional reform and discusses attempts at monitoring and implementing them with a view to laying the foundations to inform the harmonization of constitutional law on the continent. This section proposes a shift in the policy, strategy, and engagement of the continent and its Regional Economic Communities (RECs) from reactive condemnation of regressive moves to the proactive prevention of regressive constitutional and democratic changes, the encouragement and enablement of democratic progress, and the provision of technical support to constitutional reform processes.

Section 4 focuses both on the idea of national consensus as an Africa-wide foundation for constitutional reform and on its judicial application, based on case law, by domestic and continental judicial bodies. Section 5 proposes a novel way of enhancing the role of the opposition in constitutional reform—and, broadly, in constitutional and democratic governance—in order to operationalize the principle of national consensus and, in the process, incentivize African aspirations for 'consensus democracy'[9] and a cooperative and deliberative democratic dispensation that tames a pervasive, destabilizing, winner-takes-all politics. The overall aim thereof would be to enhance democratic resilience and ward against threats of backsliding. The last section offers some concluding remarks.

2. Patterns of constitutional change: Progress, resilience, and regression

Constitution-making and change are critical in laying the foundational rules for the democratic game. Democratic constitution-making affirms the acceptance of democracy as the 'only game in town'[10] and seeks to set out the normative, institutional, and procedural frameworks to enable it. At the same time, constitutional rules are not necessarily neutral, and constitutions are often made within a context of limited information as to the consequences of specific choices and their interaction with other choices.[11] Accordingly, when political interests and power balances shift, and when new understandings and knowledge come to light, debates on constitutional reform emerge, particularly in situations where the rules of the democratic game have not taken root and are continually contested. Political conflict then plays out over the constitutional framework itself rather than within the constitution.

[9] See Nic Cheeseman and Sishuwa, 'African Studies Keyword: Democracy' (2021) 64(3) African Studies Review 704. According to the authors, Africans prefer 'consensual democracy', which 'places limits on the extent of political competition, but without compromising the principle of political accountability'.

[10] Adam Przeworski, 'Democracy as Equilibrium' (2005) 3(4) Public Choice 253.

[11] Tom Ginsburg and Sumit Bisarya, 'Introduction' in Tom Ginsburg and Sumit Bisarya (eds), *Constitution Makers on Constitution Making* (CUP 2022) 2–4.

Constitutional change is a constant process: in fact, some have suggested the propriety of reconsidering constitutional frameworks at regular intervals while still ensuring constitutional stability.[12] More commonly, constitutions establish amendment procedures to establish a predictable and orderly mechanism to adapt the rules of the game. While amendment rules are meant to enable improvements in the constitutional framework in a way that reflects new thinking and information,[13] such processes can be, and have been, used to reverse fundamental compromises that were reached at the time of constitution-making.

The history of constitution-making and change in Africa since the wave of democratization in the 1990s reflects a record of progress and resilience but also of regression. The making of new constitutions and amendments may represent fundamental progress in a country's democratic trajectory, such as the Constitution of Kenya (2010), the Constitution of Niger (2010), the Constitution of Senegal (2002) and its 2016 amendments, and the 1997 amendments of the Constitution of Botswana establishing an independent election management body.

Some constitutional frameworks have also proved resilient despite attempts at undermining key aspects of them. Notably, efforts at removing term limits in Zambia (2001), Malawi (2003), Nigeria (2006), and Benin (2017) were defeated thanks to the relatively competitive democratic context of these countries. In Burkina Faso, attempts at removing term limits led to popular protests that forced the incumbent to flee in 2014. In addition, term limits have remained intact in several other countries—including those with dominant ruling parties, such as Tanzania, South Africa, Mozambique, and Botswana—largely due to the strength of their political parties, which, remarkably, have avoided (so far) the personalization of politics.[14]

In some cases, courts have also invalidated constitutional amendments on procedural as well as substantive grounds. Perhaps the most prominent example is the Constitutional Court of Benin. The Court has not only protected and expanded the unamendable provisions, notably in relation to presidential term limits,[15] but also popularized the principle of 'national consensus'[16] as both a substantive and procedural standard to evaluate the constitutionality of constitutional amendments (in addition to limits on the amendment power in the form of unamendable provisions). On this basis, the Court invalidated a constitutional amendment extending the term of Parliament from four to five years in a closed legislative session as unconstitutional.[17] While it may be argued that the Court has not applied the principle of national consensus consistently—particularly following the appointment of President Patrice Talon's former private lawyer as president of the Court, a person who resigned in July 2022 to rejoin the ruling party—the principle offers an important normative foundation for protecting constitutional democracy.

[12] See generally Zachary Elkins, Tom Ginsburg, and James Melton, *The Endurance of National Constitutions* (CUP 2012).

[13] Tom Ginsburg, Zachary Elkins, and James Melton, 'The Lifespan of Written Constitutions' (*The University of Chicago: The Law School*, 15 October 2009) https://www.law.uchicago.edu/news/lifespan-written-constitutions accessed 14 June 2022.

[14] Christof Hartmann, 'Authoritarian Origins of Term Limit Trajectories in Africa' (2022) 29(1) Democratization 57–73. The author argues that single-party authoritarian regimes create a favourable context for the enforcement of term limits, whereas personalistic regimes make their circumvention likely.

[15] Constitutional Court of Benin, Decision No DCC 11-067, 20 October 2011; Constitutional Court of Benin, Judgment No DCC 14-199, 20 November 2014.

[16] Constitutional Court of Benin, Decision No DCC 06-074, 8 July 2006.

[17] Ibid.

In Niger, the Constitutional Court, in 2009, rejected the plan to hold a constitutional referendum to adopt an ostensibly new constitution and thereby bypass the constitutional prohibition of amendment of presidential term limits by resetting the term count of the then president, who was serving his second and last term.[18] The president's subsequent decision to suspend the Constitutional Court and Parliament led to a military coup and the subsequent reinstatement of constitutional governance via the adoption of a new constitution.[19]

On a few occasions, the South African Constitutional Court has also invalidated constitutional amendments for their failure to comply with the constitutional requirement of meaningful public consultation in the amendment process.[20] The Court is yet to determine whether it has the mandate to review the substance of constitutional amendments.[21] In 2020, the Constitutional Court of the Central African Republic confirmed that unamendable constitutional provisions may not be subject to amendments even in an emergency situation.[22] The Court appeared to open the possibility of a process of national consensus to determine ways of complying with the Constitution in emergency situations where compliance with unamendable provisions is rendered impossible. Nevertheless, in 2022, it invalidated an attempt by the president to resort to the making of an ostensibly new constitution to bypass the prohibition against amendment of presidential term limits.[23]

In 2022, the Kenyan Supreme Court reversed the findings of lower courts that the Kenyan Constitution recognizes a basic structure that cannot be amended through the amendment procedures established in the Constitution.[24] The lower courts had outlined a four-step process—involving public education, consultation, establishment of and deliberation in a constituent assembly, and approval in a referendum—to amend provisions affecting the basic structure. Although the Supreme Court rejected the applicability of the basic structure doctrine in the specific case, it found the proposed constitutional amendment unconstitutional and invalid on the ground that the president did not have the power to propose amendments through public initiation, one of the three amendment procedures anticipated in the Constitution.[25]

Finally, the Tanzanian Court of Appeal, while finding that it did not have the mandate to review the substance of constitutional amendments, advised the government that a proposed amendment that sought to ban independent candidates from all elections may be

[18] Mamane Dalatou, 'Niger to Hold Constitutional Referendum on 3rd Term' (*Associated Press*, 6 June 2009) https://www.taiwannews.com.tw/en/news/969122 accessed 14 June 2022.

[19] See generally Virgine Baudais and Gregory Chauzal, 'The 2010 Coup d'état in Niger: A Praetorian Regulation of Politics?' (2011) 110(439) African Affairs 295.

[20] Karen Syma Czapanskiy and Rashida Manjoo, 'The Right of Public Participation in the Law-Making Process and the Role of the Legislature in the Promotion of this Right' (2008) 19(1) Duke Journal of Comparative and International Law 1; Linda Nyati, 'Public Participation: What Has the Constitutional Court Given the Public?' (2010) 12(2) Law, Democracy & Development 102.

[21] See Adem Kassie Abebe, 'The Substantive Validity of Constitutional Amendments in South Africa' (2014) 131 (3) South African Law Journal 656.

[22] Sonia Vohito, 'Covid-19 and the Unamendable Limits on Duration of Presidential and Legislative Terms in the Central African Republic' (*ConstitutionNet*, 22 June 2020) https://constitutionnet.org/news/covid-19-and-unamendable-limits-duration-presidential-and-legislative-terms-central-african accessed 14 June 2022.

[23] Sonia Vohito, 'Courts vs Incumbents: Guaranteeing Alternation of Power in the Central African Republic' (*ConstitutionNet*, 29 September 2022) https://constitutionnet.org/news/courts-vs-incumbents-central-african-republic accessed 20 December 2022. Nevertheless, the president unconstitutionally altered the composition of the court and organized a referendum in July 2023 which led to the adoption of a constitution without presidential term limits.

[24] *David Ndii and others v Attorney General and Others*, Petition No E282 of 2020; *Attorney General and Others v David Ndii and Others*, Civil Appeal Nos E291, E292, E293, and E294 of 2021.

[25] *The Attorney General and 2 Others v David Ndii and 79 others*, SC Petition No 12 of 2021, 31 March 2022.

incompatible with Tanzania's international human rights obligations.[26] The amendment was adopted following a decision by the High Court that the legislative ban on amendments was unconstitutional. As will be seen below, the African Court on Human and Peoples' Rights (African Court) ultimately found the ban incompatible with the right to association guaranteed in the African Charter on Human and Peoples' Rights (African Charter).[27]

However, despite these snippets of stories of progress and resilience in relation to constitutional amendments, on many occasions new constitutions and amendments have pursued objectives that are regressive from the perspective of democratic constitutionalism, the notion of checks and balances and separation of powers, and concerns with the concentration of power in the presidency, centralization of power in the national government, and the protection of fundamental rights.

Prior to the 1990s, liberal Independence Constitutions and multiparty democratic systems were obliterated through a combination of *coups d'état* and constitutional amendments that resulted in one-party dictatorships.[28] Since the 1990s, attempts at removing or otherwise tampering with term limits have been successful more often than not.[29] Incumbents across the continent have managed to change the number or duration of constitutional term limits on the presidency, whether through constitutional amendments (for example, Guinea in 2001, Togo in 2002, Gabon in 2003, Uganda in 2005, Chad in 2005, Cameroon in 2008, Algeria in 2008, Djibouti in 2010, Rwanda in 2015, Egypt in 2019, and Senegal in 2008), the adoption of ostensibly new constitutions to bypass unamendable term limits or change term-limit counts (for example, Republic of Congo in 2015, Comoros in 2018, Guinea in 2020, Côte d'Ivoire in 2020, and the Democratic Republic of the Congo in 2016), or through judicial interpretations allowing incumbents to run for third terms (for example, Namibia in 1998, Burkina Faso in 2003, Senegal in 2012, Burundi in 2015, and Côte d'Ivoire in 2020). Term-limit provisions have been reinstated by amendments in Togo (2019), Chad (2018), Algeria (2016), and Uganda (2017).

Beyond term limits, constitutional amendments in some countries have also sought to undercut democratic competition, centralize power in the presidency, or otherwise undermine checks on government power. For instance, in 2018 Benin introduced a party sponsorship system requiring candidates to obtain the endorsement of at least sixteen members of the National Assembly (of which there are 83 members) or mayors (of which there are 77).[30] While the number may seem relatively low, the requirement came after opposition parties boycotted the 2018 legislative elections owing to alleged repressive tactics and changes to the electoral law establishing, among other rules, a requirement for political parties to receive a 'certificate of conformity' from the Ministry of Interior and to secure at least

[26] *Attorney General v Reverend Christopher Mtikila*, Civil Appeal No 45 of 2009, 17 June 2010.

[27] *Christopher R Mtikila and Others v Republic of Tanzania*, Application Nos 009/2011 and 011/2011, Judgment of 14 June 2013.

[28] Lawrence Zimba, 'The Origins and Spread of One-Party States in Commonwealth Africa' in Muna Ndulo (ed), *Law in Zambia* (East African Publishing House 1984) 3–41; John Hatchard, 'Perfecting Imperfections: Developing Procedures for Amending Constitutions in Commonwealth Africa' (1998) 36(3) Journal of Modern African Studies 381, 382.

[29] See generally Julia Grauvogel and Charlotte Heyl, 'The Study of Term Limits in Sub-Saharan Africa: Lessons on Democratisation and Autocratisation' (2021) 55(3) Africa Spectrum 215–27.

[30] David Zounmenou, Jeannine Ella Abatan, and Michael Matongbada, 'A Third Election without Main Opposition Parties in Benin' (*Institute for Security Studies*, 8 April 2021) https://issafrica.org/iss-today/a-third-election-without-main-opposition-parties-in-benin accessed 28 April 2022.

fifteen members from each municipality of Benin, as well as banning party alliances from presenting a list of candidates for elections. This change came after the country changed the electoral code imposing, among other requirements, a 10 per cent threshold for winning seats in the National Assembly.[31] The implementation of these changes favoured the incumbent leadership and led to an opposition boycott of the 2019 legislative elections. Indeed, following its observation of the elections, the African Union Election Observation Mission noted that the 10 per cent threshold 'appears to contradict the fundamental principles of fairness and equal suffrage'.[32]

The Benin experience demonstrates the importance of regulating fundamental aspects of the electoral law in the constitution rather than leaving it to legislative regulation—the latter creates the possibility of unilateral alteration of the rules of the game by one of the players (the transient majority), which is ill-advised regardless of the merits of the reforms.[33] The rules in Benin were adopted ostensibly to stem the fragmentation and proliferation of candidates and parties (in a country of about 12 million people which was reportedly home to more than 200 parties before the changes) by encouraging nationwide and ideological political formations rather than regionalized identity-based formations. Nevertheless, this meant, in effect, that opposition presidential candidates needed the endorsement of Members of Parliament and mayors aligned with the ruling coalition.

These reforms have thus proven extremely controversial, partly because the issues are not regulated at the constitutional level and are hence seen as opportunistic—even capricious—moves by a transient political majority. Benin, once a paragon of democracy in francophone Africa, was downgraded in 2019 and 2020 to a hybrid or partly democratic system in all major democracy rankings, and there are concerns that President Talon may use his dominance to remove or otherwise alter term limits to run again despite his promise that he would not run for a third term[34] and the fact that the Constitution expressly makes the term-limit provision unamendable.

In Zimbabwe, the ruling party removed crucial aspects of the 2013 Constitution in order to enhance the president's appointment powers over the judiciary, this in spite of carefully crafted checks and balances in the initial inclusive drafting process that led to the adoption of the Constitution.[35] The Constitution subjects key judicial appointments to a public interview process. The first amendment exempted appointments of the Chief Justice, Deputy Chief Justice, and Judge President of the High Court from public interviews, with the president making appointments after non-binding consultations with the Judicial Service

[31] Tim Hirschel-Burns, 'Benin's King of Cotton Makes its Democracy a Sham' (*Foreign Policy*, 8 April 2021) https://foreignpolicy.com/2021/04/08/benin-election-democracy-sham-patrice-talon/ accessed 14 June 2022.

[32] African Union, 'Mission D'observation Electorale de L'union Africaine pour les Elections Legislatives du 28 Avril 2019 en Republique du Benin: Conclusions Preliminaires' (*African Union*, 30 April 2019) https://bit.ly/46rURXz accessed 1 October 2023.

[33] Adem Kassie Abebe, 'The Winner Shall Not Take It All: Constitutional Regulation and Empowerment of Opposition Parties in Africa' in Tom Ginsburg, Aziz Huq and Tarun Khaitan (eds), *The Constitutional Law of Democracy Around the World: How Elections, Parties and the Right to Vote are Enshrined Globally* (Cambridge University Press, 2024).

[34] 'Benin President Talon Pledges Not to Seek Third Mandate' (*RFI*, 30 April 2021) https://www.rfi.fr/en/africa/20210430-benin-president-patrice-talon-pledges-not-to-seek-third-mandate-elections-violence-protests-democracy-governance-africa accessed 28 April 2022.

[35] D Tinashe Hofisi, 'Clawing Back the Gains of Popular Participation – The First Amendment to the Constitution of Zimbabwe (2013)' (*ConstitutionNet*, 26 September 2017) http://www.constitutionnet.org/news/clawing-back-gains-popular-participation-first-amendment-constitution-zimbabwe-2013 accessed 28 April 2022.

Commission.[36] The second amendment exempted the promotion of judges from the public competition process, instead leaving their promotion at the behest of the president on the advice of the Commission. In addition, the amendment removed the presidential running-mate clause, which required presidents and two vice presidents to run on the same ticket. Instead, the president, after his or her election, will continue to appoint the vice president. This procedure empowers the president and his or her party at the expense of the people.

Interestingly, the provision on the replacement of the president in the event of death, impeachment, or resignation, which allows the first vice president to finish the remaining term and appears to assume the election of vice presidents on the same ticket, was not similarly reformed to require elections in the event of presidential death, incapacity, resignation, or removal. The tradition of abusive amendments preceded the adoption of the 2013 Constitution—prior to the adoption of this Constitution, several constitutional amendments were introduced to reverse decisions of the Supreme Court.[37] For instance, Amendment No 17 reversed the decision in *Chirwa v Registrar General*[38] which invalidated vague restrictions on the freedom of persons to leave Zimbabwe.

As these examples indicate, constitution-making and amendment processes in Africa have led in several instances to improvements in constitutional frameworks. In addition, the traditional bulwarks against regressive amendments, such as supermajorities, unamendable provisions, referendums, and judicial interventions, have proved relevant and resilient in some cases, especially in contexts of relatively competitive politics, and even in countries with dominant but internally well-organized parties (and thus have not been subverted and personalized by a dominant leader). Nevertheless, on many crucial occasions these same traditional mechanisms have also failed to safeguard against regressive amendments. In other words, the assumptions of competitive democracy—for example, that no single party controls a supermajority, or enjoys a level of dominance sufficient to enable it to amend the constitution unilaterally—that underlie traditional constitutional amendment rules do not always obtain, partly because of skewed electoral rules and partly because of repression and electoral rigging. Moreover, even the protection of such provisions as unamendable has not always prevented regressive changes—in the case of term limits, such protection has been bypassed, particularly through resort to making ostensibly new constitutions.

3. African standards on constitutional reform

Traditionally, the content and contours of the rules for constitutional reform are defined in the constitutional framework itself, as interpreted by the relevant constitutional adjudicators and reinforced by (unwritten) political conventions. Constitutional reform is a quintessentially domestic affair. At the same time, increasingly, beyond domestic actors and stakeholders, constitution-making and amendment processes—whether representing

[36] D Tinashe Hofisi, 'In the Shadow of Robert Mugabe? Twists and Turns in the First and Second Amendments to the Constitution of Zimbabwe' (*ConstitutionNet*, 30 April 2021) https://constitutionnet.org/news/twists-and-turns-in-zimbabwe accessed 3 June 2022.

[37] See Zimbabwe Lawyers for Human Rights, 'Amendments to the Constitution of Zimbabwe: A Constant Assault on Democracy and Constitutionalism' http://www1.umn.edu/humanrts/research/constitution%20statement-sunday%20mirror.pdf accessed 3 June 2022.

[38] 1993 (1) ZLR 291 (S).

progress, resilience, or regression—interact in diverse ways with international norms, processes, and institutions. For instance, constitutional change in one country could be triggered by developments in others, particularly neighbouring or otherwise historically linked countries. Constitutional change may also occur in line with the decisions and recommendations of supranational political and judicial actors.

More specifically, standards bearing on both the content and process of constitution-making and change have increasingly been internationalized, particularly with the notable emergence of the international bill of rights, international trade law, and the globalization of markets, ideas, and networks, all of which incentivize certain behaviours while imposing costs, and therefore limits, on the political choices and freedoms of domestic actors.

In addition to these general international standards, the AU and its RECs have developed a number of standards focused directly on constitution-making and change. In this regard, the shift from the principle of non-interference and non-indifference that marked the transformation of the Organisation of African Unity into the AU is perhaps best reflected in two key matters: peace and the prevention of atrocities, and the Africanization of fundamental values and objectives, including in relation to continental integration and constitutional rules and governance.[39] The AU has emerged as a critical norm-setter, monitor, enforcer, and enabler through its political support for the implementation of its norms and provision of technical support and capacity enhancement.[40]

Normatively, the African human rights system contains not only a broad and comprehensive set of rights—including civil and political rights, socio-economic and cultural rights, and group rights—but also institutional guarantees in regard to the rule of law, democracy, separation of powers, judicial independence, free and fair elections, independent election management bodies, and the depoliticization of the security establishment.[41] Furthermore, apart from human rights instruments, the 2000 Lomé Declaration recognizes political pluralism, democratic change of government, and recognition of a role for the political opposition as fundamental principles.[42] The Declaration also provides that countries must adopt constitutions the content of which is 'in conformity with generally acceptable principles of democracy'. The Declaration recognizes that compliance with these substantive principles and the strengthening of democratic institutions considerably reduce the risk of unconstitutional changes of government in the form of *coups d'état*.

Building on the Declaration, the 2007 African Charter on Democracy, Elections and Governance (ACDEG), in its article 23(5), prohibits 'any amendment or revision of the constitution or legal instruments which is an infringement on the principles of democratic change of government'. The application of these standards involves three separate but cumulative assessments: the use of an amendment to a constitution or law; whether it enables access to or maintenance of power; and whether the amendment constitutes an infringement of 'principles of democratic change of government'.[43] While the Charter had been

[39] Adem Kassie Abebe and Charles Fombad, 'The African Union and the Advancement of Democracy: The Problem of Unconstitutional Retention of Government Power' in Charles Fombad and Nico Steytler (eds), *Democracy, Elections and Constitutionalism in Africa* (OUP 2021).

[40] See generally Wiebusch (n 6).

[41] Adem Kassie Abebe, 'Taming Regressive Constitutional Amendments: The African Court as a Continental (Super) Constitutional Court' (2019) 17(1) International Journal of Constitutional Law 89, 109.

[42] Lomé Declaration of July 2000 on the Framework for an OAU Response to Unconstitutional Changes of Government (AHG/Decl.5 (XXXVI).

[43] Abebe and Fombad (n 39).

ratified by only 36 of the 55 member states of the AU as at December 2022,[44] considering that 46 states have signed it, and noting the substantive guarantee of democratic principles in several African instruments, it can be argued that the rule against revising constitutions and laws such that they undermine principles of democratic change of government applies to all member states. Indeed, in the Lomé Declaration and subsequent decisions, the AU has rejected 'violations of democratic standards', the persistence and recurrence of which could result in unconstitutional changes.[45] The AU has also called on all member states to 'ensure that constitutional amendments are done in accordance with the provisions of the ACDEG, as a baseline'.[46]

In recognition of the centrality of constitution-making to addressing the root causes of conflict, the AU Peace and Security Council (PSC) has adopted a policy framework guaranteeing a number of substantive and procedural safeguards related to constitution-making.[47] With a view to establishing stable and effective political governance frameworks, the policy emphasizes the importance of political participation, the rule of law, independent civil oversight, the separation of powers, and inclusive politics and pluralism, and calls, in paragraph 36, for 'a constitutional, democratic governance framework that guarantees periodic contestation for political office, based on the rule of law'.

To this end, the PSC has the mandate to promote checks and balances in public governance structures; to ensure the establishment of independent institutions such as election commissions and offices of the ombudsperson; to ensure the separation of powers between the executive, judiciary, and legislature, the decentralization of power over decision-making and management of resources, and the representation of women in decision-making positions in public institutions; and to ensure the existence of a constitutionally protected effective and independent media. Crucially, the policy requires that national constitutions must be congruent with the AU Constitutive Act.

In addition to the above *substantive* standards relating to constitutional reform, there are continental standards relating to the *process* of constitutional reform. The Lomé Declaration provides that both the preparation and revision of constitutions should be compatible with 'accepted principles' of democracy. More specifically, article 10(2) of the ACDEG provides that the process of amendment or revision of constitutions should repose 'on national consensus, obtained if need be, through referendum'. An AU Decision of 2016 reiterates the importance of complying with the standards outlined in the ACDEG but also requires that constitutional amendments involve the active participation of citizens.[48] The same decision calls on member states to establish 'permanent, impartial and independent national Constitutional Review Commissions'. Furthermore, in the context of post-conflict in particular, the PSC policy requires states to ensure the provision of

[44] For the status of ratification of the Charter, see https://bit.ly/3Q8EjOs accessed 28 October 2023.

[45] African Union, 'Decision on the Prevention of Unconstitutional Changes of Government and Strengthening the Capacity of the African Union to Manage such Situations', Assembly/AU/Dec.269(XIV) Rev.1, 2 February 2010, para 5.

[46] African Union, 'Decision on Governance, Constitutionalism and Elections in Africa' (2016) Assembly/AU/Dec.592 (XXVI).

[47] African Union Peace and Security Council, 'Policy on Post-Conflict Reconstruction and Development' (2006) https://www.peaceau.org/uploads/pcrd-policy-framwowork-eng.pdf accessed 1 October 2023.

[48] African Union, 'Decision on Governance, Constitutionalism and Elections in Africa' (2016) Assembly/AU/Dec.592 (XXVI).

opportunities and mechanisms that enhance popular participation in, and access to, the process of constitution-making.[49]

The substantive and process standards for constitutional change at the continental level have been reinforced through regional standards. Notably, the Economic Community of West African States (ECOWAS) Protocol on Democracy and Good Governance requires respect for the principles of, inter alia, the separation of powers; judicial independence; free, fair, and transparent elections; secularism and religious neutrality; decentralization of power; and non-partisan and apolitical armed, police, and security forces, and their subordination to civilian authorities.[50] In terms of process, the Protocol requires popular participation in decision-making, which would include constitutional reform, and, in article 2(1), specifically bans changes to electoral rules within six months of an election, 'except with the consent of a majority of political actors'.

Unlike ECOWAS, the East African Community (EAC), the Southern African Development Community (SADC), and other RECs recognized by the AU do not yet have protocols dedicated to democracy and good governance. Nevertheless, the treaties establishing the communities recognize democracy, human rights, and gender equality as fundamental principles and objectives.[51] In combination with the continental standards, these principles can provide a basis to monitor, inform, and possibly challenge constitution-making and amendment processes.

The implications of the applicable continental and regional rules for both the substance and process of constitutional change and revision are yet to be clarified authoritatively. Nonetheless, the standards arguably apply to both the making of new constitutions and the amendment of existing ones. To help clarify the standards, the AU PSC in 2018 mandated the AU Commission to prepare 'guidelines for constitutional amendment'.[52] Almost five years later, the guidelines are yet to materialize. In 2022, a declaration by the AU, regional organizations, and other stakeholders denounced unconstitutional changes of government, including the 'manipulation of democratic processes to effect constitutional amendments or revisions for entrenching power of the incumbent in violation of the national democratic principles'.[53] The declaration called, furthermore, for the finalization and adoption of AU guidelines on the amendment of constitutions based on:

> the AU's existing laws, policies and practice relating to constitutionalism and rule of law, with particular reference to the African Charter on Democracy, Election and Governance, to guide constitutional amendment processes [to] adhere to formal rules and procedures ... taking place in a peaceful environment, fully respecting democratic rights and ... based on a national consensus.[54]

[49] African Union Peace and Security Council (n 47) para 37.

[50] art 1(a) of the Protocol on Democracy and Good Governance Supplementary to the Protocol Relating to the Mechanism for Conflict Prevention, Management, Resolution, Peacekeeping and Security.

[51] For example, arts 6(d) and 7(2) of the EAC Treaty and arts 4(c) and 5(1)(b) and (c) of the SADC Treaty.

[52] African Union, 'PSC Press Statement of the 791st Meeting on 22 August 2018' (PSC/PR/BR (DCCXCI) (22 August 2018) https://www.peaceau.org/uploads/psc.791.press.statement.africa.charter.on.democracy.22.08.pdf accessed 29 June 2022.

[53] African Union, 'Declaration on Unconstitutional Changes of Government in Africa', adopted on 17 March 2022, para 16.

[54] Ibid.

Wiebusch and Murray have argued similarly that the continental standards on constitutional change may be clustered into four elements, keeping in mind the political, social, and economic contexts in which amendments occur rather than focusing only on a formal, rule-based assessment: adherence to formal rules and procedures (rule of law); a peaceful environment (stability); respect for democratic rights (legality); and national consensus (legitimacy).[55] While these elements provide a useful framework, they are arguably narrow and overlook a plethora of substantive and process standards for constitution-making and amendments that go beyond 'democratic rights', such as the separation of powers or judicial independence.

Overall, the standards for constitutional amendment at the African and regional level provide helpful guidance in monitoring and assessing constitutional reform processes, but they remain extremely vague principles, both at the normative and process levels. What is clear is that the assessment of the legality, validity, and legitimacy of constitution-making and revision processes in Africa can no longer be confined to the applicable rules at the national level. In effect, therefore, the continental and regional standards constitute an additional layer of guidance and constraint on constitutional reforms over and above that provided in domestic constitutional, legislative, judicial, and conventional standards.

Given the AU's large number of member states and the diversity of their legal systems and experience, the broadness of the continental substantive and procedural requirements guiding constitutional reform is unavoidable and may be even desirable, in that it allows for innovative approaches to constitutional change and enables adaptation in line with evolution in political thinking, frameworks, and national and continental experience. Nevertheless, the vagueness also creates challenges in regard to monitoring, enforcement, and the existence of competing interpretations. Indeed, some countries have rejected the interpretations of the African Court in reviewing and invalidating constitutional amendments based on continental standards.[56]

In this context of broad legal uncertainty about the exact content and implications of the continental standards, the vagueness of the principles may make the proactive engagement of the AU and regional organizations critical in ensuring compliance with the principles through early support to constitution-making and amendment processes rather than through post-enactment review or criticism of amendments incompatible with continental standards. The AU needs to enhance its capacity in this regard to ensure it monitors constitution-making and amendment processes across the continent; avail and familiarize domestic actors with the relevant continental standards and expectations; and provide advice and technical assistance based on continental and comparative experience.

Such proactive engagement would not only be more effective than reactive and post-enactment criticism or judicial challenge but would also involve a less adversarial mechanism expanding the horizon of choices for the parties. It is thus more likely to be welcomed and be impactful. Proactive engagement could be undertaken through existing institutions, such as the African Governance Architecture, which monitors compliance with the

[55] Micha Wiebusch and Christina Murray, 'Presidential Term Limits and the African Union' (2019) 63(1) Journal of African Law 131, 157.

[56] For instance, the government of Benin rejected the power of the African Court to review constitutional amendments on the ground that it is beyond its mandate. See the submission of Benin in *XYZ v Republic of Benin*, Application No 010/2020, 27 November 2020. The country did not implement the decision of the Court to abandon the amendments and postpone elections.

ACDEG, or through the establishment of a dedicated panel of experts, potentially consisting of African professionals acting on a voluntary basis, to monitor critical constitutional and legal reform processes across the continent and to offer direct engagement and support (akin to the role of the Council of Europe's Commission for Democracy through Law, also known as the Venice Commission).[57]

Judicial organs at the African continental and domestic levels have had to grapple with cases involving the compliance of constitution-making and amendment processes with democratic principles. Courts in Benin, the Gambia, Kenya, Niger, the Central African Republic, and South Africa have on different occasions invalidated constitutional amendments on procedural and/or substantive grounds.

At the continental level, the African Court has invalidated constitutional amendments on both substantive and procedural grounds. As regards substance, following a decision of the High Court of Tanzania invalidating a legislative amendment banning independent candidates from running for office, the Tanzanian government amended the Constitution to implement the same, thereby seeking to insulate the amendment from judicial review on constitutional grounds. The High Court again found the constitutional amendment unconstitutional,[58] but the Court of Appeal, the apex court, reversed the High Court decision and found that constitutional amendments adopted through the provided constitutional procedure cannot be reviewed or invalidated on substantive grounds.[59] The Court nevertheless indicated that the amendment may be incompatible with Tanzania's international responsibilities. Indeed, subsequently, the African Court found that the amendment banning independent candidates from contesting presidential and other elections is incompatible with the right to political participation.[60]

The African Court has also found the composition of the electoral commission of Côte d'Ivoire—whose membership was based on share of representation of the political groups, with higher representation for the party of the president—incompatible with requirements of independence and impartiality of election management bodies as guaranteed in the ACDEG.[61]

As regards procedural grounds, the African Court found an amendment to the Constitution of Benin invalid on the grounds of its violation of the principle of 'broad consensus' because the Parliament that approved the amendment was constituted entirely of parties affiliated with the president of the republic, and due to failure to ensure broad consultation.[62] The constitutional amendment was adopted following a boycott of parliamentary elections by the opposition in response to legislative changes which it claimed

[57] Abebe and Fombad (n 39).

[58] *Mtikila v Attorney General* [2006] TZH 5 (5 May 2006).

[59] *The Honourable Attorney General v Reverend Christopher Mtikila*, Civil Appeal No 45 of 2009 (17 June 2010).

[60] *Christopher R Mtikila and Others v Republic of Tanzania*, Application Nos 009/2011 and 011/2011, Judgment of 14 June 2013.

[61] *Actions Pour la Protection des Droits de L'Homme (APDH) v The Republic of Côte d'Ivoire*, App No 001/2014, Judgment of 18 November 2016. It is important to note that the composition of the electoral commission in Côte d'Ivoire is defined not in the Constitution but in organic laws. It has been included in this discussion because such matters are increasingly regulated at the constitutional level, and also to show that leaving matters critical to the rules of the game for legislative regulation could lead to transient majorities altering the rules to favour their interests. Indeed, the Constitutional Council of Côte d'Ivoire has entertained cases involving the constitutionality of the law. See Segnonna Horace Adjolohun, 'The Making and Remaking of National Constitutions in African Regional Courts' (2018) 1 African Journal of Comparative Constitutional Law 35–70.

[62] *XYZ v Republic of Benin*, Application No 010/2020, 27 November 2020.

undermined its operationality and even its existence. The boycott enabled the ruling coalition to win all the seats in Parliament, which in turn allowed it to amend the Constitution with a four-fifths majority, thereby obviating the need for a referendum, which is necessary only if a four-fifths majority is not obtained.[63]

Overall, constitutional amendment processes in Africa can no longer be seen solely in terms of domestic process and substantive requirements. Accordingly, domestic constitution-makers and reformers should seek to understand and consider African continental—and, as the case may be, regional—standards linked to the theme of constitutional reform. The AU and regional organizations should also provide clear guidance on the standards for constitutional change, promote them, and seek to identify reform processes and offer support to them. In this regard, the adoption of guidelines on constitutional amendment is critical and long overdue.

Such proactive consideration of supranational standards could reduce the need to resort to the African Court to challenge constitutional reforms. In view of the politically sensitive nature of constitutional amendments, the African Court could take these proactive considerations into account and show more deference to constitutional amendments, perhaps doing so on the basis of the margin of appreciation doctrine. Without such a cautious approach, the African Court's perceived aggressive engagement in the review of constitutional amendments could exacerbate the state backlash it has been facing.

Indeed, following the African Court's decision invalidating the amendments and ordering the suspension of preparations for elections, Benin withdrew the declaration allowing individuals and non-governmental organizations to submit cases to the African Court.[64] In a decision that arguably undermines the standing and relevance of the African Court, the AU chose to send observers to the elections despite the failure of the Benin government to comply with the decision of the African Court to rework the constitutional amendment and halt the election preparations.

4. Reimagining constitutional reform through inclusive majoritarianism

As the AU works towards developing and implementing guidelines on constitutional amendments, this section offers some suggestions on operationalizing the principle of 'national consensus' which is recognized as a critical foundation for the legality and legitimacy of constitutional reforms. The discussion also offers ideas for constitution-makers to consider in designing constitutional reforms as well as drafting new constitutions.

The requirement of national consensus assumes the existence of differing ideas, interests, passions, and social and political groups. Considering that constitutions set the ground rules and frameworks within which the democratic game can be played on a level playing field, the requirement of national consensus is intended to ensure that no single

[63] Under the Constitution of Benin, amendments require either a three-quarters majority in Parliament and then approval in a referendum, or approval with a four-fifths majority. See arts 154–56 of the Constitution of Benin (1990).

[64] Apollin Koagne Zouapet, 'Victim of its Commitment... You, Passer-by, a Tear to the Proclaimed Virtue: Should the Epitaph of the African Court on Human and Peoples' Rights be Prepared?' (*EJIL:Talk!*, 5 May 2020) https://www.ejiltalk.org/victim-of-its-commitment-you-passerby-a-tear-to-the-proclaimed-virtue-should-the-epitaph-of-the-african-court-on-human-and-peoples-rights-be-prepared/ accessed 14 June 2022.

transient political group, however dominant it may be, should be able unilaterally to change the rules of a game in which it is but one participant.[65] In addition, national consensus entails the identification and consideration of diverse views not only among political parties but also in broader civil society and among the public. Accordingly, seriously factoring in the principle of national consensus requires that constitutional designers set requirements that there be public education and participation—including, in certain cases, in the form of approval in a referendum—ahead of political deliberation and any adoption of amendments. In this regard, the constitutions of South Africa and Kenya provide examples worthy of emulation, with exemplary features including the allowance these constitutions make for the judicial invalidation of constitutional amendments for failure to comply with public participation requirements.[66]

At the same time, national consensus does not imply unanimity among the public or political forces, which is infeasible in a context of a plurality of interests and political viewpoints as well as of inevitably constrained levels of knowledge and imagination. Nevertheless, the principle of national consensus requires political deliberation, time, and a level of agreement that extends beyond the circles of a ruling party or coalition, especially in relation to constitutional rules governing democratic competition, such as election regulations, including presidential terms, political parties, and the organization of institutions that protect and promote democracy and the rule of law (for example courts, the bureaucracy, and fourth-branch institutions such as human rights and election commissions).

In view of this, it is argued that the principle of national consensus entails the reimagination of the historical reliance on supermajorities and/or referendums for the approval of constitutional amendments. Instead, constitution-makers would recognize deliberation and consensus among political groups as the point of departure. Such a procedure would be centred on the 'separation of *parties*' rather than traditional separation of *powers*,[67] which would necessitate a shift from reliance on supermajorities to 'inclusive majoritarianism' where the procedure of amendment of certain fundamental constitutional provisions would require approval by groups beyond the governing party or coalition.[68] Inclusive majoritarianism is a new approach that transcends the traditional reliance on supermajorities, referendums, unamendable provisions, and judicial review of amendments to reduce the chances of regressive change and limit the ability of democratically elected governments to undermine democracy from within. Instead, the new procedure would recognize and enhance the relative value and role of opposition forces in constitutional governance and decision-making.

The Lomé Declaration already recognizes, as one of the shared values and principles of democratic governance, 'the principle of democratic change and *recognition of a role for the opposition*'.[69] In addition, it specifically calls for 'guaranteeing access to the media for all political stake-holders'. While the recognition of the role of the opposition has wide implications beyond constitutions, the proposed idea of inclusive majoritarianism in relation to constitutional reform would require that amendments receive approval from a

[65] Abebe (n 5).
[66] S 59 of the Constitution of South Africa and art 118 of the Constitution of Kenya impose a duty on state institutions to ensure popular consultation in the amendment process.
[67] Levinson and Pildes (n 7).
[68] Abebe (n 5).
[69] Principle v. Emphasis added.

certain number of political groups. The exact rules and means of operationalization of the idea of inclusive majoritarianism would defy general prescriptions applicable to different contexts, and would have to be imagined and crafted in view of the specific context of each country, depending, for instance, on the degree of sociocultural and political pluralism, the party system (whether two-party or multiparty), and the electoral system (pluralist, majoritarian, or proportional), all of which impact on the number of parties required. Nevertheless, fundamentally, inclusive majoritarianism entails that certain fundamental constitutional amendments should require the support of groups beyond the ruling party or coalition.

This proposed amendment procedure is rare but not without precedent. Perhaps a notable example is the ECOWAS Democracy Protocol's prohibition of changes to electoral rules within six months of elections, 'except with the consent of a majority of political actors'.[70] The provision applies to constitutional but also other electoral rules. While the restriction applies only within a certain time from elections, the basic idea is to exclude any single political force from unilaterally altering the rules of the democratic game. It is important to note that the ECOWAS rule also applies to non-constitutional rules (meaning that it is thus broader than the suggestion in this chapter, which focuses on constitutional reform alone).

At the domestic level, another precedent is offered by Thailand. Under its 2017 Constitution, constitutional amendments must in the final reading be approved by an absolute majority in a joint sitting of the National Assembly, composed of the House of Representatives (500 elected members) and the Senate (200 appointed members).[71] In addition, the amendment must receive support from at least 20 per cent of members of opposition parties—that is, parties in the House of Representatives whose members do not hold the positions of minister, president, or vice president of the House of Representatives. Moreover, not less than one-third of the members of the Senate must approve the amendment. For certain amendments, the Constitution also requires approval in a referendum.

The Thai Constitution in general, and the amendment provision in particular, were designed by the military regime under whose auspices it was drafted in such a way as to limit any single political group from pursuing constitutional amendments.[72] The combination of a relatively low legislative majority and support from opposition parties was preferred to a higher supermajority requirement as a more effective way to balance the anticipated need for reform with broad political consensus in constitutional change.

The Thai amendment process may be seen as part of the military's plan to bake its own design choices into a constitution which it, in effect, imposed. The process is thus founded on a distrust of electoral politics and political parties, which is reflected in the Constitution's establishment of a non-partisan Senate and a slew of independent institutions so as to guarantee military influence.[73] Undertaken in combination with these non-elected institutions and a non-partisan Senate, the amendment process could make constitutional change

[70] art 2(1).

[71] Constitution of Thailand, art 256(6).

[72] On the dominance of Shinawatra, Thailand's prime minister, see Siripan Nogsuan Sawasdee, 'The Conundrum of a Dominant Party in Thailand' (2018) 4(1) Asian Journal of Comparative Politics 102.

[73] On the 'post-political' constitutional tradition in Thailand, see Tom Ginsburg, 'Constitutional Afterlife: The Continuing Impact of Thailand's Postpolitical Constitution' (2008) 7(1) International Journal of Constitutional Law 83.

particularly difficult. Nevertheless, despite their origins, the amendment requirements are achievable, while ensuring that no one political player can alter the constitutional rules single-handedly. The consequence of a cross-party approval requirement is not so much to make change impossible as to encourage a culture of compromise and engagement, which in turn could benefit democracy and constitutionalism. Even if the process makes constitutional change harder, it may be justified considering Thailand's history of political manipulation and dominance—situations which are also familiar in the African context.

Another country that, in effect, requires cross-party approval of constitutional amendments is Jamaica. Amendments to certain provisions of the Jamaican Constitution require two-thirds approval in the House of Representatives and Senate.[74] Because eight of the 23 senators (about 35 per cent of them) are appointed by the governor-general with the advice of the leader of the opposition,[75] constitutional amendments to key provisions cannot be enacted without support from at least one member nominated by the leader of the opposition, regardless of the dominance of the ruling party in the House of Representatives. Although this is a low threshold for opposition concurrence, it can still force cross-party engagement and compromise. Other Caribbean constitutions have similar provisions where a share of senators are appointed on advice of the opposition and other professional or business groups, acting together, which would necessitate that constitutional amendments receive support beyond the ruling parties.[76]

In countries with politically salient linguistic, ethnic, or religious cleavages, constitutional amendments may require cross-community approval, which amounts in effect to cross-party approval. In Cyprus, for instance, constitutional amendments require the approval of two-thirds of the elected representatives of the Turkish community and two-thirds of those of the Greek community.[77] In Africa, the Constitution of Burundi (2018) guarantees the Tutsi minority 40 per cent of seats in the National Assembly.[78] Amendments require a four-fifths approval in the National Assembly and a two-thirds approval in the Senate,[79] effectively allowing the Tutsi minority to block amendments.

While cross-community approval requirements can be good proxies for cross-party approval, this may not always be the case, as dominant cross-ethnic parties could enact amendments unilaterally. For instance, in Burundi political parties are not allowed to organize along ethnic lines; as such, each party must have membership from across communities. A dominant party may, therefore, have the needed numbers to push amendments forward, as the provisions are intended to empower social groups, rather than designed to empower opposition parties. Crucially, the Burundian Constitution allows the president to put constitutional amendments to a referendum[80] without the need for legislative approval. This undermines the consociational political arrangement and allows the president to bypass elite and political party consensus. Indeed, the president used a similar provision in

[74] Constitution of Jamaica (1962/2011), art 49(4)(a). (The author thanks Elliot Bulmer for this example.).

[75] ibid art 35.

[76] Elliot Bulmer, 'Her Majesty's Precarious Opposition: "Clean Sweep" Elections and Constitutional Balance in Commonwealth Caribbean States' in International IDEA, *Annual Review of Constitution Building Processes* (International IDEA 2019).

[77] Constitution of Cyprus (1960), art 182(3). Note that, given the practical division of the Greek and Turkish parts of Cyprus, the Constitution is effectively obsolete.

[78] art 169.

[79] art 287.

[80] arts 203 and 285.

the 2005 Constitution[81] to propose the current Constitution of 2018, which was approved in a referendum.

A hypothetical application of the idea of inclusive majoritarianism to certain constitutional amendments in Africa would show that many of the regressive reforms of the past decades, particularly those removing presidential term limits, would have been formally impossible. For instance, the 2020 constitutional reform that allowed Alpha Conde of Guinea to run for a third term was supported exclusively by his supporters, while the opposition unanimously rejected the initiative. In Zimbabwe, amendments that undermined the independence of the judiciary were also supported only by the ruling party.

It is important to note, though, that inclusive majoritarian amendment procedures might not necessarily have prevented the changes. Some dictators have invoked the constituent power to ignore the formal amendment procedure and hold rigged referendums to adopt seemingly new constitutions. Ruling parties might also establish bogus opposition parties or co-opt opposition parties. Even so, a formal requirement for cross-party approval of reforms would have denied the legitimacy that can emanate from procedural legality and/or have forced incumbents to make efforts to deliberate and compromise with the opposition, in the process offering nominal concessions even to a bogus opposition.

Cross-party approval requirements could be justified on the grounds of both legitimacy and practicality. Because an amendment would require inter-party engagement and compromise, the outcome is likely to approximate popular sentiment, which is the principal determinant of democratic legitimacy. It could also have practical benefits. First, the process encourages better deliberation and the consideration of the passions, interests, and arguments of diverse groups of people. In the African context, the requirement of inter-party approval of constitutional amendments would help curb the almost reflexive resort to capricious and often self-serving constitutional amendment. In addition to preventing certain self-serving amendments, the process would encourage groups to develop a culture of regular engagement and compromise and to recognize the legitimacy of each other's existence. These experiences, considered in the long term, can engender a politics of moderation even in daily political discourse.

The proposal may also provide a more defensible, and potentially more effective, alternative to protecting fundamental substantive principles than incorporating unamendable provisions or enabling judicial review of the substantive validity of amendments.[82] Unamendable provisions are justified on the basis of hard-to-delineate normative or substantive grounds that impose excessive limits on contemporary politics and, therefore, democracy. The elegant reliance instead on a process that can ensure consensus among a cross-range of parties representing diverse constituencies and ideas could make unamendable provisions less urgent or necessary.

The proposed cross-party approval requirement may be challenged on different grounds. First, the process could make constitutional change more difficult. Accordingly, it favours the status quo, privileging the judgements of past generations at the expense of the right to self-governance of the contemporary generation. The proposal could hence result in a situation where the fear of unilateral and illegitimate amendments leads to the continuity of an

[81] Constitution of Burundi (2005), art 198.

[82] On unamendable provisions and judicial role, see Yaniv Roznai, *Unconstitutional Constitutional Amendments: The Limits of Amendment Powers* (OUP 2019).

illegitimate constitutional framework.[83] Nevertheless, as noted, the process would ensure that change occurs only where there is genuine majoritarian will, and would be deployed in regard to a limited set of core constitutional rules related to the essence of democratic constitutionalism. Moreover, the experience of abusive constitutional amendments in Africa may justify the establishment of a process that slows down or precludes certain amendment efforts. The difficulty involved in amendments would, therefore, constitute an acceptable trade-off.

Similarly, it may be argued that the process proposed in this chapter empowers smaller political groups excessively. Nevertheless, the formal share of seats of the opposition often understates their level of popular support, as electoral processes in Africa often favour the incumbent and exaggerate the level of popular support they enjoy. Moreover, to avoid the possible 'tyranny of the minority', where a large number of small parties could force constitutional change, the total number of votes for the constitutional amendment should constitute an absolute legislative majority, in addition to there being support for it from a cross-section of parties.

It may also be argued that reliance on political parties as representatives of public views is elitist, especially at a time where representative democracy, political parties and, broadly, the political 'establishment' are facing a crisis of legitimacy. This is a challenge that even traditional amendment procedures face. It is argued that the reliance on cross-party consensus is a more reliable proxy of measuring popular preferences in all their diversities than supermajorities or other traditional amendment rules. At the same time, the increasing introduction of mechanisms to directly engage the people in the reform process could complement cross-party political consensus with direct public consensus. This is acceptable as the proposal is intended to cover a limited set of constitutional provisions. It is argued that referendums should not be relied upon as alternatives to the proposed amendment process, as they are vulnerable to manipulation and might not ensure that the amendment enjoys the genuine broad consensus necessary for its legitimacy. Accordingly, to the extent to which referendums are deployed, they should come after approval in cross-party forums.

This chapter does not propose that all political groups, or even the majority of them, should approve a constitutional reform. The bare minimum is that the incumbent party alone should not be allowed to adopt constitutional changes to core aspects of democratic constitutionalism. Beyond this core minimum, the procedure of amendment could range from requiring supermajority approval in more than half of political parties to majority approval by most (or a defined lower number) of the parties, while ensuring that the total number of votes in the legislature supporting reform constitute an absolute majority. The possible combinations of the majorities required in each party are endless, but the rules would need to be defined considering specific contexts.

Looking beyond constitutional reform, the idea of instituting inclusive majoritarianism through the recognition of the role of the opposition in governance could extend to the public funding of opposition parties (specifically the office of the leader of the opposition), the provision of regular access to publicly owned or funded media (particularly to respond

[83] This criticism may be especially pertinent in the case of constitutions that clearly lack sufficient democratic pedigree. For instance, in Myanmar, where the military holds 25% of parliamentary seats, the more than 75% approval requirement for constitutional amendments gives the military a veto on any reform. But the proposal made in this chapter empowers political parties and not the military.

to major statements of ruling party policies and to express the position of opposition parties during crucial public occasions), and the granting of roles to the opposition in the establishment of, and appointment of members to, institutions for the protection and promotion of democracy and the rule of law, such as courts, electoral commissions, and broadly the bureaucracy. In this regard, constitutions increasingly recognize the rights and financing of political parties, including the right of access to public finance,[84] and establish the office of the opposition—including recent constitutional developments towards recognizing an opposition leader in Senegal and other francophone African countries.[85]

Notably, the Constitution of Seychelles (1993/1996) recognizes the leader of the opposition, according him or her a status, salary, and benefits at least equal to a minister,[86] and provides for a Constitutional Appointments Authority composed of five members: two appointed each by the president and the leader of the opposition, and a fifth appointed by the four of them.[87] The Authority has significant powers in appointing members of institutions monitoring, protecting, and promoting institutions—such as senior judges, the Attorney General, members of the Electoral Commission, and the ombudsperson—which support the maintenance of a democratically level playing field. The members of the Authority serve guaranteed seven-year terms and may be removed only under strictly defined processes. In addition to these constitutional powers, under the Standing Orders of the Seychelles National Assembly, the leader of the opposition provides a response to the message of the president on the state of the nation (rule 28(3)), conventionally leads the finance and public accounts committee (rule 88(5)), and is a member of the Assembly Business Committee (rule 92(2)).[88]

In sum, the implementation of the proposed idea of inclusive majoritarianism would necessitate cross-party support for amendments to core constitutional rules of the democratic game, as well as enhanced recognition of the role of the opposition. This would not only lower the risk of regressive constitutional change[89] but also foster a tradition of cooperation among diverse political actors. Although democracy is founded on the twin ideals of democratic cooperation and competition, the focus of institutional design tends to be on competitive factors and checks and balances. By necessitating cross-party deliberation and cooperation, the actualization of the principle of national consensus, which should be understood as something that extends beyond the confines of constitutional change, seeks to reorient attitudes and redirect focus, among practitioners as well as scholars, towards designing institutions geared to encouraging cooperation and taming the pervasive problem of winner-takes-all politics.

[84] Charles Fombad, 'Political Party Constitutionalization in Africa: Trends and Prospects for Deepening Constitutionalism' in Rosalind Dixon, Tom Ginsburg, and Adem Abebe (eds) (n 6).

[85] Constitution of Senegal (2001/2016), art 58(2).

[86] The leader of the opposition is elected by National Assembly members who are not from the party of the incumbent president and hence could be from the legislative majority or minority. The salary, allowance, gratuity, and pension payable to the leader of the opposition are determined by legislation but 'shall be not less than those payable to a Minister and shall be a charge on the Consolidated Fund' (art 84(5)). The recognition and empowerment of the opposition eschews the purely majoritarian conception of democracy and espouses a richer vision of the fair democratic representation of all voices in decision-making.

[87] Constitution of the Republic of Seychelles (1993/1996) arts 139–42.

[88] The rules are available at https://bit.ly/3LS8A1A accessed 9 October 2023.

[89] Christina B Jensen, Michelle Kuenzi, and Jonathan-Georges Mehanna, 'Changing the Rules: Institutions, Party Systems and the Frequency of Constitutional Amendments in Africa' (2022) Africa Spectrum 1–21, 5, where the authors argue that 'partisan veto players have a powerful effect on the likelihood of constitutional amendment'.

5. Concluding remarks

Constitutional reform, through amendments or the making of entirely new constitutions, remains a constant feature of African politics. Unlike pre-1990, when constitutional change almost always served as a means to curb formal post-independence democratic gains, post-1990 constitutional changes have had a mixed impact, with some amendments and new constitutions clearly representing an advancement for constitutional democracy and others entrenching incumbent leaders, groups, and dynastic families without formally establishing one-party systems. While a number of factors have contributed to these divergent outcomes, key among them are the process of constitutional change and level of political competitiveness, which in turn are consequences of the relative freedom and fairness of elections.

In recognition of the occasional domestic constitutional and political failures to preclude self-serving and capricious amendments that undermine constitutional democracy, which in the long term adds to fragilities in peace, governance, and development, the AU (and some regional organizations) have developed standards relevant to the substantive content and process of constitutional reform. The substantive standards primarily take the form of fundamental rights and recognized democratic principles such as free elections, judicial independence, separation of powers, and the political neutrality of security institutions. These continental principles are more robust than anywhere in the world, and are, if properly monitored and implemented, arguably sufficient to ensure the resilience of a constitutional democratic system.

In terms of process, African standards require national consensus in the negotiation and adoption of constitutional amendments. This principle does not outline specific procedures but simply seeks to gauge the overall process of amendment. In combination, the continental normative and procedural standards for constitutional reform require, in addition to (1) compliance with the letter and spirit of national and continental legal requirements (legality), (2) a genuinely consultative and participatory amendment process (participation) providing opposition groups, civil society, and the broader public sufficient opportunities to present their cases. The overall context of constitutional change should also occur in (3) a relatively free and stable political environment (stability) that allows individuals and groups genuine freedom to critique and mobilize against incumbent proposals and present their alternative ideas. This chapter further argues that the principle of national consensus should be understood (4) to require approval of constitutional reforms to core rules of the democratic game by political groups beyond the ruling party or coalition, regardless of the size of the majority the party enjoys in Parliament (inclusive majoritarianism).

The continental substantive and process standards for constitutional change in Africa, as clustered into the four elements enumerated above, are arguably sufficient. Nevertheless, they need to be elaborated, popularized, and communicated to decision-makers, political parties, civil society, and public intellectuals across Africa. The AU and regional organizations should also broadly encourage the adoption of constitutional and legal provisions to recognize and enhance the status and role of the opposition, so as to enable the 'consensus democracy' Africans aspire to and as an effective antidote to the exclusionary winner-takes-all politics central to many of the stability and governance ills facing African countries. The AU and regional organizations also need to enhance their capacity to monitor constitutional reform processes, communicate and secure buy-in for the continental standards, and offer technical assistance and capacity-building drawing on comparative African experiences and insights. Such proactive engagement would not only ensure higher chances of compliance with continental standards but also create the conditions for strengthening a culture of deliberation and participation at the national level while enabling intra-African learning.

In the end, an important caveat: the chapter has focused, in line with the theme of this volume, on continental rules on constitutional change. Nevertheless, constitutions exist within the overall political, social, and political ecosystem. Without simultaneous improvement in the broader political system—from popular consciousness of, and support for the value of, democratic constitutionalism, to the quality and strength of political parties, to the economic fortunes of more than a billion Africans—constitutions will remain vulnerable to manipulation and even outright overthrow, regardless of the strength of the formal limits to their change imposed at the domestic, regional, African, or global levels. Nevertheless, rules still matter, and the ideas proposed in this chapter are aimed at contributing to advancing the horizon of conversations, in Africa and beyond, to enhance the prospects for strengthening the resilience of democratic constitutionalism.

Bibliography

Abebe A.K., 'The Substantive Validity of Constitutional Amendments in South Africa' (2014) 131 (3) South African Law Journal 656–94

Abebe A.K., ' ' in International IDEA, *Annual Review of Constitution Building Processes* (International IDEA 2019) https://www.idea.int/publications/catalogue/annual-review-constitution-building-2018 accessed 10 February 2025

Abebe A.K., 'Taming Regressive Constitutional Amendments: The African Court as a Continental (Super) Constitutional Court' (2019) 17(1) International Journal of Constitutional Law 89

Abebe A.K., 'The Vulnerability of Constitutional Pacts: Inclusive Majoritarianism as Protection against Democratic Backsliding' in International IDEA, *Annual Review of Constitution-Building: 2019* (International IDEA 2020) https://constitutionnet.org/sites/default/files/2021-01/annual-review-of-constitution-building-2019.pdf accessed 20 June 2023

Abebe A.K., 'The Winner Shall Not Take It All: Constitutional Regulation and Empowerment of Opposition Parties in Africa' in Ginsburg T., Huq A. and Khaitan T and others (eds.), *The Constitutional Law of Democracy Around the World: How Elections, Parties and the Right to Vote are Enshrined Globally* (CUP 2024)

Abebe A. and Fombad C., 'The African Union and the Advancement of Democracy: The Problem of Unconstitutional Retention of Government Power' in Fombad C.M. and Steytler N. (eds.), *Democracy, Elections and Constitutionalism in Africa* (OUP 2021)

Adjolohun S.H., 'The Making and Remaking of National Constitutions in African Regional Courts' (2018) 1 African Journal of Comparative Constitutional Law 35–70

African Union, 'Decision on Governance, Constitutionalism and Elections in Africa' (2016) Assembly/AU/Dec.592(XXVI)

African Union, 'Decision on the Prevention of Unconstitutional Changes of Government and Strengthening the Capacity of the African Union to Manage such Situations, Assembly/AU/Dec.269(XIV) Rev.1', 2 February 2010

African Union, 'Declaration on Unconstitutional Changes of Government in Africa, adopted on 17 March 2022'

African Union, 'Mission D'observation Electorale de L'union Africaine pour les Elections Legislatives du 28 Avril 2019 en Republique du Benin: Conclusions Preliminaires' (African Union, 30 April 2019) https://bit.ly/46rURXz accessed 1 October 2023

African Union, Peace and Security Council, 'Policy on Post-Conflict Reconstruction and Development' (2006) https://www.peaceau.org/uploads/pcrd-policy-framwowork-eng.pdf accessed 1 October 2023

African Union, Peace and Security Council, 'Press Statement of the 791st Meeting on 22 August 2018 (PSC/PR/BR (DCCXCI)' (22 August 2018) https://www.peaceau.org/uploads/psc.791.press.statement.africa.charter.on.democracy.22.08.pdf accessed 29 June 2022

Baudais V. and Chauzal G., 'The 2010 Coup d'état in Niger: A Praetorian Regulation of Politics?' 2011 110(439) African Affairs 295

'Benin President Talon Pledges Not to Seek Third Mandate' (*RFI*, 30 April 2021) https://www.rfi.fr/en/africa/20210430-benin-president-patrice-talon-pledges-not-to-seek-third-mandate-elections-violence-protests-democracy-governance-africa accessed 28 April 2022

Bulmer E., 'Her Majesty's Precarious Opposition: "Clean Sweep" Elections and Constitutional Balance in Commonwealth Caribbean States' in International IDEA, *Annual Review of Constitution Building: 2018* (International IDEA 2020)

Cheeseman N. and Sishuwa S., 'African Studies Keyword: Democracy' (2021) 64(3) African Studies Review 704

Czapanskiy K.S. and Manjoo R., 'The Right of Public Participation in the Law-Making Process and the Role of the Legislature in the Promotion of this Right' (2008) 19(1) Duke Journal of Comparative and International Law 1–40

Dalatou M., 'Niger to Hold Constitutional Referendum on 3rd Term' (*VoA*, 2 November 2009) https://www.voanews.com/a/a-13-2009-05-29-voa67-68801277/361821.html accessed 1 October 2023

Economic Community of West African States (ECOWAS), Protocol A/SP1/12/01 on Democracy and Good Governance Supplementary to the Protocol Relating to the Mechanism for Conflict Prevention, Management, Resolution, Peacekeeping and Security

Elkins Z., Ginsburg T., and Melton J., 'The Lifespan of Written Constitutions' (*The University of Chicago: The Law School*, 15 October 2009) https://www.law.uchicago.edu/news/lifespan-written-constitutions accessed 14 June 2022

Elkins Z., Ginsburg T., and Melton J., *The Endurance of National Constitutions* (CUP 2012)

Fombad C.M., 'Some Perspectives on Durability and Change under Modern African Constitutions' (2013) 11(2) International Journal of Constitutional Law 382–413

Fombad C.M., 'Political Party Constitutionalization in Africa: Trends and Prospects for Deepening Constitutionalism' in Dixon R., Ginsburg T., and Abebe A. (eds.), *Comparative Constitutional Law in Africa* (Edward Elgar 2022).

Ginsburg T., 'Constitutional Afterlife: The Continuing Impact of Thailand's Postpolitical Constitution' (2008) 7(1) International Journal of Constitutional Law 83–105

Ginsburg T. and Bisarya S., 'Introduction' in Ginsburg T. and Bisarya S. (eds.), *Constitution Makers on Constitution Making* (CUP 2022) 2–4

Grauvogel J. and Heyl C., 'The Study of Term Limits in Sub-Saharan Africa: Lessons on Democratisation and Autocratisation' (2021) 55(3) Africa Spectrum 215–27

Hartmann C., 'Authoritarian Origins of Term Limit Trajectories in Africa' (2022) 29(1) Democratization 57

Hatchard J., 'Perfecting Imperfections: Developing Procedures for Amending Constitutions in Commonwealth Africa' (1998) 36(3) Journal of Modern African Studies 381

Hirschel-Burns T., 'Benin's King of Cotton Makes its Democracy a Sham' (*Foreign Policy*, 8 April 2021) https://foreignpolicy.com/2021/04/08/benin-election-democracy-sham-patrice-talon/ accessed 14 June 2022

Hofisi D.T., 'Clawing Back the Gains of Popular Participation – The First Amendment to the Constitution of Zimbabwe (2013)' (*ConstitutionNet*, 26 September 2017) http://www.constitutionnet.org/news/clawing-back-gains-popular-participation-first-amendment-constitution-zimbabwe-2013 accessed 28 April 2022

Hofisi D.T., 'In the Shadow of Robert Mugabe? Twists and Turns in the First and Second Amendments to the Constitution of Zimbabwe' (*ConstitutionNet*, 30 April 2021) https://constitutionnet.org/news/twists-and-turns-in-zimbabwe accessed 3 June 2022

International IDEA, *The State of Democracy in Africa and the Middle East 2021: Resilient Democratic Aspirations and Opportunities for Consolidation* (International IDEA 2021) https://www.idea.int/publications/catalogue/state-democracy-africa-and-middle-east-2021 accessed 3 June 2022

International IDEA, *The Global State of Democracy 2021: Building Resilience in a Pandemic Era* (International IDEA 2021) https://www.idea.int/publications/catalogue/global-state-democracy-2021 accessed 14 June 2022

Jensen C., Kuenzi M., and Mehanna J.-G., 'Changing the Rules: Institutions, Party Systems and the Frequency of Constitutional Amendments in Africa' (2022) Africa Spectrum 1

Landau D., 'Abusive Constitutionalism' (2013) 47(1) UC Davis Law Review 189

Levinson D. and Pildes H., 'Separation of Parties, Not Powers' (2006) 119(8) Harvard Law Review 2311

Lomé Declaration of July 2000 on the framework for an OAU response to unconstitutional changes of government (AHG/Decl.5 (XXXVI)

Nyati L., 'Public Participation: What Has the Constitutional Court Given the Public?' (2008) 12(2) Law, Democracy & Development 102

Przeworski A., 'Democracy as Equilibrium' (2005) 3(4) Public Choice 253

Roznai Y., *Unconstitutional Constitutional Amendments: The Limits of Amendment Powers* (OUP 2019)

Sawasdee S., 'The Conundrum of a Dominant Party in Thailand' (2018) 4(1) Asian Journal of Comparative Politics 102

Vohito S., 'Covid-19 and the Unamendable Limits on Duration of Presidential and Legislative Terms in the Central African Republic' (*ConstitutionNet*, 22 June 2020) https://constitutionnet.org/news/covid-19-and-unamendable-limits-duration-presidential-and-legislative-terms-central-african accessed 14 June 2022

Vohito S., 'Courts vs Incumbents: Guaranteeing Alternation of Power in the Central African Republic' (*ConstitutionNet*, 29 September 2022) https://constitutionnet.org/news/courts-vs-incumbents-central-african-republic accessed 20 December 2022

Wiebusch M., 'Africanization of Constitutional Law' in Dixon R., Ginsburg T., and Abebe A. (eds.), *Comparative Constitutional Law in Africa* (Edward Elgar 2022)

Wiebusch M. and Murray C., 'Presidential Term Limits and the African Union' (2019) 63(1) Journal of African Law 131

Zimba L., 'The Origins and Spread of One-Party States in Commonwealth Africa' in Ndulo M. (ed.), *Law in Zambia* (East African Publishing House 1984)

Zimbabwe Lawyers for Human Rights, 'Amendments to the Constitution of Zimbabwe: A Constant Assault on Democracy and Constitutionalism' http://www1.umn.edu/humanrts/research/constitution%20statement-sunday%20mirror.pdf accessed 3 June 2022

Zouapet A., 'Victim of its Commitment … You, Passer-by, a Tear to the Proclaimed Virtue: Should the Epitaph of the African Court on Human and Peoples' Rights be Prepared?' (*EJIL:Talk!*, 5 May 2020) https://www.ejiltalk.org/victim-of-its-commitment-you-passerby-a-tear-to-the-proclaimed-virtue-should-the-epitaph-of-the-african-court-on-human-and-peoples-rights-be-prepared/ accessed 14 June 2022

Zounmenou D., Abatan J.E., and Matongbada M., 'A Third Election without Main Opposition Parties in Benin' (*Institute for Security Studies*, 8 April 2021) https://issafrica.org/iss-today/a-third-election-without-main-opposition-parties-in-benin accessed 28 April 2022

4

Making and Amending Federal Constitutions in Africa

Nico Steytler, Zemelak Ayitenew Ayele, and Henry Paul Gichana

1. Introduction

According to federal orthodoxy, one of the characteristics of a federation is that its constitution cannot be changed unilaterally by either its federal or subnational governments.[1] Thus, the constituent units must participate in any amendment of the constitution, or at least as far as the federal aspects are concerned. Specific rules have been developed to prescribe how such participation should take place.

At a theoretical level, a link has been established between how federations are formed and the content of constitutional amendment procedures. Notably, where a federation is formed by the integration of pre-existing states (a 'coming-together' federation) through a *foedus* (a compact), the constituent units retain a key role in amending that *foedus*. This has been shown to be the case in the first federations of the modern era to come about by integration, namely the 'classic' federations of the United States (US), Switzerland, Canada, and Australia.[2] However, this link is decried when federations are formed by disaggregation—the dominant manner of federation-making since the Second World War[3]—when, in a previously unitary state, significant powers are devolved to subnational governments.[4] The amendment procedures in such federations also include a strong participation role for constituent units so formed by the constitution, and they are often very similar to those of the classic federations.

Over the past three decades since the end of the Cold War, many if not most African countries have adopted new constitutions. Among these countries, a number have adopted federal or hybrid-federal constitutions in an attempt to deal with deep ethnic cleavages, imperial presidencies, a lack of equitable development, and superficial democracy.[5] The main federations or hybrid federations are Nigeria, Ethiopia, South Africa, the Democratic

[1] Ronald L Watts, 'The Federal Idea and Its Contemporary Relevance' in TJ Courchene and others (eds.), *The Federal Idea: Essays in Honour of Ronald L. Watts* (McGill-Queen's University Press 2011) 16.
[2] Nicholas Aroney, 'Formation, Representation and Amendment in Federal Constitutions' (2006) 54(2) American Journal of Comparative Law 277–336.
[3] Francesco Palermo and Karl Kössler, *Comparative Federalism: Constitutional Arrangements and Case Law* (Hart 2017) 180.
[4] Nico Steytler, 'The Relationship between Decentralisation and Constitutionalism in Africa: Concepts, Conflicts, and Hypotheses' in Charles Fombad and Nico Steytler (eds.), *Decentralisation and Constitutionalism in Africa* (OUP 2019) 25–52, 27–31.
[5] See generally Fombad and Steytler (n 4).

Nico Steytler, Zemelak Ayitenew Ayele, and Henry Paul Gichana, *Making and Amending Federal Constitutions in Africa*
In: *Constitutional Change and Constitutionalism in Africa*. Edited by: Charles M. Fombad and Nico Steytler, Oxford University Press.
 DOI: 10.1093/9780198957034.003.0006

Republic of the Congo, Comoros, Kenya, Sudan, South Sudan, and Somalia. Some have dealt successfully with the underlying reasons for a federal dispensation and others have not. The process of federal constitution-making is, at the time of writing (2023), still under way in Somalia, Sudan, and South Sudan—all failed or failing federations.[6]

The topic of constitutional amendments in federal or hybrid-federal countries in Africa has not yet been examined in the literature. Moreover, we do not have any comparative studies on how African federations have been formed and whether the manner in which they were formed correlates in any way with the procedures for constitutional amendment. Furthermore, there is little understanding of the specific rules pertaining to constitutional amendments in federations, how they were framed, and how they have operated in practice.

This chapter addresses two questions. First, has the manner in which African federations (or hybrid federations) have been formed—either by integration or disaggregation—had any influence on the mode of protection relating to the amendment of the constitution in general and/or of the federal arrangements in particular? More specifically, does the formation of a federation by integration through a *foedus* (a compact) by constituent units create a greater participatory role for such units than when the federation occurs through disaggregation? Or does the distinction between the manner of formation and the amendment procedures have little explanatory significance?

Second, what do these amendment rules mean in practice? Do they advance the basic principles of constitutionalism and have they done so in practice—by advancing democracy, limiting the central government's habit of unilaterally amending constitutions, and upholding the rule of law by ensuring compliance with and/or judicial enforcement of the amendment rules? These questions will be answered with reference to South Africa, Ethiopia, Nigeria, and Kenya. The four cases are selected because they represent the most significant devolved systems of government in Africa that, to varying degrees, operate as such. Nigeria and Ethiopia are self-proclaimed federations, while South Africa and Kenya have shied away from that label: although they have pronounced federal features, they are usually labelled as quasi-federal systems. On the federal spectrum, all four countries show a high level of centralized federalism.[7]

It is argued that the neat distinction between 'coming-together' and 'holding-together' federations does not hold much water; in a single state, federation-formation through disaggregation is usually a mixture of both—there is a continuum between integration, at the one end, and disaggregation, at the other, along which federations can be plotted. Federations emerging after conflict or civil war will exhibit many features of a 'coming-together' federation. Consequently, there is some link between the nature of federation-forming and the consequent amendment procedures. But, on whole, the modes of subnational participation developed in the classic federation have become orthodoxy and are found in most African federations. While these constitutional amendment rules advance the basic principles of constitutionalism, their application in practice is, however, dependent on the practice of constitutionalism, with some courts playing an important role in this regard.

[6] Charles M Fombad, Assefa Fiseha, and Nico Steytler (eds.), *Contemporary Governance Challenges in the Horn of Africa* (Routledge 2023).

[7] Nico Steytler and Jaap de Visser, '"Fragile Federations": The Dynamics of Devolution' in Francesco Palermo and Elisabeth Alber (eds.), *Federalism as Decision-Making* (Brill/Nijhoff 2015) 79–101.

2. Subnational participation in constitution-making and amendment

Inasmuch as it is federal orthodoxy that there are two (or more) orders of government, each having 'some areas of genuine autonomy', a further defining structural feature is, in Ronald L Watts' words, '[a] supreme written constitution, not unilaterally amendable by one order, and requiring the consent not only of the federal legislature but also of a significant proportion of constituent units through assent by their legislatures or by referendum majorities.'[8] This defining structural feature is oft-repeated but seldom explained. Watts based this structural feature on the following reasoning:

> In federations it is the constitution that defines the authority of each of the orders of government so that neither level is constitutionally subordinate to the other. It follows that the written constitution, at least in those respects defining and affecting the relative powers of the orders of government, must not be unilaterally amendable by just one order of government since that would potentially subordinate the other level of government to it. But providing for special procedures to amend the constitution raises the issue of balancing the requirements for both rigidity and flexibility in the operation of the constitution in a federation.[9]

Requiring the participation of both orders of government in amending the constitution preserves the heart of federalism—the orders of government coexist, with neither of them subordinate to the other. Thus, as little as the federal government can change the federal arrangements on its own, so as little can a subnational unit undo the federal structure unilaterally, for example by seceding.[10] Two principal formal legal measures are used to secure the participation of constituent units in constitutional amendments: (1) the agreement of a second house of parliament representing the units; and (2) the participation of the units in their own right, which have been referred to as 'institutional veto players' when their consent is required.[11]

What explains the particular amendment rules in addition to the usual ones requiring special majorities in Parliament and sometimes popular referenda? Nicholas Aroney has argued that the nature of the formation of a federation influences both the representative institutions and, interlinked with them, the amendment procedures.[12] To support his case, he selected the four oldest functioning federations, all of which came about by the integration of previously separate independent states: the US (1789), Switzerland (1848), Canada (1867), and Australia (1900) (although in the case of the latter two, the constituent units were not fully independent but dominions of Britain with a high degree of self-government).[13] In each instance, a unit (or the population of that unit) had to agree to its

[8] Watts (n 1) 13–28, 16.

[9] Ibid. 102.

[10] David Haljan, *Constitutionalising Secession* (Hart 2014) 288. There is, however, much controversy around this issue, with arguments about the right to self-determination being advanced by separatist movements. See in general Eva Maria Belser and others (eds.), *States Falling Apart? Secessionist and Autonomy Movement in Europe* (Stämpfli Verlag 2015).

[11] Arthur Benz, Jörg Kemmerzell, and Bettina Petersohn, 'Ratification and Ratification Failure: The Impact of Amendment Rules' in Arthur Benz (ed.), *Constitutional Policy in Multilevel Government: The Art of Keeping the Balance* (OUP 2016) 153–76, 154.

[12] Aroney (n 2) 277–336.

[13] Ibid. 314.

inclusion in a new federal state. Sovereignty, then, did not fall exclusively under the federal umbrella but was shared with the federal units.

At the base lies the 'compact' theory of federal constitutions: the word 'federalism' is, after all, derived from the Latin *foedus*, meaning 'treaty' (or 'compact').[14] Commencing with the US Constitution of 1789, the thirteen independent states, which had come into being after the American War of Independence against colonial Britain, shed, through the compact, some of their sovereignty. Furthermore, the compact could not be altered without the agreement of a large majority of the constituent states. For the founding fathers, as articulated by James Madison, the act of establishing the constitution would be 'a federal act' because the assent and ratification would not be given by the people of America as a whole but by each of 'the distinct and independent states'.[15]

Once a federation has been so established, the amendment requirements of the federal constitution show strong linkages with the establishment process but are not identical with it. The US amendment procedure is that any constitutional change requires an initial two-thirds' support in both houses of Congress (or similar support in two-thirds of the states) and three-quarters of state legislatures or state conventions.[16] According to the founding fathers, amending the US Constitution would have both 'national' and 'federal' characteristics. If the constitution were 'national', it would be amended by a national vote; if it were of 'federal' character only, consensus by all states would be needed. The amendment procedure is thus of both characters, as ratification by all states is not required, only ratification by a high majority of them.[17] In the event, a constitutional amendment required popular approval and the assent of ten of thirteen states (75 per cent) in preference to nine of the thirteen states (a two-thirds majority).[18]

The formation of the US, Aroney argues, also influenced the structure of the federal order of government. The central element of the shared-rule component of federalism was the second house of the federal legislature, the Senate, with equal representation of each of the founding units. Any amendment of the Constitution thus also required the approval of two-thirds of the members of the Senate. However, if equal Senate representation were to be altered, consent would have to be secured from states whose equal suffrage would be affected negatively by the proposed change.[19]

Where there was a coming together of independent states to form a new federal state—as in Switzerland, Canada, and Australia—a similar result occurred, albeit with minor variations. First of all, in Canada and Australia the consent of each participating unit was required for the formation of the federation.[20] With regard to the second house of the federal parliament, in Australia the principle of equality was implemented, but in Canada, that of proportionality; Switzerland saw a mixture of both with its recognition of 'half-cantons'. In Switzerland and Australia, the approval of the majority of voters in the federation and the

[14] See Daniel J Elazar, *Exploring Federalism* (University of Alabama Press 1987) 158. See also Glenn A Moots, 'The Covenant Tradition of Federalism: The Pioneering Studies of Daniel J Elazar' in Ann Ward and Lee Ward (eds.), *The Ashgate Research Companion to Federalism* (Routledge 2020) 385–90; Aroney (n 2) 307.

[15] Alexander Hamilton, James Madison, and John Jay, 'No. 39 [Madison]' in Terence Ball (ed.), *The Federalist with Letters of 'Brutus'* (CUP 2003) 184.

[16] Constitution of the United States, art V.

[17] Hamilton, Madison, and Jay (n 15), 'No. 39 [Madison]' 186.

[18] Ibid., 'No. 85 [Hamilton]'.

[19] Constitution of the United States, art V.

[20] Aroney (n 2) 300.

majority of voters in the majority of states is required for an amendment.[21] Any amendment to the constitution must also have the support of both houses of the federal parliament, as well as a high percentage of support in each unit (which can be obtained in the legislature or through popular support in a referendum). In Canada and Australia, provisions regarding a state's representation in the federal legislature cannot be amended without the consent of all the units or those which are directly affected thereby.[22] A similar rule applies in Canada and Australia with regard to the protection of boundaries.[23]

Aroney's argument is thus that there is 'a recurrent, systematic relationship between the contingent modes of formation of federal constitutions [and] the representative and amendment formula that emerge[s] from such processes'.[24] This theory, based explicitly on the 'coming-together' federations, therefore does not apply *ipso facto* when a unitary state disaggregates into subnational units: such units come into existence through the constitution and thus a fortiori cannot have been part of its establishment. As most post-Second World War federal formations were the result of acts of disaggregation (or more colloquially, the 'holding together' of a country), the broader applicability of Aroney's thesis is questionable.

In later studies, Aroney found that the line between aggregation and disaggregation is not always clear: 'a recognisably federal system may come into being through processes intermediate between these two possibilities'.[25] But the difference remains crucial. He argues that 'those who hold institutional power at the founding are likely to use that power to ensure that they will continue to exercise power under the new dispensation'.[26] Consequently, the depth of entrenchment of the federal features is influenced by the manner in which a federation comes into existence.[27] In a devolved federation, the legislature of the original unitary state is thus likely to retain an essential role in constitutional amendments.[28]

However, federations that came about through disaggregation show modes of constitutional amendment that are similar to those of the classic federations. First, a requirement is the approval of the second house, representing the constituent units on the basis of equality, though not always.[29] Second, a further requirement is the consent of a significant majority of constituent units. In Germany, for example, a constitutional amendment requires only two-thirds support in the second house of the federal parliament, the Bundesrat.[30] Although based on the principle not of equality among the *Länder* but proportionality, the Bundesrat is directly representative of *Länder* executives and thus reflects the majority view in the *Land* legislatures.[31]

21 Ibid. 298.
22 Ibid. 329.
23 Palermo and Kössler (n 3) 187.
24 Aroney (n 2) 335.
25 Nicholas Aroney, 'Constituent Power and the Constituent States: Towards a Theory of the Amendment of Federal Constitutions' (2017) 17(1) Jus Politicum: Thinking about Federalism(s) 1–31, 14. Aroney examined four federations (Canada, Australia, India, and the United Kingdom) to answer the same question: does the original design of a federation—by aggregation or devolution—make a difference in the amendment procedures? He concluded that the categorization of federal systems as either aggregative or devolutionary is 'usually a matter of degree'. See also Nicholas Aroney, 'The Formation and Amendment of Federal Constitutions in a Westminster-derived Context' (2018) 16(1) International Journal of Constitutional Law 42.
26 Aroney, 'Constituent Power and the Constituent States' (n 25) 18.
27 Ibid. 27.
28 Ibid. 29.
29 Aroney (n 2) 327.
30 Basic Law art 79(2).
31 Watts (n 1) 103.

A singular difference in modern federal constitutions is the principle of differentiating amendment procedures depending on the substance of the provision at stake.[32] While in some federations the entire constitution is protected, in others only those provisions specifying federal arrangements require subnational participation.[33] Watts observed that, with amendments to the distribution of powers and the integrity of the constituent units, approval of both houses of parliament is usually required.[34] What is, however, almost uniform is the requirement that, where a unit's boundaries are to be changed, its individualized consent is required.[35]

As Palermo and Kössler explain, '[s]uch procedures are quite telling about the essence of the federal compact, which would suggest in principle a veto right of subnational entities as to their existence and territorial integrity.'[36] A rule of this kind does not appear, though, in the Indian Constitution, where ordinary legislation may create a new state or amend existing boundaries after the states have expressed their views.[37] The most striking difference, perhaps, is the presence in a very few federations (all formed by disaggregation) of the prohibition against changing the fundamental federal nature of the country:[38] in Germany, the federal structure is beyond amendment by force of a constitutional provision,[39] and in India the same result is achieved by the judicial invention of the basic structure doctrine, which also pertains to federalism.[40]

Is there, then, any significance to the manner in which a federation was formed and the nature of its amendment procedures? What explains the similarities and differences? Very little has been theorized about this. Is it the case that, once a federation has come about by disaggregation, subnational participation in amendment procedures follows as a matter of principle and design? More fundamentally, are the origins of a federation merely of historical and not legal consequence, as Palermo and Kössler argue? The aim of this chapter is thus to examine these issues in the context of the formation of federations in Africa, the constitutional amendment procedures, and the practice of changing constitutions.

3. Case studies

The history of federalism in Africa has incidences of both the coming-together federations and those formed by disaggregation. Of the first kind, none has survived to the present day. Federation by disaggregation has been the dominant mode of non-centralizing, and is also the mode for quasi-federations.

Of the coming-together federations, one early example was the Federation of Rhodesia and Nyasaland (the self-governing colony of Southern Rhodesia and the two British protectorates of Northern Rhodesia and Nyasaland, 1953–63). Another example arose in Cameroon when the two trust territories of British and French Cameroon were united in a

32 See Palermo and Kössler (n 3) 180.
33 Watts (n 1) 102.
34 Ibid.
35 Ibid 104.
36 Palermo and Kössler (n 3) 186.
37 Indian Constitution 1949, art 3.
38 Palermo and Kössler (n 3) 185.
39 Basic Law art 79(3).
40 *Kesavananda Bhariti Sripadagalvaru v State of Kerala* 1973 AIR 1461.

federation (1961–72), albeit one regarded as 'a sham federation'.[41] Similar instances are the countries that were 'put together' during decolonialization. An example of this was seen when the Italian trust territory of Eritrea was added to Ethiopia under a federal arrangement, one that ended in 1962 when Ethiopia annexed Eritrea as a province. In contrast, when the Trust Territory of Somaliland (the former Italian Somaliland) and the former British Somaliland united to form the Somali Republic, no federal structure was adopted.

This chapter focuses on four functioning contemporary federations—South Africa, Ethiopia, Nigeria, and Kenya. These are the four largest African states (in terms of both territorial and population size). South Africa, Ethiopia, and Nigeria revised their constitutions to introduce or restructure their federal or quasi-federal systems in the post-Cold War period and within a span of a decade; Kenya pursued 'devolution' a decade later. All of these states adopted a federal or quasi-federal system in part to resolve or prevent identity-based conflict.

A general framework of questions is employed in this chapter. First, what was the nature of the federal constitution-making—was it by integration or disaggregation? Did regional units or interest groups participate in the federation-making? Second, in the newly established constitution, what role was given to the new constituent units in amending the constitution? Does this role include all aspects of the constitution or only those dealing with federal arrangements? Third, what is the salience of amendment rules in practice? Has constitutionalism prevailed?

3.1 South Africa

South Africa offers a unique glimpse into the two distinct processes of constitution-making. The first process ensued when the Union of South Africa was established in 1910; it followed the federal rule book but then opted against a federal dispensation. In the second, a centralized state opted to devolve power to provinces through limited federal arrangements in the 1993 and 1996 Constitutions. The amendment procedures resulting from these processes differed markedly.

3.1.1 The Union of South Africa Constitution 1910 and the possibility of federation

The formation of the Union of South Africa in 1910 followed hot on the heels of the establishment of the Australian Commonwealth in 1900. Five British dominions—the Cape of Good Hope, Transvaal, Orange River Colony, Natal, and Southern Rhodesia—enjoyed responsible government but subject to the British Colonial Law Validity Act of 1865. The main object of the Union's formation was uniting the British dominions into a single political entity—a major political event given the then recent history of war between the two Boer republics and the British Empire (Anglo-Boer War, 1899–1902). In the style of Canada and Australia, each colony was represented by elected representatives (all white males) from the respective legislatures.[42] In a grand compact, the draft constitution was submitted to

[41] Charles M Fombad, 'Cameroon and the Anomalies of Decentralisation with a Centralist Mindset' in Charles Fombad and Nico Steytler (eds.) (n 4) 326–64, 330.

[42] See HR Hahlo and Ellison Kahn, *The Union of South Africa: The Development of its Laws and Constitution* (Stevens & Son, Juta & Co 1960) 118–27; Thula Simpson, *History of South Africa: From 1902 to the Present* (Penguin 2021) 24.

each legislature for its approval. Such approval was obtained except in the case of Southern Rhodesia, which was given the option to join the Union later if there were popular approval of this in that colony. (A referendum in 1923 by white male voters shied away from joining South Africa.) The draft submitted to the imperial Westminster Parliament was adopted by the latter without any amendments, despite pleas from the disenfranchised black majority.[43]

Although the National Convention of 1908–09 had the structure for a federal compact, federalism, while proposed by some parties, was rejected. The aim was to reconcile the differences—cultural and political—between Afrikaners and English speakers, not entrench them. A limited degree of decentralized governance, in the form of provinces, was included, which allowed for coloured and African representation in the provincial legislatures in the Cape and Natal. The decentralized system entailed the continuation of the former dominions as provinces,[44] the establishment of provincial legislatures and executives, and the allocation of a list of provincial powers.

The fundamental weakness was that any provincial law had not only to be signed off by the national government but also be compatible with any national law. Although a second house of Parliament was established (the Senate), provincial representation was attenuated: for the first ten years of the Union, the governor-general nominated eight senators for each province based on their knowledge of the non-white population, while the provincial legislatures elected a further eight each. The Senate had the powers of the British House of Lords: although it had to approve a constitutional amendment by a simple majority, its vote could be overridden by the House of Assembly.[45]

When amending the provisions on coloured voters on the common voters' role in the Cape Province, a special procedure in terms of section 35(1) of the 1909 Constitution Act had to be followed: in a joint sitting of the two houses of Parliament, a two-thirds majority was required.[46] When the two houses, by an ordinary majority in each house, purported to repeal section 35(1) on the basis that it had lapsed, the Appellate Division invalidated the amendment, holding that the constitutional entrenchment clauses were still operative.[47] The court wavered, however, when the strident National Party (NP), elected to power in 1948, concocted strategies for circumventing the amendment requirements and eventually secured the approval of the amendment.[48]

No specific role was given to the provincial legislatures on amending the constitution, which, in the mould of the Westminster notion of parliamentary supremacy, could be amended by a simple majority in Parliament. While the former colonial legislatures (now called provincial councils) were retained, they had no original powers and any national law would automatically override any contradictory provincial law. However, given the rule that Parliament could alter any provincial boundary or the division of a province on the

[43] Tembeka Ngcukaitobi, *The Land is Ours: South Africa's First Black Lawyers and the Birth of Constitutionalism* (Penguin 2018) 233.

[44] Similar to the position of the Australian dominions in becoming states of the Commonwealth of Australia.

[45] Only two provisions required a two-thirds majority of both houses sitting together: that relating to the recognition of Dutch and English as official languages, and that of the protection of coloured voters in the Cape Province (s 152).

[46] Read with s 152.

[47] *Harris v Minister of Interior* 1952 (2) SA 428 (AD).

[48] Isabeau Steytler, '"Striking Back" and "Clamping Down" in South Africa: Responding to Adverse Judicial Decisions under Systems of Parliamentary Sovereignty and Constitutional Supremacy' (2020) 12(2) Hague Journal on the Rule of Law 363–86.

petition of the province concerned,[49] it could be argued that, without such a petition, such an amendment could not take place.

3.1.2 1993 and 1996 Constitutions

After a hiatus of 80 years, federalism was again on the negotiating table when the white minority government unbanned the African National Congress (ANC) and other liberation movements in 1990. Despite the ANC's opposition to federalism, the 1993 and 1996 Constitutions both contained several federal arrangements. The emergence of these arrangements at this particular 'constitutional moment' was a complex mix of integration and disaggregation, one result of which was that the newly established provinces were given a crucial say in constitutional amendment procedures.

Since the advent of the 1910 Constitution, racial segregation and oppression had been key leitmotifs in governance in South Africa. Particularly after the NP came to power, segregation was explicitly pursued in the policy of grand apartheid, in terms of which each of the black ethnic communities would be granted full independence.[50] In the event, four such territories, dismissively called 'Bantustans', became 'independent' countries: Transkei, Ciskei, Bophuthatswana, and Venda. They were recognized as such only by South Africa, and remained dependent on it for financial transfers. A further six self-governing territories were established, the most prominent of which was KwaZulu. However, this divide-and-rule strategy was rejected by the ANC, which, after years of peaceful agitation, embarked in 1961 on a strategy seeking the violent overthrow of the apartheid regime.

In 1983, a crack in the apartheid edifice appeared when a type of consociational Constitution was adopted, bringing together three race groups—white, coloured, and Indian. A tricameral parliament was instituted and composed of a chamber for each group; each chamber dealt with its 'own affairs', while on 'general affairs' they would sit as one chamber. Where they could not find unanimity on legislation on 'general affairs', a conflict-breaking further chamber, the President's Council, weighted in favour of whites, made the final decision.[51]

The reason for this discursus is to raise the following question: when the 'constitutional moment' arrived after 1990, did any of these apartheid-created institutions become negotiating partners in the making of the 1993 Constitution? In the first round of negotiations in 1991—the Convention for a Democratic South Africa (CODESA)—all interested parties were represented, including most of the four 'independent' Bantustans (but none of the six self-governing territories) and nineteen political parties. The main protagonists were the ANC and the NP, neither of which had a specific territorial base, as their supporters were spread across the country, and both of which had strong views on federalism. The ANC was vehemently opposed to it, as it would have perpetuated the past grand apartheid set-up; the NP became a convert to federalism, partly perhaps because it had majority support in certain places (the Western Cape and Northern Cape), and largely because federalism would weaken a central government under the ANC.[52] This was also the

[49] s 149 of Constitution Act of 1909.

[50] See generally Leonard Thompson, *A History of South Africa* (4th edn, Jonathan Ball 2014).

[51] Hercules Booysen and Dawid Hercules van Wyk, *Die '83 Grondwet* (Juta 1984).

[52] Nico Steytler, 'The Withering Away of Politically Salient Territorial Cleavages in South Africa and the Emergence of Watermark Ethnic Federalism' in George Anderson and Sujit Choudhry (eds.), *Territory and Power in Constitutional Transitions* (OUP 2019) 219–36.

reason advanced by the small liberal party, the Democratic Party (DP). The federal idea was also strongly propagated by the Inkatha Freedom Party (IFP), the governing party in KwaZulu, with Zulu nationalism its *raison d'être*. Of the 'independent' states, two (Ciskei and Bophuthatswana) collapsed and were taken over by the South African government, while the other two (Transkei and Venda) aligned themselves with the ANC.

After the ANC and NP agreed upon the Constitution, which was adopted by the existing tricameral Parliament in December 1993, continued violence in Natal and threatened violence by Afrikaner nationalists resulted in constitutional amendments to accommodate the relevant interests. Through direct negotiations with the Freedom Front, representing a faction of the Afrikaners, a Volkstaatraad (People's Council), functioning as a lobby and consultative body, and the notion of self-determination were inserted in the Constitution in 1994. Stronger federal features were added, though not as a result of direct negotiations with the IFP but in an attempt to lure it into the first democratic elections, an entreaty which, after further minor changes, it eventually accepted just three days before the elections.[53]

Despite the fact that territorially based entities were not the main drivers of the Interim Constitution, the newly created provinces—of which seven of the nine included the former self-governing territories[54]—became a vital part of constitutional amendments. First, amending any provision of the Constitution, barring two provisions, required a two-thirds majority in the joint sitting of the National Assembly and the Senate. The latter house was composed of ten senators from each of the nine provinces, nominated by the political parties in the provincial legislatures on the basis of proportionality.[55] Where the amendment affected the provincial legislatures or executives, the two houses had to sit separately and each had to pass such an amendment with a two-thirds majority.[56]

An important proviso was added: 'the boundaries and legislative and executive competences of *a* province shall not be amended without the consent of a relevant provincial legislature'.[57] The other exception was that, because the 1993 Constitution was only an interim constitution, the constitutional principles that were to frame the new 'final' constitution and the process of its drafting were unamendable.[58] At the heart of the continuing constitution-writing process lay the 34 constitutional principles, reflecting a true compact agreed to by the major political parties; the then-existing Bantustans played no constitutive role in this regard.

The Constitutional Assembly, comprising both houses of Parliament (400 Members of Parliament and 90 senators) had to adopt a final Constitution with a two-thirds majority. Provincial participation was thus confined to the 90 votes: no ratification process by the provincial legislatures was required. However, the senators secured a concession on provisions relating to the boundaries, powers, and functions of provinces: their two-thirds majority consent was required separately from the overall Constitutional Assembly's vote.[59]

The 1996 Constitution introduced a different concept of the second house. Termed the National Council of Provinces (NCOP), this second house comprises nine delegations,

[53] Ibid.

[54] Although the aim of demarcating provincial boundaries was to avoid any ethnic or linguistic boundaries, in seven of the nine provinces there were linguistic majorities. The ten previously self-governing territories and their administrations were absorbed into seven provinces and their newly established provincial administrations.

[55] Interim Constitution, s 48(1).

[56] Ibid. s 48(2).

[57] Ibid. s 48(2) proviso (emphasis added).

[58] Ibid. s 74.

[59] Ibid. s. 73(2).

consisting of ten members each—these delegations, as the term 'delegation' itself suggests, carry out the mandate of their provincial legislatures. A delegation comprises six members directly elected by the provincial legislature according to the party proportionality, and four members of the provincial executive led by the provincial premier.

The NCOP plays a differentiated role with regard to constitutional amendments. First, section 1 of the Constitution, containing the founding values and the amendment clause (section 74(1)), may be amended only with a supporting vote in the National Assembly of at least 75 per cent of its members, and, in the NCOP, with a supporting vote of at least six provinces (a two-thirds majority).[60] Second, amendments to the Bill of Rights need a two-thirds majority in the National Assembly and six NCOP votes.[61] Third, for all other amendments, only the two-thirds majority in the National Assembly is required, unless the amendment bill '(i) relates to a matter that affects the [NCOP], (ii) alters provincial boundaries, powers, functions or institutions, or (iii) amends a provision that deals specifically with a provincial matter'; then, the support of six NCOP voters is needed.[62] Fourth, where an amendment affects a specific province or provinces, the NCOP may not pass the bill if the bill has not been passed by the affected province or provinces' legislatures.[63] The vote of the NCOP delegation from the affected province(s) is thus not sufficient: the provincial legislature must apply its attention to the matter, a situation which (as is shown below) allows for public participation.

3.1.3 Practice: Constitutional amendments and constitutionalism

In a context of overall adherence to constitutionalism in South Africa,[64] the seventeen amendments to the 1996 Constitution thus far (2023) have followed due procedures. Some required the NCOP's participation, while others did not. The Constitution Eleventh Amendment Act of 2003, which altered the procedure for intervention by the national government in a failing provincial government, received the unanimous support of the NCOP.[65] The Constitution Twelfth Amendment Act of 2006, which was pertinent to provinces as it changed provincial boundaries, raised constitutional controversy despite its having been passed by the NCOP.

The provincial boundaries demarcated for the 1993 Constitution, using magisterial districts and Bantustan borders, were retained in the 1996 Constitution but produced anachronistic outcomes because in some places they cut through communities on the basis of race. To ensure integrated municipalities, the 1996 Constitution was amended to allow for cross-border municipalities.[66] When this arrangement proved impossible to administer, a constitutional amendment of 2005 redefined provincial boundaries according to municipal district boundaries, which entailed changes to provincial boundaries.

[60] Constitution of 1996, s 74(1).
[61] Ibid s 74(2).
[62] Ibid. s 74(3).
[63] Ibid. s 74(8).
[64] Nico Steytler, 'The Dynamic Relationship between Devolution and Constitutionalism in South Africa' in Charles Fombad and Nico Steytler (eds.) (n 4) 151–82.
[65] In comparison, the Constitution Eighteenth Amendment Bill—seeking to amend s 25 of the Bill of Rights, which protects property rights by making expropriation without compensation explicitly possible—was destined for the NCOP, but failed to garner the necessary support in the National Assembly in December 2021.
[66] Constitution Third Amendment Act of 1998.

Furthermore, two pieces of Eastern Cape territory (the Transkei), which were islands in KwaZulu-Natal (KZN) for historical reasons, were reallocated to KZN. In compensation, an area which was historically part of KZN—the Matatiele municipal area—was transferred to the Eastern Cape. This swap of land was readily consented to by the two provincial legislatures concerned, but the Matatiele municipality and community would have none of it. They argued before the Constitutional Court that the consent given by the KZN provincial legislature was not preceded by proper consultation with them and that the KZN legislature's affirmative vote was thus void. The Constitutional Court agreed and invalidated the Twelfth Amendment for not following the prescribed amendment procedure correctly.[67]

Parliament re-enacted the amendment as the Thirteenth Amendment Act of 2007, after the KZN legislature had gone through the motions of public consultation and yet again approved the amendment of the boundary, despite hints from the Court that it would be the right thing to listen to the community.[68] By inserting public participation as a vital ingredient of lawmaking in a democracy, the Court expanded the scope of constitutionalism.

3.1.4 Concluding remarks

Although the format of the constitution-making in the National Convention was typical of coming-together federations, the decision not to adopt a federal constitution resulted in a limited role for the Senate in constitutional amendments (except for the entrenched clauses) and the disappearance of provincial legislatures as 'institutional veto players' (except for boundary changes). Although the 1993 and 1996 Constitutions were not, in the main, the product of a compact between different territorially based polities, their federal arrangements gave the newly established provinces a participatory role in constitutional amendments affecting the vital features of the Constitution (the founding values and the Bill of Rights) and provincial matters. This was done through the NCOP: as a house of delegates from the provincial legislatures and executives, it obviated the need for the engagement of provincial legislatures except when the interests of one or more particular provinces were affected.

3.2 Ethiopia

In the course of its political history, Ethiopia has had four constitutions, including its present-day one. They are the 1931 and 1955 Constitutions, promulgated by Haile Selassie

[67] *Matatiele Municipality and Others v President of the Republic of South Africa and Others (2)* [2006] ZACC 12.

[68] In a scandalous footnote to the ANC's history, the Matatiele issue resurfaced in 2016. In the local government elections of that year, the ANC lost control of the two metropolitan councils in Gauteng Province (Johannesburg and Tshwane), while a third (Ekurhuleni) teetered on a knife-edge—the ANC needed the four votes of a microparty, the African Independent Congress (AIC), to retain control of this council. In terms of a coalition agreement between the ANC and AIC, the former had to return Matatiele Local Municipality to KZN. Thus, for the sake of political power in a metro in a different province 700 kilometres away, the ANC sought to change the Constitution when it had previously rejected the municipality's plea. The ANC reneged on its undertaking to the AIC, however, much to the latter's chagrin. See Aphiwe Deklerk, '"ANC Duped Us into a Coalition Agreement They Never Fulfilled," says AIC Leader Mandla Galo' (*Sowetan Live*, 13 June 2021) https://www.sowetanlive.co.za/news/south-africa/2021-06-13-anc-duped-us-into-a-coalition-agreement-they-never-fulfilled-says-aic-leader-mandla-galo/ accessed 15 August 2022.

I; the 1987 Constitution adopted by the Derg (the military junta that ruled the country for seventeen years); and the 1995 Constitution, which is currently in force. The 1931 and 1955 Constitutions were meant chiefly to provide a constitutional foundation for the then absolute monarchical system, define the manner of succession to the imperial throne, centralize power in the person of the emperor, and build a nation state (arguably, one privileging the Amhara language and culture).[69] The 1987 Constitution formally abolished the monarchical system and introduced a republican form of government.[70] It also constitutionalized a socialist system, reinforced the unitary system, and introduced a one-party system, with the Workers' Party of Ethiopia (WPE) the only party accorded the constitutional right to exist.[71]

The three Constitutions were all promulgated in a top-down manner, with no input from subnational political units or forces. In the case of the 1931 and 1955 Constitutions, they were 'granted' to the public by Emperor Haile Selassie, a point stated clearly in the preamble of the 1955 Revised Constitution.[72] The 1987 Constitution, as Tsegaye Ararsa aptly puts it, was 'more like a revolutionary manifesto with socialist overtones in its fundamental values and was, at least theoretically, made by "we, working people of Ethiopia"'.[73] At the times when each of these three Constitutions were adopted, there were thus no subnational political entities in existence to play a role in their making or revision.

3.2.1 The Ethiopian Federal Democratic Constitution of 1995

The 1995 Constitution of Ethiopia, which entrenched the country's federal system, was meant to respond to the so-called 'nationality question' which the previous constitutions had supposedly failed to address.[74] It was adopted in the aftermath of a seventeen-year civil war in which ethnically mobilized rebel groups—especially those organized under the Ethiopian People's Revolutionary Democratic Front (EPRDF), with the Tigray People's Liberation Front (TPLF) the dominant group within it—emerged victorious.[75] The 1995 Constitution was hence adopted in a constitution-making process defined and dominated by the EPRDF and, to a lesser extent, other ethnically based political organizations.[76]

The process that culminated in the promulgation of the 1995 Constitution began with the approval of the 1991 Transitional Period Charter (TPC) by 'the Peaceful and

[69] Abera Jembere, *An Introduction to the Legal History of Ethiopia* (Lit Verlag 2000) 165–80; Abera Degefa, 'Birth-defects of a Constitution and Its Impacts on Outcome: Reflection on Ethiopian Constitution Making Experience' 2019 8(1) Oromia Law Journal 9.

[70] Constitution of the People's Democratic Republic of Ethiopia of 1987, preamble.

[71] Ibid. arts 1(3), 2, and 6.

[72] The Revised Constitution of Ethiopia (1955), preamble.

[73] Constitution of 1987 (n 70), preamble. See also Tsegaye Regassa, 'The Making and Legitimacy of the Ethiopian Constitution: Towards Bridging the Gap between Constitutional Design and Constitutional Practice' (2010) 23(1) Afrika Focus 85, 98.

[74] 'The question of nationalities' was one of the principal issues raised by the Ethiopian Students Movement (ESM) of the 1960s. The ESM rejected the claim that Ethiopia was a nation state. It asserted, rather, that it was made up of many nations, each of whose right to self-determination, up to the point of secession, should be recognized. This issue was articulated for the first time in Wallelign Mekonnen, 'On the Question of Nationalities in Ethiopia' (1969) Marxists.org., https://www.marxists.org/history/erol/ethiopia/nationalities.pdf accessed 2 August 2022.

[75] Regassa (n 73).

[76] Ibid.; Theodore M Vestal, 'An Analysis of the New Constitution of Ethiopia and the Process of Its Adoption' (1996) 3(2) Northeast African Studies 21, 22–26.

Democratic Transitional Conference of Ethiopia'.[77] This conference was held in June 1991, a few weeks after the Derg were ousted from power by the EPRDF, and mainly 'national liberation fronts' (as ethnic-based rebel groups were referred to) were allowed to attend. The Charter which the conference produced was thus 'more like a pact negotiated between ethno-nationalist liberation fronts'.[78] In other words, the Charter itself was a result of political negotiation among subnational political entities and no central government was a party to its adoption. The Charter served as a constitutional document between 1991 and 1995 and laid the foundation for the current ethnic-based federal system. It recognized the right to self-determination of ethnic communities, provided for the restructuring of the country's subnational units along ethnic lines, defined the structure of the national transitional government, and provided for the representation of all ethnic communities in the central government.[79]

Importantly, the Charter provided the general framework for drafting the 1995 Constitution.[80] It established a Council of Representatives (CoR), which was composed of 87 members who represented 'national liberation movements' such as the EPRDF and Oromo Liberation Front (OLF), and a few non-ethnic political parties that were allowed to take part in government during the transitional period under the Charter.[81] The CoR, which served as the legislative organ during the transition, had the power to oversee the constitution-making process.[82] To this end, it was authorized to establish a Constitutional Commission (CC) that was to draft a constitution.[83] The CoR issued Proclamation 24 (1992), which established the said CC.[84] According to the Charter, the CC would prepare a draft constitution which was to be endorsed by the CoR; the version of the draft endorsed by the CoR would then be presented to the public for discussion. The draft that incorporated input from public discussion would then finally be adopted by a constituent assembly elected in accordance with the procedure laid down in the final draft of the constitution.

Accordingly, the members of the CC were elected in August 1992, and on 8 April 1994 the CC submitted the draft constitution to the CoR.[85] The CoR endorsed the draft constitution after some discussion but without incorporating any input from non-EPRDF members.[86] On 5 June 1994, an election was held for the constituent assembly on a multiparty basis. The EPRDF won 484 of the 547 seats in the constituent assembly. The latter, which convened on 28 October 1994, endorsed the draft constitution with barely any changes.[87]

Clearly, the constitution-making process was defined and controlled by subnational ethnic-based political groups, especially the TPLF-EPRDF, the predominant group at the time. The Charter did not indicate how and of whom the CC would be composed. However, the CoR, which was dominated by the EPRDF, had the power to establish a CC.[88] The CC

[77] Kinfe Abraham, *Ethiopia from Bullets to the Ballot Box: The Bumpy Road to Democracy and the Political Economy of Transformation* (Red Sea Press 1994) 21.
[78] Regassa (n 73) 99.
[79] Transitional Period Charter of Ethiopia 1 (1991), preamble, arts 2, 6–9.
[80] Ibid. arts 10–12.
[81] Ibid. art 10. See also Vestal (n 76).
[82] Transitional Period Charter of Ethiopia 1 (1991) (n 79) art 10.
[83] Ibid.
[84] See Constitutional Commission Establishment Proclamation (No 24 of 1992).
[85] Vestal (n 76) 23.
[86] Ibid. 25.
[87] Ibid.
[88] Abera Degefa (n 69) 16.

was in turn regulated by Proclamation 24 (1992), which was enacted by the CoR and provided that the CC would be composed of 'various sections of the population'. The CC had 27 members, most of whom were members of the EPRDF.[89] This meant, as Meaza Ashenafi (the former President of the Federal Supreme Court and then a member of the CC) put it, that 'the EPRDF, the ruling party, always dominated when an issue came to a vote as it had the largest delegation'.[90] Moreover, the CoR decided on the budget of the CC and oversaw its operations. The CC also had to submit a periodic report to the CoR, while the latter was charged with endorsing the draft constitution which it developed.

The CC was set up and began its work after the regions were established and elections for regional councils had been held. As will be seen later, the nine regions that were established during the transitional period were later entrenched as the subnational units of the Ethiopian federation. The proclamation establishing the CC implied that the regions would play a role in the constitution-making process and enjoined the CC to seek and receive comments from regional councils. The CC also had a department entitled the Regional Affairs Coordination Department.[91] Composed of representatives of the then existing nine regions and the Addis Ababa city government, this department was meant to promote the interests of the regions.[92]

Nevertheless, the role of regions in the constitution-making should not be overemphasized. The regional councils were dominated by junior members of the EPRDF, so one would not expect comments or suggestions from them to the effect of introducing provisions in the draft constitution that differed materially from those that were endorsed by the CC. The latter was, in turn, subject to article 4 of Proclamation 24 (1992), which enjoined it to prepare a draft constitution that was 'in conformity with the spirit of the Charter'. The CC could, thus, not have introduced a system in the draft constitution that was essentially different from the one established by the Charter, nor could it have overlooked the most fundamental principles entrenched in it, such as the right to self-determination of ethnic communities and the right to secession. As Regassa maintains, 'the constitution was meant to be an instrument of advancing the aspirations of those who negotiated the Charter. To that extent, then, it was the extension, a natural historical outgrowth, of the Charter.'[93]

In summary, the 1995 Constitution, unlike Ethiopia's preceding constitutions, was adopted in a process dominated by subnational political forces that sought to guard their subnational autonomy from overreach by the central government. Thus, in some sense the Constitution was not imposed by the central government; rather, it was a federal compact among the ethnic communities of the country, as represented by the ethnically organized political parties and 'national liberation fronts'. Yet, in another sense, the Constitution was, in precisely the same vein as the previous constitutions, the result of a top-down approach, given that not all subnational political forces played an equal role in its adoption. The TPLF-EPRDF, which controlled the national transitional government and drafted the transitional-period Charter, dominated the entire process of drafting the 1995 Constitution. One may safely assume that there is not a single provision in it that was not endorsed by the EPRDF.

[89] Vestal (n 76).
[90] Meaza Ashenafi, quoted in Abera Degefa (n 69).
[91] Assefa A Lemu, 'The Making of Ethiopian Constitution of 1995' (*Aiga Forum*, 11 February 2018) http://aigaforum.com/article2018/The-Making-of-Eth-Constitution-1995.htm accessed 2 August 2022.
[92] Ibid.
[93] Regassa (n 73) 102.

3.2.2 Amendment of the 1995 Constitution and the role of states

The amendment procedure of the Constitution is prescribed in its articles 104 and 105, which accord two important roles to the federal government and states in an amendment process. The first is linked to *initiating* an amendment process. A constitutional amendment may be initiated by the federal government, or, more specifically, by either of the houses of Parliament, namely the House of Peoples' Representatives (HPR) and the House of Federation (HoF). It is important to note that the HPR is composed of directly elected representatives, whereas the HoF is composed of representatives of the ethnic communities of the country—each ethnic community is represented by a single representative and by an additional representative for each one million people belonging to it. Thus, the role of the HoF as the house of ethnic communities is somewhat attenuated since, so far, the state governments select the representatives of the ethnic communities within their jurisdiction.

Either of the two federal houses may initiate a constitutional amendment with a resolution adopted with a two-thirds majority vote.[94] The states can also initiate constitutional amendments.[95] A resolution initiating a constitutional amendment must be endorsed by one-third of the state councils.[96] Each of the states can adopt the resolution initiating a constitutional amendment with a simple majority.[97] A proposed amendment, once endorsed by the HPR, HoF, or two-thirds of the states, is 'submitted for discussion and decision to the general public and to those whom the amendment of the Constitution concerns'.[98] It is unclear, though, what role the general public or those who are specifically affected by the constitutional amendment would play in a constitutional amendment.[99]

This brings us to the second role the federal government and states play in the amendment of the Constitution—the adoption of a proposed constitutional amendment. Article 105 of the Constitution provides that, as a rule, a constitutional amendment comes to effect when a bill is endorsed with a two-thirds majority of the joint session of the HPR and HoF, and when two-thirds of the states approve the amendment with a simple majority.[100] However, an extra-special procedure is required for amending certain provisions in the Constitution, namely the Bill of Rights[101] and the Constitution's amendment procedure.[102] For an amendment of these parts of the Constitution to come into effect, in the first place each of the two houses of Parliament must in separate session approve the amending bill with a two-thirds majority.[103] Secondly, the amending bill must be approved with a simple majority by the legislative council of *every* state.[104]

94 Constitution of the Federal Democratic Republic of Ethiopia 1995, art 104.
95 Ibid.
96 Ibid.
97 Ibid.
98 Ibid.
99 The Constitution indeed uses 'discussion and decision'. Could the general public, or those who are affected by the proposed constitutional amendment, thus stop the amendment if they are displeased with it? Does this imply holding a referendum at national or subnational level? Art 105(2), however, seems to suggest that the role of the public is simply to discuss the proposed amendment and provide input; as such, the final say on constitutional amendment appears to have been left to the federal government and the states.
100 Constitution of the Federal Democratic Republic of Ethiopia 1995, art 105(1).
101 Ibid.
102 Ibid. arts 104 and 105.
103 Ibid. art 105(1)(b) and (c).
104 Ibid. art 105(1)(a).

It is important to note that the right to self-determination of ethnic communities and the right to secession form part of the Bill of Rights, and that an amendment impacting on these rights would thus require this extra-special procedure—as such, a single state could veto the amendment of these parts of the Constitution. Again, it is key to note that only amendment of the provisions recognizing the right to self-determination up to and including secession of the ethnic communities requires the consent of every state. As regards the act of secession, both internal (the creation of a new regional state) or external (leaving the federation), this is a unilateral act that does not depend on the consent of other states or ethnic communities and, therefore, a formal constitutional amendment, namely the addition or removal of a regional state from the list of states in article 47(1).

The federation is conceptualized as a federation of the ethnic communities of the country.[105] As mentioned, in practice the Constitution was simply a compact among ethnically organized political forces.[106] However, it is conceived of as a federal compact entered into by and among the ethnic communities; a compact they adopted on the basis of their 'right to self-determination' recognized in the Charter. This is clear from the preamble of the Constitution, which begins with the words, 'we the nations, nationalities and peoples'. Moreover, the Constitution recognizes these ethnic communities as holders of 'sovereign power', and itself, as the Constitution they supposedly authored, as the expression of their sovereignty.[107] It is also the case that the power to interpret the Constitution is vested in the HoF.

However, the Constitution recognizes the states, not the ethnic communities, as members of the federation.[108] Also, as noted above, it is the states, not the ethnic communities, that are involved in a constitutional amendment. Indeed, six of Ethiopia's eleven states have an ethnic community which is in the majority, with these states being considered as their homelands. The communities in these states could be considered as being involved, through the state councils, in a constitutional amendment. However, the rest of the states have multi-ethnic populations in which no single ethnic community is in the majority (even states with an ethnic majority are not ethnically homogeneous). The ethnic communities that are in the minority in one of the eleven states thus cannot be directly involved in constitutional amendment, even when they have their own local councils.

3.2.3 Constitutionalism and amendments in practice

In the nearly three decades since the 1995 Constitution was adopted, it has been amended only once. This was in 1997 and in regard to article 98, which deals with the concurrent taxing powers of the states and the federal government. Previously, the article provided that both levels of government could impose and collect revenue from concurrent taxes. It was amended to the effect that the federal government may levy and collect a concurrent tax and share the revenue with the state from whose jurisdiction the revenue is collected.

[105] Alemante Gebre-Sellasie, 'Ethnic Federalism: Its Promise and Pitfalls for Africa' (2003) 28(1) Yale Journal of International Law 51, 56.

[106] Yonatan Fessha, *Ethnic Diversity and Federalism: Constitution Making in South Africa and Ethiopia* (Ashgate 2010) 193.

[107] Constitution of the Federal Democratic Republic of Ethiopia 1995, art 8.

[108] art 47(1).

Some have deemed this amendment as 'unconstitutional' or 'unofficial' because it was not officially published in the *Negarit Gazette*, Ethiopia's official law gazette.[109]

Moreover, since the adoption of the Constitution, two states, Sidama and South-West, have been officially established, and the birth of the country's twelfth state is imminent. The establishment of Sidama and South-West states did not lead to a constitutional amendment. Although the two new states are not included in the list of states in the Constitution, they function as separate states. Does this mean that the creation of a new state requires no constitutional amendment?

The answer to this question is in the affirmative, for two reasons. First, the right of an ethnic community to its own state is constitutionally guaranteed and inherent in the right to self-determination of an ethnic community. If the formation of a new state were to require a constitutional amendment, it would put the right to self-determination of the ethnic community demanding its own state at the mercy of the existing states or other ethnic communities. Second, the constitution provides that, once the procedural requirements for the formation of a new state are met, the new state 'automatically' becomes a member of the federation, without the need for a constitutional amendment. It should be noted, though, that the inclusion of the names of the new states in the Constitution, something which has important symbolic value, entails a constitutional amendment.

3.2.4 Concluding remarks

The 1995 Constitution is conceived of as a federal compact among Ethiopia's 80 or so ethnic communities. This is partly so because the constitution-making from which it arose was dominated by subnational ethnic political parties and ethnic 'liberation organizations', among them the TPLF, which exercised disproportionate influence in the process. These ethnic communities, as the contracting parties of the federal compact, are assigned an important role in constitutional amendments through their representation in the HoF, which plays the role of initiating and endorsing constitutional amendments. However, it is the states that play the most decisive role of all in constitutional amendments, since an amendment needs the consent of at least two-thirds of the states to come into effect; as regards the amendment of any provision in the Bill of Rights and the procedure for a constitutional amendment, a single state could veto it.

Nevertheless, a significant consideration is that the states are not uniformly each identical with a particular ethnic community, even though six of the eleven have an ethnic community which is in the majority. The veto power of the states in relation to the amendment of the Bill of Rights—which entrenches, among other things, the right to self-determination of ethnic communities and the procedure for a constitutional amendment—cannot be seen in isolation from the dominant role that the TPLF played in the constitution-making process. While the TPLF was indeed a dominant political force at the time of the making of the 1995 Constitution, it was clear that its political dominance would wane in time, considering that it represented only a small region (Tigray) and merely six per cent of the entire population. It thus would seem that the TPLF sought to obtain a veto power that would allow it to prevent any constitutional change impacting on the autonomy of its political base, namely the Tigray region and the people of Tigray.

[109] Assefa Fiseha and Zemelak Ayele, 'Constitutional Adjudication and Constitutional Governance in the Horn: Ethiopia, Somalia, and South Sudan' in Charles Fombad, Assefa Fiseha, and Nico Steytler (eds.) (n 6) 246.

3.3 Nigeria

Nigeria is the oldest federation in Africa, with its federal system predating independence; it also has a long history of constitution-making. It had five constitutions before independence, and since independence, has had three more, not to mention two constitutions that were not put into effect. This makes Nigeria the country with one of the highest 'turnover[s] of national constitutions'.[110] Almost all of these constitutions were introduced in the name of establishing a 'democratic' and 'true' federal system, yet constitution-making barely met the minimum as a democratic process, let alone the requirements of constitution-making leading to the establishment of a federal system. The making of all the constitutions of Nigeria was dominated either by the British colonial governors or the various military governments that assumed power in coups and counter-coups.[111]

3.3.1 Colonial constitutions

The five pre-independence constitutions, after having brought together the two Nigerian colonies and protectorates (the north and the south) under a single colony, gradually transformed the colony 'into a parliamentary federation of three major ethnic regions'.[112] The 1914 Constitution, the first pre-independence constitution, amalgamated the northern and southern colonies and protectorates of Nigeria into a single colony. The 1922 (Clifford) Constitution 'consolidated' the unification of the north and the south regions by establishing a Legislative Council of Nigeria which, composed mainly of appointed members, could enact laws for the entire territory of the country. This Constitution considered the two regions as a single political unit for financial purposes. In 1939, the British colonial administration divided the Nigerian colony into three ethnically aligned regions in the north, east, and west regions, while the 1946 Constitution used the three regions to introduce regionalism—the precursor of Nigerian federalism with three states.

The 1951 Constitution (Macpherson Constitution) gave the three regions, hitherto mere administrative regions, political status, thereby introducing a 'quasi-federal' system in Nigeria. Until that point, Nigeria had been a unitary state.[113] The last pre-independence constitution, adopted in 1954, consolidated the parliamentary federal arrangements of the 1951 Constitution. It provided self-government to the three regions, made Lagos a federal territory, and defined the power of the central government, leaving residual powers to the three regions.

As may be seen from the above, Nigeria's pre-independence constitutions laid the foundation for its present-day federal system. Yet both the constitutions and the quasi-federal system had been conceived and implemented by the British colonial administration to serve its administrative convenience rather than any democratic purpose. In fact, each of the first three constitutions was known as 'a governor's constitution' since they were drafted by the

110 'Nigeria: Nine Constitutions in 24 Years of Democracy!' (*New African*, 25 November 2013) https://newafricanmagazine.com/4073/ accessed 9 August 2022.

111 IM Oraun, 'The Military and Constitution-Making: The Nigerian Experience' (*Dullah Omar Institute*, undated) https://bit.ly/3S48hVq accessed 1 October 2023.

112 Rotimi Suberu, 'Nigeria's Permanent Constitutional Transition: Military Rule, Civilian Instability and "True Federalism" in a Deeply Divided Society', Forum of Federations: Occasional Paper Series No 34 (2019) 5.

113 Ignatius Akayaar Ayua and CJ Dakas, 'The Republic of Nigeria' in John Kincaid and G Alan Tarr (eds), *Constitutional Origins, Structures, and Change in Federal Countries* (McGill-Queen's University Press 2005) 240–79.

colonial governors with little or no input by the people and then endorsed by the British Parliament. As Abioye puts it, these constitutions 'imposed a foreign system of governance, and foreign laws' in Nigeria without making any effort 'to accommodate the foundational values of constitutionalism, namely to embody the hopes and aspirations of the people, and to reflect their societal values and traditions'.[114] Indeed, while the 1951 Constitution, which conferred political status on the three regions, was partly a result of negotiation with political parties which were formed along ethnic and regional lines,[115] it came into effect only after the British Parliament enacted it into law.

3.3.2 Post-independence constitutions

The Independence Constitution of 1960, the result of an inter-party conference, came into effect after being enacted by the British Parliament.[116] However, it was replaced three years later by another Constitution, this time adopted by Nigeria's federal Parliament, which declared Nigeria a republic and introduced a fourth region in the country. Representatives of political parties, mostly organized along ethnic and regional lines, drew up the 1963 Constitution. The latter can thus be considered as a Constitution drawn up by civilian political actors and, to a degree, as a federal compact among the political actors concerned.

As a result of the series of coups and counter-coups, Nigeria remained under military rule from 1966 to 1999, with intermittent civilian rule. The military governments introduced new constitutions in 1979, 1989, 1995, and 1999. Through these constitutions, the army initiated what Suberu calls 'mega constitutional changes', which impacted directly on the country's federal dispensation.[117] The changes increased the number of states, expanded the power of the central government at the expense of the power and autonomy of the states, and replaced the parliamentary form of government with a presidential system.[118]

The army controlled the drafting and promulgation of these constitutions and, as such, the latter were imposed rather than 'processed'.[119] For instance, the 1979 Constitution, which introduced an 'American-style Presidential Federal Model' and recognized the existing nineteen states,[120] was drafted by a constitutional drafting committee composed of 49 members all appointed by the Supreme Military Council (SMC). A constituent assembly, composed of individuals who were elected by electoral college members made up of local government councils, made minor changes to the draft constitution and submitted it to the SMC for approval.[121] The SMC inserted its own decree into the draft constitution and promulgated it. The military cancelled the 1989 Constitution, which sought to introduce a greater local government autonomy, after local and state gubernatorial elections were held

[114] Funmi T Abioye, 'Constitution-making, Legitimacy, and Rule of Law: A Comparative Analysis' (2011) 44(1) Comparative and International Law Journal of Southern Africa 67.

[115] Attoh Nonso Robert, Edith Nwosu, and Festus Okechukwu Ukwueze, 'Nigeria's Constitution Making Experience Since 1914: An Evaluation' in CA Omaka (ed.), *Law in Nigeria at 100: Reviewing the Past, Projecting the Future: Proceedings of the 47th Annual Conference of the Nigerian Association of Law Teachers (2–6 June 2014, Ebonyi State University, Abakaliki, Nigeria)* (Nigerian Association of Law Teachers 2015).

[116] Ibid.

[117] Suberu (n 112) 5.

[118] Ibid.

[119] Julius O Ihonvbere, 'How to Make an Undemocratic Constitution: The Nigerian Example' (2000) 21(2) Third World Quarterly 349; Agha Eresia-Eke, 'The Contradictions of Constitution-making in Nigeria' (2012) 6(4) African Research Review 76–92; Abioye (n 114).

[120] Suberu (n 112).

[121] Attoh, Ogonnaya Nwosu, and Okechukwu Ukwueze (n 115).

prior to presidential elections. The 1995 Constitution, which sought to introduce ethnic power-sharing and greater decentralization (with 30 states), was never implemented.

3.3.3 The 1999 Constitution

Even the making of the 1999 Constitution, which is currently in force and has ushered in Nigeria's longest period of civilian rule, was dominated by the military. General Abdulsalami Abubakar, as the head of the military government, established a team of 25 experts called a 'Constitutional Debate and Coordinating Committee'.[122] The Committee used the 1995 draft constitution as a starting point and invited groups and individuals to give their comments on it. The Committee submitted the report to the Provisional Ruling Council (PRC), the ruling military council, which ignored the 1995 draft constitution and redrafted the 1979 Constitution based on the recommendations of the Committee. Through Decree No 24 of 1995, the PRC promulgated the 1999 Constitution.

The states played no role in the making of the Constitution, even though it directly affects them. For instance, the army reorganized the territorial structure of the states in five rounds, increasing the number of states from only four regions in 1966 to twelve states in 1967, 19 in 1976, 21 in 1987, 30 in 1991, and 36 in 1996.[123] The increases were prompted by the fact that the three regions, extremely large and populous, rendered the federal territorial structure 'unbalanced' since they competed with, or even undermined, the 'weak and fragmented' federal government.[124] In addition, the three regions had scores of ethnic minorities that felt marginalized by regional majorities and demanded their own states.[125] At any rate, the existing states never consented to the creation of new states. In fact, the creation of these states did not follow any prescribed constitution-making process. The states were created by military decree and recognized only in subsequent constitution-making processes. Given the absence of the states in the making of the 1999 Constitution, are they part of its amendment procedures?

Like all legislative bills, a bill seeking to alter the Constitution may be initiated by members of the National Assembly, as well as by the executive, the judiciary, or private interest groups.[126] A bill to amend any part of the Constitution other than its section 8 or chapter IV needs to pass as an Act of Parliament supported by two-thirds of all members of each of the two houses of the National Assembly.[127] This means the bill amending the Constitution must be supported at least by 72 of the 109 members of the Senate and 240 of the 360 members of the House of Representatives.[128] The states play a critical role in constitutional amendment too, since such amendment must also be endorsed as a resolution by two-thirds of the 36 state legislative councils.[129] Here, this means that at least 24 of the 36 states must support the bill amending the Constitution by a simple majority.[130]

122 Ibid. 91.
123 Suberu (n 112) 9.
124 Ibid. 5.
125 Ibid.
126 Nigerian Constitution of 1999, s 9. Policy and Legal Advocacy Centre (PLAC), 'A Step-by-step Process of Amending the Nigerian Constitution' (*PLAC*, 2019) https://placng.org/i/wp-content/uploads/2021/05/Step-by-Step-Guide-to-the-Process-of-Amending-the-Nigerian-Constitution.pdf accessed 28 July 2022.
127 Constitution of 1999 (n 126) s 9(2).
128 PLAC (n 126).
129 Constitution of 1999 (n 126) s 9(2).
130 PLAC (n 126).

By contrast, the amendment of section 8 and chapter IV of the Constitution, as well as 'the constitutional amendment formula', require a more rigid procedure.[131] Section 8 deals with the creation of new states, the modification of any existing state boundaries, the creation of new local governments, and the alteration of local government boundaries. As for chapter IV of the Constitution, it contains a Bill of Rights. A bill amending these parts of the Constitution may pass only if it is supported by four-fifths of all members of each house of Parliament and endorsed by two-thirds of the states.[132]

The strong standing of the Senate and the state legislatures in constitutional amendment does not seem to flow from their role in the constitution-making processes (where they have been almost absent). The 1999 Constitution, replicating the 1979 Constitution (which, as noted, introduced an American-style presidential federal model), copied these procedures from the US Constitution rather than being the outcome of state pressure from below.

3.3.4 Practice: Amendments and constitutionalism

Three groups of modifications have been made to the 1999 Constitution since its adoption, with the amendments adhering to the constitutional procedure and meeting the demanding requirements for a constitutional amendment.[133] These alterations had no direct or indirect impact on the boundaries or powers of states, as they focused on matters such as electoral administration. Nonetheless, other constitutional amendment bills with a direct bearing on the states were subsequently approved by the federal Parliament and requisite number of states. For instance, in 2014 a bill that sought to introduce changes regarding, among other things, local government autonomy was approved by the federal and state legislatures.[134] However, the then president, Goodluck Jonathan, refused to sign these changes into law.

The federal legislature has also adopted bills seeking to alter the Constitution, including ones seeking to give local government enhanced autonomy—these have not come to fruition so far, partly because the president has declined to assent to them.[135] According to Suberu, there are extra-constitutional initiatives that seek to introduce fundamental changes to the federal system, among them the Sovereign National Conference, which is supported by the southern states and ethnic communities. These, however, have not resulted in any changes to the 1999 Constitution.[136]

3.3.5 Concluding remarks

The subnational territorial units of Nigeria played barely any role in the making of the numerous constitutions of the country, including the 1999 Constitution, currently in force. Indeed, most of the states were not even created in a constitution-making process but sprang into existence by military decree, after which they were simply entrenched in subsequent constitutions. Yet the 1999 Constitution, in keeping with the logic of federalism, accords them a key role in constitutional amendments in that no constitutional amendment

[131] Suberu (n 112) 17.
[132] Constitution of 1999 (n 126) s 9(3).
[133] Suberu (n 112) 17.
[134] Ibid.
[135] A federal high court declared that a constitution-amending bill cannot come into effect without the president's assent. See PLAC (n 126) 13.
[136] Ibid.

can come into effect unless endorsed by two-thirds of them. The role of the states in a constitutional amendment was not, that is to say, a response to the states' demand to have a say in changing the federal constitution. It seems, rather, that the drafters of the Constitution, aware that they were drafting a Constitution establishing a federal system, assumed that the mere fact that Nigeria was a federation required the states' involvement in a constitutional amendment.

3.4 Kenya

Kenya underwent processes of constitution-making at two critical 'constitutional moments' in its history that resulted in the creation of federal-type governance structures. The first took place between 1960 and 1963 and gave rise to the Independence Constitution, which created regional governments (*majimbo*, meaning 'provinces' or 'states'). The second, a culmination of previous constitutional review processes, unfolded between 2008 and 2010 and resulted in the current Constitution, which establishes the country's system of devolution.

At each of these junctures, Kenya had a highly centralized unitary government, as a consequence of which the subnational units created under its newly adopted constitutional frameworks were products of the disaggregation of the existing territory in a holding-together constitutional arrangement. Although ethnic accommodation was the central premise for the push to adopt *majimbo* at independence, what in turn generally underlay the push for self-governance were the objectives of checking the imperial powers exercised by the executive, entrenching democratic rule, and facilitating equitable development.[137] The same objectives, while informed by different sets of circumstances and historical bases, underlay the drive for, and adoption of, devolution under Kenya's Constitution of 2010.

3.4.1 Independence Constitution of 1963

Kenya's Independence Constitution was the product of negotiations at three constitutional conferences—the Lancaster House Conferences—held in London in 1960, 1962, and 1963.[138] The negotiations relating to the structure of the state and the question of whether to adopt a federal-type form of government pitted the Kenya African National Union (KANU), whose membership consisted of the larger ethnic tribes, against the Kenya African Democratic Union (KADU), whose membership was drawn mainly from Kenya's smaller ethnic groups.[139] While KANU adopted a centralist stance and pushed for a majoritarian system of democratic rule, KADU advocated for a form of decentralization and the sharing of power by communities at the national level.[140] The negotiations involving these two parties and overseen by the British eventually settled on regionalism, which was then entrenched in the Independence Constitution.

Given the ethnic basis of the negotiating parties, the ethnic basis of the territorial demarcation adopted by the British, and the fact that the regions which were eventually adopted

[137] Yash Pal Ghai, 'Devolution in Kenya: Background and Objectives' in Nico Steytler and Yash Pal Ghai (eds.), *Kenyan-South African Dialogue on Devolution* (Juta 2015) 69–70.
[138] Ibid. 62–65.
[139] Ibid. 68–69.
[140] Ibid. 69.

were demarcated largely on the basis of ethnicity, it is arguable, then, that while subnational units were not in existence to take part in the process of making the Independence Constitution, regional interests were indeed represented by the participating national political parties. Seeing as regionalism was adopted through a constitutional process of disaggregation, a clear compact between the ethnic communities cannot be said to have informed its formation. The adoption of regionalism may, however, be argued to have resulted from a compact of the leading political parties: a compact based on the need to secure minority interests (and also egged along by political nudging from colonial interests).[141]

To determine the boundaries of the regions that would be the basis for *majimbo*, a boundaries commission was set up. With its membership consisting of British nationals, the commission assessed the existing provincial boundaries and consulted communities, which preferred that some boundaries be redrawn to allow ethnic homogeneity in the demarcation process.[142] In the end, therefore, ethnicity constituted the basis for the demarcation of regional boundaries.

Despite Kenya's constitutional disaggregation background, provision was made for the involvement of regions and regional interests in constitutional amendment. This was achieved through the following: the requirement for the participation of the Senate and the imposition of high thresholds for approval of constitutional amendment bills in Parliament; the constitutional requirement for direct participation of regions in amendments touching on specific matters; and the requirement of a referendum in specified circumstances.

The second chamber of Parliament, the Senate, which was made up of elected representatives drawn from districts within the regions,[143] provided the first platform for the participation of regional (district-level) interests in the constitutional amendment process. While it may be argued that basing senatorial membership on districts rather than regions weakened the Senate's link to regions and its inclination to protect regional interests, its, as well as the regions', ethnic foundations, coupled with Okoth-Ogendo's description of the Senate at the time as a forum for tribal representation,[144] provide a basis for arguing that the Senate nonetheless represented regional interests in the legislative process.

The Independence Constitution imposed a high threshold of three-quarters (75 per cent) of members of both the Senate and the House of Representatives for a constitutional amendment bill to be passed.[145] A referendum was required prior to the reintroduction of a defeated constitutional amendment bill in Parliament with a requirement that the proposed changes obtain the support of two-thirds of the votes cast in the referendum.[146] While the threshold at the House of Representatives remained at three-quarters of the members for amendments touching on entrenched constitutional provisions, it was increased to a rather prohibitive nine-tenths (or 90 per cent) for the Senate.[147] These entrenched provisions included those relating to the procedure for constitutional amendment under sections 71

[141] Githu Muigai and Dan Juma, *Power, Politics & Law: Dynamics of Constitutional Change in Kenya, 1887–2022* (Kabarak University Press 2022) 164–88.

[142] Ghai (n 137) 7.

[143] Constitution of Kenya (1963) s 36(1).

[144] Hastings Okoth-Ogendo, 'Politics of Constitutional Change in Kenya since Independence, 1963 to 1969' (1972) 71(282) African Affairs 9–34.

[145] 1963 Constitution (n 143) s 71(1) and (2).

[146] Ibid. s 71(3).

[147] Ibid. s 71(6) and (7).

and 156 of the Constitution, those relating to the Senate, and those touching on the regions, including matters to do with regional boundaries and powers.[148]

In addition to participation through the institution of the Senate, regions were required to give consent to some amendments. The Constitution made provision for the periodic review and possible adjustment of the constitutional provisions relating to the financing of regions by the central government.[149] While Parliament was allowed to enact a constitutional amendment where this was proposed under the review, the Constitution required that such amendments come into operation only once at least four out of the seven regions (that is, 57 per cent) had signified (through their regional assemblies) their consent for the amendments.[150] This was intended to ensure that the central level of government did not unilaterally undertake amendments that would destabilize the second level of government, namely the regions.

Despite the seemingly high threshold for constitutional amendment in Parliament, the Independence Constitution was amended 29 times between 1963 and 2010.[151] These amendments watered down constitutional provisions, abolished the system of *majimbo*, and entrenched a highly centralized state under an imperial president. While safeguards were built into the Constitution to limit unilateral amendments to it at the instance of the central government, the foundation of these safeguards lay in the assumption that there would always be an opposition in Parliament that would make attainment of the high thresholds for amendment difficult. This assumption inadvertently failed to envision a one-party state where the central government controls both houses of Parliament, thereby rendering thresholds for amendment moot.

This 'unforeseen' event came to pass shortly after independence. KADU, the official opposition in Parliament, declared itself dissolved on 10 November 1964, both as a party and the official opposition, and indicated that it was to join and vote with the government in Parliament.[152] While this made the subsequent parliamentary adoption of constitutional amendments, including those touching on entrenched provisions, 'near unanimous',[153] it came shortly after the first amendment, which while not touching on specially entrenched provisions, had started the move to abolish regionalism.[154] It would thus appear that defenders of regionalism yielded to KANU's push for a centralized unitary state immediately after independence, aligned themselves with the central government, and did not put up a fight in Parliament to resist the initial amendments.[155] The erstwhile defenders are said to have attributed their change of tune to '[the] demands of the people themselves'.[156]

3.4.2 Constitution of 2010

Kenya's postcolonial centralization of power and the resulting increased concentration of state power in the person of the president resulted in the diminution of democratic space,

[148] Ibid. s 71(7) as read with sch 4.
[149] Ibid. ss 137(2), 138(1), and 140(1).
[150] Ibid. s 156(4)(d) & proviso (c).
[151] Kenya Law, 'The Amendments of the Constitution of Kenya from 1963 to 2019' http://kenyalaw.org/kl/index.php?id=9631 accessed 4 August 2022.
[152] Githu and Juma (n 141) 195–96.
[153] Ibid. 196.
[154] Ibid. 197.
[155] Ibid. 196.
[156] Ibid. 197.

underdevelopment (selective development),[157] and ethnic conflict. As a result, the political opposition, civil society organizations, and religious groups, among other collectives, began agitating for constitutional reform. This gave rise to two separate constitutional review and constitution-making phases. The first began in 1998 with the enactment of the Constitution of Kenya Review Act of 1997 (CKRA)[158] and culminated in a new draft constitution (the Wako Draft) that was defeated in the referendum of 2005.[159] The second was initiated following the 2007–08 post-election violence and resulted in the adoption of Kenya's current Constitution after a national referendum in 2010. Although separate, the second phase drew on, and was a harmonization of, the issues and proposals gathered in the first phase.[160]

The participatory nature of the constitution-making process that preceded the adoption of the 2010 Constitution through the various stages and drafts of the proposed Constitution ensured that the views of the regional interest groups that were represented at district fora were taken into account in the formulation of the country's system of government.[161] More specifically, with regard to the devolution of power, the people proposed a strengthened system of local governance that would enable them to determine their own choice of lifestyle, including undertaking their own budgeting at the local level; would have financial autonomy; would be accountable to the people; would be free of interference from the centre; and would be represented in national decision-making through the Senate.[162] On the basis of these proposals, recommendations were made for the entrenchment of devolution and devolved structures in the new Constitution, measures that included the design of clear, independent functions and powers for the various levels of government.

Although proposals had been made during the constitution-making process for the adoption of federal-like strong regional governments akin to the independence *majimbo*, a majority of Kenyans preferred a devolved system of government within a unitary state.[163] The 2010 Constitution, therefore, adopted a hybrid multilevel form of government: one with two levels of government made up of the national government and 47 county governments (moulded on the 47 administrative boundaries of pre-existing districts).[164] With this, Kenya departed from its historically centralized system of government and, much like South Africa, adopted a hybrid of both federal and unitary features.

While the adoption of the Constitution did not arise out of a compact between Kenya's ethnic communities, whose majorities made up the disaggregated units that constituted

[157] The absence of checks and balances on central power made the presidency the decision-maker regarding which parts of the country received which kind of development, with the result that some parts of the country were comparatively more developed while others underwent little to no development.

[158] Constitution of Kenya Review Act (CKRA) 13 of 1997.

[159] Formally, the process began in April 2001 with the establishment of the Constitution of Kenya Review Commission (CKRC). See Conrad Bosire, 'Devolution for Development, Conflict Resolution, and Limiting Central Power: An Analysis of the Constitution of Kenya 2010' (LLD thesis, University of the Western Cape 2013) 154.

[160] CKRA of 2008, ss 23, 30, and 32. See John Mutakha Kangu, 'An Interpretation of the Constitutional Framework for Devolution in Kenya: A Comparative Approach' (LLD thesis, University of the Western Cape 2014) 118.

[161] Jill Cottrell and Yash Pal Ghai, *The Role of Constitution Building Process in Democratization: Case Study – Kenya* (International IDEA 2004).

[162] Constitution of Kenya Review Commission, 'The Final Report of the Constitution of Kenya Review Commission' (CKRC 2005) 239–41; Mutakha Kangu (n 160) 114.

[163] Bosire (n 159) 156.

[164] s 2 of the Districts and Boundaries Act of 1992 established and demarcated the boundaries of Nairobi Area and 46 other districts. These districts (as demarcated under the Act) were the same ones that were renamed as 'counties' and listed as such under the 2010 Constitution. These pre-existing districts were historically demarcated such that each contains an ethnic majority.

the second level of government, the highly participatory approach to its making ensured that broad group interests were taken into account in its formulation. The common ground shared across the board was the need for devolution as an antidote to the imperial presidency, among other ills.

The Constitution established county governments as a level of government which, though interdependent with the national government, is distinct and has its own functions and powers. To protect the interests of counties at the national level, the Constitution established the Senate, the membership of which is directly elected and represents each of the counties. As such, the Senate is made up of 67 members, with these consisting of 47 members elected from each of the counties, sixteen nominated women members drawn from party lists, two members of opposite genders representing the youth, and two members of opposite genders representing persons with disabilities.

Although counties did not take part directly in the formulation of the constitutional compact that established them, their participation, as well as the protection of their interests, is provided for in instances where constitutional amendments are contemplated. This is achieved through the participation of the second chamber of Parliament, the Senate, in national-level legislative processes, as well as through the imposition of thresholds for county-level participation in constitutional amendments.

Under articles 255, 256, and 257 of the Constitution, amendments may be initiated either by Parliament (parliamentary initiative) or the people (popular initiative). The process to be followed in adopting an amendment depends on whether it touches on the constitutional provisions that are entrenched under article 255(1):

- Where an amendment originates from Parliament but does not touch on the entrenched provisions, it requires a two-thirds majority in Parliament for it to pass.
- Where an amendment originates from Parliament but touches on the entrenched provisions, it is required to be supported by a two-thirds majority in Parliament, after which it is then submitted to a referendum for approval before being assented to. To be approved in a referendum, the amendment has to gain a simple majority of the total votes cast and also be supported by at least 20 per cent of voters in at least half of the counties.
- Where an amendment originates from the people but does not touch on the entrenched provisions, it is required first to be supported by the signatures of a million registered voters; it then has to obtain majority approval in Parliament as well as the approval of a majority of county assemblies.
- Where an amendment originates from the people but touches on the entrenched provisions, it is required to obtain the following in order to pass: a million signatures of registered voters; the approval of a majority of county assemblies; majority approval in Parliament, as well as majority approval in a referendum, with at least 20 per cent of the votes cast in at least half of the counties.

The Senate, as a house of Parliament, is involved in approving bills relating to amendment of the Constitution.[165] Article 256(1) of the Constitution provides for amendments to

[165] Constitution of Kenya (2010) art 255(3).

non-entrenched provisions through a parliamentary initiative. Processes under this method of amendment follow the ordinary parliamentary processes for passing ordinary bills. In this regard, the Senate, which is mandated to represent and protect county interests,[166] is mandatorily required to be consulted and to concur with any bills that concern counties.[167] The equality of the powers of concurrence between the two houses of Parliament thus grants power to the Senate to ensure the protection of the interests of counties in amendments brought through a parliamentary initiative.

Where an amendment originates in Parliament but touches on entrenched provisions such as the objects, principles, and structure of devolved government, then county interests are taken care of at two levels: the level of deliberations in the Senate, and the level of a referendum, which is required for amending entrenched provisions.[168] County-level interests are catered for at the referendum stage by imposing minimum participation quotas for county-level voters. In the latter regard, for the amendment to be approved, the Constitution requires at least 20 per cent of registered voters in at least half of the counties to vote in that referendum.[169] This ensures that, should such an amendment pass, it has support across most of the counties.

More substantively, the Constitution requires direct participation and approval by a majority of the counties in amendments sought to be brought by way of a popular initiative.[170] In this regard, the Independent Electoral and Boundaries Commission is required, upon ascertaining that the initiative has met the numerical threshold for signatures, to submit the draft amendment bill to county assemblies for consideration and approval.[171] This applies to any amendment proposed through a popular initiative, regardless of whether or not it touches on matters relating to devolution. However, where such an amendment does indeed touch on devolution, a referendum with county-level participation quotas is required, over and above the direct involvement of counties, for it to be approved.

3.4.3 Practice: Constitutional amendment attempts

Since the adoption of the Constitution of Kenya of 2010, two attempts have been made to amend it, the first under the banner of the civil society-sponsored Punguza Mizigo Initiative (2019) and the second as part of the state-sponsored Building Bridges Initiative (BBI) (2018–22). Both of these amendments were proposed by way of a popular initiative and touched on matters relating to devolution.

The 'Punguza Mizigo' Constitutional Amendment Bill sought to amend the Constitution to, inter alia, reduce the parliamentary wage bill and address the question of gender equality in political representation by abolishing the country's 290 constituencies—which are the basis for electing members of the National Assembly—and in their place having only a male and female representative from each of the 47 counties.[172] In order to reduce the wage bill, the bill sought to abolish nominations of senators and members of county assemblies, as well as abolish the position of deputy governor. It also sought to limit the presidential

[166] Ibid. art 96(1).
[167] Ibid. art 109(4).
[168] Ibid. art 255(1)(d) and (i).
[169] Ibid. art 255(2)(a).
[170] Ibid. art 257.
[171] Ibid.
[172] Punguza Mizigo (Constitution of Kenya Amendment) Bill of 2019.

tenure term to a seven-year non-renewable term.[173] Of the counties that considered the bill, only two approved it, while a total of 25 rejected it,[174] doing so on the grounds that, among other things, it offended the objects and spirit of devolution.[175] The bill was thus defeated.

The Constitution of Kenya (Amendment) Bill of 2020 (BBI Bill) sought to, inter alia, expand the executive through the inclusion of additional positions, including that of a prime minister and deputies, as well as a leader of the opposition, and introduce a judicial ombudsman nominated by the president and empowered to investigate complaints against judges and judicial officers. The BBI Bill was challenged in court on various grounds, including its having originated from the executive rather than being a popular initiative by the people; offending constitutional principles, among them judicial independence; and offending what was regarded as the 'basic structure' of the Constitution. The Supreme Court found against the bill's constitutionality, thereby leading to its defeat.[176] At the point of its defeat, and despite its alleged impact on the principles of devolution, the bill had already obtained the approvals required from county assemblies for it to qualify for a referendum.

While counties were lauded for failing to approve the Punguza Mizigo Amendment Bill on grounds such as its alleged contravention of the object and spirit of devolution, their conduct in the BBI amendment arguably undermined the expectation that, in processes like these, they would exercise objectivity, make substantive contributions, and be effective as checks against proposals that are contrary to the interests of the devolved governments. Members of county assemblies are reported to have demanded car grants from the national government in exchange for their support of the BBI Constitutional Amendment Bill.[177] A majority of them then proceeded hastily to grant their approval without so much as giving the bill or its impact careful consideration, let alone engaging members of the public in meaningful participation, as required by law. This reduced the county assemblies' participation to a rubber-stamping exercise that undermined the provisions that the Constitution makes for their participation.

Although the adoption of the federation in Kenya was by disaggregation and came about without any specific compact by constituent units, amendments touching on the federation nonetheless require the participation of the constituent units. This requirement has had the effects of furthering democracy through the requirement for counties to participate in amendments; of preventing unilateral amendments by the central government; and of advancing constitutionalism and the rule of law through judicial pronouncements that have safeguarded the letter and spirit of the Constitution as regards procedures for constitutional amendment.

[173] Ibid.

[174] Parliament of Kenya, 'Communications from the Chair: Regarding the Resolutions of County Assemblies on the Draft Punguza Mizigo (Constitution Amendment) Bill, 2019' (2020) http://surl.li/lqnkw accessed 29 August 2022.

[175] Kitui County Assembly, 'Punguza Mizigo Bill, 2019 Rejected' (*Kitui Assembly*, 16 October 2019) https://kituiassembly.go.ke/2019/10/16/punguza-mizigo-bill-2019-rejected/ accessed 4 August 2022.

[176] See Migai Akech, in Chapter 9 of this volume.

[177] Patrick Lang'at, 'SRC Approves Car Grants for MCAs and County Assembly Speakers' (*Daily Nation*, Nairobi, 10 February 2021) https://nation.africa/kenya/news/src-approves-car-grants-for-mcas-and-county-assembly-speakers-3285704 accessed 4 August 2022.

3.4.4 Practice: Concluding remarks

The adoption of multilevel systems of government in Kenya, both at independence and in 2010, was achieved through disaggregation as a mechanism for holding together the country's various ethnic and regional interests. As such, the emerging subnational units owed their very existence to the 1963 and 2010 Constitutions. They were, therefore, not involved in the development of the compacts that created them. Nevertheless, each of the compacts bestowed a critical role on the units in constitutional amendment processes, especially those affecting the structure and integrity of multilevel systems of government in the form of either regionalism (at independence) or devolution (under the Constitution of 2010).

The fear of centralization of power by a few majority groups to the exclusion of minority groups—a fear which informed the push for, and adoption of, regionalism at independence—seems to have motivated the need for the involvement of regions and their national representatives in these constitutional amendment processes. Similarly, with the Constitution of 2010, the fear of a repetition of Kenya's experience of centralization of power and marginalization of communities at the behest of an imperial president seems to have motivated the entrenchment of subnational involvement in any constitutional amendment process touching on devolution.

4. Comparative trends

The first question this chapter posed is whether or not the manner of federation-making, be it 'coming together' or 'holding together', has an impact on how federal arrangements are protected in amendment procedures. On the face of it, the question seems of little relevance to Africa. Barring a few historical cases, such as the Union of South Africa (1910, then only a federal possibility), the Federation of Rhodesia and Nyasaland (1953–62), and Cameroon (1961–72), in all cases the starting point has been a single independent country which, through disaggregation, moved from a unitary to a multilevel form of government.

However, in some cases the process of holding a country together reflects much the same dynamics present in 'coming-together' federations, namely the dynamics that arise where the formation of a federal form of government has been the response to a territorially based conflict or civil war. Areas in a country operate outside the control of the central government; rebel groups are in charge and come to the negotiating table to bargain for a federal dispensation, often as the informal governors of those areas. The federations (and proto-federations) in the Horn of Africa—Somalia, South Sudan, and Sudan—are examples.[178] The other federations fall more squarely in the mould of a centralized system of disaggregation. We thus argue that, within the broad category of 'holding-together' federations, there is a continuum along which the federations can be plotted, with integration at the one end and disaggregation at the other.

Of the four case studies, Ethiopia is the closest to a 'coming-together' federation. After the overthrow of the centrist Derg government, there was no central government holding the country together. The war against the Derg was waged by an alliance of ethnic-based

[178] See generally Charles M Fombad, Assefa Fiseha, and Nico Steytler (eds.) (n 6).

liberation movements, each with their particular territorial basis. The Transitional Period Charter of 1991 was a classic compact between different '"independent" nations, peoples, and nationalities', which then formed the baseline of the subsequent federal Constitution of 1995.

The other federations lie more on the top-down disaggregation side of the spectrum. In South Africa, the threat of Zulu secession and the prevailing violence deepened the federal characteristics even though the IFP was never formally part of any compact. The threatened insurrection by militarized Afrikaner nationalists saw the inclusion of the prospect of a *volkstaat* (people's state) and the notion of the right of self-determination. Overall, as the principal negotiating partner, the outgoing NP's interest in federal arrangements was premised mainly on securing a weak centre. The eventual compromise resulted in a weak form of federalism, which was preserved in the constitutional principles enshrined in the Interim Constitution of 1993; these laid down the framework for the 1996 Constitution.

Nigeria and Kenya, too, are examples of 'holding-together' federations: there was no compact between different territorially based ethnic groups, but rather the reverse. In the case of Nigeria, it was usually a military-imposed federal constitution (so too in 1999), with Biafra's effort to secede brought to an end by violence and not by agreement. In Kenya, a compact between major ethnic groups was attempted in 1963 but then purposely avoided in 2010. The 'federal' constitutions in both countries sought to split up the major ethic governance structures into small units (36 states in Nigeria and 47 counties in Kenya) which individually were not the sole representatives of any ethnic group in particular.

The question, then, is, did the different shades of federation formation have any impact on the way the federal compact is protected from amendments? As noted above, Aroney's argument is that the origins of a federation give form and shape to amendment procedures. One can then hypothesize that federations formed by integration provide greater protection of the federal structure in amendment procedures, insofar as constituent units have a significant role in the second house of parliament and as individual entities. In the African examples, then, the federations leaning towards the integration side of the continuum may have stronger protective amendment procedures to secure the federal compact than those found on the disaggregation side of the continuum. It would appear that there may be evidence supporting such a hypothesis. While the federations show similar protective amendment procedures, the differences are linked to their originating dynamics.

All the federations have a second house of parliament that represents the constituent units and usually plays a significant role in deciding upon constitutional amendments. In South Africa, a two-thirds majority is required in the NCOP, as is the case in the senates of Nigeria and Kenya. Ethiopia's HoF becomes part of the process if the amendment clauses and Bill of Rights are to be amended: then, a two-thirds majority is also required in the HoF. The latter case points to a further similarity. In Ethiopia, South Africa, Nigeria, and Kenya, the second houses of parliament have differentiated roles depending on the nature of amendment, but at a minimum they all have a say in changes to the federal arrangements.

The greatest variation, though, is seen when it comes to the participatory role of constituent units. In Nigeria, two-thirds of the states' legislatures must endorse a constitutional amendment. In South Africa, the provincial legislatures play no such role; however, since the NCOP is composed of nine delegations, the mandates of which come directly from the nine provincial legislatures and executives, there is no need for such a requirement. In Kenya, the 47 county legislatures play but a minor role in constitutional amendment: only if, by popular initiative, a proposed amendment deals with the core of devolution is the support of a majority of counties needed. To an even lesser extent, when a national referendum is required, popular support of at least 20 per cent of voters in at least half of the counties is required.

The focus on popular support through referenda reflects the nature of that country's federation formation: as the driving force was not large ethnic and territorial entities, but a range of civil society organizations, amendments revert back to their support. The reason must surely be that the units created by the federal constitution do not have an a priori claim to veto any change to their collective status. In the words of Madison, the amendment process, then, has more of a 'national' than a 'federal' character. However, where the direct existence or powers of particular units are affected (for instance, by boundary changes), these units have a veto, as in the cases of South Africa, Nigeria, and Kenya.

In sharp contrast is Ethiopia, where the constitutional basis was settled by a compact between ethnic and territorially based groups. Any changes to the amendment clauses and the Bill of Rights (which includes the right to secession) requires that *all* the state legislatures, by a majority vote, must approve. With regard to the other provisions, two-thirds of state legislatures must approve by a majority vote. What also sets Ethiopia apart from the other African federations (and most other federations in the world) is the right to a unilateral amending of internal and external boundaries. Giving effect to the right of self-determination, any 'nation, nationality, and people' may establish their own territory (by changing existing boundaries) and even secede from the country.

It is thus submitted that Aroney's argument has validity, too, in the context of 'holding-together' federations. While Aroney explains how amendment procedures in the classic federations were strongly correlated to their being federations by integration, what may account for the similarities in the amendment procedures of the new federations that have a strong element of disaggregation? Although the variation in constitutional arrangements among African federations is clear, equally apparent are their similarities to the old federations. It is suggested that such arrangements are not born of the soil but are part of what has become the orthodoxy of federalism. Inasmuch as Australia, in 1900, based its federal structure on the US model, so too did African countries scratch around in the federal toolbox. The German model of executive federalism greatly influenced South Africa's system of multilevel government, which in turn was copied in Kenya. Similarly, the US Constitution was the model for the 1979 Nigerian Constitution, on which the current 1999 Constitution is based.

What do these amendment procedures mean in practice? Do they advance the basic principles of constitutionalism and have they done so in practice? Certainly, in theory, these rules advance constitutionalism. They deepen democracy by bringing into the process both subnational legislatures and, at times, their local constituencies. Giving constituent units a role in constitutional amendments is also a strong indicator of limited government. Having a second house with participatory decision-making powers equal to those of the popular house of parliament can place a restraint on a ruling party dominating the first house. Even where both houses are dominated by the national executive, the executive cannot always ride roughshod over the protected interests of subnational governments: support at subnational government level is also necessary. Moreover, when the interests of a particular constituent unit are at stake, its consent is required. Finally, the rule of law requires meticulous adherence to the detail of the amendment procedures. Because such amendments often occur under volatile political conditions, non-compliance is but kindling for a conflagration.

The constitutionalism's rub comes to the fore when the amendment rules must be applied. Where there are operative courts with the power of constitutional review, they are asked to adjudicate whether the formal amendment rules have been complied with.[179] In South Africa, the Constitutional Court invalidated an amendment bill because the formal requirements were not substantially complied with. In Kenya, the Supreme Court was also willing to annul a constitutional amendment act. These cases are, however, the exceptions: so-called 'informal amendments' by courts in the face of a clear constitutional text are much more the rule. The Ethiopian HoF, for instance, approved the postponement of federal and regional elections when there was no textual support for it.

This analysis of constitutional amendments relating to federal arrangements again affirms the argument about the symbiotic relationship between constitutionalism and federalism: amendment rules and their application advance constitutionalism, while the practice of constitutionalism makes compliance with such amendment rules possible.[180]

Bibliography

Abioye F.T., 'Constitution-making, Legitimacy, and Rule of Law: A Comparative Analysis' (2011) 44(1) Comparative and International Law Journal of Southern Africa 59–79

Abraham K., *Ethiopia from Bullets to the Ballot Box: The Bumpy Road to Democracy and the Political Economy of Transformation* (Red Sea Press 1994)

Al-Shahi A., 'Traditional Politics and a One-party System in Northern Sudan' (1979) 6(1) Bulletin (British Society for Middle Eastern Studies) 3–12

Aroney N., 'Formation, Representation and Amendment in Federal Constitutions' (2006) 54(2) American Journal of Comparative Law 277–336

Aroney N., 'Constituent Power and the Constituent States: Towards a Theory of the Amendment of Federal Constitutions' (2017) 17(1) Jus Politicum: Thinking About Federalism(s) 1–31

Aroney N., 'The Formation and Amendment of Federal Constitutions in a Westminster-derived Context' (2018) 16(1) International Journal of Constitutional Law 17–53

Attoh N., Nwosu E.O., and Ukwueze F.O., 'Nigeria's Constitution Making Experience Since 1914: An Evaluation' in Omaka C.A. (ed.), *Law in Nigeria at 100: Reviewing the Past Projecting the Future: Proceedings of the 47th Annual Conference of the Nigerian Association of Law Teachers* (2–6 June 2014, Ebonyi State University Abakaliki, Nigeria)

Ayele Z., 'Constitutionalism: The Missing Element in South Sudan's Elusive Quest for Peace through Federalism?' in Steytler N. and Fombad C.M. (eds.), *Decentralisation and Constitutionalism in Africa* (OUP 2019)

Ayua I.A. and Dakas D.C.J., 'The Republic of Nigeria' in Kincaid J. and Tarr A. (eds.), *Constitutional Origins, Structures, and Change in Federal Countries* (McGill-Queen's University Press 2005) 239–75

Belser E.M. and others (eds.), *States Falling Apart? Secessionist and Autonomy Movement in Europe* (Stämpfli Verlag 2015)

Benz A., Kemmerzell J., and Petersohn B., 'Ratification and Ratification Failure: The Impact of Amendment Rules' in Benz A. (ed.), *Constitutional Policy in Multilevel Government: The Art of Keeping the Balance* (OUP 2016)

Booysen H. and Van Wyk D.H., *Die '83 Grondwet* (Juta 1984)

Bosire C., 'Devolution for Development, Conflict Resolution, and Limiting Central Power: An Analysis of the Constitution of Kenya 2010' (LLD thesis, University of the Western Cape 2013)

[179] See Nico Steytler, 'The Symbiotic Relationship between Decentralisation and Constitutionalism in Africa' in Charles Fombad and Nico Steytler (eds) (n 4) 543–99.

[180] Ibid.

Constitution of Kenya Review Commission, 'The Final Report of the Constitution of Kenya Review Commission' (CKRC 2005)

Cottrell J. and Ghai Y.P., *The Role of Constitution Building Process in Democratisation: Case Study – Kenya* (International IDEA 2004)

Degefa A., 'Birth-defects of a Constitution and its Impacts on Outcome: Reflection on Ethiopian Constitution Making Experience' (2019) 8(1) Oromia Law Journal 9

De Klerk A., '"ANC Duped Us into a Coalition Agreement They Never Fulfilled," says AIC leader Mandla Galo' (*Sowetan Live*, 13 June 2021) https://www.sowetanlive.co.za/news/south-africa/2021-06-13-anc-duped-us-into-a-coalition-agreement-they-never-fulfilled-says-aic-leader-mandla-galo/ accessed 15 August 2022

Elazar D.J., *Exploring Federalism* (University of Alabama Press 1987)

Eresia-Eke A., 'The Contradictions of Constitution-making in Nigeria' (2012) 6(4) African Research Review 76–92

Fadlall A.S., 'Constitution-Making in the Sudan: Past Experiences' (paper presented at the Constitution-making Forum: A Government of Sudan Consultation 24–25 May 2011 Khartoum, Sudan)

Fessha Y., *Ethnic Diversity and Federalism: Constitution Making in South Africa and Ethiopia* (Ashgate 2010)

Fiseha A. and Ayele Z., 'Constitutional Adjudication and Constitutional Governance in the Horn: Ethiopia, Somalia, and South Sudan' in Fombad C.M., Fiseha A.F., and Steytler N. (eds.), *Contemporary Governance Challenges in the Horn of Africa* (Routledge 2023)

Fombad C.M., 'Cameroon and the Anomalies of Decentralisation with a Centralist Mindset' in Fombad C.M. and Steytler N. (eds.), *Decentralisation and Constitutionalism in Africa* (OUP 2019)

Fombad C.M., Fiseha A., and Steytler N. (eds.), *Contemporary Governance Challenges in the Horn of Africa* (Routledge 2023)

Fombad C.M. and Steytler N. (eds.), *Decentralisation and Constitutionalism in Africa* (OUP 2019)

Ghai Y.P., 'Devolution in Kenya: Background and Objectives' in Steytler N. and Ghai Y.P. (eds.), *Kenyan-South African Dialogue on Devolution* (Juta 2015)

Gebre-Sellasie A., 'Ethnic Federalism: Its Promise and Pitfalls for Africa' (2003) 28(1) Yale Journal of International Law 56

Government of Somalia, 'Somalia's National Constituent Assembly Adopt a New Provisional Constitution' (*ReliefWeb*, 1 August 2012) https://reliefweb.int/report/somalia/somalia%E2%80%99s-national-constituent-assembly-adopt-new-provisional-constitution accessed 4 August 2022

Hahlo H.R. and Kahn E., *The Union of South Africa: The Development of its Laws and Constitution* (Juta 1960)

Haljan D., *Constitutionalising Secession* (Hart 2014)

Hamilton A., Madison J., and Jay J., 'No. 39 [Madison], No. 85 [Hamilton]' in Ball T. (ed.), *The Federalist with Letters of 'Brutus'* (CUP 2003)

Ihonvbere J.O., 'How to Make an Undemocratic Constitution: The Nigerian Example' (2000) 21(2) Third World Quarterly 343–66

Intergovernmental Authority on Development, 'The Revitalized Agreement on Resolution of the Conflict in the Republic of South Sudan, Addis Ababa, Ethiopia' (2015)

Jembere A., *An Introduction to the Legal History of Ethiopia* (Lit Verlag 2000)

Kangu J.M., 'An Interpretation of the Constitutional Framework for Devolution in Kenya: A Comparative Approach' (LLD thesis, University of the Western Cape 2014)

Kenya Law, 'The Amendments of the Constitution of Kenya from 1963 to 2019' http://kenyalaw.org/kl/index.php?id=9631 accessed 4 August 2022

Kitui County Assembly, 'Punguza Mizigo Bill, 2019 Rejected' (*Kitui Assembly*, 16 October 2019) https://kituiassembly.go.ke/2019/10/16/punguza-mizigo-bill-2019-rejected/ accessed 4 August 2022

Kouroutakis A.E., 'The Constitution of Somalia on Paper and the Constitutional Reality' (*SSRN*, 1 January 2018) http://dx.doi.org/10.2139/ssrn.3098969 accessed 9 August 2022

Lang'at P, 'SRC Approves Car Grants for MCAs and County Assembly Speakers' (*Daily Nation*, 10 February 2021) https://nation.africa/kenya/news/src-approves-car-grants-for-mcas-and-county-assembly-speakers-3285704 accessed 4 August 2022

Lemu A.A., 'The Making of Ethiopian Constitution of 1995' (*Aiga Forum*, 11 February 2018) http://aigaforum.com/article2018/The-Making-of-Eth-Constitution-1995.htm accessed 2 August 2022

Mekonnen W., 'On the Question of Nationalities in Ethiopia' (1969) *Marxists.org.*, https://www.marxists.org/history/erol/ethiopia/nationalities.pdf accessed 2 August 2022

Moots G.A., 'The Covenant Tradition of Federalism: The Pioneering Studies of Daniel J Elazar' in Ward A. and Ward L. (eds.), *The Ashgate Research Companion to Federalism* (Routledge 2020)

Muigai G. and Juma D., *Power, Politics & Law: Dynamics of Constitutional Change in Kenya, 1887–2022* (Kabarak University Press 2022)

Ngcukaitobi T., *The Land is Ours: South Africa's First Black Lawyers and the Birth of Constitutionalism* (Penguin 2018)

Okoth-Ogendo H.W.O., 'Politics of Constitutional Change in Kenya since Independence, 1963 to 1969' (1972) 71(282) African Affairs 9–34

Oraun I.M., 'The Military and Constitution Making: The Nigerian Experience' (*Dullah Omar Institute*, undated) https://bit.ly/3S48hVq accessed 1 October 2023

Palermo F. and Kössler K., *Comparative Federalism: Constitutional Arrangements and Case Law* (Hart 2017)

Parliament of Kenya, 'Communications from the Chair: Regarding the Resolutions of County Assemblies on the Draft Punguza Mizigo (Constitution Amendment) Bill, 2019' (2020) http://surl.li/lqnkw accessed 29 August 2022

Policy and Legal Advocacy Centre, 'A Step-by-step Process of Amending the Nigerian Constitution' (*PLAC*, 2019) https://placng.org/i/wp-content/uploads/2021/05/Step-by-Step-Guide-to-the-Process-of-Amending-the-Nigerian-Constitution.pdf accessed 28 July 2022

Regassa T., 'The Making and Legitimacy of the Ethiopian Constitution: Towards Bridging the Gap between Constitutional Design and Constitutional Practice' (2010) 23(1) Afrika Focus 85–118

Shinn D.H., 'Addis Ababa Agreement: Was it Destined to Fail and Are There Lessons for the Current Sudan Peace Process?' (2004) 20(1) Annales d'Ethiopie 239–59

Simpson T., *History of South Africa: From1902 to the Present* (Penguin 2021)

Steytler I., '"Striking Back" and "Clamping Down" in South Africa: Responding to Adverse Judicial Decisions under Systems of Parliamentary Sovereignty and Constitutional Supremacy' (2020) 12(2) Hague Journal on the Rule of Law 363–86

Steytler N., 'The Dynamic Relationship between Devolution and Constitutionalism in South Africa' in Fombad C. and Steytler N. (eds.), *Decentralisation and Constitutionalism in Africa* (OUP 2019)

Steytler N., 'The Symbiotic Relationship between Decentralisation and Constitutionalism in Africa' in Fombad C. and Steytler N. (eds.), *Decentralisation and Constitutionalism in Africa* (OUP 2019)

Steytler N., 'The Withering Away of Politically Salient Territorial Cleavages in South Africa and the Emergence of Watermark Ethnic Federalism' in Anderson G. and Choudhry S. (eds.), *Territory and Power in Constitutional Transitions* (OUP 2019)

Steytler N. and De Visser J., '"Fragile Federations": The Dynamics of Devolution' in Palermo F. and Alber E. (eds.), *Federalism as Decision-Making* (Brill/Nijhoff 2015) 79–101

Suberu R., 'Nigeria's Permanent Constitutional Transition: Military Rule, Civilian Instability and "True Federalism" in a Deeply Divided Society' Forum of Federations, Occasional Paper Series No 34 (2019)

The New Humanitarian, 'Somalia: Peace Conference Passes New Charter' (*ReliefWeb*, 16 July 2000) https://reliefweb.int/report/somalia/somalia-peace-conference-passes-new-charter accessed 9 August 2022

Thompson L., *A History of South Africa* (4th edn, Jonathan Ball 2014)

Vestal T.M., 'An Analysis of the New Constitution of Ethiopia and the Process of its Adoption' (1996) 3(2) Northeast African Studies 21–38

Watts R.L., 'The Federal Idea and Its Contemporary Relevance' in Courchene T.J. and others (eds.), *The Federal Idea: Essays in Honour of Ronald L Watts* (McGill-Queen's University Press 2011)

PART 3

ETERNITY CLAUSES, CONSTITUTIONAL UNAMENDABILITY, CONSTITUTIONAL CHANGE, AND CONSTITUTIONALISM

5

Eternalized Core Provisions in the Constitutions of the Lusophone Countries in Africa and Their Uncertain Destinies

André Thomashausen

1. Introduction

This chapter traces the origins of constitutional provisions designed to shield certain fundamental principles or provisions against amendment or outright abolition. Known as 'eternity clauses', they are meant to eliminate the risk of procedurally lawful amendments that nevertheless void the original nature and foundations of a constitution. Unlike in the common law tradition, 'eternity clauses' are the rule rather than the exception in the constitutions of countries belonging to what is often characterized as the 'civil law' family of legal systems, inspired chiefly by French and German constitutionalism.

The chapter concentrates on five African countries that have retained Portuguese as their official language, namely Angola, Cabo Verde, Guinea–Bissau, Mozambique, and São Tomé and Príncipe. The eternity clauses in each country will be introduced, explained, and discussed. The five distinct eternity clauses are similar in content and wording, but their fates have differed since their introduction during the constitutional reforms of the early 1990s that abolished the post-independence one-party-state constitutions. Because the eternity clauses in the lusophone countries in Africa were modelled after the eternity clause contained in the Portuguese Constitution of 1976, this clause is briefly examined at the outset.

The overall quest is to identify whether eternity clauses have succeeded in, or could succeed in, improving the stability of constitutional law and the protection of constitutionalism against extremism and the usurpation of political power. An answer can be found in the constitutional reality of each country, its constitutional jurisprudence, and its evolution of constitutionalism over time. This requires examining the eternity clauses country by country rather than thematically.

All five lusophone countries have succeeded in preserving the formal rule of constitutional law, but in the case of Angola and Guinea–Bissau, this has not prevented manipulation of the due process of constitutional law and has weakened the substantive or material authority of their constitutions. In the case of Guinea–Bissau, the constitution survived despite the vicissitudes of extreme political conflict, and the elevated legal force of its eternity clause has proved useful in taming and normalizing political blows.

In all five lusophone countries, their eternity clauses have helped to establish a 'constitutional canon', meaning a set of core values and principles that are a common, unquestionable

André Thomashausen, *Eternalized Core Provisions in the Constitutions of the Lusophone Countries in Africa and Their Uncertain Destinies* In: *Constitutional Change and Constitutionalism in Africa*. Edited by: Charles M. Fombad and Nico Steytler, Oxford University Press. © André Thomashausen 2025. DOI: 10.1093/9780198957034.003.0007

reference or standard that even the most avaricious political ambitions would hesitate to question. This theme is considered in a wider context at the end of the chapter.

2. Origins of material limitations of constitutional review or amendment provisions

Elevating certain core provisions in a constitution to a higher level of legal authority by imposing thresholds for their removal or amendment, or by prohibiting such amendments altogether, is a technique that was first introduced in the newly constituted United States of America (US). Article 5 of the US Constitution of 1787 (the year of its approval) stipulates as follows:

> The Congress, whenever two thirds of both houses shall deem it necessary, shall propose amendments to this Constitution . . . provided that no amendment which may be made prior to the year one thousand eight hundred and eight shall in any manner affect the first and fourth clauses in the ninth section of the first article; and that no state, without its consent, shall be deprived of its equal suffrage in the Senate.

In continental Europe, limitations to constitutional amendments were first introduced in the French Constitution of 1848, in its article 2(2): 'The republican form of government shall not be at the disposition of any proposals of amendment.' This was the first formal statement of the special authority assumed by a constitution-making body as opposed to a derived 'constituted' authority. Ever since the days of the French Revolution, the distinction has been expressed in the uniquely French concepts of *pouvoir constituant* and *pouvoir constitué*, meaning the authority to make a constitution as opposed to authority derived and exercised under a given constitution.

The constitutions of Brazil (1891), Portugal (1911), China (1923), and Turkey (1924) followed the American and French notion that the constitution-making authority can prevail over authority derived from a given constitution by declaring certain fundamentals as 'irremovable' or of perpetual validity. In 2008, the Council of Europe's Venice Commission listed a total of sixteen European constitutions containing limitation clauses to constitutional amendments.[1] Following the Brazilian precedent of 1891 and the Portuguese precedents of 1911 and 1976, all Portuguese-language, or 'lusophone', countries in Africa currently contain eternity clauses in their constitutions. These are known by the Portuguese concept of *limites materiais*, meaning substantive or material review limitations.

3. Eternity clauses in lusophone Africa: The influence of Portuguese constitutionalism

The Portuguese Constitution of 1976 (last amended in 2005),[2] in its article 288 (originally, in the 1976 text, article 290), made a choice in favour of safeguarding what the leading

[1] European Commission for Democracy through Law (Venice Commission), 'Constitutional Provisions for Amending the Constitution – Limits to Constitutional Amendments', Study No 469 (2008). A study in 2017 by Yaniv Roznai found that, globally, 28% of a total of 742 constitutions contained eternity clauses. See Yaniv Roznai, 'Amendment Power, Constituent Power, and Popular Sovereignty: Linking Unamendability and Amendment Procedures' in Richard Albert, Xenophon Contiades, and Alkmene Fotiado (eds.), *The Foundations and Traditions of Constitutional Amendment* (Hart Publishing 2017) 23–49.

[2] English text at http://www.tribunalconstitucional.pt/tc/conteudo/files/constituicaoingles.pdf accessed 12 June 2022.

Portuguese scholar Gomes Canotilho termed 'the integrational norms of the Constitution' from any revisions of the constitutional text. No review would be capable of altering the 'constitutional system', namely the political-philosophical foundations of the Constitution, or negating the 'identity of the constitutional order'.[3] Another equally acclaimed constitutional scholar, Jorge Miranda, criticized the eternity clause that had been introduced into the constitution-making process as part of the 'Constitutional Pact' between the political parties represented in the Constituent Assembly and the Revolutionary Military Council which had governed Portugal since the overthrow of its authoritarian regime on 25 April 1974.[4]

In one of his first writings on the 'eternity clause', Miranda remarked that such clauses safeguard principles rather than specific provisions[5] and raised lengthy objections to their undemocratic nature and imposition of 'constitutional prophetism' on future generations of citizens.[6] Miranda became the main scholar opining in favour of the possibility and legality of constitutional reviews altering the extent and content of eternity guarantees. His views were heeded in the 1989 review of the Constitution that altered the eternity clause.[7] Nevertheless, the adherence to the theory of the possibility of 'unconstitutional norms of the constitution'[8] continues to enjoy general support in academic literature in Portugal.[9]

The Portuguese eternity clause is extensive, covering (in this order) the national independence and unity of the state; the republican form of government; the separation of church and state; citizens' rights, freedoms, and guarantees; the rights of workers, workers' committees, and trade unions; the coexistence of the public, private, and cooperative and social sectors of ownership of the means of production; the existence of economic plans within the framework of a mixed economy; the appointment of the elected office holders of the entities that exercise sovereignty, of the organs of the autonomous regions, and of local government organs by universal, direct, secret, and periodic suffrage; the proportional representation system; pluralist freedom of expression and political organization, including political parties, and the right of democratic opposition; the separation and interdependence of entities that exercise sovereignty; the submission of legal norms to review of their positive constitutionality and of their unconstitutionality by omission; the independence of the courts; the autonomy of local authorities; and the political and administrative autonomy of the Azores and Madeira archipelagos.

The provisions of the eternity clause reveal the temporal problem of such clauses. Catarina Santos Botelho recently argued that the Portuguese eternity clauses were a manifestation of 'constitutional narcissism'.[10] Indeed, in 1989 an unopposed broad majority in Parliament saw the need to unclutter the list of 'eternal guarantees'. The current wording that refers to 'the coexistence of the public, private and cooperative and social sectors of ownership of the means of production' was adopted during the 1989 revision to replace

[3] JJ Gomes Canotilho and Vital Moreira, *Constituição da República Portuguesa Anotada* (vol 2, 2nd edn, Coimbra Editora 1985) 500.

[4] For detail, see André Thomashausen, *Verfassung und Verfassungswirklichkeit im Neuen Portugal* (Duncker & Humblot 1981) 189–211.

[5] Jorge Miranda, *Manual de Direito Constitucional* (vol 2, 2nd edn, Coimbra Editora 1983) 155.

[6] Ibid. 161.

[7] Jorge Miranda, 'A Evolução da Constituição de 1976 ao Século XXI' (2016) 76(1) Revista da Ordem dos Advogados 7–23.

[8] Originating in Otto Bachoff, *Normas Constitucionais Inconstitucionais?* (JMM Cardoso da Costa tr, first published 1951, Almedina 1994).

[9] JJ Gomes Canotilho, *Direito Constitucional e Teoria da Constituição* (5th edn, Almedina 2003) 1051–55; Jorge Bacelar Gouveia, *Manual de Direito Constitucional* (vol 1, 2nd edn, Almedina 2007) 749–759.

[10] Catarina Santos Botelho, 'Narcisismo Constitucional' (*Observador*, 2 December 2018) https://observador.pt/opiniao/narcisismo-constitucional-mude-se-a-constituicao-ii/ accessed 12 June 2022.

the original wording, which read: 'the principle of collectivisation of the main means of production and land and of natural resources and the abolition of monopolies and large estates'. Similarly, the current reference to 'the existence of economic plans, within the framework of a mixed economy' replaced the original wording, 'the democratic planning of the economy', while an additional guarantee, reading 'participation by local people's organisations in local government', was simply deleted.[11] An earlier revision in 1982 had removed the right of the president to refuse to enact and publish any Act reviewing the Constitution.

What is by now a constitutional tradition in Portugal—retaining an eternity clause even if its wording needs to be realigned with constitutional reality—has been adopted in all five lusophone countries in Africa.

4. Angola

Article 236 of the Constitution of Angola of 2010 (as last amended in August 2021)[12] provides that no review of the Constitution may encroach upon the guarantee of human dignity, the territorial integrity and independence of the state and its national unity, the republican form of government, the principle of unity of the state, and the core values contained in the fundamental rights and freedom guarantees.

The provision reads as follows:

Article 236	*Artigo 236*
(Material limits)	*(Limites materiais)*
Amendments to the Constitution must safeguard the following:	*As alterações da Constituição têm de respeitar o seguinte:*
a) The dignity of the human person;	*a) A dignidade da pessoa humana;*
b) National independence, territorial integrity and unity;	*b) A independência, integridade territorial e unidade nacional;*
c) The republican nature of government;	*c) A forma republicana de governo;*
d) The unitary nature of the State;	*d) A natureza unitária do Estado;*
e) The essential core of the rights, freedoms and guarantees;	*e) O núcleo essencial dos direitos, liberdades e garantias;*
f) The rule of law and of pluralist democracy;	*f) O Estado de direito e a democracia pluralista;*
g) The secular nature of the state and the principle of the separation of church and state;	*g) A laicidade do Estado e o princípio da separação entre o Estado e as igrejas;*
h) The universal, direct, secret and periodic suffrage for the election of officeholders of the organs of sovereign and local authority;	*h) O sufrágio universal, directo, secreto e periódico para a designação dos titulares electivos dos Órgãos de Soberania e das Autarquias Locais;*
i) The independence of the Courts;	*i) A independência dos Tribunais;*
j) The separation and interdependence of the organs exercising sovereign authority;	*j) A separação e interdependência dos Órgãos de Soberania;*
k) Local autonomy.	*k) A autonomia local.*

[11] Only the Communist Party objected to the formal violation of the eternity clause in art 290. See Partido Comunista Português, 'Resolução do Comité Central do PCP Sobre a revisão da Constituição (1989)' (30 May 1989) https://www.pcp.pt/sobre-revisao-da-constituicao-1989 accessed 12 June 2022. For detail, see JFGC Oliveira, *A Revisão Constitucional e a Tutela de Princípios Fundamentais Considerações sobre os Limites Materiais do Poder de Revisão* (Universidade de Lisboa, 2018).

[12] Lei 18/21 (Angola), *Diário da República (DR)*, 1ª Série No 154, 16-08-2021. For background on the 2010 reform, see André Thomashausen, 'Constitutional Law in Extreme Emergencies' in Jürgen Bröhmer and others (eds), *Internationale Gemeinschaft und Menschenrechte – Festschrift für Georg Ress* (Heymanns 2005) 1295–304.

The Angolan Constitutional Court has ruled on two occasions on the limitations clause in article 236.[13]

4.1 Constitutional Court judgment on the 2010 constitutional review

The first ruling concerned the constitutional reform of 2010. On 3 February 2010, the National Assembly approved far-reaching constitutional amendments that included the provision for what was in effect the indirect appointment of the president by way of simple reference to the first-listed candidate in the winning list of candidates for Members of Parliament.[14] The Constitutional Court, in its Judgment 111/2010 of 30 January 2010, ruled that the limitations clause, numbered article 159 of the Constitution before its text was amended, had not been encroached upon.[15] The Court examined each eternity principle in the limitation clause one by one.[16] It ruled that the intended amendments did not affect the eternity clause on national independence, territorial integrity and unity, and the secular nature of the state, as the related 'ordinary' provisions in the Constitution regarding these principles had been retained.

The Court also ruled that the specially safeguarded core of the fundamental rights guarantees remained unaffected, given that the systematic rearrangement of the relevant provisions, the extension of some guarantees, and the introduction of new ones had strengthened rather than diminished this protection. As regards the limitation imposed on amendments affecting the rule of law and multiparty democracy, the Court reasoned that the amendment had reaffirmed these principles.

In regard to the limitation guarantee of universal, direct, secret, and periodic suffrage for the election of office holders of the organs of sovereign and local authority, the Constitutional Court observed that the proposed new system for the election of the president differed from the system of direct election provided in the 1992 text of the Constitution in that it now provided that the first-listed candidate of the winning party's list of candidates for election to Parliament would be deemed to have been elected president.

The question, however, was whether the new system could still be considered as conforming to the 'eternal' guarantee of a 'direct' election. The Court answered by finding that an election is considered 'direct' as long as no intermediary process or body, such as an electoral college, intervenes. It found that, by not having provided for any vote or confirming act in Parliament, the new constitutional dispensation continued to attribute the election and appointment of the president directly to the voters.

According to the Court, the fact that this was now done by way of a mandatory combination of the vote for the list of candidates for Parliament and for the president could not deprive this particular mode of selecting the president from being 'direct'.

[13] See André Thomashausen, 'The Constitutional Court of Angola: Judicial Restraint in a Dominant-Party State' in Charles M. Fombad (ed.), *Constitutional Adjudication in Africa* (OUP 2017) 97–112.

[14] André Thomashausen, 'Super-presidentialism in Angola and the Angolan Judiciary' in Charles M. Fombad, (ed.), *Separation of Powers in African Constitutionalism* (OUP 2016) 182–204.

[15] Acordão 111/2010 (30 January 2010)

[16] Ibid. paras 16–88.

The Constitutional Court also found that the principle of the separation of powers was not offended either by a combined vote for both Parliament and the president, stating that a separate voting round for each of the two organs was not required by the principle of the separation of powers. Similarly, the Court found that, while the implied limitation of candidacies for election to president to those included in a political party list (to the detriment of would-be independent candidates) might be regrettable and a derogation from the original text in article 54 of the Constitution, it did not violate the material review limitation guarantees, considering that the new wording of article 111(2) provided for the possibility of political party lists to include independent (non-party-affiliated) candidates.

However, the Constitutional Court found that the lack of a specific identification of the candidate first listed in the list of candidates for election to Parliament as the person who would automatically become president should the list win violated the requirement of legal clarity, which is an integral component of the rule of law, as well as the rule-of-law requirement of electoral certainty. The Court ruled that these requirements would have to be satisfied.

A further point on which the Court found the proposed amendment wanting was the proposed appointment of the deputy president, by the president, as an 'auxiliary' of the president. The Court found that another provision—one contained in article 132(1) (in the new text) and providing that the deputy president would assume and exercise all the authority and duties of the president in the case of the position of president becoming vacant—conditionally attributed sovereign powers to the deputy president, who, however, was no longer a 'sovereign organ' of the state (as required), because in terms of the new constitutional text, the deputy president was simply to be chosen and appointed by the president. In the reasoning of the Court, this contradicted the characterization of the deputy president as a sovereign organ of the state. Consequently, the Court saw this mode of appointment of the deputy president as a violation of the amendment limitation clause that safeguards 'the universal, direct, secret and periodic suffrage for the election of officeholders of the organs of sovereign authority'.[17]

Within days, the two violations were amended by the National Assembly, which provided for the designation of the name appearing on the list of candidates as a candidate for president and stipulated that the second candidate's name so appearing would be proposed (and elected) as the person assuming the office of deputy president. The constitutional amendment thus entered into force on 10 February 2010, after implementation of the Constitutional Court judgment on the limitation to amendments clause.[18] The document became known as the Angolan 2010 Constitution and is viewed as a 'new' constitution rather than a further amendment of the 1992 Constitution.[19]

[17] JB Gouveia, 'O Constitucionalismo de Angola e a sua Constituição de 2010' (2017) 9(3) Revista de Estudos Constitucionais, Hermenêutica e Teoria do Direito (RECHTD) 221–39, 231.

[18] Generally on the Constitution, see André Thomashausen, 'The Constitutions of Angola' in Rüdiger Wolfrum and Rainer Grote (eds.), *Constitutions of the Countries of the World—Oxford Constitutions Online* http://oxcon.ouplaw.com accessed 12 June 2022

[19] André Thomashausen, 'O Desenvolvimento, Contexto e Apreço da Constituicão de Angola de 2010' in MR de Sousa and others (eds.), *Estudos de Homenagem ao Prof Doutor Jorge Miranda* (vol I, Coimbra Editora 2012) 323–48.

4.2 Constitutional Court judgment on the 2021 constitutional review

The second case in which the Constitutional Court examined whether the material review limitation clause had been violated was the recent Judgment of 8 August 2021, Case No 688/2021.[20] The judgment of 2021 dealt with the first far-reaching constitutional amendment of the 2010 Constitution. The amendment introduced changes to the jurisdiction and organization of the superior courts, including the Court of Audits (functioning as Auditor General), and the statutory organization of the attorney's profession. It also reviewed the constitutional status of the central bank, as well as creating a legal authority to expropriate private property without compensation, thereby affecting the guarantee of the right to private ownership of property. Furthermore, new limitations were applicable in states of emergency, and a permanent electoral register for voters was introduced. There was also clarification in regard to the application of the two-term limitation for presidential mandates, along with clarifications regarding presential powers; alterations regarding the composition of the consultative Council of the Republic, the voting rights of Angolans living abroad, and the parliamentary rights of control and investigation of the executive; and amendments regarding local autonomy and local authorities.

In its judgment of 8 August 2021, the Constitutional Court found that the amendments were not objectionable, except in regard to the attempted introduction of an administrative reporting duty of the superior courts to the superior council entrusted with judicial administration. In an introductory section, the Court summarized several of the theoretical foundations for the existence of material review limitations, including a citation of article 28 of the French Constitution of 24 June 1793, better known (and referenced) as the French Declaration of the Rights of Men and Citizens of 26 August 1789 (subsequently repeated in the preamble to the 1793 Constitution): '[A] people always have the right to review, reform and change [their] own constitution. One generation may not subject future generations to its laws.'

This somewhat emotive citation, taken out of its historical context as part of a core document of the French Revolution,[21] revealed that the Constitutional Court was divided about testing the 2021 constitutional amendments against the material review limitation clause of the Constitution. Four of the eleven judges dissented and two of them appended their dissenting reasons. One of them, Judge President Manuel Aragão, resigned from his position immediately after the judgment.

The fallout was aggravated on 6 September 2021 by the appointment, within a few days and without preceding consultations, of Laurinda Cardoso as the new Judge President. A labour law attorney and public servant without postgraduate qualifications, the new Judge President was best known as a controversial real estate investor and business partner of Kassim Tajideen, a Lebanese businessman listed in the US as a financier of Hezbollah, a

[20] Acordão 688/2021 (8 August 2021). The amendment and the justifications for it are found in República de Angola, *Relatório e Fundamentação, Proposta de Lei de Revisão Constitucional* (Imprensa Nacional Angola, Luanda 2021) 40.

[21] At p 5, para 3 of the judgment Acordão 688/2021 (see n 20 above), which, unusually, is rendered without numbered paragraphs.

group designated by many countries as a terrorist organization.[22] The appointment seemed to confirm the view of Judge President Aragão, who exclaimed in his dissenting vote that the 2021 amendment and its endorsement by the Constitutional Court constituted the 'suicide of the rule of constitutional law'.[23] Likewise, the principal author of the 2010 Constitution, Carlos Feijó, declared that the August 2021 judgment of the Constitutional Court was unconstitutional.[24]

The dissenting reasons focused on three areas: first, the violation of the core content of the right to ownership of private property, with the introduction of expropriation without a guarantee of compensation; second, the introduction of new disqualifications for candidates for election to president, as well as the amendment of the succession rules in case of an impediment of the president; and, third, the violation of the guarantee of an independent judiciary with the introduction both of fixed retirement ages for judges and of a definition of the superior courts as hierarchically equal courts, which thereby derogated the constitutional supreme authority of the Constitutional Court.[25]

Both of the judgments, in 2010 and in 2021, dealing with amendments to the Constitution show a formalistic or positivist approach to the Angolan amendment limitation clause. In addition, in more than 700 judgments, the Constitutional Court never applied the interpretation method of attributing a stronger level of legal authority to guarantees included in the listing of 'eternal' provisions, let alone contemplated the possibility of unconstitutional provisions of the Constitution. Known in Germany as the *Wertordnungslehre*, this is the method of distinguishing ordinary constitutional provisions from those norms that enjoy elevated protection as 'eternally protected' principles or provisions.[26]

Finally, the Angolan Constitutional Court saw no cause for concern when the constitutional provision containing the eternity guarantees was moved within the systematic order of the constitutional text, assuming that as long as nothing was subtracted from the most fundamental and irremovable guarantees, editorial changes or additions were not to be questioned, never mind censured. In the case of the constitutional reform of 2010, the fiction that the then elected Parliament had been given 'constituent' powers helped overcome, again in a rather positivist manner of interpretation, any possible objections to changing the systematic position of the eternity clause. Implicitly, this approach accepts the proposition that eternity clauses can be amended in a double amendment process, first by tacitly revoking the amendment limitation and thereafter by amending them like any other provision in the constitution.

[22] Soares Kaboloca, 'Escândalo Juíza Laurinda Cardoso: E Agora, Senhor Presidente?' (*Club-K*, 7 September 2021) https://www.club-k.net/index.php?option=com_content&view=article&id=45635:caso-nacionalidade-portuguesa-de-laurinda-e-agora-senhor-presidente-soares-kaboloca&catid=41013&Itemid=1080&lang=pt accessed 12 June 2022.

[23] At p 34, para 2 in Acordão 688/2021.

[24] Manuel José, 'Demissão de Presidente do Tribunal Constitucional Angolano Provoca Debate' (*Voice of America*, 16 August 2021) https://www.voaportugues.com/a/demiss%C3%A3o-de-presidente-do-tribunal-constitucional-angolano-provoca-debate-/6004582.html accessed 12 June 2022.

[25] Judgment, following p 15, newly numbered pp 1–12 and 1–9.

[26] Famously postulated in one of the first judgments of the German Constitutional Court, BVerfGE 2, 1 (12), and expanded in BVerfGE 39, 1 (67). This is discussed in the Angolan context in Waldemar Bartolomeu De Freitas Diogo, *Limites Materiais de Revisão Constitucional no Direito Angolano* (Universidade de Lisboa, Faculdade de Direito, 2016) 102.

5. Cabo Verde

Cabo Verde enacted a first formal constitution on 7 October 1980, five years after attaining independence from Portugal on 5 July 1975. Until 1980, the country was governed in terms of an Interim Law on Political Organisation passed on the day of independence.[27] The radically Marxist Independence Constitution was replaced on 28 September 1990 by a Constitutional Law 2/III/90 to allow for multiparty elections. A new 1992 Constitution entered into force on 25 September 1992 and was amended in 1995, 1999, and, lastly, on 3 May 2010.

In Cabo Verde, article 290 of the 2010 Constitution (with identical wording to article 285 of the 1992 Constitution) removes from the constitutional review powers what are basically the same principles already found in article 236 of the Angolan eternity clause, albeit in a slightly different order:

Article 290
(Material limits of the revision)
1. The following may not be the object of revision:
   a) The national independence, integrity of the national territory and unity of the State,
   b) The republican form of Government;
   c) The universal, direct, secret and periodic suffrage for the election of the holders of office in sovereign organs and local government;
   d) The separation and interdependence of the sovereign organs;
   e) The autonomy of the local government power;
   f) The independence of the courts;
   g) The pluralism of expression and of political organization and the right of opposition.
2. The revision laws may also not restrain or limit the rights, liberties and guarantees established in the Constitution.

Artigo 290
(Limites materiais da revisão)
1. *Não podem ser objecto de revisão:*
   a) A independência nacional, a integridade do território nacional e a unidade do Estado;
   b) A forma republicana de Governo;
   c) O sufrágio universal, directo, secreto e periódico para a eleição dos titulares dos órgãos de soberania e do poder local;
   d) A separação e a interdependência dos órgãos de soberania;
   e) A autonomia do poder local;
   f) A independência dos tribunais;
   g) O pluralismo de expressão e de organização política e o direito de oposição.
2. *As leis de revisão não podem, ainda, restringir ou limitar os direitos, liberdades e garantias estabelecidos na Constituição.*

The Cabo Verde review limitation clause is crafted in broad terms, leaving a generous margin of appreciation to the legislature and Constitutional Court to determine how, for instance, a 'right of opposition' may have been 'respected' or not, in a particular piece of legislation under review. In 2009 and 2010, during the constitutional review debates, Cabo Verde came close to following the Portuguese precedent of 'adapting' or 'updating' the wording of its eternity clause. The issue was the originally absolute prohibition of the extradition of Cabo Verde nationals to a foreign jurisdiction in article 37 of the 1992 Constitution. Pressured by the Rome Statute, which had created the International Criminal Court, Cabo Verde felt compelled to allow for the extradition of its nationals, at least under some circumstances.

[27] JO da Rocha Nascimento, 'Nação e Estado na Constituição da Republica de Cabo Verde' 4 https://www.ces.uc.pt/lab2004/pdfs/JoaoNascimento.pdf accessed 12 June 2022. See also Luis Roberto Barroso and Richard Albert, 'Cabo Verde' in Luis Roberto Barroso and Richard Albert (eds.), *The 2020 International Review of Constitutional Reform* (Program on Constitutional Studies at the University of Texas at Austin in collaboration with the International Forum on the Future of Constitutionalism 2021) 60, <https://papers.ssrn.com/sol3/papers.cfm?abstract_id=3917596> accessed 25 April 2023.

Parliamentarians and scholars were opposed to this, arguing that such an (ordinary) constitutional amendment would offend the eternity guarantees in article 290(2) (at the time, still article 285(2)).

However, casting aside such concerns, the 2010 amendment ended up crafting the new article 38 of the 2010 Constitution, which forbids the extradition of Cabo Verde nationals who face a lifelong or undetermined period of imprisonment in the requesting country, unless assurances are given that such a penalty will not be enforced. The new article 38 allows, furthermore, for the extradition of nationals charged with 'terrorism' or 'organised international criminality' offences who acquired or reacquired their Cabo Verde nationality after the commission of their criminal acts, on condition of certain conditions of reciprocity, as well as generally under the provisions of the Rome Statute. The complex and convoluted review of the non-extradition of nationals clause was never tested in the Constitutional Court against the eternity guarantees in article 290(2).[28]

Contrary to the Angolan Constitutional Court, the Constitutional Court in Cabo Verde has used and referred to the review limitation clause in adjudicating issues regarding the constitutionality of ordinary legislation. Until the most recent judgment, 50/2022, it steered clear of the German doctrine of a hierarchy of constitutional norms based on different levels of immutability introduced by an eternity clause. In its judgment 24/2016, concerning the constitutionality of an amendment to the law governing promotion requirements for career magistrates, the Constitutional Court reflected that, '[i]n a democratic State, given its nature and for the reasons already stated, trust in the immutability of legal norms can only be absolute in respect of the material limitations of constitutional review.' In the same judgment, the Court invoked the 'realisation of the democratic principle in the Cabo Verde constitutional system', and stated that:

> [T]the democratic principle means that the fundamental decisions of the political community must be taken by the People, the original and sovereign entity, be it by means of referenda or through its representatives, during special occasions of constitutional review, or when ordinary legislation is approved within the confines of the due process in a rule of law country, or, further, on the taking of any other decisions that are crucial for the State, but in this first instance subject to the material limitations of constitutional amendments as provided for in article 290, with observance of the normative constitutional values, in regard to the manner and extent to which protection is afforded. That being so and within these limitations, the *volonté general* is to be determined in a legitimate manner on the basis of the process created for the articulation of the will of the majority.[29]

The philosophical-poetic reasoning and expression is typical of the Cabo Verde Constitutional Court, the judgments of which often run close to 100 pages or more in length. The Court regularly refers to and cites the great philosophers, among them Cicero,

[28] José Pina Delgado, Jorge Carlos Fonseca, and Liriam Tiujo Delgado (eds.), *Aspectos Polêmicos da Extradição em Cabo Verde e no Espaço Lusófono* (Imprensa Nacional Cabo Verde 2009); Direito e Cidadania, 'Revisão Constitucional' Special Edition (2009) (IX) 28 258. The author is much indebted to Judge José Pina Delgado of the Constitutional Court for his engagement on the thorny extradition of nationals debate in Cabo Verde.

[29] Acordão 24/2016, 11.

Aquinas, Mirandola, Spinoza, and Kant, as well as foreign constitutions and constitutional law scholars.[30] Many judgments comprehensively cite international conventions and treaties, and special mention can be made of the exceptionally comprehensive judgment 1/2017, regarding the constitutionality of an environmental protection tax.[31]

In Opinion 1/2021, the Court confirmed and repeated its earlier interpretations. At the request of the President, it gave an opinion on amendments of the Criminal Procedure Code. It referred to and quoted from its judgment 27/2017, which in turn cites verbatim the passage from judgment 24/2016, quoted above. It added:

> In a rule of law country where the principle of constitutionalism applies, which postulates the primacy of the Constitution as the measure of validity of acts undertaken by public authority, the ordinary laws must be interpreted in accordance with the Constitution and not the other way around.

Most recently, in its Judgment 50/2022, the Cabo Verde Constitutional Court engaged extensively with this reasoning, referring to the German constitutionalists Otto Bachof and Gustav Radbruch, among others. The complainant had referred to these constitutionalists in his arguments that a constitutional review of an infringement by omission should be allowed in the particular case of a trial judge who had been involved in overseeing criminal investigations that resulted in the indictment and trial of the accused before him, including the ordering of detention pending trial. It was argued that the judge in question should have recused himself, and by not doing so, had violated the Constitution by omission.

In a first step, after extensive consideration of the notion of core and implied values in a constitutional text, the Court stated that the concept of unconstitutional norms of the constitution could be applied to the Constitution of Cabo Verde, in particular in the case of a lacuna, but that this could happen only by reference to norms contained in the Constitution itself rather than to some supra- or extra-constitutional norms based on doctrines of 'natural law' and the like.[32] The Court proceeded on this basis to reject the proposition that Cabo Verdean constitutionality could be determined by reference to, in particular, Portuguese standards of due process in criminal proceedings.[33] It rejected the reasoning presented by the complainant with the trenchant claim that 'arguments bordering on self-imposed intellectual neo-colonialism . . . cannot diminish the authority of our Parliament and our Courts'.[34]

The jurisprudence of the Cabo Verde Constitutional Court thus acknowledges the concept of a hierarchy of norms, as proposed by German teachings and case law, yet without embracing the references of such a doctrine to universal concepts of human rights and normative paradigms of justice. The Cabo Verde Constitutional Court opted for cautious self-restraint and resisted the temptation of placing the judiciary above the legislative choices made by Parliament and in the actual text of the Constitution. There is no doubt that

[30] See eg Acordão 7/2016.

[31] Acordão 01/2017, 112; see also Acórdão 50/2022, 68.

[32] Acordao 50/ 2022, para 3.2.6, 25.

[33] Ibid paras 8.1–8.6, 49–57.

[34] Ibid paras 8.1, 49.

Cabo Verde's constitutional jurisprudence occupies a position of excellence in lusophone constitutionalism.

6. Guinea-Bissau

In Guinea-Bissau, the Constitution of 1996[35] provides in article 130 that no review process may affect the unitary structure and the republican form of the state; the secular nature of the state; the integrity of the national territory; the national symbols, flag, and national anthem; citizens' rights, freedoms, and guarantees; the fundamental rights of workers; universal, direct, equal, secret, and periodic suffrage in the appointment of holders of elective positions of the constitutional organs; political pluralism, the freedom of expression of political parties, and the right to democratic opposition; the separation and interdependence of the organs of sovereignty; and the independence of the courts.

Article 130
No draft revision may affect:
a) The unitary structure and the republican form of the State;
b) The secular nature of the state;
c) The integrity of the national territory;
d) The national symbols, the flag and the national anthem;
e) The rights, liberties and guarantees of citizens;
f) The fundamental rights of workers;
g) The direct, equal, secret and regular universal suffrage for deciding the holders of sovereign elected positions;
h) Political pluralism and pluralism of expression, the political parties and the right to democratic opposition;
i) The separation and interdependence of sovereign bodies;
j) The independence of tribunals.

Artigo 130
Nenhum projecto de revisão poderá afectar:
a) A estrutura unitária e a forma republicana do Estado;
b) O estatuto laico do Estado;
c) A integridade do território nacional;
d) Símbolos nacionais e Bandeira e Hino Nacionais;
e) Direitos, liberdades e garantias dos cidadãos;
f) Direitos fundamentais dos trabalhadores;
g) O sufrágio universal, directo, igual, secreto e periódico na designação dos titulares de cargos electivos dos órgãos de soberania;
h) O pluralismo político e de expressão, partidos políticos e o direito da oposição democrática;
i) A separação e a interdependência dos órgãos de soberania;
j) A independência dos tribunais.

There is no known case law that would have referred to the Guinea-Bissau eternity clause. The country's severe tensions and internal strife during the past two-and-a-half decades, with intermittent periods of state capture by some of South America's most powerful drug cartels, have repeatedly challenged constitutionalism, even though, remarkably, most of the political strife has concerned constitutional amendments.

Shortly after the adoption of the 1996 Constitution, a military junta challenged the elected government on 7 June 1998, as a result of which the Abuja Accord was brokered by the Economic Community of West African States (ECOWAS) to suspend ongoing

[35] It is an ongoing debate whether the 1996 Constitution was 'only' a consolidation of the earlier 1984 Constitution and its subsequent changes in 1993. See António E Duarte Silva, 'O Constitucionalismo da Guiné-Bissau' in AA Fernando Mourão, Walter C Porto, and Thelmer M Mantovanini (eds), *As Constituições dos Países de Língua Portuguesa Comentadas* (Edições do Senado Federal Brasilia 2008) 477–530.

civil war; this also led to the partial suspension of the Constitution and the setting of 28 November 1999 as the date for general elections. The appointment of an interim president on 14 May 1999 facilitated the signing of a political transition pact between the embittered political factions, but renewed dissent broke out when the interim president tried to enact a new constitutional law that would have changed the electoral system.

Elections took place from 28 November 1999 until 16 January 2000, and a new Parliament, constituted on 28 January 2000, confirmed the unconditional reinstatement of the 1996 Constitution. On 5 April 2001, Parliament approved the text of a new Constitution, but on 23 May 2001, the president refused to promulgate it. In September 2003, a military coup ousted the government. Legislative elections, held in March 2004, and presidential elections, in June 2005, returned the independence liberation party PAIGC (African Party for the Independence of Guinea and Cape Verde) to power under its 'historic' president, João Bernardo Vieira. However, Vieira was assassinated on 2 March 2009. The succeeding government, under Vieira's political rival Malam Sanhá, was toppled on 12 April 2012, leading to a transitional government under José Maria Vaz, who eventually failed to win the presidential elections in 2019 and had to concede victory to Umar Sissoco Embalo, the first president not representing the PAIGC. An attempt during the first week in February 2022 to remove Embalo in yet another coup was thwarted with the help of ECOWAS.[36]

The 1996 Constitution survived the decades-long instability. But it must be underlined that much of the political strife arose in relation to the Constitution, with the warring parties seeking legitimacy by reference to the Constitution, or an alternative constitution, as the supreme law of the land.

7. Mozambique

Article 300 of the Constitution of Mozambique (2018) provides material review limitations. These were first introduced in article 292 of Mozambique's 2004 Constitution, and, as in the case of the constitutions of the other Portuguese-language countries in Africa, follow the model found in article 288 of the Portuguese Constitution of 1976.

The provision in article 300 excludes the following from constitutional review: the independence and sovereignty and unity of the state; the republican form of government; the secularity of the state; fundamental rights and freedoms; the universal, direct, secret, personal, and regular right to elect the elected members of the constitutional organs of the state, the provinces, and the local authorities; pluralism of political organization, including political parties, and the right of democratic opposition; the separation of powers and the interdependence of the organs of the state; the review of constitutionality; the independence of judges; the autonomy of decentralized levels of government; the rights of workers and their unions; and the preservation of the laws governing the acquisition or loss of nationality, with amendments to any of these exclusions subject to submission to a referendum.

[36] See the detailed account in Silva (n 35).

Article 300
(Restrictions as to subject matter)
1. Constitutional amendment laws shall safeguard:
   a) the independence, the sovereignty and the unity of the State;
   b) the republican form of government;
   c) the separation between religious denominations and the state;
   d) the fundamental rights, freedoms and guarantees;
   e) universal, direct, secret, personal, equal and periodic suffrage for the appointment of elective sovereign public offices and elective offices of local administration;
   f) pluralism of expression and of political organization, including political parties and the right of democratic opposition;
   g) the separation and interdependence of the sovereign public offices;
   h) the scrutiny of constitutionality;
   i) the independence of the judiciary;
   j) the autonomy of the organs of the decentralized government on provincial, district and local authority levels;
   k) the rights of workers and trade unions;
   l) the rules governing nationality, which cannot be amended in such a way as to restrict or remove rights of citizenship.
2. Amendments pertaining to the matters listed [in] paragraph 1 must, obligatorily, be submitted to a referendum.

Artigo 300
(Limites materiais)
1. *As leis de revisão constitucional têm de respeitar:*
   a) a independência, a soberania e a unidade do Estado;
   b) a forma republicana de Governo;
   c) a separação entre as confissões religiosas e o Estado;
   d) os direitos, liberdades e garantias fundamentais;
   e) o sufrágio universal, directo, secreto, pessoal, igual e periódico na designação dos titulares electivos dos órgãos de soberania das províncias e do poder local;
   f) o pluralismo de expressão e de organização política, incluindo partidos políticos e o direito de oposição democrática;
   g) a separação e interdependência dos órgãos de soberania;
   h) a fiscalização da constitucionalidade;
   i) a independência dos juízes;
   j) a autonomia dos órgãos de governação descentralizada provincial, distrital e das autarquias locais;
   k) os direitos dos trabalhadores e das associações sindicais;
   l) as normas que regem a nacionalidade, não podendo ser alteradas para restringir ou retirar direitos de cidadania.
2. *As alterações das matérias constantes do número 1 são obrigatoriamente sujeitas a referendo.*

Mozambique is the only lusophone country in Africa that has actually amended the wording of its review limitation clause. The latest constitutional amendment, in 2018,[37] replaced the original version in paragraph (j), 'autonomy of local authorities', with 'the autonomy of the organs of the decentralized government on provincial, district and local authority levels'.

The amendment of the eternity clause passed through the National Assembly without debate, objections, or, indeed, the referendum that was required in terms of section 2 of article 300. The primary reason given for this was that the amendment had been included in the compromise package on 'decentralization' that arose from extra-parliamentary negotiations between the government and the rebellious opposition party, Renamo.[38] The problematic requirement of a referendum for any amendments

[37] Lei 1/2018, Boletim da Republica (BR) 1ª Série, No 115.

[38] On the decentralization debate, see André Thomashausen, 'The Concept and Implementation of "Gradual Decentralisation" in Mozambique' in Charles M. Fombad and Nico Steytler (eds.), *Decentralisation and Constitutionalism in Africa* (OUP 2019) 384–408; on the protracted Renamo rebellion, see André Thomashausen, 'Preventive Diplomacy in the Mozambique Transition' in H Solomon (ed.), *Towards Sustainable Peace: Reflections on Preventive Diplomacy in Africa* (Africa Institute of South Africa 2003) 270–309.

of the eternity clause was noted in the technical drafting sessions but no record of any debate exists. The rule in article 300(2) was discarded on the grounds that the new wording of paragraph (j) did not subtract anything from the old guarantee but instead added to it.[39]

Legal academics in Mozambique have suggested a further justification. It applies the reasoning put forth in 2003 by Jorge Miranda.[40] Here, the eternity clauses cannot bind the constituent or original constitution-maker (the *pouvoir constituant*) but only the constituted authority amending a constitution. According to Miranda, the original material limitations are those unwritten rules of natural law and justice that bind even a constituent (constitution-making) authority, while the written limitation clauses are merely declaratory articulations of those principles. Therefore, they can be subjected to amendments and modernization, just like any other provision in a constitution.[41]

However, Miranda's reasoning that an eternity clause is capable of amendment, if necessary, by first removing any barring of its amendment (also referred to as 'two-step amendment') has been disputed. It suited scholars who supported the 2018 reform of Mozambique's Constitution to rely on Miranda's suggestion that clauses limiting the review of certain principles and provisions should be considered as having a merely declaratory as opposed to normative nature. But the ease with which the limitation clause regarding the autonomy of local authorities was rewritten—arguably, in the process, becoming more narrowly confined to a specific arrangement of decentralized levels of government—reveals that Mozambique's lawmakers (like their Angolan counterparts) do not easily accept being bound by an original constitution-making determination which declares certain principles to be irrevocable.

8. São Tomé and Príncipe

The small island state of São Tomé and Príncipe did not include any substantive review limitations in its 1990 Constitution but included such a clause later, in the 2003 revision of the Constitution.[42] The omission in 1990 can be attributed largely to the direct involvement in the drafting process of Jorge Miranda, a known sceptic and opponent of 'eternity clauses'. The 2003 revision was also strongly influenced by a Portuguese constitutional law scholar, in this case Bacelar Gouveia.[43]

[39] As confirmed to the author by Professor Oscar Monteiro, 11 June 2022.

[40] Carlos Pedro Mondlane, 'Os Limites na Revisão Constitucional em Moçambique' (*Jus.com.br*, 23 June 2013) 2 https://jus.com.br/artigos/24761/os-limites-na-revisao-constitucional-em-mocambique accessed 12 June 2022.

[41] Jorge Miranda, *Teoria do Estado e da Constituição* (1st edn, Forense 2002) 421.

[42] Lei 1/2003.

[43] Gerhardt Seibert, 'Instabilidade Política e Revisão Constitucional: Semipresidencialismo em São Tomé e Príncipe' in Marina Costa Lobo and Octávio Amorim Neto (eds.), *O Semipresidencialismo nos Países da Lingua Portuguesa* (Lisboa ICS 2009) 201–31, 205–6.

Article 154
(Material review limits)
The following may not be [the] subject of constitutional amendment:

a) the independence, integrity of the national territory and the unity of the State;
b) the secular status of the State;
c) The republican form of Government;
d) the rights, freedoms and guarantees of citizens;
e) universal, direct, secret and periodic suffrage for the election of the holders of the organs of sovereignty and regional and local authorities;
f) the separation and interdependence of the organs of sovereignty;
g) the autonomy of regional and local authorities;
h) the independence of the courts;
i) pluralism of expression and political organization, including political parties and the right of democratic opposition.

Artigo 154
(Limites materiais da revisão)
Não podem ser objecto de revisão constitucional:

a) A independência, a integridade do território nacional e a unidade do Estado;
b) O estatuto laico do Estado;
c) A forma republicana de Governo;
d) Os direitos, liberdades e garantias dos cidadãos;
e) O sufrágio universal, directo, secreto e periódico para a eleição dos titulares dos órgãos de soberania e do poder regional e local;
f) A separação e interdependência dos órgãos de soberania;
g) A autonomia do poder regional e local;
h) A independência dos tribunais;
i) O pluralismo de expressão e de organização política, incluindo partidos políticos e o direito de oposição democrática.

No jurisprudential references to the material review limitation clause can be found. It is important to note that São Tomé and Príncipe did not have an autonomous constitutional court until 2018. The 2003 amendment of the 1990 Constitution provided for a constitutional court, but between 2005 and 2018 the jurisdiction in constitutional matters was entrusted to a special division of the Supreme Court.

However, in 2006 an attempt by then President Fradique de Menezes to amend the Constitution by way of a referendum and introduce a third term for the office of president failed in Parliament in view of the strength of the argument that holding a referendum to amend the Constitution was expressly forbidden by its article 71(3). This prohibition was introduced in the 2003 revision of the Constitution, which abrogated a rule to the contrary in article 47(2) of the original Independence Constitution of 1975. Even though the prohibition was not included in the eternity clause in article 154, the majority in Parliament held that any tampering with the 2003 prohibition of an amendment of the Constitution by way of a referendum was a dangerous proposition that would upset the specially protected balance and separation of the interdependent sovereign organs of the state.[44]

9. Relevance of the review limitations and eternity clauses

All five lusophone constitutions in Africa were inspired by, and follow the model of, the Portuguese Constitution of 1976. Nonetheless, there are subtle differences in the articulation of the constitutional prohibition of amendments affecting the guarantees expressed in the respective eternity clauses.

The Portuguese model clause states, '[l]aws revising the Constitution must safeguard—'. In Angola, the wording '[a]mendments to the Constitution must safeguard the following'

[44] José Paquete d'Alva Teixeira, 'Comentário à Constituição Política Santomense' in FAA Mourão, Walter C Porto, and Thelmer M Mantovanini (eds.) (n 35) 773–830, 779.

is identical, and the same is true for Mozambique, where the text reads '[c]onstitutional amendment laws must safeguard'. Cabo Verde chose the phrasing, '[t]he following may not be the object of revision', while the Guinea–Bissau Constitution contains the briefest formulation of all: 'No draft revision may affect: —'. São Tomé preferred '[t]he following may not be subject of constitutional amendment'.

The variations in drafting styles do not detract from the common meaning of all the clauses, namely that the stipulations of the eternity guarantee are meant to protect the principles enumerated in those clauses. It is clear that what are shielded from amendment are not specific provisions of the constitutions but, rather, the principles they seek to serve and uphold. Evidently, there is a wide margin of appreciation in regard to the scope and meaning of those principles.

A comparison of the five lusophone eternity clauses (see Table 5.1 below) reveals only one distinct difference: in the case of Mozambique, a section 2 of the clause introduced a modern relativization of the eternity clause by providing that 'amendments pertaining to the matters listed [in] paragraph 1 must, obligatorily, be submitted to a referendum'. By implication, the clause acknowledges that eternity clauses can be amended, albeit in a two-step amendment process in which, first, the eternity clause is removed and, second, amendments are carried out that may have been problematic had the eternity clause not been derogated first. The Mozambican recourse to a referendum acknowledges that an ordinary legislature alone might, indeed, not have the authority to remove an eternity clause and that this would necessitate the direct intervention of the deemed origin of all political power: the electorate itself.

Regardless of the verbatim exception in the Mozambican eternity clause which allows explicitly for a review of the clause (albeit it subject to referendum), all the lusophone eternity clauses in Africa by implication accept the possibility of amendment, simply by not having explicitly forbidden such amendment. The reasons for such an omission of a formal amendment prohibition in regard to the eternity clauses are interesting both in theory and in terms of their implications for the practice of constitutionalism.

Over time, eternity clauses were introduced in the lusophone countries under review after the abandonment of the one-party-state model that applied in all of these five countries until the early 1990s. In all cases except Cabo Verde, one can discern that their courts were wary in their reception of the Portuguese eternity clause. The Constitutional Court of Angola even felt the need recently (in 2021) to cite (in the context of an appreciation of the country's eternity clause) the passage from the 1789 French Declaration of the Rights of Men and Citizens stating that 'a people always have the right to review, reform and change its own constitution. One generation may not subject future generations to its laws.'[45] Even the Cabo Verde Constitutional Court, clearly the most dedicated and sophisticated of the Portuguese-language constitutional courts in Africa, refrained from commenting on the proposition that eternity clauses might be amendable in a 'two-step' amendment process, thus leaving this controversial question open for future debate.

Against this background, the main practical purpose of material review limitation clauses remains that they can serve as a powerful tool of constitutional interpretation if they are seen as establishing a normative hierarchy of fundamental constitutional values. However, the potential this holds to strengthen constitutionalism is compromised when

[45] See n 21.

Table 5.1 Eternity clauses in the constitutions of lusophone Africa

Angola	Cabo Verde	Guinea-Bissau	Mozambique	São Tomé and Príncipe
Article 236 (Material limits) Amendments to the Constitution must safeguard the following: a) The dignity of the human person; b) National independence, territorial integrity and unity; c) The republican nature of government; d) The unitary nature of the state; e) The essential core of the rights, freedoms and guarantees; f) The rule of law and of pluralist democracy; g) The secular nature of the state and the principle of the separation of church and state; h) The universal, direct, secret and periodic suffrage for the election of officeholders of the organs of sovereign and local authority; i) The independence of the Courts; j) The separation and interdependence of the organs exercising sovereign authority; k) Local autonomy.	Article 290 (Material limits of the revision) 1. The following may not be the object of revision: a) The national independence, integrity of the national territory and unity of the state; b) The republican form of government; c) The universal, direct, secret and periodic suffrage for the election of the holders of office in sovereign organs and local government; d) The separation and interdependence of the sovereign organs; e) The autonomy of the local government power; f) The independence of the courts; g) The pluralism of expression and of political organization and the right of opposition. 2. The revision laws may also not restrain or limit the rights, liberties and guarantees established in the Constitution.	Article 130 No draft revision may affect: a) The unitary structure and the republican form of the state; b) The secular nature of the state; c) The integrity of the national territory; d) The national symbols, the flag and the national anthem; e) The rights, liberties and guarantees of citizens; f) The fundamental rights of workers; g) The direct, equal, secret and regular universal suffrage for deciding the holders of sovereign elected positions; h) Political pluralism and pluralism of expression, the political parties and the right to democratic opposition; i) The separation and interdependence of sovereign bodies; j) The independence of tribunals.	Article 300 Restrictions as to Subject Matter 1. Constitutional amendment laws shall safeguard: a) the independence, the sovereignty and the unity of the State; b) the republican form of Government; c) the separation between religious denominations and the State; d) the fundamental rights, freedoms and guarantees; e) universal, direct, secret, personal, equal and periodic suffrage for the appointment of elective sovereign public offices and elective offices of local administration; f) pluralism of expression and of political organisation, including political parties and the right of democratic opposition; g) the separation and interdependence of the sovereign public offices; h) the scrutiny of constitutionality; i) the independence of the judiciary; j) the autonomy of the organs of the decentralized government on provincial, district and local authority levels; k) the rights of workers and trade unions; l) the rules governing nationality, which cannot be amended in such a way as to restrict or remove rights of citizenship. 2. Amendments pertaining to the matters listed paragraph 1 must, obligatorily, be submitted to a referendum.	Article 154 (Material review limits) The following may not be [the] subject of constitutional amendment: a) the independence, integrity of the national territory and the unity of the state; b) the secular status of the state; c) The Republican form of government; d) the rights, freedoms and guarantees of citizens; e) universal, direct, secret and periodic suffrage for the election of the holders of the organs of sovereignty and regional and local authorities; f) The separation and interdependence of the organs of sovereignty; g) the autonomy of regional and local authorities; h) the independence of the courts; i) pluralism of expression and political organization, including political parties and the right of democratic opposition.

the eternity clause is verbose and all-embracing instead of limited to what are truly the most important and fundamental norms. The differences between the eternity clause in article 79(3) of the German Constitution and that in article 288 of the Portuguese Constitution illustrate this point.[46]

The eternity guarantees in article 79(3) of Germany's Constitution of 1949 (known as the Grundgesetz) are limited to the federal organization of the state, the participation of the federal states in the exercise of legislative authority, the dignity of the human person, and the principles of a constitutional rule of law. On the basis of these 'eternity guarantees', the German Constitutional Court developed its hierarchy of imperative principles as yardsticks for finding ordinary legislation or administrative acts constitutional or unconstitutional.[47] The German method fails, however, where eternity clauses are crafted widely and become all-embracing, for instance by including all and any fundamental rights and freedoms instead of just some of the most fundamental ones, such as the guarantee of human dignity and of the rule of law.

In common law jurisdictions, a reception of the German *Wertordnungslehre*[48] can be found in India, in its 'basic structures doctrine'. However, Charles Fombad argues aptly in the introductory chapter to this volume that the practical relevance and usefulness of the Indian 'basic structures doctrine' has not been remarkable.

The theoretical dispute as to whether it is possible to distinguish between a 'constituent' or 'original' constitutional legislator and a constituted or 'derived' and amending legislator cannot resolve the difficulties arising from the inevitable ageing of legal provisions over time and the fact that subsequent generations will tend to rebel against the choices made by generations before them.

The Angolan Parliament which was elected in 2008 simply attributed 'constituent powers' to itself and, without changing a single seat or the nature of any mandate, switched at will from being a constitution-making 'constituent' legislator to an 'ordinary' legislator, thus demeaning the distinction between *'pouvoir constituant'* and *'pouvoir constitué'* to a mere labelling exercise. In South Africa, it is arguably the case that, aside from its ordinarily elected Parliament, the country has never had a body specifically elected to serve as a 'constituent' constitution-making body.[49]

'Constituent assemblies', meaning assemblies of representatives specially elected to draft constitutions, are the exception rather than the rule and have seldom been successful, with consensus often being reached outside such assemblies via understandings and agreements reached between political parties.[50]

[46] See, however, the tools developed earlier by the Portuguese Constitutional Court: André Thomashausen, 'Basic Rights, Liberty and their Protection under the New Portuguese Constitution of 1976' (1981) 1 Human Rights Law Journal 182–208 and 416–28. See also André Thomashausen, 'Der Einfluß des Grundgesetzes auf Ausländisches Verfassungsrecht: Portugal' in K Stern (ed.), *40 Jahre Grundgesetz – Entstehung, Bewährung und Internationale Ausstrahlung* (Beck 1990) 243–58; 'Der Grundrechtsschutz in Portugal' in E Grabitz (ed.), *Grundrechte in Europa und USA – Band I: Strukture nationaler Systeme* (P Engel Verlag 1986) 591–650.

[47] RC Van Ooyen and MHW Möllers, 'Ordnungsdenken in der Rechtsprechung des Bundesverfassunggerichts' in RC Van Ooyen and MHW Möllers (eds), *Handbuch Bundesverfassunggericht im Politischen System* (Springer 2015) 479–95; T Maunz, 'Der Streit um das Rechte Verfassungsverständnis' (1974) 21(2) Zeitschrift für Politik 138–47; Horst Dreier, 'Grenzen Demokratischer Freiheit im Verfassungsstaat' (1994) 49(15/16) Juristenzeitung 741–52.

[48] *Kesavananda Bharati Sripadagalvaru & Ors v State of Kerala & Anr* (1973) 4 SCC 225.

[49] André Thomashausen, 'Demokratie und Rechtsstaatlichkeit in Südafrika' in U Battis and others (eds), *Das Grundgesetz im Prozess Europäischer und Globaler Verfassungsentwicklung* (Baden Baden 2000) 163–88.

[50] For example, in the case of Portugal, see André Thomashausen, 'Constituição e Realidade Constitucional' (1977) 37(2) Revista da Ordem dos Advogados 471–91; see also Thomashausen (n 4) 503.

German constitutional scholars have suggested the idea of rationalizing a binding and irremovable authority of material limitation of review clauses on the basis of an application of the legal principles of self-commitment (by the legislature) or estoppel. Accordingly, an interpretation of the eternity clause that would allow for a review of the eternity clause itself would offend basic legal hermeneutics, as this would entail interpreting a clause in such a manner as to defeat its application. A less formalistic view is that the authority of a people to write and review a constitution is absolute and therefore cannot be conditioned or relinquished.

According to this line of reasoning, a law passed in Parliament to irrevocably transfer its sovereign authority to the executive, such as the German Ermächtigungsgesetz of 24 March 1933, is not only unconstitutional but, in terms of legal logic, null and void.[51] In Africa, the same should have applied to the constitutional dictate imposed in the former Zaire by Laurent Kabila in his Décret-loi Constitutionel de la RDC du 28 May 1997,[52] article 5 of which stated:

The President of the Republic exercises legislative authority by means of decree-laws deliberated by the Council of Ministers.	*Le président de la République exerce le pouvoir législatif par décrets-lois délibérés en conseil des ministres.*

The German answers to the challenge of determining the authority to review material review limitations *('Revisionsrevisionskompetenz')* overlooks the much older, and indeed compelling, distinction made by Dicey in 1885 when he resorted to the notion of the rule of law to bind the original constituent authority:

> [I]f a sovereign (prince) grants a constitution, binding himself not to make laws except with the consent of an elected legislature, and if that rule is law, any subsequent rule made by the prince alone abolishing the legislature, will not be law.[53]

The notion of 'sovereignty' was defined originally by Jean Bodin in 1576 by reference to 'the supreme power over citizens and subjects unrestrained by law'.[54] Following this logic, a constitution-making, and therefore constituent, authority can declare that no subsequent rule shall be 'lawful' if it encroaches upon certain guarantees and principles or procedures.

The conclusion that can be drawn from the review of, and reflection on, the eternity clauses in the Portuguese-speaking countries in Africa, but also in regard to constitutional eternity clauses generally, is that the preservation and defence of a constitution against radical politically driven changes to, or voidance of, its original content and identity lies in the strength of the constitutional rule of law in each particular country. Such rule of constitutional law can result simply from the strength of a tradition of constitutionalism or it can be

51 K Stern, *Das Staatsrecht der Bundesrepublik Deutschland* (vol 1, 2nd edn, CH Beck Verlag 1984) 115; Z Giacometti, *Das Staatsrecht der Kantone* (Polygraphischer Verlag AG 1941) 449; Hans Kelsen, *Allgemeine Staatslehre* (Mohr Siebeck 1925) 249; Hans Kelsen, *Das Problem der Souveränitat und die Theorie des Völkerrechts* (Mohr Siebeck 1920) 119 f; U Matthée, *Die Legalität des Ermächtigungsgesetzes vom 24 März 1933 und die Schranken der Verfassungsrevision in der Weimarer Verfassung* (Kiel 1971) 87.

52 Décret-Loi constitutionnel No 003 du 27 mai 1997 relatif à l'organisation et à l'exercice du pouvoir en République Démocratique du Congo (DRC).

53 AV Dicey, *Study of the Law of the Constitution* (9th edn, Macmillan 1945) 66; Ivor Jennings, *The Law and the Constitution* (5th edn, University of London Press 1959) 152.

54 Jean Bodin Angevin, *Les Six Livres de la République* (Jacques du Puy 1576).

articulated explicitly within a constitutional text, in terms of an 'eternity clause', to act as a deterrent against constitutional adventurism.

Bibliography

Bachoff O., *Normas Constitucionais Inconstitucionais?* (tr Cardoso da Costa J.M.M., first published 1951, Almedina 1994).

Barroso L.R. and Albert R., 'Cabo Verde' in Barroso L.R. and Albert R., *The 2020 International Review of Constitutional Reform* (Program on Constitutional Studies at the University of Texas at Austin in collaboration with the International Forum on the Future of Constitutionalism 2021)

Bodin J., *Les Six Livres de la République* (Jacques du Puy 1576)

Botelho C.S., 'Narcisismo Constitucional' (*Observador*, 2 December 2018) https://observador.pt/opiniao/narcisismo-constitucional-mude-se-a-constituicao-ii/ accessed 12 June 2022

d'Alva Teixeira J.P., 'Comentário à Constituição Política Santomense' in Mourão F.A.A., Porto W.C., and Mantovanini T.M. (eds.), *As Constituições dos Países de Língua Portuguesa Comentadas* (Edições do Senado Federal Brasilia 2008) 773–830

De Freitas Diogo W.B., *Limites Materiais de Revisão Constitucional no Direito Angolano* (Universidade de Lisboa, Faculdade de Direito Lisboa 2016) 102

Delgado J.P., Fonseca J.C., and Delgado L.T. (eds.), *Aspectos Polêmicos da Extradição em Cabo Verde e no Espaço Lusófono* (Imprensa Nacional Cabo Verde 2009)

Dicey A.V., *Study of the Law of the Constitution* (9th edn, Macmillan 1945)

Dreier H, 'Grenzen Demokratischer Freiheit im Verfassungsstaat' (1994) 49(15/16) Juristenzeitung 741–52

Duarte Silva A.E., 'O Constitucionalismo da Guiné-Bissau' in Mourão F.A.A, Porto W.C., and Mantovanini T.M. (eds.), *As Constituições dos Países de Língua Portuguesa Comentadas* (Edições do Senado Federal Brasilia 2008) 477–530

Gomes Canotilho J.J. and Moreira V., *Constituição da República Portuguesa Anotada* (vol 2, 2nd edn, Coimbra Editora 1985)

Gomes Canotilho J.J., *Direito Constitucional e Teoria da Constituição* (5th edn, Almedina 2003)

Giacometti Z., *Das Staatsrecht der Kantone* (Polygraphischer Verlag A.G. 1941)

Gouveia J.B., *Manual de Direito Constitucional* (vol 1, 2nd edn, Almedina 2007)

Gouveia J.B., 'O Constitucionalismo de Angola e a sua Constituição de 2010' (2017) 9(3) Revista de Estudos Constitucionais, Hermenêutica e Teoria do Direito (RECHTD) 221–39

European Commission for Democracy through Law (Venice Commission), 'Constitutional Provisions for Amending the Constitution – Limits to Constitutional Amendments', Study No. 469 (2008)

Jennings I., *The Law and the Constitution* (5th edn, University of London Press 1959)

José M., 'Demissão de Presidente do Tribunal Constitucional Angolano Provoca Debate' (*Voice of America* 16 August 2021) https://www.voaportugues.com/a/demiss%C3%A3o-de-presidente-do-tribunal-constitucional-angolano-provoca-debate-/6004582.html accessed 12 June 2022

Kaboloca S., 'Escândalo Juíza Laurinda Cardoso: E Agora, Senhor Presidente?' (*Club-K*, 7 September 2021) https://www.club-k.net/index.php?option=com_content&view=article&id=45635:caso-nacionalidade-portuguesa-de-laurinda-e-agora-senhor-presidente-soares-kaboloca&catid=41013&Itemid=1080&lang=pt accessed 12 June 2022

Kelsen H., *Das Problem der Souveränitat und die Theorie des Völkerrechts* (Mohr Siebeck 1920)

Kelsen H., *Allgemeine Staatslehre* (Mohr Siebeck 1925)

Matthée U., *Die Legalität des Ermächtigungsgesetzes vom 24 März 1933 und die Schranken der Verfassungsrevision in der Weimarer Verfassung* (CAU Universität Kiel 1971)

Maunz T., 'Der Streit um das Rechte Verfassungsverständnis' (1974) 21(2) Zeitschrift für Politik 138–47

Miranda J., *Manual de Direito Constitucional* (vol 2, 2nd edn, Coimbra Editora 1983)

Miranda J., *Teoria do Estado e da Constituição* 1ed (Forense 2002)

Miranda J., 'A Evolução da Constituição de 1976 ao Século XXI' (2016) 76(1) Revista da Ordem dos Advogados 7–23

Mondlane C.P., 'Os Limites na Revisão Constitucional em Moçambique' (*Jus.com.br*, 23 June 2013) https://jus.com.br/artigos/24761/os-limites-na-revisao-constitucional-em-mocambique 2 accessed 12 June 2022

Nascimento J.O., 'Nação e Estado na Constituição da Republica de Cabo Verde' https://www.ces.uc.pt/lab2004/pdfs/JoaoNascimento.pdf accessed 12 June 2022

Oliveira J.F.G.C., *A Revisão Constitucional e a Tutela de Princípios Fundamentais Considerações sobre os Limites Materiais do Poder de Revisão* (Universidade de Lisboa 2018)

Partido Comunista Português, 'Resolução do Comité Central do PCP Sobre a revisão da Constituição (1989)' (30 May 1989) https://www.pcp.pt/sobre-revisao-da-constituicao-1989 accessed 12 June 2022

República de Angola, *Relatório e Fundamentação, Proposta de Lei de Revisão Constitucional* (Imprensa Nacional Angola, Luanda 2021)

Roznai Y., 'Amendment Power, Constituent Power, and Popular Sovereignty: Linking Unamendability and Amendment Procedures' (30 April 2017) in Albert R., Contiades X., and Fotiado A. (eds.), *The Foundations and Traditions of Constitutional Amendment* (Hart Publishing 2017) 23–49

Seibert G., 'Instabilidade Política e Revisão Constitucional: Semipresidencialismo em São Tomé e Príncipe' in Lobo M.C. and Neto O.A. (eds.), *O Semipresidencialismo nos Países da Lingua Portuguesa* (Lisboa ICS 2009)

Stern K., *Das Staatsrecht der Bundesrepublik Deutschland* (vol 1, 2nd edn, CH Beck 1984)

Thomashausen A., 'Constituição e Realidade Constitucional' (1977) 37(2) Revista da Ordem dos Advogados 471–91.

Thomashausen A., *Verfassung und Verfassungswirklichkeit im neuen Portugal* (Duncker & Humblot 1981)

Thomashausen A., 'Basic Rights, Liberty and their Protection under the New Portuguese Constitution of 1976' (1981) 1 Human Rights Law Journal 182–208

Thomashausen A., 'Der Grundrechtsschutz in Portugal' in Grabitz E. (ed.), *Grundrechte in Europa und USA - Band I: Strukturen nationaler Systeme* (P Engel Verlag 1986) 591–650

Thomashausen A., 'Der Einfluß des Grundgesetzes auf ausländisches Verfassungsrecht: Portugal' in Stern K. (ed.), *40 Jahre Grundgesetz - Entstehung, Bewährung und internationale Ausstrahlung* (Beck 1990) 243–58

Thomashausen A., 'Demokratie und Rechtsstaatlichkeit in Südafrika' in Battis U. and others (eds.), *Das Grundgesetz im Prozess Europäischer und Globaler Verfassungsentwicklung* (Baden Baden 2000) 163–88

Thomashausen A., 'Preventive Diplomacy in the Mozambique Transition' in Solomon H. (ed.), *Towards Sustainable Peace: Reflections on Preventive Diplomacy in Africa* (Africa Institute of South Africa 2003) 270–309

Thomashausen A., 'Constitutional Law in Extreme Emergencies' in Bröhmer J. and others (eds.), *Internationale Gemeinschaft und Menschenrechte - Festschrift* für Georg Ress (Heymanns 2005) 1295–304

Thomashausen A., 'O Desenvolvimento, Contexto e Apreço da Constituicão de Angola de 2010' in de Sousa M.R. and others (eds.), *Estudos de Homenagem ao Prof Doutor Jorge Miranda* (vol 1, Coimbra Editora 2012) 323–48

Thomashausen A., 'Super-presidentialism in Angola and the Angolan Judiciary' in Charles M. Fombad (ed.) *Separation of Powers in African Constitutionalism* (OUP 2016) 182–204

Thomashausen A., 'The Constitutional Court of Angola: Judicial Restraint in a Dominant-Party State' in Charles M. Fombad (ed.) *Constitutional Adjudication in Africa* (OUP 2017) 97–112

Thomashausen A., 'The Concept and Implementation of "Gradual Decentralisation" in Mozambique' in Charles M. Fombad and Nico Steytler (eds.) *Decentralisation and Constitutionalism in Africa* (OUP 2019) 384–408

Thomashausen A., 'The Constitutions of Angola' in Wolfrum R. and Grote R. (eds.), *Constitutions of the Countries of the World—Oxford Constitutions Online* http://oxcon.ouplaw.com accessed 12 June 2022

Van Ooyen R.C. and Möllers M.H.W., 'Ordnungsdenken in der Rechtsprechung des Bundesverfassunggerichts' in Van Ooyen R.C. and Möllers M.H.W. (eds.), *Handbuch Bundesverfassunggericht im Politischen System* (Springer 2015) 479–95

6

Eternity Clauses in African Constitutionalism: A Case Study of CEMAC Countries

Abdou Khadre Diop

1. Introduction

One of the prominent features shared by the Central African Economic and Monetary Community (CEMAC) countries[1] is constitutional instability. In a study published in 2014, Charles Fombad analysed the frequency with which constitutions in the Central Africa region are amended and found that, among them, CEMAC countries hold the record. He noted that, apart from Angola and São Tomé and Príncipe, 'the rest of the countries have rewritten and adopted new constitutions on average every ten and a half years during the last 52 years, with Chad, the Central African Republic, and Congo doing this almost every seven years'.[2]

A constitution loses its value as the supreme law if it is changed frequently and arbitrarily to suit the convenience of ruling elites. Furthermore, constitutional stability and the certainty and predictability that go with it are important elements of constitutionalism and respect of the rule of law.[3] Indeed, the wish to limit and control the ability of leaders to alter the constitution easily and often (as they had done before the 1990s) seemed to be in the minds of constitutional reformers in all the CEMAC countries. In this regard, there are three formal means of limiting the possibilities to amend the constitution.

First, the constitution cannot be amended at any time (temporal restrictions). In the CEMAC countries, constitutional provisions prohibit the amendment of the constitution in specified circumstances, such as during periods when there is an emergency or in the event that the presidency is vacant due to death, resignation, or temporary or indefinite incapacity.[4] It is understandable why there is a need to ensure that no leader or acting leader exploits a crisis to change a constitution in ways that serve to perpetuate his or her stay in power.[5]

[1] CEMAC (Communauté Economiques des États de l'Afrique Centrale) is an economic and monetary zone comprising six countries in Central Africa: Cameroon, Central African Republic, Republic of the Congo, Gabon, Equatorial Guinea, and Chad.

[2] Charles M Fombad, 'Strengthening Constitutional Order and Upholding the Rule of Law in Central Africa: Reversing the Descent towards Symbolic Constitutionalism' (2014) 14(2) African Human Rights Law Journal 428.

[3] Ibid.

[4] See eg art 228 of the Constitution of Chad (2018); art 240 of the Constitution of Congo (2015); and art 116 of the Constitution of Gabon (1991).

[5] Charles M Fombad, 'Limits on the Power to Amend Constitutions: Recent Trends in Africa and their Potential Impact on Constitutionalism' (2007) 6 University of Botswana Law Journal 57.

Abdou Khadre Diop, *Eternity Clauses in African Constitutionalism: A Case Study of CEMAC Countries* In: *Constitutional Change and Constitutionalism in Africa*. Edited by: Charles M. Fombad and Nico Steytler, Oxford University Press.
DOI: 10.1093/9780198957034.003.0008

Second, other provisions stipulate that the constitution cannot be amended without observing a particular procedure. Constitutional amendment procedures, which have gained increasing attention in recent scholarship in Africa[6] and elsewhere,[7] are an important tool to prevent abusive revisions[8] of the fundamental text. Instituting constitutional amendment procedures which are more cumbersome than the regular lawmaking process is fundamental to buttressing claims of constitutional supremacy. It is regarded as one of the core elements of constitutionalism[9] and the aim thereof is not to block constitutional amendment entirely but to ensure that the process is reasonably difficult and thereby impose a check against any arbitrary or whimsical constitutional changes that may defeat the will of the people.[10]

In this regard, the CEMAC countries have set up certain procedural requirements. Informed by borrowing from the French constitutional tradition, the initiative to amend the constitution is vested in public authorities, either Parliament or the president—solely[11] or through the Council of Ministers.[12] Regarding the adoption by Parliament, high thresholds are usually required for amendments[13] or, in the case of referendums, a simple majority is required.

[6] Charles M Fombad, 'Some Perspectives on Durability and Change under Modern African Constitutions' (2013) 11(2) International Journal of Constitutional Law 382–413; Adem K Adebe, 'Taming Regressive Constitutional Amendments: The African Court as a Continental (Super) Constitutional Court' (2019) 17(1) International Journal of Constitutional Law 89–117; Sègnonna H Adjolohun, 'The Making and Remaking of National Constitutions in African Regional Courts' (2018) 1 African Journal of Comparative Constitutional Law 35–70; Mouhamadou M. Aïdara, 'Le Juge Constitutionnel Africain et le Contrôle des lois Portant Révision de la Constitution: Contribution à un Débat' (2011) (*Afrilex*, March 2021) https://afrilex.u-bordeaux.fr/wp-content/uploads/2021/03/Article_Aidara_Le_juge_constitutionnel_1_-1.pdf accessed 20 July 2022; Francisco M Djedjro, 'La Révision des Constitutions dans les États Africains Francophones: Esquisse de Bilan' (1992) 1 Revue de Droit Public 111–34; Abraham H Diompy, 'Les Dynamiques Récentes de la Justice Constitutionnelle en Afrique Francophone' (*Afrilex*, 2014) https://afrilex.u-bordeaux.fr/wp-content/uploads/2021/03/JOURNEE_DE_LA_JEUNE_RECHERCHE_EN_DROIT_CONSTITUTIONNEL.pdf accessed 20 July 2022; Ibrahima Diallo, 'Pour un Examen Minutieux de la Question des Révisions de la Constitution dans les États Africains Francophones' https://afrilex.u-bordeaux.fr/wp-content/uploads/2021/03/POUR_UN_EXAMEN_MINUTIEUX_DE_LA_QUESTION_DES_REVISIONS_DE_LA_CONSTITUTION_DANS_LES_ETATS_AFRICAINS_FRANCOPHONES.pdf (*Afrilex*, 2015) accessed 20 July 2022; Karim Dosso, 'Les Pratiques Constitutionnelles dans les Pays d'Afrique Noire Francophone: Cohérences et Incohérence' (2012) 90(2) Revue Française de Droit Constitutionnel 57–85; Abdoulaye Soma, 'Le Contrôle de Constitutionnalité des lois Constitutionnelles en Afrique Noire Francophone' (2011) 5 Pratique Juridique Actuelle 619–40.

[7] Sanford Levinson, 'Designing an Amendment Process' in John Ferejohn and others (eds), *Constitutional Culture and Democratic Rule* (CUP 2001) 275; Richard Albert, 'The Expressive Function of Constitutional Amendment Rules' (2013) 59(2) McGill Law Journal 230; Carlos Bernal, 'Unconstitutional Constitutional Amendments in the Case Study of Colombia: An Analysis of the Justification and Meaning of the Constitutional Replacement Doctrine' (2013) 11(2) International Journal of Constitutional Law 339; Yaniv Roznai, 'Unconstitutional Constitutional Amendments – The Migration and Success of a Constitutional Idea' (2013) 61(3) American Journal of Comparative Law 657.

[8] In this chapter, the terms 'revision' and 'amendment' are used interchangeably.

[9] See John Hatchard, 'Perfecting Imperfections: Developing Procedures for Amending Constitutions in Commonwealth Africa' (1998) 36 (3)The Journal of Modern African Studies 381; Djedjro (n 6) 111.

[10] Charles M Fombad, 'Constitutional Reforms and Constitutionalism in Africa: Reflections on Some Current Challenges and Future Prospects' (2011) 59(4) Buffalo Law Review 1018.

[11] Examples are Cameroon (see art 63 of the 1996 Constitution), Equatorial Guinea (art 133 of the 1991 Constitution), and the Central African Republic (art 151 of the 2016 Constitution).

[12] Examples are Chad (art 226 of the 2018 Constitution), Gabon (art 116 of the 1991 Constitution), and Republic of the Congo (art 240 of the 2015 Constitution).

[13] In Cameroon, the requirement is for an absolute majority or, if the president requests a second reading, a two-thirds majority (art 63(3)); a majority of two-thirds is required in Chad (art 226(3)), in Gabon (art 116(7)), and in the Central African Republic (art 151); a majority of three-quarters is required in Equatorial Guinea (art 133(3)) and in the Republic of the Congo (art 241(3)).

Third, not all provisions of the constitution are amendable (material restrictions). All the CEMAC constitutions contain a category of matters that are expressly designated as not subject to amendment. These unamendable provisions, also known as 'eternity clauses', are intended to guarantee the durability of certain values, principles, or concepts which the constitutional designer believed should never be threatened or changed. Eternity clauses can be understood as a legal standard declaring certain principles, values, or specific constitutional provisions to be unalterable and irrevocable. Put differently, they are a special mechanism of constitutional entrenchment: one that might be termed indefinite or limitless.

While a factual examination of the CEMAC countries shows that there is a huge gap between the text providing for eternity clauses and the practice in reality, it must be assumed nonetheless that there is an increasing trend of unamendability in global constitutionalism. According to Yaniv Roznai, between 1789 and 1944, only 17 per cent of the world's constitutions included unamendable provisions. However, between 1945 and 1988, 27 per cent of constitutions enacted worldwide included such provisions, and of the constitutions enacted between 1989 and 2013, some 53 per cent included them.[14] More recently, both the Tunisian Constitution, adopted by referendum on 25 July 2022, and Nepal's Constitution of 2015 incorporated formally unamendable clauses.

Moreover, in Africa, and in particular in francophone African countries, unamendable provisions, or eternity clauses, are a common feature of constitutional design. Eternity clauses became an especially attractive tool for constitution-makers in African francophone countries during the so-called third wave of democratization that began in the early 1990s. Almost all African francophone countries have borrowed the concept of unamendable provisions from the Constitution of the Fifth French Republic.[15]

The focus of this chapter is on the countries of the CEMAC region, which have seldom been discussed either in the English or French literature on the subject of eternity clauses. The analysis is comparative and encompasses six countries: Gabon, the Republic of the Congo (hereafter referred to as Congo), Equatorial Guinea, the Central African Republic, Cameroon, and Chad. Apart from their belonging to the same zone, the countries have the commonality of being francophone and, as such, have adopted the Gaullist model of constitutional order. Although Equatorial Guinea, which is lusophone, seems to be an exception, its constitutional system has been influenced in many respects by the civil legal system within which the other countries operate. Another common feature of these countries is the frequency with which they undergo constitutional amendments, some of which directly or indirectly affect core principles or values that are supposed to be protected eternally by the so-called eternity clauses.

The argument in this chapter is that an empirical study of the CEMAC countries shows that unamendable provisions or eternity clauses are irrelevant both in theory and in practice as a means for ensuring the entrenchment of constitutional values. As designed in the post-1990 constitutions, the eternity clauses in the various countries seem on the whole to be declarative in nature rather than enforceable. The provisions, indeed, have an aspirational

[14] See Yaniv Roznai, *Unconstitutional Constitutional Amendments: The Limits of Amendment Powers* (OUP 2017) 20.

[15] See Constitution of Senegal, art 103; Constitution of Benin, art 156; Constitution of Niger, art 175.

quality, given that the practical realities appear to be at odds with the notion of entrenched values or perpetual principles. Moreover, due to the influence of the French constitutional review model, the countries lack a judicial power that is vested with the ability to undertake a proper review of constitutional amendments.

As Abbott Lawrence Lowell notes, 'the device of providing that a law shall never be repealed is an old one, but I am not aware that it has ever been of any avail'.[16] Similarly, Benjamin Akzin has expressed scepticism about the usefulness of eternity clauses: if 'the demand for change were to become so strong . . . it is hardly imaginable that its protagonists would renounce their objectives only because the Constitution says that the provision is inviolable'.[17] These statements fit the situation perfectly in the CEMAC countries, where eternity clauses enjoy a formal existence but are in reality no more than a pipe dream.

The discussion that follows is divided into three sections. The first (section 2) is an overview of the scope of eternity clauses in the CEMAC countries. Here, we will provide an analysis of the values or principles enshrined in the eternity clauses in order to gain a better understanding of their meaning as well as the way they are formulated. The next section (section 3) provides an overview of the practices that CEMAC countries have engineered for circumventing the eternity clauses. In that section, the rationale for eternity clauses is juxtaposed, via an empirical analysis, with the stratagems that have been devised to circumvent them.

Thereafter, the chapter examines the lack of judicial enforcement of eternity clauses, doing so through an analysis of the jurisdiction and interpretations of the constitutional courts or councils of the six countries. In this section (section 4), it is argued that eternity clauses are not judicially enforceable and that, at worst, the interpretation of the constitution by constitutional courts or councils reinforces the weakness of such clauses.

The last section (section 5) contains concluding remarks. It is argued that, given the aspirational and non-enforceable nature of eternity clauses in the countries under study, a more effective alternative to them is to better secure the amendment process of the core values of the constitution rather than to regard these values as eternal—that is to say, to consider 'rigidity' rather than 'eternity'.

2. The scope of eternity clauses: Merely aspirational

Comparative law reveals that eternity clauses may be used to safeguard three types of values or principles that are relevant to a nation's constitutional identity. The first group is composed of universal values such as democracy, natural and inalienable human rights, and the rule of law. The second group is made up of particular features relating to the structural characteristics of the state (such as federalism),[18] the role of religion in the given society,[19] or certain principles concerning the division of powers. The third group consists of

[16] Abbott L Lowell, *Greater European Governments* (Harvard University Press 1918) 103.

[17] Benjamin Akzin, 'The Place of the Constitution in the Modern State' (1967) 2(1) Israel Law Review 12.

[18] For example, the Basic Law of Germany clearly states that '[a]mendments affecting the division of the Federation into Länder, their participation in principle in the legislative process . . . shall be inadmissible' (art 79).

[19] For example, the Constitution of Morocco clearly states that '[n]either the State system of monarchy nor the prescription relating to the Islamic religion are subject to constitutional revision.'

principles relating to sovereignty or the protection of the state's independence (territorial and/or national integrity).

An examination of all the constitutions of the CEMAC countries shows that all three types of values or principles are formally protected by eternity clauses: the republican form of the state, the secular form of the state, territorial integrity or national unity, and democratic values. But should this limitation on the ability to amend the constitution, as stipulated in the eternity clauses in the six countries, truly be regarded as an eternity clause? The question arises because the unamendability clauses are formulated as principles—in other words, as general guidelines rather than as rules requiring strict compliance.[20] Due to its elasticity and semantic openness, unamendability formulated as a general principle allows for balancing and flexibility. Thus, it must be assumed that by choosing to consider broad principles or values rather than specific provisions in the design of the eternity clauses, the constitutional drafters sought to invest them merely with an aspirational or declarative function. This assumption is borne out by, and demonstrated in, an analysis of the concepts used in the eternity clauses in the six countries, with these concepts including republicanism, secularism, sovereignty (national integrity, national unity), and democracy.

2.1 The republican form of the state

If there is one commonality in all the eternity clauses in the CEMAC countries' constitutions, it is the protection of the republican form of the state. In their eternity clauses, all of these constitutions expressly exclude this form of the state from any procedure of revision.[21]

The core meaning of 'the republican form of the state' is, at first glance, not hard to understand. Most scholars would agree that a republican state is, at the very least, one in which the people control their rulers.[22] As James Madison wrote:

> We may define a republic to be . . . a government which derives all its powers directly or indirectly from the great body of the people, and is administered by persons holding their offices during pleasure, for a limited period, or during good behavior. It is essential to such a government, that it be derived from the great body of the society.[23]

Similarly, the US Supreme Court ruled in 1891 that 'the distinguishing feature of the republican state is the right of the people to choose their own officers for governmental administration, and pass their own laws'.[24] It is, therefore, obvious that locating sovereignty within the people is the essence of the republican form of the state. Indeed, the provisions declaring the republican form of state are in line with the articles dealing with national sovereignty

[20] On the distinction between principles and rules, see Ronald Dworkin, 'The Model of Rules' (1967–1968) 35(1) University of Chicago Law Review 14; Ronald Dworkin, *Taking Rights Seriously* (Harvard University Press 1977) 24; Robert Alexy, 'On the Structure of Legal Principles' (2000) 13(3) Ratio Juris 294–95.

[21] See art 153 of the Constitution of the Central African Republic; art 227 (Chad); art 64 (Cameroon); art 117 (Gabon); art 240 (Congo); art 134 (Equatorial Guinea).

[22] See Deborah J Merritt, 'Republican Government and Autonomous State: A New Role for the Guarantee Clause' (1994) 65(4) University of Colorado Law Review 815–34.

[23] James Madison, *The Federalist* (Jacob E. Cooke ed, Wesleyan University Press 1961) 251.

[24] In re Duncan, 139 US 449, 461 (1891) (United States Supreme Court, Lawyers' Co-operative Publishing Co)

in the constitutions of the CEMAC countries. For instance, article 2 of the Cameroonian Constitution provides that:

> National sovereignty shall be vested in the people of Cameroon who shall exercise same either through the President of the Republic and Members of Parliament or by way of referendum ... The authorities responsible for the management of the State shall derive their powers from the people through election by direct or indirect universal suffrage.

In the same vein, articles 24 and 26 of the Constitution of the Central African Republic provide, respectively, that 'the form of the State is the Republic' and that '[n]ational sovereignty belongs to the people'.[25]

The inclusion of the republican form of the state in all of the selected constitutions is inspired largely by the French constitutional design. Such a clause was inserted for the first time in the French Constitution by the law of 14 August 1884 on the partial revision of the Constitution.[26] This form of government was a symbol of victory over an authoritarian, monarchical past.[27] Later, the same provision was subsumed in article 95 of the French Constitution of 1946 and paragraph 5 of article 89 of the French Constitution of 1958. Subsequently, the inclusion of the republican form of the state as an intangible provision was replicated in many constitutional orders in Europe and Africa. This choice was justified by the wish to put an end to the tyranny of monarchs, though it is worth noting that in certain constitutions the eternity clause refers to the monarchic rather than the republican form, as is the case in Morocco.[28]

The specification of the republican form of the state in the CEMAC countries seems important. The adoption of constitutional law in these countries was intended to prevent a return to traditional monarchies and to unify the different traditional political societies into a modern political form. Thus, in a sense, this was the only way to preserve the unity of the territories that had been reconquered from the colonizers. Furthermore, the inclusion of the republican form of the state in an eternity clause meant that the constituent power sought to prevent constitutional coups, military coups, and all other forms of breakdown of constitutional order.

All in all, the republican form of state is a broad concept that entails numerous constitutional requirements, such as the right to vote; the right to free and fair elections; the separation of powers; and the ban on clientelism, the personalization of power, and *coups d'état*. Thus, a practical question arises: how to concretely protect the substance of this clause? Andrew Friedman, analysing the republican form as an entrenched provision under the French Constitution, concludes that the common interpretation of the provision is that it is simply a guide for the legislature and not really an enforceable one.[29] Its function, that is

[25] See also Constitution of Congo, art 5; Constitution of Equatorial Guinea, art 2; Constitution of Chad, art 3; Constitution of Gabon, art 3.

[26] See Michel Verpeaux, 'La République, la Constitution de 1958 et le Conseil Constitutionnel' in Pierre Avril (ed), *La République* (Montchrestien 2001) 129–39.

[27] Eivind Smith, 'Les Fonctions Symboliques des Constitutions' in Michel Troper (ed), *Traité International de droit Constitutionnel: Théorie de la Constitution* (Dalloz 2012) 767–95; see also Kemal Gözler, *Le Pouvoir de Révision Constitutionnelle* (Presses Universitaires du Septentrion 1997) 137.

[28] According to art 175 of the Constitution of Morocco, '[n]o revision may infringe the provisions relative to the Muslim religion, on the monarchic form of the State.'

[29] Andrew Friedman, 'Dead Hand Constitutionalism: The Danger of Eternity Clauses in New Democracies' (2011) 4(1) Mexican Law Review 88.

to say, is merely aspirational and idealistic. The same conclusion can be drawn in regard to the CEMAC countries, especially since the value of such a principle in court has never been determined.

Besides the republican form of the state, some CEMAC countries also refer to the secular form of the state, which is discussed below.

2.2 The secular form of the state

Three of the six member states of CEMAC include the secular form of the state as one of the salient points of the eternity clause provisions. According to article 153 of the Constitution of the Central African Republic, 'the republican and secular form of the state' is expressly excluded from revision. Similarly, article 227 of the Chadian Constitution provides that no procedure of revision may be implemented or pursued when it infringes on 'the republican form of the state, the principle of the separation of power and secularity'. In the same vein, article 240 of the Congolese Constitution stipulates that 'the republican form and the secular character of the state may not be made the subject of revision'.

Although the other three CEMAC countries do not include secularity in their eternity clauses, they mention it as one of the elements that characterize the state. For instance, article 1 of the Cameroonian Constitution provides that the state 'shall be one and indivisible, secular, democratic, and dedicated to social service',[30] while the Gabonese Constitution affirms the separation of state and religion.[31] Similarly, the French Constitution of the Fifth Republic also affirms the secular form of the state, though it does not include this in the eternity clause.

Constitutional protection of secularism is common in francophone African countries. However, there are exceptions. In Morocco,[32] Algeria,[33] and Tunisia,[34] provisions relating to Islam are unamendable. In the Central African Republic, Chad, and Congo, the introduction of the principle of secularity in the eternity clause can be explained by reference to the relationship between religion and the state. In the case of Chad, the country is geographically divided by a religious border, with a predominantly Muslim community in the north and a predominantly Christian community in the south. This 'threatening religious border' is, according to some scholars, a ticking time bomb for the stability of the country. The Chadian population is marked by this north–south divide and the religious sentiments that have characterized each of these historically antagonistic regions for several decades.

The existence of this geographical and historical context serves to explain why the constitutional drafters declared in the preamble that political, ethnic, and religious tolerance, pardons, interreligious dialogues, and cultural dialogues constitute fundamental values contributing to the consolidation of national unity and cohesion. For the drafters of the Chadian Constitution, secularism appeared to be the only way to guarantee diversity and

[30] Constitution of Cameroon, art 1.
[31] Constitution of Gabon, art 2.
[32] Constitution of Morocco (2011), art 175.
[33] Constitution of Algeria (2016), art 212.
[34] Constitution of Tunisia (2014), art 1.

pluralism, as well as peace and stability; accordingly, enshrining the secular form of the state in the eternity clause implies that it is a value to be protected in perpetuity.

In the case of the Central African Republic, the history of the country has been fraught with sectarian violence and targeted killings motivated by religion, particularly so after the 2013 coup. In 2014, the International Commission of Inquiry on the Central African Republic released a report confirming, on the one hand, that there had been a 'pattern of ethnic cleansing' committed by the anti-Balaka in the areas where Muslims had been living, and, on the other, noting an increased targeting of the Christian population by Seleka elements. This context, among other reasons, may explain why the constitutional drafters in 2004,[35] and later, in 2016,[36] considered secularism as an eternal value necessary for maintaining peace in the country.

Be that as it may, the crux of the matter remains the meaning of 'secularism' and its normative value as the topic of an eternity clause. As Andre Cabanis points out, the concept of secularism is dynamic and cannot be subject to a universal definition.[37] Its meaning depends on the context in which it is invoked. This is why Souleymane Bachir Diagne has argued that Western secularism is not relevant to understanding the meaning of secularism in sub-Saharan Africa.[38] Against this background, the fact that the constitutional drafters regarded a contingent concept like secularism as an eternal value yet refrained from offering any further specification would suggest either that they did not envisage it as an enforceable value or at least that they left wide discretion to judges to determine what is secular and what is not—as was the situation with the Turkish Constitutional Court in the case of the so-called 'headscarf decision'.[39]

2.3 Territorial integrity and national unity

Territorial integrity, national integrity, national unity, or independence find expression in the eternity clauses of the constitutions of Cameroon,[40] Chad,[41] and Equatorial Guinea.[42] In the other three countries, territorial integrity and national unity are not considered unamendable provisions, albeit that there is an express prohibition against amending the constitution in the particular circumstances where territorial integrity would be placed in jeopardy.[43]

[35] Constitution of the Central African Republic (27 December 2004).

[36] Constitution of the Central African Republic (30 March 2016).

[37] André Cabanis, 'La Laïcité dans les Constitutions de l'Afrique de Succession Coloniale Française' (2020) 8(12) Revue Internationale des Francophones. http://rifrancophonies.com/index.php?id=1193 accessed 3 August 2022.

[38] Souleymane B Diagne, 'The Constitution of a "Laic" African and Muslim Country: Senegal' in Ali U Bâli and Hanna Lerner (eds), *Constitution Writing, Religion and Democracy* (CUP 2017) 131.

[39] Constitutional Court of Turkey, Decision No 2008/116 of 5 June 2008; Official Gazette No 27032, 22 October 2008; see also Yaniv Roznai and Serkan Yolcu, 'An Unconstitutional Constitutional Amendment – The Turkish Perspective: A Comment on the Turkish Constitutional Court's Headscarf Decision' (2012) 10(1) International Journal of Constitutional Law 175; Ergun Özbudun, 'Judicial Review of Constitutional Amendments in Turkey' (2009) 15(4) European Public Law 533, 537 f.

[40] Constitution of Cameroon, art 64.

[41] Constitution of Chad, art 227.

[42] Constitution of Equatorial Guinea, art 134.

[43] See Constitution of Gabon, art 116; Constitution of Congo, art 240(2); Constitution of the Central African Republic, art 152. This is also the case in France (art 89 of the Constitution), Senegal (art 103 of the Constitution), Togo (art 144 of the Constitution), and Côte d'Ivoire (art 178 of the Constitution).

According to Charles Fombad, these concepts, as used by constitutional designers as part of unamendable provisions, are obscure.[44] Indeed, constitutional drafters use the terms 'territorial integrity' and/or 'national unity' without providing further clarification.

As regards the concept of territorial integrity, it is common to find it as an unamendable provision in other African countries[45] and elsewhere.[46] This unamendability typically appears in the constitutions of many states that were formerly colonial territories or under foreign rule. Given the centrality of the principle of territorial integrity in international law, it is not surprising that countries engaged in state-building would seek to incorporate it in their basic laws. But no definition is provided so as to afford a clear understanding of the meaning of 'territorial integrity' under constitutional law. As Denis Baranger remarks with reference to the French Constitution, 'there is nothing objective or merely procedural about such a standard as the "integrity of the territory"'.[47]

Two arguments may be put forward to justify the inclusion of territorial integrity as an unamendable provision in the countries under study. On the one hand, it may be argued that the commitment to territorial integrity as an unamendable provision refers purely to securing the country's external borders. From the point of view of constitutional theory, 'territory' is one of the elements that make a state, and it is thus a crucial element of state authority. Because every polity wants to preserve its own existence and identity, it seems clear on the face of it why a state would wish to protect its territorial integrity, alongside other core constitutional and democratic commitments, from possible incursions through constitutional amendments.

As such, the fact that provisions regarding territorial integrity are unamendable in Cameroon, Chad, and Equatorial Guinea indicates that the constitutional drafters in each case sought to protect the state's sovereignty and 'right to exist',[48] as well as the *uti possidetis juris* principle as adopted by African countries in the 1960s.[49] In the case of Cameroon, the boundary dispute with Nigeria over the peninsula of Bakassi is a perfect illustration of a dispute over territorial integrity.[50] Further examples are, in the case of Chad, the long-standing border dispute with Libya,[51] and in the case of Equatorial Guinea, the border dispute with Gabon.[52]

[44] Fombad (n 10) 1018.

[45] See eg the Constitution of Algeria (1996), art 223; Constitution of Angola (2010), art 236(b); Constitution of Cabo Verde (1992), art 313; Constitution of Comoros (2018), art 115; Constitution of Mauritania (1991), art 99(3).

[46] Constitution of Portugal (1976), art 288; Constitution of Turkey (1982) arts 3 and 4; Constitution of Ukraine (1996), art 157.

[47] Denis Baranger, 'The Language of Eternity: Judicial Review of the Amending Power in France (or the Absence Thereof)' (2011) 44(3) Israel Law Review 404.

[48] See John Mukum Mbaku, 'International Law and Limit of Sovereignty of African States' (2018) 30(2) Florida Journal of International Law 43–68.

[49] See the separate opinion of Judge Abdulqawi A Yusuf in the case *Frontier dispute (Burkina Faso v Niger)*, ICJ Report, 2013, 94; Jean M Sorel and Rostane Mehdi, 'L'uti Possidetis entre la Consécration Juridique et la Pratique: Essai de Réactualisation' (1994) 40(1) Annuaire Français de Droit International 11–40.

[50] International Court of Justice (ICJ), *Case Concerning the Land and Maritime Boundary between Cameroon and Nigeria (2002)* (ICJ Report 2002) 303.

[51] See Robert W McKoeon, 'The Aouzou Strip: Adjudication of Competing Territorial Claims in Africa by the International Court of Justice' (1991) 23(1) Journal of International Law 147–70.

[52] See Arpita G Sachdeva, 'Case Concerning a Mysterious Maritime Delimitation Treaty: Why the Dispute before the ICJ in Gabon/Equatorial Guinea Is Not about Delimitation' (*Völkerrechtsblog*, 23 April 2021) https://voelkerrechtsblog.org/case-concerning-a-mysterious-maritime-delimitation-treaty/ accessed 30 July 2022.

On the other hand (and turning to the second justification), seen from an internal, in-country perspective, the unamendability of territorial integrity expresses the state's prioritization of national integrity over any claims to self-determination that may arise. Accordingly, it is a way to prohibit any form of secession through constitutional amendment. States are, indeed, reluctant to legitimize secessionist claims because they have a general interest in preserving their own territorial integrity. The will to self-preservation and the fear of a country's disintegration are often reflected in the constitutional unamendability of territorial integrity or indivisibility. This seems to make sense in the case of Cameroon, in view of the so-called anglophone crisis in the southern part of the country,[53] or, in the case of Equatorial Guinea, in view of the secessionist dynamic ignited by the movement for the self-determination of Bioko.[54] Against this background, the introduction of territorial integrity as an unamendable provision is a clear message prohibiting arrangements that could lead to any form of secession or separation.

As regards the concept of national unity, it is mentioned as an unamendable provision in the constitutions of Chad, Cameroon, and Equatorial Guinea. Much like the concept of territorial integrity, 'national unity' has a defensive function. It is closely linked to the indivisibility of the nation mentioned in most francophone African constitutions.[55] The reference to national unity as a value which is protected perpetually may be understood as the adoption of a unitary form of state, pursuant to which any procedure that has the effect of altering this form should be declared unlawful.[56] In other words, it formalizes the rejection of federalism as a form of government in these countries.

The anglophone crisis in Cameroon is a fitting illustration of the aspirational character of the commitment to national unity. The reality in Cameroon, as in almost all the countries under study, is that the commitment to national unity as an eternal value is just a pipe dream given the aspiration of the anglophone part of the country either to secede or to return to a two-state federation. As Fombad notes, 'the bi-cultural character of the country is not only a historical fact but a daily reality that cannot be ignored or wished away'.[57] A constitutional amendment is indeed needed to recognize, as is the case in Canada,[58] the two distinct cultures in the country and, consequently, to design the country's institutional architecture in conformity with that reality. Conversely, it is worth noting that,

[53] See Laura-Stella E Enonchong, *The Constitution and Governance in Cameroon* (Routledge Studies on Law in Africa 2021) 178; Ngwa Nfobin and Nchotu V Minang, 'The Cameroon Anglophone Question in International Law' (2014) 22(2) African Journal of International and Comparative Law 234–52; Alain D Olinga, 'La Question Anglophone dans le Cameroun d'aujourd'hui' (1994) 48(3) Revue Juridique et Politique 292; Roxana Mates, 'The Internationalisation of the Secessionist crisis in Cameroon' (2021) 66(2) Studia Europaea 5–22.

[54] See Ibrahim Sundiata, 'Engaging Equatorial Guinea: Bioko in the Diasporic Imagination' (2009) 28(2) Afro-Hispanic Review 131–40.

[55] Alain Ondoua, 'La Population en Droit Constitutionnel: le Cas des Pays d'Afrique Francophone' (2012) 2(242) Afrique Contemporaine 87.

[56] See, for instance, the decisions of the Constitutional Council in France protecting the principle of national unity: Decision No 91-290 DC of 9 May 1991, Loi portant statut de la collectivité territoriale de Corse, *Rec* p 50; Decision No 99-412 DC du 15 June 1999, Charte européenne des langues régionales ou minoritaires, *Rec* p 71.

[57] Charles M Fombad, 'Developments in Cameroon Constitutional Law: The Year 2016 in Review' (*I. CONnect blog*, November 2017) http://www.iconnectblog.com/2017/11/developments-in-cameroonian-constitutional-law-the-year-2016-in-review/ accessed 27 July 2022. See further Carlson Anyangwe and Charles M Fombad, 'Cameroon and the Crisis of Constitutional Identity: Is Anglophone Identity Incompatible with a Cameroonian Constitutional Identity?' in Charles M Fombad and Nico Steytler (eds.), *Constitutional Identity and Constitutionalism in Africa* (Oxford University Press 2024) 214-247.

[58] See Canadian Supreme Court, Secession of Quebec, [1998] 2 SCR 217.

in other countries, it is the federal form of government which is considered an eternal value.[59]

But the crux of the matter is how to protect territorial integrity or national unity effectively against any form of formal or informal revision. For instance, if the state fears the voluntary ceding of territory under external pressure or coercion, what is the use of an unamendability clause on territorial integrity? A noted by Theodore Christakis, secession (or annexation) is a matter of fact rather than law.[60] Thus, in an analysis of the case of Ukraine in the light of the Crimean crisis, Yaniv Roznai and Silvia Suteu argue that the unamendable protection of territorial integrity is an especially ineffective type of eternity clause.[61] The same may be said of the preservation of national unity as an eternal value. If the aspiration of the people is to adopt a federalist system in order to better manage the diversity that characterizes most African states—notably Cameroon, Chad, and Equatorial Guinea—what would be the value of the eternity clauses protecting the unitary form of state?

Regarded from this perspective, the inclusion of these concepts in eternity clauses may be seen as a risk. According to Andrew Friedman, given the nature of constitutional dynamics, unamendability might achieve the exact opposite of its original purpose: not only does it not prevent certain changes, but by blocking any chance of effectuating them through peaceful and political means, it encourages the realization of these changes in an extra-constitutional manner.[62]

Be that as it may, the concepts of territorial integrity and national unity are dynamic and obscure, and in practical terms it is difficult to enforce them as constitutional values. The same observation can be made when constitutions seek to entrench the broad principle of democratic values as an eternal provision.

2.4 The democratic values

The eternity clauses in the constitutions under study refer also to democratic values. The Cameroonian Constitution prescribes that 'no procedure for the amendment of the Constitution affecting the republican form, unity, and territorial integrity of the state and *the democratic principles* which govern the Republic shall be accepted'.[63] It is not clear what these 'democratic principles' are—the Constitution does not make this apparent, and there is no known case law in Cameroon providing insights as to the intention of the legislator.

Similarly, the Constitution of Gabon merely provides that the 'pluralistic character of the state and democracy are intangible traits that cannot be the object of a constitutional revision', without offering any further specification. Likewise, the Constitution of Equatorial Guinea refers simply to the 'democratic regime of the state' in its eternity clause.

[59] This is the case in Germany: see art 79 of the Basic Law.

[60] Théodore Christakis, 'La Sécession: Une Question de Simple Fait?' (2007) European Society of International Law 15.

[61] Yaniv Roznai and Silvia Suteu, 'The Eternal Territory? The Crimean Crisis and Ukraine's Territorial Integrity as an Unamendable Constitutional Principle' (2015) 16(3)German Law Journal 542.

[62] Friedman (n 29) 77–96.

[63] Emphasis added.

In contrast, the Constitution of Congo does not mention democratic values or principles.[64] Only the constitutions of Chad and the Central African Republic give more detail, thus limiting the scope of the eternal democratic values being granted perpetual protection. In the case of the latter, article 153 refers to 'the number and duration of the presidential mandates; the conditions of eligibility; the incompatibilities with the functions of President of the Republic; [and] the fundamental rights of the citizen' as democratic values to perpetuate. For its part, the Chadian Constitution refers to 'the freedoms and fundamental rights of the citizen and the policy of pluralism'.

The protection of democratic values through the tools of eternal provision is not the preserve of the CEMAC countries. Needless to say, the concept of democracy is a fuzzy one which has been subject to a variety of interpretations. It may thus be interpreted broadly as including the separation of powers, the protection of human rights, the independence of the judiciary, the holding of free and fair elections, pluralism, and the setting of presidential term limits.

In the CEMAC region, the Central African Republic is currently the only country that refers to presidential term limits and the conditions of eligibility for the office of the presidency as perpetual democratic values. Such a provision is popular elsewhere in francophone African countries.[65] In the other countries under study, the provision either has existed in the past but been removed,[66] or it currently exists but without being mentioned in the eternity clause.[67] By and large, presidential term limits in constitutional law in Africa are a never-ending debate.[68] Without a doubt, they have become a key feature in the definition of democracy, as they promote the alternation of elected public office holders and serve to prevent a regime from descending into tyranny.[69] Term limits, indeed, are a part of the institutional design repertoire that has characterized Africa's third wave of democratization.

The Constitution of Chad also includes pluralism as a democratic value to be perpetuated through the eternity clause. Pluralism, or the multiparty system, was commonly included in constitutions after the Second World War. As Fombad notes, one of the most significant constitutional developments in the 1990s was the reintroduction, in all the constitutions in the region, including the CEMAC countries, of provisions recognizing multipartyism.[70] While the constitutions of Cameroon and Gabon merely mention democracy, the constitutions of Chad and the Central African Republic explicitly include the protection of human rights in their eternity clauses.

The inclusion of human rights as entrenched provisions is not particularly common in Africa. Apart from the two countries mentioned, the Namibian Constitution prohibits

[64] See Constitution of Congo (2015), art 240.

[65] It is the case, for instance, in Senegal (art 103 of the Constitution), in Madagascar (art 163), in Guinea (art 154), and in Algeria (art 234).

[66] See the next section for further discussion.

[67] This is the case in the Constitution of Chad (2018) and the Constitution of Equatorial Guinea (1991/2011).

[68] Jack R Mangala, 'Presidential Term Limit, the Never Ended Debate' in Jack R Mangala (ed.), *The Politics of Challenging Presidential Term Limits in Africa* (Palgrave Macmillan 2020) 1–37.

[69] See Tom Ginsburg, James Melton, and Zachary Elkins, 'On the Evasion of Executive Term Limits' (2011) 52(6) William & Mary Law Review 1806–18.

[70] Charles M Fombad, 'Conceptualising a Framework for Inclusive, Fair and Robust Multiparty Democracy in Africa: The Constitutionalisation of the Rights of Political Parties' (2015) 48(1) Verfassung und Recht in Übersee VRÜ 3–27; Charles M Fombad, 'Challenges to Constitutionalism and Constitutional Rights in Africa and the Enabling Role of Political Parties: Lessons and Perspectives from Southern Africa' (2007) 55(1) American Journal of Comparative Law 1–45.

any amendment that 'diminishes or detracts from the fundamental rights and freedoms';[71] similarly, the constitutions of Algeria, Angola, Cabo Verde, and Mozambique provide that amendments must respect fundamental rights.[72]

It follows from the preceding discussion that the scope of the eternity clauses is very broad. It covers all of the values or principles which the constitutional drafters regarded as part of a country's national identity at some point in history. However, the way in which these clauses are expressed or formulated is noticeably vague, which leads one to wonder whether they are, strictly speaking, rules with an increased normativity or merely principles that serve as general guidelines, as is the case with socio-economic rights in certain constitutions.[73] In the light of the analysis that has been conducted, it must be assumed that, given the way in which such clauses are formulated, they are more aspirational in nature than enforceable. This deduction, as we shall see, is confirmed once we confront the eternity clauses with the practical realities that obtain within the CEMAC countries.

3. Eternity clauses' promises vs the practical realities: Merely illusory

It is quite clear that the objective of preventing the abuse of powers to amend constitutions has not been attained in the Central African region,[74] notwithstanding the inclusion of unamendable provisions in the constitutions of the six countries under study. Furthermore, the frequency of *coups d'état* naturally leads to a suspension of the constitutional order,[75] thus undermining the letter and spirit of the eternity clauses. Confronting eternity clauses with the practical realities in the CEMAC countries leads to the conclusion that such clauses are merely illusory. Indeed, certain practices, such as unconstitutional constitutional change and unconstitutional changes of government, call into question the effectiveness of eternity clauses.

3.1 Unconstitutional constitutional change

Constitutional change, whether through the revision of an existing constitution or the adoption of a new one, has been the predominant strategy among the CEMAC countries for overcoming unamendable provisions. A factual examination of 'unconstitutional constitutional change'[76] in these countries justifies such a statement. This is illustrated by the practice either of replacing one constitution with another in order to circumvent the eternity clauses or of amending a constitution while ignoring these clauses.

[71] Constitution of Namibia (1990), art 131.

[72] Constitution of Algeria (2016), art 210; Constitution of Angola (2010), art 236; Constitution of Cabo Verde (1992), art 313; Constitution of Mozambique (2004), art 292.

[73] See David Kenny and Lauryn M McCann, 'Directive Principles, Political Constitutionalism, and Constitutional Culture: The Case of Ireland's Failed Directive Principles of Social Policy' (2022) 18(2) European Constitutional Law Review 207–36.

[74] Fombad (n 2) 429.

[75] Moussa Zaki, 'Petites Constitutions et Droit Transitoire en Afrique' (2012) 6(6) Revue du Droit Public 667.

[76] Roznai (n 14).

3.1.1. Replacement: The case of Congo

The replacement of the constitution has been used in Congo to overcome the eternity clause prohibiting any amendment relating to presidential term limits. Indeed, President Denis Sassou Nguesso ruled the country from 1979–92 and returned to the presidency in 1997. By 2015, the long-reigning president was nearing the term limitations enshrined in the 2002 Constitution of the Republic of the Congo, article 57 of which states that the 'President of the Republic is elected for seven years by universal direct suffrage' and is 're-eligible one time'. Furthermore, article 58, which lists the requirements for being a candidate for the presidency, establishes a maximum age limit for running for the office. The limit serves as an additional safeguard against lifelong presidents and is set at 70 years of age.[77] Above all, article 185 expressly stated that the provision limiting the mandates of the president of the republic shall not be the object of any amendment.[78]

However, the president sought to overcome this provision by initiating a new Constitution. In July 2015, he held a 'national forum' at which the possibility of extending his right to run for office was discussed. In September 2015, these discussions eventuated in a proposal for adopting a new Constitution, initiated by the president. The proposed document would remove both the term-limit restriction and the maximum age limit for holding the presidency. Invoking the democratic legitimacy of a referendum, the president stated that he had 'decided to directly give a voice to the people in order for them to decide on the draft law formulating the fundamental principles of the Republic'.

Despite fierce resistance, the referendum proceeded and was successful, with a 92 per cent majority voting in favour of the new constitution. As a result, the president is allowed to seek two further presidential terms, a situation made possible by the adoption of a new constitutional order and, correlatively, the abrogation of the previous one containing the eternity clause. The presidential term limit was duly removed from the eternity clause, which nevertheless still entrenches the 'integrity of the republican and secular form of the state'.[79]

As various scholars have rightly argued, while the aim of eternity clauses is to prevent abusive amendments, what they cannot prohibit is constitutional replacement. According to Georges Vedel and Louis Favoreu, the so-called constituent power *(pouvoir constituant* or *pouvoir constituant originaire)*, which is the extraordinary power to form a constitution, is free and independent of any formal bonds of positive law created by the constitution.[80] By contrast, the constituted power *(pouvoir constitué or pouvoir constituant derivé)*, which is a power created by an existing constitution, functions according to the forms and the mode that the nation grants it in positive law. Thus, the distinction between amendment and replacement of the constitution[81] is based on the nature of the power that intervenes.

[77] See also the Constitution of Senegal, art 28 of which sets a maximum age limit of 75 years old on the day of the ballot.

[78] The same provision is found in art 178 of the Constitution of Congo (1992).

[79] Constitution of Congo (2015), art 240. See generally Charles M Fombad and Nathaniel A Inegbedion, 'Presidential Term Limits and their Impact on Constitutionalism in Africa' in Christina Murray and Charles M Fombad (eds), *Fostering Constitutionalism in Africa* (Pretoria University Law Press 2010) 1–29.

[80] Georges Vedel, *Manuel Élémentaire de Droit Constitutionnel* (Dalloz 2002) 149; Louis Favoreu, 'Le Droit Constitutionnel, Droit de la Constitution et Constitution du Droit' (1990) 1 Revue Française de Droit Constitutionnel 71-89.

[81] David S Law and Ryan Whalen, 'Constitutional Amendment versus Constitutional Replacement: An Empirical Comparison' in Xenophon Contiades and Alkmene Fotiadou (eds), *Routledge Handbook of Comparative*

According to this formalistic way of thinking, the replacement of the Congolese Constitution in 2015 with a new text removing the term limits in the eternity clause cannot be considered an unconstitutional change since the expression of the constituent power cannot be limited. But from a substantive point of view, it must be assumed that, more often than not, replacements are inconsequential and amount in substance to overblown amendments. In the case of Congo, the objective of the constitutional replacement was not to make any genuine change to the political system, the form of the state, or other critical matters, but merely to allow the incumbent to run for further terms.[82] Thus, in this case the exercise of the constituent power was merely a diversion: a stratagem to overcome the unamendable provisions. By contrast, other countries seeking the same end often go ahead with the constitutional amendment process merely by ignoring the requirements of the eternity clauses.

3.1.2. Amendment: The cases of Cameroon, Gabon, and Equatorial Guinea

As noted, another stratagem is simply to amend the existing constitution, including its unamendable provisions. For instance, in Cameroon, a theoretical debate arose on the issue of the 2008 constitutional amendment in view of the eternity clause in the 1996 Constitution. Indeed, the 1996 constitutional amendment, regarded by many scholars as a new Constitution,[83] introduced presidential term limits into the country's constitutional framework. Two presidential elections were held subsequently, in 1997 and 2004, with Paul Biya winning what was described in both instances as a tainted victory.[84] The implication of the term-limit provision was that the second mandate of President Biya, who has been in power since 1982, was due to end in 2011. Before then, the incumbent initiated a constitutional amendment to remove the term-limit provision and allow him to rule for further terms in spite of popular discontentment.[85] To little surprise, Law No 2008/001 of 14 April 2008, amending and supplementing certain provisions of Law No 96/6 of 18 January 1996 (to amend the Constitution of 2 June 1972), was adopted and promulgated.

However, even if the procedural amendment of the Constitution were to be considered regular in a purely formalistic way,[86] it was clearly in breach of 'the democratic principles' protected by the eternity clause. In a recent study, Laura-Stella Enonchong argues that,

Constitutional Change (Routledge 2020) 1–49; Donald S Lutz, 'Toward a Theory of Constitutional Amendment' (1994) 88(2) American Political Science 55; Georges Tsebelis and Dominic J Nardi, 'A Long Constitution is a (Positively) Bad Constitution: Evidence from OECD Countries' (2016) 46(2) British Journal of Political Science 457.

[82] Vivien R Manangou, 'La Constitution Congolaise du 6 Novembre 2015: Entre Influence Française et Affirmation Identitaire' (2019) 13(13) Les Annales de Droit 121.

[83] See Maurice Kamto, 'Révision Constitutionnelle ou Écriture d'une Nouvelle Constitution' (1996) 23–24 Lex Lata 17–20.

[84] Freedom House, 'Freedom in the World 2010 – Cameroon' (*Refworld*, 3 May 2010) https://www.refworld.org/docid/4c0ceafec.html accessed 12 July 2022.

[85] More than 200 people who demonstrated against the changes were killed by security forces. See 'Cameroon Parliament Extends Biya's Term Limit' (*France 24 News*, 11 April 2008) https://www.france24.com/en/20080411-cameroon-parliament-paul-biya-term-limit-extension accessed 1 October 2023; Tansa Musa, 'Update 1 – Cameroon's Biya Signs Law Allowing Third Term Bid' (*Reuters*, 15 April 2008) https://www.reuters.com/article/cameroon-constitution-idUKL1529602420080415 accessed 1 October 2023.

[86] See Constitution of Cameroon (1996), art 63.

despite the absence of a normative understanding of what the 'democratic principles' mentioned in the eternity clause entail, in a historical, theoretical, and contextual analysis the provision may be understood to include presidential term limits.[87] This position seems entirely correct. The introduction of term-limit provisions as one of the prominent features of the third wave of democratization in sub-Saharan Africa was, along with other things, aimed at consolidating a transition to democratic governance.[88] It is thus difficult to see how a constitutional change that enables one individual to remain in office indefinitely can be said to promote and enhance democracy. Furthermore, as Fombad and Inegbedion note, 'term limits reduce the barriers to entry to politics, facilitate the process of developing a culture of political competition, and enhance the prospects for political development and the consolidation of democracy'.[89]

An interpretation by the country's Constitutional Council would have been invaluable in clarifying the situation. However, given that Cameroon has inherited the constitutional jurisdiction model from France,[90] the Council has been unable to play a significant role in the process of constitutional change. Indeed, although the leader of an opposition party not represented in Parliament attempted to challenge the constitutionality of the amendment and Parliament's competence to amend the Constitution, this petition was dismissed due to the absence of *locus standi*.[91]

Another example of the circumvention of the eternity clause is provided by Gabon. Through a strategy of repeated constitutional amendment, Gabonese leaders have succeeded in maintaining a lifelong presidency and quasi-hereditary monarchy,[92] even though the eternity clause protects the republican, pluralistic, and democratic character of the state.[93]

With the adoption of its Constitution of 1991 after a number of national conferences, Gabon, like almost all countries in sub-Saharan Africa, chose to incorporate the core elements of constitutionalism in its new constitutional order. One of the salient features of this was the introduction of multipartyism and presidential term-limit provisions. Against this background, article 9 of the Constitution limited the presidential term to five years and enshrined the impossibility of anyone's running for more than two terms.[94]

However, in 1997, and then in 2003, this provision was amended with the specific purpose of rolling back democratic features of the 1991's Constitution, thus undermining

[87] Laura-Stella E Enonchong, 'Unconstitutional Constitutional Amendment or Constitutional Dismemberment? A Reappraisal of the Presidential Term Limit Amendment in Cameroon' (2022) 11(2) Global Constitutionalism 283.

[88] See H Kwasi Prempeh, 'Africa's Constitutionalism Revival: False Start or New Dawn?' (2007) 5(3) International Journal of Constitutional Law 487.

[89] Fombad and Inegbedion (n 79) 17.

[90] Charles M Fombad, 'The New Cameroonian Constitutional Council in a Comparative Perspective: Progress or Retrogression?' (1998) 42(2) Journal of African Law 172–86; Jean Louis Amougou, 'La Constitutionnalisation du Droit en Afrique: l'exemple de la Création du Conseil Constitutionnel Camerounais' (2004) 19 Annuaire Internationale de Justice Constitutionnelle 45–63.

[91] See Arrêt No 01/CC du 17 avril 2008, decision of the Joint Benches of the Supreme Court of Cameroon sitting as the Constitutional Council. In 2008, the Constitutional Council had not been created, and as such the Supreme Court was exercising temporary constitutional jurisdiction in terms of art 67(4) of the Constitution.

[92] Andy Moses, *La République Monarchique* (Edi Livres 2015).

[93] This eternity clause was introduced into the Gabonese Constitution of 1991 but then never removed despite the frequency with which constitutional amendment has occurred.

[94] See art 9 of the initial version of the 1991 Constitution.

principles that were considered perpetual values under the eternity clause (that is to say, pluralism and democracy). The first amendment sought to extend the duration of the mandate from five to seven years, but still maintained the two-term-limit rule.[95] The 2003 amendments, though, went further than that.

The first noticeable change to came out of these amendments had to do with the voting procedure. The amendment introduced a one-round relative-majority electoral system that replaced the two-round absolute-majority system. This meant essentially that a candidate could now win a presidential election in Gabon after receiving only 5 per cent of the votes if this 5 per cent represented 'the most votes' against candidates who received less than 5 per cent. One may surmise that Omar Bongo, faced with growing unpopularity, devised this stratagem as a way of securing easy victories for himself.[96]

In addition to this first stratagem, another amendment was introduced in order to remove the two-presidential-term limit, which derived from the National Conference in the 1990s,[97] at which point Gabon was primed for the possibility of being encumbered by the same president for life. These subsequent changes, naturally, paved the way for a presidency for life for Omar Bongo until his death in 2009, but also eased the succession of his son, Ali Bongo, to the same office.

Ali Bongo was declared the winner of the 2009 presidential elections with just 41.79 per cent of the vote, in the context of a 54 per cent abstention rate.[98] The fact that only 46 per cent of the electorate voted in 2009, and of that, only 41.79 per cent voted for Ali Bongo whereas a clear majority of 58.21 per cent voted against him, has raised the question of Ali Bongo's legitimacy as the president of Gabon as well as the conformity of the 2003 constitutional amendment with the eternity clause enshrining democracy, republicanism, and pluralism as perpetual values. The results of these amendments are lifelong presidency and dynastic succession, which have been characterized as a constitutional coup[99] rather than an instantiation of the democracy, pluralism, and republican values that are protected as unamendable provisions.

The third case to highlight is the practice of constitutional amendment in Equatorial Guinea vis-à-vis the eternal values enshrined in the Constitution. As is the case in Cameroon with Paul Biya, and in Gabon with the Bongo family, Equatorial Guinea is characterized by a lifelong presidency and family reign. Here, the Nguema family has ruled the country since its independence from Spain in 1968. The current president, Teodoro Obiang Nguema, deposed his uncle, Francisco Macias Nguema, in a bloody coup on 3 August 1979 before taking over the reins. Today, he is the longest-serving president in the world.

[95] According to art 11 as amended, 'the term of office of the President of the Republic begins on the day of his taking the oath and ends upon the expiration of the seventh year following his election'.

[96] See Daniel Mengara, 'The Making of Monarchical Republic: The Undoing of Presidential Term Limits in Gabon under Omar Bongo' in Jack R Mangala (ed.), *The Politics of Challenging Presidential Term Limits in Africa* (Palgrave Macmillan 2020) 81.

[97] The new version of art 9 reads as follows: 'The President of the Republic is elected for a presidential term of seven (7) years, by universal and direct suffrage. The President is re-electable.'

[98] Levi M Midepani, 'Pratiques Électorales et Reproduction Oligarchique au Gabon. Analyses à Partir des Élections Législatives de 2006' (2009) 115(3) Politique Africaine 48.

[99] John M Mbaku, 'Threats to Democracy in Africa: The Rise of the Constitutional Coup' (*Brookings*, 30 October 2020) https://www.brookings.edu/blog/africa-in-focus/2020/10/30/threats-to-democracy-in-africa-the-rise-of-the-constitutional-coup/ accessed 30 July 2022.

Notably, one of the main tools he uses to remain in power is constitutional amendment, even though the Constitution prohibits any amendment affecting the republican form of the state or the democratic regime. For instance, in 2011 the Constitution was amended to impose a presidential term limit, which was welcomed by the media and civil society. According to the new version of the Constitution, 'the mandate of the President of the Republic is limited to two consecutive periods, not being able to present himself for a third mandate until an alternation is produced'.[100] However, this provision was seen as non-retrospective, which meant that President Obiang was allowed to run for two more constitutional terms. This is a trick that Yoweri Museveni also pulled off in Uganda by changing the Constitution and setting the clock back to zero.[101]

Most importantly, there were two other provisions undermining the principles of a republican state and democratic regime as enshrined in the eternity clauses. First, the 2011 amendment removed the presidential age limit, allowing Obiang Nguema to become one of the oldest and longest-serving presidents in the world.[102] Second, another provision with a dynastic flavour was the change to the presidential vacancy rules. Under the 1991 version of the Constitution:

> [I]n the event of vacancy of the Presidency, a college comprising the President of Parliament, who presides over it, the Prime Minister, the President of the Supreme Court and a member of the Constitutional Council designated by its president shall ensure the interim management of the state.[103]

But in 2011, as Tom Ginsburg notes, the vacancy rules were modified to clear the way for the ageing dictator to hand-pick his successor through the creation of a new vice-presidential position[104] that would assume the functions of president in a case of vacancy (death, permanent physical or mental incapacity, or resignation). Unsurprisingly, the president appointed his eldest son, who would become the legal successor to the presidency should the incumbent step down, die, or become incapacitated while in office.

In the examples of Cameroon, Gabon, and Equatorial Guinea, we have seen that no matter what principles or values are enshrined in eternity clauses, the practice of unconstitutional constitutional amendment can easily undermine them without check or review. Furthermore, in the cases of these three countries, the eternity clauses have remained intact in the constitutions despite the frequency of revisions. In other words, unlike in the Congolese case, where the eternity clause was completely removed, none of the provisions within the eternity clauses of these three countries were explicitly repealed. However, constitutional amendments have effectively undermined their substance, leaving them formally in place but significantly weakened due to the lack of judicial enforcement.

[100] art 36(2) of the Constitution of 1991, amended in 2011.

[101] See Ajifowoke Michael Gbenga, 'Africa's "President for Life" Trend Continues as Museveni Seeks Reelection' (*Ventures Africa*, 19 March 2019) https://venturesafrica.com/museveni-seeks-reelection/ accessed 1 October 2023.

[102] Under art 33 of the Constitution of 1991, the age limit for presidential candidates was 75 years. This provision was removed in 2011 when President Nguema was 69 years old.

[103] art 43(2) of the Constitution of 1991 as amended by Constitutional Law No 1/1995 of 17 January 1995.

[104] Tom Ginsburg, 'Voting Underway in Equatorial Guinea' (*I.CONnect blog*, 11 November 2021) http://www.iconnectblog.com/2011/11/voting-underway-in-equatorial-guinea/ accessed 2 August 2022.

3.1.3 Suspension: The cases of Chad and the Central African Republic

The practice of unconstitutional change of government,[105] considered a crime under the Malabo Protocol,[106] undoubtedly constitutes a suspension of the republican form of the state, which in all the CEMAC countries is held as an eternal value.

By and large, unconstitutional changes of government—defined as the commission, or ordering to be committed, of a number of specified acts with the aim of illegally accessing or maintaining power, including a putsch or *coup d'état* against a democratically elected government[107]—are one of the common challenges the African continent is still facing. This is evident, for instance, in the recent wave of *coups d'état* in the Economic Community of West African States (ECOWAS) region,[108] leading Oumarou Narey to wonder whether they have not become a new mode of accession to power.[109] In the CEMAC countries, this phenomenon can be understood as a practical way to undermine what are considered eternal values under the constitution.

In the case of a *coup d'état*, the state loses the inviolability of its eternity clauses, which are thereby neutralized: consequently, none of the principles and values of the eternity clauses can be asserted, even if a political transition takes place to pave the way back to constitutional order.[110] During the transitional period, even if the new authorities are appointed by consensus, they do not have the democratic legitimacy necessary to run a republican form of state as enshrined in the eternity clauses. Therefore, unamendable provisions seem merely illusory in the context of the suspension of the constitutional order. This is confirmed by a factual analysis of the practice of unconstitutional change of government in Chad and the Central African Republic.

In the case of the Central African Republic, the country has been linked historically with *coups d'état* ever since its independence from France,[111] a practice which has led to the suspension of the constitutional order and consequently the eternity clauses. In the case of Chad, a recent *coup d'état* followed the death of President Idriss Déby when the military seized power and installed his then 37-year-old son, Mahamat Idriss Déby, a military commander, as interim president. Parliament and the government were dissolved, and the Constitution was suspended.

The Constitution stipulates that, upon the death of the president, their duties are exercised provisionally by the president of the National Assembly, who is to lead the country to

[105] See Oumarou Narey, 'Les Changements Anticonstitutionnels de Gouvernement: Mode ou Contre-mode?' (*ACL-AIDC Blog*, 28 June 2022) https://blog-iacl-aidc.org/transformations/2022/6/28/les-changements-anticonstitutionnels-de-gouvernement-mode-ou-contre-mode accessed 3 July 2022; Charles M Fombad, 'Countering the Scourge of Unconstitutional Changes of Government in Africa' (*IACL-AIDC Blog*, 16 June 2022) https://blog-iacl-aidc.org/transformations/2022/6/16/countering-the-scourge-of-unconstitutional-changes-of-government-in-africa accessed 2 August 2022.

[106] Harmen Van Der Wilt, 'Unconstitutional Change of Government: A New Crime within the Jurisdiction of the African Criminal Court' in Charles C Jalloh, Kamari M Clarke, and Vincent O Nmehielle (eds.), *The African Court of Justice and Human and Peoples' Rights in Context: Development and Challenges* (CUP 2019) 619–42; Abdoulaye Soma, 'Le Crime International de Changement Anticonstitutionnel de Gouvernement' (2016) 26(3) Revue Suisse de Droit International et Européen 417.

[107] See Protocol on Amendments to the Protocol on the Statute of the African Court of Justice and Human Rights, STC/Legal/Min7(1) Rev I, African Union; First Meeting of the Specialised Technical Committee on Justice and Legal Affairs, 15–16 May 2014, Addis Ababa, Ethiopia.

[108] The affected ECOWAS member states are Burkina Faso, Guinea, Mali, and Niger.

[109] See Narey (n 105).

[110] Valérie E Soma Kaboré, 'La Forme Républicaine de l'État comme Clause d'éternité Constitutionnelle' (2019) 58 Revue Burkinabè de Droit 96.

[111] See Francis Laloupo, 'Coup d'État réussi en Centrafrique' (2003) 11 Géopolitique Africaine 141–49.

elections within 90 days.[112] The Constitution also states that any candidate for president must be at least 45 years old and a civilian, thus excluding Mahamat Idriss Déby, who was 37 at the time and an army general. Moreover, the eternity clause provides that the republican form of state and the principle of the separation of powers are values which are protected perpetually. The military ignored these provisions. In suspending the Constitution, they thus suspended its eternal values; these include the republican form of state, in terms of which it is the right of the people to choose their own officers for governmental administration and to pass their own laws.

It follows from this discussion that the use of eternity clauses as a tool to entrench constitutional values and principles is unable to prevent the abusive practice of unconstitutional constitutional change. Likewise, eternity clauses are neutralized in cases of coups leading to the suspension of the constitutional order. The frequency of coups and abusive unconstitutional constitutional change challenge the purpose of eternity clauses, especially since their judicial enforcement is not guaranteed.

4. Judicial enforcement: The weakness of eternity clauses

Eternity clauses are meaningless as tools for entrenching constitutional values if there are no measures to ensure their enforceability by way of a genuine judicial review. As Michael Hein rightly points out, when the constitutionality of constitutional amendments is under review, it is an obvious choice for courts to refer to a constitutional entrenchment clause since provisions like these set explicit limits to constitutional change.[113] Thus, the first means of enforcing eternity clauses is to undertake a judicial review of compliance with the constitutional amendment requirements. However, an examination of the constitutional framework for judicial review in the CEMAC countries shows that courts do not have explicit authority to rule on constitutional amendments. More importantly, on the rare occasions when they have intervened in the constitutional amendment process, their interpretations have served to weaken rather than bolster the eternity clauses.

4.1 The constitutional framework for judicial review of compliance

In general, constitutions and organic laws in francophone and lusophone countries in Africa do not explicitly empower constitutional or supreme courts to hear cases related to constitutional amendment laws. Theoretically, this trend may be explained by the influence in such countries of the French Constitution and French doctrine generally. As Georges Vedel notes, 'the amending power is the expression of sovereignty in all its plenitude',[114]

[112] art 81 of the Constitution of Chad reads as follows: 'In case of vacancy of the Presidency of the Republic for any cause, or of definite incapacity as declared by the Supreme Court, referred to by the Government, and deciding with the absolute majority of its members, the duties of the President of the Republic, with the exception of the powers specified in Articles 85, 88, 95 and 96, are provisionally exercised by the President of the National Assembly and, in case of incapacity of the latter, by the First Vice President.'

[113] Michael Hein, 'Do Constitutional Entrenchment Clauses Matter? Constitutional Review of Constitutional Amendment in Europe' (2020) 18(1) International Journal of Constitutional Law 82.

[114] Georges Vedel, 'Schengen et Maastricht (à propos de la décision no 91-294 DC du Conseil constitutionnel du 25 Juillet 1991)' (1992) 8(2) Revue Française de Droit Administratif 173–78.

and therefore it cannot be subject to constitutional scrutiny—a position which is regularly recalled by the French Constitutional Council in its jurisprudence.[115] Constitutional justice institutions in African countries such as Senegal[116] and the Comoros[117] consistently declare their incompetence to rule on the constitutionality of constitutional amendments. However, other constitutional courts, such as those of Benin,[118] Mali,[119] and Niger,[120] take the opposite approach and interpret their constitutions, albeit by different lines of reasoning, as allowing them to review constitutional amendments.[121]

In the CEMAC countries, constitutions are, by and large, drafted without expressly recognizing the power of constitutional courts, councils, or supreme courts to rule on constitutional amendments. In most cases, constitutional judicial bodies have jurisdiction over the constitutionality of ordinary laws, organic laws, and international treaties.[122] Constitutional amendment bills, though, are generally not mentioned, with the exception being the Constitution of the Central African Republic, which provides that the Constitutional Court is competent to give its opinion on bills or proposals relating to constitutional revision.[123]

Nevertheless, it would be to the benefit of certain provisions in the constitutions of the CEMAC countries if the jurisdiction of constitutional courts to rule on constitutional amendments could be determined. Courts such as the Constitutional Tribunals of Equatorial Guinea or Gabon could rely on vague wording such as 'other categories of laws'[124] or 'any other matters'[125] to declare their competence on constitutional amendment. It would not be ingenious to do so, since the Constitutional Court of Mali has adopted such reasoning.[126] Other provisions give power to constitutional courts to interpret the constitution or to serve as an advisory body at the behest of public authorities such as the president or Members of Parliament.

In the case of Congo, for instance, the Constitutional Court relied on its power to interpret the Constitution in order to give an opinion on a presidential initiative in 2015 to change the Constitution by referendum.[127] It must be admitted that the 2002 Constitution of Congo did not expressly provide for the Constitutional Court's competence in matters

[115] See eg French Constitutional Council, Decision No 92-312 of 2 September 1992; Decision No 2003-469DC of 26 March 2003.

[116] See Decision No 1/C/2003 of 11 June 2003; Decision No 3/C/2005 of 18 January 2006; Decision No 2/C/2009 of 18 June 2009.

[117] See Constitutional Court of Comoros, Judgement No 09-009/CC of 6 May 2009.

[118] Constitutional Court of Benin, Judgement No DCC 06-074, 8 July 2006; Constitutional Court of Benin, Judgement No DCC 11-67, 11 October 2011.

[119] Constitutional Court of Mali, Decision No 01-128 of 11 and 12 December 2001.

[120] Constitutional Court of Niger, Decision No 002/2009/CC of 25 May 2009.

[121] See Charles M Fombad, 'An Overview of the Legal Framework for Amending Modern African Constitutions', in Chapter 1 of this volume.

[122] See Constitution of Equatorial Guinea (2012), art 101; Constitution of Gabon (2011), art 84; Constitution of Cameroon (2008), art 47; Constitution of Congo (2015), art 175.

[123] Constitution of the Central African Republic (2016), art 95.

[124] art 85 of the Constitution of Gabon provides as follows: 'Other categories of law as well as regulatory acts may be deferred to the Constitutional Court either by the President of the Republic, the Prime Minister, the presidents of the Chambers of Parliament or a tenth of members from each Chamber, the presidents of the Supreme Court, the Council of the State and the Court of Accountancy, or any citizen or moral person damaged by the law or act in dispute.'

[125] According to art 101(2)(h) of the Constitution of Equatorial Guinea, the Constitutional Tribunal is competent to address 'any other matters that the laws attribute to it'.

[126] Constitutional Court of Mali, Decision No 01-128 of 11 and 12 December 2001.

[127] Constitutional Court, Decision No 002-ACC-SVC/15 of 17 September 2015.

of interpretation. But in the 2015 case, the Court invoked the organic law on its organization and functioning, which expressly provided, in article 36, for the possibility of the Constitutional Court's being seized by the president of the republic and the presidents of the two parliamentary chambers with a view to interpreting a constitutional provision.[128] Likewise, the Court added that the organic law allows it to give an opinion on any matters within its competence.

These two provisions were thus considered, notwithstanding the Court's lack of an express power in the Constitution to rule on constitutional amendments, to be the legal basis for the Court to give an opinion on the proposal of the president to introduce a constitutional change with the effect of removing the presidential term limit. The problem with this mechanism, though, is that it would depend on a referral by political actors, who are often unconcerned with the application or interpretation of the law. It must be recognized that this reasoning sought to legitimize the decision of the president by giving him a judicial go-ahead rather than to determine the justiciability of constitutional amendment laws before the Court.

Similarly, the Constitutional Council of Chad, in 2004, accepted to rule on the constitutionality of a constitutional amendment introduced by the president of the republic.[129] The Council was seized by Members of Parliament to examine the constitutional amendment initiated by President Idriss Déby allowing him to stand for elections again. Surprisingly, the Council, without indicating the basis on which it accepted to rule on constitutional amendment, declared that the request should be declared admissible. Arguably, it may be surmised that the Court did not differentiate between organic, ordinary, and constitutional law, since the 1996 Constitution simply provided that 'the constitutional council is competent to rule on the constitutionality of laws, treaties, and international agreements'[130] without giving further detail. The same reasoning was adopted by the Constitutional Court of Burundi when it declared that the powers conferred on it to review the constitutionality of laws implicitly also gave it the powers to review the regularity of laws amending the Constitution.[131] Be that as it may, the Court dismissed the request, declaring that the constitutional amendment was in conformity with the Constitution, and thereby giving the president the green light to amend the Constitution.

In the light of the above, it is clear that judicial enforcement of eternity clauses is not guaranteed by the wording of the constitutions of the countries under study, seeing as the review of constitutional amendments is not a power expressly in the hands of the constitutional courts. However, through the power of consultation (in the Central African Republic), or interpretation of the constitution (in Congo and Chad), courts can intervene in constitutional revisions before their adoption. But the crux of the matter remains: when courts intervene in the review of the constitution, do they do so with the effect of enforcing the eternity clauses or weakening them?

[128] According to Organic Law No 1-2003 of 17 January 2003 on the Organization and Functioning of the Constitutional Court, '[t]he Constitutional Court may be seized for interpretation of constitutional provisions by the authorities referred to in article 35 of the present law.'

[129] Constitutional Council of Chad, Decision No 001/CC/SG/04 of 11 June 2004, on the proposal of 31 March 1996 to revise the Constitution.

[130] Constitution of Chad (1996), art 161.

[131] Constitutional Court of Burundi, RCCB/40 of 18 April 1994.

4.2 Judicial interpretation of eternity clauses

On two occasions, constitutional jurisdictions in the CEMAC region have ruled on constitutional amendments, thereby interpreting the principles and values enshrined in the eternity clauses. In the first case, ruled on in 2015, the Constitutional Court of Congo avoided the eternity clause, while in the second, in 2020, the Constitutional Court of the Central African Republic admitted the possibility of circumventing the eternity clause.

4.2.1. The Constitutional Court of Congo

In 2015, the Constitutional Court of Congo issued a decision pertaining to constitutional change in which it simply ignored the requirements stemming from the eternity clause.[132] The Court had to examine the legal basis of the referendum held at the behest of the president of the republic. According to the Congolese Constitution of 2001, referendums can be decreed under two different procedures. The first one relates to article 110, which is part of Title VI of the Constitution regulating legislative power and containing the structure and function of Parliament. According to this provision, Parliament 'has the initiative of referendums, concurrently with the President of the Republic'. The second provision is article 186, which is part of Title XVIII relating to the revision of the Constitution.[133] Within this Title, article 185 contains an eternity clause that entrenches the presidential term limit and the republican and secular forms of the state.

Given this constitutional framework, the president sought to introduce a constitutional change to remove the presidential term limit by resorting to article 110, relating to the legislative referendum, and not article 186, dealing with constitutional revision. Thus, the Court had to give an opinion on the constitutionality of the legal basis invoked by the president in order to consult the people by way of a referendum 'on the evolution of the institutions of the Republic'. This question is similar to the one raised before the Constitutional Court of Niger six years earlier.[134] In 2009, the Constitutional Court of Niger ruled that the legislative referendum procedure provided for in article 49 of the Constitution cannot be utilized as a legal basis to amend the Constitution. The only way to amend the Constitution is by recourse to articles 134, 135, and 136, which contain the eternity clause.

Welcomed by scholars[135] and rejected by the president of Niger,[136] this reasoning was not followed by the Constitutional Court of Congo, which ruled that such a referendum was in the power of the president and in complete conformity with the Constitution. The Court accepted the president's use of a legislative referendum rather than the constitutional amendment process, as a means to effect constitutional change. In doing so, it merely ignored the eternity clause prohibiting any change seeking to remove or extend the

132 Constitutional Court, Decision No 002-ACC-SVC/15 of 17 September 2015.

133 The article provides as follows: 'When it emanates from the President of the Republic, the bill of revision is submitted directly to referendum, after the opinion of conformity of the Constitutional Court. When it emanates from the Parliament, the proposal of revision must be voted by two thirds of the members of the two chambers of the Parliament meeting in Congress, after the opinion of conformity of the Constitutional Court. In the two cases, the revision is only definitive after being approved by referendum.'

134 Constitutional Court of Niger, Decision No 002/2009/CC of 25 May 2009.

135 Fabrice Hourquebie and Wanda Mastor, 'Les cours Constitutionnelles et Suprêmes Étrangères et les Élections Présidentielles' (2012) 34 Nouveaux Cahiers du Conseil Constitutionnel 143-162.

136 After this ruling, he dissolved Parliament and the Court, holding a referendum in August 2009 that approved the extension of the term.

presidential term limit. What is more, surprisingly enough, it made no mention of constitutional revision or replacement in its opinion, instead choosing to use the term 'evolution of the institutions of the Republic'.

This choice is far from trivial. Referring to 'constitutional change' would mean that the legal basis could not be article 110 but Title XVIII regulating the procedure of revision and mentioning the eternity clause. Referring to 'constitutional replacement' would have been likely to lead to the reasoning of the Constitutional Court of Niger, according to which, unless a new state is being formed or a similarly revolutionary occurrence is undeniable, a new constitution must be seen as emanating from the revision procedures present in the old. In effect, a new constitution should be seen as the simultaneous revision of most or all of the provisions of the old one.

Thus, introducing the concept of 'the evolution of the institutions of the Republic' was perceived as a novel approach, which prompted a creative interpretation of the Constitution to navigate away from the constitutional deadlock caused by the eternity clause. This interpretation led the Court to rule that the president possesses 'the privilege to use this constitutional prerogative', which allows him or her to 'initiate proceedings with the aim of submitting to the general public, for approval or rejection, a text or any other matter of national interest, as the one for the evolution of the institutions of the republic'. This reasoning is proof once again that eternity clauses are merely aspirational: here, a court interpreted a constitutional change that had the effect of infringing them, yet made its interpretation without any reference to these clauses.

4.2.2 The Constitutional Court of the Central African Republic

On 5 June 2020 and 23 September 2022, the Constitutional Court of the Central African Republic issued two landmark decisions pertaining to the constitutional amendment and eternity-clause requirement.[137]

4.2.2.1 The 2020 opinion

During the upheaval of the Covid-19 pandemic, the president of the National Assembly of the Central African Republic introduced a bill seeking to amend the Constitution.[138] In terms of the bill, the president and Members of Parliament would be allowed to continue their mandate due to the pandemic, the argument being that the country would not be able to hold an election by the end of the year (December 2020). In the process, the constitutional amendment bill introduced the possibility of postponing the presidential and parliamentary elections in a case of *force majeure*. The government argued that the proposed amendment would be beneficial in filling a void in the Constitution given that the current constitutional framework was silent on the issue of holding elections under unprecedented circumstances such as those associated with the Covid-19 pandemic; at the same time, article 153 of the Constitution has a clause that explicitly prohibits any revision relating to the number and duration of presidential mandates.

[137] Constitutional Court of the Central African Republic, Decision No 15/CC/20 of 5 June 2020 and Decision No 009/CC/22 of 23 September 2022.

[138] See Seni M Ouédraogo and Djibrinah Ouédraogo, 'Les Élections Présidentielles et Législatives à l'épreuve de la COVID-19: Une Mise en Lumière en Afrique de l'Ouest Francophone' (*Afrilex*, 2020) https://base.afriquegouvernance.net/docs/afrilex_les_elections_presidentielles_et_legislatives_covid_seni_m_djibrihina_ouedraogo_21_04_2020.pdf accessed 23 July 2022.

Against this background, the key issue was the conformity of the amendment bill to the eternity clause. Article 105 of the Constitution declares as follows:

> The bills or proposals of constitutional law are referred for [its] opinion to the Constitutional Court by the President of the Republic, the President of the National Assembly, or the President of the Senate before being submitted to a vote of the Parliament or to a referendum.

It was on this basis that the Constitutional Court was asked to give an opinion on the constitutionality of the amendment bill, which would have an impact on the duration of the presidential term and on the eternity clause prohibiting any amendment relating to it. Surprisingly, the Court opined that the constitutional amendment was unconstitutional, in that:

> Considering that the combined examination of these constitutional provisions indicates that the people have unequivocally expressed their will to establish a constitutional safeguard regarding the term limit of the President of the Republic— a safeguard that no one, not even their representatives, the deputies, may alter or remove without betraying this sovereign will.[139]

The Court added that the proposed amendment would necessarily have an impact on article 35[140] and lead to a modification of the duration of the presidential term, which is protected as an unamendable provision. More interestingly, although the eternity clause refers explicitly to presidential term limits, the Court, through a progressive interpretation, considered that any amendment impacting on the mandate of the Members of Parliament would also be unconstitutional. Therefore, any attempt to postpone the national elections (presidential or legislative) through a constitutional amendment is a violation of the so-called eternity clause under article 135 of the Constitution.

Furthermore, the Constitutional Court used another means to entrench the current constitution and, by extension, the unamendable presidential term limits. It interpreted the presidential oath, which appears in article 38 and includes an obligation for the president 'to respect and uphold the Constitution which the people have freely given themselves'. The Court concluded that a president who seeks to amend the Constitution in this regard would be violating their oath.

This opinion had the effect of halting the amendment process. The presidential election was indeed held in December 2020, as initially planned in accordance with the electoral calendar. This shows that the Constitutional Court of the Central African Republic is courageously standing up for the respect of the rule of law and demonstrating its ability to uphold

[139] Author's translation. The original text in French states: '*Considérant que l'examen combiné de ces dispositions constitutionnelles indiquent que le peuple a clairement manifesté sa volonté d'instituer un verrou constitutionnel en ce qui concerne le mandat du Président de la République, verrou que nul ne peut, pas même ses représentants, les députés, sauf à trahir cette volonté, ni supprimer, ni modifier.*'

[140] art 35 provides as follows: 'The President of the Republic is elected by universal direct suffrage and by secret majority ballot, in two (2) rounds. The duration of the mandate of the President of the Republic is of five (5) years. The mandate is renewable one sole time. In no case, may the President of the Republic exercise more than two (2) consecutive mandates or extend it for whatever motive that may be.'

the eternity clause, as other jurisdictions in francophone African countries have already done.[141] However, the Court has gone further and opened the door to the possibility of circumventing the so-called eternity clause. It pointed out hypothetical means of adapting the Constitution without violating the eternity clause.

The first means would be to adapt the Constitution to the realities of the pandemic through a referendum. The Court argued that only the people could decide whether exceptional circumstances circumvent the unamendable presidential term limit that they instituted. Put simply, the people, through a referendum, could decide to unlock the unamendable provisions.[142] Nevertheless, the Court did not clarify whether the referendum should be held in accordance with the process of constitutional amendment, as stipulated by the Constitution itself,[143] or whether it is about a referendum to adopt a new constitution (replacement).[144] But, relying on the reasoning of the Constitutional Court of Niger, there are only two possibilities for arriving at a new constitution: first, through the creation of a new state; and, second, when the constitution of an existing state has been suspended or abrogated as a result of an extra-constitutional de facto situation.[145] None of these contingencies applied in the present case.

We may think that the Constitutional Court of the Central African Republic was referring to a constitutional amendment through a referendum, as provided by article 152. In this regard, it would mean that the eternity clause is never eternal. The unamendable provision can be unlocked by the people under certain circumstances without replacing the current constitution. In other words, whatever the people do, they can undo.

All in all, the Constitutional Court recognizes that the constitutional amendment undermining the eternity clause can be effected through a particular procedure leading to a referendum. However, it must be noted that this reasoning is somewhat problematic: the Court seems to completely gloss over the fact that a referendum under article 152 is an option and not an obligation. In other words, the Constitution envisages a referendum as a secondary, and not the primary, method of approval of a constitutional amendment. The Court seems to change the Constitution through this judicial interpretation, making a referendum mandatory when it comes to amending a provision protected by the eternity clause.

As it happened, though, the Court concluded that this way of circumventing the eternity clause was not possible in this particular case, as it would be difficult to hold a referendum timeously (that is, before the planned date of the presidential election). It then explored another means of circumventing the eternity clause at issue in order to adapt the Constitution to the realities of the Covid-19 pandemic. The second option involved an informal constitutional amendment. According to the Court:

[141] See eg Constitutional Court of Niger, Decision No 002/2009/CC of 25 May 2009; Constitutional Court of Mali, Decision No 01-128 of 11 and 12 December 2001; Constitutional Council of Burkina Faso, Decision No 2015-046/CC of 5 November 2015; Court Constitutional of Benin, Judgment No DCC 06-074 of 8 July 2006; Constitutional Court of Benin, Judgment No DCC 11-67 of 11 October 2011.

[142] See art 6 of the opinion: '*est d'avis que la Constitution ne peut être révisée dans le sens d'introduire des dispositions pouvant permettre de reporter les élections ou d'autoriser un glissement du calendrier électoral qui impacterait la durée du mandat du Président de la République, sauf à recourir au référendum*.'

[143] See art 152. According to this article, '[t]he revision intervenes when the bill presented in complete form *[a l'état]* has been voted by the Parliament meeting in Congress with a majority of three-quarters (3/4) of the members who compose it or has been adopted by referendum.'

[144] As was the case with the adoption of the current Constitution.

[145] Constitutional Court of Niger, Decision No 002/2009/CC of 25 May 2009.

> if the constitutional and legal deadlines for the electoral process cannot be respected, and will obviously lead to the date of 31 March 2021 being exceeded, it is necessary, *without proceeding to a revision of the constitution*, to resort to a consensual approach through a national consultation carried out within a short period of time, bringing together in one place the various entities, notably the executive, the legislature, the political parties, the civil society, the former presidents of the republic, the former heads of state, the institutions of the republic (except the Constitutional Court), this in order to reach a consensual solution that can frame the postponement of the elections and the shift of the electoral calendar that has become unavoidable.[146]

This national consultation, according to the Court, should be led by the executive and the results reviewed by the Court in order to affirm their conformity to the Constitution. By way of this reasoning, the Court admitted the possibility of amending the Constitution through an agreement between political, institutional, and social actors, given the circumstances.

The Constitutional Court's proposal lends support to Hans Kelsen's observation that 'there is no legal possibility of preventing a constitution from being modified by way of custom, even if the constitution has the character of statutory law'[147] or, one may add, if it includes a number of unamendable provisions. What Kelsen refers to as 'custom' is, according to Richard Albert, what we understand as a 'constitutional convention': a rule that creates an obligation, confers rights or powers, or otherwise governs the conduct of political actors.[148] Indeed, it is generally acknowledged that eternity clauses can be circumvented through unwritten understandings and conventions.

Taking inspiration from this assessment, the Constitutional Court of the Central African Republic has explored a practical solution that does not involve a formal amendment to the Constitution. What the Constitutional Court proposed is what Richard Albert called the 'informal constitutional change by incorporation, more exactly incorporation by void-filing'.[149] Indeed, the crux of the matter, in this case, is that the Constitution is silent on the possibility of postponing elections under exceptional circumstances, such as Covid-19. Thus, through an agreement, political actors as well as civil society can fill the void in the existing constitution without amending it formally. At the same time, the national consultation would have the effect of neutralizing the presidential term limit as an eternity clause and suspending it until the holding of the next elections.

In sum, as the analysis shows, this opinion of the Constitutional Court of the Central African Republic is proof, once again, that constitutions are not documents cast in stone. Despite the presence of eternity clauses, there is always a way, if necessary, to amend the

[146] Author's translation, emphasis added. The original text in French is as follows: '*si les délais constitutionnels et légaux du processus électoral ne peuvent être respectés, et conduisent manifestement au dépassement de la date du 31 mars 2021, il est nécessaire, sans procéder à une révision de la constitution, de recourir à une approche consensuelle à travers une consultation nationale réalisée dans un délai court, réunissant en un même lieu les différentes entités, notamment le pouvoir exécutif, le pouvoir législatif, les partis politiques, la société civile, les anciens présidents de la république, les anciens chefs d'État, les institutions de la république, ceci afin de parvenir à une solution consensuelle pouvant encadrer le report des élections et le décalage du calendrier électoral devenu inévitable*'.

[147] Hans Kelsen, *General Theory of Law and State* (Anders Wedberg tr, Harvard University Press 1945) 259.

[148] Richard Albert, 'How Unwritten Constitutional Norms Change Written Constitutions' (2015) 38(2) Dublin University Law Journal 387–417, 390.

[149] Ibid.

constitution by referendum or to adapt it through constitutional conventions or political agreement as a result of a national consultation. Put simply, nothing is immune from change.

4.2.2.2 The 2022 ruling

On 23 September 2022, at the request of Central African citizens and the country's legally constituted political parties, the Constitutional Court ruled on the president of the republic's attempt to write a new constitution with the view to resetting the presidential term count, a move that clearly would contravene the term-limit rule protected by the eternity clause.[150] As was the case before the Constitutional Court of Niger in 2009,[151] the Constitutional Court of the Central African Republic maintained that neither the president of the republic nor the president of the National Assembly has the right to initiate the repeal of the current constitution and its replacement by another one, even by referendum. The Court argued that 'the repeal of a constitution occurs after a violent event profoundly affecting the functioning of the State, such as a coup d'état, or when it is necessary to change the nature of the political regime'.[152] Since this was not the case in the circumstances at hand, the resort to the repeal of the Constitution was contrary to the constitutional order and amounted to an unconstitutional change.

Moreover, in its analysis of the eternity clause, the Court held that this remained immune from change. Contrary to its opinion in 2020, it adopted a firmer tone by noting that:

> the constitution of March 30, 2016, excludes the revision of the intangible provisions set forth in Article 153 of the Constitution, that these exclusions are binding on the current President of the Republic by the oath he took at his installation, and that he cannot contravene them in his favor even by resorting to a referendum.[153]

Two elements require particular attention here. The first is the oath of the president of the republic, which, according to the Court, constitutes an essential foundation for his (or her) respect of the eternity clause. The second is that, contrary to its 2020 opinion, the Court maintained that the eternity clause cannot be violated even by referendum. Here, the Court did not explore the option of a national consultation, as it did in its 2020 opinion. Thus, in its 2022 decision, it reinforces the normativity and absolute nature of the eternity clause, which cannot be subject to revision by parliamentary or referendum means, and underlines that such an obligation arises from the oath of the president of the republic.

The Constitutional Court's avowed commitment to protecting the eternity clause is laudable, but this raises the question of how its judicial decisions are received by the political authorities. While it is true that Constitutional Court decisions are not subject to appeal and are binding on public authorities, the reaction of the Central African authorities has been to weaken the Court's jurisdiction. In response to this decision, the president of the Court was forced to retire early, paving the way for the president of the republic to retable the

[150] Constitutional Court of the Central African Republic, Ruling No 009/CC/22 of 23 September 2022.
[151] Constitutional Court of Niger (n 145).
[152] Constitutional Court of the Central African Republic, Ruling No 009/CC/22 of 23 September 2022 11.
[153] Ibid. 16.

reform.[154] Indeed, the president submitted a request to the Constitutional Court in January 2023 to validate his proposal to convene a referendum notwithstanding the decision of 23 September 2022, which the Court, in turn, proceeded to authorize on 20 January 2023.[155]

5. Concluding remarks: Better to think of 'rigidity' than 'eternity'

The preceding discussion has shown that recourse to eternity clauses as a tool for entrenching constitutional values is a common feature in all of the countries in the CEMAC region. Such clauses were touted as a legal means to curb the fever of frequent, abusive, and opportunistic constitutional manipulation that has wracked every CEMAC state without exception. Thus, during the third wave of democratization in the post-1990 era constitution-makers have borrowed the concept of unamendable provisions from the Constitution of the Fifth French Republic.

The result has been twofold. On the one hand, certain principles have been enshrined in the constitutions as immutable or perpetual principles or values, among them republicanism, secularism, democracy, national unity, and territorial integrity. On the other, none of the constitutions of the six countries currently contain specific provisions that are declared unamendable, as is the case in Germany[156] or Tunisia.[157] The Constitution of Congo (2001) provided an eternity clause seeking to entrench the rights enunciated in its Titles I and II, but these were removed from the eternity clause under the 2015 Constitution. The Constitution of the Central African Republic considers the provision of article 153 as unamendable—but, here, it is a legal tool designed to protect the eternity clause itself from being amended, as is also the case in the Constitution of Senegal.[158]

These results notwithstanding, it can be concluded from the empirical study presented in this chapter that eternity clauses in CEMAC countries are, in sum, a matter of much ado about nothing. On the one hand, their presence has not prevented frequent and abusive constitutional amendments that alter the principles or values protected in such clauses. State leaders, sometimes with the complicity of constitutional courts, have developed a variety of strategies to circumvent so-called eternity clauses through either 'unconstitutional constitutional change' (replacement or revision) or the suspension of the constitutional order itself. On the other hand, the wording of the eternity clauses in the CEMAC countries is highly ambiguous, given that the scope and substance of the entrenched principles and values is not easy to characterize. The concepts of republicanism, secularism, democracy, national unity, and territorial integrity are far from precise—indeed, they are excessively broad and flexible, as a result of which they may be interpreted in one way or another depending on who is doing the interpretation and when. The clauses are thus more aspirational or declarative in nature than they are enforceable.

[154] Adem K Adebe, 'Africa's Next Wannabe Third-term Presidents Must Be Stopped' (*Opinion, Al Jazeera* 21 October 2022) https://www.aljazeera.com/opinions/2022/10/21/africas-next-wannabe-third-term-presidents-must-be-stopped accessed 25 January 2023.

[155] See 'Centrafrique: la Cour Constitutionnelle Autorise F.A Touadera à Convoquer un Référendum' (*Radio Ndekeluka*, 20 January 2023) https://www.radiondekeluka.org/actualites/politique/39874-centrafrique-la-cour-constitutionnelle-autorise-f-a-touadera-a-convoquer-un-referendum.html accessed 27 April 2023.

[156] art 79(3) of the Constitution of Germany prohibits any amendment of the rights enshrined in arts 1–20.

[157] arts 1 and 2 of the 2014 Constitution.

[158] See Constitution of Senegal (2001), art 103.

It follows from the above that the concept of unamendability merely creates the illusion of protection against manipulation of constitutional amendment powers and nothing more. This conclusion, arrived at through an empirical study of CEMAC countries, confirms once more the prevailing assumption in the literature that such provisions are 'a mere dormant declaration, a theoretical concept without any real practical implications',[159] or, as Jon Elster put it, 'the purpose of such unamendable clauses is, I believe, mainly symbolic'.[160] Other scholars have gone further, arguing that these clauses are not illusory but potentially dangerous.[161]

This being so, what is the alternative? If we agree that the aim of the concept of eternity clauses is to protect fundamental values and principles then, as scholars such as Charles Fombad[162] and Michel Louis Martin[163] have argued, there is no need to resort to the notion of unamendability to achieve that aim. A more realistic approach is what Michel Martin calls 'controlled revisability at scale'. According to him, it is advisable to differentiate, or hierarchize, the provisions of the fundamental law according to a scale of constitutionality determined by the constituent.[164] The idea, as reflected by the Ghanaian constituent power, would be to distinguish between entrenched provisions and especially entrenched provisions, and to make the process of amending the latter particularly difficult and protracted.[165]

This idea, oddly enough, emerges from the opinion issued by the Constitutional Court of the Central African Republic (as previously analysed), in which it stated that the amendment infringing the eternity clause could not be made through the process of approval before Parliament but only through the process of approval by referendum. Put differently, the Court seems to distinguish between the provisions amendable through the normal process (either by the Parliament or by referendum discretionarily decided by the president) and provisions that are amendable only by referendum.

In sum, the experience of eternity clauses in CEMAC countries prompts us to rethink the practicality of unamendability. It suggests that alternative mechanisms for safeguarding fundamental values and principles, such as controlled revisability at scale, may offer a more effective and flexible approach. This would align better with the dynamic nature of constitutional governance and the evolving needs of nations in the region.

Bibliography

Adebe A.K., 'Taming Regressive Constitutional Amendments: The African Court as a Continental (Super) Constitutional Court' (2019) 17(1) International Journal of Constitutional Law 89–117

Adebe A.K., 'Africa's Next Wannabe Third-term Presidents Must Be Stopped' (*Opinion, Al Jazeera*, October 2022) https://www.aljazeera.com/opinions/2022/10/21/africas-next-wannabe-third-term-presidents-must-be-stopped accessed 25 January 2023

159 Ladislav Vyhnánek, 'The Eternity Clause in the Czech Constitution as Limit to European Integration' (2015) 9(2) Vienna Journal on International Constitutional Law 240–52.

160 Jon Elster, 'Constitutionalism in Eastern Europe: An Introduction' (1991) 58(2) University of Chicago Law Review 471.

161 Fombad (n 5) 57; Friedman (n 29) 93–96.

162 Fombad (n 5) 27–60.

163 Michel L Martin, 'Pour un Constitutionnalisme de Quatrième Génération? Présidences Reconductibles, Prévisibilité Maitrisée à Échelle' in Oumarou Narey (ed.), *La Constitution* (L'Harmattan 2018) 91–125.

164 Ibid. 121.

165 Fombad (n 5) 58.

Adjolohun S.H., 'The Making and Remaking of National Constitutions in African Regional Courts' (2018) 1 African Journal of Comparative Constitutional Law 35–70

Aïdara M.M., 'Le Juge Constitutionnel Africain et le Contrôle des lois Portant Révision de la Constitution: Contribution à un Débat' (*Afrilex*, 2011) https://afrilex.u-bordeaux.fr/wp-content/uploads/2021/03/Article_Aidara_Le_juge_constitutionnel_1_-1.pdf accessed 20 July 2022

Albert R., 'The Expressive Function of Constitutional Amendment Rules' (2013) 59(2) McGill Law Journal 225–81

Albert R., 'Constitutional Amendment and Dismemberment' (2018) 43(1) Yale Journal of International Law 1–84

Albert R., 'How Unwritten Constitutional Norms Change Written Constitutions' (2015) 38(2) Dublin University Law Journal 387–417

Alexy A., 'On the Structure of Legal Principles' (2000) 13(3) Ratio Juris 294–304

Amougou, J.L.A., 'La Constitutionnalisation du Droit en Afrique: L'exemple de la Création du Conseil Constitutionnel Camerounais' (2004) 19 Annuaire Internationale de Justice Constitutionnelle 45–63

Akzin B., 'The Place of the Constitution in the Modern State' (1967) 2(1) Israel Law Review 12

Anyangwe C. and Fombad C.M., 'Cameroon and the Crisis of Constitutional Identity: Is Anglophone Identity Incompatible with a Cameroonian Constitutional Identity?' in Fombad C.M. and Steytler N. (eds.), *Constitutional Identity and Constitutionalism in Africa* (forthcoming)

Baranger D., 'The Language of Eternity: Judicial Review of the Amending Power in France (or the Absence Thereof)' (2011) 44(3) Israel Law Review 404

Bernal C., 'Unconstitutional Constitutional Amendments in the Case Study of Colombia: An Analysis of the Justification and Meaning of the Constitutional Replacement Doctrine' (2013) 11(2) International Journal of Constitutional Law 339

Bockenforde M. and others, *Judicial Review Systems in West Africa: A Comparative Analysis* (International IDEA 2016)

Cabanis A., 'La Laïcité dans les Constitutions de l'Afrique de Succession Coloniale Française' (2020) 8 Revue Internationale des Francophones http://rifrancophonies.com/index.php?id=1193 accessed 3 August 2022

Christakis T., 'La Sécession: Une Question de Simple Fait?' (2007) European Society of International Law 15

Diagne S.B., 'The Constitution of a "Laic" African and Muslim Country: Senegal' in Bâli A.U. and Lerner H. (eds.), *Constitution Writing, Religion and Democracy* (CUP 2017) 131

Diallo I., 'Pour un Examen Minutieux de la Question des Révisions de la Constitution dans les États Africains Francophones' (*Afrilex*, 2015) https://afrilex.u-bordeaux.fr/wp-content/uploads/2021/03/POUR_UN_EXAMEN_MINUTIEUX_DE_LA_QUESTION_DES_REVISIONS_DE_LA_CONSTITUTION_DANS_LES_ETATS_AFRICAINS_FRANCOPHONES.pdf accessed 20 July 2022

Diompy A.H., 'Les Dynamiques Récentes de la Justice Constitutionnelle en Afrique Francophone' (*Afrilex*, 2014) https://afrilex.u-bordeaux.fr/wp-content/uploads/2021/03/JOURNEE_DE_LA_JEUNE_RECHERCHE_EN_DROIT_CONSTITUTIONNEL.pdfaccessed 20 July 2022

Djedjro F.M., 'La Révision des Constitutions dans les États Africains Francophones: Esquisse de Bilan' (1992) 1 Revue de Droit Public 111–34

Dosso K., 'Les Pratiques Constitutionnelles dans les Pays d'Afrique Noire Francophone: Cohérences et Incohérence' (2012) 90 Revue Française de Droit Constitutionnel 57–85

Dworkin R., 'The Model of Rules' (1967–1968) 35 (1)University of Chicago Law Review 14

Dworkin R., *Taking Rights Seriously* (Harvard University Press 1977) 24

Enonchong L.S.E., *The Constitution and Governance in Cameroon* (Routledge Studies on Law in Africa 2021)

Enonchong L.S.E., 'Unconstitutional Constitutional Amendment or Constitutional Dismemberment? A Reappraisal of the Presidential Term Limit Amendment in Cameroon' (2022) 11(2) Global Constitutionalism 274–96

Elster J., 'Constitutionalism in Eastern Europe: An Introduction' (1991) 58(2) University of Chicago Law Review 471

Favoreu L., 'Le Droit Constitutionnel, Droit de la Constitution et Constitution du Droit' (1990) Revue Française de Droit Constitutionnel

Fombad C.M., 'The New Cameroonian Constitutional Council in a Comparative Perspective: Progress or Retrogression?' (1998) 42(2) Journal of African Law 172–86

Fombad C.M., 'Challenges to Constitutionalism and Constitutional Rights in Africa and the Enabling Role of Political Parties: Lessons and Perspectives from Southern Africa' (2007) 55(1) American Journal of Comparative Law 1–46

Fombad C.M., 'Limits on the Power to Amend Constitutions: Recent Trends in Africa and their Potential Impact on Constitutionalism' (2007) 6 University of Botswana Law Journal 55–56

Fombad C.M. and Inegbedion N.A., 'Presidential Term Limits and their Impact on Constitutionalism in Africa' in Murray C. and Fombad C.M. (eds.), *Fostering Constitutionalism in Africa* (Pretoria University Law Press 2010) 1–29

Fombad C.M., 'Constitutional Reforms and Constitutionalism in Africa: Reflections on Some Current Challenges and Future Prospects' (2011) 59(4) Buffalo Law Review 1007–108

Fombad C.M., 'Some Perspectives on Durability and Change under Modern African Constitutions' (2013) 11(2) International Journal of Constitutional Law 382–413

Fombad C.M., 'Strengthening Constitutional Order and Upholding the Rule of Law in Central Africa: Reversing the Descent Towards Symbolic Constitutionalism' (2014) 14(2) African Human Rights Law Journal 412–48

Fombad C.M., 'Conceptualising a Framework for Inclusive, Fair and Robust Multiparty Democracy in Africa: The Constitutionalisation of the Rights of Political Parties' (2015) 48(1) Verfassung und Recht in Übersee VRÜ 3–27

Fombad C.M. (ed.), *The Implementation of Modern African Constitutions: Challenges and Prospects* (Pretoria University Press 2016)

Fombad C.M., 'An Overview of Contemporary Models of Constitutional Review in Africa' in Fombad C.M. (ed.), *Constitutional Adjudication in Africa* (OUP 2017) 17–50

Fombad C.M., 'Developments in Cameroon Constitutional Law: The Year 2016' in Albert R. and others (eds.), 'The I·CONnect-Clough Center 2016 Global Review of Constitutional Law' (3 August 2017), available at SSRN: https://ssrn.com/abstract=3014378

Fombad C.M., 'Countering the Scourge of Unconstitutional Changes of Government in Africa' (*IACL-AIDC Blog*, 16 June 2022) https://blog-iacl-aidc.org/transformations/2022/6/16/countering-the-scourge-of-unconstitutional-changes-of-government-in-africa accessed 2 August 2022

France 24 News, 'Cameroon Parliament Extends Biya's Term Limit' (*France 24 News*, 11 April 2008) https://www.france24.com/en/20080411-cameroon-parliament-paul-biya-term-limit-extension accessed 1 October 2023

Freedom House, 'Freedom in the World 2010 – Cameroon' (*Refworld*, 3 May 2010) https://www.refworld.org/docid/4c0ceafec.html accessed 12 July 2022.

Friedman A., 'Dead Hand Constitutionalism: The Danger of Eternity Clauses in New Democracies' (2011) 4(1) Mexican Law Review 77–96

Gbenga A.M., 'Africa's "President for Life" Trend Continues as Museveni Seeks Reelection' (*Ventures Africa*, 19 March 2019) https://venturesafrica.com/museveni-seeks-reelection/ accessed 1 October 2023

Ginsburg T., Melton J., and Elkins Z., 'On the Evasion of Executive Term Limits' (2011) 52 (6)William & Mary Law Review 1806–18

Gözler K., *Le Pouvoir de Révision Constitutionnelle* (Presses Universitaires du Septentrion 1997) 137

Hatchard J., 'Perfecting Imperfections: Developing Procedures for Amending Constitutions in Commonwealth Africa' (1998) 36 (3) Journal of Modern African Studies 381

Hein M., 'Do Constitutional Entrenchment Clauses Matter? Constitutional Review of Constitutional Amendment in Europe' (2020) 18(1) International Journal of Constitutional Law 82

Hourquebie F. and Mastor W., 'Les Cours Constitutionnelles et Suprêmes étrangères et les élections Présidentielles' (2012) 34 Nouveaux Cahiers du Conseil Constitutionnel 143-162

International Court of Justice, 'Case Concerning the Land and Maritime Boundary between Cameroon and Nigeria (2002)' (ICJ Report, 2002) 303

Kamto M., 'Révision Constitutionnelle ou Écriture d'une Nouvelle Constitution' (1996) 23–24 Lex Lata 17–20

Kelsen H., *General Theory of Law and State* (Wedberg A tr, Harvard University Press 1945) 259

Kenny D. and McCann L.M., 'Directive Principles, Political Constitutionalism, and Constitutional Culture: The Case of Ireland's Failed Directive Principles of Social Policy' (2022) 18(2) European Constitutional Law Review 207–36

Laloupo F., 'Coup d'État réussi en Centrafrique' (2003) 11 Géopolitique Africaine 141–49

Law D.S. and Whalen R., 'Constitutional Amendment versus Constitutional Replacement: An Empirical Comparison' in Contiades X. and Fotiadou A. (eds.), *Routledge Handbook of Comparative Constitutional Change* (Routledge 2020) 1–49

Levinson S., 'Designing an Amendment Process' in Ferejohn J. and others (eds.), *Constitutional Culture and Democratic Rule* (CUP 2001) 275

Lowell A.L., *Greater European Governments* (Harvard University Press 1918) 103

Lutz D.S., 'Toward a Theory of Constitutional Amendment' (1994) 88 (2)American Political Science 55

Madison J., *The Federalist* (Jacob E. Cooke ed, Wesleyan University Press 1961)25

Manangou V.R., 'La Constitution Congolaise du 6 Novembre 2015: Entre Influence Française et Affirmation Identitaire' (2019) 13 (13)Les Annales de Droit 121

Mangala J.R., 'Presidential Term Limit, the Never Ended Debate' in Mangala J.R. (ed.), *The Politics of Challenging Presidential Term Limits in Africa* (Palgrave Macmillan 2020) 1–37

Martin M.L., 'Pour un Constitutionnalisme de Quatrième Génération? Présidences Reconductibles, Prévisibilité Maitrisée à Échelle' in Narey O. (ed.), *La Constitution* (L'Harmattan 2018) 91–125.

Mates M., 'The Internationalisation of the Secessionist Crisis in Cameroon' (2021) 66(2) Studia Europaea 5–22

Mbaku J.M., 'International Law and Limit of Sovereignty of African States' (2018) 30(2) Florida Journal of International Law 43–68

Mbaku J.M., 'Threats to Democracy in Africa: The Rise of the Constitutional Coup' (*Brookings*, 30 October 2020) https://www.brookings.edu/blog/africa-in-focus/2020/10/30/threats-to-democracy-in-africa-the-rise-of-the-constitutional-coup/ accessed 30 July 2022

McKoeon R.W., 'The Aouzou Strip: Adjudication of Competing Territorial Claims in Africa by the International Court of Justice' (1991) 23(1) Journal of International Law 147–70

Mengara D., 'The Making of Monarchical Republic: The Undoing of Presidential Term Limits in Gabon under Omar Bongo' in Mangala J.R. (ed.), *The Politics of Challenging Presidential Term Limits in Africa* (Palgrave Macmillan 2020) 81

Merritt D.J., 'Republican Government and Autonomous State: A New Role for the Guarantee Clause' (1994) 65(4) University of Colorado Law Review 815–34

Midepani L.M., 'Pratiques Électorales et Reproduction Oligarchique au Gabon. Analyses à Partir des Élections Législatives de 2006' (2009) 115(3) Politique Africaine 48

Musa T., 'Update 1 – Cameroon's Biya Signs Law Allowing Third Term Bid' (*Reuters*, 15 April 2008) https://www.reuters.com/article/cameroon-constitution-idUKL1529602420080415

Narey O., 'Les Changements Anticonstitutionnels de Gouvernement: Mode ou Contre-mode?' (*ACL-AIDC Blog*, 28 June 2022) https://blog-iacl-aidc.org/transformations/2022/6/28/les-changements-anticonstitutionnels-de-gouvernement-mode-ou-contre-mode accessed 13 July 2022

Nfobin N. and Minang N.V., 'The Cameroon Anglophone Question in International Law' (2014) 22(2) African Journal of International and Comparative Law 234–52

Ouédraogo S.M. and Ouédraogo D., 'Les Élections Présidentielles et Législatives à l'épreuve de la COVID-19: Une Mise en Lumière en Afrique de l'Ouest Francophone' (*Afrilex*, 2020) https://base.afriquegouvernance.net/docs/afrilex_les_elections_presidentielles_et_legislatives_covid_seni_m_djibrihina_ouedraogo_21_04_2020.pdf accessed 23 July 2022.

Olinga A.D., 'La Question Anglophone dans le Cameroun d'aujourd'hui' (1994) 48(3) Revue Juridique et Politique 292

Ondoua A., 'La Population en Droit Constitutionnel: le Cas des Pays d'Afrique Francophone' (2012) 2(242) Afrique Contemporaine 87

Özbudun E., 'Judicial Review of Constitutional Amendments in Turkey' (2009) 15(4) European Public Law 533–38

Prempeh H.K., 'Africa's Constitutionalism Revival: False Start or New Dawn?' (2007) 5(3) International Journal of Constitutional Law 469–506

Radio Ndekeluka, 'Centrafrique: la Cour Constitutionnelle Autorise F.A Touadera à Convoquer un Référendum' (*Radio Ndekeluka*, 20 January 2023) https://www.radiondekeluka.org/actualites/politique/39874-centrafrique-la-cour-constitutionnelle-autorise-f-a-touadera-a-convoquer-un-referendum.html accessed 27 April 2023

Roznai Y., 'Unconstitutional Constitutional Amendments – The Migration and Success of a Constitutional Idea' (2013) 61(3) American Journal of Comparative Law 657–719

Roznai Y., 'Towards a Theory of Unamendability' (24 February 2015) NYU School of Law, Public Law Research Paper No 15–12 http://dx.doi.org/10.2139/ssrn.2569292 accessed 20 September 2022

Roznai Y., *Unconstitutional Constitutional Amendments: The Limits of Amendment Powers* (OUP 2017)

Roznai Y., 'Necrocracy or Democracy? Assessing Objections to Constitutional Unamendability: Unamendability in Constitutional Democracies' in Albert R. and Oder B.E. (eds.), *An Unamendable Constitution? Unamendability in Constitutional Democracies* (Springer Link 2018) 29–61

Roznai Y. and Suteu S., 'The Eternal Territory? The Crimean Crisis and Ukraine's Territorial Integrity as an Unamendable Constitutional Principle' (2015) German Law Journal 542–80

Roznai Y. and Yolcu S., 'An Unconstitutional Constitutional Amendment – The Turkish Perspective: A Comment on the Turkish Constitutional Court's Headscarf Decision' (2012) 10(1) International Journal of Constitutional Law 175–207

Sachdeva A.G., 'Case Concerning a Mysterious Maritime Delimitation Treaty: Why the Dispute before the ICJ in Gabon/Equatorial Guinea Is Not about Delimitation' (*Völkerrechtsblog*, 23 April 2021) https://voelkerrechtsblog.org/case-concerning-a-mysterious-maritime-delimitation-treaty/ accessed 30 July 2022

Smith E., 'Les Fonctions Symboliques des Constitutions' in Troper M. (ed.), *Traité International de droit Constitutionnel; Théorie de la Constitution* (Dalloz 2012) 767–95

Soma A., 'Le Contrôle de Constitutionnalité des lois Constitutionnelles en Afrique Noire Francophone' (2011) 5 Pratique Juridique Actuelle 619–40

Soma A., 'Le Crime International de Changement Anticonstitutionnel de Gouvernement' (2016) 26(3) Revue Suisse de Droit International et Européen 417

Soma Kaboré V.E., 'La Forme Républicaine de l'État comme Clause d'éternité Constitutionnelle' (2019) 58 Revue Burkinabè de Droit 96

Sorel J.M. and Mehdi R., 'L'uti Possidetis entre la Consécration Juridique et la Pratique: Essai de Réactualisation' (1994) 40(1) Annuaire Français de Droit International 11–40

Sundiata I., 'Engaging Equatorial Guinea: Bioko in the Diasporic Imagination' (2009) 28(2) Afro-Hispanic Review 131–40

Suteu S., *Eternity Clauses in Democratic Constitutionalism* (OUP 2021)

Tsebelis G. and Nardi D.J., 'A Long Constitution is a (Positively) Bad Constitution: Evidence from OECD Countries' (2016) 46 (2) British Journal of Political Science 457

Van Der Wilt H., 'Unconstitutional Change of Government: A New Crime within the Jurisdiction of the African Criminal Court' in Jalloh C.C., Clarke K.M., and O Nmehielle V. (eds.), *The African Court of Justice and Human and Peoples' Rights in Context: Development and Challenges* (CUP 2019) 619–42

Vedel G., 'Schengen et Maastricht (à propos de la décision no 91-294 DC du Conseil constitutionnel du 25 Juillet 1991)' (1992) 8(2) Revue Française de Droit Administratif 173–78

Vedel G., *Manuel Élémentaire de Droit Constitutionnel* (Dalloz 2002) 149

Verpeaux M., 'La République, la Constitution de 1958 et le Conseil Constitutionnel' in Avril P (ed.), *La République* (Montchrestien 2001) 129–39

Vyhnánek L., 'The Eternity Clause in the Czech Constitution as Limit to European Integration' (2015) 9(2) Vienna Journal on International Constitutional Law 240–52

Zaki M., 'Petites Constitutions et Droit Transitoire en Afrique' (2012) 6(6) Revue du Droit Public 667

PART 4
THE JUDICIARY, CONSTITUTIONAL CHANGE, AND CONSTITUTIONALISM

7

The Trouble with Judicial Amendments: Lessons from Ghana

*Maame A.S. Mensa-Bonsu**

1. Introduction

The law of the Medes and Persians had the unique distinction among legal codes that it enjoyed unrivalled sanctity. But the very reason it was so hallowed is why it is no longer with us. For, once enacted, a rule joined the body of the 'law of the Medes and Persians which altereth not'.[1]

While that must have impressed on their emperors the need to be circumspect in passing law, it committed their constitutions to increasing rigidity and therefore irrationality.[2] A constitution stands no chance of multigenerational longevity if it is incapable of being changed by the generation which, for the moment, constitutes the people.[3] Conversely, if every whim can find its way into the constitution, it would have to be as frequently amended to exclude the whims of the past as to include the whims of the present, and consequently would lose its sanctity.

A constitution must, therefore, admit of change but none too easily. The process by which this change is wrought—that is, constitutional amendment—is crucial because it has the potential to undermine the entire constitutional project. Is this a danger triggered when the constitution is amended by judicial decision? This is a critical question for African constitutions, which are wont to grant their judiciary the power of judicial review (without which no decision of a court could touch the constitution).

This chapter examines the experience of Ghana under its Constitution of 1992 in order to discuss the thorny issue of judicial amendment of constitutions. I take the position that this practice is wrong and undermines the constitutionalist effort, regardless of outcome. I therefore discuss both cases where the amendment improves the outcomes or operation of the Constitution and cases where it exacerbates existing problems or creates new ones. The chapter is in 5 sections. Following this introduction is section 2, which provides an overview of the current Constitution of Ghana. Section 3 discusses relevant case law in this regard, and section 4 extrapolates from the Ghanaian experience to argue against

* I am indebted to Joojo Afun for invaluable research assistance.

[1] Daniel 6:12.

[2] Timothy Endicott, 'The Impossibility of the Rule of Law' in Timothy Endicott (ed.), *Vagueness in Law* (OUP 2000).

[3] This chapter takes as axiomatic Rubenfeld's view that 'we the people' comprise the whole of the people over the lifespan of a nation. See Jed Rubenfeld, *Freedom and Time* (Yale University Press 2001) 153.

Maame A.S. Mensa-Bonsu, *The Trouble with Judicial Amendments: Lessons from Ghana* In: *Constitutional Change and Constitutionalism in Africa*. Edited by: Charles M. Fombad and Nico Steytler, Oxford University Press.
 DOI: 10.1093/9780198957034.003.0009

constitutional amendments proceeding from the bench in African democracies. The final section (section 5) reminds African academics particularly, and African peoples generally, of the importance of our role as the countervailing power to constitutionally entrenched judicial review.

2. The Constitution of Ghana (1992) and the judiciary: The backstory

This section explains the antecedents and origins of the Constitution of Ghana (1992), in order that the place which the judiciary occupies in the small-c constitution may be appreciated. It also explains the powers that the constitutional text allocates to this arm of the state.

On 31 December 1981, Ghana's Third Republic fell in a coup led by Jerry John Rawlings. It was his second successful coup.[4] From then until 7 January 1993, Rawlings and his Provisional National Defence Council (PNDC) ruled Ghana with an iron fist.[5] Human rights abuses, including indiscriminate confiscation of property, sudden disappearances, and trials by panels unseen based on secret evidence, created what became known as 'a culture of silence'.[6] By the time Ghana began its fourth attempt at republican statehood, deference to authority had become deeply ingrained.

As with many African constitutions, the origins of the Constitution of 1992 are less democratic than its preamble suggests, with its enactment process having been heavily manipulated by the Rawlings government.[7] The Assembly which drafted it was consultative rather than constituent; that is, it had no promulgating power. It remains unclear by which criteria certain groups (among them the Market Women Association, the Bakers Association, and the Ghana Hairdressers and Beauticians Association)[8] came to be represented in the Assembly and others not. Public reaction to the Assembly's composition was mixed. Some (government sympathizers in particular) hailed it as inclusive and evincing respect for all social strata; others saw it as evidence of the PNDC's machinations to control the process, given that literacy rates among many of these groups was especially low.

The decree which established the Consultative Assembly to draft the Constitution not only reserved to the PNDC the power to insert any clause it wished into the final draft but also expressly denied immunity for anything said or done against Chairman Rawlings or any of his Secretaries,[9] raising much doubt that the Assembly would be a forum of free and candid deliberation.[10] In protest, the Bar boycotted the proceedings, which succeeded in making a noble point of principle but meant that the process had little input from the

[4] The first was on 4 June 1979. The regime was called the Armed Forces Revolutionary Council.

[5] Kevin Shillington, *Ghana and the Rawlings Factor* (Macmillan 1992).

[6] Albert Adu Boahen, *The Ghanaian Sphinx: Reflections on the Contemporary History of Ghana 1972–1987* (GAAS 1989); Paul Nugent, *Big Men, Small Boys and Politics in Ghana: Power, Ideology and the Burden of History, 1982–1994* (Pinter 1995).

[7] Bluwey calls it the PNDC's 'preparation to succeed self': Gilbert Bluwey, 'Obstacles to an Orderly Transition to Constitutional Rule under the PNDC' in Kwame Ninsin and Francis Drah (eds.), *Ghana's Transition to Constitutional Rule* (Ghana Universities Press 1991).

[8] Wilson Kwame Yayoh, 'Resurgence of Multi-Party Rule in Ghana, 1990–2004: A Historical Review' (2006–2007) 10 Transactions of the Historical Society of Ghana 125, 131–34.

[9] Provisional National Defence Council (PNDC) Law 253, s 14(3).

[10] E Gyimah-Boadi described it as a '"grant" of the PNDC'. See E Gyimah-Boadi, 'Notes on Ghana's Current Transition to Constitutional Rule' (1991) 38(4) Africa Today 5, 16.

echelons of legal experts, who have since had to practice, advocate, litigate, and generally live within the constitutional order that emerged from it.[11]

Owing to the contrived process by which the Constitution of 1992 was developed and promulgated, it has been argued—erroneously—that it cannot properly be called an expression of the will of the people and nor can they have been its constituent power.[12] While government manipulation of the process is undeniable, it is equally a fact that the Constitution could not have come into force without the overwhelming approval it received from the people in the referendum that was held. A 92 per cent vote in support of a constitution is no casual endorsement, especially when one considers that this was its outcome in spite of the government's undisguised preference for the opposite result. A better view, then, is to see the endorsement as relocating the authority of the document to the people, such that whoever assented to the Constitution thereafter did so as their authorized agent.

Despite its complicated genesis, the Constitution makes a claim of supremacy in the legal order, which it reiterates throughout the text. Yet, mindful that it must, of necessity, admit of change, it sets out in Chapter 25 an elaborate methodology by which changes can be made to its text. During the eleven years of the Rawlings dictatorship, the two incontrovertible facts about Ghana's small-c constitution were that, first, the rule of recognition was 'what the PNDC says is law, no matter the form or medium' and, second, that this rule could be changed only by those who overcame the PNDC by violence.

Needless to say, the PNDC exerted itself to prevent any such Samson from emerging. That period was, for Ghanaians, a pure experience.[13] But, as the case of *Ekwam v Pianim* shows,[14] even a cowed people will eventually act on the need for their Constitution to respond to their present realities, plans, and aspirations. A rule of recognition that does not include the people's agency can only last so long. The 1992 Constitution, therefore, creates a forked path to constitutional change: one road leads to the amendment of an unentrenched provision and the other, slower, bumpy, and more difficult road leads to the amendment of an entrenched provision.[15] In both cases, the people must be the force behind the constitutional change, either through their representatives, in the case of unentrenched provisions, or by referendum, for entrenched provisions.

That the supremacy of the Constitution is a testament to, and product of, the people's agency does not *ipso facto* prevent it from being disregarded. After all, once the president is invested with power—even if only for the duration of his or her term—who is to stop him or her from arrogating powers unto himself or herself that the Constitution has granted to another, turning the constitutional distribution of powers and protection of rights, as Madison put it, into 'parchment soldiers'? Under no illusion that Ghana is that noble society of whom Waldron's four assumptions are true,[16] the Constitution underwrites its

[11] The Bar in any case had been allotted only two seats—a fact that by itself would have been eyebrow-raising. Juxtaposed with the ten allotted to the Butchers Association, for example, it was bewildering and (not unjustifiably) seen as an effort to keep competence to a minimum in the Assembly. See Yayoh (n 8) 125, 131–34. Thus, while it is argued that the point about the boycott is valid, it is, admittedly, unclear that the Bar would have been able to make much of an impact on the final form.

[12] Joseph Aryee, 'Ghana's Return to Constitutional Rule under the Provisional National Defence Council (PNDC)' (1996) 29(4) Verfassung und Recht in Übersee 434.

[13] Carl Schmitt, *Political Theology: Four Chapters on the Concept of Sovereignty* (George Schwab tr, UCP 2005).

[14] *Ekwam v Pianim* (No 1) [1996–97] SCGLR 117.

[15] ch 25 of the Constitution of Ghana (1992) sets out the procedure for amending both entrenched and unentrenched provisions.

[16] Jeremy Waldron, 'The Core of the Case against Judicial Review' (2006) 115(6) Yale Law Journal 1346.

supremacy with a (perhaps overly) robust judicial review mechanism. The Supreme Court is appointed by article 2 to 'interpret and enforce' the Constitution, including over the executive and the legislature. To give bite to their bark, the Supreme Court is empowered to make such orders as necessary to secure constitutional compliance. Article 2 creates the offence of a 'high crime', which consists in disregarding a Supreme Court order and, in the case of the president or vice president, can be grounds for impeachment.

In a long history of harassment and insecurity, incidents that loom large in the institutional memory of Ghana's judicial arm include, in the First Republic, President Nkrumah's firing of Korsah CJ[17] and arrest of several respected judges for judgments he disliked;[18] in the Second Republic, Prime Minister Busia's public bluster that no court could force him to do something against his will;[19] during the second military regime, General Acheampong's dissolution of the Supreme Court;[20] and, during the second Rawlings junta, the abduction and murder of three High Court judges after they reversed decisions of the kangaroo courts of the Armed Forces Revolutionary Council.[21]

With these and many other less well-known incidents in its memory, the judiciary created by the 1992 Constitution was most unlikely to have found the courage or confidence that enabled the American Supreme Court to seize the power of judicial review. The very powerful executive would have inevitably overrun the Constitution itself, and in its first two terms the military-turned-civilian government would have been little different from the eleven-year full-blown dictatorship immediately preceding it. The judicial review mechanism of the 1992 Constitution sought (rightly so) to produce and sustain a monumental change in the balance of power in executive–judiciary relations, and the (self-) perception of the judiciary and its role in the state.

Drawing on these powers, the Court made immense gains for Ghana's constitutionalism effort in the first decade of the Constitution's life, primarily in the sphere of fundamental human rights. As WK Wilson and others have noted, the military government did not accede to constitutional governance out of a new-found commitment to constitutionalist ideals. Indeed, that Rawlings had not intended, when he took office in January 1993, to make any changes to his modus operandi was evident in the frequent complaints he made about the Constitution hampering his actions.[22] Judicial review has been crucial to changing the state's ethos and tackling the executive high-handedness to which the country's long history of unfettered power had acclimated its people.

However, the main duty of judicial review under the 1992 Constitution was not merely to restrain executive or legislative action. It was, as noted earlier, to *interpret and enforce* the Constitution. If the consequence has been the restraint of the executive, it is only because the executive has become accustomed to that total lack of constraint which GK Chesterton refers to as 'unfreedom'.[23] But this should not distract from its real purpose. Whatever the

[17] Geoffrey Bing, *Reap the Whirlwind: An Account of Kwame Nkrumah's Ghana from 1950–1966* (MacGibbon & Kee 1968).

[18] Ibid.

[19] SO Gyandoh, CEK Kumado and J Griffiths, 'Dr Busia's Radio Broadcast on the Sallah Decision', 2 G & G 739 (2d)' 1374.

[20] PNDC (n 9).

[21] Mike Oquaye, *Politics in Ghana, 1982–1992: Rawlings, Revolution and Populist Democracy* (Tornado Publications and Thomson Press India Ltd 2004).

[22] E Gyimah-Boadi, 'Ghana's Uncertain Political Opening' (1994) 5(2) Democracy 75, 80.

[23] GK Chesterton, 'Mr Bernard Shaw' in David Dooley (ed.), *The Collected Works of G.K. Chesterton, vol 1* (Ignatius Press 1986) 67.

outcomes of judicial review, if it is not itself constrained by the boundaries of the constitutional text: it is, at best, illegitimate and, at worst, the tool of judicial supremacy.

To be sure, some of the longest leaps forward in Ghana's constitutionalism effort have been achieved via judicial review. It gave substance to the freedoms of assembly,[24] association,[25] information,[26] and expression;[27] and the rights to liberty,[28] fair trial,[29] the vote,[30] and administrative justice.[31] It has compelled the executive,[32] legislature,[33] and independent institutions, such as the Commission on Human and Administrative Justice (CHRAJ)[34] and the Electoral Commission,[35] to stay *intra vires*. Even the judicial arm itself has been challenged before the Court.[36] That judicial review has added momentum to the country's forward march is beyond dispute.[37]

But that is not the only metric by which the Court's performance should be measured. In the next section, we assess whether the Court has been able to patrol the borders of the Constitution *without* trying to change it in ways that the Constitution never asked it to.

3. Amending the Constitution from behind the gavel

Not every constitutional decision handed down by the Court is properly called an act of judicial review, though by rights, if the Court were respecting its own fetters, it would be. The Court may not always admit, or in some cases even realize, what it is doing. Thus, it is important, in an analysis of the Court's output, to look beyond its rhetoric and assess what it does rather than what it says it does.

To that end, it is worth taking a moment to delineate what references to 'judicial amendment' mean in the context of this chapter. Emmet McFarlane provides a helpfully clear definition which is adopted here with slight reservation.[38] A judicial amendment is:

> a judicial decision that effectively adds to, removes from, or modifies the constitution in a manner that is inconsistent with, or not plausibly contemplated by, the text in its original

24 *New Patriotic Party v Inspector General of Police* [1993–94] 2 GLR 459.
25 *Mensima v Attorney-General* [1996–97] SCGLR 67.
26 *Ghana Independent Broadcasters Association (GIBA) v Attorney-General* (J1 4 of 2016) [2016] GHASC 91.
27 *New Patriotic Party v Ghana Broadcasting Corporation* [1993–94] 2 GLR 354.
28 *Martin Kpebu (No 2) v Attorney-General* (J1 13 of 2015) [2016] GHASC 15.
29 Ibid.
30 *Ramadan and Another v Electoral Commission and Another* [2016] GHASC 19.
31 *Awuni v West African Examination Council* [2003–04] SCGLR 471; *Aboagye v Ghana Commercial Bank* 1 [2001–02] SCGLR 797.
32 *Banful v the Attorney-General* [2017] GHASC 21; *GBA v A-G* [2016] GHASC 43.
33 *JH Mensah v Attorney-General* [1996–97] SCGLR 320.
34 *Ex parte CHRAJ (Richard Anane Interested Party)* [2007–2008] SCGLR 213.
35 *Tehn-Addy v Electoral Commission* [1996–97] SCGLR 589; *Apaloo v Electoral Commission* [2001–02] 2 GLR 372.
36 *GBA v Attorney-General (Abban case)* [2003–04] SCGLR 250.
37 See eg Maame AS Mensa-Bonsu, 'Forging Forward Introspectively as Ghana's Constitution Turns Thirty' (*IACL-AIDC Blog*, 11 October 2021) https://blog-iacl-aidc.org/2021-posts/2021/10/11/forging-forward-introspectively-as-ghanas-constitution-turns-thirty accessed 1 October 2023; SY Bimpong-Buta, *The Role of the Supreme Court in the Development Of Constitutional Law In Ghana* (Advanced Legal Publications 2007).
38 The wider political community's response is arguably a component of judicial amendment. Of course, those expectations are embedded in the small-constitution and so matter very much; nevertheless, they are evidence of judicial amendment rather than a component thereof.

or modern meaning, the intent or purposes of the relevant provisions, and the expectations of the broader political community as to what the constitution contains.[39]

In this chapter, therefore, I will not tackle judicial review decisions on the merits of the decision. Rather, I will focus on how they meet the important components of that definition; that is, whether they depart substantially from what the Constitution could have intended and thereby modify it.

Courts sometimes fall prey to the seductive arguments of counsel, which they couch in the purple prose of 'doing the right thing' and keeping the Constitution 'a living organism'. In the cases discussed in this section, the Court let itself be lured into the trap of believing it is entitled to 'do the right thing' rather than the constitutionally mandated thing, and so handed down decisions that had the effect of changing the constitutional text itself. Admittedly, these cases are reassuringly few; indeed, there have been only four, thus far, in the lifespan of the 1992 Constitution.[40] But that is cold comfort. Improper amendment of even a single subparagraph of a provision of the Constitution so thoroughly upsets the constitutional agreement the document represents that it is no consolation to find its occurrence minimal in frequency or even impact. Therefore, though few, the cases in this section cause much unease and merit grave introspection by supreme courts everywhere on the continent.

Sam (No 2) v A-G[41] was the first case to change the text of the Constitution of Ghana. In that case, the Solicitor-General raised a preliminary objection to the action on grounds of standing, arguing that the plaintiff was in no way personally affected by the divestiture of state property that was the subject matter of the action. Holding that an article 2 action did not require such proximity to the challenged act, the Court dismissed the objection. Article 2 of the 1992 Constitution gives to 'any person' the right to invoke the Supreme Court's original constitutional jurisdiction. Bamford-Addo and Akuffo JJSC, with whom Acquah, Atuguba, and Ampiah JJSC all concurred, basing themselves on the proposals in the draft Constitution on which the Consultative Assembly's debates were centred, held that the person needed also to be a citizen. Article 2, as a result of this case, now begins: '2(1) A Ghanaian person who alleges that'.

The Court's first conscious foray into constitutional amendment was the case of *Agyei-Twum v AG*.[42] In that case, a petition seeking the removal of the Chief Justice was presented by the second defendant to the president, who announced that he was setting up a committee to investigate the merits of the petition in accordance with article 146(6) of the 1992 Constitution. The plaintiff then sought a declaration, which the Supreme Court granted,

[39] Emmett Macfarlane, 'Judicial Amendment of the Constitution' (2021) 19(5) International Journal of Constitutional Law 1894, 1896.

[40] The case of *Ghana Bar Association v Attorney-General (Supreme Court Justices)* [2016] GHASC 43 is frequently viewed as an instance of judicial amendment. However, closer study of the decision leads to the conclusion that it did not amend the Constitution and is indeed correct. The misfortune is that it was most inarticulate, and therefore, without a very close reading, appears to take the incoherent position (which a large portion of the legal fraternity understood it as) that the president is not bound to act on the advice of the Judicial Council but cannot disregard it either. On a close reading, though, it becomes clear that what the court meant is that the president is not bound to nominate at all upon receiving the Judicial Council's advice, but should they choose to nominate, they are limited to the advice offered by the Judicial Council. This does not alter the constitutional text. Seeeg pp 4 and 24 of the judgment.

[41] *Sam (No 2) v Attorney-General* (2000) SCGLR 305.

[42] *Frank Agyei-Twum v Attorney-General* (2006) JELR 68390 (SC).

that on a proper interpretation of the whole of article 146, the president could not set up a committee to investigate such a petition unless there was, prima facie, a case for the Chief Justice to answer, even though the text of the article does not anywhere mention this 'prima facie case' condition precedent to the committee's appointment. *Agyei-Twum* thus created a new article 146(6) that reads:

> Where the petition is for the removal of the Chief Justice, the President shall, *acting in consultation with the Council of State, and being satisfied that there is a prima facie case*, appoint a committee consisting of two Justices of the Supreme Court, one of whom shall be appointed chairman by the President, and three other persons who are not members of the Council of State, nor members of Parliament, nor lawyers.[43]

Ransford France (No 3)[44] was the next and, as will be shown later, most indefensible instance of judicial amendment in Ghana's history. The plaintiff asserted that the Electoral Commission's power to create new constituencies under article 47 of the 1992 Constitution was a discretionary power and therefore caught by article 296(c), which obliges public officers vested with discretionary power to publish, in a constitutional or legislative instrument, regulations detailing how that discretion will be deployed. The Court, speaking through Date-Bah JSC with undivided voice, held that a literal reading of article 296(c) would cause the 'grave mischief' of 'a nuclear melt-down, so to speak, of government, as we have known it since 1969'.[45] Consequently, the Court held, the terms of the clause were, although unequivocal, 'thoroughly impractical'[46] and hence to be disregarded in this instance. The Court thus rewrote article 296(c) to render the mandatory 'shall' into an optional 'may'. The clause now reads:

> [W]here the person or authority is not a judge or other judicial officer, there *may, when appropriate*, be published by constitutional instrument or statutory instrument, regulations that are not inconsistent with the provisions of this Constitution or that other law to govern the exercise of the discretionary power.[47]

Occupy Ghana v Auditor-General[48] is the final case this section engages with. It is a case in which the plaintiff asked the Court for an interpretation of article 187(7)(b)(i),(ii), and (iii). The question arising from these provisions was whether or not Ghana's Auditor-General, who, in their annual report to Parliament, is required to identify monies lost to the state through inefficiencies and mismanagement by public officials, is also obliged to thereafter recover such sums. While the plaintiff asserted that they were, the Auditor-General considered that they had the discretion, not the obligation, to so recover. The Court had no difficulty identifying the power as a discretionary one. But it then held that, in the light of the principles animating the Constitution, the 'may' should be read as a 'shall' and treated as mandatory. The new article 187(7)(b) now reads as follows:

[43] Emphasis added.
[44] *Ransford France (No 3) v Electoral Commission & Attorney-General* [2012] 1 SCGLR 705.
[45] Ibid.
[46] Ibid.
[47] Emphasis added.
[48] *Occupy Ghana v Auditor-General* (J1 19 of 2016) [2017] GHASC 24.

In the performance of his functions under this Constitution or any other law the Auditor-General

b. shall disallow any item of expenditure which is contrary to law.[49]

Sam (No 2) stands in a category of its own. For though it, like all the other cases in this section, results in an amendment of the Constitution, it appears to be the only one in which the trespass is unintentional. While the inadvertence does not mitigate its effect, it does stand as a powerful reminder of two things: first, courts are not always consciously and malignantly power-grabbing when they overreach; second, judicial review jurisprudence must be studied very carefully, and even accidental blunders denounced, so that the Court, while accepting that inevitably it will err, will be so protective of its record that it will treat every occasion of judicial review as one capable of being its hamartia and therefore approach the event with the greatest degree of thoroughness and circumspection.

The Court seems to have completely overlooked the fact that the expressed desire of the Committee of Experts[50] to limit article 2 actions to citizens was not acceded to by the Constituent Assembly, and so the wording in article 2 does not, in fact, contain this limitation. In the result, article 2, the very article which the Court called 'one of the most important provisions of the Constitution' and 'one of the most crucial built-in mechanisms' for protecting the integrity of the Constitution,[51] was inopportunely amended by a ruling on a mere preliminary objection.

That the Court was neither purporting nor intending to impose its idea of what was better or more useful is obvious from the two judgments. These professed no opinion as to whether the Committee of Experts was right or wrong to hold that preference. The judgments simply accepted that view to be the meaning intended by the framers of the Constitution and upheld it. The Court clearly meant well but also clearly got it wrong. Had the academy lived up to its role and drawn attention to the error of the Court, this erroneous position could have been corrected. But, as it went without comment, it has since been applied in two further cases.[52]

Of the three cases of deliberate judicial amendment, the rhetoric of the Court in *Occupy Ghana* is the least frightening. The Court betrays its own discomfiture with its actions by the prolix, apologist oration with which it prefaces this constitutional rewrite. Dotse JSC, giving examples of cases in which rules of statutory construction were decided, reminds us that the rules of interpretation are judge-made—a fact neither party had challenged. He then observes that courts in the Commonwealth have increasingly adopted the modern purposive approach (MOPA) towards constitutional interpretation. He cites three cases in which the Court had, endorsing MOPA and considering it 'appropriate, abandoned the strict constructionist view of interpretation' before proceeding to amend the Constitution under this guise of interpretation.

[49] Emphasis added.

[50] Committee of Experts, 'Report of the Committee of Experts (Constitution) on Proposals for a Draft Constitution of Ghana' (Republic of Ghana 1991).

[51] Ibid. 371.

[52] *Federation of Youth Association of Ghana (FEDYAG) v Public Universities of Ghana & Ors* [2011] GHASC; *New Patriotic Party v Attorney-General* (CIBA Case) [1996–97] SCGLR 729.

His Lordship would have been more accurate to have admitted that he had abandoned construction as, strictly speaking, the task of interpretation. A 'broad purposive approach' to finding meaning is, in general, a Humpty Dumpty approach[53] to the exercise. What a word means and what one wants it to mean are hardly the same thing. Deciphering the former could scarcely be the same exercise as determining the latter. The purpose of a constitutional or statutory text is to be found in the language of the text, not in the divination of the good society that the court gleans from it. Perhaps it is the erroneous belief, widespread in the Ghanaian legal fraternity, that the judges in *Re Akoto*[54] were timorous souls who let their people down[55] that has spawned in Ghanaian Supreme Court judges the egregious belief that a purposive approach is the mark of judicial intrepidness. Be that as it may, the fact remains that when the Court adopts a purposive approach, it has *ipso facto* chosen to find what it wants the words to mean. The correct term for that sort of activity in relation to the text of a Constitution is not, as His Lordship said, constitutional interpretation but rather constitutional amendment. It does not change the nature of the act that one calls it something less pernicious.

The salubrious outcome of the *Occupy Ghana* decision caused it to be undeservedly praised. In the first year alone after its handing down, the Auditor-General recovered USD 12 million for the persistently stretched Ghanaian public coffers. But the ruling's impact does not ameliorate its constitutional indefensibility. The Court decided upon the values that this part of the Constitution should actively pursue, then undertook the legislative-drafting task of determining how the clause should be worded and, finally, in issuing the relevant declarations, enacted the new article 187(7)(b).

The rhetoric of *Agyei-Twum* was less equivocal. The Court examined the equivalent provisions in respect of other superior court judges and took the position that the omission of the requirement of a prima facie case was a mistake. It eluded the Court that the drafters might have deliberately set a lower bar for public objections to the administration of a Chief Justice than for those of every other judge. The Court acknowledged that the Report of the Committee of Experts recommended the phrase be inserted and the power to set up the investigative committee be given to the Council of State.[56] It also admitted that the Consultative Assembly responded to that recommendation in the negative and deliberately assigned that power to another. Nevertheless, it came to the conclusion that the phrase it wanted to insert was left out inadvertently and that it had the power to remedy that accident.

Much of the judgment is dedicated to explaining why the interpretation the Court chose was correct. But the justification offered is entirely outcome-based, the conclusions incompatible with the reasoning. For example, how does the conclusion that the drafters meant to insert the 'prima facie' requirement, but somehow overlooked to do so, follow naturally from the observation that they expressly inserted the phrase in the case of judges below the apex court? Indeed, it is an easy argument to make that the lower threshold is a deliberate

[53] In Lewis Carroll's *Through the Looking-Glass*, Humpty Dumpty says to Alice that words he uses mean what he chooses them to mean—nothing more, nothing less.

[54] *Re Akoto & 7 Others* [1961] GLR 523, Justices Van Lare, Akiwumi, and Korsah CJ.

[55] CEK Kumado, 'Forgive Us Our Trespasses: An Examination of the Indemnity Clause in the 1992 Constitution of Ghana' (1993–1995) 19 University of Ghana Law Journal 83.

[56] Committee of Experts (n 50) para 286.

method of engendering higher public accountability between the public and the executive head of the judiciary. What it shows is simply how little regard the judges have for the parameters of their power under article 2 of the 1992 Constitution. The appearance of thoroughness the decision wears serves only to distract one from its entirely *ultra vires* nature.

Finally, and most disturbingly, there is *Ransford France*. It is rare that a court is as unabashed in its arrogation of power as it was in this case. The Court did not claim that there were multiple possible interpretations of that clause and that it was just preferring one; it did not even claim that the only possible interpretation was the position it was taking. It plainly admitted what it took the Constitution to mean but then boldly declared that it knew better and was going to overrule it on this occasion. It did not even bother to articulate a general principle of when a discretionary power might be taken to be beyond article 296(c). That step would have at least provided some yardstick for measuring the Court's later use of this self-allocated constitutional overrule power. It is hard to say that a court behaving in this manner considers itself bound by any parameters other than its will. This is what makes *Ransford France* so frightening: it is not only an instance of judicial amendment but also unapologetically stakes a claim of judicial supremacy.

Wherever the Court changes the text of a provision, no matter how minor the change, it also adjusts the content of article 2 upwards. The result is that, instead of the judicial review being limited to assessing an act or omission for its compliance with the text, it is expanded to include a value assessment of the act or omission's outcome. Article 2, as these cases have amended it, consequently now reads as follows:

> 2 (1) A *Ghanaian* person who alleges that
> (a) an enactment or anything contained in or done under the authority of that or any other enactment; or
> (b) any act or omission of any person is inconsistent with or is in contravention of a provision of this Constitution, *or results in an undesirable outcome*, may bring an action in the Supreme Court for a declaration to that effect.

The Constitution makes a good-faith, albeit flawed, attempt at separating and limiting power in predictable ways, but in giving a veto over the state's every operational move to the judiciary it has concentrated power in that arm and subverted the attempt. The Supreme Court's meddling with the constitutional text has only exacerbated the problem.

4. What Ghana teaches us about judicial activism in constitutional interpretation

There is an outcome-based, as well as, principle-based objection to constitutional amendments emanating from the bench—and Ghana's experience bears out both such objections.

4.1 The objection based on outcome

There is no reason whatsoever to believe that interpreting and enforcing the law positions judges to make the best decisions about constitutional design. At the outset, one can accept their particular suitability to ascertaining the limitations of a constitutional text.[57] Years of successfully practising family law might not make lawyers better spouses, but it does make them rather more familiar than their clients with what the law says in that field and what that means in practice. Similarly, judges, by virtue of deciphering statutes, delegated legislation, and precedents are inordinately more familiar with what interpreting legislation entails than those in any other arm or office of state. Whatever the deficiencies of the judicial arm, we are better off having its specialized skill set applied to the highest norms of the jurisdiction than relying on the bona fides or democratic credentials of the other two arms. If these sufficed, we would not need a Constitution in the first place.

Furthermore, the superiority of the judicial claim of competence in constitutional interpretation would seem to be augmented by the socio-economic circumstances of Ghana in particular and the Global South in general. Functional literacy rates in many parts of sub-Saharan Africa are very poor.[58] This means the majority cannot read the Constitution. How then could they assess their representatives' interpretation of the limits that the Constitution places on them? A (representative) democracy runs on the premise of mandates being periodically assessed. If there is no one to assess the use of the mandate, there is no democracy, no matter how many ways or times elections are held. An illiterate populace might be able to assess its elected officials' performance based on their collective experience of the economy, security, education, and so on. But the tangible effects of power arrogation are felt only after the power grab has succeeded, and this is so irrespective of whether the power grab was achieved by force or cunning. Judges offer a disadvantaged populace the only means of holding their elected officers to the fine print of their mandate. As we saw in section 1, the Court's ability to patrol the borders of the power distribution of the Constitution of 1992 is what kept the dictator-turned-president from ruling under its authority as he did when he ruled absolutely.

There is, however, no necessary connection between judicial work and adeptness at power distribution or rights creation. Creating a right involves multiple ancillary matters that must be resolved. For example, Hohfeldian correlatives dictate that the duty-holder for every claim-right be identified.[59] If duty-holders require infrastructural support to be able to carry out their new duties then they acquire a second-order right to the provision of that infrastructure, and the second-order duty-holder must also be identified.

[57] Even this is contested. Scholars such as Ekins do not think that judicial work advantages the Constitutional Court in any way as the final voice in constitutional interpretation. For a fuller understanding of his objection, see the Judicial Power Project https://judicialpowerproject.org.uk/ accessed 7 February 2025.

[58] 'Functional' here means the ability to digest complex documents such as leases, contracts, or even newspapers. Owing to discrepancies in the definitions of literacy used by African censuses, reported rates of literacy are artificially high. For example, in censuses in Ghana in 2010 and Malawi in 2018, the adopted definition was 'able to read and write a simple sentence in any language'. See Ghana 2010 Population & Housing Census Summary Report of Final Results, xi https://statsghana.gov.gh/gssmain/storage/img/marqueeupdater/Census2010_Summary_report_of_final_results.pdf accessed 7 February 2025; Malawi Population and Housing Census Report 2018, 21 https://malawi.unfpa.org/sites/default/files/resource-pdf/2018%20Malawi%20Population%20and%20Housing%20Census%20Main%20Report%20%281%29.pdf accessed 7 February 2025; in Sierra Leone, the Gambia, and Madagascar, respondents were counted as literate if they were able to read all or part of a typed sentence they were shown. See Sierra Leone Demographic and Health Survey (2019) 34 Sierra Leone Demographic and Health Survey (2019) last accessed 07/ 02/ 2025; Gambia Demographic and Health Survey 2019–20, 32 https://dhsprogram.com/pubs/pdf/FR369/FR369.pdf accessed 7 February 2025; Madagascar Enquête Démographique et de Santé 2021, 40 https://dhsprogram.com/pubs/pdf/GF54/GF54.pdf accessed 7 February 2025.

[59] Wesley Newcomb Hohfeld, 'Fundamental Legal Conceptions Applied in Judicial Reasoning' in Walter Wheeler Cook (ed), *Fundamental Legal Conceptions Applied in Judicial Reasoning and Other Legal Essays* (Yale University Press 1923).

An illustration will be helpful. In 2021, Justice Gifty Agyei-Addo ruled correctly that Tyron Marghuy, an incoming high school freshman whom Achimota School had refused to register on account of the dreadlocks he wore as a manifestation of his Rastafarian religion, was entitled to attend the school and practice his religion there.[60] If his religious practice involves dietary requirements, he is entitled to observe this diet at school. This is his first-order right, and the school must enrol him and provide the dietary needs of his first-order right as the first-order duty-holder. As a state-funded school, Achimota has, by virtue of Justice Agyei-Addo's decision, acquired a second-order right to the funding it needs to fulfil its first-order duty to meet Tyron Marghuy's dietary needs, and the state now holds the second-order duty to provide that funding.

The burdens created by this decision are legitimate only because Tyron Marghuy's right to manifest his religion were granted, not by Justice Agyei-Addo, but by the Constitution. The Court has no ability to foresee all the implications of any of its decisions. Indeed, while it must be mindful always of the consequences of its methodology, the consequences of its decision proper are not its problem. As Hayfron-Benjamin J put it so well, 'all that [they] are concerned with is to give effect to these provisions and carry out their manifest purposes without regard to temporary or passing expediency'.[61]

A forum whose task is indifferent to where the chips fall is, by that token, incapable of foreseeing all the chips, or all the ways, or all the places, they may fall. For that reason, it should never wade into policy or governance matters. It should especially not seek to amend the Constitution to improve outcomes, given its limited understanding and foresight of them. As noted earlier, even *Agyei-Twum*, which seemed to improve the operationalization of the Constitution by reducing the chances of frivolous petitions (which would cost the judiciary in time, money, and output), overlooked the important consideration that the Constitution may have been creating a more direct accountability loop between the executive head of the third arm and the people.

In short, the knock-on effects of constitutional amendments provide a compelling outcomes-based reason as to why these amendments should never emanate from the judiciary. They require such a bird's-eye view of the present and future, policy and practice, the essential and the aspirational, and other implications that, as Gibson points out, 'no nine people, however wise and well informed, possess the individual or collective powers of imagination necessary'[62] to properly evaluate that task. Constitutional amendment must needs be the product of a process capable of being as fully informed as the limitations of human vision allow[63]—or at least as poorly informed as the people choose it to be.

Additionally, and by dint of the myopia discussed above, judicial amendments aimed at improving outcomes invariably end up undermining the rule of law. An official who in good faith wants to exercise their discretion in line with the Constitution will, faced with *Ransford France* and *Occupy Ghana*, be unable to tell whether regulations are needed in their particular circumstance or whether the discretion they have been assigned is to

[60] *Tyron Iras Marghuy v Board of Governors Achimota Senior High School & Attorney-General*, 2021, unreported case, Suit No HR/0055/2021.

[61] *People's Popular Party v Attorney-General* [1971] 1 GLR 138–52 at 138.

[62] Dale Gibson, 'Founding Fathers-in-Law: Judicial Amendment of the Canadian Constitution' (1992) 55(1) Law & Contemporary Problems 262.

[63] Larry Alexander, 'What are Constitutions, and What Should (and Can) They Do?' (2011) 28(1) Social Philosophy and Policy 1.

be treated as mandatory. Nor will they be able to take instruction from the decisions of other similarly positioned officials or even their predecessor in office. Similarly, a citizen encountering any of the many holders of discretionary power will no longer be able to predict how any of those encounters would turn out now. There is no longer a pre-emptive way of identifying which instances of 'may' will be interpreted by that official as being covered by *Ransford France* or *Occupy Ghana* and—crucially—whether the Court will agree with that official or not.

The value of the rule of law is that it makes the journey from encounter with state power to the outcome of said encounter reasonably predictable.[64] In so doing, it empowers citizens to make choices about how and when to bring themselves into contact with state power.[65] Therefore, when the Court begins to play fast and loose with its interpretive parameters in the interests of outcomes, it erodes the certainty of the law. Any gain in outcome is defeated by the loss in judicial restraint. A clearly defined rule gives predictability to its outcome. That is the purpose of a written constitution and indeed of setting out the methodology for changing its terms. Judicial decision is not one of the methods provided for in Chapter 25 of the Constitution. Whether this is wise or not, it is the provision Ghanaians have made. The Court makes the stability and reliability of the entire Constitution shaky when it amends the document by fiat.

4.2 The objection based on principle

The objection in principle is even more fundamental. The people's claim to self-government, and therefore to freedom, consists in their being the constituent power of their constitution. As Ekins notes, freedom is self-government.[66] A people as large as the citizenry of the modern state cannot practice direct democracy: necessarily, they must delegate their participation to their representatives. It is by their agents acting within the terms of reference of the agency agreement that their authority and autonomy is retained. The constitution is that agency agreement. The judges are agents under the agreement.

But if the agent should *suo motu* be able to review the terms of the agreement, updating it according to their own understanding of what their principal needs are they still an agent? If the so-called principal is bound by changes to the terms of reference made unilaterally by the agent, are they still principal? Judicial amendment hollows out the claim to self-government that democratic governance is. Regardless of how frequently they hold elections, a people are no longer in charge of who they are or in what direction they are heading—and are, therefore, not free even if they live under an increasingly improving constitution.

Judicial review is a justified practice even within a democratic order. But judicial amendment is irreconcilably opposed to it. Interpreting the constitution means ascertaining its meaning. Admittedly, this can be tricky. There are, in fact, situations where the text does not offer clarity as to its intentions and judges cannot be a Pilate[67] and look away. But the need

[64] Joseph Raz, 'The Rule of Law and Its Virtue' (1977) 93 Law Quarterly Review 195.

[65] John Finnis, *Natural Law and Natural Rights* (OUP 1980) 270–72.

[66] Richard Ekins, 'How to Be a Free People' (2013) 58(2) American Journal of Jurisprudence 163.

[67] As described in the Book of Matthew, Pontius Pilate was the consul who presided over the Jews' accusation of treason to Jesus. Unconvinced, but unwilling to risk a backlash, he simply washed his hands of the dispute.

for them to have authority to resolve the dispute does not equate to the authority to update or improve its unambiguous meaning.[68]

4.3 So how should the courts behave?

Their lofty tones notwithstanding, living constitutionalist arguments are invariably calls to judicial amendment. The two cases that will be discussed in this section stand in praise of judicial discernment and definitively answer the question of the correct posture judges should adopt when exhorted by counsel to assume powers they were not constitutionally assigned. These cases are not the only instances in the 30-year life of the 1992 Constitution that the Court has resisted counsel's effort to entice it into amending the constitutional text. They are, however, the most recent occasions thereof, and thus demonstrate the sophistication with which these pernicious calls are made and how easily the Court might be distracted by them.

The first, *Asare v AG (CRC case)*, is an especially clear example of the phenomenon of the excessive faith in judicial review that misapprehends the Court as a rights-creating forum. The Court's refusal to do what was not its job was not fully appreciated. Thus, it was castigated for being too deferential to the executive. In truth, however, the decision is unassailable, for it merely recognizes that the updating of constitutions is not the business of the Court.

The facts bear retelling. President Mills, apparently in fulfilment of a manifesto promise,[69] exercised his powers under article 278 and established a commission of inquiry called the Constitutional Review Commission (CRC). By the time the Commission's report was ready, President Mills had died and his vice president had thereby assumed the presidency. On receiving the report, the now President Mahama also established a commission of inquiry, this time called the Constitutional Review Implementation Committee (CRIC), whose task was to implement the recommendations of the CRC. Perhaps it was the opacity of CRIC's methodology which caused such public anxiety[70] that the Supreme Court was seen as the last chance to prevent the executive from riding roughshod over the people. The court's decision was, therefore, judged unkindly only out of disappointment and despair.

The determinative questions in the case were: (1) whether Parliament has exclusive jurisdiction over all stages of the legislative process; and (2) whether the president's power to appoint commissions of inquiry is limited to the affairs of a public entity and to public interest activities or occurrences. The plaintiff cited jurisprudence from the Kenyan and Iranian Constitutions, and, based thereon, urged the Court to hold that, as Parliament is the only institution with amendment power under Chapter 25 of the Constitution, it was the only one that could undertake activities preparatory to constitutional amendment.

[68] Jeffrey Goldsworthy, 'Constitutional Interpretation: Originalism' (2009) 4(4) Philosophy Compass 682, 683.

[69] Government of Ghana, *White Paper on CRC Report* (2012) 2.

[70] See eg Maame AS Mensa-Bonsu, 'Forty-one in One Blow! Thoughts on the Proposed Single Question Referendum to Decide the Amendment of Ghana's Constitution' (2016) 24(1) African Journal of International and Comparative Law 1; Justice Srem-Sai and others, 'Taking the Process of Amending the Entrenched Provisions of the 1992 Constitution: A Comprehensive Legal Perspective' <https://www.myjoyonline.com/taking-the-process-of-amending-the-entrenched-provisions-of-the-1992-constitution-a-comprehensive-legal-perspective/> accessed 7 February 2025

The Court, adopting the terminology of the plaintiff, identified three clear phases through which a matter passes before a legislation ensues—front end, middle end, and back end—and held that only the latter two stages were legislative, properly so-called. For that reason, only activities within those two stages could encounter the exclusive jurisdiction of Parliament. Speaking through Benin JSC, the majority held that, since none of the activities that happened before the first reading required Parliament to even consider a bill for the purpose of enactment, no such activity was legislative. Sadly, the majority decision did not discuss the constitutional amendment implications of the interpretation they were being invited to share. Wood CJ's concurring judgment, however, turned almost entirely on the amendment implications of the plaintiff's reading. Thus, while the reasons concurred in by the majority are Benin's, Wood CJ's is the one in focus in this chapter.

Her ladyship (Wood CJ) held that the constitutions that were being urged on her as guidance made express provision for frontend activities, whereas Ghana's did not. To determine whether this was an intentional choice (thus limiting interpretation) or a matter of no fundamental importance to the constitutional design (and so amenable to clarification via interpretation), she relied on *McCulloch*.[71] Wood CJ accepted its position that a constitution must, by its nature, set out only 'its great outlines' and 'most important objects', leaving its minor details to be deduced from the parameters thus provided.

She then asked whether the initiating power of frontend activities were minor details or important objects. She held that conferring exclusive pre-legislative power is not a minor detail and noted that it was precisely for this reason that the constitutions being urged on her had specified the mode by which they could be initiated. Wood CJ pointed out the level of detail in the methodology for amending entrenched provisions under Ghana's Constitution, and concluded that the non-mention of the frontend activities was no minor matter but, rather, an express constitutional design choice which it did not lie in the Court's competence to correct.

The second case of this section is *Ghana Independent Broadcasters Association (GIBA) v Attorney-General*,[72] in which the Court was invited to strike down twelve of the regulations made by the National Media Commission (NMC) in 2015. The regulations were challenged on two grounds. The first was that they were beyond the competence of the NMC and therefore unconstitutional; and second, that they were draconian. The Court did strike them down but only on the first ground. It emphasized that it was doing so not because of their harshness—undeniable though that was—but because the NMC has no authority to create criminal offences under its enabling legislation. The Court reminded the parties that article 2 allows it to review legislation for its compatibility with the Constitution; on the wisdom, or lack thereof, of a piece of legislation, however, it is not empowered to rule.

4.4 What is right about these decisions?

When the Court amends the Constitution by the express insertion of specific words or phrases, the amending nature of the decision is easy to spot. Thus, even a minimally vigilant

[71] *McCulloch v Maryland*, 17 US (4 Wheat) 316 (1819).

[72] *Ghana Independent Broadcasters Association (GIBA) v Attorney-General* (J1 4 of 2016) [2017] GHASC 45.

society would be alerted to the judiciary's overreach in such cases and, though it may by its inaction acquiesce in this judicial aggrandizement, it cannot say it did not know that it had ceded this power to its Court.

The greater danger is presented by cases like *Asare*[73] and *GIBA* for the amendments they would have sponsored would not have been by insertion of specific words. In the case of *Asare*, it would have been by way of excluding from the scope of executive (and civic) power the ability to prepare an informed piece of legislation for the consideration of Parliament. That, in effect, would have redefined the ambit of several articles, including articles 289 (on amending the Constitution), 108 (on bills with financial implications), 179 (on the budget), and 181(2) (on state loans). Accepting the plaintiff's interpretation would, therefore, have entailed a major rewrite of the Constitution. As Gibson notes, there are limits to what any constitutional sentence is capable of meaning: 'elephant' cannot mean 'mouse'; 'banana' cannot mean 'apple'; 'direct tax' cannot mean 'indirect tax'. Judicial rulings that go beyond those outer limits cannot be fairly considered to be interpretive exercises.'[74]

In his lucid metaphor, Conor Gearty likens the public sphere to a swimming pool, with policy at the deep end and legislation at the shallow. He maintains that judges should not swim in the deep end just because they can, since their swimming prowess is neither here nor there. The core issue is the court's legitimacy to decide a matter, and legitimacy is a question of trust.[75] To whom have the people entrusted a matter? This, not competence, is the real determiner of legitimacy. In any case, as contended above, the judiciary does not win this battle even on competence. The court was right to decline to wade into those policy waters in the first place because it is unlikely to navigate them well.

But the point to underscore is that the two cases show the deference that courts should display if invited to amend the Constitution. When the people have clearly made a choice in a matter, whether by the distribution of power or the content of the constitutional text, the judiciary cannot possibly, as mere caretaker thereof, be the proper forum by which these arrangements are changed. A court that understands this, when faced with a tempting opportunity for constitutional amendment, displays not even restraint, but deference. As Gearty succinctly explains, 'restraint and deference are not the same: the first is about knowing your job, the second about knowing your place'.[76]

There are those scholars who believe some amount of judicial constitutional amendment is necessary and even beneficial to a constitution.[77] The reasons cited for this necessity include that politicians may lack the incentive for needed constitutional amendments (as, for instance, where there is no groundswell seeking the change) and that the formal amendment procedures may be too slow to respond to an emergency situation.[78] These arguments, however, are not persuasive at all. A reasonably functional democracy depends on the premise that the people will call their agents—executive and legislative—to heel and ensure that matters important to society are attended to. If they cannot mind the health of

[73] *Asare Baah III v Attorney-General* (2010–2012) 1 GLR 427.
[74] Gibson (n 62) 261 at 272.
[75] Conor Gearty, 'Are Judges Now out of Their Depth? Tom Sargant Memorial Annual Lecture 2007' (London, 17 October 2007) https://files.justice.org.uk/wp-content/uploads/2015/02/06172430/Are-Judges-now-out-of-their-Depth.pdf accessed 1 October 2023.
[76] Ibid.
[77] For example, Gibson (n 62) 277–78; Kate Glover Berger, 'Judicial Amendment and Our Constitutional Lives: A Reply to Emmett Macfarlane' (2021) 19(5) International Journal of Constitutional Law 1925, 1931.
[78] Gibson (n 62) 277–78.

their constitution through this mechanism, then perhaps democracy is not the governance configuration that suits them. Self-government is as much a duty as it is a right.

As to the emergency example, it seems inconceivable that a constitutional emergency would not rouse the people to action. By their nature, matters grave enough to be constitutional emergencies are also hardly ever unanticipated and unforeseeable. As the Covid-19 pandemic has reassured us, a democratic society will always have time to respond through its elected officials, even to emergencies. When, in Ghana, it was deemed that legislative authority was required for the president to act in response to Covid, Parliament met and issued the needed legislation under a certificate of emergency.[79]

Even if constitutional amendment procedures have to be abandoned for sake of the emergency, it does not follow that the task should then accrue to the judiciary. The view loses what little attractiveness it may have held when Gibson cautions thus:

> [C]ourts should exercise self-restraint in these matters, permitting themselves to engage in constitutional amendment only when it is either inevitable that they do so, or when it would clearly be detrimental to the nation to leave the matter to the formal amendment process. In all other circumstances, judges should restrict their interpretation to the (rather generous, after all) forms of judicial review that fall within the scope of fair construction.[80]

When is it inevitable? Was *Agyei-Twum* such an instance? Would it have been clearly detrimental for the courts to have left the changing of the verb in *Occupy Ghana* to the formal amendment procedures? As for *Ransford France*, which of these two categories of permissibility does it fall under? There seems no simpler way to avoid judicial usurpation of constituent authority and the attendant challenges than to strictly follow the rule that the amendment of the Constitution be reserved to the method chosen by the Constitution.

What the Court did entirely correctly in *Asare* and *GIBA* was that it accepted, or at least remembered, its assigned place in the Constitution and stayed in its lane. It is the deference—the knowledge of its place—which the Court showed that lends these cases the glow of propriety, because in constitutional amendment matters, deference is owed as of right to the constituent power: the people.

4.5 How should the people themselves behave?

Because the courts in Ghana have, by enforcing the Constitution, materialized rights, it has come to be believed, erroneously, that they have created these rights and that what they have done previously is answer the difficult questions of what rights should exist in society, when, in fact, all they have done is explain the scope or implications of the rights that do exist by express pronouncement of the Constitution. This misconceived view of the Court's judicial review activities led the CRC, tasked with conducting an exhaustive review of the

[79] There are, of course, multiple issues with the Imposition of Restrictions Act. See Maame AS Mensa-Bonsu, 'Ghana' in Luis Roberto Barroso and Richard Albert (eds), *The 2020 International Review of Constitutional Reform* (Program on Constitutional Studies at the University of Texas at Austin in collaboration with the International Forum on the Future of Constitutionalism 2021) 121. Still, they do not negate the point that the democratic process is able to respond to emergencies and that there is no pretext for judicial amendment.

[80] Gibson (n 62) 27.

Constitution and proposing amendments for the sake of improvement, to take the position that questions of gay rights should be left to the Supreme Court to decide.[81] By abandoning themselves to judicial review in this way, Ghanaians have naturally lured the Court into expanding its mandate and amending the Constitution. In frequency, judicial amendments have been few and far between (2000, 2005, 2012, 2017), but in constitutionalism, they have proven very expensive. If the other arms of state and the public continue to leave hard and unpleasant questions about who they should be and what their Constitution should say to the Court, judicial amendments will increase both in incidence and in cost.

The people must be willing to shoulder the weight of the responsibility of being a democratic society. They must view judicial review with suspicion and subject its output to intense scrutiny, so that the Court, when called to interpret the Constitution, will be extremely wary about doing anything more than that. It is an indictment on the people of Ghana that the Court they have empowered only to interpret their Constitution can say its meaning is thoroughly impractical and therefore to be disregarded. A more vigilant and engaged society would have responded to *Agyei-Twum* with such fervour that the Court would have hesitated to do it again, never mind do it in such insouciant tones.

Less famous than the story of *Marbury v Madison*[82] is the backlash that followed it, and which was so severe that the court did not exert this implicit right of judicial review again for the next 50 years.[83] If we do not wish to return to being the helpless subjects of an all-powerful ruler, we cannot afford to abandon ourselves to the choices of the judiciary. Tyranny is no less tyrannical for being judicial.

5. Conclusion

This chapter has examined judicial amendment under the Constitution of Ghana (1992) and argued strenuously against it. It has been shown that neither in terms of outcome nor in principle can judicial amendment aid the country's journey to constitutionalism. That clarity and predictability are two chief second-order values of the constitutional amendment procedures captured in Chapter 25 is effortlessly discerned from a study of that chapter.

Article 290, which entrenches certain parts of the Constitution, provides an easy example. Rather than using an unenlightening phrase such as 'a provision affecting a right or a fundamental governance structure shall be entrenched', the article specifically lists every entrenched provision. It could be argued that, as only Parliament may amend the Constitution, it would cause no confusion in the wider society for there to be some flexibility in the scope of entrenchment. Yet in the cost–benefit analysis, this flexibility did not persuade the framers. The Supreme Court's boldness is neither welcome nor forgivable. For, as *Ransford France* amply demonstrates, this form of judicial overreach leads only to inconsistent jurisprudence that confuses and disorganizes public affairs. The outcome it sought by its interference it cannot achieve—precisely because its act was interference.

[81] Constitutional Review Commission of Ghana, 'Report of the Constitutional Review Commission of Ghana' (2010) 654.

[82] *Marbury v Madison* 5 US 137 (1803), the landmark American case in which the court declared that enforcing the law entitled it to have the final say what the law meant.

[83] Wallace Mendelson, 'Sectional Politics and the Rise of Judicial Supremacy' (1947) 9(2) Journal of Politics 255.

The grandiloquent celebration of 'the constitution as a living organism' is not justification of an approach that allows its express terms to be disregarded in favour of other terms not contained therein. Absent the Constitution, there is no reason why the judiciary's pronouncement on any matter should be received as more than the opinions of a small selection of citizens. It therefore cannot take the benefit of the wider society's respect for the constitutional arrangement and itself disregard the demarcations of its power per that arrangement. The boundary of judicial interpretation of the Constitution is the text of the Constitution; it is not the needs of the society. However, the courts will not be able to accept this as long as the people abdicate their supervisory role. Only if they scrutinize and patrol the judiciary's use of its constitutionally allotted judicial review powers will they be able to keep judicial review from turning into amendment and so be able to live by the terms of the Constitution that they adopted for themselves.

In this scrutiny exercise, academics bear the duty to lead the charge. It is because we failed with *Agyei-Twum* that we now have *Ransford France* perverting the functioning of the Constitution. What Ghana's story should impress on African constitutional academics is that we owe it to our constitutions and our own constitutional experience to monitor, analyse, and critique every judicial decision so that the Court will gain and maintain the circumspection without which judicial review will turn our democracies into juristocracies[84] and thereby defeat the very point of leaving military rule behind.

Bibliography

Adu Boahen A., *The Ghanaian Sphinx: Reflections on the Contemporary History of Ghana 1972–1987* (GAAS 1989)

Alexander L., 'What are Constitutions, and What Should (and Can) They Do?' (2011) 28(1) Social Philosophy and Policy 1

Aryee J., 'Ghana's Return to Constitutional Rule under the Provisional National Defence Council (PNDC)' (1996) 29(4) Verfassung und Recht in Übersee 434

Berger K.G., 'Judicial Amendment and Our Constitutional Lives: A Reply to Emmett Macfarlane' (2021) 19(5) International Journal of Constitutional Law 1925

Bimpong-Buta S.Y., *The Role of the Supreme Court in the Development of Constitutional Law in Ghana* (Advanced Legal Publications 2007)

Bing G., *Reap the Whirlwind: An Account of Kwame Nkrumah's Ghana from 1950–1966* (MacGibbon & Kee 1968)

Bluwey G., 'Obstacles to an Orderly Transition to Constitutional Rule under the PNDC' in Ninsin K. and Drah F. (eds.), *Ghana's Transition to Constitutional Rule* (Ghana Universities Press 1991)

[84] 'Judiocracy', coined in Everett M Dirksen, 'The Supreme Court and the People' (1968) 66 Michigan Law Review 837, is the earliest term used to describe the phenomenon. But 'juristocracy' is more common in recent literature. See eg Carlo Guarneri and Patrizia Pederzoli, *From Democracy to Juristocracy? The Power of Judges: A Comparative Study of Courts and Democracy* (OUP 2002); Ran Hirschl, *Towards Juristocracy: The Origins and Consequences of the New Constitutionalism* 2006 4(3) International Journal of Constitutional Law 581–86; Alec Stone Sweet, *Governing with Judges: Constitutional Politics in Europe* (OUP 2000); Ran Hirschl, 'Juristocracy'—Political, not Juridical' (2004) 13(3) The Good Society 6; James Grant, 'The Rise of Juristocracy' (2010) 34(2) The Wilson Quarterly 16; Martin Loughlin, 'Toward a Juristocracy' in Martin Loughlin (ed.), *Against Constitutionalism* (Harvard University Press 2022) 124. The trend is, in fact, a growing global phenomenon that goes beyond judicial amendment. In Ghana, as in the constitutionalist world, the other symptoms of juristocracy appear to be creeping into the country's jurisprudence. This includes the politicization of judicial appointments and the judicialization of politics, for example through the prosecution of opponents for corruption, first under the offence of causing financial loss to the state, and, more recently, by the Office of the Special Prosecutor. These prosecutions have generally been pursued against former government officials from the opposition party.

Chesterton G.K., 'Mr Bernard Shaw' in Dooley D. (ed.), *The Collected Works of G.K. Chesterton, vol 1* (Ignatius Press 1986)

Committee of Experts, 'Report of the Committee of Experts (Constitution) on Proposals for a Draft Constitution of Ghana' (Republic of Ghana 1991)

Constitutional Review Commission of Ghana, 'Report of the Constitutional Review Commission of Ghana' (2010)

Dirksen E.M., 'The Supreme Court and the People' (1968) 66 Michigan Law Review 837

Ekins R., 'How to Be a Free People' (2013) 58(2) American Journal of Jurisprudence 163

Endicott T., 'The Impossibility of the Rule of Law' in Endicott T (ed.), *Vagueness in Law* (OUP 2000)

Finnis J., *Natural Law and Natural Rights* (OUP 1980)

Gambia Demographic and Health Survey 2019–20 32 https://dhsprogram.com/pubs/pdf/FR369/FR369.pdf accessed 23 March 2025

Gearty C., 'Are the Judges Now out of their Depth? Tom Sargant Memorial Annual Lecture 2007' (London, 17 October 2007) https://files.justice.org.uk/wp-content/uploads/2015/02/06172430/Are-Judges-now-out-of-their-Depth.pdf accessed 1 October 2023

Ghana 2010 Population and Housing Census Summary Report of Final Results, xi https://statsghana.gov.gh/gssmain/storage/img/marqueeupdater/Census2010_Summary_report_of_final_results.pdf accessed 23 March 2025

Gibson D., 'Founding Fathers-in-Law: Judicial Amendment of the Canadian Constitution' (1992) 55(1) Law & Contemporary Problems 261

Goldsworthy J., 'Constitutional Interpretation: Originalism' (2009) 4(4) Philosophy Compass 682

Government of Ghana, *White Paper on the CRC Report*, 2012

Grant J., 'The Rise of Juristocracy' (2010) 34(2) The Wilson Quarterly 16–27

Guarneri C. and Pederzoli P., *From Democracy to Juristocracy? The Power of Judges: A Comparative Study of Courts and Democracy* (OUP 2002)

Gyandoh S.O., Kumado C.E.K., and Griffiths J., 'Dr Busia's Radio Broadcast on the Sallah Decision, 2 G & G 739 (2d)' 1374

Gyimah-Boadi E., 'Notes on Ghana's Current Transition to Constitutional Rule' (1991) 38(4) Africa Today 5–17

Gyimah-Boadi E., 'Ghana's Uncertain Political Opening' (1994) 5(2) Democracy 75

Hirschl R., '"Juristocracy" – Political, not Juridical' (2004) 13(3) The Good Society 6–11

Hirschl R., 'Towards Juristocracy: The Origins and Consequences of the New Constitutionalism' (2006) 4(3) International Journal of Constitutional Law 581–86

Hohfeld W.N., 'Fundamental Legal Conceptions Applied in Judicial Reasoning' in Cook W.W. (ed.), *Fundamental Legal Conceptions Applied in Judicial Reasoning and Other Legal Essays* (Yale University Press 1923)

Kumado C.E.K., 'Forgive Us Our Trespasses: An Examination of the Indemnity Clause in the 1992 Constitution of Ghana' (1993–1995) 19 University of Ghana Law Journal 83–101

Loughlin M., 'Toward a Juristocracy' in Loughlin M. (ed.), *Against Constitutionalism* (Harvard University Press 2022)

Macfarlane E., 'Judicial Amendment of the Constitution' (2021) 19(5) International Journal of Constitutional Law 1894–924

Madagascar Enquête Démographique et de Santé 2021

Malawi Population and Housing Census Report 2018, 21 https://malawi.unfpa.org/sites/default/files/resource-pdf/2018%20Malawi%20Population%20and%20Housing%20Census%20Main%20Report%20%281%29.pdf, last accessed 23/3/2025

Mendelson W., 'Sectional Politics and the Rise of Judicial Supremacy' (1947) 9(2) Journal of Politics 255

Mensa-Bonsu M.A.S., 'Forty-one in one Blow! Thoughts on the Proposed Single Question Referendum to Decide the Amendment of Ghana's Constitution' (2016) 24(1) African Journal of International and Comparative Law 1

Mensa-Bonsu M.A.S., 'Ghana' in Barroso L.R. and Albert R. (eds.), *The 2020 International Review of Constitutional Reform* (Program on Constitutional Studies at the University of Texas at Austin in collaboration with the International Forum on the Future of Constitutionalism 2021) 121

Mensa-Bonsu M.A.S., 'Forging Forward Introspectively as Ghana's Constitution Turns Thirty' (*IACL-AIDC Blog*, 11 October 2021) https://blog-iacl-aidc.org/2021-posts/2021/10/11/forging-forward-introspectively-as-ghanas-constitution-turns-thirty accessed 1 October 2023

Nugent P., *Big Men, Small Boys and Politics in Ghana: Power, Ideology and the Burden of History, 1982–1994* (Pinter 1995)

Oquaye M., *Politics in Ghana, 1982–1992: Rawlings, Revolution, and Populist Democracy* (Tornado Publications and Thomson Press India Ltd 2004) 6
Raz J., 'The Rule of Law and its Virtue' (1977) 93 Law Quarterly Review 195
Rubenfeld J., *Freedom and Time* (Yale University Press 2001) 153
Schmitt C., *Political Theology: Four Chapters on the Concept of Sovereignty* (George Schwab tr, UCP 2005)
Shillington K., *Ghana and the Rawlings Factor* (Macmillan 1992)
Sierra Leone Demographic and Health Survey 2019, https://dhsprogram.com/pubs/pdf/FR365/FR365.pdf last accessed 23/3/2025
Srem-Sai J., Dzah D.E., and Acheampong K.O., 'Taking the Process of Amending the Entrenched Provisions of the 1992 Constitution: A Comprehensive Legal Perspective' (*Ghanaweb*, 17 July 2014) https://myjoyonline.com/taking-the-process-of-amending-the-entrenched-provisions-of-the-1992-constitution-a-comprehensive-legal-perspective/ accessed 20 July 2022
Stone Sweet A, *Governing with Judges: Constitutional Politics in Europe* (OUP 2000)
Waldron J., 'The Core of the Case against Judicial Review' (2006) 115(6) Yale Law Journal 1346
Yayoh W.K., 'Resurgence of Multi-Party Rule in Ghana, 1990–2004: A Historical Review' (2006–2007) 10 Transactions of the Historical Society of Ghana 125–47

8

Time to Reduce Judicial Adventurism: Reflections on *Glenister II* and *Sonke Gender Justice* through the Lens of the Separation of Powers and Proposals for Reform

Lauren Kohn

1. Introduction

We are living in an era of constitutional flux. Throughout Africa and across the globe, many previously well-functioning constitutional democracies are in decline, and there is now extensive literature on the causes and dynamics of this process. For example, writing in 2018 in the context of the first Trump administration, Ginsburg and Huq identified two key ways in which constitutional democracies can be 'lost': via 'authoritarian reversion' and 'constitutional retrogression'.[1] The former entails a sweeping, expedited 'collapse into authoritarianism' and the latter a less visible, more gradual erosion of the tenets of constitutional democracy, including the 'adjudicative and administrative rule of law'.[2]

Arguably, the second process is under way in South Africa. The cases discussed in this chapter—*Glenister v President of the Republic of South Africa*[3] and *Sonke Gender Justice NPC v President of the Republic of South Africa*[4]—bookend the 'Zuma years'[5] and are pertinent illustrations of this process. They entail innovative judicial reasoning in an endeavour to protect the principles of legality and public accountability (coupled with public integrity), yet they also represent a threat to these principles due to reasoning which is, in part, flawed. Ultimately, these judgments result in informal constitutional amendment.[6] Like all public power, judicial power must be exercised lawfully and rationally—it must be justified.[7] This speaks to the 'adjudicative rule of law' as a core component of constitutional

1 Aziz Huq and Tom Ginsburg, 'How to Lose a Constitutional Democracy' (2018) 65 UCLA Law Review 78, 83.
2 Ibid.
3 2011 (3) SA 347 (CC) *(Glenister II)*.
4 2021 (3) BCLR 269 (CC) *(Sonke)*.
5 Richard Calland, *The Zuma Years – South Africa's Changing Face of Power* (Zebra Press 2014).
6 For a definition of informal (or judicial) constitutional amendment, see Emmett Macfarlane, 'Judicial Amendment of the Constitution' (2021) 19(5) International Journal of Constitutional Law 1984, 1896. For a comprehensive overview of the different kinds of constitutional amendment, see Charles M Fombad, 'An Overview of the Legal Framework for Amending Modern African Constitutions' (Chapter 1 of this volume).
7 Cora Hoexter, *Administrative Law in South Africa* (2nd edn, Juta 2012) 147. See also Cora Hoexter and Glenn Penfold, *Administrative Law in South Africa* (3rd edn, Juta 2021) 188, who contend that, '[j]udicial activism, the unashamed liberal credo of the old era, is simply not an adequate response to the challenges posed by constitutional democracy and its central demand that the use of public power, including judicial power, be justified.'

Lauren Kohn, *Time to Reduce Judicial Adventurism: Reflections on* Glenister II *and* Sonke Gender Justice *through the Lens of the Separation of Powers and Proposals for Reform* In: *Constitutional Change and Constitutionalism in Africa*. Edited by: Charles M. Fombad and Nico Steytler, Oxford University Press. © Lauren Kohn 2025. DOI: 10.1093/9780198957034.003.0010

democracy and the related matter of *how* constitutional change—or, at least, refinement—should, and should not, occur if we care about all the values in 'the rule of law's basket of ideals'.[8]

It is true that the South African judiciary has been confronted by the immense challenges of corruption—and state capture as a disturbing species of it—and maladministration. These problems have beset the country palpably over the last fifteen years,[9] and, as *Glenister II* and *Sonke* reveal, the judiciary has responded at times by interpreting the Constitution creatively to derive from it ambitious constitutional requirements and remedies.[10] Furthermore, these cases are illustrative of a particular kind of tinkering with the constitutional text. Not all modes of judicial activism are fundamentally problematic: one should imagine a spectrum with various categories of intervention. These categories can overlap with each other, and are thus not watertight, yet an appreciation of their distinctiveness is important in guiding the appropriate level of activism to avoid the inclination towards arbitrary[11] judicial action.

At one end of the spectrum is the most generous allowance for judicial creativity—the category of rights adjudication proper.[12] Within this domain of assessing the nature, content, and limitation of open-textured human rights, courts inevitably have a greater degree of interpretative leeway. As the Constitutional Court noted in *Walters*, 'both the rights and the enactment . . . must be interpreted so as to promote the value system of an open and democratic society based on human dignity, equality and freedom'.[13] This approach accords with 'transformative constitutionalism'[14] and the kind of legal adjudication it entails. However, as Langa rightly remarked:

> [W]hile it is vital that we embrace the idea of substantive adjudication, there is a distinct limit to how far we can go. Judges do not have a free rein to determine what the law is . . . [since laws,] including the Constitution, do not mean 'whatever we wish them to mean'.[15]

[8] Raisa Cachalia and Lauren Kohn, 'The Quest for "Reasonable Certainty": Refining the Justice and Equity Framework Remedial Framework in Public Procurement Cases' (2020) 137(4) South African Law Journal 659, 661.

[9] See Hoexter and Penfold (n 7) 132 on 'the continuing menace of public corruption' being 'one of the greatest challenges currently confronting South Africa'.

[10] Note that the focus of this chapter is on judicial innovation when it comes to substantive requirements. For a discussion of judicial remedial innovation, see Helen Taylor, 'Forcing the Court's Remedial Hand: Non-Compliance as a Catalyst for Remedial Innovation' (2019) 9(1) Constitutional Court Review 247.

[11] Arbitrariness is the converse of rationality. See *Pharmaceutical Manufacturers Association of South Africa and Another: In re Ex Parte President of the Republic of South Africa* 2000(2) SA 674 (CC) *(Pharmaceutical Manufacturers)* para 85: 'It is a requirement of the rule of law that the exercise of public power . . . should not be arbitrary. Decisions must be rationally related to the purpose for which the power was given, otherwise they are in effect arbitrary and inconsistent with this requirement.' On arbitrariness and 'tempering power', see further Martin Krygier, 'Tempering Power' in Maurice Adams, Anne Meuwese, and Ernst Hirsch Ballin (eds), *Constitutionalism and the Rule of Law: Bridging Idealism and Realism* (CUP 2017) 34–59.

[12] The qualifier 'proper' is used to describe cases where a right is squarely at issue and thus subjected to proper interpretation (and limitations analysis) by the court, as compared with the likes of *Glenister II* and *Sonke*, where a mishmash of possibly implicated rights was invoked shotgun-style and no proper limitations analysis was conducted. See sections 2 and 3 below.

[13] *Ex Parte Minister of Safety & Security and Others: In Re S v Walters and Another* 2002 (4) SA 613 (CC) [26].

[14] Karl Klare, 'Legal Culture and Transformative Constitutionalism' (1998) 14(1) South African Journal on Human Rights 146; Pius Langa, 'Transformative Constitutionalism' (2006) 17(3) Stellenbosch Law Review 351.

[15] Langa (n 14) 357.

This separation-of-powers cautionary note takes one to the other end of the spectrum and to two further categories of judicial activism. These kinds of judicial interpretation and innovation are such that they actually alter the constitutional text. They are flip sides of the same coin: one involves reading-out and/or obviously altering explicit textual provisions, and the other involves the reading-in of provisions. The courts should tread carefully and avoid these extreme interventions; certainly, they should not engage in this mode of constitutional tweaking in the absence of persuasive judicial reason-giving.

Both *Glenister II* and *Sonke* entail the judicial reading-in to the constitutional text of a public accountability-based institutional requirement to establish independent oversight structures where a background mix of rights is concerned. Furthermore, in both cases this was done pursuant to unclear, and hence largely unpersuasive, reasoning. Issacharoff described *Glenister II*'s innovation as a 'far-reaching' and 'structural alteration in overall governmental accountability'.[16] We should be wary of such informal structural changes to the constitutional text and not forget that, for sound democratic reasons, there are carefully calibrated constitutional amendment procedures.[17] While the judiciary—in particular, the Constitutional Court—plays a vital role in South Africa's constitutional democracy, like the other branches of state, the judiciary must be mindful of its institutional limitations and thus the necessary limits on its powers to preserve its legitimacy and integrity.[18] Langa's insights on transformative constitutionalism are again compelling:

> Were the courts to completely discard any adherence to the text they would enter squarely into the domain of the legislature as creators rather than interpreters of the law. That is clearly not what the Constitution envisages.[19]

Careful reflection upon *Glenister II* and the judicial resonance it continues to have—as illustrated by the likes of *Sonke*—reveals a Constitutional Court acting qua legislature, which is certainly cause for pause. Of course, this is not to say that this twinset of judgments is without virtue: aspects of both majority judgments[20] are laudable. First, they reveal a sound appreciation of the Constitution's separation-of-powers design, with its structurally implied 'integrity and accountability' fourth branch.[21] Second, they elucidate a litmus test for 'independence' and the application of this standard in assessing the oversight bodies in question—the anti-corruption unit in *Glenister II*, and the Judicial Inspectorate of Correctional Services (JICS) in *Sonke*. Third, the judgments' leveraging of the founding constitutional value of public accountability (coupled, as it is, with openness and responsiveness)[22] is to be welcomed.

[16] Samuel Issacharoff, 'Constitutional Courts and Consolidated Power' (2014) 62(3) American Journal of Comparative Law 585, 606.

[17] Constitution of the Republic of South Africa (1996) (the Constitution), s 74. See Richard Albert, *Constitutional Amendments – Making, Breaking, and Changing Constitutions* (OUP 2019), 269–70 on the 'democracy-enhancing virtues' of formal amendment and its legitimacy deriving not 'from its content alone but also the process by which it comes into existence'. See also Yaniv Roznai, *Unconstitutional Constitutional Amendments – The Limits of Amendment Powers* (OUP 2017).

[18] Lauren Kohn, 'The Burgeoning Constitutional Requirement of Rationality & The Separation of Powers: Has Rationality Review Gone Too Far?' (2013) 130(4) South African Law Journal 810, 818–24.

[19] Langa (n 14) 357–58.

[20] This chapter focuses on the majority judgments in both cases.

[21] See Lauren Kohn, 'The National Prosecuting Authority as Part of South Africa's Integrity & Accountability Branch and the Related Case for an Anti-Corruption Redress System' (2022) 12(1) Constitutional Court Review 1.

[22] Constitution (n 17) s 1(d).

After all, the principle of 'legality-cum-rationality'[23] born of the rule of law[24]—courtesy of the bold finding in *Fedsure*[25]—does a lot of the work a lot of the time[26] when it comes to checking abuses of public power.[27]

In short, however, while the outcomes in *Glenister II* and *Sonke* pass constitutional muster insofar as they are aimed at ensuring the accountability and legality of public power, the manner in which the judicial reasoning proceeds to reach these outcomes is neither sufficient nor necessarily sustainable. Disconcertingly, the reasoning, and attendant adventurism, displayed in these judgments may exacerbate some of the problems South Africa has been facing for some time now[28] by stretching the limits of the judicial function within the separation of powers. It is thus important to develop an awareness of how, why, and in what form such stealthy judicial amendment occurs. This, in turn, reveals why we need to think carefully about informal constitutional change and, conversely, consider what kind of change may be needed to help 'save' a constitutional democracy in gradual decline, as is arguably so in South Africa—a country still feeling the shockwaves of state capture.[29] To this end, the cases discussed in this chapter are important for two interrelated reasons.

The first reason is that both *Glenister II* and *Sonke* entail informal constitutional change in which the judiciary responds to a governmental failure to ensure the adequate independence—and hence integrity and accountability—of the oversight bodies in question and, in turn, the integrity and accountability of the wielders of public powers who are subject to their oversight. In *Glenister II*, the Court found that disbanding the erstwhile Directorate of Special Operations (the DSO, commonly referred to as 'the Scorpions') and replacing it with the Directorate of Priority Crime Investigation (the DPCI, commonly referred to as 'the Hawks') within the South African Police Services (SAPS) was an 'unreasonable step'.[30] The Scorpions were housed within the office of the National Prosecuting Authority (NPA)—not the SAPS—and the text of the Constitution; read with applicable Constitutional Court jurisprudence; the National Prosecuting Authority Act 32 of 1998; and its subsidiary legislation and policy directives, clearly reveal the NPA to be an

[23] Lauren Kohn, 'Time to Go Back to First Principles: A Critical Analysis of the 2017 Procurement Regulations Reveals Them to be Short of the Legality-cum-rationality Mark' (2019) 6(1) African Public Procurement Law Journal 1. This term flows from the Constitutional Court's collapsing of these rule-of-law concepts. See eg *Masetlha v President of the Republic of South Africa* 2008 (1) SA 566 (CC) [42] paras 77–78.

[24] Constitution (n 17) s 1(c).

[25] *Fedsure Life Assurance Ltd & Others v Greater Johannesburg Transitional Metropolitan Council and Others* 1999 (1) SA 374 (CC) *(Fedsure)*.

[26] Aziz Z Huq, 'A Tactical Separation of Powers Doctrine' (2019) 9(1) Constitutional Court Review 19, 40 regarding the courts' response to state capture having put 'pressure' on 'the value of "legality"'.

[27] This is particularly so due to the expansion of rationality review. See eg Michael Bishop, 'Rationality is Dead! Long Live Rationality! Saving Rational Basis Review' (2010) 25(2) South African Public Law 312; Kohn (n 18).

[28] Shortly after *Glenister II* was handed down, the Department of Justice and Constitutional Development published a Discussion Document that made perturbing references to the role and place of the judiciary within the separation of powers. See Department of Justice and Constitutional Development, 'Discussion Document on the Transformation of the Judicial System and the Role of the Judiciary in the Developmental South African State' (February 2012) https://www.justice.gov.za/docs/other-docs/20120228-transf-jud.pdf accessed 24 October 2022. For commentary on this document, see Jonathan Klaaren, 'Transformation of the Judicial System in South Africa, 2012–2013' (2015) 47(3) George Washington International Law Review 481.

[29] 'State capture' is not a series of isolated corrupt acts but the execution of a carefully orchestrated project to pillage state funds for private gain. For evidence of state capture in South Africa, see the *Report of the Judicial Commission of Inquiry into Allegations of State Capture, Corruption and Fraud in the Public Sector Including Organs of State* (2021–2022) https://www.gov.za/documents/judicial-commission-inquiry-state-capture-report-part-3-viii-1-mar-2022-0000 accessed 22 October 2022 (better known as the *Zondo Report*).

[30] *Glenister II* (n 3) para 194.

integrity-and-accountability body within South Africa's four-branched model of the separation of powers.[31] This is not the case for the SAPS.

In *Sonke*, the establishment of the JICS 'without ensuring that it has an adequate level of independence from the Department over which it is to exercise oversight' was similarly held not to be 'a reasonable step'.[32] In both cases, the Court reached its conclusion by way of doctrinally loose reasoning. Essentially, 'the scheme of the Constitution'[33] was relied upon to create 'a weak constitutional principle based on an *amalgam*'[34] of: (1) international law and the 'constitutional principle of cooperation';[35] (2) the value of public accountability; (3) the Bill of Rights (with a 'conglomerate'[36] of implicated rights including, in both instances, that of human dignity); and (4) the general section 7(2) mandate of the state to 'respect, protect, promote and fulfil' these rights.

The second reason these judgments are important is that in illustrating the kind of constitutional change that is *not* a sustainable solution—far-reaching, informal judicial change that relies on amorphous high-order constitutional principles—they bring to mind the kind of change that is indeed required. As alluded to above, while the judgments reveal a lack of appreciation of the judicial role within the separation of powers, they equally reveal an insightful understanding of the role of the fourth-branch public integrity-and-accountability institutions within South Africa's constitutional model of the separation of powers.

This foregrounds the need to contemplate the big-picture issue of a constitutional amendment explicitly to entrench this four-branched model. This would, in turn, reduce the possibility, however remote it may seem, of the judicial dilution of this sensible contemporary fourth-branch appreciation of the separation of powers. As Huq has noted, 'legal rules matter because the process of institutional decomposition happens over time' and the rules, as 'institutional shelters', can enable 'resistance to backsliding',[37] particularly where they are explicitly and clearly entrenched. A sturdy shelter for the separation of powers is something for South Africa's Parliament to contemplate as the country navigates the state capture which has been glaringly brought to light in the *Zondo Report*.[38]

Finally, this duo of 'public integrity-and-accountability' cases—*Glenister-II* and *Sonke*—highlights the adverse implications for human dignity where the integrity-and-accountability body in question (the Hawks and the JICS, respectively) is not adequately independent. Integrity and accountability have been flouted by state capture, and more generally by corruption and maladministration. As people, we cannot live a dignified life if we live in the fear that the state is not only failing to work for us[39] but is, in fact, often deliberately acting against us with little regard for our basic human rights.

[31] Kohn (n 21). See also Lauren Kohn, 'State Capture in South Africa: Time to Think Differently About Redress and Recovering the Stolen Loot' (*The Conversation*, 8 February 2023) https://theconversation.com/state-capture-in-south-africa-time-to-think-differently-about-redress-and-recovering-the-stolen-loot-199219 accessed 22 May 2023.

[32] *Sonke* (n 4) para 129.

[33] *Glenister II* (n 3) para 200; *Sonke* (n 4) para 46.

[34] Nico Steytler, 'Towards Understanding and Combatting the Crime of Corruption in Africa' in Charles M Fombad and Nico Steytler (eds.), *Corruption and Constitutionalism in Africa* (OUP 2020) 457, 478 (emphasis added).

[35] Ibid.

[36] *Sonke* (n 4) para 68.

[37] Huq (n 26) 25.

[38] *Zondo Report* (n 29).

[39] The Constitutional Court underscored the essence of integral and accountable governance in *MEC for Health, Eastern Cape & Another v Kirland Investments (Pty) Ltd* 2014 (3) SA 481 (CC) para 82, where it noted that

This raises, for brief consideration, the possibility of recalibrating the constitutional section 10 right to human dignity via the properly prescribed constitutional amendment process to render it an individual justiciable right with enhanced substantive bite. This approach would free up space for the courts in navigating complex public integrity-and-accountability cases within the separation of powers, as the judicial reasoning could then shift from the realm of reading-in tenuous structural requirements to the category of rights Public adjudication proper. In turn, this would reduce pressure on the judiciary and its resultant inclination to resolve serious cases with reasoning that cannot be taken entirely seriously.

The chapter rounds off discussion of *Glenister II* and *Sonke* (in sections 2 and 3, respectively) with a brief comparison, in section 4, of other categories of judicial amendment that are more appropriate. Section 5 gives consideration to grander-scheme constitutional change to make South Africa's *implied* constitutional model of the separation of powers *express*. This is coupled with a proposal for an amendment to the right to dignity. Section 6 concludes the chapter's analysis. In analysing the pair of public integrity-and-accountability cases that are in focus here—*Glenister II* and *Sonke*—this contribution seeks to convey a message about what *not* to do, and about what should perhaps indeed be done. This message is fundamentally Dworkinian in nature: it is about 'law as integrity'[40] and hence about making the implicit *explicit* through clear, candid judicial reasoning—and, therefore, about making constitutional amendments that respect the Constitution itself.

2. *Glenister II*: Judicial adventurism in pursuit of public integrity and accountability

2.1 Facts and finding

Glenister II is the second and central judgment in a Constitutional Court trifecta[41] initiated by Hugh Glenister, a Johannesburg-based businessman acting in the public interest.[42] Mr Glenister was concerned about the deleterious impact of corruption and its likely increase following the decision to disband the effective corruption-busting unit, the Scorpions (housed under the NPA), and replace it with the Hawks (within the SAPS). This

'there is a higher duty on the state to respect the law, to fulfil procedural requirements and to tread respectfully when dealing with rights. Government ... is the Constitution's primary agent. It must do right, and it must do it properly.'

[40] Ronald Dworkin, *Law's Empire* (Belknap Press of Harvard University Press 1986) 262.

[41] The prequel to *Glenister II*—that is, *Glenister v President of the Republic of South Africa* 2009 (1) SA 287 (CC) (*Glenister I*)—entailed an unsuccessful challenge by Mr Glenister to the Cabinet decision to initiate these statutes. See *Glenister II* (n 3) para 11: '[T]his Court, in *Glenister I*, dismissed the challenge, holding that it had not been established that it would be appropriate ... [for it to] intervene in the affairs of Parliament nor that material and irreversible harm would result if the Court did not intervene at that stage.' The sequel to *Glenister II* is *Helen Suzman Foundation v The President of the Republic of South Africa* [2014] ZACC 32 *(Glenister III)*, which entailed a follow-up challenge to the amended legislation. Mogoeng CJ penned the majority judgment. The crisp question addressed was whether 'the South African Police Service Act (SAPS Act), as amended again ... [complied with] the constitutional obligation to establish an adequately independent anti-corruption agency' See para 2 of *Glenister III*. The Court held that several provisions were unconstitutional and invalid, but, according to Tushnet, adopted a more 'deferential' approach than in *Glenister II*. See Mark Tushnet, 'Fourth-Branch Institutions: South Africa' in David S Law, *Constitutionalism in Context* (CUP 2022) 426, 436.

[42] Constitution (n 17) s 38.

controversial policy decision was made in 2007 in Polokwane (the capital city of Limpopo Province) at the 52nd national conference of the ruling African National Congress (ANC), prior to Jacob Zuma's taking office as president and—as is now known with the benefit of hindsight—the commencement of an era of state capture of staggering proportions.

The so-called Polokwane Resolution was given effect to via the legislation that created the Hawks and at the same time sounded the Scorpions' death knell, namely the South African Police Service Amendment Act 57 of 2008 and the National Prosecuting Authority Amendment Act 56 of 2008 (the impugned laws). This move was made in spite of the recommendation by the Khampepe Commission (Report of 3 February 2006) that the Scorpions remain in existence within the NPA—a body constitutionally committed to serving 'without fear, favour or prejudice'[43]—and notwithstanding the South African Cabinet's apparent approval of the Report.[44] The *Glenister-II* litigation commenced after the impugned laws came into force.

In a close split indicative of the complexities of the case and the concomitant complexities in the majority's reasoning, the Court was divided five-to-four. Moseneke DCJ and Cameron J penned the 'bold'[45] judgment for the majority, and Ngcobo CJ the more deferential one for the minority. The majority judgment in *Glenister II* remains worthy of reflection even now, since it continues to have judicial ripple effects more than a decade later, at a time when the country is still grappling with its corruption crisis. It is also opportune to analyse *Glenister II* afresh for a further reason: some of its significance appears to have been missed when the judgment was handed down. While there was, at the time, some analysis of the implications of the majority judgment's creative harnessing of international law on the domestic plane,[46] there was nonetheless a lack of detailed critical engagement with the remarkable constitutional 'divination'[47] made by Cameron and Moseneke JJ for the majority.

In short, the justices amended the Constitution by reading-in a constitutional requirement on the state to take reasonable measures to combat and prevent corruption by establishing an adequately independent oversight body. To this end, the majority employed the general constitutional requirement in section 7(2) – that the state 'respect, protect, promote and fulfil the rights in the Bill of Rights' – to establish an overarching standard of reasonableness in terms of which to scrutinize the impugned legislative acts. In turn, the majority found that 'the statutory structure creating the DPCI'[48] (the Hawks)

[43] Ibid. s 179(4).

[44] *Glenister II* (n 3) paras 6–7.

[45] Mark S Kende, 'Enforcing the South African Constitution: The Fight for Judicial Independence and Separation of Powers' (2014) 23(35) Transnational Law & Contemporary Problems 35, 44.

[46] Ibid. 43–45; Issacharoff (n 16) 606–08, and see 607 where he notes that '[p]lacing responsibility for its decision on international law is an interesting judicial expedient'. See further Samuel Issacharoff, 'The Democratic Risk to Democratic Transitions' (2013) 5(1) Constitutional Court Review 1, 27–30; Juha Tuovinen, 'The Role of International Law in Constitutional Adjudication: *Glenister v President of the Republic of South* Africa' (2013) 130(4) South African Law Journal 661; Juha Tuovinen, 'What to Do With International Law? Three Flaws in Glenister' (2013) 5(1) Constitutional Court Review 434; Ziyad Motala, 'Divination through a Strange Lens' (*Times Live*, 26 March 2011) https://www.timeslive.co.za/ideas/2011-03-27-divination-through-a-strange-lens/ accessed 24 October 2022. Edwin Cameron himself mounted a defence of the *Glenister-II* majority judgment (which he penned with Moseneke DCJ). His article focuses, too, on the international-law development which the case presents. See Edwin Cameron, 'Constitutionalism, Rights, and International Law: The *Glenister* Decision' (2013) 23(2) Duke Journal of Comparative and International Law 389. This chapter does not deal with the use of international law by the *Glenister-II* and *Sonke* majority judgments but focuses on the development they present in relation to s 7(2)'s reasonableness standard.

[47] *S v Zuma and Others* 1995 (2) SA 642 (CC) para 18.

[48] *Glenister II* (n 3) para 248.

offended this implied 'constitutional obligation resting on Parliament to create an independent anti-corruption entity'[49]—an obligation unreservedly drawn from the 'heart'[50] of the Constitution. The question, then, is how exactly did the majority reach this decision?

2.2 The reasoning: From the heart of the Constitution

The court in *Glenister II* had to answer two interrelated questions, and on both scores the majority and minority were strongly divided. The first was whether 'the Constitution imposes an obligation on the state to establish and maintain an independent body to combat corruption and organised crime'.[51] The majority's answer was a firm 'yes', but one built on the foundations of faulty judicial reasoning. The second question was whether 'the specialised unit which the impugned legislation ... established'—the Hawks—'[met] the requirement of independence'. The majority's answer to this second question was a definitive 'no', this time based on more persuasive legal reasoning. As for how the Court went about finding as it did on these two issues, it is best to start where the Court itself started—with a context-setting elucidation of corruption that reveals it to be the inverse of integrity[52] and accountability:[53]

> There can be no gainsaying that corruption threatens to fell at the knees virtually everything we hold dear and precious in our hard-won constitutional order. It blatantly undermines the democratic ethos, the institutions of democracy, the rule of law and the foundational values of our nascent constitutional project. It fuels maladministration and public fraudulence and imperils the capacity of the state to fulfil its *obligations to respect, protect, promote and fulfil all the rights* enshrined in the Bill of Rights. When corruption and organised crime flourish, sustainable development and economic growth are stunted. And in turn, the stability and *security of society* is put at risk.[54]

As the italicized phrases suggest, right at the outset of its reasoning, the majority was laying the (tenuous) foundations for its (drastic) development of a general constitutional obligation to take reasonable and effective legislative steps in pursuit of the protection, promotion, and fulfilment of the full suite of rights in the Bill of Rights. The judgment proceeded to traverse the international and regional instruments on corruption, and South Africa's domestic mandate to tackle it as detailed in the Preamble to the Prevention and Combatting of Corrupt Activities Act 12 of 2004 (PRECCA).

Two key points emerge from the judgment on this score. The first is that corruption is the antithesis of good governance insofar as it 'undermines the principles of accountability and transparency'.[55] The second is that, to the extent that corruption undermines good governance, it necessarily also undermines human-rights realisation—whenever public money is

[49] Ibid.
[50] Ibid. paras 178, 189.
[51] Ibid. para 163.
[52] For fuller discussion, see Kohn (n 21) 34.
[53] For fuller discussion, see ibid 32.
[54] *Glenister II* (n 3) para 166 (emphasis added).
[55] Ibid. para 169.

funnelled off for corrupt, self-serving purposes, there is necessarily less money to build houses, provide education, ensure municipal service delivery, and so on. Ultimately, when corruption reigns, 'we, the people' are less able to live a dignified human existence.

The Court, accordingly, emphasised extracts from the judgments in *Heath* and *Shaik* which noted, respectively, that corruption undermines 'the constitutional commitment to human dignity, [and] the achievement of equality'[56] and (thus) 'negatively affects development and the promotion of human rights'.[57] This is indeed so and deserving of emphasis—so far, so good. Then, having established the dangers of corruption and the resultant 'need and rationale' for combating it,[58] the majority moved to the core issue, namely 'the source of the obligation to establish and maintain a corruption-fighting unit' and the 'structural and operational attributes' such a unit must have.[59] It is at this point that the majority reasoning began to falter, and for the primary reason that there is in fact *no* such express obligation in the text of the Constitution.[60]

2.2.1 Vices in the majority reasoning

Had the constitutional drafters intended to make provision for a permanent anti-corruption body, presumably they would have been explicit in establishing it,[61] likely alongside other 'institutions supporting constitutional democracy' in the Constitution's Chapter 9—a proudly South African innovation, which is now an international benchmark on matters fourth-branch.[62] This was not the case, however, and so to conjure up a constitutional basis for such a body in the absence of the requisite constitutional scaffold is not only to employ sketchy foundational reasoning but also tantamount to showing inadequate respect for the constitutional text itself, and indeed its design. It is, in other words, to change the Constitution by judicial fiat.

The majority was at least candid about the Constitution's silence on the need to establish an independent corruption-fighting unit: Moseneke DCJ and Cameron J noted that the Constitution 'does not in express terms command' the establishment of such a unit, nor does it prescribe its 'operational and other attributes'.[63] Yet, in the same breath, the majority baldly asserted, without 'doubt', that the Constitution's 'scheme taken as a whole imposes a pressing duty on the state to set up a concrete and effective mechanism to prevent and root out corruption and cognate corrupt practices'.[64]

[56] *South African Association of Personal Injury Lawyers v Heath* 2001 (1) SA 883 (CC) para 4 (emphasis added), by the *Glenister II* (n 3) majority, para 172.

[57] *S v Shaik* 2007 (1) SA 240 (SCA) para 223 (emphasis added), by the *Glenister II* (n 3) majority, para 173.

[58] *Glenister II* (n 3) para 166.

[59] Ibid. para 174.

[60] Kende (n 45) 43: '[N]othing in the Constitution actually specified that there must be such an agency.'

[61] For a proposal on the form, role, functions, and structural and operational attributes of this body, see Lauren Kohn, 'Integrity & Accountability Commissions of Inquiry: A South African Perspective' (2024) 20(4) Utrecht Law Review 98-119, section 3.5, where a case is made for the establishment of 'a permanent anti-state-capture and corruption commission' – more or less along the lines suggested in the *Zondo Report* (n 29) pt VI(4), para 252. See also, Lauren Kohn and Theunis Roux, 'The 21st Constitution Amendment Bill's proposed Anti-corruption Commission Needs a Rethink' (*Mail & Guardian*, 25 August 2024) <https://mg.co.za/thought-leader/opinion/2024-08-25-proposed-anti-corruption-commission-needs-a-rethink/> accessed 14 February 2025.

[62] The Constitution's elucidation of state institutions that 'strengthen constitutional democracy in the Republic' has become a blueprint of sorts globally in discussion of the fourth branch of the state. For further detail, see eg Tushnet (n 41) and Mark Tushnet, *The New Fourth Branch: Institutions for Protecting Constitutional Democracy* (CUP 2021).

[63] *Glenister II* (n 3) para 175.

[64] Ibid.

This statement should give us pause. First, it certainly enables us to breathe a sigh of relief, for of course we need such a duty to exist and to be respected and given meaningful effect to: corruption is a societal epidemic that threatens us all. Yet, equally, this kind of judicial reasoning should make us wonder: what other duties could the judiciary *mero motu* bring into definitive constitutional existence, and in the absence of a concrete rights challenge? Moreover, what does this mean for the judicial role and the preservation of this significant role within the separation of powers in a constitutional democracy?

All of this points to a possible cause of the Court's flawed reasoning: instead of grounding the matter in a distinctive rights infraction and then ascertaining a clear correlative duty on this basis,[65] the Court adopted a back-to-front approach. Thus, the majority began by asserting the 'incontestable' and 'uncontested'[66] existence of a constitutional duty to fight corruption, and then, in the absence of a clear breach of a particular right, fumbled in trying to source the duty's constitutional provenance and sketch its remit. This may explain why the purported 'limitations analysis' in the judgment is no more than a paragraph long[67] and, in fact, not an analysis of any limitation of a right at all. The majority paraphrased section 36, centred as it is on an assessment of the nature of the right vis-à-vis the nature and extent of the limitation thereof, but then misapplied this test by focusing on a duty in the absence of a flip-side right. According to the majority, '[t]he respondents offered no attempt to justify *any limitation of the duty* to create an independent anti-corruption unit.'[68]

Without a clear right to give content to this duty, the Court became creative and the analysis turned into a slippery effort to join the dots. To enumerate, these dots were: (1) South Africa's anti-corruption obligations under international law;[69] (2) the principle of co-operation;[70] (3) the constitutional commitment to accountability; (4) the assertion that the 'failure on the part of the state to create a sufficiently independent anti-corruption entity' infringed a mix of rights;[71] and (5) the overarching section 7(2) requirement that the state 'respect, protect, promote and fulfil the rights in the Bill of Rights'.

According to the majority, and on a 'common sense approach' in view of the 'scheme' of the Constitution,[72] these dots could be joined to render an implicit[73] constitutional duty, housed in section 7(2), to take 'reasonable and effective steps': in this case, to 'establish an anti-corruption entity with the necessary independence'.[74] The Court put this so plainly and boldly—it described (its own ascertainment of) this implied obligation as 'unequivocal',[75] 'cardinal',[76] 'patent',[77] and 'incontestable'[78]—that it is perhaps no wonder

[65] On rights and duties as 'jural correlatives', see Wesley Hohfeld, 'Some Fundamental Legal Conceptions as Applied in Judicial Reasoning' (1913) 23(1) Yale Law Journal 28.

[66] *Glenister II* (n 3) para 177.

[67] Ibid. para 203.

[68] Ibid. (emphasis added).

[69] Read with the constitutional provisions governing the application of international law in the domestic realm. See Constitution (n 17) s 39(1); s 231(2), which was 'of prime significance' (*Glenister II* (n 3) para 194); and s 233, which demands 'any reasonable interpretation that is consistent with international law when legislation is interpreted' (*Glenister II* (n 3) para 202).

[70] Steytler (n 34) 478.

[71] *Glenister II* (n 3) para 198.

[72] Ibid. para. 200.

[73] Ibid. paras 189, 194–95.

[74] Ibid. para 192.

[75] Ibid.

[76] Ibid. para 200.

[77] Ibid. para 203.

[78] Ibid.

readers of the judgment were lulled into a sense of analytical complacency at the time it was handed down. For if the judges themselves believed this specific duty to be so patent (notwithstanding its textual invisibility) surely we should too? The allegory of the emperor and his new clothes comes to mind here.

Cameron J himself acknowledged the 'dramatic'[79] effect of the judgment two years later. He highlighted the two 'major substantive innovations of *Glenister*' as 'first, the domestication of international law' and 'second' (the focus of this chapter), 'the reaffirmation that governmental measures in pursuance of the section 7(2) obligation to respect, protect, promote and fulfil rights in the Bill of Rights *must be reasonable*'.[80] This latter innovation—which was under-recognised, and thus undertheorised, at the time (and arguably still is)—he predicted 'may yet have a significant impact'.[81] The likes of *Sonke*[82] reveal that it is indeed having such an impact, which raises a number of complexities.

The first complexity is *Glenister II*'s introduction of a general positive obligation to take 'reasonable and effective steps' through 'laws and structures'[83] into section 7(2) in relation to *any* of the rights in the Bill of Rights. The second, and related, complexity is that the constitutional drafters' deliberate choice of tying particular rights (the so-called qualified socio-economic rights) to an express reasonableness standard, and resultant 'internal' limitations analysis, is rendered somewhat meaningless. This is because, according to the majority, the reasonableness standard apparently applies across the spectrum of rights. This in turn raises the question, what of section 36, with its careful calibration of factors to be weighed in the balance in assessing the justifiability or otherwise of a rights infringement? Do we simply apply a globular reasonableness test when it comes to the assessment of legislative acts that infringe rights and allow section 36 to pale into insignificance, as both *Glenister II* and *Sonke* seem to suggest? And how does this fit with the applicability and use of the legality-cum-rationality standard for assessing the constitutionality of Acts?

As the literature underscores,[84] there are sound reasons for subjecting administrative acts (compared with, say, legislative acts) to the more onerous review standard of reasonableness rather than 'mere' rationality. After all, had the constitutional architects intended a generally applicable reasonableness standard to apply to *all* acts (legislative, executive, administrative, and so on), they presumably would have inserted this qualifier into section 7(2). They did not—and for good separation-of-powers reasons.[85] And so, with *Glenister II*, one sees both the judicial reading-in of a standard that vitiates sound doctrines[86] underpinning South Africa's constitutional order, and a reading-out—or, at any rate, an incipient hollowing-out—of clear terms and tests within the Bill of Rights.

This is problematic, for it amounts to a form of 'constitutional retrogression' to the extent that it erodes the 'adjudicative rule of law'[87] with its ambitions of clarity, certainty,

[79] Cameron (n 46) 404.
[80] Ibid. 408 (emphasis added).
[81] Ibid. 409.
[82] *Sonke* (n 4).
[83] *Glenister II* (n 3) para 189.
[84] See eg Hoexter and Penfold (n 7) 483 ff; Kohn (n 18) 827.
[85] Kohn (n 18) 827.
[86] For an exposition of the notion of 'doctrine' and 'doctrinal analysis', see Helen Scott, 'The Death of Doctrine: Private-law Scholarship in South Africa Today' in Jurgen Basedow, Holger Fleischer, and Reinhard Zimmermann (eds.), *Legislators, Judges, and Professors* (Mohr Siebeck 2016) 223.
[87] Huq and Ginsburg (n 1) 83.

accessibility, and thus precision in legal reasoning.[88] These constituents of the rule of law chime with those other crucial constitutional values of '*accountability*, responsiveness and openness'.[89] We cannot *account* for behaviour if we do not know its bounds, and the same applies to the judiciary. These rule-of-law requirements are important in enabling state and societal actors to plan their lives, predict legal outcomes, and ensure that their conduct adheres to what is required of them: to adhere to the law. As Ginsburg and Versteeg trenchantly note, '[t]he rule of law is the central political ideal of our time, a lynchpin of democracy, justice and development.'[90] It is important that its constituent principles—including 'compliance, consistency and congruence'[91]—are respected by all, including the judiciary.

In seeking to vindicate the rule of law and the value of accountability, the *Glenister-II* majority reasoning (in addressing the 'first' question before the Court) arguably does a disservice to these very values. It takes creative, transformative adjudication a bit too far,[92] and so may in fact 'disturb the finely-balanced ordering of society and endanger the ideals of transformation'.[93] Thankfully, the Court does somewhat better in addressing the second question.

2.2.2 Towards more virtuous judicial reasoning

The second question the Court had to address was whether the Hawks, as the specialised unit established under the impugned laws and in lieu of the disbanded Scorpions, met the 'requirement of independence'. More particularly, the Court had to determine whether the Hawks enjoyed 'an adequate level of structural and operational autonomy, secured through institutional and legal mechanisms, to prevent undue political interference'.[94] The majority found that this was not the case. While it again fudged its reasoning in places—for example, the majority oscillated between the use of the more lenient yardstick of 'sufficient' independence[95] and the more onerous one of 'adequate' independence[96]—its reasoning in addressing question two is generally commendable.

Having already traversed the international instruments on combating corruption and the notion of 'independence'—and having already made the intriguing leap from the realm of the international to South Africa's domestic Constitution—the Court then distilled, and applied, certain markers of independence. These markers, or factors, include: (1) 'security of tenure', with a solemn 'oath or undertaking' a noteworthy element of it;[97] (2) security of 'remuneration'; and (3) 'mechanisms for accountability and oversight'.[98] To this list the Court

[88] See Lon L Fuller, *The Morality of Law* (Yale University Press 1969) 33–39 on the core (procedural) requirements of the rule of law: generality, publicity, prospectivity, clarity, consistency, possibility of compliance, stability, and congruence.

[89] Constitution (n 17) s 1(d) (emphasis added).

[90] Tom Ginsburg and Mila Versteeg, 'Constitutional Correlates of the Rule of Law' in Adams, Meuwese and Ballin (eds) (n 11) 506–25, 506.

[91] Ibid. 507.

[92] For example, Kende (n 45) correctly notes that '*Glenister* has problems when examined using formalist constitutional methodology'. See also Tushnet (n 62) 117–18. cf Theunis Roux, 'The South African Constitutional Court's Democratic Rights Jurisprudence' (2013) 5 Constitutional Court Review 33, 73: 'The judges must thus continually seek refuge in the clear terms of their mandate, even if that approach on occasion, *as it did in Glenister, leads to strained formalistic reasoning*' (emphasis added). As this chapter shows, the reasoning in *Glenister II* cannot accurately be described as 'formalistic'.

[93] Langa (n 14) 358.

[94] *Glenister II* (n 3) para 206.

[95] *Glenister II* (n 3) para 196.

[96] Ibid. paras 194, 206.

[97] Ibid. para 218.

[98] Ibid. para 210.

added the consideration of (4) whether or not Parliament has created 'an institution that appears from the reasonable standpoint of the public to be independent'. After all, public confidence in an institution's independence is a key 'constituent' of that independence.[99]

Importantly, in giving meaning to the concept of independence, the Court considered South Africa's 'uniquely South African constitutional structure'[100] and the need to look to 'the courts, to Chapter 9 institutions, to the [National Director of Public Prosecutions] NDPP' and 'the now-defunct DSO'.[101] This grouping of institutions signals a proper understanding of the Constitution's 'implied' version of the separation-of-powers doctrine with its integrity-and-accountability fourth branch.[102] It is surprising that this judicial groundwork was not adequately noted – be it in ensuing case law or academic literature – around the time the judgment was handed down.

A few years later, cases such as *Nkandla*[103] and *Corruption Watch*[104] made the roles and constitutional positionality of public integrity-and-accountability bodies (such as the Public Protector and NPA) within the South African state system all the more patent. However, one should not forget that the *Glenister-II* court made the first strides here. Only in recent years have commentators recognised as much, perhaps due in part to the growing global momentum in matters fourth-branch.

For example, following the *Nkandla* judgment, Klug in 2017 referred to *Glenister II* as an example of a judgment 'recognising independent institutions alongside the traditional *trias politica* as significant contributors to South Africa's particular form of the separation of powers'.[105] In a 2019 contribution,[106] he again noted *Glenister II* as a case indicative of the rising role of 'integrity institutions'.[107] However, as in his 2017 article,[108] Klug's focus appears to be on the establishment of the obligation to create an independent anti-corruption body as the 'integrity institution' in question.[109] Klug thus overlooks the *Glenister II* majority's unpacking of the role and place of the *NPA* as a fourth-branch body within the separation of powers.

Tushnet's recent scholarship on fourth-branch institutions also focuses on *Glenister-II*'s separation-of-powers reasoning on anti-corruption agencies.[110] But again, the Court's appreciation of a *textually entrenched*, but often under-appreciated, integrity-and-accountability body, namely the NPA,[111] is what is really commendable. It has been

[99] Ibid. para 207.
[100] Ibid. para 216.
[101] Ibid. paras 211, 205.
[102] Kohn (n 21).
[103] *Economic Freedom Fighters v Speaker of the National Assembly and Others; Democratic Alliance v Speaker of the National Assembly and Others* 2016 (3) SA 580 (CC) *(Nkandla)*.
[104] *Corruption Watch NPC and Others v President of the Republic of South Africa and Others; Nxasana v Corruption Watch NPC and Others* 2018 (2) SACR 442 (CC) *(Corruption Watch)*.
[105] Heinz Klug, 'Institutional Integrity and the Promise of Constitutionalism: Justice Moseneke, Judicial Authority and the Separation of Powers' (2017) 1 Acta Juridica 3, 22.
[106] Heinz Klug, 'Transformative Constitutions and the Role of Integrity Institutions in Tempering Power: The Case of Resistance to State Capture in Post-Apartheid South Africa' (2019) 67(3) Buffalo Law Review 701, 723–24; 739–40.
[107] Ibid.
[108] Klug (n 105) 24.
[109] Klug (n 106) 740.
[110] Tushnet (n 41) 439; Tushnet (n 62) 118.
[111] Kohn (n 21) 36 and 44–53, and, as early as 2016 Kohn noted in, Lauren Kohn, 'Mbeki Guilty of Misinterpreting the Law' (*Mail & Guardian*, 17 February 2016) that, '[t]he NPA is a *hybrid* constitutional beast (emphasis added) <https://mg.co.za/article/2016-02-17-mbekis-defence-of-npa-decision-wont-wash/> accessed 14 February 2025.

stated erroneously in the literature that the NPA forms part of the executive.[112] In fact, it is a 'hybrid'[113] constitutional body that straddles the 'administration of justice'[114] and the executive—it is an integrity-and-accountability body in South Africa's constitutional democracy.[115]

In comparing the defunct Scorpions (housed, as they were, under the NPA) with the Hawks, in order to assess the independence of the latter, the *Glenister II*'s majority shines a light on the special constitutional status of the NPA, headed by the NDPP, which plays a vital role at the office's helm. This comparative exercise formed a key basis for the Court's conclusion that the 'statutory structure creating the DPCI' missed the mark on independence. Ultimately, the *Glenister II* court concluded as follows:

> The absence of specially secured conditions of employment; the imposition of oversight by a committee of political executives, and the subordination of the DPCI's power to investigate at the hands of members of the executive, who control the DPCI's policy guidelines, are inimical to the degree of independence that is required.[116]

As a result, the majority declared Chapter 6A of the South African Police Service Act 68 of 1995 to be inconsistent and invalid for failing to secure an adequate degree of independence for the Hawks. The Court gave Parliament eighteen months to remedy this defect. As Tushnet has rightly remarked, what the majority did in *Glenister II* amounted to 'forcing a desirable outcome into an ill-fitting doctrinal framework'.[117] For the reasons previously noted, one might go even further and argue that, in fact, the Court created a framework to accommodate its finding, but in the absence of compelling doctrinal reason-giving.

3. *Sonke Gender Justice*: *Glenister II* reloaded and rebooted

3.1 Facts and finding

The *Sonke* case was decided on 4 December 2020, nearly a decade after *Glenister II* was handed down. The majority judgment was penned by Theron J,[118] and there were two dissenting views: those of Jafta J and Victor AJ.[119] *Sonke* relied strongly on the *Glenister-II* line of reasoning and took it even further—even though the Court could easily have

[112] See eg DW Freedman, 'The National Prosecuting Authority' in *LAWSA – Constitutional Law: Structures of Government* (vol 7(2), 3rd edn, LexisNexis South Africa 2020), para 352; Huq (n 26) 41.

[113] On the 'hybrid' nature of certain integrity-and-accountability institutions, see Kohn (n 18) 833 regarding the Judicial Services Commission (JSC) and Kohn (n 21) and (n 111) regarding the NPA. This term, 'hybrid', has since gained traction in academic literature in matters fourth-branch. See Charles M Fombad, 'Corruption and the Crisis of Constitutionalism in Africa' in Charles M Fombad and Nico Steytler (eds) (n 34) 45, where several 'hybrid institutions' are enumerated. See further Charles M Fombad, 'The Role of Emerging Hybrid Institutions of Accountability in the Separation of Powers Scheme in Africa' in Charles M Fombad (ed.), *Separation of Powers in African Constitutionalism* (OUP 2016) 325.

[114] The office of the NPA is provided for alongside the judiciary in ch 8 of the Constitution, entitled 'Courts and Administration of Justice'.

[115] For discussion, see Kohn (n 21); *Corruption Watch* (n 104) para 19.

[116] *Glenister II* (n 3) paras 248, 249–50.

[117] Tushnet (n 62) 119.

[118] Five of the other justices concurred in her majority judgment.

[119] The majority judgment is the focus of the analysis in this chapter.

adopted less invasive means of reaching the same outcome. *Sonke* concerned a challenge to certain sections of the Correctional Services Act 111 of 1998 (the Act) on the basis that they failed to ensure 'an adequate level of independence to the Judicial Inspectorate for Correctional Services [JICS]'.[120] Unlike *Glenister II*—with the hodgepodge of background rights that it raised—*Sonke* invoked a particular rights bundle: the section 35 rights of arrested, detained, and accused persons.[121] Indeed, the judgment commenced by noting that '[t]he treatment of incarcerated persons and the conditions in which they are held lie at the heart of this application.'[122]

Intriguingly however, given the section 35 rights stated to be at issue, the Court could simply have assessed the constitutionality of the impugned legislative provisions by way of the standard limitations analysis under section 36, rather than paying mere lip service to this provision and instead[123] applying the *Glenister-II* approach, almost by rote. In adopting this somewhat misguided approach, the Court concluded that:

> Section 7(2), read with sections 10, 11, 12 and 35 of the Constitution, impose a positive obligation on the State to establish and maintain a correctional centre oversight mechanism that is independent . . . Establishing the Judicial Inspectorate without ensuring that it has an adequate level of independence from the Department over which it is to exercise oversight cannot be considered a reasonable step.[124]

The Court found that the statutory formulation of the JICS rendered it neither financially nor operationally independent[125] and said this lack of independence 'would leave the rights of inmates under sections 10, 11, 12 and 35 of the Constitution vulnerable to infringement'.[126] As such, the majority held that, in enacting the impugned sections 88A(1)(b) and 91 of the Act, Parliament had failed to act 'reasonably and effectively as required by section 7(2) of the Constitution'.[127] Parliament was given 24 months to remedy this constitutional invalidity.

3.2 The reasoning: *Glenister II* déjà vu

Before the judicial reasoning in *Sonke* is summarized, two main differences between it and *Glenister II* should be noted. The first is that, unlike the (impliedly) *constitutionally* created anti-corruption unit in *Glenister II*, the JICS is a *statutorily* created oversight body 'tasked with monitoring and reporting on the treatment of inmates and conditions in correctional centres'.[128] Secondly, the Correctional Services Act itself explicitly establishes the JICS 'as

[120] *Sonke* (n 4) para 1.
[121] Most notably, in s 35(2), the right 'to conditions of detention that are consistent with human dignity, including at least exercise, and the provision, at state expense, of adequate accommodation, nutrition, reading material and medical treatment'.
[122] *Sonke* (n 4) para 1.
[123] s 36 of the Constitution (n 7) gets a brief, one-time mention at para 32: 'All the rights in the Bill of Rights apply to inmates, save where justifiably limited in terms of section 36 of the Constitution.'
[124] *Sonke* (n 4) para 129.
[125] Ibid. para 130.
[126] Ibid. para 129.
[127] Ibid. para 130.
[128] Ibid. para 18.

an independent office under the control of the Inspecting Judge'[129]—its *raison d'être* is to be an independent oversight body that fulfils this legislative mandate.

This raises the question, why did the Court not just scrutinise the legislative means employed in the Act to ascertain whether these surmounted the established rationality standard in achieving the desired end (or legislative purpose)? Simple application of the legality-cum-rationality test—even in its minimally conceived original guise[130]—would have revealed that, without affording the JICS the necessary financial and operational independence, the legislative means cannot be rationally related to the attainment of the desired end. This would have been the end of the story: no threat to the separation of powers, and no need to recapitulate the doctrinally dubious reasoning employed in *Glenister II*. Instead, the latter course of action is precisely what the Court opted to take.

As in *Glenister II*, the majority in *Sonke* framed the issues to be addressed as two-pronged in nature: first, 'whether the Constitution imposes an obligation on the State to ensure that the Judicial Inspectorate, as the body tasked with monitoring and reporting on the treatment of inmates and conditions in correctional centres, has an adequate level of independence'; and second, 'whether the impugned provisions of the Act ensure an adequate level of independence to the Judicial Inspectorate'.[131] Again, as in *Glenister II*, the majority answered 'yes' and then 'no' to these questions, respectively—and, once more as in *Glenister II*, the reasoning in addressing question one was fundamentally problematic. The majority reasoning in *Sonke* likewise commenced with a detailed contextual prelude to the legal arguments, however in this instance, it was an overture at odds with the way in which the Court ultimately proceeded. This is because little ended up turning on the rights of incarcerated persons.

After sketching out the relevant provisions in the Act, the Court went on to provide an overview of the 'historical context of correctional centres in South Africa'[132] and the 'constitutional rights of inmates'.[133] At this point, the Court took a page out of the *Glenister-II* playbook and invoked a 'conglomerate of implicated rights of inmates'[134] rather than focusing on section 35. Dignity was added to the mix, along with life and freedom and security of the person.[135] Then—and rather ironically, given the Court's caution that 'the State's obligations in section 7(2) is [*sic*] *a matter of rights interpretation*'[136]—the Court did not follow through with this approach, and to the extent that it did engage in something akin to 'rights interpretation', its attempt was muddled.

For example, Theron J noted that '[s]ection 35 is unqualified',[137] which should mean that any limitation of it, and appreciation of the duties flowing from it, is assessed through the prism of section 36. Yet, to reiterate, no proper limitations analysis was actually conducted by the Court. Instead, and notwithstanding the fact that none of the implicated rights contain an explicit reasonableness standard,[138] the Court went through the *Glenister-II*

[129] Ibid.; see ch IX of the Act, especially ss 85–91 regarding the objects of the JICS.

[130] As developed by the Constitutional Court in the 'seminal trio of cases': *Fedsure* (n 25); *Pharmaceutical Manufacturers* (n 11); and *President of the Republic of South Africa & Others v South African Rugby Football Union & Others* 2000 (1) SA 1 (CC) *(SARFU)*.

[131] *Sonke* (n 4) para 16.

[132] Ibid. paras 23–9.

[133] Ibid. paras 29–39.

[134] Ibid. para 68.

[135] Ibid. paras 33–39.

[136] Ibid. para 29 (emphasis added).

[137] Ibid. para 38.

[138] As is the case, eg with the qualified socio-economic rights in ss 26–27 of the Constitution (n 17).

motions[139] and applied the implicit section 7(2) reasonableness standard to the impugned provisions of the Act. The reasoning thus essentially followed the same formula: (1) the value of public accountability provided the springboard;[140] (2) international law[141] was relied upon (in particular as regards the need 'to establish oversight bodies for the prevention of torture and degrading treatment'), and then; (3) the crucial section 7(2) ingredient was added, with a fleeting reference to the 'conglomerate of implicated rights of inmates'.[142]

Another intriguing aspect of the majority judgment in *Sonke* is that it builds on a reference in *Glenister II* to the case of *Rail Commuters*,[143] and does so in a way that introduces a further peculiarity into its reasoning. *Rail Commuters* is a carefully reasoned, unanimous judgment that concerned responsibility for the safety of passengers travelling on commuter trains.[144] The applicants in that case argued that the state respondents bore a positive obligation under the South African Transport Services Act 9 of 1989, read in light of the Constitution, to take steps to protect the safety and security of rail commuters. In *Sonke*, the majority inserted a paragraph from *Rail Commuters* to the effect that section 7(2) of the Constitution 'requires the bearer of constitutional obligations to perform them in a manner which is reasonable'.[145] The *Sonke* majority then blended this with reference to the socio-economic rights case of *TAC*[146] and the latter's enunciation of the reasonableness criterion in *such cases*.

However, this mode of judicial reasoning by the Court in *Sonke* amounts to an oversimplification, and in fact a misreading, of *Rail Commuters* and the Court's doctrinal work in socio-economic rights cases. Having cited these cases, buttressed with the constitutional value of accountability, the Court in *Sonke* leapt, without properly looking, to its conclusion. In short, this conclusion was that, '[t]he vulnerability of inmates in correctional centres and the real possibility'—rather than actual occurrence—'of the infringement of their rights to life, dignity, bodily security and conditions consonant with human dignity *imposes a positive obligation* on the State to provide *appropriate*[147] protection to inmates "through laws and structures designed to afford such protection"'.[148]

This assertion is quite staggering. In *Rail Commuters*, the Court was clear in its analysis of the constitutional and legislative provisions, such that it was sensibly able to ascertain a public-law duty to ensure reasonable measures to provide for the safety of rail commuters.[149]

[139] *Sonke* (n 4) paras 42–47.

[140] Ibid. para 49 on 'the value of accountability' and 'requiring the State to account for the steps that it takes to respect, protect, promote and fulfil the rights in the Bill of Rights'; according to the Court, 'the value of accountability is served by requiring the State to show that the measures that it adopts to fulfil its section 7(2) obligations are reasonable and effective'.

[141] Ibid. paras 58–70, with the Court focusing on 'the Optional Protocol', 'the Convention', and 'the Paris Principles'.

[142] Ibid. para 68.

[143] *Rail Commuters Action Group v Transnet Ltd t/a Metrorail* 2005 (2) SA 359 (CC) *(Rail Commuters)*, referred to at fn 175 of *Glenister II* (n 3) para 190 in summarizing the general ss 7 and 8 Bill of Rights obligations.

[144] *Rail Commuters* (n 143) para 1.

[145] Ibid. from para 87, and referred to in *Sonke* (n 4) para 48.

[146] *Minister of Health v Treatment Action Campaign (No 2)* 2002 (5) SA 721 (CC) *(TAC)*.

[147] cf *Government of the Republic of South Africa and Others v Grootboom and Others* 2001 (1) SA 46 (CC), the socio-economic rights judgment on the s 26 housing right. In refuting the argument for recognition of a minimum core obligation for housing, the Court was at pains not to adopt international law without more. It distinguished, amongst others, the Constitution's choice of the softer qualifier 'adequate' from the term used in the International Covenant on Economic, Social and Cultural Rights, namely 'appropriate'.

[148] *Sonke* (n 4) para 50 (emphasis added).

[149] Ibid. para 84.

Indeed, O'Regan J cautioned that the ambit of positive state duties would need to be drawn in 'an incremental and context-driven manner'.[150] In *Rail Commuters*, the Court made a sound assessment with reference to various factors, including the 'intensity of the harm' and 'relevant human and financial constraints'.[151] There is no such judicial justification in *Sonke*, but perhaps this was to be expected given the Court's almost myopic reliance on the *Glenister-II* style of reasoning.

The court in *Sonke* then echoed *Glenister II* again in asserting that international law obligations, in this case 'to create a correctional centre oversight mechanism that has the necessary independence',[152] are *sourced in the Constitution itself*.[153] Similarly, it seems to come down to the 'heart' of the Constitution rather than an appreciation of its text. The overall result may be relatively constitutionally satisfying—the Court is ultimately filling 'an accountability vacuum'[154] left by the democratic arms of state—but the means employed to reach it are less so. This makes one wonder whether the Court itself is adhering to the basics of rationality and sound reason-giving.

Fortunately, as in in *Glenister II*, the Court fared somewhat better in dealing with question two.[155] Here, it began by summarizing its own jurisprudence on independence and drawing the distinction between 'individual and institutional independence',[156] the latter being germane in *Sonke*, as in *Glenister II*. The Court highlighted the 'markers of institutional independence': (1) structural independence (with its element of financial independence); (2) operational independence (which includes the appointment and accountability of staff and operational decisions); and (3) the public perception of independence, given that public confidence in an institution's independence is 'an indispensable part' thereof.[157] The Court then applied these markers in its assessment of sections 88A(1)(b) and 91 of the Act.

What is interesting is that, in doing so, it bolstered its analysis with reference to case law dealing with the independence of other integrity-and-accountability bodies—but, distinguishably, bodies established under the Constitution itself. For example, the Court considered the meaning of financial independence[158] with reference to *New National Party*[159] on the funding of the Electoral Commission and referred to *Glenister III*—dubbed the '*Helen Suzman Foundation* case'[160]—which considered, among others, the funding of the Hawks.

Using these comparators, the majority in *Sonke* concluded that it was problematic that, rather than being appropriated exclusively by Parliament, the JICS' budget 'is both determined and controlled by the very Department over which it is meant to exercise oversight', which has 'an unfettered discretion' over the JICS' level of funding.[161] The Court, correctly,

[150] Ibid. para 85.
[151] Ibid. para 88.
[152] Ibid. para 69.
[153] Ibid.
[154] Hoexter (n 7) 248.
[155] *Sonke* (n 4) para 71 ff: 'Do the impugned provisions ensure the Judicial Inspectorate an adequate level of independence?'
[156] Ibid. para 72.
[157] Ibid. paras 76–80.
[158] Ibid. paras 88–90.
[159] *New National Party of South Africa v Government of Republic of South Africa* 1999 (3) SA 191 (CC) *(New National Party)*.
[160] *Glenister III* (n 41).
[161] *Sonke* (n 4) paras 90–91.

found it wholly inappropriate for a government department to be in control 'of the funding of an independent institution like the Judicial Inspectorate ... for this seriously undermines its independence'.[162]

The majority was also correct in its recognition of the constitutional integrity-and-accountability bodies. As noted above, these bodies should rightly be appreciated as comprising the fourth branch of state in South Africa. As in *Glenister II*, the Court grouped the likes of the Chapter 9 institutions, the judiciary, and the NPA, in comparing their financial independence to that of the JICS.[163] Where the Court faltered, however, was in its leap from *constitutionally* established integrity-and-accountability bodies to *legislatively* created integrity-and-accountability bodies, such as the JICS.

To this end, Theron J for the majority simply held that the conclusion that sections 88A(1)(b) and 91 'undermine the independence' of the JICS is 'bolstered by a consideration of the legislative provisions governing the financing of other independent institutions' (such as the judiciary and the NPA), as well as statutes pertaining to the Chapter 9 institutions.[164] While South Africa's constitutional text makes it clear that these independent institutions are important in the pursuit and protection of constitutional democracy, there is no catch-all provision for the creation of similar entities via legislation. This is not to say that bodies like the JICS should not be created, and created independent and so maintained—these are, after all, interventions valuable to the Constitution's integrity-and-accountability mission. But to equate these bodies with the constitutionally created integrity-and-accountability bodies, without more, arguably shows a lack of judicial appreciation for the country's supreme law itself.

Finally, the majority saw no issue with section 88A(4) of the Act. This section requires '[a]ny matters relating to misconduct and incapacity of the [CEO] to be referred to the National Commissioner by the Inspecting Judge'.[165] The Court held that this provision could be read to be constitutionally congruent. As for sections 88A(1)(b) and 91 of the Act, their constitutional invalidity was confirmed on the basis that these provisions did not ensure the JICS an adequate level of independence from the department over which it exercises oversight. This, in turn, meant that the legislation fell short of being a 'reasonable and effective step', as (implicitly) required by section 7(2) of the Bill of Rights.[166]

The upshot of *Sonke*, in the wake of *Glenister II*, can be summarised as follows: it has strengthened a judicially established *structural requirement* in the Constitution to ensure independent oversight entities in furthering the accountability and integrity of public power. This *requirement* is assessed against the potentially far-reaching standard of reasonableness combined with effectiveness. Furthermore, this assessment is now applicable to legislative acts *even in the absence of a clear socio-economic rights infringement*. This outcome seems a victory for constitutionalism—and it is, no doubt, a powerful foil against corruption—but it may be a hollow victory, especially given the *manner* of its creation. That is to say, it is not an entirely satisfactory outcome if one cares about all the elements of constitutionalism.[167]

[162] Ibid. para 92.
[163] Ibid. paras 106–07.
[164] Ibid. para 107.
[165] Ibid. paras 109–28.
[166] Ibid. para 129.
[167] Constitutionalism is best understood as a prescriptive concept in terms of which a constitutional system adheres to at least the following basic norms and values: the rule of law; the separation of powers; the existence of

3.3 The *Glenister-II* momentum continues

Since *Sonke*'s revival of the *Glenister II* innovation—in particular, its judicial development of the implied section 7(2) reasonableness standard for assessing the state's legislative (and other) measures—*Glenister II* has gathered more momentum. In 2022, the judgment of *AmaBhungane Centre for Investigative Journalism NPC v President of the Republic of South Africa*[168] was handed down by the Constitutional Court. It, too, built on the legacy of *Glenister II* and the 'constitutional and statutory dictates of transparency, *accountability* and openness'[169] in finding that, '[c]oncomitant with the need to enact legislation to fight corruption, is the need to regulate the funding of candidates and political parties by legislative means.'[170]

Again, as in *Glenister II*, reinforced by *Sonke*—though, oddly, without any reference to the latter case—the finding in *AmaBhungane* was premised on 'both international and domestic obligations'.[171] *AmaBhungane* employed *Glenister II*'s development of the implied constitutional obligation to tackle corruption via independent structures[172] to conclude that the Executive Ethics Code[173] was unconstitutional insofar as it excluded 'from disclosure donations for internal party elections'. To this extent, it undermined 'the Ethics Act and the conflict of interest regime that is essential to promote transparency and to deal with the pervasive corruption bedeviling us'.[174] The *Glenister-II* methodology is thus now seemingly being applied to corruption concerns more generally. The Court in *AmaBhungane* stated:

> In *Glenister II*, this Court extensively explicated on the state's international commitments and obligations in section 7(2) of the Constitution, to combat and prevent corruption ... in the context of the need to establish an independent anti-corruption unit, *but equally relevant here*.[175]

This development is, in principle, good and necessary, especially in the state-capture context, but it does require one to think critically about what judges are doing and how they are doing it—any constitutional 'culture of justification'[176] demands as much.

an independent judiciary; democratic self-government; and the protection of human rights. For a detailed discussion on, in particular, the positive dimension of constitutionalism, see Kohn (n 61) 102–04. See also Okon Akiba, 'Constitutional Government and the Future of Constitutionalism in Africa' in Okon Akiba (ed), *Constitutionalism and Society in Africa* (Routledge 2004) 5. See also Nick Barber, *The Principles of Constitutionalism* (OUP 2018) 1, who provides a compelling case for 'positive constitutionalism' as requiring 'the creation of an effective and competent set of state institutions'.

168 [2022] ZACC 31 *(AmaBhungane)*.

169 Ibid. para 70, and see para 39, where emphasis is placed on the value of accountability.

170 Ibid. para 42.

171 Ibid.

172 Ibid. para 39. The starting point in the analysis is *Glenister II*'s ascertainment that the Constitution establishes 'a requirement on the state, including the President, to take reasonable measures to combat and prevent corruption'.

173 The Executive Ethics Code (published in Proclamation No R41 of 2000) was enacted in 2000 by the then president, under s 96(1) of the Constitution (n 17).

174 *AmaBhungane* (n 168) para 70.

175 Ibid. para 41 (emphasis added).

176 Etienne Mureinik, 'A Bridge to Where? Introducing the Interim Bill of Rights' (1994) 10(1) South African Journal on Human Rights 31, 32.

4. Shaky judicial foundations and the backsliding risk

Glenister II is an undeniably important judgment. It is a brave one that, during the Zuma era, set the tone for an emboldened Constitutional Court to hand down a series of strong judgments in an effort to protect public integrity and accountability.[177] Tushnet has suggested that the likes of 'the Scorpions litigation' and the decisions for which it paved the way 'kept the issue of Zuma's corruption on the public agenda and may well have contributed to the gradual, then rapid, erosion of support for Zuma in the public and then within the ANC'.[178] There can be no denying the constitutional importance of this feat, and, as illustrated in section 3 above, *Glenister II*'s ripple effects continue today. But the question that remains to be determined—one not easy to ask and answer—is whether the judicial means can definitively be said to justify the ends. There is room for some scepticism on this score.

In section 1, this chapter cautioned that, while judicial adventurism, broadly speaking, is not necessarily a bad thing—particularly not in the category of rights-adjudication proper—there are certain categories of it that are more nocuous than others, which thus require more rigorous judicial justification. An appreciation of these different categories of intervention can, in turn, foster a deeper understanding of what may (or should) permissibly be done by the unelected judiciary: how so, and why so.

To this end, the *Glenister II* and *Sonke* twinset entails the reading-in to the Constitution of a structural requirement with positive state obligations attached. This was done in the absence of a clear rights infringement such that the Court was outside the more textured, and thus flexible, realm of rights interpretation and proper limitations analysis. The reasoning (and findings) in *Glenister II* and *Sonke* essentially oust the need for careful scrutiny in terms of the section 36 limitations clause, given these judgments' establishment of an (implied) overarching reasonableness standard. This judicial diptych can be compared with other cases where the constitutional text also does not unequivocally invite judicial adventurism, but where the constitutional interpretation and reasoning, in light of the facts, render the outcomes more satisfactory from a judicial justification—and thus separation-of-powers—perspective.

An example is the majority judgment in *Doctors for Life*.[179] This 2006 case concerned the constitutional duty on Parliament[180] and provincial legislatures to facilitate public involvement in the lawmaking process, in view of the section 19 bundle of political rights. The majority judgment—interestingly, penned by Ngcobo J, who wrote *Glenister II*'s more cautious dissent—read the qualifier 'reasonable' into section 72(1)(a) of the Constitution[181] and held that the legislature had failed to satisfy this standard. The result is that, since *Doctors for Life*, the constitutional manner-and-form provision on public involvement in lawmaking entails a reasonableness standard *not* explicitly contemplated by the constitutional drafters, and notwithstanding their explicitly requiring as much in the sister provision on public access to the legislatures.[182] But this was not so much a judicial leap as a necessary step: one

[177] See eg *Nkandla* (n 103); *Corruption Watch* (n 104).

[178] Tushnet (n 41) 439.

[179] *Doctors for Life International v The Speaker of the National Assembly* 2006 (6) SA 416 (CC) *(Doctors for Life)*.

[180] In particular, what was at issue was this duty on the part of the National Council of Provinces (NCOP).

[181] And thereby its twin provisions pertaining to the National Assembly (s 59(1)(a)) and the provincial legislatures (s 118(1)(a)). See *Doctors for Life* (n 179) para 74.

[182] ss 59(1)(b), 72(1)(b), and 118(1)(b) of the Constitution (n 17) explicitly require legislatures to conduct their business 'in an open manner' and hold their 'sittings, and those of [their] ... committees, in public', subject to

relatively carefully justified in the context of a detailed analysis of both the representative and participatory elements of South Africa's constitutional democracy and grounded in the context of the nature and scope of the right to participate in public affairs, as developed locally and in international and foreign law.[183]

Another example of a case of judicial reading-in which is constitutionally palatable is that of *Fedsure*,[184] in which the Constitutional Court developed the principle of legality as a carve-out (implied) component of the rule of law,[185] which is explicitly entrenched in section 1(c) of the Constitution. It is unlikely that the Court would have anticipated the 'burgeoning'[186] of legality as a substantive review ground—one which, in many respects, has come to mimic administrative-law review.[187] This expansion of legality review has, in large part, been due to the unenviable need to catch executive excesses within the review-net. However, the judicial intervention by the *Fedsure* court itself was not a far-fetched one, but a doctrinally sustainable one that should not be conflated with respective courts' actual application of it.

Aside from these instances of 'read-in', the other controversial category of judicial adventurism which may be problematic is where the court is asked to read-out explicit constitutional requirements and/or alter them in a palpable way. The case of *Electoral Commission v Minister of Cooperative Governance & Traditional Affairs*[188] comes to mind. This was an urgent application for the postponement of local government elections in the midst of the Covid-19 pandemic and lockdown. The section 19(2) right to free and fair elections was raised in support of this application, but it cuts two ways—when it comes to elections, regularity[189] and accessibility[190] are both ambitions of the right. The *Electoral Commission* judgment brought the section 19 right, with its varied inherent goals, into tension with the explicit constitutional requirement in section 159(2) that, on the dissolution of a municipal council, 'an election must be held within 90 days'.

'reasonable measures' being permissible to regulate public access. The respective sub-ss (2) echo this explicit reasonableness standard in relation to decisions to limit public access. Given these textual indicia, Yacoob J for the minority made the following observation in *Doctors for Life* (n 179) para 317: 'Section 72(1)(a) does not employ the concept of reasonableness. It is impossible to explain, if the constitutional purpose is to oblige Parliament to take reasonable measures to facilitate public involvement in all its processes, why the section does not say so in so many words. It seems that the concept of reasonableness is deliberately employed twice in other parts of section 72. This points strongly to the conclusion that a deliberate choice was made and a deliberate decision taken to employ the words in two other parts of the section but not to employ them in subsection (1)(a).'

183 *Doctors for Life* (n 179) para 101.

184 *Fedsure* (n 25).

185 Ibid. para 58: 'It seems central to the conception of our constitutional order that the legislature and executive in every sphere are constrained by the principle that they may exercise no power and perform no function beyond that conferred upon them by law. At least in this sense, then, the principle of legality is *implied within the terms* of the interim Constitution.' (emphasis added).

186 Kohn (n 18).

187 Since the controversial judgment of *State Information Technology Agency SOC Limited v Gijima Holdings (Pty) Limited* 2018 (2) SA 23 (CC), state self-reviews on administrative law grounds must now (if rather disingenuously) be assessed via the principle of legality-cum-rationality in any event, expanding the 'parallel universe' of administrative law well beyond the remit of the Promotion of Administrative Justice Act 3 of 2000.

188 *Electoral Commission v Minister of Cooperative Governance and Traditional Affairs* [2021] ZACC 29 (*Electoral Commission*).

189 Ibid. para 154 (d).

190 The Commission's case for deferral was motivated primarily by the fact that the Covid-19 lockdown regulations rendered it 'not possible to hold free, fair and safe elections on 27 October 2021' and, relatedly, 'because no voter registration weekend was held before the Minister's proclamation of 3 August 2021, many . . . people would be disenfranchised'. See ibid para 167.

The majority judgment, delivered by Rogers AJ, provides a good illustration of sound judicial reason-giving in the spirit of public accountability, responsiveness, and openness. Having given clear reasons for his finding, Rogers AJ held that '[t]he constitutional duty imposed on the Commission . . . is to hold the elections within the 90-day-limit and make them as free and fair as circumstances reasonably permit.'[191] After all, as he noted, while there may have been good reasons to delay the elections, the 'mechanism' for making such calls and contingency plans 'is not judicial': 'let Parliament decide what to do about it', because even though '[t]he Constitution can be amended', for 'sound reasons this must follow an exacting procedure'.[192]

This is quite right, and brings to mind the kind of constitutional change that may be required to address the dilemmas which the likes of *Glenister II* and *Sonke* pose in the South African context of flagrant corruption, maladministration, and resultant deficiencies in state structures and services. Before this chapter provides some insights in this regard, it is worth reiterating part of the reason the Constitutional Court stepped into the democratic breach as it did in these public integrity-and-accountability cases.

The cases discussed in sections 2 and 3 show that constitutional challenges pegged to 'higher-order norms'[193] and (implied) overarching standards make the stretching (and thus straining) of the constitutional text all the more likely, given the inherent malleability of these norms and standards. We need to remember the power of 'crisp and readily available focal points'[194] to reduce adjudicatory—and textual—strain. The analysis of 'the what' and 'the how' of the informal constitutional changes brought to the fore by the jurisprudence in sections 2 and 3 in turn illuminates the need for focal clarity, rigour, and refinement. Writing in the US context, Issacharoff and Pildes distinguished between 'first-order' and 'second-order' constitutional adjudication in a 'dominant-party democracy', with the former directed at the 'foreground' of constitutional rights and the latter tackling 'the background rules that structure partisan political competition'.[195] Choudhry recalibrated this to fit the South African context and noted, among other things, that '[a] first-order approach would check those consequences of the ANC's political domination that manifest themselves *as violations of rights*.'[196]

Within this first-order realm, there is the promise of both enhanced individual, and related judicial, empowerment vis-à-vis the traditional arms of state, especially when compared with the resort to more ephemeral second- and higher-order norms such as the rule of law, a general (implied) standard of reasonableness, and so on. This nebulous terrain is especially taxing for judicial navigation where the higher-order constitutional norms are unwritten. And yet, as opposition parties, non-governmental organizations, and the likes of Mr Glenister have scrambled to address executive malfeasance and maladministration,

191 Ibid. para 196.

192 Ibid. para. 201.

193 See Issacharoff (n 16) 589, where he cautions that 'such appeals to first-order principles put . . . [the courts] on a stronger collision course with the governing authorities'.

194 Huq (n 26) 39.

195 Richard H Pildes, 'The Theory of Political Competition' (1999) 85(8) Virginia Law Review 1605; Samuel Issacharoff, 'Gerrymandering and Political Cartels' (2002) 116(2) Harvard Law Review 594; Richard H Pildes and Samuel Issacharoff, 'Politics as Markets: Partisan Lockups of the Democratic Process' (1998) 50(3) Stanford Law Review 643; Richard H Pildes, 'Foreword: The Constitutionalization of Democratic Politics' (2004) 118(1) Harvard Law Review 28.

196 Sujit Choudhry, 'He Had a Mandate: The South African Constitutional Court and the African National Congress in a Dominant Party Democracy' (2009) 2(1) Constitutional Court Review 1, 19 (emphasis added).

the judiciary has had to do the bulk of the heavy lifting and, as illustrated above, often via a kind of gap-filling resort to nebulous values or requirements rather than concrete justiciable rights (or even express constitutional requirements). This is where creative judicial interpretation risks becoming a vice rather than a virtue.

The judicial role is meant simply to be adjudicative; therapeutic; prophylactic. It should not have to entail informal constitutional amendment in the form of reading-in (or reading-out) in tension with the text itself. Aside from the separation-of-powers concerns flowing from such a judicial approach, there are the additional concerns that even insofar as these changes (embodied in the judicial outcomes) may be substantively good or necessary, given the mode of their creation, such changes will likely lack legitimacy, and furthermore, may not necessarily be enduring. When it comes to constitutional change—and the democratic backsliding risk—we are at a precipitous moment in the country, on the continent, and across the globe.[197]

On the latter score, the 2022 judgment of the US Supreme Court in *Dobbs*[198] bears reference. This case aptly illustrates that judicial colouring outside the lines is not the way to go about constitutional change, especially where the lines should properly be drawn by the democratic branches of state. With shifts in the bench can follow shifts in judicial ideology, and so judicial colouring, and line-drawing, can in turn be wiped out. In short, the majority in *Dobbs*, per Justice Alito, overturned the seminal case of *Roe*,[199] followed by *Casey*,[200] which duo entrenched a woman's right to abortion on a 'trimester-based framework'[201] in the US Constitution. In *Roe*, this entrenchment was accomplished by virtue of an implied right to privacy flowing from the First, Fourth, Fifth, Ninth, and Fourteenth Amendments. The *Casey* court took a more singular approach and relied solely on the Due Process Clause in the Fourteenth Amendment.

As for how *Dobbs* overruled this cardinal jurisprudential duo—one whose seminal *ratio* was perhaps taken for granted—Roux gives a succinct synopsis of the majority's reasoning:

> Since the right to abortion (according to the majority) *was plainly not such a 'deeply rooted' right*, its recognition in *Roe* had been erroneous. Rather than a legitimate act of constitutional interpretation, that decision, as claimed by Justice Byron White in dissent at the time, had been an '*exercise of raw judicial power*'... [and] in failing to address that problem, the *Casey* court had simply compounded the error.[202]

Dobbs patently reveals the danger of the exercise of 'raw judicial power' through, among others, the reading-in of implied constitutional terms and rights. The right to abortion was carved out of an implied right to privacy and, as if with the sweep of a wand, it has since vanished with a change in the bench and a related change in judicial ideology. Constitutional change can be important, especially in a country such as South Africa whose Constitution

[197] Huq and Ginsburg (n 1) 121, Table 2.
[198] *Dobbs v Jackson Women's Health Organization* 597 US (2022) *(Dobbs)*.
[199] *Roe v Wade* 410 US 113 (1973) *(Roe)*.
[200] *Planned Parenthood of Southeastern Pa. v Casey* 505 US 833 (1992) *(Casey)*.
[201] Theunis Roux, 'What does the US Supreme Court's Decision in *Dobbs* Tell Us about the Virtues of Australia's Approach to Protecting Fundamental Rights?' (*Australian Public Law*, July 2022) https://www.auspublaw.org/blog/2022/07/what-does-the-us-supreme-courts-decision-in-dobbs-tell-us-about-the-virtues-of-australias-approach-to-protecting-fundamental-rights accessed 22 October 2022.
[202] Ibid. (emphasis added).

is transformative in nature. We are not living in statis, but rather in extremely fluid—even catalytic—times,[203] and such times can certainly call for extraordinary measures. The right kind of constitutional change may just be the measure.

Albert has noted that '[f]ormal amendment has its own democracy-enhancing virtues'[204] and is validated 'not [by] its content alone but also the process by which it comes into existence', as well as 'by the sociological legitimacy of the relevant publics accepting it'.[205] Section 5 of this chapter proposes two formal constitutional amendments that would ensure such democracy enhancement and sociological legitimacy. These proposed amendments are, in part, informed by the lessons that *Glenister II* and *Sonke* provide. After all, stealthy judicial interventions aside, the judgments do have certain redeeming features in common which may indicate where to start with the needed context-responsive refinement of the Constitution in a country afflicted by state capture, corruption, maladministration and diminishing levels of professionalism. These redeeming features of the judgments have been noted in sections 2 and 3, but bear emphasis again here.

First, *Glenister II* and *Sonke* are cases that sought to vindicate the public integrity-and-accountability mission of the Constitution. They thus drew explicitly on the value of accountability—an, as yet, relatively untapped constitutional check for all exercises of public power. Second, they underscored the value, and right to, human dignity—a right which is a cornerstone of South Africa's constitutional dispensation and yet one which lacks substantive specificity, and thus, practical potential. Third, *Glenister II* and *Sonke* revealed a sound appreciation of the Constitution's structural calibration of the separation-of-powers doctrine with its integrity-and-accountability fourth-branch bodies, particularly insofar as they have a crucial complementary role to play in addition to the judiciary, in checking abuses of executive, and other public, powers.

5. Constitutional amendments that could curb backsliding

5.1 Making separation of powers constitutionally explicit

In the *Electoral Commission* case, Rogers AJ noted that '[t]here may be competing proposals for constitutional amendment, and the choices should be made by the democratically elected representatives of the people in Parliament, not the courts'.[206] This is an important starting point in reflecting on the kind of constitutional amendment(s) that should be considered in addressing the public integrity-and-accountability deficit in South Africa. The first consideration is big-picture in nature. It entails 'the more idealistic reflection of down-the-line "largescale institutional transformation" by way of constitutional amendment . . . in particular, the need to consider making the separation of powers, with its integrity and accountability component, an *express* constitutional principle'.[207]

[203] Stu Woolman, 'A Politics of Accountability: How South Africa's Judicial Recognition of the Binding Legal Effect of the Public Protector's Recommendations Had a Catalysing Effect that Brought Down a President' (2016) 8(1) Constitutional Court Review 155, 181.
[204] Albert (n 17) 269.
[205] Ibid. 270.
[206] *Electoral Commission* (n 188) para 201.
[207] Kohn (n 21) 11.

The separation of powers is structurally implied in the architecture of the Constitution with: (1) its chapter-by-chapter division of legislative, executive, and judicial authority; and (2) the likes of Chapter 9—which establishes the independent state institutions supporting constitutional democracy—as well as, among others; (3) the explicit entrenchment of the prosecuting authority (NPA) and the JSC in Chapter 8, and the likes of the Public Service Commission (PSC) in Chapter 10, and the Financial and Fiscal Commission (FFC) in Chapter 13.[208] South Africa's constitutional structure and text therefore indicates the adoption of a version of the separation of powers that goes beyond a mere tripartite division of core state authority. The Constitution in fact contemplates 'a more contemporary, and thus appropriate, model [of the doctrine of the separation of powers]'.[209] This is a model that includes the fourth branch, which is best described as the 'integrity and accountability branch'.[210]

Structural clarity aside, however, the textual invisibility of the separation of powers has pros[211] as well as cons. In the latter respect, *Dobbs* illustrates[212]—albeit in relation to women's right to abortion—that insofar as terms, rights, and requirements are (judicially) read in to a constitution, there is always the possibility (however remote) that they can similarly be read out. There is something to commend a degree of textual specificity, at least in regard to the fundamentals. In seeking to illustrate that 'constitutional democracy' is not a 'twentieth-century phenomenon whose time has passed', Loughlin cautions against the 'view of the cosmopolitans' who argue for 'the ideal "*invisible* constitution"'.[213] In terms of this paradigm, 'the constitution no longer has ultimate authority since it is now subject to the creative powers of judicial interpretation'—a context in which, Loughlin argues, '[s]uper-legality reigns'.[214]

Constitutional design should militate against such super-legality as far as possible. If we are serious about fostering and maintaining, particularly *public*, integrity and accountability, and tackling the state capture that flies in the face of it, then civic and political will should be garnered in favour of grander-scheme consideration of constitutional amendment explicitly to entrench the constitutional principle of the separation of powers, along with its fourth-branch component.

The constitutional architects already provided the scaffolding for such a provision in the form of Constitutional Principle (CP) VI.[215] This principle stated that, '[t]here shall

[208] The Constitution (n 17).

[209] Kohn (n 21) 26.

[210] Ibid, pt IIB on the 'core concepts' of both public 'accountability' and 'integrity' and why the bodies grouped under this rubric are best described as part of the integrity-and-accountability fourth branch. See also Kohn (n 61) 104–06, especially at n 87 on why the qualifier, 'public', is becoming increasingly important as the courts have recently began to misread—and thus claw back—the finding in *Nkandla* (n 103). On matters fourth-branch, see also Tushnet (n 41) and (n 62); Klug (n 105) and (n 106); Heinz Klug, 'Accountability and the Role of Independent Constitutional Institutions in South Africa's Post-Apartheid Constitutions' (2015) 60(1) New York Law School Review 153.

[211] Huq (n 26) 40. See Karl Klare, 'Self-realisation, Human Rights, and Separation of Powers: A Democracy-seeking Approach' (2015) 26(3) Stellenbosch Law Review 445, on the value of a 'democracy-seeking approach' to the separation of powers.

[212] *Dobbs* (n 198).

[213] Martin Loughlin, *Against Constitutionalism* (Harvard University Press 2022) 200–01 (emphasis added).

[214] Ibid.

[215] The Constitutional Principles (CPs) formed the blueprint in terms of which the Constitutional Court had to assess the Constitution during the certification process. These principles were set out in sch 4 to the Interim Constitution (Constitution of the Republic of South Africa, 1993) and incorporated into it via s 71(1)(a). The Preamble to the Interim Constitution encapsulated the significance of the CPs: 'The elected representatives of all

be a separation of powers between the Legislature, Executive and Judiciary, with appropriate checks and balances to ensure accountability, responsiveness and openness.' The separation of powers is undoubtedly a core, if unwritten, constitutional value of South Africa's legal order.[216] The express guarantee of it should thus, as a matter of logic, find its home in the section 1 founding values provision.[217] An additional subparagraph should simply be added and worded along the following lines: 'A separation of powers between the Legislature, Executive, Judiciary, *and the Integrity-and-Accountability Branch of State*, with appropriate checks and balances to ensure accountability, responsiveness and openness.'

The italicised words reflect the suggested addition of the South African fourth branch to the originally formulated CP VI, the better to encapsulate the actual (structurally) constitutionally-contemplated division of state authority. As noted above,[218] the fourth branch includes the likes of the NPA, JSC, and Chapter 9 institutions.[219] Among other things, the proposed constitutional amendment would clarify and enhance the functioning of the integrity-and-accountability bodies, as well as reduce the possibility of judicial adventurism or—as in *Dobbs*, albeit in relation to a right—denialism in regard to the separation of powers.[220]

5.2 Amending the section 10 right to human dignity

The second formal constitutional amendment that should proceed, and would likely reduce state capture and corruption, entails refinement of the section 10 right to human dignity.[221]

the people of South Africa should be mandated to adopt a new Constitution in accordance with *a solemn pact* recorded as Constitutional Principles' (emphasis added). In *Certification of the Constitution of the Republic of South Africa, 1996* 1996 (4) SA 744 (CC) para 15 *(First Certification Judgment)*, the Court confirmed that these CPs 'constitute the formal record of the "solemn pact"'.

[216] The court in the *First Certification Judgment* (n 215) paras 106–13 held that the Constitution complied with CP VI in ensuring the constitutional separation of powers. The court also emphasized at para 111 that, '[a]s the separation of powers doctrine is not a fixed or rigid constitutional doctrine, it is given expression in many different forms and made subject to checks and balances of many kinds.' This point underscores the contemporary relevance of the integrity-and-accountability bodies as some of the many 'checkers and balancers' in the constitutional system.

[217] Or in such other constitutional location Parliament deems fit. Of course, to effect the suggested amendment of s 1, the required 75% majority vote in Parliament would need to be attained as per s 74(1) of the Constitution.

[218] See Kohn (n 21) 35–38 on the different integrity-and-accountability bodies.

[219] See ibid 38–40, and Kohn (n 61), for my original theorization of the 'key distinguishing features of the integrity-and-accountability bodies', which features, collectively considered, provide a sound unifying theory pursuant to which these bodies can be identified, grouped, recognized, respected, and themselves checked and balanced by the other arms of state.

[220] Judicial adventurism (or denialism) is inevitably exacerbated where gaps, or textual invisibility of principles and requirements, exist in the constitutional text—as *Glenister II* (n 3) and *Sonke* (n 4) so powerfully illustrate. These cases show that such invisibility increases the likelihood of judicial creativity and resultant indirect constitutional amendment, which places strain on the judiciary within the separation of powers. In a similar vein, Tushnet (n 62) 33 cautions against 'the risks associated with [the judiciary] making megapolitical decisions', as these 'might induce an overly strategic cast of mind in the judges, which might affect them even in their core work ... [o]r, in the other direction, the judges might be overly legalistic, discounting political consequences too much'. Tushnet explains the net result thus: 'These effects might be especially troubling if they have the effect of reducing support for the constitutional court when it seeks to guard the constitution against the effects of party politics on constitutional structures and individual rights.'

[221] Constitution (n 17) s 10: 'Human Dignity – Everyone has inherent dignity and the right to have their dignity respected and protected.'

This right is seminal to South Africa's constitutional ordering[222] but was crafted in circular terms and consequently, it has been invoked as the primary right in constitutional litigation only where it has been required to house more specific rights that lack explicit constitutional homes.[223]

The right to dignity has both individual and collective dimensions.[224] In the latter respect, one untapped aspect of the right is its potential to enhance democracy by bolstering, particularly *public* integrity and accountability. As O'Regan observes, the right to dignity is not only 'foundational to other fundamental rights, but to democracy itself'.[225] The *Zondo Report*[226] indisputably reveals that state capture, and corruption generally, entail the removal of power from 'we, the people' (acting through our freely elected representatives) when the public purse is exploited for private (illegal) gains.[227] This renders democracy a dead letter as integrity and accountability dissipate and, in turn, civic and individual dignity are undermined. Dworkin has noted that, 'because we honour dignity, we demand democracy'[228]—the two go hand in hand.[229] The question remains how better to ensure their mutually reinforcing potential.

The Constitution's section 10 formulation of the right to dignity lacks textual specificity and thus, substantive bite. Aside from the practical reasons to leverage this right's potential, there are therefore also doctrinal reasons for its amendment. Bird has commented that a contemporary appreciation of the right to dignity entails a 'new kind of political criticism' pursuant to which we can better assess 'social practices, institutional routines and forms of life'.[230] There is promise in this apt observation.

The Court in *Glenister II* made it clear that corruption is an affront to human dignity and adversely impacts one's ability to enjoy all other human rights.[231] *Glenister II* and *Sonke* are also useful illustrations of the increased likelihood of doctrinally unpersuasive reasoning, and hence judicial activism, where cases end up pegged to higher-order norms. In comparison, first-order rights adjudication proper—where a clear and express right is plainly at issue—opens the space for judicial interpretation which is less likely to fall foul of the separation of powers.

The Constitution itself provides a clue as to the kind of substantive refinement of the right to dignity that may go some way in addressing the foregoing concerns. Section 198

[222] *S v Makwanyane and Another* 1995 (3) SA 391 (CC) *(Makwanyane)* para 329 on dignity as 'the touchstone of the new political order'.

[223] *Dawood and Another v Minister of Home Affairs and Others* 2000 (3) SA 936 (CC) *(Dawood)*; *Nandutu and Others v Minister of Home Affairs and Others* 2019 (5) SA 325 (CC). In both cases, the right to dignity was used to carve out recognition of a right to family life which is not mentioned in the Constitution.

[224] Ibid, eg *Dawood* (n 223) para 30: 'human beings are social beings whose humanity is expressed through their relationships with others'.

[225] *Makwanyane* (n 222) para 330: 'human dignity is important to all democracies'; and quoting *Kindler v Canada* (1992) 6 CRR (2nd) 193 (SCC) 237: 'It is the dignity and importance of the individual which is the essence and the cornerstone of democratic government.'

[226] *Zondo Report* (n 29).

[227] Rather than the public good. See Nico Steytler, 'The "Financial Constitution" and the Prevention and Combatting of Corruption: A Comparative Study of Nigeria, South Africa, and Kenya' in Charles M Fombad and Nico Steytler (eds.) (n 34) 386, 399.

[228] Ronald Dworkin, 'Life's Dominion: An Argument about Abortion and Euthanasia' (Philip A Hart Memorial Lecture, 1993) 19 https://scholarship.law.georgetown.edu/hartlecture/19 accessed 27 October 2022.

[229] For more recent scholarship on this synergy, see Colin Bird, *Human Dignity and Political Criticism* (CUP 2021) 247: 'the protection of human dignity is a common responsibility with specifically political import'.

[230] Ibid., ch 15, 'Dignity and Political Criticism'.

[231] *Glenister II* (n 3) paras 172, 198, and 200.

contains the'[g]overning principles' on the 'security services' in the Republic. In terms of section 198(a), '[n]ational security must reflect the resolve of South Africans, as individuals and as a nation, *to live as equals, to live in peace and harmony, to be free from fear and want and to seek a better life*.'[232] Corruption is a crime that diminishes the ability to live in peace and harmony, free from fear and want, and as long as it continues, the section 198 aspiration rings hollow. This aspiration should be better harnessed within the constitutional text.

The proposed amendment to the section 10 right to human dignity thus proceeds along similar lines to section 198, with the right reading something like this:

> (1) Everyone has inherent dignity and the right to have their dignity respected and protected. This includes, amongst others –
> (a) the right to live free from fear and want and to be able to seek a better life; and
> (b) the right to live in a South Africa that is free of state capture, corruption, and maladministration, and which is committed to the tenets of public integrity and accountability.
> (2) The state must take reasonable legislative and other measures, within its available resources, to achieve the progressive realization of this right.

The addition of the positive state duty in the proposed subsection (2) would maintain the standard of reasonableness entrenched in the likes of *Glenister II* and *Sonke* for assessing state efforts (or failures) to establish (among others) independent oversight structures, while simultaneously enhancing and legitimising this judicially developed, overarching constitutional standard. It would make the constitutionally 'implicit' explicit, free up space for *proper* judicial interpretation in this respect, and so reduce judicial adventurism that comes with the straining of the constitutional text, and resultantly, the judiciary's position within the separation of powers. Such an amendment is the kind of means that would justify the desirable constitutional end of enhancing (public) integrity and accountability in South Africa's constitutional democracy.

6. Conclusion

It is fitting to come full circle and note the words of former Chief Justice, Pius Langa:

> Widespread transformation of economic and social conditions is *beyond the powers of the courts alone*. Only when our judicial commitment is *coupled with legislative reform and appropriate executive action* can the vast disparities that continue to exist in South Africa be eradicated.[233]

This chapter has provided a detailed analysis of a significant diptych of (majority) judgments, *Glenister II* and *Sonke*. They reveal a judicial commitment to fostering public integrity and accountability, underscored by the goal of transforming state functioning, and thus society, for the better. Equally, however, they reveal the difficulties that arise when the

[232] Constitution (n 17) s 198(a) (emphasis added).
[233] Langa (n 14) 358 (emphasis added).

courts try to go it alone and fill the accountability vacuum where the democratic arms of state fail.

State capture is a massive failure of the state; corruption, maladministration, and resultant deficiencies in state structures and services are failures of the state. But the courts alone cannot, and should not, have to remedy such dilemmas—and certainly they should not be doing so in the manner in large part revealed by *Glenister II* and *Sonke*. That is to say, the courts should not be engaging in precarious judicial reasoning and the reading-in of potentially far-reaching constitutional requirements that ultimately, as in the cases analysed, structurally alter governmental accountability.[234] However satisfied one may be with the outcomes of these judgments, these outcomes were not reached pursuant to the sound application of the 'law as integrity',[235] and one should be candid about this. The judicial signalling in *Glenister II* and *Sonke* to the effect that their rather drastic developments did not flout the separation of powers and the constitutional text itself is thus disingenuous. It is time for the emperor to put on some well-fitting clothes.

To this end, this chapter not only traverses the question of what should *not* be done when it comes to constitutional change but also highlights the kind of change that is indeed needed to address the public integrity-and-accountability deficit in South Africa, while simultaneously reducing the pressure on the judiciary within the separation of powers. Two distinguishable, but interrelated, constitutional amendments have thus been briefly proposed: one to ensure the explicit entrenchment of the separation of powers (with its public integrity-and-accountability fourth branch of state), and another to render the right to human dignity a right with enhanced substantive, and thus adjudicatory, potential.

This chapter has not only cautioned against the pitfalls of excessively creative judicial reasoning, as illustrated in *Glenister II* and *Sonke*, but has also leveraged the positive aspects of the reasoning in these cases by making concrete proposals for how South Africa might better start tackling corruption. The suggested changes would reduce 'democratic backsliding' and enhance the 'adjudicative rule of law';[236] they would further the right kind of 'judicial commitment'—one coupled, as it should be, with the appropriate 'legislative reform and . . . executive action',[237] and so help restore power to 'we, the people'.

Bibliography

Akiba O., 'Constitutional Government and the Future of Constitutionalism in Africa' in Akiba O. (ed.), *Constitutionalism and Society in Africa* (Routledge 2004)

Albert R., *Constitutional Amendments – Making, Breaking, and Changing Constitutions* (OUP 2019)

Barber N., *The Principles of Constitutionalism* (OUP 2018)

Bird C., *Human Dignity and Political Criticism* (CUP 2021)

Bishop M., 'Rationality is Dead! Long Live Rationality! Saving Rational Basis Review' (2010) 25(2) South African Public Law 312–45

Cachalia R. and Kohn L., 'The Quest for "Reasonable Certainty": Refining the Justice and Equity Framework Remedial Framework in Public Procurement Cases' (2020) 137(4) South African Law Journal 659–97

Calland R., *The Zuma Years – South Africa's Changing Face of Power* (Zebra Press 2014)

234 Issacharoff (n 16) 606.
235 Dworkin (n 40).
236 Huq and Ginsburg (n 1) 83.
237 Langa (n 14) 358.

Cameron E., 'Constitutionalism, Rights, and International Law: The *Glenister* Decision' (2013) 23(2) Duke Journal of Comparative and International Law 389–409

Choudhry S., 'He Made a Mandate: The South African Constitutional Court and the African National Congress in a Dominant Party Democracy' (2009) 2(1) Constitutional Court Review 1–86

Department of Justice and Constitutional Development, 'Discussion Document on the Transformation of the Judicial System and the Role of the Judiciary in the Developmental South African State' (February 2012) https://www.justice.gov.za/docs/other-docs/20120228-transf-jud.pdf accessed 24 October 2022

Dworkin R., *Law's Empire* (Belknap Press of Harvard University Press 1986)

Dworkin R., 'Life's Dominion: An Argument about Abortion and Euthanasia' (Philip A. Hart Memorial Lecture, 1993) 19 https://scholarship.law.georgetown.edu/hartlecture/19 accessed 27 October 2022

Fombad C.M., 'The Role of Emerging Hybrid Institutions of Accountability in the Separation of Powers Scheme in Africa' in Fombad C.M. (ed.), *Separation of Powers in African Constitutionalism* (OUP 2016) 325

Fombad C.M., 'Corruption and the Crisis of Constitutionalism in Africa' in Fombad C.M. and Steytler N. (eds.), *Corruption and Constitutionalism in Africa* (OUP 2020) 45

Freedman D.W., 'The National Prosecuting Authority' in *LAWSA – Constitutional Law: Structures of Government* (vol 7(2), 3rd edn, LexisNexis South Africa 2020)

Fuller L.L., *The Morality of Law* (Yale University Press 1969)

Ginsburg T. and Huq A., *How to Save a Constitutional Democracy* (University of Chicago Press 2018)

Ginsburg T. and Versteeg M., 'Constitutional Correlates of the Rule of Law' in Adams M., Meuwese A., and Ballin E.H. (eds.), *Constitutionalism and the Rule of Law: Bridging Idealism and Realism* (CUP 2017) 506–25

Hoexter C., *Administrative Law in South Africa* (2nd edn, Juta 2012)

Hoexter C. and Penfold G., *Administrative Law in South Africa* (3rd edn, Juta 2021)

Hohfeld W., 'Some Fundamental Legal Conceptions as Applied in Judicial Reasoning' (1931) 23(1) Yale Law Journal 16–59

Huq A.Z. and Ginsburg T., 'How to Lose a Constitutional Democracy' (2018) 65 UCLA Law Review 78

Huq A.Z., 'A Tactical Separation of Powers Doctrine' (2019) 9(1) Constitutional Court Review 19–44

Issacharoff S., 'Gerrymandering and Political Cartels' (2002) 116(2) Harvard Law Review 593–648

Issacharoff S., 'The Democratic Risk to Democratic Transitions' (2013) 5(1) Constitutional Court Review 1–31

Issacharoff S., 'Constitutional Courts and Consolidated Power' (2014) 62(3) American Journal of Comparative Law 585–612

Kende M.S., 'Enforcing the South African Constitution: The Fight for Judicial Independence and Separation of Powers' (2014) 23(35) Transnational Law and Contemporary Problems 35

Klare K., 'Legal Culture and Transformative Constitutionalism' (1998) 14(1) South African Journal of Human Rights 146–88

Klare K., 'Self-realisation, Human Rights, and Separation of Powers: A Democracy-seeking Approach' (2015) 26(3) Stellenbosch Law Review 445–70

Klaaren J., 'Transformation of the Judicial System in South Africa, 2012–2013' (2015) 47(3) George Washington International Law Review 481–508

Klug H., 'Accountability and the Role of Independent Constitutional Institutions in South Africa's Post-Apartheid Constitutions' (2015) 60(1) New York Law School Law Review 153

Klug H., 'Institutional Integrity and the Promise of Constitutionalism: Justice Moseneke, Judicial Authority and the Separation of Powers' (2017) 1 Acta Juridica 3–28

Klug H., 'Transformative Constitutions and the Role of Integrity Institutions in Tempering Power: The Case of Resistance to State Capture in Post-Apartheid South Africa' (2019) 67(3) Buffalo Law Review 701

Kohn L., 'Integrity & Accountability Commissions of Inquiry: A South African Perspective' (2024) 20(4) Utrecht Law Review 98–119

Kohn L., 'Mbeki Guilty of Misinterpreting the Law' (*Mail & Guardian*, 17 February 2016) https://mg.co.za/article/2016-02-17-mbekis-defence-of-npa-decision-wont-wash/ accessed 14 February 2025

Kohn L., 'The Burgeoning Constitutional Requirement of Rationality & The Separation of Powers: Has Rationality Review Gone Too Far?' (2013) 130(4) South African Law Journal 810–36

Kohn L. and Roux, T 'The 21st Constitution Amendment Bill's proposed Anti-corruption Commission Needs a Rethink' (*Mail & Guardian*, 25 August 2024) https://mg.co.za/thought-leader/opinion/2024-08-25-proposed-anti-corruption-commission-needs-a-rethink/ accessed 14 February 2025

Kohn L., 'Time to go Back to First Principles: A Critical Analysis of the 2017 Procurement Regulations Reveals Them to be Short of the Legality-cum-rationality Mark' (2019) 6(1) African Public Procurement Law Journal 1

Kohn L., 'The National Prosecuting Authority as Part of South Africa's Integrity & Accountability Branch and the Related Case for an Anti-Corruption Redress System' (2022) 12(1) Constitutional Court Review 1–58

Krygier M., 'Tempering Power' in Adams M., Meuwese A., and Ballin E.H. (eds.), *Constitutionalism and the Rule of Law: Bridging Idealism and Realism* (CUP 2017) 34–59

Langa P., 'Transformative Constitutionalism' (2006) 17(3) Stellenbosch Law Review 351–60

Loughlin M., *Against Constitutionalism* (Harvard University Press 2022)

Macfarlane E., 'Judicial Amendment of the Constitution' (2021) 19(5) International Journal of Constitutional Law 1894–924

Motala Z., 'Divination through a Strange Lens' (*Times Live*, 26 March 2011) https://www.timeslive.co.za/ideas/2011-03-27-divination-through-a-strange-lens/ accessed 24 October 2022

Mureinik E., 'A Bridge to Where – Introducing the Interim Bill of Rights' (1994) 10(1) South African Journal of Human Rights 31–48

Pildes R.H., 'The Theory of Political Competition' (1999) 85(8) Virginia Law Review 1605–26

Pildes R.H., 'Foreword: The Constitutionalization of Democratic Politics' (2004) 118(1) Harvard Law Review 28

Pildes R.H. and Issacharoff S., 'Politics as Markets: Partisan Lockups of the Democratic Process' (1998) 50(3) Stanford Law Review 643–717

Report of the Judicial Commission of Inquiry into Allegations of State Capture, Corruption and Fraud in the Public Sector Including Organs of State (2021–2022) https://www.gov.za/documents/judicial-commission-inquiry-state-capture-report-part-3-viii-1-mar-2022-0000 accessed 22 October 2022

Roux T., 'The South African Constitutional Court's Democratic Rights Jurisprudence' (2013) 5 Constitutional Court Review 33–73

Roux T., 'What Does the US Supreme Court's Decision in *Dobbs* Tell Us about the Virtues of Australia's Approach to Protecting Fundamental Rights?' (*Australian Public Law*, July 2022) https://www.auspublaw.org/blog/2022/07/what-does-the-us-supreme-courts-decision-in-dobbs-tell-us-about-the-virtues-of-australias-approach-to-protecting-fundamental-rights accessed 22 October 2022

Roznai Y., *Unconstitutional Constitutional Amendments – The Limits of Amendment Powers* (OUP 2017)

Sadurski W., *Poland's Constitutional Breakdown* (OUP 2019)

Scott H., 'The Death of Doctrine: Private-law Scholarship in South Africa Today' in Basedow J., Fleischer H., and Zimmermann R. (eds.), *Legislators, Judges, and Professors* (Mohr Siebeck 2016) 223

Steytler N., 'Towards Understanding and Combatting the Crime of Corruption in Africa' in Fombad C.M. and Steytler N. (eds.), *Corruption and Constitutionalism in Africa* (OUP 2020) 457

Steytler N., 'The "Financial Constitution" and the Prevention and Combatting of Corruption – A Comparative Study of Nigeria, South Africa, and Kenya' in Fombad C.M. and Steytler N. (eds.), *Corruption and Constitutionalism in Africa* (OUP 2020) 386

Taylor H., 'Forcing the Court's Remedial Hand: Non-Compliance as a Catalyst for Remedial Innovation' (2019) 9(1) Constitutional Court Review 247–81

Tuovinen J., 'The Role of International Law in Constitutional Adjudication: *Glenister v President of the Republic of South* Africa' (2013) 130(4) South African Law Journal 661–72

Tuovinen J., 'What to Do With International Law? Three Flaws in Glenister' (2013) 5(1) Constitutional Court Review 434–49

Tushnet M., *The New Fourth Branch – Institutions for Protecting Constitutional Democracy* (CUP 2021)

Tushnet M., 'Fourth-Branch Institutions: South Africa' in Law D.S., *Constitutionalism in Context* (CUP 2022) 426

Woolman S., 'A Politics of Accountability: How South Africa's Judicial Recognition of the Binding Legal Effect of the Public Protector's Recommendations Had a Catalysing Effect that Brought Down a President' (2016) 8(1) Constitutional Court Review 155

9

The Basic Structure Doctrine and the Politics of Constitutional Change in Kenya: A Case of Judicial Adventurism?

Migai Akech

1. Introduction

Kenya held a hard-fought presidential election on 8 August 2017. Following a declaration by the Independent Electoral and Boundaries Commission (IEBC) on 11 August 2017 that Uhuru Kenyatta, the incumbent, had won the election, Raila Odinga, the runner-up, filed a petition in the Supreme Court challenging the result. The petitioners claimed that the election had not been conducted by the law. The Supreme Court agreed with the petitioners and nullified the election. A repeat poll was subsequently held on 25 October 2017. Odinga boycotted this poll, which Kenyatta won, thereby retaining office.

But retaining power in these circumstances meant that President Kenyatta had no mandate to govern legitimately. Accordingly, in early 2018, President Kenyatta sought out Odinga in a bid to reach a political settlement to enable him to govern a divided country. The two leaders announced their rapprochement in March 2018, shaking hands in public and declaring their commitment to creating a programme that would ensure inclusivity in governance and stem the culture of divisive elections. Not long afterwards, the president appointed the Building Bridges to Unity Advisory Taskforce (BBI Taskforce) to evaluate these national challenges and, after considering the views of citizens, suggest how they could be addressed to build lasting unity.[1]

The BBI Taskforce developed the Constitution of Kenya Amendment Bill 2020 (BBI Bill) and set in motion a process to enact it. While the National Assembly was considering the BBI Bill, several citizens moved to the High Court. The petitioners in *David Ndii & others v Attorney General & others*[2] claimed that the BBI Bill contained 'unconstitutional amendments' and asked the High Court to protect the Constitution's basic structure from these amendments. The High Court obliged. Unhappy with the High Court's decision, the respondents, including the IEBC and Attorney General, appealed to the Court of Appeal. In *Independent and Electoral Boundaries Commission v David Ndii & others*,[3] the Court of

[1] Gazette Notice No 5154, 31 May 2018.

[2] *Ndii & others v Attorney General & others*, Nairobi High Court Constitutional Petition No 282 of 2010 as consolidated with Petition Nos 397 of 2020, E400 of 2020, E401 of 2020, E402 of 2020, E416 of 2020, E426 of 2020, and E2 of 2021.

[3] *Independent and Electoral Boundaries v Ndii & others*, Nairobi Court of Appeal Civil Appeal Nos E291 and E293 of 2021.

Migai Akech, *The Basic Structure Doctrine and the Politics of Constitutional Change in Kenya: A Case of Judicial Adventurism?*
In: *Constitutional Change and Constitutionalism in Africa*. Edited by: Charles M. Fombad and Nico Steytler, Oxford University Press.
 DOI: 10.1093/9780198957034.003.0011

Appeal upheld the judgment of the High Court. The IEBC and the Attorney General then moved to the Supreme Court, which in its decision disagreed with the two lower courts. In *Attorney General & 2 others v David Ndii & others*,[4] the Supreme Court determined that the basic structure doctrine was not applicable in Kenya.

In essence, the BBI Bill and the three court cases on its constitutionality were about who—between the people and the courts—gets to make decisions about constitutional change. These are the questions at the heart of the concept of unconstitutional constitutional amendments (UCA), of which the so-called basic structure doctrine forms a part.[5] The UCA concept holds that some constitutional amendments are unconstitutional because they undermine core principles—or basic structures or features—that are either explicitly stated in a constitution or may be inferred from it by a court. In the latter scenario, the court asserts the power to read in implied limitations on the amendment power. The exercise of this power can be controversial, and it raises the question of the proper role of courts in a constitutional democracy.

This chapter has two objectives. First, it evaluates the application of the basic structure doctrine by three Kenyan courts to determine the constitutionality of the BBI Bill. It contends that, while the High Court and the Court of Appeal were unduly adventurous and wrongly asserted that the basic structure doctrine was applicable in Kenya, thereby frustrating an arguably necessary process of constitutional change, the Supreme Court adopted a restrained approach which appreciated that courts should limit their role to facilitating political processes like these and ensuring that they are participatory and deliberative. From this perspective, courts should invalidate constitutional amendments only where they are enacted in processes that do not adhere to a constitution's provisions on how it may be amended.

Second, the chapter analyses how the three courts dealt with the question of public participation in constitutional amendment initiatives. In this respect, the chapter argues that the Kenyan Supreme Court's test for the adequacy of public participation in such initiatives is unclear and could be used to frustrate participatory constitutional amendment processes or approve amendment processes that are not sufficiently participatory, depending on the inclination of the judges. In either case, the test therefore enables the courts to inappropriately approve or decline amendments to the Constitution.

The chapter is organized as follows: section 2 provides a conceptual framework and examines the basic structure doctrine from the perspective of the role of courts in constitutional change processes. Section 3 examines the politics of the Building Bridges Initiative (BBI) and the rationale for constitutional change in Kenya. Section 4 evaluates the judgments of the High Court, the Court of Appeal, and the Supreme Court on the applicability of the basic structure doctrine in Kenya. Section 5 reflects on the impact of the BBI decisions on the future of constitutional change in Kenya, while section 6 concludes the chapter.

[4] *Attorney General & 2 others v Ndii & others*, Supreme Court Petition No 12 of 2021 as consolidated with Petitions Nos 11 and 13 of 2021.

[5] Strictly speaking, the so-called basic structure doctrine is not a doctrine, given that, as several Supreme Court judges pointed out in the *BBI* case, it is not a legal principle to which there is wide adherence.

2. The basic structure doctrine, courts and constitutional change

Courts play an important role in a democracy. By exercising their power of judicial review appropriately, they can keep the other branches of government within the limits assigned to their authority and ensure that majorities do not oppress minorities. Yet, while the power of judicial review is a necessary mechanism for controlling the power of government and limiting majority will, courts may abuse this power, thus undermining their legitimacy. This power is also bound to be controversial, considering that the judges who exercise it are appointed and therefore not accountable to the people in the same manner as the members of the executive and legislature.

Courts must, therefore, walk a fine line. On the one hand, they may be accused of overreaching where their judicial review decisions are perceived to constitute policy-making that ought to be reserved for the political branches of government, as ordained by the separation-of-powers doctrine. On the other, courts may be accused of conservatism and encouraging tyranny by majorities where they are unduly restrained in exercising the power of judicial review.

Accordingly, they must develop principles and mechanisms that enable them to exercise the power of judicial review in a manner that preserves their legitimacy while allowing the other branches of government to perform their functions without undue hindrance.

These concerns arise, for example, in the context of constitutional change. Should courts exercise their power of judicial review to prevent the people from amending their constitution or limit the extent to which they can do so? Constitutional amendments can be, and often have been, used to undermine commitments to constitutional democracy. Governments can use such amendments to hold on to power when they should not, to strengthen their power, to remove or undermine constitutional checks on their power, to overturn limits on their term in office, or even to prevent themselves from being ousted from power. Electoral majorities, too, for their part, can use constitutional amendments to oppress minorities. In such circumstances, it is arguably the case that courts should intervene to help check the abuse of the constitutional amendment power, thereby safeguarding democracy by ensuring the stability of its governance arrangements and the protection of vulnerable groups.

Conversely, it must be appreciated that change is inevitable and existing institutions should be open to adaptation. We should thus appreciate that constitutions are time-bound. What is more, no generation has the right to impose its values on later generations, for whom a constitution needs to reflect their current predicaments and preoccupations. Thus, courts should not stand in the way of constitutional change by preventing or unduly limiting the exercise of the power of constitutional amendment.

Hence, constitutional amendments are a necessary continuation of the dialogue initiated by the writers of a constitution.[6] This explains why constitutions typically establish formal amendment procedures that regulate how they may be amended, modified, repealed, or replaced.[7] Such procedures are necessary to allow constitutions to adapt to pressing

[6] Catalina Torres-Artunduaga and Santiago Garcia-Jaramillo, 'Democratizing the Doctrine of Unconstitutional Constitutional Amendments: The Puzzle of Amending the Judiciary Branch' (2020) 14(1) ICL Journal 1, 14.

[7] Adem Kassie Abebe, 'The Substantive Validity of Constitutional Amendments in South Africa' (2014) 131(3) South African Law Journal 656, 657.

needs, lived experiences, and new ways of thinking.[8] Above all, they constitute a recognition that the people have the power and the right to alter their constitution.[9] A constitution risks becoming irrelevant to the lives of the people, and may provoke violent change through revolutionary means, if it cannot be amended or if its amendment procedures are overly cumbersome. Indeed, amendment procedures are a peaceful alternative to revolutions, which are often violent.[10] We should, therefore, see such procedures as a means of channeling revolutions through legal means.[11] For this reason, practicable amendment procedures are necessary because they ensure a constitution's continuous existence and effectiveness.[12]

In evaluating constitutional amendments, we thus need to balance the equally important but competing considerations of stability and change. While constitutions should not be too easy to amend, amending them should not be arduous either.[13] But how should a polity go about ensuring this critical balance? The typical balancing method is for a constitution to establish procedures for its amendment that either make it easy or difficult to amend. Thus, 'flexible constitutions' are those that are easy to amend because they can, for example, be amended through the use of the ordinary legislative process. Conversely, 'rigid constitutions' are those that are difficult to amend because they can be amended only through the use of special procedures such as a supermajority or special majority in the legislature, the involvement of various institutions in the amendment process, approval by an absolute or special majority of voters in a referendum, or a combination of such special procedures.

A constitution can also establish a tiered amendment procedure by which it provides different amendment rules for different parts of the constitutional order.[14] With this method, the constitution demands exacting demonstrations of popular will for the amendment of provisions that are deemed to require special protection, thus raising the costs of dangerous forms of constitutional change.[15] One formulation of this approach is to require supermajorities and the involvement of various institutions in the amendment process.[16] Another common requirement is that a popular referendum has to be held before an amendment can take effect. In yet another formulation, the proposed amendment must be supported by a special—and not just a mere absolute—majority of voters in a referendum.

In using such devices that establish several veto players in the amendment process, constitutions seek to prevent the enactment of partisan and regressive amendments.[17] The South African Constitution, for example, adopts this approach. While it does not expressly

[8] Ibid.

[9] Raymond Ku, 'Consensus of the Governed: The Legitimacy of Constitutional Change' (1995) 64(2) Fordham Law Review 535, 542.

[10] John R Vile, 'The Amending Process: Alternative to Revolution' (1983) 11(2) South Eastern Political Review 49.

[11] Mark Tushnet, 'Peasants with Pitchforks, and Toilers with Twitter: Constitutional Revolutions and the Constituent Power' (2015) 13(3) International Journal of Constitutional Law 639.

[12] Abebe (n 7) 658.

[13] See Sanford Levinson (ed), *Responding to Imperfection: The Theory and Practice of Constitutional Amendment* (Princeton University Press 1995).

[14] Rosalind Dixon and David Landau, 'Transnational Constitutionalism and a Limited Doctrine of Unconstitutional Constitutional Amendment' (2015) 13(3) International Journal of Constitutional Law 606, 613.

[15] Ibid.

[16] See Charles Fombad, 'Some Perspectives on Durability and Change under Modern African Constitutions' (2013) 11(2) International Journal of Constitutional Law 382.

[17] Bjorn Erik Rasch and Roger D Congleton, 'Amendment Procedures and Constitutional Stability' in Roger D Congleton and Birgitta Swedenborg (eds.), *Democratic Constitutional Design and Public Policy: Analysis and Evidence* (MIT Press 2006) 319.

insulate any of its provisions from amendment, it establishes institutional and procedural safeguards against abusive amendments.[18] Similarly, the Ghanaian Constitution makes it difficult to amend entrenched provisions. By means of these special procedures, constitutions demand exacting demonstrations of popular will for the amendment of their fundamental principles, thus raising the costs of dangerous forms of constitutional change.

Other constitutions, such as the German Constitution,[19] go so far as precluding the amendment of certain constitutional rules or explicitly empowering courts to review the form or even substance of constitutional amendments.[20] In this approach, constitutions create 'eternity clauses', meaning that the clauses are entrenched (that is, immune from amendment) for some time, or for eternity. In other cases, constitutions may explicitly empower courts to review the substance of constitutional amendments and determine whether they violate fundamental constitutional principles.

The concept of unconstitutional constitutional amendment is the second method for balancing the competing considerations of constitutional change and stability. Here, the power to amend a constitution is subject to implied substantive limits. In this judicial method, courts assert an implied power to invalidate constitutional amendments that, in their view, violate or undermine the fundamental provisions of a constitution. This power is asserted on various extra-constitutional grounds which are said to precede and outlive extant constitutional rules even if these rules are supported by an overwhelming majority of the people and their representatives.

One claim is that constitutional amendments should not undermine the essentials of a constitution, even though they can 'correct imperfections'.[21] A second claim is that constitutions, particularly liberal ones, recognize higher-order principles of natural law and rights that set normative limits on the amendment power.[22] On this basis, certain moral principles and norms are deemed unalterable. A third claim, also based on liberal political thought, is that there are certain inherent limits to the power of government that constitutional amendments must not violate. A fourth, interrelated, claim is that fundamental liberties are entrenched constitutional values, since they are the quintessence of self-government, and hence any attempt to amend them would be 'unintelligible and revolting'.[23]

These claims have been recognized in the decisions of courts in various countries. For example, in the case in India of *Kesavananda Bharati v State of Kerala*,[24] the Supreme Court held that the power to amend the Constitution did not include the power to abrogate it or otherwise obliterate basic constitutional norms. According to the Court, the basic structure of the Constitution—consisting of certain principles founded on individual dignity and freedoms—was fundamental and therefore immutable. The Court 'discovered' these basic features from the preamble of the Constitution as well as the history and composition of the constituent assembly which adopted this Constitution. It is these findings of the Indian Supreme Court that some scholars have claimed constitute a doctrine.

[18] Abebe (n 7) 659.

[19] Basic Law of the Federal Republic of Germany (1949), art 79.

[20] See Kemal Gözler, *Judicial Review of Constitutional Amendments: A Comparative Study* (Ekin Press 2008).

[21] See eg John Rawls, *Political Liberalism* (Columbia University Press 1993) 238–39.

[22] See eg Walter F Murphy, 'Merlin's Memory: The Past and Future Imperfect of the Once and Future Polity' in Sanford Levinson (ed.) (n 13) 177.

[23] Stephen Macedo, *Liberal Virtues: Citizenship, Virtue and Community in Liberal Constitutionalism* (Clarendon Press 1990) 183.

[24] *Kesavananda Bharati v State of Kerala* [1973] AIR 161 (SC).

Let us now review the BBI: why did it deem constitutional change to be necessary, what changes did it propose, and how did it go about amending the Constitution?

3. Amending the Kenyan Constitution: The Building Bridges Initiative

The BBI sought to unite Kenya in the wake of the divisive presidential elections of 2017. Following their handshake in March 2018, Kenyatta and Odinga issued a joint communiqué in which they observed that, despite constitutional reforms, Kenyans continued to be bitterly divided, and gave their commitment to 'offer the leadership that [would prevent] future generations inheriting dangerous division and [offer] them a path to a bright future for all'.[25] President Kenyatta then appointed the BBI Taskforce in May 2018. The Taskforce presented its report to President Kenyatta in October 2019, in which it made various recommendations.[26] Concerning ethnic antagonism, competition, and divisive elections, the Taskforce recommended the substitution of the 'winner-take-all model for the presidency' with a consociational model more suitable for an ethnically divided society.[27] In addition, it recommended a system of government that would address Kenya's unique needs, especially in forging a home-grown national executive structure.

Secondly, the BBI Taskforce observed that Kenyans were discontented with the current system under which the Cabinet comprises individuals who are not Members of Parliament (MPs). It recommended a Cabinet made up of both MPs and technocrats, with the latter being *ex officio* MPs.[28] Thirdly, it proposed that: 'the runner-up of a presidential election should become an ex-officio member of Parliament and the leader of the Official Opposition if his or her party is not represented in the Government, or of a coalition of Parliamentary parties not represented in the Government'.[29]

The BBI Taskforce also made recommendations in regard to enhanced representation in the electoral system, inclusivity in the allocation of national resources, economic transformation, tackling corruption, enhancing the effectiveness of the devolved system of government, improving the safety and security of citizens, and strengthening the criminal justice system.[30]

However, although the BBI sought to unite the country, it quickly created a rift between President Kenyatta and his deputy, William Ruto, who saw it as 'the beginning of a new political alliance intended to isolate and sideline him in the 2022 elections'.[31] Ruto vehemently opposed the BBI and soon 'led a group of legislators from the ruling Jubilee party—including a majority from President Kenyatta's Central Kenya stronghold—to defect *en masse* to a new outfit, the United Democratic Alliance [UDA Party]'.[32] The proponents of

[25] Joint Communique of Building Bridges to a New Kenyan Nation (9 March 2018) 2.

[26] Presidential Taskforce on Building Bridges to Unity Advisory, 'Building Bridges to a United Kenya: From a Nation of Blood Ties to a Nation of Ideals' (BBI Taskforce Report October 2019).

[27] Ibid. 10.

[28] Ibid. 11.

[29] Ibid. 12.

[30] Ibid. 12–16.

[31] Macharia Gaitho, 'How Kenyatta Won over a Foe and Lost His Deputy' (*Al Jazeera*, 21 June 2022) <https://www.aljazeera.com/features/2022/6/21/analysis-how-kenyas-president-won-over-a-foe-and-alienated-his> accessed 21 June 2022.

[32] Ibid.

the BBI made little or no effort to accommodate Ruto and his supporters,[33] who accordingly opposed the recommendations of the BBI Taskforce.[34]

Thus, a segment of the populace perceived the BBI as an instrument for the regime to prevail in the presidential succession war and not as a genuine effort to address national governance challenges, especially the divisive elections.[35] According to its critics, the BBI was a ploy to secure positions for its proponents in an expanded executive.[36] They also claimed it would undermine the independence of the judiciary and marginalize sparsely populated areas of the country.[37]

Despite the opposition, President Kenyatta and Odinga pressed on. After the BBI Taskforce presented its recommendations, the president appointed a steering committee to validate the Taskforce report through consultations with citizens and propose policy and legal changes.[38] The steering committee made various proposals, including a bill to amend the Constitution. Accordingly, the Constitution of Kenya (Amendment) Bill 2020 (BBI Bill) sought to amend the Constitution:

> to address issues arising from its implementation, specifically the need to resolve issues of divisive elections and promote gender equity in governance; strengthen the structure of devolution and increase resource allocation to the counties; broaden mechanisms for the people of Kenya to benefit from economic growth; harmonise certain roles and functions of the bicameral legislature; fortify [the] national ethos by specifying the responsibilities of citizens; and strengthen accountability on public resources and the fight against corruption.[39]

In particular, the BBI Bill sought to broaden the structure of the executive by introducing the office of prime minister and two deputy prime ministers, who would all be appointed by the president and have leadership roles in the executive and Parliament. It also proposed that Cabinet ministers could be appointed from among members of the National Assembly. Secondly, it proposed to enhance the impartiality of the public service by removing the requirement for vetting of the principal secretaries by the National Assembly.

Thirdly, the BBI Bill proposed to enhance the transparency of the judiciary by introducing the office of Judiciary Ombudsman—who would be a non-voting member of the Judicial Service Commission—to handle complaints about the judicial process from

[33] See eg Laban Wanambisi, 'DP Ruto Calls for Inclusivity in the Building Bridges Initiative' (*Capital News*, 16 February 2020) https://www.capitalfm.co.ke/news/2020/02/dp-ruto-calls-for-inclusivity-in-the-building-bridges-initiative/ accessed 10 July 2021.

[34] See eg Morris Kiruga, 'Kenya: Building Bridges Initiative Deepens Ruto-Odinga Rivalry' (*Africa Report*, 4 December 2019) https://www.theafricareport.com/20845/kenya-building-bridges-initiative-deepens-ruto-odinga-rivalry/ accessed 8 August 2020.

[35] See eg Akoko Akech, 'BBI: A Ploy to Subvert Democracy through Deception' (*Elephant*, 13 December 2019) https://www.theelephant.info/features/2019/12/13/bbi-a-ploy-to-subvert-democracy-through-deception/ accessed 5 February 2020; Odhiambo Jamwa, 'Jubilee Fight Contemptuous of Kenyans' Plight' (*The Star*, 15 April 2020) https://www.the-star.co.ke/amp/opinion/star-blogs/2020-04-15-jubilee-fight-contemptuous-of-kenyans-plight/?utm_term=Autofeed&utm_medium=Social&utm_source=Twitter&__twitter_impression=true accessed 5 October 2020.

[36] Emmy Auma and Ivan Campbell, 'Why Peace Remains Elusive as Kenya Prepares for the 2022 General Elections' (*Saferworld*, August 2021) https://www.saferworld.org.uk/long-reads/why-peace-remains-elusive-as-kenya-prepares-for-the-2022-general-elections accessed 10 February 2022.

[37] Ibid.

[38] Gazette Notice No 264, 10 January 2020.

[39] Constitution of Kenya (Amendment) Bill 2020, Memorandum of Objects and Reasons.

members of the public. In terms of this proposal, the Judiciary Ombudsman could initiate a motion to remove a judge from office on account of complaints received from the public. Still in regard to the judiciary, the BBI Bill proposed that advocates representing the Law Society of Kenya in the Judicial Service Commission would be prohibited from practising in the courts and tribunals, to minimize potential conflicts of interest. This provision also sought to provide a mechanism to enable the Judicial Service Commission to discipline judicial officers, including judges.

Fourthly, the BBI Bill sought to strengthen devolution by, among other things, anchoring the Constituencies Development Fund in the Constitution, to facilitate the performance of national government functions within the constituencies; in regard to devolution, the bill proposed to establish a County Assembly Fund and a Ward Development Fund.

Fifthly, it aimed to strengthen accountability by empowering the Cabinet secretary responsible for finance to stop the transfer of funds to a state organ or other public entity or a county government where there are serious and persistent material breaches of established financial control measures. Yet another key feature of the bill was the proposal to include the Director of Public Prosecutions as an independent office to enhance its independence and budgetary autonomy. As regards corruption, the bill proposed a mechanism for the expeditious investigation, prosecution, and trial of corruption-related matters.

The Constitution provides for two modes of amending itself, namely a parliamentary initiative under article 256 or a popular initiative under article 257. In either case, however, amendments relating to ten specified matters require the approval of the people in a referendum.[40] These matters are: the supremacy of the Constitution; the territory of Kenya; the sovereignty of the people; the national values and principles of governance; the Bill of Rights; the president's term of office; the independence of the judiciary and commissions and independent offices; the functions of Parliament; the objects, principles, and structure of devolved government; and the amendment provisions. An amendment relating to any of these matters can pass only if at least 20 per cent of the registered voters in each of at least half of the 47 counties vote in the referendum, and it is supported by a simple majority of the citizens voting in the referendum.[41]

An initiative by Parliament to amend the Constitution must meet several requirements.[42] First, each house of Parliament (the National Assembly and Senate) must pass the bill, in both its second and third readings, by not less than two-thirds of all the members of that house. Second, Parliament must publicize the bill and facilitate public discussion of it. Third, after the two houses have passed the bill, their speakers have to jointly submit it to the president for assent and publication. The president is then required to assent to the bill and cause it to be published within 30 days of Parliament having enacted it. If the bill proposes to amend a provision that requires the people's approval in a referendum, the Constitution requires the president, before assenting to it, to request that the IEBC conduct a national referendum within 90 days for approval of the bill.[43]

By contrast, a popular initiative to amend the Constitution must, in the first place, be signed by at least one million registered voters.[44] The Constitution requires the promoters

[40] Constitution of Kenya (2010), art 255.
[41] Ibid. art 255(2).
[42] Ibid. art 256(1)–(4).
[43] Ibid. art 256(5).
[44] Ibid. art 257(1).

of the popular initiative to formulate it into a draft bill and deliver the bill and the supporting signatures to the IEBC, which has to verify that the initiative is supported by at least one million registered voters. If the IEBC is satisfied that the initiative meets these requirements, the Constitution requires it to submit the bill to each county assembly for consideration. A county assembly that approves the bill then delivers a copy of the bill to the two houses of Parliament. Once a majority of the county assemblies have approved the bill, it is introduced in Parliament. The bill passes if it is supported by a majority of the members of each house of Parliament, the Speaker of the National Assembly shall submit it to the president for assent. However, if either house of Parliament fails to pass the bill, or it relates to a matter specified in article 255(1), it shall be submitted to the people in a referendum.

Fearful that they would not marshal the majority required to pass the BBI Bill through a parliamentary initiative, given the strong opposition from Ruto's UDA Party, the promoters of the BBI Bill opted for the popular initiative route. The BBI secretariat therefore put in motion the process of collecting the required signatures of registered voters who supported the initiative. Having obtained these signatures, it submitted them to the IEBC, which verified them and submitted the bill to the county assemblies for consideration. A majority of the county assemblies approved the bill, which was then introduced in the National Assembly.[45]

4. The BBI goes to court

4.1 The High Court

While the county assemblies were considering the BBI Bill, various individuals filed a petition against it in the High Court. Essentially, they wanted the High Court to declare that the basic structure doctrine and corollary doctrines as regards unconstitutional constitutional amendment and eternity clauses were applicable in Kenya. Further, they wanted the High Court to declare that these doctrines protected certain provisions of the Constitution, which in their view constituted its basic structure, from amendment, either by Parliament or through a popular initiative. These were the provisions on the sovereignty of the people, the supremacy of the Constitution, the Republic, the Bill of Rights, the executive, and the judiciary. Furthermore, they wanted the High Court to declare that Parliament could not pass an amendment that destroyed or altered the basic structure of the Constitution.

The Attorney General, Parliament, and the BBI secretariat opposed the petition. They contended that every provision of the Constitution was amendable and that the power of the people to amend the Constitution was unlimited, provided that the people adhered to the stipulated amendment procedures. Moreover, they argued that the petition was premature, as it anticipated that Parliament would pass a bill that was yet to be introduced.

[45] See eg 'Kenya Set for Referendum as over 30 Counties Pass BBI' (*Business Daily*, 23 February 2021) <https://www.businessdailyafrica.com/bd/news/kenya-over-30-counties-pass-bbi-3301258> accessed 23 February 2021.

4.1.1 The High Court on the basic structure doctrine

In a unanimous decision, the High Court agreed with the petitioners on the applicability of the basic structure doctrine in Kenya. In its view, the basic structure of the Constitution consisted 'of the foundational structure of the Constitution as provided in the Preamble; the eighteen chapters; and six schedules of the Constitution'.[46] Essentially, the High Court thought that the entire Constitution comprised its basic structure, and could not 'be amended without recalling the Primary Constituent Power of the people'.[47]

As the High Court saw it, the exercise of the people's primary constituent power—that is, the power to make the constitution—entailed four mandatory procedures: civic education, public participation, constituent assembly debate, and a referendum.[48] The Court concluded that certain provisions of the Constitution were 'eternity clauses' and thus insulated from any amendment at all.[49] However, it did not indicate which provisions of the Constitution were eternity clauses, stating only that identifying them would be based on a court's 'fact-intensive determination'.[50] Nevertheless, the Court acknowledged that some provisions of the Constitution could be amended by the stipulated procedures as long as they did not change its basic structure.[51]

On the basis that the people may amend the basic structure and eternity clauses of the Constitution only by using their primary constituent power, the High Court determined that the process culminating in the BBI Bill was unconstitutional. Having made this determination, it deemed it unnecessary to interrogate the BBI Bill. The Court faulted the process that produced the bill because it did not entail the use of the four procedures which it had claimed were mandatory.

In arriving at these determinations, the High Court stated that it was guided by the nature of the 2010 Constitution, the history of its making, and the question of how the extent and limits of the constitutional amendment powers it allows for should be interpreted given its nature and the history of its making.[52] For the High Court, the historical context was 'imperative for giving proper meaning' to the text of the Constitution.[53] History, therefore, formed the primary basis for the High Court's determinations as to the applicability of the basic structure 'doctrine' in Kenya and its implications for constitutional amendment.

The High Court next described how a 'culture of hyper-amendment' had destroyed the identity of the Independence Constitution and led to Kenya's transformation into an autocratic state.[54] As the Court noted, it was in reaction to the excesses of the state that citizens began clamouring for change in the early 1980s, events that culminated in the initiation of a constitutional review in 2001 after the merger of government-led and civil society-driven efforts in the so-called Ufungamano Initiative.[55] What followed was a 'strong people-driven' and participatory constitutional review under a legislative framework the

[46] *Ndii & others v Attorney General & others* (n 2) para 474(f).
[47] Ibid.
[48] Ibid. paras 474(c) and (e), and 784(i)(c).
[49] Ibid. para 474(g).
[50] Ibid.
[51] Ibid.
[52] Ibid. para 395.
[53] Ibid. para 395(i).
[54] Ibid. paras 405–09.
[55] Ibid. paras 410–11.

objective of which was 'to facilitate the comprehensive review of the Constitution by the people'.[56]

As the High Court further noted, the legislative framework established four organs of review: the Constitution of Kenya Review Commission (CKRC), the District Constitutional Forums, the National Constitutional Consultative Forum, and the National Assembly.[57] It was the responsibility of these organs of review to ensure that the people participated meaningfully in generating and debating proposals to alter the Constitution, as well as to ensure that the outcome reflected the wishes of the people.[58] The CKRC produced a draft constitution in October 2002 that 'was a reflection of the true will of the people of Kenya'.[59] However, President Moi dissolved Parliament before it could adopt it.

Kenya then held a general election in 2002 that ushered in the National Rainbow Coalition (NARC) administration, with Mwai Kibaki as president. Afterwards, the National Constitutional Consultative Forum (or National Constitutional Conference) convened in 2003 and commenced debate on the CKRC draft constitution (commonly known as the Bomas Draft Constitution). Although the proceedings of the conference were, as the High Court put it, 'often acrimonious', they resulted in the delivery in 2004 of a draft constitution.[60] The Court noted that, as the conference was concluding its work, the High Court, in *Timothy Njoya & Others v Attorney General & Others* (*Njoya*),[61] held that any new constitution had to be ratified by a referendum. In response, Parliament amended the Constitutional Review Act 1997 to provide for such a referendum.

According to the High Court, the Kibaki government then unilaterally altered the Bomas Draft Constitution, in the process creating the so-called Wako Draft Constitution, which it put to a referendum in 2005. The people rejected this draft constitution in the referendum. This ended the constitutional review process, and it was only resuscitated with the intervention of the African Union's Panel of Eminent African Personalities, which had helped Kenya mediate the post-election crisis of 2007–08. The resulting mediation agreement, the National Accord, identified constitutional reform as one of the key long-term strategies for durable peace. The Constitution of Kenya Review Act 2008 was then enacted to facilitate the completion of constitutional reform.

The Constitution of Kenya Review Act 2008 established five organs of review: the Committee of Experts (CoE); the Civil Society Reference Group; the Parliamentary Select Committee; the National Assembly; and the referendum.[62] The Act required the CoE to build on the work of the CKRC and identify contentious and non-contentious issues.[63] Having identified these issues, the CoE: (1) published a harmonized draft constitution; (2) sought the views of the public on it and incorporated them; (3) presented the revised draft to the Parliamentary Service Commission 'for deliberation and consensus building on contentious issues'; and (4) revised the draft, taking into account the consensus achieved by the Parliamentary Service Commission, and returned it to the Parliamentary Service Commission. The Parliamentary Service Commission then submitted the draft to the

[56] Ibid. para 414.
[57] Ibid. para 415.
[58] Ibid. para 426.
[59] Ibid. para 427.
[60] Ibid. para 429.
[61] *Timothy Njoya & others v Attorney General & others* [2004] eKLR.
[62] Ibid. para 442.
[63] Ibid. para 444.

National Assembly for approval, after which the Attorney General published the draft constitution and the Interim Independent Electoral Commission proceeded to conduct the referendum.[64]

From this account of the history of the making of the 2010 Constitution, the High Court concluded that 'Kenyans were clear that they wanted a Constitution in which the ordinary [citizen] took center-stage in *debating and designing*'.[65] In the Court's view, the people rejected the Wako Draft Constitution in 2005 'because it failed the public participation process test and, instead, verged on political elite consensus'.[66] The High Court went on to state that Kenyans bequeathed themselves the 2010 Constitution 'in spite of, and, at times, against the political and other elites'.[67] It thus characterized the 2010 Constitution as having been initiated and drafted by ordinary citizens and, furthermore, as replete with content largely of their making, and hence, by implication, as content unaffected by the involvement of elites, whether political or otherwise.

As it happens, the High Court's reading of the history of the making of the 2010 Constitution was not only selective but erroneous. It made five fundamental errors in its reading of this history. The first of these is that, contrary to what the Court asserted, political elites did indeed play an instrumental role in the making of the 2010 Constitution, as is demonstrated by the composition and the work of the organs of review in both phases of the process, namely Bomas (2000–05) and the National Accord (2008–10).

The two phases of the constitutional review process were initiated by elites, the government, and civil society, in the case of Bomas; and, in the case of the National Accord process, the coalition government. In both instances, elites constituted the bodies that generated the draft constitutional documents. While these bodies represented all segments of society, their members were invariably educated elites, whether at the national or local level.[68] For example, many were politicians, civil society elites, and professionals. To qualify for an appointment as a member of the CKRC, for example, one had to be 'educated up to a minimum of "O" level standard or its equivalent'.[69] Significantly, such elites initiated the process of constitutional review. Similarly, the second phase was also dominated by political elites.[70]

Furthermore, political elite consensus was instrumental to the realization of the Constitution. As various commentators have noted, the first phase of the constitutional review process failed due to lack of agreement among the political elite on two contentious issues: the system of government, and devolution.[71] While the Odinga wing of the NARC coalition government had championed the Bomas Draft Constitution's provisions on these contentious issues, given that they preferred a parliamentary system of government and

[64] Ibid. para 448.

[65] Ibid. para 469 (emphasis added).

[66] Ibid. para 471.

[67] Ibid. para 473.

[68] See eg Alicia L Bannon, 'Designing a Constitution-Drafting Process: Lessons from Kenya' (2007) 116(8) Yale Law Journal 1849, where the author observes that 'many different elites—from business interests to human rights groups—were involved in Kenya's review process'.

[69] Constitution of Kenya Review Act 1997, s 4A(1)(c).

[70] Constitution of Kenya Review Act 2008, s 5.

[71] See eg Godwin R Murunga, 'Elite Compromises and the Content of the 2010 Constitution' in Godwin R Murunga, Duncan Okello, and Anders Sjogren (eds.), *Kenya: The Struggle for a New Constitutional Order* (Zed Books 2014) 144; Bannon (n 68) 1824; Christina Murray, 'Political Elites and the People: Kenya's Decade Long Constitution-Making Process' (2018) https://papers.ssrn.com/sol3/papers.cfm?abstract_id=3147154 accessed 12 June 2021; Abrak Saati, *The Participation Myth: Outcomes of Participatory Constitution Building Processes on Democracy* (Umea University 2015).

an extensive devolution of power, President Kibaki's wing vehemently opposed them, as it favoured a presidential system.[72]

The Bomas National Constitutional Conference (NCC) produced a draft constitution in 2004. But before the conference could adopt this draft, the High Court in the *Njoya* case stopped the process, on the basis that the draft could be adopted only after the people had approved it in a referendum. At much the same time, other individuals who had issues with the constitutional review process went to the High Court, asking it to stop the CKRC from preparing the draft bill and to prohibit the Attorney General from receiving the final draft bill from the Commission.[73] The Court obliged in *Kung'u & others v Republic & others*, with the result that, although the *Njoya* court decided that a referendum had to be held, there was now no document upon which such a referendum could proceed.[74]

The constitutional review process stalled for some months until the Parliamentary Select Committee on the Constitutional Review Process revived it in 2005 through a bipartisan initiative (the first Naivasha Accord) that culminated in a new agreement to review the then Constitution. But differences between the government and opposition soon emerged, with the government declaring it would not honour the Naivasha Accord. Subsequently, Parliament enacted a law that empowered itself to amend the Bomas Draft Constitution, before submitting it for the people's approval in a referendum. The Attorney General, Amos Wako, prepared a draft constitution, which Parliament debated, adopted, and put to the people in a referendum. The people rejected the Wako Draft Constitution (as it was known). The constitutional review process was thus put on the back burner for some two years until the post-election violence of 2007–08 necessitated its revival.

This is the context in which Parliament passed the Constitutional Review Act of 2008. Notably, the Act did not establish a constituent assembly. The second phase of the constitutional review process deliberately incorporated a requirement for political elite consensus, as it was appreciated that a new constitution would not be realized without an elite compact.[75] This explains why the Parliamentary Select Committee was tasked with building consensus on the contentious issues.[76] Once the Committee had gained the required consensus, the CoE would produce a draft incorporating the consensus, before sending it back to the Committee, which would present it to the National Assembly for discussion, albeit that the latter could not amend it. The National Assembly would then submit the draft to the Attorney General for publication, after which it would be put to a referendum. Thus, the Constitution of Kenya Review Act of 2008 was designed to compel the political elite to agree on the contentious issues.[77]

Accordingly, the High Court failed to appreciate that the draft constitution subjected to referendum in 2010 was not a product of the people's constituent assembly. As the Court determined in *Njoya*, the National Constitutional Consultative Forum, the key organ in the first phase of constitution-making, was not a constituent assembly in that the people had

[72] Jill Cottrell and Yash Ghai, 'Constitution Making and Democratization in Kenya (2000–2005)' (2007) 14(1) Democratization 1, 16; Beth Elise Whitaker and Jason Giersch, 'Voting on a Constitution: Implications for Democracy in Kenya' (2009) 27(1) Journal of Contemporary African Studies 6.

[73] *Karenge & another v Republic and others*, Nairobi High Court Misc Application No 309 of 2004.

[74] Republic of Kenya, 'Report of the Committee of Eminent Persons on the Constitution Review Process' (30 May 2006) 29.

[75] See eg Murunga (n 71) 158.

[76] Constitution of Kenya Review Act 2008, s 32(c).

[77] Murray (n 71) 7.

not directly elected two-thirds of its members; conversely, the second phase did not have a similar organ, meaning that the 2010 Constitution was not the product of a constituent assembly.

A related error of the High Court was its claim that the people could exercise their constituent power only through four mandatory and sequential procedures—as previously noted, these are civic education, public participation, constituent assembly debate, and a referendum. However, this claim does not find support in constitution-making practice in general, or the history of the making of the 2010 Constitution in particular. The Constitution came into being neither by means of these four procedures nor in the sequence that the High Court purported to prescribe for the exercise of the constituent power.

Indeed, the question of whether a constituent assembly and a referendum are *both* necessary mechanisms remains contested among constitutional theorists.[78] In *Njoya*, for example, Kubo J in his dissent argued that there are several alternative ways of legitimating a constitution: ways which include relying on a constituent assembly, holding a mandatory referendum, or trusting in the legislature. The issue of legitimating a constitution, he said, was 'predominantly political' and required a political solution. In his view, therefore, if the people preferred one specific mode, they should provide for it explicitly in their constitution or other law.

Kubo J's view finds support in constitution-making practice. Ergo, while some jurisdictions insist on a referendum, for others it suffices that the people elect a constituent assembly that then makes decisions on their behalf.[79] For example, in South Africa, Uganda, and Tunisia, directly elected constituent assemblies were tasked with adopting the final constitutional text.[80] In the three cases, a referendum was included only as an option of last resort in case the assemblies failed to adopt the text by the required majority.[81] In a nutshell, the people should determine how they wish to exercise their constituent power: it was not open to the High Court to dictate to the people how they should exercise this power.

Fourth, the High Court failed to appreciate that the draft constitution which was subjected to a referendum in 2010 differed in fundamental respects from the Bomas Draft, with the political elites having altered it through a pact at Naivasha in 2010. In its harmonized draft constitution, the CoE had recommended a hybrid presidential and parliamentary system of government. However, when the Parliamentary Select Committee received this draft, it opted for a presidential system. It based this decision on its mandate under the Constitutional Review Act 2008 'to build consensus on the Reviewed Harmonized Draft Constitution'.[82] The consensus enabled the process to move forward, culminating in the ratification of the draft constitution in the referendum held in August 2010.[83] Ultimately,

[78] Markus Bockenforde, 'Letting the Constituent Power Decide? Merits and Challenges of Referenda in Constitution Making Processes in Africa' in Tania Abbiate, Markus Bockenforde, and Veronica Federico (eds.), *Public Participation in African Constitutionalism* (Routledge 2018) 26, 30.

[79] Saati (n 71) 34.

[80] Bockenforde (n 78) 34.

[81] Ibid.

[82] Republic of Kenya, National Assembly, 'Report of the Parliamentary Select Committee on the Review of the Constitution on the Reviewed Harmonized Draft Constitution' (29 January 2010) 6.

[83] Murray (n 71) 11, where the author notes that the consensus was 'achieved not because political elites were convinced by it but because this time the perceived costs of not agreeing were too high socially, politically and economically'.

therefore, the 2010 Constitution was a compromise document that bore 'the imprint of elite machinations', 'like most constitutions around the world'.[84]

Finally, the High Court failed to appreciate that the question of how the proposed new constitution would be amended was extensively deliberated upon and resolved in the first phase of the constitutional review. Indeed, the question of how the constitution would be amended was never a contentious issue. The historical record clearly shows that the National Consultative Forum was aware of the dangers of the culture of hyper-amendments that had defined the Independence Constitution.[85] Equally, the NCC was wary of overly rigid amendment procedures.[86] It is clear from the *Final Report of the Constitution of Kenya Review Commission* that the people gave due consideration to the matters they wanted to be entrenched in the Constitution and how the Constitution should be amended. Moreover, the people sought to limit the power of Parliament to amend the Constitution and wanted to be involved in changing 'certain provisions of the Constitution through referenda'. More significantly, the people stated that:

> a distinction should be made between entrenched and non-entrenched provisions of the Constitution, with [a] stringent mechanism being set up for amending the former entrenched provisions which should include supremacy of the Constitution, the Bill of Rights, land, the judiciary, finance, the system of government.[87]

For this reason, the Constitution of Kenya Review Commission concluded as follows:

> There is [a] need to protect the Constitution against indiscriminate amendments. If the amendment procedure is too simple, it reduces public confidence in the Constitution. The converse, however, is also true. If the amendment procedure is too rigid, it may encourage revolutionary measures to bring about change instead of using the acceptable constitutional means. Thus, a balance must be struck between these two extremes.[88]

To attain this balance, the Constitution of Kenya Review Commission recommended amendment procedures that were neither too simple nor too rigid.[89] Significantly, all the four draft constitutions adopted this approach to constitutional amendments and contained virtually the same provisions on this issue, in what is now contained in Chapter 16 of the 2010 Constitution.[90]

4.1.2 The High Court on public participation

Two related petitions that were consolidated with the main petition[91] contended that the county assemblies had not carried out public participation on the BBI Bill and had passed

[84] Murunga (n 71) 144, 160.
[85] Republic of Kenya, 'Final Report of the Constitution of Kenya Review Commission' (2004) 74.
[86] Ibid.
[87] Ibid. 75.
[88] Ibid. 74.
[89] Ibid.
[90] See ch 19, Revised Zero Draft Constitution (Ghai Draft) (2002); ch 19, Bomas Draft Constitution (2004); ch 19, Proposed New Constitution (Wako Draft) (2005); ch 19, Harmonized Draft Constitution (2009); ch 16, Revised Harmonized Draft Constitution (2010).
[91] Petition Nos E400 and E416 of 2020.

it hurriedly and clandestinely. The petitions also averred that the promoters of the bill had collected the signatures of supporters before giving them copies of it.

On this question of public participation, the BBI secretariat and BBI Steering Committee held that, because the petitioners had failed to submit their views to the task force, the petitioners could not complain that public participation was inadequate; in any case, they said, there was no specific complaint by any individual of being prevented from participating in the process of considering the bill. They submitted that the bill was instead a 'product of a wide, comprehensive and broad consultative engagement and public involvement all over Kenya, which process entailed voluntary nationwide public participation'.[92] In their estimation, the magnitude of public participation could be ascertained only at the end of the process once the county assemblies, the National Assembly, and the Senate had concluded their deliberations.

The BBI secretariat and BBI Steering Committee also contended that it would have been premature to solicit public participation before submitting the bill to the county assemblies for consideration. They added that the process of constitutional amendment was, in any event, subject to a referendum, which is a form of public participation: the latter had to be seen as a continuum—in other words, one beginning with the collection of a million signatures and ending in the referendum.

In response, the High Court took the view that the Constitution requires the promoters of a constitutional amendment bill to provide voters with adequate information at every stage of the process so that they can make informed decisions.[93] According to the Court:

> the voters were entitled, at a minimum, to copies of the . . . Bill [so as to be able] to read and understand what the Promoters were proposing to amend . . . At the very least, the copies ought to have been in constitutionally required languages, namely English, Kiswahili, and Braille . . . and Kenya Sign Language.[94]

In the High Court's view, any attempt to provide information that did not meet this threshold would not suffice.[95] Based on this test, the Court concluded that the BBI Steering Committee had not printed the bill in Kiswahili or any other languages, and had made no effort to make copies of the bill available to the public. In the end, the High Court determined that the exercise of signature collection in support of the bill was constitutionally flawed given the absence of meaningful public participation and sensitization of the people before the collection of signatures.[96] Moreover, it held that the IEBC had a duty to ensure that the promoters of the bill had complied with the public participation requirements before determining that the bill had met the constitutional requirements for transmittal to the county assemblies for consideration.[97]

92 *Ndii & others v Attorney General & others* (n 2) para 134.
93 Ibid. paras 566 and 567.
94 Ibid. para 572.
95 Ibid.
96 Ibid. para 576.
97 Ibid. para 577.

4.2 The Court of Appeal

The respondents appealed to the Court of Appeal, which, for the most part, upheld the judgment of the High Court. Six of the seven judges of the Court of Appeal agreed with the High Court that the basic structure doctrine was applicable in Kenya, while five of them held that it limited the amendment power. Four judges also affirmed the decision of the High Court that the basic structure of the 2010 Constitution could be altered only through the exercise of the primary constituent power, an exercise which had to include the four sequential processes of civic education, public participation, constituent assembly debate, and a referendum.

As regards public participation, the Court of Appeal was unanimous that neither the president nor the BBI Steering Committee had the power to initiate changes to the Constitution. It was also unanimous that the BBI Bill was unconstitutional and amounted to a usurpation of the people's sovereign power. Five of the seven judges agreed that the collection of signatures had not been conducted transparently and that there had been no civic education on the BBI Bill or public participation before the signature collection. According to the minority, no evidence was presented to prove that any voter who supported the initiative had *not* been provided with copies of the bill or had given his or her signature before comprehending the nature of the bill. However, the Court of Appeal did not make a specific declaration in regard to whether the Bill had been subjected to public participation or in regard to the roles of the promoters and the IEBC in the process.

4.2.1 The Court of Appeal on the basic structure doctrine

On the question of the basic structure doctrine, the Court of Appeal, in the first place, made the same errors as the High Court in regard to the history of the making of the 2010 Constitution. Indeed, the three judges of the Court of Appeal who considered the matter of history simply endorsed the High Court's selective and erroneous reading of it. Thus, Kiage JA did not consider it necessary to go into a detailed analysis of this history[98] but then contradicted himself by saying that '[a]ny court interpreting the Constitution must perforce be alive to the historical background if it is to do justice to the text of the Constitution'.[99] Significantly, even though he did not attempt to set out the historical background to which he alluded, he could still assert that the Constitution 'was the product of phenomenal public participation and driven by [ordinary citizens]', thereby minimizing the role of the political elite.[100]

Moreover, and contrary to the fact that the people sought to balance flexibility and rigidity in amending the Constitution, he stated erroneously that 'it is the people themselves who preferred rigidity over flexibility', and that the people were only 'bothered by hyper-amendability' and did not decide on the question of hyper-rigidity.[101] Again, Kiage JA wrongly asserted that '[t]he recorded history is crystal clear that the people of Kenya conceived, composed and constituted their constitution which they birthed in 2010'.[102]

[98] *Independent Electoral and Boundaries Commission v Ndii & others* (Court of Appeal at Nairobi, Civil Appeal No E291 of 2020) 492 (*IEBC v Ndii & others*).
[99] Ibid. 495.
[100] Ibid. 494.
[101] Ibid. 555.
[102] Ibid. 510.

Similarly, Nambuye JA wrongly claimed that the history clearly demonstrated that 'Kenyans . . . intended to insulate the Constitution against hyper-amendability'.[103] The judge thus failed to appreciate that the people were not only aware of the dangers of the culture of hyper-amendments which had defined the Independence Constitution but also cautious about overly rigid amendment procedures (as indicated in this chapter's earlier critique of the High Court's decision).

Kairu JA endorsed the High Court's incorrect finding 'that in the making of the Constitution . . . Kenyans were *insistent* on the four sequential processes in the form of civic education, public participation and collation of views, constituent assembly debate, consultations, and public discourse and ultimately a referendum to ratify the Constitution'.[104] Kairu JA understood the High Court 'to have meant that in making the Constitution . . . Kenyans adopted a rigorous process involving the four steps [and] to remake it or to fundamentally alter it, an equally rigorous process, as was used in making it, must be undertaken'.[105] But having endorsed the High Court's determination on the four-step process, Kairu JA inexplicably concluded that there was 'no requirement under article 257 for a constituent assembly'.[106] Furthermore, while Tuiyott JA reasoned that the history of the making of the Constitution '[gave] colour to the text of the provisions of Chapter 16 on amendments',[107] he entirely ignored the fact that these provisions seek to attain a balance between flexibility and rigidity.

Nevertheless, two judges of the Court of Appeal read the history correctly. Okwengu JA noted that, inasmuch as the framers of the 2010 Constitution had sought to deal with the 'hyper-amendment culture that resulted in the mutilation of the former Constitution', they incorporated a chapter in the Constitution dealing with amendment, thereby accepting that 'there will be situations in which there will be need to amend the Constitution'.[108] For Okwengu JA, the Constitution resolved the issue of Kenya's hyper-amendment culture by establishing 'appropriate safeguards including the people's participation and final decision on amendments'.[109] On this basis, the judge reasoned that, as regards amendments, the 2010 Constitution of Kenya is 'explicit and self-sufficient'.[110]

Sichale JA reasoned likewise that Chapter 16 of the Constitution contains explicit amendment provisions, making it unnecessary to look outside the Constitution and import the basic structure 'doctrine'.[111] Moreover, she considered that the framers of the Constitution had 'balanced between flexibility and rigidity'.[112] In her view, it was important to give the people room to amend a constitution, since no society is static and '[what was] good for one generation may not necessarily be good for the next'.[113] She thus faulted the High Court's findings for not being 'supported by the context, structure, and history of the Constitution'.[114]

[103] Ibid. 236.
[104] Ibid. 682 (emphasis added).
[105] Ibid. 683.
[106] Ibid. 744.
[107] Ibid. 876.
[108] Ibid. 388–89.
[109] Ibid. 389.
[110] Ibid.
[111] Ibid. 789.
[112] Ibid. 795.
[113] Ibid. 796.
[114] Ibid. 806.

Secondly, although a few of the judges of the Court of Appeal considered how some of the provisions of the BBI Bill altered the Constitution's fundamental principles, they conflated these values with questions of institutional design. For example, according to Musinga JA:

> The people of Kenya in promulgating the 2010 Constitution opted for a pure presidential system, and in my view, the proposal [to replace it with a hybrid one, where there will be a Prime Minister, Deputy Prime Minister, Cabinet Ministers, Attorney General and Leader of the Opposition, who will also sit in Parliament] interferes with the concept of separation of powers as members of the executive will also be members of the legislature.[115]

This is a superficial statement devoid of critical analysis. The separation-of-powers doctrine does not dictate the absolute or rigid separation of governmental powers. While the doctrine seeks to prevent the concentration of power in one arm of government, the arms of government can share powers, provided there are checks and balances.[116] As South Africa's Constitutional Court observed in the *First Certification Judgment*, there is no universal model of this doctrine, and '[n]o constitutional scheme can reflect a complete separation of powers; the scheme is always one of partial separation.'[117] Here, this court reasoned that the overlap between the membership of the executive and the legislature provided 'a singularly important check and balance on the exercise of executive power' as it made the executive more directly answerable to the elected legislature'[118] Thus, Musinga JA fails to appreciate that the separation-of-powers doctrine accommodates different institutional designs of the system of government, including the BBI Bill's hybrid system. In addition, Musinga JA's assertion is historically incorrect, since the people opted for a hybrid system of government.

Furthermore, for a majority of the judges of the Court of Appeal, it was deemed unnecessary to demonstrate how exactly the BBI Bill altered or dismembered the Constitution's fundamental principles. As far as they were concerned, it was sufficient that they believed that the bill threatened the Constitution. Thus, for Kiage JA, it sufficed that '[t]he amendments proposed by the BBI Bill *have the potential* to alter by one fell swoop, the fundamental pillars that define and [undergird] our Constitution.'[119] For Nambuye JA, it was enough that '[t]he impugned Bill *attempts* to alter fundamental aspects of the Constitution' and that, if it were passed, it *would have* 'explicitly changed' this Constitution and given it a new identity.[120] Kairu JA did not attempt to analyse the BBI Bill. According to him, whether a proposal for amendment was strictly that or a dismemberment of the Constitution was a matter for judicial interpretation.[121] However, he did not apply this test to the BBI Bill to determine whether or not it constituted a dismemberment. Similarly, Tuiyott JA assumed that 'fundamental alterations to the core of the Constitution [require] the exercise of the primary constituent power of the people', without indicating whether or how the provisions of the BBI Bill would alter the Constitution.[122]

[115] Ibid. para 290.
[116] *Certification of the Constitution of the Republic of South Africa*, 1996 1996 (4) SA 744 (CC) para 111.
[117] Ibid. paras 108 and 109.
[118] Ibid. para 111.
[119] *IEBC v Ndii & others* (n 98) 550 (emphasis added).
[120] Ibid. para. 63 (emphasis added).
[121] Ibid. 684.
[122] Ibid. 875.

Thirdly, the Court of Appeal was self-serving in making the claim that the BBI Bill's proposal to create the office of the Judiciary Ombudsman was unconstitutional. In this respect, Musinga JA asserted that the bill's provision that the president appoints the Judiciary Ombudsman would entrench executive control of the Judicial Service Commission and judiciary.[123] At present, however, the judiciary dominates the membership of this Commission,[124] so to claim that one additional presidential appointee would 'entrench' executive control of it is an alarming overstatement. In any case, in making the 2010 Constitution, Kenyans also wished for an accountable judiciary. It is arguable, though, that, as presently constituted, the Judicial Service Commission is neither sufficiently accountable to the people nor any enhancement of the judiciary's accountability. For example, the Commission does not have the power to discipline judges. Musinga JA ignores this reality.

As Sichale JA stated in her dissenting opinion, judges should not arrogate unto themselves the unfettered power to validate or invalidate amendments based on their preferred reading of the Constitution.[125] She was particularly troubled by the subjectivity of the basic structure 'doctrine', given the High Court's conclusion that whether or not a provision of the Constitution is an unamendable clause would be decided on a case-by-case basis. For Sichale JA, the people, not unelected judges, should determine whether a provision of the Constitution is unamendable.[126]

On the question of whether certain provisions of the 2010 Constitution are unamendable, Okwengu JA disagreed with the High Court's position that the Constitution contains eternity clauses. While she admitted that the core parts of the Constitution are amendable, she thought that there was 'an implied limitation that amendments will only be permissible if compliant with the purport and spirit of the Constitution'.[127] As she saw it, 'any proposed constitutional amendment must pass both the procedural and the substantive test'.[128] According to her, an amendment in the latter category would include amendments to divide Kenya into two, abolish the judiciary, deny the right of an accused person to a hearing, or relinquish control of Kenya to a foreign power.

4.2.2 The Court of Appeal on public participation

A majority of the judges of the Court of Appeal determined that there was no public participation in respect of the BBI Bill, but the Court did not pronounce itself on whether the Constitution requires the IEBC to verify that the promoters of a constitutional amendment bill have complied with the Constitution's public participation requirements.

According to Musinga JA, although there was a degree of public participation in the development and passing of the BBI Bill, it was not in accordance with the Constitution.[129]

[123] Ibid. para 288.

[124] The Judicial Service Commission consists of the Chief Justice as chairperson; a Supreme Court judge elected by the judges of the Supreme Court; a Court of Appeal judge elected by the judges of the Court of Appeal; a High Court judge and a magistrate elected by the members of the association of judges and magistrates; the Attorney General; two advocates elected by the Law Society of Kenya; a person nominated by the Public Service Commission; and one woman and one man to represent the public, appointed by the president. The Chief Registrar of the Judiciary is the secretary to the Judicial Service Commission. See Constitution of Kenya (2010), art 171.

[125] *IEBC v Ndii & others* (n 98) 798.

[126] Ibid. 801–02

[127] Ibid. 401.

[128] Ibid. 401–02.

[129] Ibid. para 345.

For Kiage JA, the speedy passage of the bill through the county assemblies without the involvement of the people indicated that 'there was a measure of cynical disregard for the very opportunities and timelines intended to facilitate public participation'.[130] As Okwengu JA saw it, a popular initiative must 'start with sensitisation and engagement with the people' so that they 'know what the initiative entails before they can support it'.[131] In her view, public participation in a constitutional amendment through a popular initiative is 'particularly crucial at the commencement of the initiative'.[132] Applying this reasoning to the case, she concluded that there was no meaningful public participation before the collection of signatures in support of the BBI Bill, given the absence of a programme for civic education or sensitization in regard to the Bill.

However, Kiage JA thought that the High Court had established an onerous, unattainable threshold for public participation. He reasoned that, at the stage preceding the collection of the one million signatures, the promoters of a popular initiative were only required to disseminate information about the nature of the proposed amendment to the Constitution and its rationale.[133] As he saw it, the promoters' duty is 'one of sensitization with candour and disclosure as opposed to one of full broadcast by all means, in all languages, to all voters of the particulars [of the amendment bill]'.[134] Nambuye JA agreed, stating that fulfilling the Constitution's public participation requirements entails civic education, namely explaining the rationale of proposed amendments to the people so that they can understand the ramifications of the amendments.[135] Similarly, Kairu JA thought that the Constitution imposed a duty on the promoters of a popular initiative to supply voters with adequate information so as to enable them to make informed decisions.[136] However, he was not persuaded that the promoters of the BBI Bill had not fulfilled this duty.

Tuiyott JA did not agree with the High Court's finding that there was a lack of meaningful public participation and sensitization of the people before the collection of signatures. He considered that 'to insist on a countrywide or full-blown civic education and public participation exercise at the time of collection of signatures [would] place a burdensome financial and logistical obligation on the promoter [of a popular initiative]', thus making it difficult for citizens to drive the process.[137] He concluded that, at the signature-collection stage, the promoters only needed to give the voter 'such information about the draft Bill as would enable him/her [to] decide whether or not to sign in support'.[138] However, he stated that public participation was required in the four stages of the constitutional amendment process (signature collection, county assemblies, Parliament, and the referendum), and that a 'flaw in one phase of the process renders the entire process defective'.[139]

130 Ibid. 594, 595.
131 Ibid. 416.
132 Ibid.
133 Ibid. 591.
134 Ibid.
135 ibid 249.
136 ibid 701.
137 Ibid. 1045.
138 Ibid.
139 Ibid. 1045–46.

4.3 The Supreme Court

Dissatisfied with the decision of the Court of Appeal, the Attorney General and IEBC appealed to the Supreme Court. In essence, they faulted the Court of Appeal for disregarding the clear text of the Constitution on amendment and misconstruing the historical context of the Constitution's provisions on amendment. As regards public participation, they faulted the Court of Appeal for failing to appreciate that this issue was not ripe for consideration, given that the amendment process was still at the preliminary stages when the petitions against the BBI Bill were filed in the High Court. Furthermore, the IEBC contended that the High Court had erred when it held that the Constitution imposes a duty on the IEBC to ensure that the promoters of a popular initiative had undertaken public participation before submitting an amendment bill to the county assemblies.

The Supreme Court partly allowed the appeals. With respect to the basic structure 'doctrine', six of the seven judges of the Court held that it was not applicable in Kenya, and that it was not necessary to amend the Constitution using the four sequential steps pronounced by the two lower courts. According to the majority, no gaps had been identified with regard to Chapter 16 of the Constitution that could justify the application of the 'doctrine'. As for the question of public participation, five of the judges held that the popular initiative route for amending the Constitution was reserved for citizens; consequently, the BBI Bill was unconstitutional because the president had initiated it. Moreover, the judges were unanimous that the second schedule of the BBI Bill, which had been a late addition to the bill, was unconstitutional because it had not been subjected to public participation. The judges were also unanimous that the Constitution did not impose a duty on the IEBC to ensure that the promoters of the BBI Bill complied with the requirements for public participation.

Finally, by a majority of four, the Supreme Court held that there was public participation with respect to the BBI Bill. They were satisfied with the BBI Steering Committee's evidence that it had: (1) held national and regional stakeholder consultations (with civil society, faith-based organizations, women's groups, youth groups, persons-with-disability groups, cultural leaders, and the government); (2) received written submissions from citizens; and (3) engaged experts and drafters. They were also satisfied that there had been public participation in the county assemblies and the National Assembly.

4.3.1 The Supreme Court on the basic structure doctrine

The two lower courts based their determination on the applicability of the basic structure doctrine and its implications for the amendment of the Constitution on their reading of the history of the latter's making; that is, these courts used that history to 'clarify and provide interpretive guidance on the intent of the Kenyan people during the drafting of Chapter Sixteen of the Constitution'.[140] It was, therefore, important for the Supreme Court to determine whether the lower courts' reading of this history was correct.

For the majority, the history was important in determining whether the Constitution contemplated the basic structure doctrine. Thus, Koome CJ observed that the Court needed to examine 'the rationale behind the provisions of Chapter Sixteen of the Constitution as documented in the preparatory documents from the constitution-making process'.[141]

[140] *AG & 2 others v Ndii & others* (n 4) para 220.
[141] Ibid. para 118.

Lenaola SCJ concurred, stating that interpreting Chapter 16 ought to commence with tracing the history of the making of the Constitution and how the CKRC addressed the question of amending it.[142]

According to Koome CJ, the history demonstrated that, while:

> there was a strong concern that the country should adopt provisions on amendment power that are able to protect the constitutional order from abusive amendments . . . [t]here was also recognition that the Constitution must remain flexible in order to adjust to political, social, economic, technological and other changes that would take place in the polity.[143]

She considered that 'Kenyans did not want to shift from one extreme to another extreme in the amendment spectrum, that is, from hyper-amendments to ultra-rigidity'. Thus, the lower courts had 'failed to appreciate that the concern with the culture of hyper-amendment had already been taken into account during the drafting of the Constitution'.[144] This happened because the 'people's desire for a balance between the two extremes of hyper-amendability and ultra-rigidity that informed the drafting of Chapter Sixteen of the Constitution was lost [in these courts]', which 'focused solely on the past problem of hyper-amendability'.[145] For Koome CJ, it was therefore vital that 'courts should take into account exhaustive and complete accounts of historical narratives', since they would reach erroneous conclusions if they failed to do so, as the High Court and the Court of Appeal had done.[146]

For Ouko SCJ, the 'doctrine', if adopted, would make the Constitution overly rigid, 'with the courts playing the roles allocated in the express terms of the Constitution to the people directly or delegated to their elected representatives'.[147] Wanjala SCJ noted, too, that it was important not 'to stifle the growth and flowering of the Constitution for the benefit of future generations'.[148] Ndungu SCJ agreed, stating that the text of the Constitution made it clear that its drafters were mindful of the need to give future generations room to change it to suit their circumstances, and accordingly 'struck the perfect balance' between amending and protecting it.[149] Lenaola SCJ also concurred on this reading of the history.[150]

Koome CJ considered that the 'quest for a balance between rigidity and flexibility [was] evident in the "tiered" amendment provisions in Chapter Sixteen which stipulate three pathways for amending the Constitution', namely amendment by parliamentary initiative, amendment by popular initiative, and amendment of the entrenched provisions of the Constitution.[151] In this tiered amendment process, 'the core or essential features of the Constitution were accorded heightened protection' but were, nevertheless, 'open to amendment through an enhanced inclusive and participatory process that culminates in the people exercising their sovereign power through ratification in a democratic process in the form of a referendum'.[152]

142 Ibid. para 1413.
143 Ibid. para 191.
144 Ibid. para 216.
145 Ibid. para 222.
146 Ibid. paras 221 and 222.
147 Ibid. para 1811.
148 Ibid. paras 1025, 1823, and 1860.
149 Ibid. para 1160.
150 Ibid. paras 1415, 1418, and 1419.
151 Ibid. para 192.
152 Ibid. para 199.

Because Kenyans had selected the tiered amendment process as their response to the culture of hyper-amendability, it was 'difficult to justify the judicially-created fourth pathway of amending the Constitution founded on the basic structure doctrine'.[153] Koome CJ also considered that the judicial creation of a fourth pathway amounted to a usurpation of the people's sovereignty and undermined 'democratic constitutionalism and self-government by stifling the voice of present and future generations in governance'.[154] Ouko SCJ agreed, stating that the tiered amendment procedures were an adequate way of addressing the problem of abusive constitutional amendments.[155]

Furthermore, Koome CJ faulted the lower courts for not identifying the inadequacies of the three pathways for amending the Constitution that could have justified the imposition of a fourth pathway.[156] In addition, she pointed out that the lower courts had not considered:

> 'the amendment practice in the post-2010 dispensation in their analysis of Kenya's constitutional history, which showed that Chapter Sixteen of the Constitution had brought stability in the constitutional system in contrast to the culture of hyper-amendment under the former Constitution'.[157]

She contended that the fact that there had been 21 failed attempts to amend the 2010 Constitution proves that 'the tiered amendment design is an adequate bulwark against abusive amendments', and that Kenyans had attained the goal of balancing flexibility and rigidity in designing the amendment power.[158] Agreeing with the Chief Justice, Mwilu DCJ observed that Chapter 16, not the basic structure 'doctrine', was the 'mechanism expressly imported into the Constitution 2010 to protect it from hyper-amendment, dismemberment, or alteration'.[159]

As far as the majority were concerned, the people could amend any provision of the Constitution.[160] Wanjala SCJ reasoned that, given the permissive provisions of Chapter 16, it was unnecessary to recall the people so that they could exercise their primary constituent power and amend the Constitution.[161] Moreover, Ndungu SCJ found it absurd that despite acknowledging that there was no clause in the Constitution that barred amendment to any article, the High Court and the Court of Appeal 'proceeded to consider factors outside the Constitution to create *unamendable clauses!*'[162] Lenaola SCJ also thought that the two lower courts had gone overboard, remarking that 'courts should not by judicial craft or innovation impose hurdles to prevent the people from amending the Constitution provided that the procedural requirements under Chapter Sixteen are complied with'.[163] Ouko SCJ concurred, and said that the changes proposed by the BBI Bill would improve, not destroy, the Constitution.[164]

[153] Ibid. paras 197, 200, and 1811.
[154] Ibid. paras 201 and 210.
[155] Ibid. para 1803.
[156] Ibid. para 217.
[157] Ibid.
[158] Ibid. paras 211 and 212.
[159] Ibid. para 438.
[160] Ibid. para 1017.
[161] Ibid. para 1025.
[162] Ibid. para 1159.
[163] Ibid. para 1419.
[164] Ibid. paras 1797 and 1859.

Furthermore, for the majority, the four sequential steps for the amendment of the Constitution pronounced by the two lower courts were not necessary, since the Constitution does not expressly provide for them.[165] Indeed, Ouko SCJ took the view that a constituent assembly is an organ for constitution-making and not amendment, since the Constitution does not recognize it 'as one of the organs for the process'.[166] However, Lenaola SCJ thought that the four steps would apply when a new Constitution was being made, but that they needed to be anchored in legislation, as demonstrated by the Constitution of Kenya Review Acts of 1997 and 2008.[167]

For the minority, however, the basic structure doctrine was a useful device for protecting the essential characteristics of the Constitution. Thus, Ibrahim SCJ, while appreciating that the doctrine could be abused, reasoned that courts should intervene where amendments, although compliant with Chapter 16, threatened the essential characteristics of the Constitution—for example, transforming Kenya into a monarchy or fusing the three arms of government into one with the president at the helm.[168] At the same time, Ibrahim SCJ observed that the people, by exercising their primary constituent power, '[could] unmake, destroy or alter the constitutional order'.[169] He thus seems to imply that, in this fashion, the people could do whatever they fancied, including, for example, transforming Kenya into a monarchy.[170]

Wanjala SCJ was also sympathetic to the view that courts should have some power to restrain the people. He warned that it was dangerous to presume that 'a constitutional amendment in exercise of the primary constituent power cannot imperil the Constitution'.[171] Thus, he considered that a proposed amendment must pass both the procedural and substantive test. However, he based the substantive test not on the basic structure 'doctrine' but on article 259 of the Constitution, which, among other things, stipulates that it should be interpreted in a manner that promotes its purposes, values, and principles, advances the rule of law, and contributes to good governance.[172] On this basis, he reasoned that the second schedule of the BBI Bill was unconstitutional because it introduced a timeline and criteria different to that provided in article 89(2) of the Constitution for the review of constituency boundaries, in addition to purporting to direct the IEBC on how to carry out its constitutional mandate to review and delimit constituencies.[173] For him, the second schedule of the BBI Bill could not be said to be promoting the purposes, values, and principles of the Constitution, or to be contributing to good governance.[174]

Lenaola SCJ and Ouko SCJ concurred. According to Lenaola SCJ, 'any attempt at delimiting boundaries by amending Article 89(1) without consequential amendments to Article 89(2) to (12) and following the procedure in Section 36 [of the IEBC Act] defeats not just logic but is blatantly unconstitutional'.[175] Moreover, he thought that the second

165 Ibid. para 1166 (per Ndungu SCJ).
166 Ibid. para 1846.
167 Ibid. para 1485.
168 Ibid. paras 736 and 746.
169 Ibid. para 768.
170 Ibid. para 783.
171 Ibid. para 1027.
172 Ibid. para 1026.
173 Ibid. para 1062.
174 Ibid. para 1063.
175 Ibid. para 1563.

schedule was unconstitutional for purporting to direct the IEBC on how to carry out its mandate.[176]

Ouko SCJ asserted that the second schedule was unconstitutional for three reasons: (1) it provided only one criterion, namely population quota, as the basis for delimitation, contrary to the provisions of article 89; (2) it distributed the newly created constituencies to specific counties and directed the IEBC to delimit these constituencies' boundaries based on that single criterion; and (3) it set a timeline for the delimitation of boundaries, contrary to article 89(2).[177] He also thought that the BBI Bill did not contain a provision on the delimitation of constituencies on which the second schedule could have been anchored.[178]

4.3.2 The Supreme Court on public participation

As regards the functions of the IEBC, the Supreme Court was unanimous that it had no obligation to ensure that the promoters of the BBI Bill complied with the requirements for public participation before determining that the bill had met constitutional requirements for transmittal to the county assemblies. Koome CJ reasoned that the IEBC '[could] only discharge a mandate vested in it explicitly by the law', and that mandate was limited to verifying that a popular initiative was supported by at least one million registered voters.[179] Wanjala SCJ and Lenaola SCJ concurred, with the former stating that nothing in the Constitution 'places upon the IEBC an extra obligation to look beyond the names and signatures appended to the Amendment Bill'.[180]

On the question of whether there was public participation in respect of the BBI Bill, the Supreme Court was guided by the principles it established in *British American Tobacco Kenya PLC v Cabinet Secretary for the Ministry of Health & 2 others* (the '*BAT* Principles').[181] These *BAT* principles are that:

- Public participation applies to all aspects of governance.
- The public officer and/or entity charged with the performance of a particular duty bears the onus of ensuring and facilitating public participation.
- These duty-bearers must conduct public participation using reasonable means.
- Public participation must be real and not illusory.
- It must be purposive and meaningful.
- It must be accompanied by reasonable notice and reasonable opportunity, with reasonableness being determined on a case-to-case basis.
- Public participation is not necessarily a process consisting only of oral hearings—written submissions can also be made, so the fact that someone was not heard is not enough to annul the process.
- The mode, degree, scope, and extent of public participation is to be determined on a case-to-case basis.
- The components of meaningful public participation include clear subject matter that the public can understand; clear and simple structures and processes; opportunity for

[176] Ibid. para 1567.
[177] Ibid. paras 1938 and 1939.
[178] Ibid. para 1940.
[179] Ibid. para 296.
[180] Ibid. paras 1089 and 1628.
[181] *British American Tobacco Kenya PLC v Cabinet Secretary for the Ministry of Health & 2 others* [2019] eKLR.

> balanced influence by the public; commitment to the process; inclusive and effective representation; integrity and transparency of the process; and the capacity of the public to engage, which entails that they must first be sensitized on the subject matter.

Applying these guiding principles, Koome CJ stated that the process of constitutional amendment, which she considered to be continuous and consisting of several phases, 'should be inclusive, enable deep public participation, and promote active involvement of the people during all the stages'.[182] These phases are the collection of signatures, passage through the county assemblies, passage through the two houses of Parliament, and the referendum campaign. Furthermore, the people should understand the choices available to them.[183]

Ibrahim SCJ and Ouko SCJ agreed, noting that public participation needed to occur in all the phases of the process.[184] For Ibrahim SCJ, the promoters of a popular initiative were obliged to be transparent and provide reasonable notice and reasonable opportunity for public participation.[185] According to Ouko SCJ, 'it is illogical to wait until the process is concluded to ascertain whether it was effective or done according to the law'.[186] He thus rejected the appellant's argument that public participation was a continuous process, the efficacy of which could be evaluated only at the end of the constitutional amendment exercise.[187]

As far as Mwilu DCJ was concerned, grievances about public participation could be raised at any stage of the process of constitutional amendment.[188] However, she agreed with the Chief Justice that the promoters of a popular initiative to amend the Constitution were not obliged to undertake any public participation prior to presenting their amendment bill to the IEBC.[189] Ndungu SCJ also agreed, stating that the promoters were not under an obligation to conduct public participation prior to collecting signatures.[190] She reasoned that imposing such a burdensome requirement would discourage prospective promoters from advancing constitutional amendments.[191] The Chief Justice and Ibrahim SCJ agreed.[192] However, Ibrahim SCJ thought that the promoters should have provided each potential supporter of the initiative with a copy of the amendment bill in a language he or she understood.[193]

On the basis of the *BAT* principles, the majority decided that there had been public participation with respect to the BBI Bill, except for its second schedule, which was a late addition to the process. For the Chief Justice, the bill was the 'product of comprehensive and consultative public engagement all over Kenya; which process entailed voluntary nationwide public participation'.[194] For Ndungu SCJ and Ouko SCJ, there was no evidence

[182] Ibid. para 302.
[183] Ibid.
[184] Ibid. paras. 855 and 2012.
[185] Ibid. paras 861, 874, and 880 (faulting the promoters of the BBI Bill for presenting a bill that had not been subjected to public participation).
[186] Ibid. para 2012.
[187] Ibid. para 2002.
[188] Ibid. para 600.
[189] Ibid. para 604.
[190] Ibid. para 1275.
[191] Ibid. para 1277.
[192] Ibid. paras 305 and 306.
[193] Ibid. paras 863 and 864.
[194] Ibid. paras 312 and 314.

to support the allegations that public participation was not conducted during the collection of signatures, in the county assemblies, or in Parliament.[195] In addition, Ndungu SCJ contended that no person complained that his or her right to participate in the making of BBI Bill had been violated.[196] In her view, a person alleging lack of public participation must specify the stage of the amendment process that he or she feels was lacking in this respect.[197] Likewise, Lenaola SCJ found that no evidence had been placed before the lower courts to prove that the voters who appended their signatures to the bill 'did so without being accorded a chance to study the Bill, or that any of their submissions or representations were not [considered]'.[198] Lenaola SCJ also reasoned that the question of public participation could be determined only at the end of the process envisaged in article 257 of the Constitution.[199]

According to Lenaola SCJ, the question of whether there had been public participation in respect of the BBI Bill was determined 'by considering the continuum of the entire process and not just specifically at the stage of signature collection'.[200] He considered that members of the public had participated: (1) by appending their signatures to the popular initiative at the amendment proposal stage; (2) indirectly through their representatives, and directly by submitting representations and submissions when the county assemblies and Parliament were considering the bill; and (3) voting in the referendum.[201]

Wanjala SCJ differed on the issue of public participation, contending that it was only logical that the people should understand the contents of an amendment bill before being asked to append their signatures to it.[202] Thus, the promoters of a popular initiative ought to undertake meaningful public participation, including civic education, before embarking on the collection of signatures in support of an amendment bill. He concluded that the promoters of the BBI Bill had failed to conduct relevant civic education.[203] Ouko SCJ also thought that the promoters of a popular initiative had a duty to carry out public participation before collecting signatures.[204]

5. The BBI decisions and the future of constitutional change in Kenya

The Supreme Court reversed the decisions of the High Court and the Court of Appeal, deciding instead that the people, either directly or through their representatives, can amend any provision of the Constitution, provided they adhere to its amendment procedures. What do the decisions portend for the future of constitutional change in Kenya in terms of the role of the courts in balancing continuity and change and policing the application of the Constitution's provisions on public participation?

195 Ibid. paras 1284, 1289, 1294, and 2030.
196 Ibid. para 1294.
197 Ibid. para 1298.
198 Ibid. para 1636.
199 Ibid. para 1637.
200 Ibid. para 1629.
201 Ibid. paras 1631, 1632, 1633, and 1635.
202 Ibid. para 1096.
203 Ibid. para 1097.
204 Ibid. para 2018.

5.1 Courts, continuity, and change

The idea that a constitution has a basic structure is useful to the extent that it protects a set of higher ideals (or fundamental principles) that are essential to the realization of constitutionalism and democratic governance in a given polity. Such ideals may include the right to self-rule, the separation of powers, the defence of human rights, and the rule of law. Indeed, a constitution must embrace such higher ideals if it is to protect the weak and the voiceless and not merely protect textual settlements attained in negotiations between dominant or powerful groups during constitution-making processes—processes in which the weak and voiceless might not have participated effectively. On the basis of this reasoning, it is arguable that the legislature and majorities should be restricted or prohibited from amending the higher ideals. The idea that a constitution has a basic structure is also useful to the extent that it aids the preservation of the identity of a constitution, inasmuch as it entails that the latter should be altered only through the exercise of the (primary) constituent power.

As we have seen, Justices Ibrahim and Wanjala of the Supreme Court expressed this viewpoint in their judgments. Ibrahim SCJ thought that, in certain situations, courts can invalidate amendments even if they have been enacted through processes that adhere to the formal requirements of the Constitution.[205] For him, such scenarios included instances where Parliament decided that Kenya should cease to be a sovereign republic and become an absolute monarchy, or fused the three arms of government into one, with the president at the helm.[206] Wanjala SCJ agreed, stating that courts should not shut their eyes to a constitutional amendment which has the potential to subvert the Constitution, even if the process of its enactment adhered to the requirements of Chapter 16.[207]

But while the basic structure doctrine evidently can be useful in such rare scenarios, it is problematic and should be approached with caution for a number of reasons. The first of these is that courts applying it have often protected institutional designs in a constitution under the guise of protecting its fundamental values. Thus, the 'doctrine' has led to the freezing of particular institutional designs in constitutional systems, with the result that past generations continue to rule present and future generations from the grave; as Torres-Artunduaga and Garcia-Jaramillo note, it 'might lead to reification of a particular institutional design within the Constitutional system, or the Court's understanding of such design'.[208] However, the constitutional writers of the past should not bar the constituent power of future generations from reconsidering the values and desirability of a constitution's principles or institutions, however apparently important.[209] Ergo, it is necessary to appreciate that questions of institutional design respond to their time.

Courts should, therefore, ensure that original institutional designs are open to change and improvement even as these courts seek to preserve a constitution's fundamental principles. For example, the principle of judicial independence can admit many concrete applications, which are context-dependent. This explains the variations in the judicial councils

[205] Ibid. para 743.
[206] Ibid. para 737.
[207] Ibid. para 1026.
[208] Torres-Artunduaga and Garcia-Jaramillo (n 6) 26.
[209] Abebe (n 7) 672.

many countries establish in order to maintain a balance between judicial independence and accountability.[210] Similarly, the separation-of-powers doctrine finds expression in presidential, parliamentary, or hybrid systems of government. Accordingly, while it is important to protect a polity's fundamental principles, there ought to be flexibility in institutional design, hence the need to recognize that constitutional institutions may take different forms, provided these forms adhere to fundamental principles.

Such flexibility prevents conflict, as its absence would mean that change could occur only through revolution. Provided that amendments are made in a democratic and deliberative manner, they should be seen as the necessary continuation of a conversation that was started by the constitution-makers—after all, no constitution is perfect. Thus, while we must protect the higher-order principles, we must equally give succeeding generations room to adapt constitutions to suit their unique circumstances. In Kenya's case, the provisions of the 2010 Constitution on the executive departed markedly from the Bomas Draft Constitution. What the people endorsed in the 2010 referendum departed from the Bomas Draft in significant respects. It would not serve the people of Kenya to deny present and future generations the possibility of changing provisions that were the outcome of a political settlement.

Indeed, political settlements on initiatives to amend the constitution should be encouraged. It is difficult to justify the claim of the two lower courts in the *BBI* cases that the people cannot amend the provisions of a constitution that in significant respects was the outcome of a political settlement. On the contrary, it should be open to the people to endorse or reject—in referendums—political settlements. The courts should, therefore, view political compromises such as the BBI from this perspective. As we have seen, the BBI Bill sought to amend the Constitution to address important governance challenges on which Kenyans remain polarized, particularly the system of government, a challenge that contributed significantly to the divisive presidential elections of 2013 and 2017. Many Kenyans agree that the winner-take-all institutional model of the presidency embodied in the 2010 Constitution is divisive, does not serve them well, and needs to be replaced with a model better suited for their ethnically divided society. In this respect, it is noteworthy that the BBI Bill sought to introduce the same system of government that the Committee of Experts had proposed in its harmonized draft constitution.[211]

Secondly, there will always be differences in power among the people at the time of constitution-making. Constitutions are never negotiated in a context of balanced powers. Inevitably, some groups and actors will have more power than others, even if this may change over time. Indeed, true constitution-making can occur only behind the mythical veil of ignorance, as John Rawls posited. But because there will always be differences in power, there must be room for the weak, as they become empowered, to amend extant constitutional settlements. Had the enslaved people of the United States participated in the making of its venerated Constitution, it would certainly have had markedly different provisions on the institution of slavery. Similarly, black South Africans should not be condemned to live forever with the Constitution of 1996. The white apartheid constituency shaped its terms in core respects, which explains, for example, why Julius Malema and others are clamouring

[210] See eg Nuno Garoupa and Tom Ginsburg, 'Guarding the Guardians: Judicial Councils and Judicial Independence' (2009) 57(1) American Journal of Comparative Law 103.

[211] See Constitution of Kenya (Amendment) Bill 2020, s 28; Harmonized Draft Constitution, arts 179, 180.

for land expropriation without compensation. It should, therefore, always be possible to amend constitutions, if only to avoid ossifying oppression.

Thirdly, the so-called basic structure doctrine is imprecise, as Ouko SCJ noted in his judgment.[212] Courts applying the doctrine have neither identified nor consistently followed a standard of review for determining whether or not an amendment is unconstitutional.[213] Essentially, the basic structure of any given constitution is what a court says it is—whether a particular feature is part of the basic structure is worked out on a case-by-case basis.[214] Accordingly, different courts have applied the label of 'basic structure' to varying provisions, and not always for convincing reasons. Some courts have been unrestrained in invoking the doctrine, and have applied it to strike down even constitutional amendments that merely *affect* protected principles.[215]

For example, the Indian Supreme Court has rightly been criticized for holding unconstitutional a constitutional amendment that sought to establish a mechanism for judicial accountability. This was in the case of the *National Judicial Appointments Commission (NJAC) Judgment*,[216] where the Court claimed that the amendment violated the basic structure of the Indian Constitution by compromising the principle of judicial independence. Consequently, there is no certainty that the interpretation a court provides will be consistent with the constitution and conform to its identity. Put differently, judicial declarations that certain provisions form part of a constitution's basic structure in many cases merely preserve the understanding that particular courts have of norms that are open to differences of interpretation.

The decisions of the High Court and the Court of Appeal in the *BBI* cases fall into this category. For these two courts, virtually the entire Constitution comprises its basic structure. Casting the basic structure as expansively as these two courts did and protecting virtually the entire Constitution from amendment would frustrate necessary democratic constitutional change. However, a reading of the text of the Constitution shows that it protects only the provisions stipulated in article 255(1) as its fundamental principles. Furthermore, the Constitution does not expressly immunize any of its provisions from amendment, as the Supreme Court affirmed. Had the drafters of the Constitution intended to entrench provisions other than those stipulated in article 255(1), or to immunize any provisions from amendment, they would have done so expressly. In the absence of such preclusion, the people should be able to amend any provision of the Constitution, following the prescribed procedures.

The two lower courts also injected 'eternity clauses' into the Constitution without indicating which of its provisions were immune from amendment, and stating only that this determination would be based on a court's 'fact-intensive determination'. The absence of clarity on what constitutes an eternity clause means that these clauses will be whatever different courts claim they are. Therefore (and as noted previously), there is no certainty that the interpretation a court provides will be consistent with the Constitution and conform to its identity.

212 *AG & 2 others v Ndii & others* (n 4) paras 1814, 1818.

213 Rehan Abeyratne, 'Giving Structure to the Basic Structure Doctrine' (2017) 1(2) Indian Law Review 189.

214 Dixon and Landau (n 14) 628, where the authors observe that the Colombian and Indian Constitutional Courts have not 'attempted to delineate a narrow or exhaustive list of fundamental constitutional principles ex ante, but instead both have sought to work these principles out on a case-by-case basis'.

215 Abeyratne (n 213) 190.

216 *Supreme Court Advocates-on-Record Association v Union of India* (2016) 4 SCC 1.

In addition, the two lower courts did not consider—or considered only perfunctorily—whether or how the BBI Bill violated the fundamental principles of the Constitution or destroyed its basic structure. The High Court simply declared that the basic structure 'doctrine' protected certain fundamental aspects of the Constitution from amendment but did not undertake a granular analysis of the BBI Bill to determine whether and how any of its provisions destroyed this basic structure. In other words, the Court nullified the BBI Bill on the grounds only that it thought—rather than demonstrated—that the bill's provisions destroyed the Constitution's basic structure insofar as the Court defined this structure.

It should also be appreciated that constitutional moments in which the people are able to exercise the primary constituent power are extremely rare events. Kenya has only had one such moment in its history, namely the Bomas Process of the early 2000s, and the product thereof was heavily contested for nearly a decade. Indeed, it was not until 2010 that the outcome of the Bomas Process was transformed into a constitution, albeit with material alterations dictated by the need for political compromise. Should the people not have had an opportunity to have their say on these alterations? As Ouko SCJ observed, '[e]ven the opponents of the [BBI] must agree that dealing with the country's divisive politics and the resultant ethnic tensions every election cycle is a public policy imperative, because everyone would like to see a united country.'[217] In these circumstances, it would be ironic to insist, as the two lower courts did, that the people could amend the Constitution only through the exercise of their primary constituent power, yet the fact is that they did not deliberate upon, and continue to disagree over, some of its provisions, particularly those regarding the executive. In Kenya's context, there is hence no guarantee that the process of exercising the primary constituent power will be orderly, will be concluded as intended, or will necessarily produce qualitatively better constitutional provisions than by way of the exercise of the amendment power.

Fourthly, the 'doctrine' can undermine the democratic process by preventing popular majorities from using constitutional amendments for ends that enhance democracy; by preventing constitutional amendments, it 'cuts off any avenue—at least short of constitutional replacement—for the public to contribute to shaping the meaning of a constitutional text'.[218] Essentially, the 'doctrine' transforms the courts into policymakers, insofar as it allows them to opt among different policies by approving or refusing an amendment to the constitution. Moreover, it gives the court an unreviewable power to determine the meaning of constitutional provisions.[219] However, constitution-making or amendment should take a bottom-up rather than top-down approach. Through deliberative and participatory processes, citizens should be able to persuade one another of the value of any proposed constitutional amendment. This would be more democratic than the courts imposing a view they derived from 'some implicit lines in the constitution'.[220]

Moreover, as we have seen with respect to the lower courts' determination that the BBI Bill's proposal to create the office of Judiciary Ombudsman violated the principle of judicial independence, courts can impose their self-serving and unjustified views on constitutional amendments on the people. Judicial control of constitutional amendments could lead to a

[217] *AG & 2 others v Ndii & others* (n 4) para 1859.
[218] Dixon and Landau (n 14) 610.
[219] Ibid. 611.
[220] Torres-Artunduaga and Garcia-Jaramillo (n 6) 42.

situation where courts effectively arrogate the role of the people and their elected representatives in defining a country's fundamental values—values over which there may be reasonable disagreement. Furthermore, the absence of clearly defined limits means that every court will have its own list of what is basic or eternal and what is not.

Rather than telling the public what constitutes the basic structure of a constitution, and in the process risking becoming 'unaccountable accountability-holders', the courts should play the limited, judicially manageable, and legitimate role of facilitating dialogue and ensuring that amendment processes are deliberative.[221] In this respect, it is worth noting that 'constitutional provisions and principles are often quite open-textured in nature, and thus open to multiple different reasonable interpretations'.[222] In such contexts, it would arguably be more democratic for the people to deliberate and agree on the interpretation of the constitution than for a court to impose its interpretation.[223] Seen from this perspective, the courts should approve amendments that change the design of constitutional institutions, provided that the amendments adhere to the fundamental values of a constitution and are enacted through participatory and deliberative methods that adhere to a constitution's amendment procedures.[224]

Given the foregoing limitations of the basic structure doctrine, many commentators have urged that it should be applied with caution, while many courts have either not embraced it or applied it with restraint. Thus, Rosalind Dixon and David Landau observe that, while the doctrine may be necessary in fragile democracies, courts often overestimate or misunderstand the threats posed by constitutional amendments.[225] In their estimation, '[c]omparative experience with the doctrine shows that it is routinely overused against constitutional changes that appear unlikely to pose a substantial threat to the fundamental values of a democratic order'.[226] They caution that '[g]iving courts unfettered power to invalidate amendments for incompatibility with their own prior preferred reading of a constitution will create a clear democratic danger or cost'.[227] Even ardent proponents of the doctrine such as Yaniv Roznai concede that courts can use it as an institutional trump card that they apply selectively to aggrandize their authority vis-à-vis the elected branches of government.[228]
To guard against misuse or abuse of the doctrine, the judicial review of constitutional amendments should be conducted with restraint and according to set standards or guidelines. To this end, Dixon and Landau suggest that: 'courts should adopt a flexible but weak approach to applying the doctrine [and] should intervene only when they are quite confident that a given constitutional amendment, either alone or in conjunction with other changes, poses a substantial threat to core democratic values'.[229] This is also the approach that Justices Ibrahim and Wanjala took in the Supreme Court.

But where amendments do not pose any such threat—and the BBI Bill, it is submitted, posed no such threat—courts should allow institutional adaptation of the fundamental

[221] Ibid.
[222] Dixon and Landau (n 14) 610.
[223] Ibid.
[224] Torres-Artunduaga and Garcia-Jaramillo (n 6) 42.
[225] Dixon and Landau (n 14) 609 and 614.
[226] Ibid. 636.
[227] Ibid. 608.
[228] Yaniv Roznai, *Unconstitutional Constitutional Amendments: The Limits of Amendment Powers* (OUP 2017) 193–96.
[229] Dixon and Landau (n 14) 608.

principles of a constitution, as the Supreme Court affirmed. In this respect, Torres-Artunduaga and Garcia-Jaramillo have argued that courts should appreciate that the fundamental principles of a constitution can admit different interpretations and, consequently, '[should] permit pragmatic activism to correct the dysfunctionalities of a specific institutional design in the future'.[230] Ergo, the people should be able to amend these principles, provided they do so through participatory, deliberative processes that involve multiple institutional actors.[231] As Roznai contends, the intensity of judicial review of constitutional amendments should vary according to the amendment procedures used.[232] Thus, amendments that are the product of 'multi-procedural, inclusive, and deliberative popular' processes should be subject to 'less intense' judicial review, since they presumably enjoy high degrees of democratic legitimacy.[233]

Since the people are sovereign, they should have the freedom to determine the terms of the social contract and how they wish to change those terms. Chapter 16 of the Constitution recognizes this sovereignty and allows the people to amend it to address important concerns of the day. Thus, as weak or marginalized segments of society become empowered, they should have the opportunity to redefine the elements of the social contract that they feel need redefining.

5.2 Policing public participation

While the Supreme Court recognized that the people can amend any provision of the Constitution, its test for the adequacy of public participation in amendment initiatives is unclear and could be used to frustrate arguably participatory constitutional amendment processes or approve amendment processes that are not sufficiently participatory, depending on the inclination of the judges.

As we saw, the High Court set an exceedingly high standard of public participation and even expanded the functions of the IEBC, which it determined had the additional responsibility of verifying that the promoters of a constitutional amendment bill complied with the Constitution's public participation requirements. It was, therefore, helpful that the Supreme Court endeavoured to lower the standard of public participation. First, the majority of the Supreme Court judges maintained that requiring the promoters of a popular initiative to amend the Constitution to carry out civic education and provide copies of an amendment bill in the languages of the supporters would be burdensome and make it difficult for ordinary citizens to advance constitutional amendments. Alternatively, as some Supreme Court judges recommended, the state should bear the burden of funding public participation once citizens declare their intention to amend the Constitution through a popular initiative. Second, the majority considered that courts should evaluate the adequacy of public participation in the political process of amending the Constitution at its conclusion rather than while it is ongoing.

Yet, while the decision of the Supreme Court in the *BBI* case is useful in providing some guidance on the problematic question of public participation, the Court's test

[230] Torres-Artunduaga and Garcia-Jaramillo (n 6) 22, 39.
[231] Roznai (n 228) 175.
[232] Ibid. 219.
[233] Ibid.

for the adequacy of public participation which it established in the *BAT* case is unclear. Unsurprisingly, therefore, the majority and minority judgments of the Supreme Court in the *BBI* case arrived at different conclusions after applying this test. For some judges, public participation was 'crucial' at the commencement of a popular initiative, and a programme of civic education on the initiative prior to its commencement was required. For these judges, public participation demanded 'deep public participation' and 'active involvement of the people during all stages'. For other judges, it sufficed that, at this stage, the promoters had sensitized the voters or supporters by giving them 'adequate information' on the initiative. Again, some judges thought that direct public participation was required in all the four stages of a constitutional amendment via the popular initiative route, while others thought that the public participated through its representatives when the county assemblies and Parliament were considering a bill. Moreover, for some judges, a flaw in one phase would render the entire process defective, while others were not prepared to go that far. Moreover, while some judges were prepared to interrogate and/or injunct an ongoing constitutional amendment process, others thought that a court should examine the process in its entirety and, should it be necessary, intervene only once the process has been concluded.

The Supreme Court failed to resolve these undoubtedly difficult questions. Accordingly, its *BAT* test could be used to frustrate arguably participatory constitutional amendment processes or approve processes that are not sufficiently participatory. The decision thus leaves it open for courts to approve or reject constitutional amendment initiatives, depending on their inclination.

Arguably, public participation in a constitutional amendment process needs to be seen as a continuum and evaluated at its conclusion, not while it is ongoing. In this process, the public has numerous opportunities to be informed about and/or interrogate a bill, should it wish to do so. First, a promoter of a constitutional amendment bill undoubtedly has to persuade voters to append their signatures to it, a process that entails informing them and responding to their questions or concerns. Second, the Constitution requires the county assemblies and the two houses of Parliament to seek the views of the public when they are considering such a bill. Hence, the public has another opportunity to participate at this stage. Third, where the bill relates to the fundamental matters specified in article 255(1) of the Constitution, the people again have an opportunity—an important one in the form of a referendum—to interrogate such a bill, and even to veto it.

In my view, therefore, the issue of public participation was not ripe for consideration, given that the BBI amendment process was merely at the preliminary stages when the petitions against it were filed. Courts should allow the amendment process to play out and evaluate it only at the end. After all, a court can always nullify an amendment process that violates the Constitution upon its conclusion.

In these circumstances, the Supreme Court needs to clarify the Constitution's requirement for public participation in amendment processes to prevent courts from using it to frustrate participatory constitutional amendment processes or approve processes that are not participatory. As various judges of the Court of Appeal and the Supreme Court recommended in this respect, Parliament needs to enact a law on public participation to guide constitutional amendment initiatives.[234]

[234] *AG & 2 others v Ndii & others* (n 4) paras 226, 493, 501, 1640, and 2036.

6. Conclusion

While the High Court and the Court of Appeal were unduly adventurous and wrongly asserted that the basic structure doctrine was applicable in Kenya, thereby frustrating an arguably necessary process of constitutional change, the Supreme Court adopted a restrained approach which appreciated that courts should limit their role to facilitating such political processes and ensuring that they are participatory and deliberative. In evaluating constitutional amendments, courts must balance the equally important but competing considerations of stability and change. Where, as in the case of the Constitution of Kenya (2010), the drafters have established amendment procedures that strive to maintain this balance, courts should not impose additional hurdles by reading in implied limitations on the amendment power. On the contrary, the judicial review of constitutional amendments should be conducted with restraint. Thus, courts should only interfere with constitutional amendments that are enacted by the amendment procedures as a last resort.

In addition, courts should not determine for the people how they should exercise their primary or secondary constituent power—it is up to the people to determine how they wish to do so. Sometimes they will express how they wish to do so, which explains the amendment procedures found in most constitutions. Where they have done so, as in the case of Chapter 16 of the 2010 Constitution, courts should not impose additional implied hurdles on the exercise of the power of amendment. In any case, and particularly where, as in Kenya's case, the ratification of constitutional amendments requires the exacting procedure of a referendum, it is open to the people to reject amendments which are the product of a process that is not participatory, are crudely identified with self-interest, or have been hijacked by political elites. Since the referendum gives the people the final authority over constitutional proposals, it is a significant mechanism that often constrains political elites and ensures that they present constitutional amendments that would be broadly acceptable to the people.

Secondly, the Supreme Court's test for the adequacy of public participation in popular initiatives to amend the Constitution is unclear and could be used to frustrate arguably participatory constitutional amendment processes or approve amendment processes that are not sufficiently participatory, depending on the inclination of the judges. In either case, the test, therefore, enables the courts to inappropriately approve or decline amendments to the Constitution. Public participation in a constitutional amendment process is a continuum that courts, as a general rule, should allow to unfold and interrogate only upon its conclusion rather than while it is ongoing.

Bibliography

Abebe A.K., 'The Substantive Validity of Constitutional Amendments in South Africa' (2014) 131(3) South African Law Journal 656

Abeyratne R., 'Giving Structure to the Basic Structure Doctrine' (2017) 1(2) Indian Law Review 189

Akech A., 'BBI: A Ploy to Subvert Democracy through Deception' (*Elephant*, 13 December 2019) https://www.theelephant.info/features/2019/12/13/bbi-a-ploy-to-subvert-democracy-through-deception/ accessed 5 February 2020

Auma E. and Campbell I., 'Why Peace Remains Elusive as Kenya Prepares for the 2022 General Elections' (*Saferworld*, August 2021) https://www.saferworld.org.uk/long-reads/why-peace-remains-elusive-as-kenya-prepares-for-the-2022-general-elections accessed 10 February 2022

Bannon A.L., 'Designing a Constitution-Drafting Process: Lessons from Kenya' (2007) 116(8) Yale Law Journal 1849

Bockenforde M., 'Letting the Constituent Power Decide? Merits and Challenges of Referenda in Constitution Making Processes in Africa' in Abbiate T., Bockenforde M. and Federico V. (eds.), *Public Participation in African Constitutionalism* (Routledge 2018) 26

Cottrell J. and Ghai Y., 'Constitution Making and Democratization in Kenya (2000–2005)' (2007) 14(1) Democratization 1

Dixon R. and Landau D., 'Transnational Constitutionalism and a Limited Doctrine of Unconstitutional Constitutional Amendment' (2015) 13(3) International Journal of Constitutional Law 606

Fombad C., 'Some Perspectives on Durability and Change under Modern African Constitutions' (2013) 11(2) International Journal of Constitutional Law 382

Gaitho M., 'How Kenyatta Won over a Foe and Lost His Deputy' (*Al Jazeera*, 21 June 2022) <https://www.aljazeera.com/features/2022/6/21/analysis-how-kenyas-president-won-over-a-foe-and-alienated-his> accessed 21 June 2022

Garoupa N. and Ginsburg T., 'Guarding the Guardians: Judicial Councils and Judicial Independence' (2009) 57(1) American Journal of Comparative Law 103

Gözler K., *Judicial Review of Constitutional Amendments: A Comparative Study* (Ekin Press 2008)

Jamwa O., 'Jubilee Fight Contemptuous of Kenyans' Plight' (*The Star*, 15 April 2020) https://www.the-star.co.ke/amp/opinion/star-blogs/2020-04-15-jubilee-fight-contemptuous-of-kenyans-plight/?utm_term=Autofeed&utm_medium=Social&utm_source=Twitter&__twitter_impression=true accessed 5 October 2020

Joint Communique of Building Bridges to a New Kenyan Nation (9 March 2018)

'Kenya Set for Referendum as Over 30 Counties Pass BBI' (*Business Daily*, 23 February 2021)<https://www.businessdailyafrica.com/bd/news/kenya-over-30-counties-pass-bbi-3301258> accessed 23 February 2021

Kiruga M., 'Kenya: Building Bridges Initiative Deepens Ruto-Odinga Rivalry' (*Africa Report*, 4 December 2019) https://www.theafricareport.com/20845/kenya-building-bridges-initiative-deepens-ruto-odinga-rivalry/ accessed 8 August 2020

Ku R., 'Consensus of the Governed: The Legitimacy of Constitutional Change' (1995) 64(2) Fordham Law Review 535

Levinson S. (ed.), *Responding to Imperfection: The Theory and Practice of Constitutional Amendment* (Princeton University Press 1995)

Macedo M., *Liberal Virtues: Citizenship, Virtue and Community in Liberal Constitutionalism* (Clarendon Press 1990) 183

Murphy W.F., 'Merlin's Memory: The Past and Future Imperfect of the Once and Future Polity' in Levinson S. (ed.), *Responding to Imperfection: The Theory and Practice of Constitutional Amendment* (Princeton University Press 1995) 177

Murray C., 'Political Elites and the People: Kenya's Decade Long Constitution-Making Process' (2018) https://papers.ssrn.com/sol3/papers.cfm?abstract_id=3147154 accessed 12 June 2021

Murunga G.R., 'Elite Compromises and the Content of the 2010 Constitution' in Murunga G.R., Okello D. and Sjogren A. (eds.), *Kenya: The Struggle for a New Constitutional Order* (Zed Books 2014) 144

Presidential Taskforce on Building Bridges to Unity Advisory, 'Building Bridges to a United Kenya: From a Nation of Blood Ties to a Nation of Ideals' (BBI Taskforce Report October 2019)

Rasch B.E. and Congleton R.D., 'Amendment Procedures and Constitutional Stability' in Congleton R.D. and Swedenborg B. (eds.), *Democratic Constitutional Design and Public Policy: Analysis and Evidence* (MIT Press 2006) 319

Rawls J., *Political Liberalism* (Columbia University Press 1993)

Republic of Kenya, National Assembly, 'Report of the Parliamentary Select Committee on the Review of the Constitution on the Reviewed Harmonized Draft Constitution' (29 January 2010)

Republic of Kenya, 'Report of the Committee of Eminent Persons on the Constitution Review Process' (30 May 2006) 29

Republic of Kenya, 'Final Report of the Constitution of Kenya Review Commission' (2004)

Rosnai Y., *Unconstitutional Constitutional Amendments: The Limits of Amendment Powers* (OUP 2017)

Saati A., *The Participation Myth: Outcomes of Participatory Constitution Building Processes on Democracy* (Umea University 2015)

Torres-Artunduaga C. and Garcia-Jaramillo S., 'Democratizing the Doctrine of Unconstitutional Constitutional Amendments: The Puzzle of Amending the Judiciary Branch' (2020) 14(1) ICL Journal 1

Tushnet M., 'Peasants with Pitchforks, and Toilers with Twitter: Constitutional Revolutions and the Constituent Power' (2015) 13(3) International Journal of Constitutional Law 639–54

Vile J.R., 'The Amending Process: Alternative to Revolution' (1983) 11(2) South Eastern Political Review 49
Wanambisi L, 'DP Ruto Calls for Inclusivity in the Building Bridges Initiative' (*Capital News*, 16 February 2020) https://www.capitalfm.co.ke/news/2020/02/dp-ruto-calls-for-inclusivity-in-the-building-bridges-initiative/ accessed 10 July 2021
Whitaker B.E. and Giersch J., 'Voting on a Constitution: Implications for Democracy in Kenya' (2009) 27(1) Journal of Contemporary African Studies 6

PART 5

CASE STUDIES: DISTINCT PROFILES OF CONSTITUTIONAL CHANGE

10

A Divided Quest for a More Perfect Union: Ethno-regionalism, Recurrent Constitutional Alterations, and the Failure of Institutional Change in Nigeria's Fourth Republic

Rotimi T. Suberu

1. Introduction

Constitutional instability is a conspicuous feature of governance in Nigeria's deeply fractionalized society. The adoption of five separate constitutions between independence in 1960 and the inauguration of the Fourth Republic in 1999 is emblematic of the country's constitutional volatility.[1] In addition, the Fourth Republic witnessed five rounds of alterations to the 1999 Constitution between 2010 and 2023. Nonetheless, the Nigerian National Assembly continued to be inundated by, and to propound, a deluge of proposals for further constitutional change. Indeed, recent official amendments and proposed alterations to the Nigerian Constitution have not pacified agitators who seek a fundamental and comprehensive restructuring of Nigeria's constitutional architecture.

This chapter analyses the ethno-regional foundations and ramifications of Nigeria's contemporary constitutional restiveness and impasse. It documents the uncompleted, unfulfilled, and iterative nature of current constitutional change in Nigeria, while demonstrating how ethno-regional cleavages have impeded the realization of more far-reaching and enduring reforms in this contentious federation. The chapter describes, but does not seek to validate, contending ethno-regionalist perspectives on constitutional change. Instead, it explores how ethno-regionalist fault lines might be bridged in order to advance consensual and constructive constitutional change. The chapter is, in essence, more concerned with the ethnopolitical contestation associated with constitutional change, and its potential resolutions, than with the purely formal or legalistic mechanics and dynamics of such change.

[1] The five constitutions are the Independence Constitution (1960); Republican Constitution (1963); Constitution of the Second Republic (1979); Constitution of the (abortive) Third Republic (1989); and the Constitution of the Fourth Republic (1999). A sixth constitution, the 1995 Draft Constitution, was announced by General Sani Abacha in 1996 but not promulgated. For a discussion of Nigeria's past and recent constitutional politics, see Rotimi Suberu, 'Managing Constitutional Change in the Nigerian Federation' (2015) 45(4) Publius: The Journal of Federalism 552–79; Ovie Omo-Agege and Ahmed Idris Wase, 'Brief on the Press Conference by the Leadership of the Senate and the House of Representatives Committees on Constitution Review on the Progress of the 44 Constitution Amendment Bills Transferred to the State Houses of Assembly' (Abuja, 18 October 2022).

Rotimi T. Suberu, *A Divided Quest for a More Perfect Union: Ethno-regionalism, Recurrent Constitutional Alterations, and the Failure of Institutional Change in Nigeria's Fourth Republic* In: *Constitutional Change and Constitutionalism in Africa*. Edited by: Charles M. Fombad and Nico Steytler, Oxford University Press. © Rotimi T. Suberu 2025. DOI: 10.1093/9780198957034.003.0012

First, a historical overview contextualizes Nigeria's contemporary constitutional politics in two contentious political settlements, namely a relatively centrifugal parliamentary federalism during the late colonial period (1954–59) and First Republic (1960–66), on the one hand, and a comparatively centripetal presidential intergovernmental system since the 1979 Constitution of the Second Republic, on the other. While the former settlement preceded the intervention of the military in Nigerian politics, the military heavily shaped the latter settlement, producing widespread strictures reflecting the authoritarian provenance of Nigeria's contemporary constitutional structure. Second, key features of successive alterations to the 1999 Constitution are discussed with a view to highlighting the failure of these changes to pacify strident agitation for restructuring the federation into a more decentralized, dynamic, durable, and robustly democratic multi-ethnic union. Third, the centrepiece of the chapter identifies how a historic north–south ethnopolitical fault line has impeded the development of political consensus on key constitutional reform issues involving fiscal decentralization, policing, local government, the very idea of political restructuring, and the procedures for constitutional amendment. Fourth, recommendations for transcending Nigeria's constitutional impasse are proffered, after which the chapter concludes with a summary of its arguments and their implications.

2. Historical analysis: Between two contentious national constitutional settlements (1960–66 and 1979 to the present)

Nigeria's contemporary constitutional travails epitomize the challenges associated with accommodating diverse ethnicities in deeply divided societies. The country has many sectional fault lines, including the division between a predominantly Muslim north (which contains 54 per cent of the national population and 75 per cent of the country's territory) and a predominantly Christian south.[2] Nigeria's other major cleavages include divisions between the country's three major ethnic groups (Muslim Hausa-Fulani, Christian Igbo, and the religiously bi-communal Yoruba); and between these three large ethnicities, on the one hand, and hundreds of smaller ethnic communities (the so-called ethnic minorities), on the other. A contemporary shorthand for Nigeria's ethno-regional diversity divides the country into six quasi-official geopolitical zones, three each in the north and south: the North West (populated by the Hausa-Fulani), North East (a mixture of Hausa-Fulani, Kanuri, and other northern Muslim groups), North Central (including the 'middle belt' of northern minorities), South West (Yoruba), South East (Igbo), and South South (southern minorities in the oil-rich Niger Delta).

The quest to accommodate these ethnic, regional, and religious divisions has produced two broad political moments or settlements: first, a pre-military constitutional settlement that enshrined a relatively decentralized parliamentary ethno-regional federalism during the late colonial period and under the First Republic's 1960 and 1963 Constitutions; and, second, a military-sponsored constitutional settlement that has entrenched a

[2] For a discussion of these demographics, see Abdul Raufu Mustapha, 'Ethnic Structure, Inequality and Governance of the Public Sector in Nigeria', United Nations Research Institute for Social Development, Program Paper No 24 (November 2006); Brian Smith, 'Federal-state Relations in Nigeria' (1981) 80(320) African Affairs 355–78.

relatively centralized presidential federalism of multiple constituent states since the 1979 Constitution. Despite Nigerian contemporary constitutional discourse's nostalgic idealization of the pre-military settlement, neither that settlement nor its successor compact were free of combustible ethno-regional divisiveness, challenges, and agitation.

Mediated by Nigeria's British colonial hegemon, Nigeria's initial constitutional settlement contained several contentious features that ultimately contributed to its violent overthrow by the military in 1966. The most problematic feature involved the establishment of a federation of three ethnic-majority-dominated regions, with the Hausa-Fulani-dominated Northern Region being larger and more populous than the two southern regions (the Yoruba-dominated Western Region and the Igbo-led Eastern Region) combined. An extensive body of literature suggests that the existence of such an 'over-mighty' constituent unit would violate a foundational principle of 'federal stability' by detracting from the legitimacy and authority of the central government through the likelihood of engendering or compounding an acute sense of ethnopolitical insecurity among smaller constituent units or groups and thereby fuelling ethno-secessionist tendencies.[3] Indeed, the structural imbalance in Nigeria's pre-military federal system aggravated fears of northern political hegemony, alienated the country's ethnic minority communities, and encouraged the mobilization of ethno-regional identities.

Federalism in the First Republic thus promoted the formation and polarization of sectional political parties, while robbing the union of the political flexibility and adaptability that would have resulted from a federal system with a multiplicity of constituent units. While it assuaged ethnic minority agitation in the Western Region, the establishment of the Midwest Region as Nigeria's fourth region in 1963 did not address minority grievances elsewhere in the federation. Instead, the creation of another region in the south, along with the retention of the Northern Region as a monolithic behemoth, accentuated the disproportionate size and power of the north. The absence of a robust Senate or federalist chamber in Nigeria's Westminster parliamentary system, the presence of disunity between the northern prime minister and southern ceremonial president, and the vulnerability of the judicial branch in a context of parliamentary sovereignty all reinforced the flagrant flaws in Nigeria's ethno-regionalist First Republic.[4]

Despite the ethnic and regional polarization that it encouraged, Nigeria's initial constitutional settlement contained some benign features. The regions enjoyed relatively extensive autonomy: separate regional constitutions, the authority to establish local police departments, entitlements to considerable amounts of federally collected revenues on the basis of the regional attribution or derivation of those revenues (the so-called derivation principle), and quasi-diplomatic representation in London.[5] Among other advantages, such autonomy enabled the regions to exercise a degree of choice and healthy competitiveness in delivering local public goods and socio-economic development. Furthermore, the parliamentary

[3] Henry Hale, 'Divided We Stand: Institutional Sources of Ethno-federal State Survival and Collapse' (2004) 56(2) World Politics 165–93; Billy Dudley, 'Federalism and the Balance of Political Power in Nigeria' (1966) 4(1) Journal of Commonwealth and Comparative Politics 16–29.

[4] Rotimi Suberu, 'Federalism and the First Republic of Nigeria, 1960–1966' in Toyin Falola and Mathew Heaton (eds.), *Oxford Handbook of Nigerian History* (OUP 2022) 377–98.

[5] See Constitution of the Federal Republic of Nigeria (1963), ss 105(7), 137–40. The following regional constitutions were attached as appendices to the 1963 Constitution: the Constitution of Northern Nigeria Law (1963); Constitution of Eastern Nigeria Law (1963); Constitution of Western Nigeria Law (1963); and Constitution of Mid-Western Nigeria Act (1964).

system of Nigeria's pre-military republic witnessed coalitional political dynamics that were more congenial than the personalized politics common among African presidential systems. These advantages of Nigeria's decentralized parliamentary ethno-regional federalism notwithstanding, the flagrant regional inequalities in the federation's territorial configuration greatly disrupted and destabilized the constitutional settlement of the First Republic, leading to inter-regional political polarization, ethno-military coups, and secessionist warfare.[6]

In a bid to contain the imminent secession of the Eastern Region, the military in 1967 divided the old regions into twelve states: six each in the north and south. This marked a milestone in Nigeria's transition from an unbalanced ethno-regionalist polity to a relatively more equilibrated multi-unit or multi-state federation. The military undertook further political reorganizations and reforms, which it entrenched in the 1979, 1989, and 1999 Constitutions. Aside from the structure of multiple constituent states (which increased to 19, 21, 30, and 36 in 1976, 1987, 1991, and 1996, respectively), Nigeria's new constitutional settlement jettisoned the parliamentary system for a United States (US)-style presidential system. The military-backed constitutional framework instituted a formal system of separation of powers while creating multiple putatively independent commissions. The settlement dramatically expanded the powers of the centre vis-à-vis the states while massively redistributing the country's expanding oil revenues vertically (between the centre and subnational governments) and horizontally (among the subnational governments). It also recognized local government as the third tier of the federal system and entrenched the number of 'local government areas in Nigeria', thereby significantly (but not entirely) constraining the prerogatives of the states over the local government system.[7] Nigeria's new constitutional framework promoted the federal character principle as a policy for ensuring broad ethnic representation in a highly centralized federal government and in the composition of the subnational state and local governments.[8]

The new constitutional settlement produced mixed results. On the one hand, the new settlement's fragmentation of major ethnic regions into multiple states, alongside the creation of several ethnic-minority-controlled states, served to consolidate central authority, cross-cut and depolarize ethnic politics, prevent a recurrence of large-scale ethno-secessionist warfare, and broaden and strengthen support for Nigerian national unity.[9] Although the new settlement did not prevent the rise of separatist, ethnonationalist, and fundamentalist movements in the Fourth Republic, such extremist centrifugal agitation generally lacked credibility among key elite constituencies. Ethno-regional secessionism or separatism, therefore, did not constitute credible or viable threats to Nigeria's unity or continuity.[10]

[6] AHM Kirk-Greene, *Crisis and Conflict in Nigeria: A Documentary Sourcebook 1966–1969*, vol 1 (OUP 1971); Larry Diamond, 'Class, Ethnicity, and the Democratic State: Nigeria, 1950–1966' (1983) 25(3) Comparative Studies in Society and History 457–89.

[7] Constitution of the Federal Republic of Nigeria (1999), ss 3(6), 7; *AG of Abia State & Ors v AG of the Federation* [2006] 16 NWLR (Part 1005) 265 (SC).

[8] Constitution (1999), s 14(3)–(4).

[9] Larry Diamond, 'Issues in the Constitutional Design of a Third Nigerian Republic' (1987) 86(343) African Affairs 209–26; Donald Horowitz, 'The Many Uses of Federalism' (2007) 55 Drake Law Review 953–66.

[10] Friday Olokor, 'Ohanaeze, Sultan, Others Condemn Secession Bid' *Punch* (Lagos, 17 November 2020); Peter Dada, 'Agitation for Yoruba Nation Won't Succeed – Akeredolu' *Punch* (Lagos, 23 December 2022).

On the other hand, the new settlement provoked much criticism and agitation that challenged its procedural legitimacy and substantive soundness.[11] Procedurally, the new settlement was the imposition of a corrupt and abusive military dictatorship: one mostly dominated by northern Nigerian military officers, who accounted for six of Nigeria's eight military heads of state between 1966 and 1999. While it periodically involved the use of civilian drafting committees and constituent assemblies, the military's constitution-making process was never democratic. The civilian participants in the process often simply ratified the military's predetermined vision, including the adoption of multi-state federalism and an executive presidential system. The military exercised the prerogatives of vetoing, amending, or rewriting any proposals or recommendations emanating from civilian constitutional committees or assemblies. What is more, the ensuing constitutional charters were never subjected to popular ratification in a referendum.

Substantively, critics challenged the new settlement for transforming Nigeria from a decentralized parliamentary federation into a 'bastardized', hyper-centralized, near-unitary presidential system.[12] They described such centralization as inimical to interethnic unity and security, pluralistic democratic politics, and developmental progress. Critics argued that the new system's emphasis on the centralized redistribution of federally collected oil revenues fostered intergroup distributional contention and impoverishment instead of promoting economically productive intergovernmental competition in line with the expectations of a market-preserving federalism.[13] Nigeria's worsening socio-economic outcomes, including the world's largest concentrations of poor people and out-of-school children and the proliferation of violent sectarian and separatist insurgencies or movements, reinforced criticism of the new federalism's dysfunctionality and corruption.

Criticism of the new constitutional settlement became particularly vociferous among 'Southern Leaders of Thought', who included Emeka Anyaoku, Ben Nwabueze, Ayo Adebanjo, Edwin Clark, and other prominent leaders of apex sociocultural organizations such as the Yoruba-based Afenifere, the Ohanaeze Ndi Igbo, and the Pan-Niger Delta Forum.[14] These southern Nigerian elites and organizations described the settlement as an elaborate design by a northern-dominated military to perpetuate northern political domination of the federation while advancing the region's economic expropriation of southern-derived oil resources. The critics pushed for the convocation of a sovereign national conference of ethnic nationalities that would return Nigeria to a more decentralized federalism. Many argued for the reconstitution of Nigeria into a union of six geopolitical zones. These zones (or constituent units of comparable scale) would, in this view, function

[11] Julius Ihonvbere, 'How to Make an Undemocratic Constitution: The Nigerian Example' (2000) 21(2) Third World Quarterly 343–66; Tunde Ogowewo, 'Why the Judicial Annulment of the Constitution of 1999 is Imperative for the Survival of Nigeria's Democracy' (2000) 44(2) Journal of African Law 135–66.

[12] Ladipo Adamolekun, 'The Nigerian Federation at the Crossroads: The Way Forward' (2005) 35(3) Publius: The Journal of Federalism 383–405; also Ihonvbere (n 11).

[13] Ladipo Adamolekun and John Kincaid, 'The Federal Solution: Assessment and Prognosis for Nigeria and Africa' (1991) 21(4) Publius: The Journal of Federalism 173–88; Emeka Anyaoku, 'Nigeria on the Brink: A Message to Our President and the National Assembly' *The Guardian* (Lagos, 18 July 2019); 'New Federal Constitution, Not a Review Needed' *Punch* (Lagos, 19 February 2020).

[14] Victor Gbonegun, 'Southern Leaders of Thought Seek Negotiated Restructuring via New Constitution' *The Guardian* (Lagos, 25 August 2017); Ben Ezeamalu, 'Nwabueze, Anyaoku, Akinrinade, Others Explain How to Restructure Nigeria' *Premium Times* (Abuja, 25 August 2017); 'Southern Leaders Unveil 5-Point Agenda for Restructuring' *PM News* (Lagos, 4 September 2017).

as more viable federalist units than the current politically weak, fiscally dependent, and military-instituted 36 states.

Agitation opposing the military's constitutional settlement persisted after the 1999 transition from military to civilian rule. It led to a national civic forum for constitutional change, multiple presidential constitutional reform panels, two major national constitutional conferences (in 2005 and 2014), a succession of federal legislative committees devoted to constitutional review, and recurrent cycles of alterations to the 1999 Constitution. Despite persistent agitation and repeated alteration, however, the basic structure of Nigeria's presidential multi-state federalism remained largely unchanged.

3. Alteration without transformation under the 1999 Constitution

During the first decade of the Fourth Republic, between 1999 and 2010, successive official initiatives to amend the 1999 Constitution failed because the National Assembly consolidated proposed changes into a single constitutional amendment bill. But the relatively rigid nature of the 1999 Constitution, along with the absence of a broad-based national consensus on comprehensive political change, placed steep hurdles in the way of enacting major constitutional reform. Under section 9 of the 1999 Constitution, a proposal to alter the Constitution must be approved by not less than two-thirds of all the members of each house of the bicameral National Assembly, or by a four-fifths majority of these members if the alteration concerns the amendment formula itself, fundamental human rights, boundary adjustments, or the creation of new states or localities. In both cases, the alteration must be approved by resolutions of the houses of assembly of two-thirds of the states and also receive presidential assent.[15]

To achieve elite consensus on constitutional change, the National Assembly abandoned a relatively holistic agenda for a more realistic or pragmatic piecemeal approach to reform. Beginning with the first series of alterations to the 1999 Constitution, in July 2010, the National Assembly prioritized less contentious constitutional reforms while deferring consideration of more contentious issues. Far from addressing demands for the transformation of Nigeria's military-derived constitutional settlement, however, these piecemeal alterations focused largely on a narrower set of exigent or emerging administrative, political, and electoral concerns.

For instance, the Constitution of the Federal Republic of Nigeria (First Alteration) Act of July 2010 enhanced the operational autonomy, budgetary independence, and oversight powers of both the Independent National Electoral Commission (INEC) and the National Assembly. The Act also formulated new guidelines and timelines for conducting and adjudicating federal and state elections, removed the powers of administrative tribunals (as distinct from more apolitical regular courts) to disqualify candidates for political office on grounds of misdemeanour, augmented the regulations for recalling national and state legislators, and introduced rules to enhance internal party democracy. Finally, in response to the political crisis, uncertainty, and void engendered in late 2009 and early 2010 by the illness, incapacitation, and eventual death of President Umaru Yar'Adua, the Act included

[15] Osita Ogbu, 'A Critical Analysis of the Constitution (First Alteration) Act' (2011–2012) 10 The Nigerian Juridical Review 49–72.

new regulations on political succession in the event of the unforeseen or abrupt absence of an incumbent president or governor.[16]

The Second Alteration Act of November 2010 incorporated further adjustments to the 1999 Constitution, including changes to the recently passed First Alteration Act. The second Act readjusted the nation's electoral calendar in order to establish an extended and more flexible time frame for organizing and adjudicating national and subnational elections. The Act augmented the procedures for adjudicating gubernatorial election petitions, beginning with the Governorship Election Tribunals and extending to the Court of Appeal and the Supreme Court.[17] The judicature was also a focus for the Third Alteration Act of March 2011, which constitutionally entrenched the National Industrial Court as a superior court of record with full jurisdiction over industrial disputes throughout the federation.[18]

Enacting three rounds of narrowly focused alterations to the 1999 Constitution in quick succession in 2010–11 did little to assuage official and societal pressures for further constitutional change. Thus, a fourth cycle of alteration to the 1999 Constitution was enacted in 2017, taking effect following presidential assent in 2018. The fourth alteration Acts contained a comparatively broader, but still limited, set of constitutional amendments. The Acts consisted of the following five components:

- Reductions in age eligibility requirements for the positions of president, member of the House of Representatives, and member of a state house of assembly from 40 to 35, 35 to 25, and 30 to 25 years, respectively (the so-called Not Too Young to Run Act).
- Constitutional guarantees of financial autonomy (from state executives) for state legislatures and judiciaries by making their budgets a direct charge on the consolidated revenue funds of the states.
- Regulations strictly enforcing the two-term limits for national and state chief political executives by restricting to only one additional term any person who was sworn in to complete the term of a president or governor.
- Provisions enhancing the authority and effectiveness of the INEC by empowering the commission to deregister political parties, while extending its time frame for conducting by-elections.
- New guidelines for effective, speedy adjudication and resolution of pre-election matters or conflicts arising from the conduct of party primaries.[19]

Reflecting the failure of the fourth alteration Acts to satiate Nigeria's constitutional agitators, a fifth cycle of changes to the 1999 Constitution received presidential assent in March 2023. The sixteen constitutional alterations enacted in this fifth round included amendments

[16] Constitution of the Federal Republic of Nigeria (First Alteration) Act of 2010, arts 1–12.

[17] Constitution of the Federal Republic of Nigeria (Second Alteration) Act of 2010, arts 13–22.

[18] Constitution of the Federal Republic of Nigeria (Third Alteration) Act of 2010, arts 23–32.

[19] The alterations relating to reduced age requirements for political office, financial autonomy for state judiciaries and legislatures, term limits for political chief executives, INEC powers to deregister parties, and the timeline for resolving pre-election matters are incorporated, respectively, in the following Acts: Constitution of the Federal Republic of Nigeria 1999 (Fourth Alteration) Act 27 of 2017; Constitution of the Federal Republic of Nigeria 1999 (Fourth Alteration) Act 4 of 2017; Constitution of the Federal Republic of Nigeria 1999 (Fourth Alteration) Act 16 of 2017; Constitution of the Federal Republic of Nigeria 1999 (Fourth Alteration) Act 9 of 2017; and Constitution of the Federal Republic of Nigeria 1999 (Fourth Alteration) Act 21 of 2017. For a succinct analysis of the five alterations, see 'The Hydra-headed Fourth Alteration' (*Law Pavilion*, 27 June 2019) https://lawpavilion.com/blog/the-hydra-headed-fourth-alteration/ accessed 14 June 2023.

transferring railways, correctional services (prisons), and national grid electricity generation, transmission, and distribution from the exclusive list of federal legislative powers to the concurrent list.[20] However, given the principle of central supremacy or paramountcy in cases of inconsistency between federal and state laws under section 4(5) of the 1999 Constitution, the expansion of the concurrent powers of the states should not be overstated. What is more, the fifth round of amendments included changes that underscored Nigeria's constitutional centralization.

For instance, seven of the sixteen amendments under the fifth alteration Acts involved changes to the names of local government areas, thereby advancing the relative unification, nationalization, or centralization of the local government system. Other centralizing amendments required state governors (along with the federal president) to nominate their cabinets within 60 days of taking office, prescribed a mandatory gender quota for federal and subnational executive Cabinets, imposed uniform regulations relating to the inaugural sessions or sittings of national and state legislative houses, entrenched new financial and administrative measures guaranteeing the autonomy of subnational legislatures and judiciaries from state executives, and reinforced the integrationist objectives and directive principles of governmental policy written into the 1999 Constitution.[21]

Overall, the successive alterations to the 1999 Constitution drew mixed responses. For their official protagonists in the National Assembly, the alterations 'undoubtedly improved our electoral management and adjudication systems, fostered political participation and addressed other fundamental good governance issues'.[22] The alterations, seen from this official perspective, were not only substantively constructive but also resulted from procedures that were participatory or inclusive. Aside from their ratifications by the required legislative supermajorities at national and subnational levels, the alterations emerged from what the National Assembly described as a consultative process that involved the Assembly's solicitation of submissions from citizens and civil society organizations; public hearings at the national level and across the six geopolitical zones; and extensive deliberation by national legislative constitutional review committees, and by conferences of speakers of state legislatures.[23]

Critics, however, denounced the alterations as half-hearted, dysfunctional, cosmetic, and ineffective legislative charades that tinkered with a 'status quo, which is a dead end', while failing to 'address fundamental issues such as the practice of true federalism, resource control, revenue allocation, the rights of minorities, ethnicity and religious tolerance, as well as crime control in the states'.[24] Even the fifth alteration Acts, which included concessions to federalist states' rights, were criticized for '[falling] short of taking Nigeria to its natural configuration of a fully functional federal polity'.[25] The amendments were challenged

[20] Olaniwun Ajayi, 'The Nigerian Constitution in Progress: Recent Amendments' (*Olaniwun Ajayi*, April 2023) https://www.olaniwunajayi.net/ accessed 1 October 2023.
[21] Ibid.
[22] Omo-Agege and Wase (n 1).
[23] Ibid.
[24] Charles Soludo, 'Reconstructing Nigeria for Prosperity' *This Day* (Lagos, 17 September 2012); Rotimi Suberu, 'Federalism and Constitutional Reform in the Fourth Nigerian Republic: Progress, Problems and Prospects' National Institute for Legislative Studies Occasional Paper Series No 1 (January 2015) 27; 'Amendment of the Constitution: Matters Arising' *The Guardian* (14 December 2022).
[25] 'Federalism: Constitution Amendment Bills Fall Short' *Punch* (Lagos, 27 March 2023).

specifically for excluding provisions on 'fiscal federalism' and decentralized policing and consequently neglecting 'core demands of the advocates of restructuring'.[26]

In essence, the five successive rounds of alteration to the 1999 Constitution barely addressed the vociferous agitation for constitutional restructuring and a more decentralized federalism in Nigeria. Instead, the amendments generally perpetuated the centralizing practice of embedding and entrenching subnational political institutions in the national constitution. In a frank admission in 2017, Senate President Sola Saraki explained that agitation for restructuring was a source of profound inter-regional 'suspicion and tension'. He added that 'there was a meeting in Kaduna [the former capital of the Northern Region] where it was clear that certain parts of the country wanted more time to understand what restructuring is'.[27] Saraki's explanation spoke to the ethno-regional fault line behind the absence of fundamental constitutional change in the Fourth Republic.

4. Ethno-regional cleavages and the elusiveness of fundamental constitutional change

The north–south cleavages and ethno-regional dissonances impeding fundamental constitutional or federalist reforms in Nigeria were especially evident in relation to fiscal federalism, policing, local government, the general idea of federal restructuring, and the procedures for achieving constitutional change.

4.1 Fiscal federalism and the economics of decentralization

Resentment in Nigeria's coastal, oil-rich south about its perceived subsidization of the poorer, landlocked, more populous, and politically more powerful north underpinned much of the southern agitation for true federalism, subnational resource control, and economic decentralization. Three issues in particular epitomized this regional economic conflict in the Fourth Republic: oil revenue allocation, the control of value added tax (VAT), and the proposal for a National Water Resources Bill.

The derivation principle, to reiterate, was a defining feature of the Nigerian revenue allocation system under the country's original federalist settlement. As oil revenues came to dominate Nigeria's public finances and political economy in the 1970s, however, the country's military rulers systematically de-emphasized the derivation rule, reducing its weight from 50 per cent of oil-mining rents and royalties during the First Republic to only 1 per cent of mineral revenues in the Account by 1999.[28] However, violent agitation for local resource control by the Ogoni and other ethnic groups in the oil-rich Niger Delta led to a

[26] Ibid; Gbenga Akinsanmi, 'Fresh Agitation after Constitutional Amendment' *This Day* (Lagos, 26 March 2023).

[27] Ezigbo Onyebuchi and Hammed Shittu, 'Saraki: Mistrust Triggered by Hate Speeches, Caused Rejection of Power Devolution Bill' *This Day* (Lagos, 30 July 2017).

[28] Constitution (1963), s 140(1); TY Danjuma, 'Revenue Sharing and the Political Economy of Nigerian Federalism' (June 1994) 1(1) Nigerian Journal of Federalism 43–68; Rotimi T Suberu, *Federalism and Ethnic Conflict* (United States Institute of Peace Press 2001) 65.

substantial restoration of the derivation rule under the 1999 Constitution. Section 162(2) of the Constitution provided that the rule should be applied to at least 13 per cent of revenues derived 'directly from any natural resources'.

The Fourth Republic's federal government adopted additional measures to alleviate tension and turbulence in the economically strategic Delta region. The initiatives included applying the derivation rule to onshore and offshore oil resources, establishing a Niger Delta Development Commission, creating a Federal Ministry of the Niger Delta, and implementing an amnesty programme for militants in the region.[29] However, these measures did not end agitation in the Niger Delta for more subnational resource control. In particular, leaders of the region proposed transferring control of natural mineral resources from the centre to the subnational level, or an increased application of the derivation rule to up to 50 per cent of centrally collected oil revenues.[30] But the non-oil-producing states in general, and northern leaders and governments in particular, resisted such proposals. Indeed, many of these leaders and governments criticized, and sought to reverse, existing concessions to the Niger Delta.[31]

In 2001, the 'permanent northern majority' in the House of Representatives voted overwhelmingly to defeat a bill on subnational resource control by House Member Temi Harimman of Delta State.[32] The bill 'sought to amend the 1969 Petroleum Act, praying that oil-producing states, local governments, and communities be granted ownership and control of resources, thus reversing the present situation where the Federal Government exercises excessive control over oil'.[33] Aside from killing Harimman's bill, northern interests spearheaded an unsuccessful legal challenge at the Supreme Court against the centre's abrogation of the onshore–offshore oil dichotomy.[34] Similarly, northern delegates to the 2005 Constitutional Conference successfully resisted a proposal by Niger Delta delegates to increase the derivation principle from 13 per cent to at least 25 per cent, leading to a walkout by the Delta delegates.[35]

Northern legislators also conspicuously rejected a proposal to increase to 10 per cent the 3 per cent of operating expenditures that the Petroleum Industry Act (PIA) of 2021 required oil industry operators to pay into a Host Community Development Trust Fund (HCDTF).[36] At the same time, the Act provided that 30 per cent of the profits of the state-owned commercial oil company, 10 per cent of rents on petroleum prospecting licences, and another 10 per cent of rents on petroleum mining leases should all be paid into a

[29] Niger-Delta Development Commission (Establishment, etc) Act of 2000; Allocation of Revenue (Abolition of Dichotomy in the Application of the Principle of Derivation) Act of 2004; Niger-Delta Development Commission (Establishment, etc) (Amendment) Act of 2017.

[30] Chris Eze, 'New Revenue Formula: Niger Delta Demands 50 Percent Derivation' *Daily Trust* (Abuja, 11 October 2013); Dennis Naku, 'South-South Wants Oil Derivation Share Increased to 50%' *Punch* (Lagos, 9 October 2021).

[31] 'Key Issues Before Northern Delegates to the 2014 National Conference' *Vanguard* (Lagos, 12–15 May 2014).

[32] Itse Sagay, 'Nigeria: Federalism, the Constitution, and Resource Control' (Text of speech delivered at the fourth sensitization programme held by the Ibori Vanguard at the Lagoon Restaurant, Lagos, 19 May 2001).

[33] Ibid.

[34] *AG Adamawa & Ors v AG Federation & Ors* (2005) 18 NWLR (Pt 958) 581.

[35] Bolanle Omonijo and Emma Aziken, 'Confab in Dilemma as Southern Delegates Walk Out' *Vanguard* (Lagos, 15 June 2005); 'Constitutional Change Conference Deadlocks over Oil Dispute' (*The New Humanitarian*, 30 June 2005).

[36] Paul Omorogbe, 'PIB: How the North Secured Funding for Frontier Basins' *Nigerian Tribune* (Ibadan, 5 July 2021). See also Marc-Antoine Pérouse de Montclos, 'The Politics and Crisis of the Petroleum Industry Bill in Nigeria' (2014) 52(3) Journal of Modern African Studies 403–24.

Frontier Exploration Fund, designed primarily to fund new oil prospecting in the north.[37] Indeed, 'the PIA was originally proposed by the executive (largely supported in the North) and passed largely along regional (North-South) lines . . . and many lawmakers from the South believe the bill advances Northern interests to the detriment of the South'.[38] In matters of oil revenue allocation, political elites from the north and south consistently adopted conflicting positions, with the former generally calling for centralized control and/or redistribution of oil resources and the latter pressing for subnational control, retention, or derivation-based allocation of such revenues.

Intergovernmental conflict over VAT revenues similarly arrayed southern decentralists against northern centralists in an ethnopolitical melee over the economics of Nigeria's constitutional federalism. The military had introduced a centrally collected VAT in 1993 as a replacement for the state-administered sales tax. Under section 40 of the Value Added Tax Act of 1993, VAT revenues are to be distributed in the proportion of 50 per cent to the states and Abuja, 35 per cent to local governments, and 15 per cent to the federal government. Fifty per cent of the revenues due to the states and local governments are shared equally by each state or locality, while relative population and the principle of derivation are respectively weighted 30 per cent and 20 per cent in the VAT horizontal distribution formula.[39]

The relatively wealthier southern states challenged the VAT scheme on numerous grounds.[40] First, the states contended that value-added, consumption, and sale taxes were not referenced in the exclusive or concurrent legislative lists of the 1999 Constitution and, therefore, remained within the exclusive (residual) authority of the states. Second, the states opposed the relatively limited weight given to derivation, which allegedly short-changed southern states with the highest VAT derivation, such as Lagos, Rivers, and Oyo. Finally, southerners criticized the fact that sharia-implementing states in the Muslim north (where consumption of alcohol was criminalized) partook in the sharing of those portions of VAT revenues derived from the production and consumption of alcohol in mostly southern states. In the words of a governor of Rivers State, '[y]ou can't destroy beer in your state in the name of Sharia, yet share from VAT on beer from other states. It is hypocrisy'.[41]

Although the Supreme Court, in 2014, declined to exercise jurisdiction in a VAT-based legal tussle between Lagos and the Federal Inland Revenue Service (FIRS), a federal high court in Rivers in 2021 affirmed the rights of the Rivers State Government to collect VAT.[42]

[37] Kasirim Nwuke, 'Nigeria's Petroleum Industry Act: Addressing Old Problems, Creating New Ones' (*Brookings*, 24 November 2021) https://www.brookings.edu/articles/nigerias-petroleum-industry-act-addressing-old-problems-creating-new-ones/ accessed 1 October 2023.

[38] Ibid.

[39] Taiwo Oyedele, 'How to Fix Nigeria's Broken VAT System' (*PWC*, undated) https://www.pwc.com/ng/en/assets/pdf/how-to-fix-nigeria-broken-vat-system.pdf accessed 14 June 2023.

[40] See Adamu Abuh, Kingsley Jeremiah, and Ameh Ochojila, 'Five Northern States Join FIRS in VAT Dispute against Rivers, Lagos' *The Guardian* (Lagos, 4 October 2021); Tunde Ajala, 'Legal Battle over VAT Collection Stirs Debates on Equity, Fiscal Federalism' *Punch* (Lagos, 3 October 2021); Akinyemi Ashade, 'VAT Controversy: The Need to Avoid Fiscal Anarchy' *Premium Times* (Abuja, 15 September 2021); Joseph Onyekwere, 'Value Added Tax (VAT): Conflict and Resolving the Question of Unbalanced Fiscal Federalism' *The Guardian* (Lagos, 7 September 2021).

[41] Okafor Ofiebor, 'Wike Vows to Begin Collection of VAT, Warns FG' *The News* (Lagos, 8 September 2021).

[42] *AG Lagos State v AG Federation* (2014) LPELR-22701 (SC); *AG Rivers State v FIRS & AG Federation*, Suit No FHC/PH/CS/149/2020.

The federal government immediately appealed the ruling, while a resolution of the northern governors and emirs attacked the judgment. As Governor Bello Masari of Katsina State claimed, '[t]hat judgment is not fair. It is other parts of the country that make Lagos and Rivers states what they are. We have to work together as a nation.'[43]

Promoting the collective interests of Nigeria as a nation was the official justification for the federal executive's National Water Resources Bill of 2020. However, the bill polarized the country, with several legislators and leaders from the far north supporting it, while southerners and their allies in the middle belt denounced and disparaged it. Among other contentious provisions, the bill established a presidentially appointed Nigeria Water Resources Regulatory Commission (NWRRC) 'for the regulation, equitable and sustainable development, management, use and conservation of Nigeria's surface water and ground water resources'.[44] The bill gave the federal executive control of all water sources affecting more than one state; limited subnational state regulation of water to 'sources occurring solely within the boundaries of the state', as may be 'guided by the policy and principles of the federal government'; and arrogated to the NWRRC the authority to issue 'rules and regulations' in relation to all borehole drilling.[45] The proposed law also empowered the NWRC to regulate or prohibit any conduct or activities in relation to an area the Commission has declared by order 'to be a groundwater conservation area'.[46] Indeed, under section 148 of the National Water Resources Bill, '[n]o person shall use water otherwise than as permitted under this Bill.'

Wole Soyinka, the author and Nobel laureate, was among the most vociferous southern Nigerian critics of the bill. He not only expressed 'full agreement with virtually every pronouncement of alarm, outrage, opprobrium, and repudiation that has been heaped upon this bill and its parentage' but also urged the bill's critics 'to move beyond denunciation, however, and embark on practical responses for its formal deactivation and permanent internment'.[47] Indeed, southerners construed the bill as part of an agenda by a Fulani presidency to commandeer grazing and watering resources, routes, and reserves in the middle belt and the south for Fulani herders, who had increasingly been involved in violent confrontations with farmers for access to these resources.[48]

For its protagonists in the federal government and northern Nigeria, however, the Water Bill was consistent with a policy of making Nigerian natural resources available for the 'equitable and affordable' access and development of all its constituent communities and citizens rather than for the parochial and unequal benefit of particular ethnic groups.[49] Such a perceived quest to advance a national against a parochial agenda was also the official justification for the centralization of policing in Nigeria.

[43] 'Lagos, Rivers Begin VAT Collection, FG, North, Disagree' *Punch* (Lagos, 15 September 2021).

[44] See Committee Report on the National Water Resources Bill 2020 https://placng.org/i/wp-content/uploads/2020/09/Committee-Report-on-the-National-Water-Resources-Bill-2020.pdf accessed 23 December 2022.

[45] National Water Resources Bill of 2020, ss 2(2), 28(g).

[46] Ibid. s 71.

[47] Wole Soyinka, 'MLK's Mighty Stream of Righteousness' *Premium Times* (Abuja, 27 August 2020).

[48] Lawrence Njoku, 'Opposition Mounts against Reintroduced National Water Resources Bill' *The Guardian* (Lagos, 7 September 2020).

[49] National Water Resources Bill (n 45) s 1(1)(c).

4.2 Policing

The military's abrogation since the 1960s of separate regionally controlled subnational policing departments epitomized Nigeria's shift from a relatively decentralized to a comparatively centralized constitutional settlement. Under the country's military-backed constitutions of 1979, 1989, and 1999, a single Nigeria Police Force (NPF) was established for the entire federation and placed under the control of a presidentially appointed Inspector General of Police. Constitutional representation in the Police Council for state governors, as well as the authority they enjoyed to give lawful directions to heads or commissioners of contingents of NPF in their states, could not detract from the over-centralization of policing in the country. The Council was largely advisory in design and moribund in practice, while central authorities could override governors' directives to state police commissioners. Indeed, there were cases of police commissioners or their subordinates disobeying gubernatorial directives.[50]

Supporters of the unitary over-centralized policing system defended the system on the following grounds: blatant politicization of regionally controlled local police bodies in the First Republic; ongoing emasculation, subversion, and manipulation by state governors of state-controlled institutions, including local governments, traditional authorities, and state judiciaries and legislatures; the financial dependency and insolvency of most state governments, leading to concerns about their ability to adequately fund and maintain professional state-level police forces; and fears that autonomous state police bodies could threaten national unity or degenerate into ethnic militias and secessionist armies.[51]

Proponents of state police, on the other hand, argued that decentralizing policing would contain Nigeria's deepening internal security challenges, respond to the overstretched NPF's glaring inability to effectively police the entire federation, revitalize the country's federalism, and institutionalize or formalize the proliferation across the federation of state-backed informal quasi-policing bodies and vigilantes.[52] The proponents contended that transferring more national revenue to the states and entrenching robust oversight mechanisms would address concerns about the underfunding and politicization of subnational police.

Ethno-regional identities shaped the contending positions on policing in Nigeria. Such ethno-regionalism was evident on many levels, including in the federal presidency, the National Assembly, the Nigerian Governors' Forum, and civil society. As the repositories and beneficiaries of centralized police powers, successive Nigerian presidents, including southern Nigerians like Goodluck Jonathan and Olusegun Obasanjo, opposed the decentralization of policing.[53] However, as the country's security crisis persisted or deepened

[50] Oluwakemi Adelagun, 'Magodo: Police Officer Disobeys Sanwo-Olu over Invasion' *Premium Times* (Abuja, 5 January 2022).

[51] Kole Shettima, 'State Policing: A Case for Concern about Devolution' in Oliver Owen (ed.), *Police Reform in Nigeria: The Devolution Debate* (CLEEN Foundation 2018) 26–29; Mohammed Adoke, *Burden of Service: Reminiscences of Nigeria's Former Attorney-General* (Clink Street 2019) 244.

[52] M Adeniji Kazeem, 'State Policing: A Case for Devolution' in Owen (ed) (n 51) 22–25; Ike Ekweremadu, 'A Vote for State Police' *This Day* (Lagos, 15 February 2018).

[53] See 'Nigeria not Ripe for State Police, Jonathan Declares' *Vanguard* (Lagos, 8 August 2012) https://www.vanguardngr.com/2012/08/nigeria-not-ripe-for-state-police-jonathan-declares/ accessed 19 February 2023; 'Obasanjo makes U-Turn, Says Nigeria Needs State Police to Tackle Insecurity' (*The Cable*, 22 April 2022) https://www.thecable.ng/obasanjo-makes-u-turn-says-nigeria-needs-state-police-to-tackle-insecurity/amp accessed 19 February 2023.

over the course of the Fourth Republic, a north–south cleavage on police (de)centralization appeared to emerge in the presidency. President Muhammadu Buhari, a northern Muslim, for instance, stridently opposed the establishment of state police. He argued that 'state police is not an option. Find out the relationship between local government and the governors. Are the third tier of government getting what they are supposed to get constitutionally?'[54] In contrast, Buhari's deputy, Vice President Yemi Osinbajo, a southern Yoruba Christian, said: 'We must accept that there is a need for greater decentralisation of the police force. I have been a frequent advocate of state policing and I believe this certainly must be the way we must go.'[55]

In the National Assembly, Ike Ekweremadu, a one-time deputy Senate president from the south-eastern state of Enugu, was the most prominent advocate of state police. Ekweremadu not only wrote extensively and thoughtfully on the merits of a decentralized policing arrangement but also crafted an elaborate legislative bill on state police.[56] The bill included provisions to make state police accountable to citizens and local communities while insulating its financing, control, and appointment from politicization. Yet, Ekweremadu's sustained and systematic advocacy in support of state policing in particular, and fundamental constitutional reform in general, proved unsuccessful. He 'regretted that vital amendments which would have helped to deepen Nigeria's democratic experience, enhance equity and justice and boost national development had perished at the altar of mutual suspicion and narrow sectional interests'.[57]

Sectional polarization on policing reform was most evident in July 2012 when the Northern Governors' Forum renounced an earlier resolution of the umbrella Nigerian Governors' Forum that 'identified the increasing need for state police as a strategy for combating the rising insecurity in the country'.[58] Disassociating itself from the resolution, the Northern Governors' Forum argued 'that the country was not ripe for state police and that the present structure of central police should remain'.[59] Nonetheless, more than a decade later, the Northern Governors' Forum and Northern Traditional Rulers Council called for a constitutional amendment 'to give legal backing to state police'.[60] The reversal of the northern governors' opposition to state police reflected Nigeria's worsening insecurity crisis and, especially, the severity of the crisis in the north. Northern embrace of decentralized policing was hailed as a major 'breakthrough' in the development of elite consensus on constitutional reform in Nigeria.[61]

Yet, the most steadfast support for state police continued to come from southern Nigeria and sections of the middle belt, where prominent political leaders and organizations alleged a 'hidden ethnic and regional agenda' to prevent police decentralization and promote

[54] 'Why State Police is Not an Option – President Buhari' *Sahara Reporters, New York* (5 January 2022) <https://saharareporters.com/2022/01/05/why-state-police-not-option-%E2%80%94president-buhari> accessed 14 February 2025.

[55] Chinedu Asadu, 'State Policing is the Way Forward – Osinbajo Speaks on Building Multi-ethnic Nigeria' *The Cable* (Lagos, 7 March 2021) <https://www.thecable.ng/building-a-nation-like-nigeria-may-appear-messy-osinbajo-admits/> accessed 14 February 2025.

[56] Ekweremadu (n 52).

[57] Nwabueze Okonkwo, 'Ekweremadu, Obiozor, Others Brainstorm on Nation's Constitution' *Vanguard* (Lagos, 7 November 2015).

[58] Henry Umoru, 'State Police: It is Northern vs Southern Governors' *Vanguard* (Lagos, 2 September 2012).

[59] Ibid.

[60] Ebenezer Obadare, 'Policing Breakthrough in Nigeria' (*Council on Foreign Relations*, 26 September 2022).

[61] Ibid.

the unitary police and security services as instruments of sectional 'subjugation'.[62] Northern suspicion of subnational policing, on the other hand, was deep-seated, even in states with the most severe internal security crises. Governor Babagana Zulum of Borno State, at the epicentre of the Boko Haram insurgency, for instance, acknowledged that Borno would mostly benefit from establishing state police, but nevertheless strongly opposed it because '[s]tate police will further polarise an already fragile system and disintegrate further our weak national unity.'[63] For many supporters of Nigeria's unitary police arrangements, internal insecurity challenges would be better managed not by police decentralization but by expanding national security institutions, bolstering the grass-roots conflict mediation roles of traditional institutions and local governments, and addressing inequality, injustice, and other underlying structural drivers of social insecurity and instability.[64]

4.3 Local government

North–South tensions coloured issues such as whether or not local governments should be organized uniformly across the federation, funded primarily by federally collected oil and other revenues from the Federation Account, have their boundaries and names listed in the federal Constitution, and designated and recognized as the third order of Nigeria's federal system (after the centre and the states). Nigeria's northern-dominated military rulers resolved these questions affirmatively, establishing a uniform, single-tiered local government system, formally allocating about 20 per cent of revenues in the Federation Account to the localities, and entrenching 774 local government areas in the federal Constitution. The military institutionalized a system of 'double devolution' and indirect centralization that recognized two levels of subnational federal governance, thereby circumventing the status of the states as sole constitutive federating units.[65]

The idea of a centrally mandated, designated, structured, and funded local government system was consistent with a centripetal constitutional vision of Nigeria as a politically and economically integrated federation. Prominent northern leaders defended Nigeria's contemporary local government system and rejected the proposal of so-called true federalists that the localities be delisted from the 1999 Constitution and fully entrusted to the states. Yakubu Gowon (a former military head of state), Auwalu Yadudu (a professor of law and former federal legal adviser), and Babachir Lawal (a former secretary to the federal government) were among prominent northern Nigerians supporting a nationally uniform or centrally ordered local government system.[66] Lawal went as far as suggesting that the states

[62] 'Arming State Security Outfits' *Vanguard* (Lagos, 4 November 2022); Rotimi Akeredolu, 'We Believe in One Nigeria: Not One Country, Two Systems' *Premium Times* (Abuja, 22 September 2022); Ejiofor Alike, 'When Danjuma Spoke as Insider in the Military' *This Day* (Lagos, 30 October 2022).

[63] Tunde Ajala, 'Foreign Interests Sponsoring Boko Haram to Recruit Northern Children – Zulum' *Punch* (Lagos, 17 January 2021).

[64] Shettima (n 51); 'Insecurity: Religious, Traditional Rulers Have Key Roles to Play, Says Buhari' *PM News* (Lagos, 22 April 2022).

[65] Richard Sklar, 'Foundations of Federal Government in Nigeria' in Adigun Agbaje, Larry Diamond, and Ebere Onwudiwe (eds.), *Nigeria's Struggle for Democracy and Good Governance* (Ibadan University Press 2004) 3–17.

[66] Yakubu Gowon, 'The Centenary of Barewa College: Reminiscences – Past, Present and Future' *Daily Trust* (Abuja, 1 April 2021); Auwalu Yadudu, 'Avoid Taking Slippery Slope Path to Constitutional Review' *This Day* (Lagos, 15 June 2021); Queen Esther Iroanusi, 'Interview: Nigerian Governors are Parasites, Wasting Nation's Resources – Babachir Lawal' *Premium Times* (Abuja, 18 February 2020).

should be scrapped and localities elevated into Nigeria's primary subnational units, thereby effectively transforming Nigeria into a unitary state.

Many centralists, including the National Union of Local Government Employees (NULGE), also argued for transferring responsibility for conducting local government elections from the State Independent Electoral Commission (SIEC) to the federal INEC; for channeling Federation Account revenues directly to the localities, thereby bypassing the current State Joint Local Government Account; and for entrenching new constitutional regulations that would curtail the ability of state governors to supplant democratically elected local councils with appointed caretaker committees.[67]

Prominent southern political and intellectual elites, however, vehemently critiqued the centralization of the local government system. For instance, Bola Ahmed Tinubu, leading southern Nigerian politician, former governor of Lagos, and official winner of the 2023 Nigerian presidential election, denounced any constitutional amendment that would sever 'the fiscal relationship between state and local government [and] . . . transfer the passage of funds to local governments from the states to the national government in Abuja'. Such an amendment, Tinubu argued, would cause local governments 'to turn their backs on their state capitals', make 'local governments susceptible to Abuja's financial control', and thus increase the power of the federal government 'at the expense of the states'.[68]

Significantly, the Tinubu-led Lagos State Government approached the Supreme Court for a validation of the constitutional rights of the states to create new local government areas beyond the 774 localities established under the 1999 Constitution. In *AG Lagos State v AG Federation* (2004), the Court ruled that new local government areas (LGAs) created by Lagos State were legal but inchoate until their ratification by the National Assembly.[69] Given the constitutional entrenchment and centralized funding of the LGAs, however, any recognition of new LGAs by the National Assembly would have wide-ranging national legal and fiscal implications. In essence, Lagos and other states in the federation downgraded their new LGAs to local council development areas (LCDAs) or comparable constitutionally unrecognized entities.[70]

With the north and south accounting, respectively, for 419 and 355 of the country's 774 LGAs, leading scholars of the local government system from southern Nigeria consistently bemoaned the fact that the 'Constitution continued to favour the North in the number of its LGAs'.[71] The scholars argued that the regional distribution of LGAs was 'arbitrary' and based on '[political] manipulation . . . while efficiency considerations were only secondary'.[72] Furthermore, according to Itse Sagay, 'the direct funding of local governments from Abuja means that the bulk of the 20% of the Federation Account that goes to local governments ends up in the North'.[73]

[67] Emmanuel Samiala, 'NULGE Lauds National Assembly for Passing LG Autonomy Bill' *The Guardian* (Lagos, 2 August 2021).

[68] Adeola Oladele-Fayehun, 'Why Insecurity Thrives in Nigeria, by Tinubu' *The Nation* (Lagos, 25 August 2012).

[69] *AG Lagos State v AG Federation* (2004) 18 NWLR (Pt 904) 1 (SC).

[70] Ayotunde David Odewale, Bisiriyu Talaet, and Olubusayo A Ajayi, 'Creation of Local Council Development Areas in Southwestern Nigeria: A SWOT Analysis' (2018) 2(1) African Journal of Stability and Development 128–39.

[71] Alex Gboyega and others, 'Political Economy of the Petroleum Sector in Nigeria' (2011) World Bank Policy Research Working Paper 5779, 12.

[72] Ibid.; Adamolekun (n 12) 389.

[73] Sagay (n 32).

Southern criticism of a perceived northern regional bias in the configuration of the Nigerian local government system often ignored the fact that the north's larger population and much vaster land mass would justify its higher number of LGAs. Such criticism of the uniform local government system, and of the place of the north in the system, contributed to giving the agenda of decentralization, true federalism, or large-scale constitutional reform or restructuring an anti-northern character. Consequently, the north became, in the words of historian Moses Ochonu, 'the epicenter of opposition to restructuring and other fundamental reforms the union needs'.[74]

4.4 Restructuring

Prominent northern Nigerians, such as Vice President Abubakar Atiku and Governor Nasir El-Rufai, embraced southern-led agitation to revisit, reform, or redesign the basic structures and foundations of Nigeria's federal constitutional architecture.[75] They shared the belief that a fundamental decentralist reform of Nigerian federal governance would enhance national unity, development, and democracy. Nonetheless, some of the most ardent and acerbic critics of restructuring, such as President Buhari and Alhaji Muhammad Sa'ad Abubakar III (the Sultan of Sokoto), came from the north.[76] At the same time, restructuring's earliest, most vociferous, and most persistent or sympathetic protagonists and analysts were southern Nigerians.[77] North–south differences over restructuring spanned issues such as the meaning, rationale, implications, and modalities of restructuring.

Critics and sceptics of the concept of restructuring, from northern and southern Nigeria alike, including Presidents Buhari and Obasanjo, highlighted its fuzziness and elusiveness.[78] Indeed, one observer outlined ten different 'schools of thought' on Nigeria's restructuring.[79] While acknowledging the concept's imprecisions, southern supporters of restructuring were more likely to define its essence as the devolution of powers and resources from the centre to the subunits in order to create a more genuinely decentralized and successful federation. The Southern Governors' Forum, for example:

> agreed that the progress of the nation requires that urgent and bold steps be taken to restructure the Nigerian federation leading to the evolution of state police, the review of

[74] Moses Ochonu, 'Atiku's Road to Damascus on Restructuring' *Premium Times* (Abuja, 16 July 2017).

[75] Atiku Abubakar, 'The Importance of Strengthening State Economic Management Systems' *Premium Times* (Abuja, 26 April 2018); Nasir Ahmad El-Rufai, 'Next Generation Nigeria: What is Restructuring and Does Nigeria Need It?' (Chatham House Africa Programme Meeting Transcript, 21 September 2017).

[76] 'Buhari's Wrong Stance on Restructuring' *Punch* (Lagos, 23 November 2018); Bashir Adefaka, 'Sultan Joins the National Question Debate: The Restructuring Nigeria Needs' *Vanguard* (Lagos, 6 November 2016).

[77] Kunle Amuwo and others (eds.), *Federalism and Political Restructuring in Nigeria* (Spectrum Books and IFRA 1998); Musa Abutudu, 'Federalism, Political Restructuring, and the Lingering National Question' in Said Adejumobi (ed.), *Governance and Politics in Post-Military Nigeria* (Palgrave Macmillan 2010) 23–60; Osy Nwebo, 'Federalism under the 1999 Constitution: The Challenge of Restructuring and Democratic Legitimacy' in Romola Adeola and Ademola Jegede (eds.), *Governance in Nigeria Post-1999: Revisiting the Democratic New Dawn of the Fourth Republic* (Pretoria University Press 2019) 43–63; Romola Adeola, Ademola Jegede, and Asikia Karibi-Whyte, 'Restructuring Nigeria's Federalism Post-1999: How Should Nigeria Federate and Share Resources' in Romola Adeola and Ademola Jegede (eds.) ibid 145–54.

[78] 'Restructure Your Mentality First Before You Talk of Restructuring Nigeria – Obasanjo Says' (*Linda Ikeji Lagos*, 26 August 2017) <https://www.lindaikejisblog.com/2017/8/restructure-your-mentality-first-before-you-talk-of-restructuring-nigeria-obasanjo-says.html#google_vignette> accessed 14 February 2025; *Punch* (n 76).

[79] Tunde Bakare, 'Pragmatic Steps Towards Restructuring Nigeria' *Premium Times* (Abuja, 1 October 2017).

> revenue allocation formula in favor of the subnational governments, and the creation of other institutions which legitimately advance our commitment to and practice of true federalism.[80]

In addition to contesting the precise meaning(s) of restructuring, proponents and opponents of restructuring often diverged on whether or not the question of Nigerian unity was settled and non-negotiable. Southern-based newspapers such as *Punch* and *Vanguard* consistently claimed that 'Nigeria should be re-negotiated' because 'Nigerian groups feel trapped in an unfair, inequitable, unworkable, unimprovable, unproductive, hate-stirring, violent, draconian and oppressive system'.[81] President Buhari and many sceptics or critics of restructuring, on the other hand, consistently proclaimed Nigerian unity to be 'settled and not negotiable'.[82] According to Usman Sarki, '[i]t never dawned on the advocates of true federalism and restructuring that all those issues have at one point or the other in the past been discussed and resolved in Nigeria's political and constitutional history'.[83]

Northern and southern Nigerians also diverged on the ramifications of restructuring for Nigerian national unity and political stability. For its southern proponents, restructuring was pivotal to national progress and, indeed, an existential imperative. In the opinion of Governor Fayemi of the south-western state of Ekiti:

> a fundamental restructuring of Nigerian federalism is an unavoidable step for the creation and sustenance of a participatory, consensus oriented, accountable, transparent, responsive, effective and efficient, equitable and inclusive national governance and one that is based on respect for the rule of law. I am convinced that this can, and will definitely happen in Nigeria and at some point in the near future.[84]

Northern religious and judicial leaders, such as Sheikh Ahmad Abubakar Gumi and Chief Justice Ibrahim Muhammad Tanko, embraced fundamental constitutional change as a pathway to a more effective legal recognition, accommodation, or integration of Islamic sharia law in the Nigerian federation.[85] For the most part, however, northern Nigerian interlocutors portrayed restructuring as a recipe for eviscerating Nigeria's national stability. Anthony Sani, a chieftain of the northern Arewa Consultative Forum, for instance, argued that 'advocates of restructuring want different countries where some sections are on the cutting edge and some others on knife edge of survival'.[86] Indeed, Usman Sarki characterized 'the real motive behind the debates [on restructuring] as nothing short of an attempt

[80] Communiqué issued after the meeting of the governors of southern Nigeria at Government House, Asaba, Delta State, 11 May 2021.

[81] 'Buhari: Nigeria Should be Re-negotiated' *Punch* (Lagos, 3 November 2020); 'Constitution Review or New Charter' *Vanguard* (Lagos, 14 September 2020).

[82] Taiwo-Hassan Adebayo, 'Nigeria's Unity is Settled and Not Negotiable – Buhari' *Premium Times* (Abuja, 21 August 2017).

[83] Usman Sarki, 'Federalism and Restructuring: The Choice for Nigerians, 1' *Intervention* (Abuja, 11 August 2020).

[84] Kayode Fayemi, 'Reviewing Nigeria's 20 Years of Democracy' *This Day* (Lagos, 24 November 2019).

[85] Alfred Olufemi, 'Nigeria's Chief Justice Wants More Sharia in Constitution' *Premium Times* (Abuja, 13 December 2019); Ben Agande, 'Sheikh Gumi to CJN: Leave Sharia Alone, Talk about Restructuring' *Vanguard* (Lagos, 22 December 2019).

[86] Godwin Isenyo, 'Advocates of Restructuring Want Different Countries – Ex-ACF Secretary' *Punch* (Lagos, 4 November 2022).

at creating widespread instability in the country that would result in the destabilization of the government and ultimate destruction of the federal system'.[87] Consequently, according to the Northern Elders' Forum, presidential powers should be used 'to protect the territorial integrity of Nigeria and its citizens' and to contain agitation for restructuring by 'secessionists' 'irredentists', 'subversives', 'chauvinists' and 'ethnic bullies'.[88]

For many critics of restructuring, the concept of a sovereign national conference (SNC) of ethnic nationalities, popular among proponents of restructuring, underlines restructuring's potential threat to national unity. For these critics, the idea of a sovereign assemblage of contending ethnic groups—one established outside the framework of the existing Constitution and governmental authority—is a recipe or 'agenda' for anarchy, chaos, confusion, or 'regional domination and secession'.[89] From this perspective, any attempt to reform Nigeria should not deviate from the amendment procedures enshrined in the country's Constitution.

4.5 Constitutional amendment procedures

Proponents of restructuring have typically critiqued, and proposed alternatives to, the constitutional alteration procedures written into the 1999 Constitution. The official constitutional alteration procedures, to reiterate, envisage amendments that are approved by supermajorities in the National Assembly, ratified by two-thirds of state assemblies, and assented to by the president. But proponents of restructuring question the credibility and legitimacy of this amendment formula on several grounds.

First, they contend that the formula is designed only to modify or tinker with a deeply flawed 1999 Constitution: the formula is thus inappropriate for creating a new or fundamentally revised Constitution. According to President Obasanjo: 'the Nigerian Constitution does not give the National Assembly the power to write a new constitution but the power to amend the existing one. What is required is a new Constitution to meet the agitation and aspiration of all Nigerians and to allay all fears'.[90]

Second, according to this critical perspective, entrusting constitutional reform primarily to sitting legislative houses, as envisaged under current rules, 'will most likely pose a formidable opposition to the people's sovereignty' by encouraging excessive self-dealing.[91] Members of the National Assembly, for instance, could not be expected to fully embrace amendments that reduce their legislative powers or prerogatives by enhancing decentralization. Thus, as Vice President Osinbajo claimed, 'we may not get very much traction if they are asked to vote themselves, as it were, out of their current relatively decent circumstances'.[92]

[87] Sarki (n 83).

[88] Lami Sadiq and others, 'You're Complicit in Secession Bid, Northern Elders Tell Southern Governors' *Daily Trust* (Abuja, 26 May 2021).

[89] Zainab Usman, 'Does Nigeria really need a Sovereign National Conference?' *African Arguments* (London, 29 January 2014) <https://africanarguments.org/2014/01/does-nigeria-really-need-a-sovereign-national-conference-by-zainab-usman/> accessed 14 February 2025.

[90] Raymod Mordi, 'Nigeria Needs a New Constitution to Forestall Another War, Says Obasanjo' *The Nation* (Lagos, 1 March 2020).

[91] Nwebo (n 77) 44.

[92] Tunde Ajala, 'Nigeria Runs Expensive Government, There's Need for National Debate – Osinbajo' *Punch* (Lagos, 20 June 2020).

Third, despite recent electoral reforms, Nigeria's electoral process has remained violent, corrupt, and contentious. Such infringements raise questions about the credibility, representativeness, or legitimacy of Nigeria's legislative houses as institutions for producing sustainable federal democratic constitutional reforms.

Finally, in view of the solid majorities the north enjoys in national and subnational legislatures, current constitutional amendment rules seem inherently skewed towards preserving northern primacy and prerogatives. Politically dominant northern legislators, in other words, could not be expected to undermine northern ethno-regional advantages or underwrite southern-led demands for restructuring. As claimed by Femi Okunrounmu, a Yoruba proponent of restructuring and chair of President Jonathan's advisory panel on constitutional reforms, the northern 'agenda' essentially entails ensuring that all reform issues 'go to the National Assembly, where the North has the numbers to frustrate those it considers antagonistic to its interests'.[93]

The alternative constitutional reform procedures that proponents of restructuring prefer include two features not provided for under the 1999 Constitution, namely 'a sovereign national conference where all the contentious issues around the demand for restructuring will be frankly and freely discussed' and 'a plebiscite or a referendum' in which the resolutions of the conference are approved by the general population.[94] A third element, an interim government of national unity to supervise the process of rewriting a Constitution, has been advocated by some proponents of restructuring, including the noted Yoruba lawyer Afe Balola, but is less widely embraced by other reformers, including the Patriots.[95]

Founded and led by southern Nigerian legal luminaries such as Rotimi Williams and Ben Nwabueze, the Patriots proposed '[a] Bill for an Act to make provisions for convening a National Conference of the People of Nigeria for the Purpose of Preparing a Constitution for consideration and adoption by the people of Nigeria at a Referendum and matters ancillary thereto.'[96] But official national constitutional conferences convened by Nigerian presidents from the south, in 2005 and 2014, as well as an unofficial conference of ethnic nationalities promoted by the Patriots and their allies in the Pro-national Conference (Pronaco) coalition, did not significantly advance the constitutional reform process.[97] The conferences raised questions about their representativeness, produced contentious recommendations, and provoked opposition from the powerful National Assembly, as a result of which they lacked political traction. However, while these extra-constitutional procedures have largely failed, the official amendment process was arguably successful in producing modest electoral reforms.

Criticizing the promotion of extra-constitutional paths to restructuring, a governor of the north-western state of Sokoto and former Speaker of the House of Representatives, Aminu Tambuwal, argued, '[y]ou cannot go outside of the constitution to amend the constitution.'[98] Indeed, according to a spokesperson for the Kaduna State Government: 'as a

[93] Seye Olumide, 'Concern over Outcome of Confab, by Okunrounmu, Olunloyo' *The Guardian* (Lagos, 29 June 2014).

[94] Nwebo (n 77) 60.

[95] 'The Call for Interim Government' *The Sun* (Lagos, 2 May 2022).

[96] 'Statement by the Patriots Following Meeting of February 13, 2005' (*Dawodu.com*, 13 February 2005) https://dawodu.com/articles/statement-by-the-patriots-following-meeting-of-february-13-2005-933 accessed 1 October 2023.

[97] Pronational Conference (Pronaco), 'Draft of the Peoples National Conference's Proposed Constitution for the Federal Republic of Nigeria' (2007).

[98] 'Restructuring Cannot Work Without National Assembly – Tambuwal' *Vanguard* (Lagos, 23 November 2020).

body of Nigerians elected from constituencies across the country, the National Assembly is the veritable Constitutional Conference. Therefore it is not helpful to seek to traduce its legitimacy by persons who do not have any electoral mandate'.[99]

In fact, extra-constitutional measures such as a sovereign conference or an interim government indirectly challenge the legitimacy of the existing legal or political order. They could, thus, lead the country down the slippery slope of democratic breakdown, constitutional coup, and promissory military re-interventionism. A more promising path to major constitutional reform would focus on building consensus on reform among the National Assembly, state legislatures, and the presidency.

5. Beyond the impasse: Towards a national consensus on major reforms

Highlighting a north–south fault line on major issues of constitutional change should not detract from the existence of significant intra-regional differences on either side of the regional cleavage nor suggest that regional positions on constitutional issues are rigid, unchanging, or permanent, let alone imply that Nigeria is exceptional or unique in the crystallization or polarization of constitutional conflict around a north–south ethno-regional fault line. The ambiguous position of the middle belt, or central Nigeria, which is located geographically in the north but culturally and politically represents an ethno-religiously mixed buffer zone between north and south, is especially emblematic of the relative fluidity of the north–south fault line. Thus, the middle belt can be conflicted on constitutional reform, identifying with northern constitutional centralism and conservatism on some issues (for instance, the inviolability and continuity of Nigerian unity; centralized resource distribution; and a uniform local government system) while embracing southern constitutional agitation on other matters (for example, decentralized policing and restrictions on the implementation of sharia).[100]

Furthermore, regional perspectives on the country's constitutional structure and federalist future are not entirely static but can respond dynamically to broader political and economic changes. Thus, for much of the 1950s and 1960s, support for a relatively centralized multi-state federalism came from ethnic and political minorities in the north, while the region's dominant Muslim Hausa-Fulani elite supported regionalist federalism and even secession.[101] Current centralist attitudes to federalism in the core north came only with military intervention, the dissolution of the northern region into multiple states, and the growing dependency of the region on centrally collected revenue derived from the south. Similarly, the Igbo in the south-east, where secessionist sentiments have remained comparatively strong since the civil war, were the major ethnicity that was most strongly associated with an integrative centralism before the war.[102]

[99] Ibrahim Hassan, 'Restructuring, Opportunity for Nation-Building, Says el-Rufai' *Vanguard* (Lagos, 2 December 2020).

[100] Pita Agbese, 'Federalism in Nigeria: Northern Nigerian Perspectives' in Ebere Onwudiwe and others (eds.), *Nigerian Federalism in Crisis: Critical Perspectives and Political Options* (Program on Ethnic and Federal Studies, University of Ibadan 2005) 127–46; Amos Tauna, 'Middle Belt Berates Presidency's Response to Calls for Restructuring' *Daily Post* (Lagos, 8 October 2020).

[101] Agbese (n 100) 142.

[102] Onwudiwe and others (eds) (n 100) 166.

In short, it is not impossible for northern opposition to far-reaching decentralization to change. Such transformation would reflect a variety of factors, including deepening separatist Islamist challenges to the failures of a secularist multireligious Nigeria, erosion of the north's national political dominance by the ongoing routinization of federal democratic ethnic power-sharing practices, and advances in current oil prospecting projects in the north.

Overall, however, a broad regional cleavage persists on matters of constitutional reform in Nigeria, with the north typically resisting, and the south generally embracing, major decentralist federal reforms. Such north–south dissonance on foundational constitutional questions is not peculiar to Nigeria. The origins and evolution of federalism in the US, for instance, were shaped by fundamental differences between the slave-holding, more rural and agrarian southern states and the more urbanized and modernized 'free' states in the north over such foundational constitutional issues as states' rights in relation to the institution of racial slavery, the balance of power in the federal government, the admission of new federating states into the union, and the right to secession. These differences culminated in a bloody civil war that abolished the institution of slavery while preserving the American union. Nonetheless, 'racially tinged' and regionally inflected inequality, domination, exclusion, and partisan polarization continue to challenge the resilience and quality of America's federal democracy.[103]

A vicious regional conflict between a predominantly Islamic and Arabic north and a mostly black African Christian and traditionalist south also plagued Sudan right from its independence in 1956. The conflict led to two periods of violent conflict (1956–72 and 1983–2004), two major internationally mediated peace agreements (the Addis Ababa Agreement (1972–83) and the 2005 Comprehensive Peace Agreement), and the eventual dissolution of the country into two sovereign entities with the independence of the Republic of South Sudan in 2011. Significantly, Sudan's dissolution reflected the unwillingness of northern Arab Muslims in control of central power to embrace southern Sudanese demands for a pluralist federation, including the 'Nigerian option of secularizing the federation and confining the Sharia law to Muslim majority states'.[104]

Despite its relative success in containing conflicts over sharia, Nigeria continues to be vexed by an underlying historical disjuncture between northern political and demographic primacy and southern socio-economic ascendancy. The duality is reflected in scientific polls and quantitative analyses that show a greater sense of Nigerian identity and loyalty in northern than in southern Nigeria.[105] Overcoming this north–south conflict is imperative if Nigeria's constitutional architecture is to be reformed to produce a more stable, sustainable, and inclusive constitutional framework.

Building consensus across Nigeria's north–south dichotomy on major constitutional reforms would involve several interrelated measures. Nigeria's constitutional reformers should, for instance, commit to working within existing constitutional amendment rules, acknowledge the relative ingenuity and resilience (despite major shortcomings) of the country's current constitutional settlement, and intentionally de-emphasize the anti-northern rhetoric of much of the current restructuring advocacy.

[103] Steven Levitsky and Daniel Ziblatt, *How Democracies Die* (Broadway Books 2018) 227.

[104] Brendan O'Leary, 'The Federalization of Iraq and the Break-up of Sudan' (2012) 47(4) Government and Opposition 511.

[105] Anna Brigevich and Emmanuel Oritsejafor, 'Ethnic Versus National Identity and Satisfaction with Democracy: The Decline of the Ethnic Cleavage in Nigeria?' (2024) 34 (4) Regional & Federal Studies 441–472.

Reformers should also do the following: build inter-regional political guarantees into major constitutional reform demands like policing and fiscal decentralization; promote constitutional reforms that are regionally neutral or reflect a Rawlsian veil of ignorance; and utilize the putatively pan-Nigerian institution of the presidency as a veritable rallying point for mobilizing and building consensus behind major constitutional change. Finally, supporters of a political reform agenda in Nigeria could benefit from exploring and advancing opportunities for non-constitutional renewal.

Although they failed to achieve far-reaching transformations, the five rounds of alteration to the 1999 Constitution showed that constitutional amendments could be achieved in the Fourth Republic. The achievement of modest electoral reforms, in particular, highlighted the promise and prudence of working within, rather than outside, current constitutional amendment rules. Working within official amendment rules should not preclude the creative use of extra-constitutional channels. However, where extra-legislative constitutional conferences or panels are constituted, they should be designed to support rather than supplant the primary responsibility of the legislatures and the presidency for constitutional reform. Such conferences or panels should be backed by legislative resolution or enactment in order to guarantee legislators' buy-in or support.

A willingness to work within current constitutional amendment rules presupposes an acknowledgement of the relative legitimacy and resiliency of Nigeria's present constitutional settlement. A revisionist over-idealization of Nigeria's initial pre-military ethnoregionalist constitutional settlement and an under-appreciation of the merits of the current multi-state federalist compact often undermine and discredit current agitation for restructuring. Despite its many flaws, Nigeria's current constitutional framework has been relatively successful in alleviating ethnopolitical instability and preventing a recurrence of large-scale national warfare. As Vice President Osinbajo has noted, '[u]nlike many other African countries, which have known protracted multigenerational strife and perpetual division, our conflict ended after three years and we have suffered no relapse into such fratricide since then.'[106] Such achievements of multi-state federalism would suggest that some of the more radical mega-constitutional reforms, such as proposals to merge the states into larger regions or geopolitical zones, should be treated with caution.[107] Instead, emphasis should be placed on exploring reforms within the current framework of multiple constituent states.

A moderation of the proposed scale of reform would serve to reassure elements in northern Nigeria who are less enthusiastic about radical constitutional change. If, as Olisa Agbakoba acknowledges, the 'South has presented restructuring in [such] a way that the North feels threatened', then reconceptualizing some of the reform demands into more moderate or less drastic proposals would be less provocative to the north.[108] The underlying goal here is to build north–south consensus on reform by reformulating constitutional reform demands in ways that could elicit 'agreement with Northern Nigeria'.[109]

[106] Yemi Osinbajo, 'Lessons from the Civil War' *Premium Times* (Abuja, 1 February 2020).

[107] Seye Olumide and Ijeoma Thomas-Odia, 'Anyaoku Calls for Devolution of Powers to Geo-political Units' *The Guardian* (Lagos, 14 August 2016); Leke Baiyewu, 'South-West Govs Propose Six Regions, Demand LG Autonomy, Resource Control' *Punch* (Lagos, 12 July 2021).

[108] Tunde Ajala, 'Without Devolution of Power, Nigeria Going Nowhere – Agbakoba' *Punch* (Lagos, 20 December 2020).

[109] Ibid.

Current demands for subnational resource control, for instance, could be reformulated as a proposal for the devolution of more federally collected revenues on the basis of a less politicized revenue sharing formula. While the current formula redistributes revenue to subunits on the basis of inter-unit equality and relative population, for instance, the revised formula should reward accountability, prudence, and commitment to social welfare and inclusive economic development on the part of subnational governments.

Similarly, incorporating robust oversight mechanisms into proposals for police decentralization could allay fears that state police will be used to oppress ethnic minorities, victimize non-indigenes, suppress the political opposition, subvert central authority, or undermine national unity. These mechanisms, for instance, could guarantee truly independent subnational police service commissions, incorporate rules on adequate representation for minorities and non-indigenes in subnational police services, insert senior federal police officers into the operations of state police, and permit federal intervention in egregious cases of abusive subnational policing.

Another way to build consensus on change is to focus constitutional reforms on proposals that are formally ethnically neutral but practically effective in promoting intergroup equity and security. Strengthening independent oversight agencies that promote well-run elections, anti-corruption measures, and human rights can indirectly protect ethnic and political minorities and, therefore, advance intergroup peace and security. Similarly, diverse regional groups could be expected to embrace a general proposal to reduce the concentration of powers in the presidency as a means of curtailing the opportunity or propensity to abuse presidential powers for sectional advantage. Indeed, given the broad commitment in Nigeria to rotating the powerful presidency on a north–south or geopolitical basis, members of each region or geopolitical zone are equally at risk of potential abuses of presidential power. Each group is thus effectively in a state of ignorance about who would be most adversely affected by such abuses. As suggested by Horowitz, such conditions of a Rawlsian veil of ignorance, wherein the 'future of all groups is uncertain', should generate support for neutral rules that protect all groups.[110]

Despite periodic calls to abandon the presidential system, however, there is no sustained and broad commitment to returning Nigeria to the more collegiate and less personalized institution of parliamentary governance. Rather, given the vote-spread requirements governing its election, the presidency remains the most prestigious political office in the federation. The office, in theory, symbolizes Nigeria's putative multi-ethnic unity. Furthermore, the presidency, via the power to assent to all amendments, wields the final veto in the constitutional reform process. The presidency, therefore, can serve as a rallying point for galvanizing broad national consensus on constitutional reforms. A presidential committee, with representation of the country's leading ethno-regional organizations, for instance, could be established to build consensus on major reforms.

Another way to generate consensus on political reform and moderate the divisiveness of constitutional politics is to focus on opportunities for non-constitutional renewal through ordinary legislation, judicial arbitration, and informal political conventions. The National Assembly has already shown a willingness to reformulate contentious constitutional politics into less intractable legislative interventions. It has, in the past, proposed deleting from the Constitution clauses entrenching laws relating to land use, national securities, public

[110] Donald Horowitz, 'Ethnic Power Sharing: Three Big Problems' (2014) 25(2) Journal of Democracy 10.

complaints, and the National Youth Service Corps.[111] Transforming these laws from entrenched constitutional provisions into ordinary legislative enactments would give the legislature the flexibility to modify them without the rancorous politics or onerous processes associated with constitutional alterations. In a similar vein, important adjustments can be made to the revenue allocation system, including adjustments to the 13 per cent minimum derivation rule, without a constitutional amendment.

Judicial arbitration could also provide an alternative path to important political change. Several Supreme Court rulings in the Fourth Republic upholding states' rights suggest that judicial intervention can supplement constitutional reform in promoting a more decentralized federalism in Nigeria. Validating the abrogation of the onshore–offshore dichotomy, voiding federal orders or laws that encroached on subnational autonomy, promoting the financial autonomy of local authorities, and upholding the rights of the states to collect taxes relating to residual matters are some of the constructive ways in which the courts have advanced 'restructuring by litigation', as claimed by the activist lawyer Femi Falana.[112]

Informal political conventions remain the most promising avenue of non-constitutional renewal in Nigeria, however. Current practices involving the regional-cum-geopolitical rotation of the presidency, the creation of new local authorities, and the establishment of subnational security arrangements highlight the promise of informality. But perverse manifestations of informal politics also abound, including outrageous political corruption, unequal patron–client relations, rampant disobedience of court orders, violent electoral contests, and several other acts bordering on criminal politics.

Informal conventions, therefore, need to develop around more constructive practices and attitudes, such as political accountability, local community development, political toleration, national social cohesion and identity, and respect for the rule of law. Ultimately, Nigeria's political future will be shaped not only by prudent formal constitutional change but also by informal norms and conventions that support good governance even in the absence of consensus on formal reforms.

6. Conclusion

Nigeria's volatile constitutional history has seen five separate constitutions, multiple rounds of alterations to the 1999 Constitution for the Fourth Republic, and two radically different mega-constitutional settlements. The country's transition from a relatively decentralized ethno-regionalist constitutional framework to a comparatively centralized multi-state arrangement has been ethno-regionally contentious, pitting northern centralists against southern decentralists. Despite a broad recognition that Nigeria's current constitutional framework is defective and requires significant reform, a north–south dichotomy on the country's constitutional architecture and future has prevented major institutional change.

North–south divisions have prevented the decentralization of the country's dysfunctional unitary policing structure while polarizing opinions on the place of local government in the intergovernmental system. These divisions have provoked contentious debates and deadlocks on resource control and revenue sharing, generated divergent perspectives on

[111] Henry Umoru, 'How the Senate Voted on Constitution Alteration' *Vanguard* (Lagos, 30 July 2017).
[112] Femi Falana, 'The Legal Battle for Restructuring' *This Day* (Lagos, 28 January 2019).

the restructuring of the federation, and undermined the development of a political consensus on appropriate procedures for re-engineering Nigeria's constitutional structure.

Nigeria's quest for a more sustainable constitution and stable union is divided and deadlocked. That struggle is not a political dead end or inexorably doomed to failure, however. This chapter has enunciated the following interlocking pathways to achieving constructive fundamental constitutional change in Nigeria: fidelity to existing constitutional amendment rules; nuanced and balanced appreciation of the resiliency and ingenuity of the country's current multi-state federal system, despite the system's significant flaws; a concerted presidentially supported initiative for bridging the north–south chasm on Nigeria's constitutional architecture; the introduction of robust guarantees of inter-regional mutual security and equity into constitutional reform proposals; a focus on the construction of independent constitutional checks and balances and other ethnically neutral reforms; and creatively exploring, advancing, or deepening opportunities for non-constitutional renewal.

Bibliography

Abubakar A., 'The Importance of Strengthening State Economic Management Systems' *Premium Times* (Abuja, 26 April 2018)

Abuh A., Jeremiah K. and Ochojila A., 'Five Northern States Join FIRS in VAT Dispute against Rivers, Lagos' *The Guardian* (Lagos, 4 October 2021)

Abutudu M., 'Federalism, Political Restructuring, and the Lingering National Question' in Adejumobi S. (ed.), *Governance and Politics in Post-Military Nigeria* (Palgrave Macmillan 2010) 23–60

Adamolekun L., 'The Nigerian Federation at the Crossroads: The Way Forward' (2005) 35(3) Publius: The Journal of Federalism 383–405

Adamolekun L. and Kincaid J., 'The Federal Solution: Assessment and Prognosis for Nigeria and Africa' (1991) 21(4) Publius: The Journal of Federalism 173–88

Adebayo T.-H., 'Nigeria's Unity is Settled and Not Negotiable – Buhari' *Premium Times* (Abuja, 21 August 2017)

Adefaka B., 'Sultan Joins the National Question Debate: The Restructuring Nigeria Needs!' *Vanguard* (Lagos, 6 November 2016)

Adelagun O., 'Magodo: Police Officer Disobeys Sanwo-Olu over Invasion' *Premium Times* (Abuja, 5 January 2022)

Adeola R., Jegede A., and Karibi-Whyte A., 'Restructuring Nigeria's Federalism Post-1999: How Should Nigeria Federate and Share Resources' in Adeola R. and Jegede A. (eds.), *Governance in Nigeria Post-1999: Revisiting the Democratic New Dawn of the Fourth Republic* (Pretoria University Press 2019) 145–54

Adoke M., *Burden of Service: Reminiscences of Nigeria's Former Attorney-General* (Clink Street 2019) 244

Agbese P., 'Federalism in Nigeria: Northern Nigerian Perspectives' in Onwudiwe E. and Suberu R. (eds.), *Nigerian Federalism in Crisis: Critical Perspectives and Political Options* (Ibadan Program on Ethnic and Federal Studies, University of Ibadan 2005) 127–46

Agande B., 'Sheikh Gumi to CJN: Leave Sharia Alone, Talk about Restructuring' *Vanguard* (Lagos, 22 December 2019)

Ajala T., 'Nigeria Runs Expensive Government, There's Need for National Debate – Osinbajo' *Punch* (Lagos, 20 June 2020)

Ajala T., 'Without Devolution of Power, Nigeria going Nowhere – Agbakoba' *Punch* (Lagos, 20 December 2020)

Ajala T., 'Foreign Interests Sponsoring Boko Haram to Recruit Northern Children – Zulum' *Punch* (Lagos, 17 January 2021)

Ajala T., 'Legal Battle over VAT Collection Stirs Debates on Equity, Fiscal Federalism' *Punch* (Lagos, 3 October 2021)

Ajayi O., 'The Nigerian Constitution in Progress: Recent Amendments' (April 2023) https://www.olaniwunajayi.net/ accessed 1 October 2023

Akeredolu R., 'We Believe in One Nigeria; Not One Country, Two Systems' *Premium Times* (Abuja, 22 September 2022)
Akinsanmi G., 'Fresh Agitations after Constitutional Amendment' *This Day* (Lagos, 26 March 2023)
Alike E., 'When Danjuma Spoke as Insider in the Military' *This Day* (Lagos, 30 October 2022)
'Amendment of the Constitution: Matters Arising' *The Guardian* (Lagos, 14 December 2022)
Amuwo K. and others (eds.), *Federalism and Political Restructuring in Nigeria* (Ibadan Spectrum Books and IFRA 1998)
Anyaoku E., 'Nigeria on the Brink: A Message to our President and the National Assembly' *The Guardian* (Lagos, 18 July 2019)
'Arming State Security Outfits' *Vanguard* (Lagos, 4 November 2022)
Asadu C., 'State Policing is the Way Forward – Osinbajo Speaks on Building Multi-ethnic Nigeria' *The Cable* (Lagos, 7 March 2021)) https://www.thecable.ng/building-a-nation-like-nigeria-may-appear-messy-osinbajo-admits/ accessed 14 February 2025
Ashade A., 'VAT Controversy: The Need to Avoid Fiscal Anarchy' *Premium Times* (Abuja, 15 September 2021)
'A Vote for State Police' *This Day* (Lagos, 15 February 2018)
Baiyewu L., 'South–West Govs Propose Six Regions, Demand LG Autonomy, Resource Control' *Punch* (Lagos, 12 July 2021)
Bakare T., 'Pragmatic Steps Towards Restructuring Nigeria' *Premium Times* (Abuja, 1 October 2017)
Brigevich A. and Oritsejafor E., 'Ethnic Versus National Identity and Satisfaction with Democracy: The Decline of the Ethnic Cleavage in Nigeria?' (2024) 34 (4) Regional & Federal Studies 441–472.
'Buhari: Nigeria should be re-negotiated' *Punch* (Lagos, 3 November 2020)
'Buhari's Wrong Stance on Restructuring' *Punch* (Lagos, 23 November 2018)
Committee Report on the National Water Resources Bill 2020 https://placng.org/i/wp-content/uploads/2020/09/Committee-Report-on-the-National-Water-Resources-Bill-2020.pdf accessed 23 December 2022
'Constitutional Change Conference Deadlocks over Oil Dispute' (*The New Humanitarian*, 30 June 2005)
'Constitution Review or New Charter' *Vanguard* (Lagos, 14 September 2020)
Dada P., 'Agitation for Yoruba Nation Won't Succeed – Akeredolu' *Punch* (Lagos, 23 December 2022)
Danjuma T.Y., 'Revenue Sharing and the Political Economy of Nigerian Federalism' (June 1994) 1(1) Nigerian Journal of Federalism 43–68
Diamond L., 'Class, Ethnicity, and the Democratic State: Nigeria, 1950–1966' (1983) 25(3) Comparative Studies in Society and History 457–89
Diamond L., 'Issues in the Constitutional Design of a Third Nigerian Republic' (1987) 86(343) African Affairs 209–26
Dudley B., 'Federalism and the Balance of Political Power in Nigeria' (1966) 4(1) Journal of Commonwealth and Comparative Politics 16–29
El-Rufai N.A., 'Next Generation Nigeria: What is Restructuring and Does Nigeria Need it?' (Chatham House Africa Programme Meeting Transcript, 21 September 2017)
Eze C., 'New Revenue Formula: Niger Delta Demands 50 Percent Derivation' *Daily Trust* (Abuja, 11 October 2013)
Ezeamalu B., 'Nwabueze, Anyaoku, Akinrinade, Others Explain How to Restructure Nigeria' *Premium Times* (Abuja, 25 August 2017)
Falana F., 'The Legal Battle for Restructuring' *This Day* (Lagos, 28 January 2019)
Fayemi K., 'Reviewing Nigeria's 20 Years of Democracy' *This Day* (Lagos, 24 November 2019)
'Federalism: Constitution Amendment Bills Fall Short' *Punch* (Lagos, 27 March 2023)
Gbonegun V., 'Southern Leaders of Thought Seek Negotiated Restructuring via New Constitution' *The Guardian* (Lagos, 25 August 2017)
Gboyega A. and others, 'Political Economy of the Petroleum Sector in Nigeria' (2011) 5779 World Bank Policy Research Working Paper 12
Gowon Y., 'The Centenary of Barewa College: Reminiscences – Past, Present and Future' *Daily Trust* (Abuja, 1 April 2021)
Hale H., 'Divided We Stand: Institutional Sources of Ethno-federal State Survival and Collapse' (2004) 56(2) World Politics 165–93
Hassan I., 'Restructuring, Opportunity for Nation-building, Says el-Rufai' *Vanguard* (Lagos, 2 December 2020)
Horowitz D., 'The Many Uses of Federalism' (2007) 55 Drake Law Review 953–66
Horowitz D., 'Ethnic Power Sharing: Three Big Problems' (2014) 25(2) Journal of Democracy 10

Ihonvbere J., 'How to Make an Undemocratic Constitution: The Nigerian Example' (2000) 21(2) Third World Quarterly 343–66

Ikeji L., 'Restructure Your Mentality First Before You Talk of Restructuring Nigeria – Obasanjo Says' (*Linda Ikeji Lagos*, 26 August 2017) https://www.lindaikejisblog.com/2017/8/restructure-your-mentality-first-before-you-talk-of-restructuring-nigeria-obasanjo-says.html#google_vignette accessed 14 February 2025

Iroanusi Q.E., 'Interview: Nigerian Governors are Parasites, Wasting Nation's Resources – Babachir Lawal' *Premium Times* (Abuja, 18 February 2020)

Isenyo G., 'Advocates of Restructuring Want Different Countries – Ex-ACF Secretary' *Punch* (Lagos, 4 November 2022)

Kazeem M.A., 'State Policing: A Case for Devolution' in Owen O. (ed.), *Police Reform in Nigeria: The Devolution Debate* (CLEEN Foundation 2018) 22–25

'Key Issues Before Northern Delegates to the 2014 National Conference' *Vanguard* (Lagos, 12–15 May 2014)

Kirk-Greene A.H.M., *Crisis and Conflict in Nigeria: A Documentary Sourcebook 1966–1969*, vol 1 (OUP 1971)

'Lagos, Rivers Begin VAT Collection, FG, North, Disagree' *Punch* (Lagos, 15 September 2021)

Levitsky S. and Ziblatt D., *How Democracies Die* (New York Broadway Books 2018)

Mordi R., 'Nigeria Needs a New Constitution to Forestall Another War, Says Obasanjo' *The Nation* (Lagos, 1 March 2020)

Mustapha A.R., 'Ethnic Structure, Inequality and Governance of the Public Sector in Nigeria' United Nations Research Institute for Social Development, Program Paper No. 24 (November 2006)

Naku D., 'South-South Wants Oil Derivation Share Increased to 50%' *Punch* (Lagos, 9 October 2021)

'New Federal Constitution, Not a Review Needed' *Punch* (Lagos, 19 February 2020)

'Nigeria not Ripe for State Police, Jonathan Declares' *Vanguard* (Lagos, August 2012)

Njoku L., 'Opposition Mounts against Reintroduced National Water Resources Bill' *The Guardian* (Lagos, 7 September 2020)

Nwebo O., 'Federalism Under the 1999 Constitution: The Challenge of Restructuring and Democratic Legitimacy' in Adeola R. and Jegede A. (eds.), *Governance in Nigeria Post-1999: Revisiting the Democratic New Dawn of the Fourth Republic* (Pretoria University Press 2019) 43–63

Nwuke K., 'Nigeria's Petroleum Industry Act: Addressing Old Problems, Creating New Ones' *Brookings* (24 November 2021) https://www.brookings.edu/articles/nigerias-petroleum-industry-act-addressing-old-problems-creating-new-ones/ accessed 1 October 2023

Obadare E., 'Policing Breakthrough in Nigeria' (*Council on Foreign Relations*, 26 September 2022)

'Obasanjo Makes U-Turn, Says Nigeria Needs State Police to Tackle Insecurity' *The Cable* (Lagos, 22 April 2022) https://www.thecable.ng/obasanjo-makes-u-turn-says-nigeria-needs-state-police-to-tackle-insecurity/amp accessed 19 February 2023.

Ochonu M., 'Atiku's Road to Damascus on Restructuring' *Premium Times* (Abuja, 16 July 2017)

Odewale A., Talaet B., and Ojayi A., 'Creation of Local Council Development Areas in Southwestern Nigeria: A SWOT Analysis' (2018) 2(1) African Journal of Stability and Development 128–39

Ofiebor O., 'Wike Vows to Begin Collection of VAT, Warns FG' *The News* (Lagos, 8 September 2021)

Ogbu O., 'A Critical Analysis of the Constitution (First Alteration) Act' (2011–2012) 10 The Nigerian Juridical Review 49–72

Ogowewo T., 'Why the Judicial Annulment of the Constitution of 1999 is Imperative for the Survival of Nigeria's Democracy' (2000) 44(2) Journal of African Law 135–66

Okonkwo N., 'Ekweremadu, Obiozor, Others Brainstorm on Nation's Constitution' *Vanguard* (Lagos, 7 November 2015)

Oladele-Fayehun A., 'Why Insecurity Thrives in Nigeria, by Tinubu' *The Nation* (Lagos, 25 August 2012)

O'Leary B., 'The Federalization of Iraq and the Break-up of Sudan' (2012) 47(4) Government and Opposition 511

Olokor F., 'Ohanaeze, Sultan, Others Condemn Secession Bid' *Punch* (Lagos, 17 November 2020)

Olufemi A., 'Nigeria's Chief Justice Wants More Sharia in Constitution' *Premium Times* (Abuja, 13 December 2019)

Olumide S., 'Concern over Outcome of Confab, by Okunrounmu, Olunloyo' *The Guardian* (Lagos, 29 June 2014)

Olumide S. and Thomas-Oida I., 'Anyaoku Calls for Devolution of Powers to Geo-political Units' *The Guardian* (Lagos, 14 August 2016)

Omo-Agege O. and Wase A.I., 'Brief on the Press Conference by the Leadership of the Senate and the House of Representatives Committees on Constitution Review On the Progress of the 44 Constitution Amendment Bills Transferred to the State Houses of Assembly' (Abuja, 18 October 2022)

Omonijo B. and Aziken E., 'Confab in Dilemma as Southern Delegates Walk Out' *Vanguard* (Lagos, 15 June 2005)

Omorogbe P., 'PIB: How the North Secured Funding for Frontier Basins' *Nigerian Tribune* (Ibadan, 5 July 2021)

Onwudiwe E. and Sklar R., 'Nigerian Federalism as Viewed by Eastern Thinkers' in Nwudiwe E. and Suberu R., *Nigerian Federalism in Crisis: Critical Perspectives and Political Options* (Ibadan Program on Ethnic and Federal Studies, University of Ibadan 2005) 166

Onyebuchi E. and Shittu H., 'Saraki: Mistrust Triggered by Hate Speeches, Caused Rejection of Power Devolution Bill' *This Day* (Lagos, 30 July 2017)

Onyekwere J., 'Value Added Tax (VAT): Conflict and Resolving the Question of Unbalanced Fiscal Federalism' *The Guardian* (Lagos, 7 September 2021)

Osinbajo Y., 'Lessons from the Civil War' *Premium Times* (Abuja, 1 February 2020)

Oyedele T., 'How to Fix Nigeria's Broken VAT System' (*PWC*, undated) https://www.pwc.com/ng/en/assets/pdf/how-to-fix-nigeria-broken-vat-system.pdf accessed 14 June 2023

Pérouse de Montclos M.A., 'The Politics and Crisis of the Petroleum Industry Bill in Nigeria' (2014) 52(3) Journal of Modern African Studies 403–24

Pronational Conference (Pronaco), 'Draft of the Peoples National Conference's Proposed Constitution for the Federal Republic of Nigeria' (Pronaco 2007)

'Restructuring cannot work without National Assembly – Tambuwal' *Vanguard* (Lagos, 23 November 2020)

Sadiq L. and others, 'You're Complicit in Secession Bid, Northern Elders Tell Southern Governors' *Daily Trust* (Abuja, 26 May 2021)

Sagay I., 'Nigeria: Federalism, the Constitution, and Resource Control' (Text of speech delivered at the fourth sensitization programme held by the Ibori Vanguard at the Lagoon Restaurant, Lagos, 19 May 2001)

Samiala E., 'NULGE Lauds National Assembly for Passing LG Autonomy Bill' *The Guardian* (Lagos, 2 August 2021)

Sarki U., 'Federalism and Restructuring: The Choice for Nigerians, 1' *Intervention* (Abuja, 11 August 2020)

Shettima K., 'State Policing: A Case for Concern about Devolution' in Owen O. (ed.), *Police Reform in Nigeria: The Devolution Debate* (CLEEN Foundation 2018) 26–29

Shettima K., 'Insecurity: Religious, Traditional Rulers Have Key Roles to Play, Says Buhari' *PM News* (Lagos, 22 April 2022)

Sklar R., 'Foundations of Federal Government in Nigeria' in Agbaje A., Diamond L., and Onwudiwe E. (eds.), *Nigeria's Struggle for Democracy and Good Governance* (Ibadan University Press 2004) 3–17

Smith B., 'Federal-state Relations in Nigeria' (1981) 80(320) African Affairs 355–78

Soludo C., 'Reconstructing Nigeria for Prosperity' *This Day* (Lagos, 17 September 2012)

'Southern Leaders Unveil 5-Point Agenda for Restructuring' *PM News* (Lagos, 4 September 2017)

Soyinka W., 'MLK's Mighty Stream of Righteousness' *Premium Times* (Abuja, 27 August 2020)

'Statement by the Patriots Following Meeting of February 13, 2005' (*Dwawodu.com*, 13 February 2005) https://dawodu.com/articles/statement-by-the-patriots-following-meeting-of-february-13-2005-933 accessed 1 October 2023

Suberu R.T., *Federalism and Ethnic Conflict* (United States Institute of Peace Press 2001)

Suberu R.T., 'Federalism and Constitutional Reform in the Fourth Nigerian Republic: Progress, Problems and Prospects' (January 2015) National Institute for Legislative Studies Occasional Paper Series No. 1

Suberu R.T., 'Managing Constitutional Change in the Nigerian Federation' (2015) 45(4) Publius: The Journal of Federalism 552–79

Suberu R.T., 'Federalism and the First Republic of Nigeria, 1960–1966' in Falola T. and Heaton M. (eds.), *Oxford Handbook of Nigerian History* (OUP 2022) 377–98

Tauna A., 'Middle Belt Berates Presidency's Response to Calls for Restructuring' *Daily Post* (Lagos, 8 October 2020)

'The Call for Interim Government' *The Sun* (Lagos, 2 May 2022)

'The Hydra-headed Fourth Alteration' (*Law Pavilion*, 27 June 2019) https://lawpavilion.com/blog/the-hydra-headed-fourth-alteration/ accessed 14 June 2023

Umoru H., 'State Police: It is Northern vs Southern Governors' *Vanguard* (Lagos, 2 September 2012)

Umoru H., 'How the Senate Voted on Constitution Alteration' *Vanguard* (Lagos, 30 July 2017)

Usman Z., 'Does Nigeria Really Need a Sovereign National Conference?' *African Arguments* (London, 29 January 2014)<https://africanarguments.org/2014/01/does-nigeria-really-need-a-sovereign-national-conference-by-zainab-usman/> accessed 14 February 2025

'Why State Police is Not an Option – President Buhari' *Sahara Reporters, New York* (5 January 2022)<https://saharareporters.com/2022/01/05/why-state-police-not-option-%E2%80%94president-buhari> accessed 14 February 2025.

Yadudu A., 'Avoid Taking Slippery Slope Path to Constitutional Review' *This Day* (Lagos, 15 June 2021)

11

Constitutional Adaptation and Change in Ethiopia

Assefa Fiseha

1. Introduction

There have been several demands for constitutional amendment in Ethiopia. Among the most common issues contested by experts and political parties are the type of federal system; constitutional dispute-resolution mechanisms (including the role of the judiciary and the mandate of the second chamber of Parliament); the rights of minorities; the protection and enforcement of human rights; relations between party and state institutions; language policy; and the country's system of government (a debate involving a possible shift to a presidential system). While there has been no formal amendment of the Constitution of Ethiopia (1995), there have been significant changes to its spirit. After an introduction that explains the instability in Ethiopia's constitutional system—largely the result of a non-inclusive political tradition—this chapter examines how the Ethiopian Constitution has been adapted since its proclamation in 1995. The South African Constitution, which is more or less the same age, has been formally amended twenty times; by contrast, Ethiopia has never formally amended its Constitution.

The question, then, is how has the Constitution been adapted over time? What are the modes of constitutional adaptation in Ethiopia? What is the level of disharmony between the Constitution and practice, and how does one account for it? Who are the main actors in this process? Could any change to the Constitution be considered a valid adaptation? Should political institutions, including parties, be given wide discretion to change essential parts of the Constitution without any restriction? If so, would the Constitution still be worth its name?

These are basic issues seldom explored in the debate on constitutional issues in Ethiopia, and it is a gap which this contribution aims to address. The chapter shows that, while there have been only two (incomplete) attempts at constitutional amendment in Ethiopia, constitutional changes by different organs remain the predominant practice. To demonstrate this, section 2 briefly sets out the political context in Ethiopia. Section 3 then describes an incomplete process of formal constitutional amendment—a rare practice in the literature on constitutional amendment. Section 4 examines constitutional interpretation as a way of adapting the Constitution. Section 5 discusses various changes that have been made to the Constitution, with the focus on a policy-design and political decision-making process that has significantly reshaped the Constitution—meaning the actual Constitution, which has come to differ in some essential respects from the written Constitution. The last section (section 6) contains a short conclusion.

Assefa Fiseha, *Constitutional Adaptation and Change in Ethiopia* In: *Constitutional Change and Constitutionalism in Africa*. Edited by: Charles M. Fombad and Nico Steytler, Oxford University Press. © Assefa Fiseha 2025. DOI: 10.1093/9780198957034.003.0013

2. Lack of political inclusivity; lack of constitutional stability

Despite its long history, Ethiopia's constitutional system demonstrates discontinuity and disruption, with each successive regime aspiring to break away from the past. In 1931, Emperor Haile Selassie (who reigned from 1930–74) proclaimed Ethiopia's first written constitution, which was revised significantly in 1955 following the United Nations' decision to 'federate' Eritrea with Ethiopia. Both constitutions were grants from the emperor and used, in effect, to consolidate his absolute power. Following the revolution in 1974 that brought the monarchy to an end, the military junta, the Derg (1974–91), ruled the country by decree until 1987. When the junta consolidated its power by eliminating its opponents, it felt it necessary to have a socialist constitution inspired by that of the USSR, its main ally. This constitution (1987–91), was a short-lived one and, as in the imperial era, served merely to legitimate and fortify Ethiopia's then ruling powers.

Opposition to the Derg soon began calling for a return to civilian rule, ethnonational accommodation, and religious and gender equality. Absent a political solution to the demands, rebel forces emerged in Eritrea and Tigray. Towards the end of 1980s, the military, representing the centrist political elite and its 'centralized nation-building' project through socialism, was losing ground. The Ethiopian People's Revolutionary Democratic Front (EPRDF) and Eritrean rebels had already succeeded in defeating the military, yet there was a last attempt, made in London in May 1991, to bring a peaceful end to the raging civil war. The conference brought together the Derg and the rebel forces, represented mainly by the Eritrean People's Liberation Front (EPLF) and Tigray People's Liberation Front (TPLF). But realizing the weakening of the Derg, its delegates lost interest in pursuing the peace process. Then, on 21 May 1991, Mengistu Haile Mariam, the president and head of the Derg, went into exile in Zimbabwe.

Following the regime's collapse, the EPRDF and EPLF were ready to fill the political vacuum by seizing control of Addis Ababa and Asmara, respectively. These groups were later joined by the Oromo Liberation Front (OLF), which was partly a product of the student movement of the 1970s that had long supported the right to self-determination of the Oromos, Ethiopia's largest ethnonational group (comprising 35 per cent of the population). The groups made a joint statement confirming the need for a broad-based Transitional Government of Ethiopia (TGE). A national conference on transition was duly convened in Addis Ababa from 1–5 July 1991, and attended by some 27 political parties.[1]

The conference led to the signing of the transitional-period Charter, which served as an interim constitution from 1991 to 1994 and was repealed with the adoption of the 1995 Constitution. As regards the early phase of the TGE (1991–92), one could state firmly that the TGE was the most inclusive government the country had had in its entire history, and although it was not elected, it was able to represent contending views and communities. Yet some centrist groups, including the former regime's party, the Workers Party of Ethiopia, and the Ethiopian People's Revolutionary Party (EPRP), were left out, allegedly for 'their unwillingness to renounce violence as a means to achieve political ends'.[2] Given

[1] For detail on the transitional period, see Sarah Vaughan, *The Addis Ababa Transitional Conference of July 1991: Its Origins, History and Significance* (Centre of African Studies, University of Edinburgh 1994).

[2] Sarah Vaughan, 'Ethnicity and Power in Ethiopia' (PhD thesis, University of Edinburgh 2003).

the marginalization of centrist parties like these, the ethnonational liberation forces, along with the chief architect of the Derg's overthrow, the EPRDF, enjoyed an easy ride into the constitution-making process and the reshaping of post-1991 Ethiopia.

The TGE faced challenges as it entered its second year. Both the principles on which the state was to be reorganized and the period of time in which regional elections, scheduled for June 1992, were to be conducted were the subject of contestation. While the OLF and the All Amhara People's Organization sought a postponement, maintaining that they needed more time to prepare for competing in the regions, the EPRDF insisted on proceeding as scheduled. The centrist elite had long advocated a centralized unitary state, and when it realized this option would make it unpopular, given the nature of political cleavages in Ethiopia, and the country's countless national liberation movements, it would often resort to 'geographic federalism'. This policy position entailed dividing major ethnonational groups into many smaller states, as is the case in Nigeria, which was a non-starter for the victorious national liberation fronts that were keen to procure self-government for their respective groups.

In addition, the OLF found itself in a deadlock with the EPRDF, which alleged that it had allied itself with another Oromo group, the Oromo People's Democratic Organization (OPDO)—a group regarded as a 'puppet' by Oromo elites. This infuriated the OLF, which saw itself as the only legitimate Oromo party[3] and withdrew from the government. Its leaders went into exile, where they remained until winds of change in the country in 2018 saw them begin to return.

Thus, while the conference of 1991 began as an inclusive affair that in turn led to a fairly inclusive TGE, the TGE became increasingly less inclusive towards the end of its term. It is hard to disagree with Marina Ottaway's characterization of the last few years of the transition: 'It [was] a formal process devoid of content. The spirit of the democratic transition was missing completely as democratization became a purely formal exercise, [with] the major contenders of power from the opposition missing throughout.'[4]

Yet, exclusion and marginalization have a long history in Ethiopia, where they are among the country's deep-seated problems. If one reflects on recent political history, the military junta (1974–91) thought it could marginalize a section of society, but it was that very section of society (Eritrean and Tigrayan rebels) that dismantled its regime in 1991. The EPRDF (1991–2018), too, thought it could marginalize a section of society, in this case the centrist elite (except, of course, during 1991–92 and then 2005–10). Ethiopia held a more open multiparty election in 2005 but the results were contested by the opposition, resulting in post-election crisis and the subsequent arrest of key opposition political party leaders. EPRDF's hegemonic and authoritarian rule continued leading to widespread protests in 2015, both in Oromia and Amhara regional states. The political developments since 2018 show that the centrist elite is in charge after dislodging the TPLF. The Prosperity Party (PP)[5] now imagines it can consolidate its power without Tigray, and by marginalizing

[3] For detail, see Merera Gudina, *Ethiopia: Competing Ethnic Nationalisms and the Quest for Democracy 1960–2000* (Shaker Publishing 2003) 102–05.

[4] Marina Ottaway, 'The Ethiopian Transition: Democratization or New Authoritarianism?' (2005) 2(3) Northeast African Studies 67, 73.

[5] The EPRDF morphed into the Prosperity Party (PP) in 2019 after the withdrawal of the TPLF and the dissolution of its former coalition members, which have been reduced to branches of the PP's headquarters in Addis Ababa. The PP also lost the class element that bound together the EPRDF. With the decline of class and ideology as touchstones of political mobilization, ethnonationalism has engulfed the PP, and the country at large, since 2018.

major political parties from Oromia such as the OLF and Oromo Federalist Congress (OFC). Thus, the cycle of exclusion and marginalization keeps turning, with those who are left out continuing to threaten the extant regime. Groups alternate power to such an extent that Ethiopia has in a way *institutionalized political fragility*.[6] Those in power marginalize other major actors, while those who are left out eventually win and come back to repeat the same mistake—and so the cycle repeats itself. Fragility has thus indeed been institutionalized in Ethiopia. The lesson this holds is that deeply divided countries such as Ethiopia cannot ensure constitutional and political stability without designing an all-inclusive constitutional and political system.

3. Formal amendment

In 1995, Ethiopia adopted a federal system with nine states. A federation arises from a bargain between centripetal and centrifugal forces. This pact has to be enshrined in a constitution which is supreme and that binds both the federal government and the states in such a way as to ensure that what has been agreed upon cannot be changed unilaterally by either level of government. To that extent, federal constitutions must be rigid, and require the participation of both the federal government and states in their amendment. If the federal constitution contains the principles governing the relationship between the federal government and states, and if the authority of both governments derives from the constitution, then it follows that, for its supremacy to be ensured, the constitution should not be subject to unilateral alteration by either order of government.

Indeed, the idea of a federation as a compact demands that, where introducing formal changes to the federal constitution is deemed necessary, both the federal government and the states (through their government or their people) must participate in the amendment process. According to Carl Friedrich, the participation of the states in the amendment of the constitution is a key feature of a federation.[7] Furthermore, if the supremacy of the constitution is to be maintained, it should not be easily changed. That the amendment procedure should be rigid is hence also a requirement.[8] Constitutions change and adapt, and an agreed method for achieving constitutional adjustments as the need arises is often the key to the continued success of a federation.

However, this broad principle aside, federal constitutions differ significantly both as regards the specific procedures they prescribe for their amendment and the degree to which states are required to participate in any such amendment. On the one hand, we have federations that require the consent of every state for any amendment, or which entrench an eternity clause;[9] on the other, we have federations where an ordinary vote of the federal parliament suffices for amending the constitution, as is the case in India.[10]

[6] For detail, see Assefa Fiseha, 'Transition to Democracy in Deeply Divided Ethiopia: Mission Impossible' (2022) 39(2) Journal of Global South Studies 257–301.

[7] Carl Friedrich, *Trends of Federalism in Theory and Practice* (Praeger 1968) 6–7.

[8] DJ Kriek, 'The Rigidity of the Constitution' in DJ Kriek (ed.), *Federalism: The Solution?* (HSRC Publishers 1992) 57–58. The term 'rigidity' means here that the procedures for amending the constitution differ from the procedures for amending an ordinary law. Often the former require a more rigorous procedure than the latter.

[9] US Constitution, art v.

[10] Indian Constitution, art 368.

The Ethiopian Constitution has a highly rigid procedure for constitutional amendment. In principle, the Constitution does not incorporate unamendable provisions, as is the case in the German Basic Law under its article 79, which requires the participation of both the federal and state governments in all amendment cases. Some of the provisions in the Ethiopian Constitution, especially those prescribing the procedure for amendment itself and those governing fundamental rights and freedoms, can be amended only if approved by a majority vote in all the states and by a two-thirds majority vote in each of the federal houses.[11] The majority of the provisions, including those governing the relationship between the federal and state governments, can be amended only if approved by a two-thirds majority vote in a joint session of both federal houses, and by a simple majority vote of the legislative councils of two-thirds of states.[12] Yet this is misleading. Political actors often find ways of making changes to the Constitution without necessarily adhering to the formal amendment procedures.[13] Thus, formal procedures alone might not give one a sufficiently detailed idea of the rigidity of the Constitution.

3.1 Incomplete process of constitutional amendment

Ethiopia has not amended its Constitution according to the procedures it has for such an exercise. There are, however, two contentious exceptions where an effort has been made to amend the Constitution but the amendment remains incomplete: one is related to concurrent tax, and the other to the number of constituent units in the Ethiopian federation.

3.1.1 Concurrent tax

Article 98 of the Constitution provides the following:

1. The Federal Government and the States shall jointly levy and collect profit, sales, excise and personal income taxes on enterprises they jointly establish.
2. They shall jointly levy and collect taxes on the profits of companies and on dividends due to shareholders.
3 They shall jointly levy and collect taxes on incomes derived from large-scale mining and all petroleum and gas operations, and royalties on such operations.

Although these clauses prescribe a concurrent tax, in practice jointly levying and collecting concurrent taxes was found to be difficult owing to the lack of reliable data at either level of government and to the problems attendant to trying to coordinate the actions of these two levels. This led to a proposal in 1997 for a formal amendment that would allow the federal government to levy and collect concurrent taxes. Under the proposal, concurrent taxes would be levied and administered (collected) by the federal government, whereas the states would share the revenue on the basis of a formula designed by the House of Federation

[11] Ethiopian Constitution, art 105(1)(a), (b) and (c).

[12] Ibid. art 105(2)(b).

[13] This is an area not well-researched in Ethiopia. The only work in this regard is Nigussie Afesha, 'The Practice of Informal Changes to the Ethiopian Constitution in the Course of Application' (2016) 10(2) Mizan Law Review 366–99.

(HoF) as per article 62(7) of the Constitution. However, there is widespread agreement among members of the HoF that the proposal for amendment was tabled before the two federal houses or regional states had endorsed it, and that it had not been proclaimed formally or promulgated in the federal *Negarit Gazetta* (the official law gazette of the federal government), as required.

At a meeting of stakeholders in Bar Dar in 2015, disagreement arose as to whether the proposal should be considered an amendment to the Constitution or not. In actuality, federal and regional states are operating on the basis of the 'amended' article, but one cannot find the proclamation of amendment in a *Negarit Gazetta.* This is odd indeed, because the then ruling party, the EPRDF, had full control of all legislative bodies at federal and regional state level and could have secured the necessary votes to proclaim the proposed amendment without difficulty—yet the process ended before it could reach completion. As a result, operative practice, along with the incomplete process of amendment, has changed the spirit, if not the letter, of the Constitution. This is an indication of reformers' disregard of the procedures set out in the Constitution. Disregard of constitutional procedures is also evident in the case of the changes that were made to the number of constituent units in the country—an issue briefly discussed below.[14]

3.1.2 The number of constituent units

Article 47 of the Constitution names and specifies the number of constituent units in Ethiopia, while article 47(3) sets out the procedures that are required for establishing a new regional state:

The right of any Nation, Nationality or People to form its own state is exercisable under the following procedures:

a) When the demand for statehood has been approved by a two-thirds majority of the members of the Council of the Nation, Nationality or People concerned, and the demand is presented in writing to the State Council;
b) When the Council that received the demand has organized a referendum within one year to be held in the Nation, Nationality or People that made the demand;
c) When the demand for statehood is supported by a majority vote in the referendum; [and]
d) When the State Council will have transferred its powers to the Nation, Nationality or People that made the demand.

In short, establishing a new regional state requires a two-thirds majority vote of the local council that represents the particular community; the request then has to be submitted to the regional state council, which, within a year of the request, has to hold a referendum in which the specified community votes by a majority for a new regional state.

Ethiopia is highly diverse and the second-most populous country in Africa; as such, nine states are certainly not enough to ensure the principle of self-government, which is one of the pillars of the Constitution. As a result, numerous demands have been made for new

[14] See Richard Albert, *Constitutional Amendments: Making, Breaking and Changing Constitutions* (OUP 2019) 110–11. Albert examines cultures of constitutional amendment and assesses whether actors adhere to procedures set out in the constitution or neglect these procedures and change the constitution by other means.

constituent units. The ruling EPRDF was, however, reluctant to concede to them, as its focus was on economic growth rather than political reform. But after the winds of change that resulted in the election of Abiy Ahmed as the leader of the party and, subsequently, as prime minister in 2018, the Southern Nations, Nationalities and Peoples' Regional State (SNNPR) faced mounting challenges related to demands for self-government.

The SNNPR is distinct because it hosts some 56 different groups, unlike other regional states, which are dominated by a single ethnonational group. In an assertion of their new-found autonomy, different subunits in the SNNPR threatened the southern-member coalition of the ruling party. During the transitional period (1991–94), the 56 ethnonational groups were organized into five states, before being merged to form what became the SNNPR in 1995. The then leaders of Ethiopia used carrot-and-stick tactics to abolish the five states and form a single entity without creating consensus. On the one hand, ethnonational groups such as the Sidama and Wolayta have long-standing claims for self-rule and thus continue to demand their own regional states.[15] On the other, affording self-rule to 56 different groups (some of them with only a few thousand people) would be a nightmare for the ruling party; nor were there enough resources and expertise to run the government, given that Ethiopia was a new federation. Instead of having too many small states, the leaders wanted a relatively bigger Southern state with possible self-rule arrangements at the local level (in the form of zones and special *woredas*).

To achieve this complex objective of making the relatively bigger ethnonational groups such as the Sidama and Wolayta happy and keeping the south unified, the ruling party reserved key positions for the Sidama and Wolayta (the second-most influential group in the south, and former Prime Minister Haile Mariam's ethnic base) and created some twenty ethnic-based local governments with elected councils as well as executive and judicial powers. The process was not necessarily entirely consensual, but certainly the elite in the south was engaged in it. The ruling party also tried to keep balance between the two bigger groups—for instance, if a Sidama became a party chair or regional state president, then a Wolayta became a deputy party chair or deputy regional state president (or vice versa). This worked reasonably well in a tight party system. Indeed, some used to call the south a federation within a federation, with this regional state being fairly peaceful and better able to build a multitude of small cities at the zonal level than other such states.

But in 2018 two factors triggered a challenge to this complex arrangement: political liberalization and power struggle. With the coming to power of Abiy Ahmed, and his promise to democratize Ethiopia, unhappy political elites in the south wanted to have their own regional states instead of staying under one regional state. The fragmentation within the ruling party was seen as a perfect time to assert new-found autonomy, and thus it was that eleven local governments decided they each wanted to have their own states. They followed the constitutional procedures and applied to the regional state council and relevant federal authorities (the HoF and the National Electoral Board of Ethiopia, or NEBE) for regional statehood.[16]

[15] For detail, see Shiferaw Muleta, 'Chronicles of Sidama People's Struggle for Self-rule' (*Addis Standard*, Special Issue, 30 May 2019) http://addisstandard.com/special-edition-chronicles-of-sidama-peoples-struggle-for-self-rule/ accessed 1 October 2023.

[16] See Samson Berhane, 'A Renewed Push for Statehood Raises More Questions than Answers' (*The Reporter*, 6 August 2022) https://www.thereporterethiopia.com/25590/ accessed 25 October 2023.

A second factor was the power struggle between Shiferaw Shigute (of the Sidama, and a former deputy chair of the party from the SNNP) and Hailemariam Desalegn (the former prime minister from Wolayta). In the bid to elect the new prime minister following the resignation of Hailemariam at the height of the political crisis in 2017 and early 2018, the EPRDF was divided.[17] Some coalition members wanted a premier from the Oromo Democratic Party (ODP), while others wanted Shiferaw Shigute from the south. When Ahmed was elected by a majority vote, Shigute was unhappy and sought to deliver at local level while presumably knowing that he would not survive the political wave. Shigute, who knew well how the SNNPR operates, asked the Sidama elite to trigger an application for regional statehood at the local level. He had been blamed for long by his ethnic group for suppressing an age-old demand for regional statehood and no doubt thought it an opportune time for payback. Shigute must have been well aware that if the Sidama began to claim statehood, other groups would invariably follow suit, which would mean the end of the south as a regional state and the emergence instead of many new regional states. That is exactly what happened: the Sidama requested statehood, after which the Wolayta—and then nine others—did the same thing.

The federal government and the new leaders of the Southern coalition did not know what to do, as the pace of change was too fast and was coming at a time when the government had promised 'political freedom and transition to democracy'. Yet, with the exception of the Sidama case—which made it all the way to NEBE—the ten other demands were withheld by the then ruling party and never tabled before the SNNPR council, as required by the federal and regional state constitutions.

Even the Sidama case did not go as planned. The federal government and NEBE, busy as they were in undergoing political reforms, failed to respond within a year, by the end of July 2019. Unhappy with the situation, Sidama youth, working in cooperation with the Sidama elite in the regional state, chose to declare regional statehood on their own and indicated mid-July 2019 as the deadline. The local political elite mobilized the youth as well as the local population at large, declaring their readiness for de facto regional statehood by mid-July 2019. Yet, many other issues remained unresolved, including the status of the capital Hawassa (a multi-ethnic city which has seen a great deal of investment by the federal and regional governments over the past three decades); border tensions that could erupt with Wolayta and Oromia when the Sidama exercised statehood; and the rights of minorities in the new Sidama regional state.

Thus, when the local political elite mobilized itself, the SNNPR and federal government were in panic. They were unprepared for the consequences, and there had been no real engagement on political solutions. The NEBE was undergoing reform and did not have the institutional wherewithal to make a decision. The result was a deadlock: local youth and the Sidama elite vying for statehood, and the SNNPR and federal government in panic.

Matters came to a head when the NEBE made a decision following the appointment of a full board, saying that it could facilitate the demand for statehood only in November 2019. Local elites lost patience and began to protest. The federal government sent in the army, and clashes between the military and protestors led to deaths and the destruction of property. An emergency was declared, and the Southern state placed under military rule. When the

[17] Interview with a member of the SNNPR Council in Hawassa, 15 November 2018.

referendum was finally held, it saw overwhelming support for a new state and the emergence in June 2020 of the Sidama Region as Ethiopia's tenth state.

Following the procedures set out in the federal and SNNPR constitutions, another new state, the South West Region, soon joined it, becoming the country's eleventh state in 2021.[18] The South West Region is diverse in its ethnic composition and the result of an unhappy compromise among the different groups. The main reason for granting it statehood was related to convenience. It was too far to be administered from the SNNPR capital of Hawassa—despite its enormous potential for growth, it remained a hotspot for various kinds of conflict, and the regional state was too far away to provide a much-needed political solution.

As a result of the birth of two new states from the SNNPR, the number of states in Ethiopia has increased from nine to twelve. Nevertheless, the federal Constitution's article 46, which declares that Ethiopia has nine states, has not been amended to reflect the four new states. Indeed, neither the federal government nor the SNNPR have shown much interest in wanting to do so. The emergence of two new states has not ended the demand for more states in the SNNPR either. Several of the zones and special *woredas* in the SNNPR have requested statehood and complied with the procedures stipulated under article 47. At the time of writing, two more new states emerged from the SNNPR.[19]

At first, the regional state council was not willing to take further steps once the Sidama and South West cases were settled. Experts indicate that the ruling party was not willing to see the proliferation of new states, and had blocked the council from making the decisions needed to facilitate a referendum.[20] However, after facing mounting pressure, the ruling party conceded to some demands, albeit only partially, as in most cases the response did not align with the demands. The ruling party resorted to what it calls 'clusters' (or small-scale replicas of the SNNPR, focusing on administrative convenience), instead of addressing the demand for self-government by ethnonational groups as promised in the Constitution. Except the Sidama, all three new states are inhabited by diverse groups and 'clustering' does not address the demand for self-government by ethno-national groups.

The party, thus, in one way or another continues to backtrack on its promises. As in the Sidama and South West cases, the federal Constitution's listing of the states as nine in number has not been amended. In actuality, Ethiopia has twelve states, but as a matter of constitutionality only nine. As noted previously, the ruling party has control of federal and

[18] Kaffa, Sheka, Bench Sheko, Dawuro, and West Omo Zones, and Konta Special Woreda are now part of the new South West State. See 'Ethiopia Gets Eleventh State with More than 96% Approval for South West Referendum' (*Addis Standard*, 9 October 2021) https://addisstandard.com/news-alert-ethiopia-gets-eleventh-state-with-more-than-96-approval-for-south-west-referendum/#:~:text=Addis%20Abeba%2C%20October%209%2F2021,Zones%2C%20as%20well%20as%20Konta accessed 1 October 2023.

[19] The Konso, Gedeo, Gamo, Gofa, South Omo, and Wolayta Zones, as well as the local council members of five special *woredas* (namely Amaro, Ale, Basketo, Burji and Derashe), voted to restructure their administrative units into a newly organized regional state. The Wolayta, Gamo, Gofa, and other diverse communities in South Omo were 'clustered' as one state, denying age-old demands by the Wolayta for their own state. Another 'cluster' state emerged for the Gurage, Hadiya, Halaba, Kembata Tmbaro, and Silte Zones, as well as the Yem Special Woreda, which voted to restructure their respective administrative units to form another new regional state. This is ironic because in the early 1990s an effort to establish a state—one inhabited by the Wolayta, Gamo, Gofa, and Dawro, under the rubric of WoGaGoDa—was rejected; now one of the states has simply brought that project back to life. See Data Dea, 'Enduring Issues in State-Society in Ethiopia: A Case Study of the WoGaGoDa Conflict in Wolaita Southern Ethiopia' (2005/2006) 2(1/2) International Journal of Ethiopian Studies 141–59.

[20] Wolayta, Hadiya, Guraghe, and Silte are some of the zones to have demanded statehood (interview with former Deputy Speaker of SNNPR in Hawassa, 15 May 2021).

regional elected bodies, and thus the failure to comply is not because it lacks a majority but because it disregards constitutional principles and procedures.

4. Adaptation through interpretation: Extending term limits beyond constitutional limits

Ethiopia, unlike many other countries, has empowered its second chamber, the HoF—a non-legislative second chamber and political organ that represents the different ethnonational groups in the country—to adjudicate constitutional disputes and umpire federalism. The Constitution is considered as the reflection of the 'free will and consent' of the nationalities. It is, in the words of the framers, 'a political contract', and therefore only the authors, namely the nationalities, are vested with the power of interpreting the Constitution. Article 61(2) of the Constitution stipulates that 'each Nation, Nationality and People shall be represented in the HoF by at least one member. Each Nation or Nationality shall be represented by one additional representative for each one million of its population.' As a result, the nationality with the largest number of people has as many seats as its size may allow in the HoF. As of 2005, state governors, the highest political figures in the states, have been among the key members sent to represent the states and nationalities in the HoF and to decide crucial issues such as constitutional interpretation and the federal subsidy allocated to each state. Political reality dictated by ethnonationalist-based mobilization and ideological commitment seem to be the explanations for this distinct constitutional design.

Given that interpreting the Constitution and resolving constitutional disputes require technical legal expertise, the HoF is assisted by the Council of Constitutional Inquiry (CCI), a body composed of eight legal experts (two of whom are the president of the Federal Supreme Court and the deputy), appointed by the president of the country, along with three members of the HoF. The role of the CCI is to provide advisory opinions to the HoF. The cases first have to be submitted to the CCI; the legal opinion, along with the case, is then submitted to the HoF for a decision when the CCI thinks that the case calls for constitutional interpretation. The HoF has the discretion to adopt, modify, or reject the CCI's opinion.

Ethiopia was scheduled to hold its sixth countrywide and regional state elections in May 2020. However, the newly appointed NEBE announced on 31 March 2020 that it could not hold the election due to restrictions imposed in response to Covid-19. The announcement triggered debate on how to engage with two major issues: managing the health crisis and addressing election-related deadlock. The ruling party issued an emergency decree followed by detailed regulations, to address the pandemic, but the postponement of the election remained a major issue, as the mandate of the federal government and the then nine regional states was due to end on the first week of October 2020. The Constitution expressly sets the term limit of the federal and regional state legislative bodies at five years, and, in article 9, prohibits any means of assuming power other than by elections.

The House of People's Representatives requested constitutional advice from the HoF, which referred the matter to the CCI. One can safely assume that the government selected this route considering the fact that it had sufficient votes to secure the kind of constitutional opinion it desired, given that the ruling party controls the HoF entirely. The CCI, after holding a public hearing that excluded those who were suspected of having opinions the government might not like, decided that the elections could be postponed until Parliament decided that Covid-19 was no longer a public health threat. It also extended the term of Parliament and regional state councils until the sixth general elections were held. This decision was endorsed by the HoF.

There is no agreement among scholars on whether the Constitution could be interpreted to allow the postponement of the elections and the extension of the term of Parliament, given that there is an express clause in the Constitution that sets a five-year term. There is, however, general agreement that the process and the decision of the CCI and HoF were deeply flawed. The public hearing was less than inclusive of diverse views on the matter. First, the CCI did not recommend putting a limit on the powers which the government could exercise during the extended period. As per the recommendations of the CCI and the decision of the HoF, the government was allowed to act as if it were within its term limit. Second, the CCI recommended that the government be in charge of deciding if and when the sixth national elections would be held. Third, the CCI did not require inclusivity in the government. The government was not enjoined to consult regional states and political parties on public matters during the extended period, including in regard to how and when the elections would be held.

Fourth, the CCI recommended that the terms of state councils should be extended, doing so without providing any detailed justification for its stance. States are autonomous levels of government and have at least some say on certain issues regarding elections for state councils, including determining the terms of state councils through their constitutions. In its one-page decision on the extension of the terms of state councils, the CCI simply ignored this and suggested that the terms of state councils be extended. There was no request to extend the terms of regional states, and the CCI/HoF's decision in this regard was uncalled for. Interestingly, the CCI/HoF decision extended the HoF's term itself, raising a clear case of conflict of interest, with the HoF becoming a judge in its own case. The HoF simply endorsed the federal government's request for an extension of its term. A political body controlled by the same party served as a rubber-stamp institution.

The decision above was partly the trigger of the war that broke out between the federal government and Tigray in November 2020. As part of its political tit for tat with the federal government and the PP, the TPLF insisted that elections be held before the expiry of the terms of Parliament. It maintained that postponing the elections was unconstitutional and would lead to a power vacuum, since, according to the TPLF, the mandate of the current Parliament would come to an end on 10 October 2020 and under no circumstances could it be extended. Importantly, it resolved to hold statewide elections in Tigray should the national elections be postponed beyond the set date, a resolution it implemented in September 2020. It claimed that holding regional state elections is part and parcel of the mandate of self-government.

In turn, the Tigray Democratic Party challenged the constitutionality of the measures by the TPLF in terms of establishing an electoral board and holding elections. The CCI decided that the action of the Tigray state government in this respect was unconstitutional; thereafter, the federal government imposed a state of emergency in the region, appointing a caretaker government. Tigray by then did not have representatives in the HoF, and the regional state's claim that holding regional state elections at a time when the NEBE had declined to conduct the elections was fully justified as part and parcel of the right to self-government was not given due consideration. This was among the many causes of the tragic war that broke out between the federal government and the regional state.

5. Informal amendments and disregard of the Constitution

The principal objective of the federal system in Ethiopia is to address what was articulated by the Ethiopian Student Movement (ESM) in the 1970s as the 'nationality question'. The ESM argued that post-Menelik (1889–1913) Ethiopia constituted a 'prison house [for] nationalities' and that the centralized nation-building project was a failure; the activists called for an end to 'national oppression' through the grant of the right to self-determination to the nationalities. Since then, the nationality question has remained a key issue for political parties in Ethiopia.[21]

Leftist in its origins, the EPRDF championed the right to self-determination of nationalities, with the 1995 Constitution promising self-government, fair representation in federal institutions, and even the right to secession for nationalities. As a result, at a formal level, the Ethiopian federation provides very generous powers to regional states. In theory, the division of power envisaged in the Constitution, specifically in articles 51 and 52, along with the right to self-rule, allows states to develop socio-economic development policies of their own to suit their local contexts, subject only to broad federation-wide standards set out in the Constitution. However, a clearer picture of the federal system in Ethiopia can be gained if one looks at the operation of the party system. Many critics point to this as the most obvious limitation of Ethiopia's federalism: in particular, they highlight the paradox that arose, especially during the period 2001–15, on the one hand, to the generously constitutional powers granted to the states, and, on the other, to the federal system's centralization in practice due to the hegemonic nature of the party system and developmental state.[22]

The guiding ideology of the EPRDF before the organization transformed itself into the PP was 'revolutionary democracy'.[23] This ideology was followed rigidly during the civil war (1975–91) and then, too, with the adoption of the 1995 Constitution, notwithstanding the latter's enshrinement of pluralism and multiparty democracy. Revolutionary democracy entails exclusive control of power (at all levels of governments) by a vanguard party that assumes a leading and hegemonic role. The effect was that the ruling party controlled not only the institutions of the federal government but also all the regional state governments, both directly through its member parties (the four coalitions each led the four relatively influential states), as well as indirectly through affiliated parties that controlled the other five states.[24] Policy formulation, along with the nomination, election, and appointment of key political figures at the federal and regional state level, was effected through the centralized party structure.

Thus, the role of federalism and the regional states were merely to serve as implementing, subservient, rubber-stamping institutions of the vanguard party at the helm of power. The implication was that the autonomy of the states was limited in practice, with the party

[21] See Vaughan (n 2); Bahru Zewde, *The Quest for Socialist Utopia: The Ethiopian Student Movement 1960–1974* (James Currey 2014) 218.

[22] Lovise Aalen, *Ethnic Federalism in a Dominant Party State: The Ethiopian Experience 1991–2000* (Chr Michelsen Institute 2002) 82-85; Assefa Fiseha, 'Federalism, Development and the Changing Political Dynamics in Ethiopia' (2019) 17(1) International Journal of Constitutional Law 353-360.

[23] For detail, see Jean-Nicolas Bach, 'Abyotawi Democracy: Neither Revolutionary nor Democratic – A Critical Review of EPRDF's Conception of Revolutionary Democracy in Post-1991 Ethiopia' (2011) 5(4) Journal of East African Studies 641.

[24] Assefa Fiseha, 'Theory versus Practice in the Implementation of Ethiopia's Ethnic Federalism' in David Turton (ed.), *Ethnic Federalism: The Ethiopian Experience in Comparative Perspective* (James Currey 2006).

structure overshadowing and weakening the federal and regional government institutions. The party structure and its decision-making procedures undermined the federal division of power and subordinated the state governments to the whims of the party.[25] In this regard, Ethiopia has not been anywhere as federal in character as promised by the Constitution. Indeed, federalism and self-government, the essential elements of the Constitution, were altered significantly even in the absence of any formal amendments.

The EPRDF also pursued the developmental state (2001–15), a centrally designed state-led structure[26] that transferred land administration powers from the states to the federal government. The Addis Ababa 'integrated development plan', which aimed to expand the city's boundary to Oromia in 2015, was particularly critical, as it triggered the Oromo protests in 2015. In reaction to weak regional state leadership and the perception of a lack of regional state autonomy—a situation that was seen as failing to ensure the rights of the Oromos in Addis Ababa—the slogan 'we want genuine self-rule'[27] gained popularity during the widespread protests that broke out in Oromia in early 2016. Self-rule and the political autonomy of regional states were thus compromised by the party apparatus and its ideology of the developmental state, as a result of which a variety of laws and policies conferred wide mandates to the federal government. The overall effect was a substantial expansion of the mandate of the federal government so as to include the power of administering urban and rural land, something which hitherto had been the mandate of local governments.

There was hope that, with the coming to power of Abiy Ahmed and his promise of political reform, centralization would come to an end and genuine self-government would be attained, but as the following sections demonstrate, there has been more continuity than change, with the drive for centralization having seen substate nationalism intensify to new levels. Indeed, the raging war between the centre and expressions of substate nationalism is making the Ethiopian state more fragile than ever.

5.1 The new trend: Continuity or change?

The new drive for centralization and change to the spirit of the Constitution takes many forms. What is new is that the drive for centralization stems more from authoritarian leadership than the party apparatus. The PP seems more disorganized, and to be facing greater internal power struggles and ideological disorientation, than the erstwhile EPRDF.

The first indicator of authoritarian centralization in Ethiopia is the federal government's removal of regional state heads. Since the new government came to power in 2018, many of the leaders of the regional states have been removed by the ruling party, disregarding regional states' mandate to self-rule and the people's right to elect their own leaders[28] and, rather, imposing its will by force, including by waging civil war in regional states.

[25] Ibid.

[26] For detail, see Assefa Fiseha, 'Ethiopia: Development with or without Freedom?' in Eva Brems, Christophe Van der Becken, and Solomon Abay (eds.), *Human Rights and Development: Legal Perspectives from and for Ethiopia* (Brill Nijhoff 2015).

[27] See René Lefort, 'Unrest in Ethiopia: The Ultimate Warning Shot?' (*Open Democracy*, 2 February 2016) https://www.opendemocracy.net/ren-lefort/unrest-in-ethiopia-ultimate-warning-shot accessed 1 October 2023.

[28] The EPRDF used to remove regional state heads, but there was some effort to follow constitutional rules. Regional state councils would at least approve party decisions. Current practice, however, points to a complete disregard of constitutional rules and procedures.

This is happening despite popular support for democracy and federalism, as indicated by Afrobarometer.[29] Instead of providing political solutions to major issues (through, for example, a more inclusive political system, more working federal languages, a transition to democracy, a fair share of resources, and genuine self-rule, all of which have been demanded in protests since 2015),[30] the new trend is to use force to suppress popular demands. The actions taken by the federal government, ranging from those in the Somali region[31] and Sidama[32] to Oromia,[33] Tigray, and Wolayta,[34] speak for themselves. It has exercised one-party military rule, including using emergency decrees to remove regional state leaders and suppress public demands; using violence and excessive force;[35] committing massive abuses of human rights;[36] sponsoring political killings and imprisoning opposition political leaders (including Jawar Mohammed,[37] Lidetu Ayalew, Bekele Gerba, Eskinder Nega, several senior Oromo leaders, and thousands of junior opposition party members); and restricting media outlets and Internet access.[38]

[29] 'Overwhelming Majority of Ethiopians Support Democracy, Seek Accountable Governance' (*Afrobarometer*, 30 October 2020) https://www.afrobarometer.org/articles/overwhelming-majority-ethiopians-support-democracy-seek-accountable-governance/ accessed 1 October 2023.

[30] René Lefort and William Davison, 'Federalist Façade for Centralist Front' (*Ethiopia Insight*, 18 August 2019) https://www.ethiopia-insight.com/2019/08/18/federalist-facade-for-centralist-front/ accessed 1 October 2023.

[31] See Tobias Hagmann, 'Fast Politics, Slow Justice: Ethiopia's Somali Region Two Years After Abdi Iley', LSE Conflict Research Programme Briefing Paper, 11 September 2020 https://www.lse.ac.uk/ideas/Assets/Documents/Conflict-Research-Programme/crp-memos/Hagmann-Two-years-after-Iley-final.pdf accessed 1 October 2023.

[32] See Morris Kiruga, 'The Sidama Crisis and Escalating Demands for Statehood Challenge Ethiopian Constitution' (*The Africa Report*, 2 August 2019) https://www.theafricareport.com/15883/the-sidama-crisis-and-escalating-demands-for-statehood-challenge-ethiopian-constitution/ accessed 1 October 2023; William Davison and Kulle Kursha, 'As Southern Nations Break Free, Pressure Mounts on EPRDF' (*Ethiopia Insight*, 28 November 2018) https://www.ethiopia-insight.com/2018/11/28/as-southern-nations-break-free-pressure-mounts-on-eprdf/ accessed 1 October 2023.

[33] See Tsedale Lemma, 'After the Postponed Elections: Ethiopia's Fragile Transition Hangs in the Balance' (*BTI Transformation Index*, 24 August 2020) https://blog.bti-project.org/2020/08/24/ethiopias-fragile-transition-hangs-in-the-balance accessed 1 October 2023; Etenesh Abera and Biah Jelan, 'Oromia Reeling from State Violence after Security Forces Kill, Injure a Staggering Number of Protesters' (*Addis Standard*, 19 August 2020) https://addisstandard.com/analysis-oromia-reeling-from-state-violence-after-security-forces-kill-injure-a-staggering-number-of-protesters/ accessed 1 October 2023.

[34] See Medihane Ekubamichael, 'Weeks after Army's Violent Crackdown in Wolaita, Prosperity Party Removes Zonal Chief' (*Addis Standard*, 2 September 2020) https://addisstandard.com/news-weeks-after-armys-violent-crackdown-in-wolaita-prosperity-party-removes-zonal-chief-administrator-others/ accessed 1 October 2023; Minyahil Tadesse, 'It's Time to Respect the Wolayta People's Constitutional Rights' (*Ethiopia Insight*, 28 August 2020) https://www.ethiopia-insight.com/2020/08/28/its-time-to-respect-the-wolayta-peoples-constitutional-rights/ accessed 1 October 2023.

[35] See Ayele Woubshet, 'Our "Protectors" in Blue: Police Brutality and Misconduct in Ethiopia' (*Ethiopia Insight*, 14 August 2020) https://www.ethiopia-insight.com/2020/08/14/our-protectors-in-blue-police-brutality-and-misconduct-in-ethiopia/ accessed 1 October 2023.

[36] See Declan Walsh, 'Ethiopia's War Leads to Ethnic Cleansing in Tigray Region, US Report Says' *New York Times* (New York, 26 February 2021) https://www.nytimes.com/2021/02/26/world/middleeast/ethiopia-tigray-ethnic-cleansing.html accessed 1 October 2023; Servet Gunergok, 'Ethnic Cleansing Being Committed in Tigray: Report' (*AA*, 27 February 2021) https://www.aa.com.tr/en/americas/ethnic-cleansing-being-committed-in-tigray-report/2158784 accessed 1 October 2023.

[37] The government charged Jawar and others with terrorism. See Elias Meseret, 'Ethiopia Charges Prominent Opposition Figure with Terrorism' *Washington Post* (Washington DC, 19 September 2020) https://www.washingtonpost.com/world/africa/ethiopia-charges-prominent-opposition-figure-with-terrorism/2020/09/19/52249eb0-fa6c-11ea-85f7-5941188a98cd_story.html accessed 1 October 2023.

[38] Since June 2020, several media houses critical of the government have been shut down (eg Asrat Media, Oromo Media Network, and Tigray TV) and various journalists sent to jail. The Internet has also been blocked in parts of Ethiopia. See Girma Gutema, 'OMN: An "Alien" Star in Ethiopia's Skewed Media Universe is "Cancelled"' (*Ethiopia Insight*, 12 August 2020) https://www.ethiopia-insight.com/2020/08/12/omn-an-alien-star-in-ethiopias-skewed-media-universe-is-cancelled/ accessed 1 October 2023.

The federal government has issued several emergency rules imposing military rule (otherwise called 'command posts') in regional states such as Oromia,[39] Tigray, Benishangul-Gumuz,[40] and parts of the Amhara and the south,[41] but only a few of these declarations have been submitted to Parliament for approval.[42] At the time of writing (May 2022), the Amhara region had been placed under military rule without a formal declaration of emergency and the federal government was arresting what it calls 'informal armed groups'. Command posts entail the suspension of civilian rule and its replacement with military rule—and, owing to the frequency and the wide geographic coverage of military rule, it has become the new normal. It is as if militarism has replaced federalism.

While there is continuity in centralized federalism both under the EPRDF and its successor, the PP, the PP's federalism is distinctive in two respects. As witnessed in the devastating wars in Tigray, the south (Sidama and Wolayta), and Oromia, the regime's determination to use violence to crush political demands for self-government and inclusion is a prominent feature of Ethiopia's recent history.[43] The PP has also shifted its narrative towards integrative federalism and, as part of that, liquidated formerly autonomous coalition and affiliate member parties, thereby turning the PP into a single national party—a trend with serious implications for federalism and the autonomy of states.

The second indicator of authoritarian centralization is the ideological framework of the new ruling party. An adviser to the government has stated that 'we will continue to implement Menelik's (1889–1913) nation-building project that was disrupted by EPRDF in 1991'.[44] This project centralized Ethiopia and liquidated quasi-autonomous kingdoms in a brutal, coercive process that was the source of the country's agony in the twentieth century. Some regarded it a normal process of nation-building,[45] while others saw it as empire-building and a form of colonialism.[46] In between the two extremes were those who described that era as a 'prison house [for] nationalities' and advocated a new social contract involving a more inclusive centre and genuine self-rule, be it via a federation or a confederation.[47]

[39] 'Amid Renewed Violence and Conflicting Accounts Army Places Oromo Special, South Wollo & North Shewa Zones of Amhara Region under Command Post' (*Addis Standard*, 19 April 2021) https://addisstandard.com/analysis-amid-renewed-violence-and-conflicting-accounts-army-places-oromo-special-south-wollo-north-shewa-zones-of-amhara-region-under-command-post/ accessed 1 October 2023.

[40] 'Metekel Zone Command Post Takes Measures against 23 Anti-peace Elements' (*Fana Broadcasting Corporate*, 8 December 2020) https://www.fanabc.com/english/metekel-zone-command-post-takes-measures-against-23-anti-peace-elements/ accessed 1 October 2023.

[41] 'Ethiopia: Army To Take over Security in Troubled South' (*TesfaNews*, 23 July 2019) https://tesfanews.net/ethiopia-army-command-post-take-over-security-sidama/ accessed 1 October 2023.

[42] The command post imposed in Benishangul Gumuz in 2020, and the countrywide state of emergency imposed in November 2021, were approved by Parliament. See 'Update: Details of Ethiopia's State of Emergency Proclamation' (*Addis Standard*, 2 November 2021) https://addisstandard.com/update-details-of-ethiopias-state-of-emergency-proclamation/ accessed 1 October 2023.

[43] According to some sources, Abiy Ahmed's recent war has caused death to millions of people in Ethiopia, and though much is said about the war in Ukraine, Tigray's war remains the world's largest one. See Mark Green, 'Ukraine Understandably the Focus, but Ethiopia's Tigray Conflict is World's Largest' (*Wilson Center*, 25 October 2022) https://www.wilsoncenter.org/blog-post/ukraine-understandably-focus-ethiopias-tigray-conflict-worlds-largest accessed 1 October 2023.

[44] See Daniel Kibret's interview, 'Meskerem Abera' (*Abay News*, 25 March 2020) https://www.youtube.com/watch?v=WZzcxrHngV4&t=1759s accessed 19 April 2021.

[45] For detail, see Donald Levine, *Greater Ethiopia: The Evolution of a Multiethnic Society* (2nd edn, University of Chicago Press 2000).

[46] Assefa Jaleta, 'Oromo Nationalism and Ethiopian Ethnocratic Politics' (2002) 20 Horn of Africa 11–45.

[47] Gudina (n 3).

The contemporary call for a return to the old nation-building era is expressed in Prime Minister Abiy Ahmed's book *Medemer*, published in 2019[48] and said to articulate the PP's ideology. According to Gemechu, '[i]t glorifies Ethiopia's past, criticizes Ethiopian federalism for promoting ethnic divisions, and imagines a very centralized Ethiopian state and national identity.'[49] *Medemer* thus distances itself from the EPRDF's policy of accommodative ethnonationalism, which it characterizes as divisive, and imagines a united, integrated Ethiopia premised on the Ethiopian people, rather than the 'Nations, Nationalities and Peoples' declared in the Constitution. The doctrine also advocates an 'Ethiopia-first nationalism'—this was an official party-state ideology under the Derg (1974–91) and has now been recycled in a new form under the PP.

Thus, since the establishment of the PP, Ethiopia has effectively become a decentralized unitary state rather than a federation. Prime Minister Abiy rejected the concept of Ethiopia as a plurinational state, as outlined in the preamble of the 1995 Constitution, and said, 'we are one people'. Hence, the critique, as aptly explained by Trueman, is that the 'imperial narrative is being recycled' in a new form through Abiy.[50] This new trend was partly tempered following the power struggle between the Amhara (via the Amhara Democratic Party, or ADP) and Oromo (via the ODP) wings of the PP, shifting the balance in favour of narrow circles of ODP after deposing senior members of ADP during the mid-2022 PP congress. It is yet to be seen what this shift means, but so far the new regime has been fully endorsing the pre-1991 narrative. This is not surprising. Abiy Ahmed's victory speech in Parliament in April 2018 included the words, 'God rest the soul of my mother who told me as a young boy that I will be Ethiopia's seventh King.'[51] Democratization and genuine self-government are unlikely under a leader who thinks he is Ethiopia's seventh king, given that a centralized kingdom is the antithesis of federalism and self-government.

The third indicator of authoritarian centralization is a new policy that regulates the regional state police. The Constitution, in article 52, empowers regional states to establish their own police to ensure peace in their territories.[52] However, a recent policy document of the federal government shows that the federal government has proposed dissolving the regional state police, alleging that it is heavily militarized against its mission and becoming a threat to peace and security.[53] The document states that the special police are becoming tools for extremist ethnic and religious groups.[54] The policy thus centralizes the process of

[48] Abiy Ahmed, *Medemer* (Tsehai Publishers 2019).

[49] Milkessa Gemechu, 'Ethiopia: Federalism, Party Merger and Conflicts' (2023) 42 Conflict Studies Quarterly 24, 35.

[50] Trevor Trueman, 'An Imperial Narrative Gets Recycled' (*Ethiopia Insight*, 24 August 2020) https://www.ethiopia-insight.com/2020/08/24/an-imperial-narrative-gets-recycled/ accessed 1 October 2023. Following the PP's congress in 2022, there has been an intense power struggle between the Oromo and Amahara wings of the ruling party, leading to dismissal of senior ADP members from the party. For now, the Oromo wing seems to dominate the ruling party, and it is not clear yet whether this will lead to a new narrative.

[51] See his speech at https://www.youtube.com/watch?v=ajjlYTbJm4U accessed 9 September 2020.

[52] Regional states have also established special police that resemble the army more than they do regular police. The states claim the special police should be seen as a manifestation of political autonomy, but the militarization of this police force has been a cause for concern, with the federal government wishing to regulate it. However, the new Police Standard does not draw a distinction between the regular and special police, and regional states thus question its constitutionality. See Police Standard of Ethiopia, December 2020, Addis Ababa, Policy Document, 61–78. Interview with expert involved in the preparation of the document, Ministry of Peace, Addis Ababa, 15 May 2021.

[53] Police Standard (n 52) 79.

[54] Ibid. 58.

recruiting regional state police by subjecting it to federal control.[55] Regional state police, according to this document, are made *accountable*[56] to the federal police while retaining administrative accountability to the regional states.[57] Reversing previous trends and violating the regional state mandate, the policy subjects the promotion and appointment of the deputy commissioner and commissioner of regional states to be made by the federal government (Ministry of Peace).[58]

Fourthly, there are signs that show a move towards the centrally designed making and unmaking of constituent unit boundaries, as part of the shift to a 'geographic federalism' that does away with the current federation. Under an apparent claim that addressing interregional state disputes has become difficult to manage and needs 'an expert' solution, the federal government established the Identity and Administrative Boundary Commission,[59] allegedly with a countrywide mandate and perhaps to dismantle the federal system, identified by the centrist elite as the 'main source of Ethiopia's political crisis'.[60] As per article 48 of the federal Constitution, disputes between two or more regional states are to be resolved amicably by the regional states. If that fails, the matter has to be submitted to the HoF—as mentioned before, a non-legislative second chamber composed of representatives of the different ethnonational groups. Yet, despite such clear constitutional principles, the federal government issued a proclamation establishing the Identity and Administrative Boundary Commission, which is accountable to the prime minister. The Commission is required to bring studies for addressing identity-based and boundary disputes to the federal executive, Parliament, and the HoF.

As per the Constitution, identity-based demands are decided by the local-elected and regional-state elected councils once the demand is submitted by the concerned community. The new body takes away the mandate of the community and the regional state councils, and ultimately the *substantive* mandate of the HoF. What has been bestowed by the *Constitution* on the regional states and the HoF is now given to the Commission by *law*. Self-government, as stipulated by articles 8 and 39 of the Constitution, is the mandate of the 'nations and nationalities', and any controversy related to self-government is adjudicated by the HoF, the house which is supposed to guard their interests. As the new body takes away the mandate of the HoF and introduces centralized decision-making disregarding regional states, experts argue that it is unconstitutional body. In addition, some of the members are well-known political activists and leaders of political parties—that is, partisan members rather than the independent ones claimed by the federal government and the law itself.[61]

[55] Ibid. 71.

[56] Ibid. The regional state police will be headed by a Commissioner whose status is one rung lower than that of the Federal Commissioner General. This introduces a new element of regional state police accountability to the federal level that violates the federal principle.

[57] Ibid. 67.

[58] Ibid. 47.

[59] See Proclamation 1101/2019, Administrative, Boundary and Identity Issues Commission. See also Assefa Fiseha, 'Federalism and Security: The Special Police in Ethiopia' (2022) 6(2) Journal of Autonomy and Security Studies 96–130

[60] One of the main opinion-makers on this issue, a former Derg official named Dawit Woldegiorgis, wrote that 'ethnic politics that has been institutionalized by the ruling party for the last 28 years was the single cause of [the] discontent and disenfranchisement that brought the country . . . to its knees'. See Dawit Woldegiorgis, 'Ethiopia: A Country on the Brinks' (*Borkena*, 10 April 2019) https://borkena.com/2019/04/10/ethiopia-a-country-on-the-brinks-by-dawit-woldegiorgis/ accessed 1 October 2023.

[61] See Staff Report, 'Drawing Lessons from Commissions' Unceremonious Demise' (*The Reporter*, 5 March 2022) https://www.thereporterethiopia.com/22344/ accessed 1 October 2023.

The nomenclature of the Commission is also controversial. In Amharic, the phrase 'Astedader Wosen' is centrist in its connotation. Regional states in Ethiopia are autonomous units, not provincial entities, as in a unitary state, and it is indeed very odd to refer to *Astedader Wosen* as if the boundary of the states could easily be made and unmade by the federal government. Any adjustment to the boundaries of regional states can be made only with the participation of the federal government and regional states, as it amounts to constitutional change. The normative assumption of the law thus speaks for itself: very centrist, and thus rightly criticized as having been designed by an '*Ahadawi*/centrist mindset'.[62] Ironically, the decision of the CCI in *Hamle* 24/2011 EC, made in response to Tigray's challenge to the constitutionality of the law establishing the Commission, cites examples from Nigeria and India to justify its decisions explaining the constitutionality of the law, rejecting the application from Tigray. In India, the federal Parliament is mandated by the Constitution to make and unmake provincial boundaries as if India were a unitary state. By contrast, the Ethiopian Constitution does not give this kind of mandate to the federal government or federal Parliament. Indeed, under its articles 8 and 39, constituent units are given a wide degree of autonomy, and this autonomy covers both political and territorial autonomy. In a genuine federation, the federal government cannot unilaterally make or unmake the boundaries of constituent units; it requires the consent of the units.

Arguably, the law could have established an independent body of experts, not political activists, to provide expert opinions to the HoF and help it make sound decisions. Ahmed's speech in July 2021, which described the contested territories (in western Tigray) as belonging to Begemidir (the old name of Gondar province of the Amhara region), also prejudges an outcome that may be made by the Commission.[63] Federal institutions are supposed to mediate impartially in disputes between regional states. Amhara and Tigray regional states have claims and counterclaims over a disputed territory. The federal army is thus given a green light to side with the Amhara region and thereby reduced to an agent of the Amhara regional state, not any more impartial Ethiopia's defence force. The outcome of the Commission is now a foregone conclusion.[64] By doing so, Abiy Ahmed has made federal institutions subservient to the interests of the centrist elite. This approach is unlikely to bring lasting solutions either to the inhabitants of the contested territories or to the regional states (Amhara and Tigray).

The overall trend is that the PP is, in effect, turning a federation into a unitary decentralized state. This remains a puzzle because the Constitution has not been formally amended. One should look into the forces that brought Ahmed to power to grasp the risks of this development. He came from Oromia, and it is well known that the core content of the protests in Oromia was demand for inclusion, genuine self-rule and end to federal government intervention in states. In other words, it was a demand for more, not less, autonomy. It is ironic, then, that Ahmed is keen to centralize power, contrary to his own social base—an irony that clearly reveals his plan. As mentioned, the Constitution has not been amended,

[62] The application by the Tigray National Regional State to the CCI, as summarized in the decision of the CCI in *Hamle* 24 July 2011 EC, demonstrates this point very well.

[63] See Abiy Ahmed, 'Speech, 1 July 2021' https://www.youtube.com/watch?v=sJPw2EwNhx4 accessed 1 October 2023.

[64] Not surprisingly, an application made by the Tigray National Regional State to quash the law establishing the Commission as unconstitutional was not accepted by the CCI. The CCI, in *Hamle* 24 July 2011 EC, ruled that the contested law is constitutional and rejected the application.

and the new ruling elite introduced these policies in violation of the political autonomy of the states.

Yet, it should be mentioned that the centralization drive is limited by deinstitutionalization of the public and security sectors, which limits the capacity of the state. Indeed, deinstitutionalization characterizes the new regime.[65] The federal government has lost a monopoly over the use of force and has not been able to ensure law and order throughout the country, the bare minimum role of any government.[66] This has affected public trust in authorities and public institutions.[67] Ethiopia has more than five million internally displaced people as a result of horizontal and vertical conflicts which the government is unable to handle—one of the highest such counts in the world.[68] Following an interethnic conflict between Amhara and Benishangul Gumuz, Deputy Prime Minister Demeke Mekonen said, 'there is no other option for residents in Metekel zone other than organizing, arming and defending themselves'.[69] The federal government has allowed the proliferation of informal forces, such as Fano, Qeerro, and regional-state special forces, and as a result has lost control of parts of Oromia, Benishangul Gumuz, Amhara, and Tigray. The Ethiopian state is thus contracting and shrinking. A former official, Dawit W Giorgis, wrote that 'Ethiopia under Abiy is officially a failed state by all indicators.'[70] Thus, alongside the drive for centralization, there is also fragmentation.

The above developments show that the party, its ideology, its key decisions, and its leadership are more impactful than the constitutional rules in Ethiopia. The party, its ideology, and the key decisions that impact the country's political system are the constitution in the narrow sense, not the written Constitution—'in the narrow sense' because, while the Constitution empowers the main political institutions, it also limits their mandate, but this latter part is missing in Ethiopia. Indeed, it is difficult to grasp political developments in Ethiopia without analysing the party system and its decision-making structure.

At this stage, one has to ask, can any change to the Constitution be considered as a valid adaptation and change? Should political institutions and the party be given wide discretion to change the essentials parts of the Constitution without any limits? If so, would the Constitution be worth its name? One possible response is to have a system of checks and

[65] While deinstitutionalization applies to many fields, foreign policy offers particularly a good illustration of it. The Constitution declares that foreign policy is the preserve of the federal government, but since the new regime came to power, regional states have been engaged, without any control from the federal government, in signing agreements with foreign countries. For instance, the Amhara and Oromia regions made deals with Eritrea before the outbreak of the war in November 2020; likewise, Somali region has strong ties with Somalia. At the time of the writing, all these deals had complicated federal–regional state relations to such an extent that the Foreign Ministry issued a new directive prohibiting regional states from entering into foreign relations.

[66] A former Derg official who returned to Ethiopia following Abiy Ahmed's grant of amnesty, and who initially advised the prime minister to scrap the existing Constitution and start a fresh transition, said, 'Ethiopia under Abiy is officially a failed state.' See '"Ethiopia is Becoming A Failed State": Major David Woldegiorgis' (*BBC News (Amharic)*, 10 April 2019) https://www.bbc.com/amharic/news-47879359 accessed 1 October 2023.

[67] Fikremariam Molla Gedefaw, 'For Prosperity, Ethiopia Needs Institutional Not Individual Strength' (*Ethiopia Insight*, 15 September 2020) https://www.ethiopia-insight.com/2020/09/15/for-prosperity-ethiopia-needs-institutional-not-individual-strength/ accessed 1 October 2023.

[68] See Jacky Habib, 'Ethiopia Set a World Record for Displacement in a Single Year: 5.1 million in 2021' (*NPR*, 28 May 2022) https://www.npr.org/sections/goatsandsoda/2022/05/28/1100469734/ethiopia-set-a-world-record-for-displacements-in-a-single-year-5-1-million-in-20 accessed 1 October 2023.

[69] Siyanne Mekonnen, 'Deputy PM Recommends Arming Civilians in Metekel, Benishangul Gumuz Region as Spate of Attacks by Armed Men Leaves Dozens Killed' (*Addis Standard*, 14 October 2020) https://addisstandard.com/news-deputy-pm-recommends-arming-civilians-in-metekel-benishangul-gumuz-region-as-spate-of-attacks-by-armed-men-leaves-dozens-killed/ accessed 14 October 2023.

[70] Woldegiorgis (n 60).

balances that checks whether the alterations made are valid in the eyes of the Constitution. The system of constitutional review is meant to limit the role of political organs when they exceed their limits, including their mandate to change the constitution.[71] Yet, as the previous sections demonstrated, Ethiopia's system of constitutional review is itself a victim of political intrigue and has not served to limit the role of political organs. None of the changes and adaptations made to the Constitution have been seriously challenged by the HoF for their constitutionality.

6. Conclusion

Although not formally amended, the 1995 Constitution has seen significant changes through policy design; through the decisions of the main political organs, including the ruling party; and through interpretation. Constitutional amendment has been pursued on two occasions, but the process has not been completed. The political practice shows that key decisions are made based on the proposed changes even if the process is incomplete. On both occasions, political actors chose to operate under the changed circumstances without completing the procedures, and this happened in a context where the ruling party had complete control of federal and regional state legislative bodies. Major adjustments and changes to the Constitution have been made through the policies and decisions of the party system. This was evident all the way up to 2015.

Centrally designed policies, including the developmental state and hegemonic party system, have become the real 'constitution' and prevailed over written constitutional principles and procedures. Since the new regime assumed power in 2018, there has been more continuity than change in this respect. As the new party lacks ideological coherence, personal rule seems to have replaced party ideology and structure. A good example of this is the drive for centralization through the transformation of the EPRDF into the PP: into a party that turned former coalition members into branches, thus enhancing central control of the branches. Regional state branches are made accountable to the centre, and by implication regional state heads remain subordinate to the federal government. The increased role of the army and security that follows command and control during emergency and 'command posts' in a federal context also reinforces the drive for centralization: so much so that Ethiopia looks more like a decentralized unitary state than a federation. All these major changes to the spirit of the Constitution have been made through informal changes rather than formal constitutional amendment. Ideology, party structure, and personal rule have displaced essential parts of the written Constitution without the need to comply with the formal amendment procedure. The constituted power has assumed the role of constituent power and managed to change the Constitution without limit. It has been a one-way process in which power-holders manipulate the Constitution and the Constitution loses its supremacy. Ethiopia is a textbook example of a country where political power is yet to be institutionalized and regulated by law.

71 The Supreme Court of India, in *Kesavananda* (Writ Petition (Civil) 135 of 1970), ruled that the amendment power could be used only as long as it did not violate the Constitution's basic structure. The concept of the basic structure was said to include the supremacy of the Constitution, the republican and democratic form of government, the secular character of the state, the separation of powers, and federalism.

Bibliography

Aalen L., *Ethnic Federalism in a Dominant Party State: The Ethiopian Experience 1991–2000* (Chr Michelsen Institute 2002)

Abera E. and Jelan B., 'Analysis: Oromia Reeling from State Violence after Security Forces Kill, Injure a Staggering Number of Protesters' (*Addis Standard*, 19 August 2020) https://addisstandard.com/analysis-oromia-reeling-from-state-violence-after-security-forces-kill-injure-a-staggering-number-of-protesters/ accessed 1 October 2023

Afesha N., 'The Practice of Informal Changes to the Ethiopian Constitution in the Course of Application' (2016) 10(2) Mizan Law Review 366–99

Ahmed A., *Medemer* (Tsehai Publishers 2019)

Ahmed A., 'Speech' https://www.youtube.com/watch?v=ajjlYTbJm4U https://www.youtube.com/watch?v=9RO6D6xPZAk accessed 9 September 2020

Ahmed A., 'Speech, 1 July 2021' https://www.youtube.com/watch?v=sJPw2EwNhx4 accessed 1 August 2023

Albert R., *Constitutional Amendments: Making, Breaking and Changing Constitutions* (OUP 2019)

Amnesty International, 'Beyond Law Enforcement: Human Rights Violations by Ethiopian Security Forces in Amhara and Oromia' (29 May 2020) https://www.amnesty.org/download/Documents/AFR2523582020ENGLISH.PDF accessed 1 August 2023

Bach J.N., 'Abyotawi Democracy: Neither Revolutionary nor Democratic – A Critical Review of EPRDF's Conception of Revolutionary Democracy in Post-1991 Ethiopia' (2011) 5(4) Journal of East African Studies 641

Barak A., *The Judge in a Democracy* (Princeton University Press 2006)

Bekele E., 'Regional Prosperity Party Leaders Need to Regain Autonomy – and Rescue Ethiopian Democracy' https://www.ethiopia-insight.com/2020/09/11/regional-prosperity-party-leaders-need-to-regain-autonomy-and-rescue-ethiopian-democracy/ accessed 1 October 2023

https://theconversation.com/ethiopias-political-crisis-plays-out-in-the-regions-why-its-a-federal-problem-144893 accessed 27 August 2020

Berhane S., 'A Renewed Push for Statehood Raises More Questions than Answers' (*The Reporter*, 6 August 2022) https://www.thereporterethiopia.com/25590/ accessed 25 October 2023

Berhe M.G., 'Ethiopia's Political Crisis Plays Out in the Regions. Why it's a Federal Problem' (*The Conversation*, 27 August 2020)

Brewer-Carías A.R., *Constitutional Courts as Positive Legislators: A Comparative Law Study* (CUP 2011)

Data D., 'Enduring Issues in State-Society in Ethiopia: A Case Study of the WoGaGoDa Conflict in Wolaita Southern Ethiopia' (2005/2006) 2(1/2) International Journal of Ethiopian Studies 141–59

Davison D., 'Kulle Kursha As Southern Nations Break Free, Pressure Mounts on EPRDF' (*Ethiopia Insight*, 28 November 2018) https://www.ethiopia-insight.com/2018/11/28/as-southern-nations-break-free-pressure-mounts-on-eprdf/accessed 1 October 2023

Ekubamichael M., 'Weeks After Army's Violent Crackdown in Wolaita, Prosperity Party Removes Zonal Chief' (*Addis Standard*, 2 September 2020) https://addisstandard.com/news-weeks-after-armys-violent-crackdown-in-wolaita-prosperity-party-removes-zonal-chief-administrator-others/ accessed 1 October 2020

'Ethiopia: Army to Take Over Security in Troubled South' (*TesfaNews*, 23 July 2019) https://www.tesfanews.net/ethiopia-army-command-post-take-over-security-sidama/ accessed 1 October 2023

'Ethiopia: IDP Population Movement – Emergency Plan of Action Final Report DREF n° MDRET019' (*ReliefWeb*, 23 July 2019) https://reliefweb.int/report/ethiopia/ethiopia-idp-population-movement-emergency-plan-action-final-report-dref-n-mdret019 accessed 11 September 2020

'Ethiopia gets Eleventh State with More than 96% Approval for South West Referendum' (*Addis Standard*, 9 October 2021) https://addisstandard.com/news-alert-ethiopia-gets-eleventh-state-with-more-than-96-approval-for-south-west-referendum/#:~:text=Addis%20Abeba%2C%20October%209%2F2021,Zones%2C%20as%20well%20as%20Konta accessed 9 October 2021

'"Ethiopia is Becoming A Failed State": Major David Woldegiorgis' (*BBC News (Amharic)*, 10 April 2019) https://www.bbc.com/amharic/news-47879359 accessed 1 October 2023

Fiseha A., 'Theory versus Practice in the Implementation of Ethiopia's Ethnic Federalism' in Turton D. (ed.), *Ethnic Federalism: The Ethiopian Experience in Comparative Perspective* (James Currey 2006)

Fiseha A., 'Federalism, Development and the Changing Political Dynamics in Ethiopia' (2019) 17(1) International Journal of Constitutional Law 353–60

Fiseha A., 'Ethiopia: Development with or without Freedom?' in Brems E., van der Becken C., and Abay S. (eds.), *Human Rights and Development: Legal Perspectives from and for Ethiopia* (Brill Nijhoff 2015)

Fiseha A., 'Transition to Democracy in Deeply Divided Ethiopia: Mission Impossible' (2022) 39(2) Journal of Global South Studies 41–82

Fiseha A., 'Federalism and Security: The Special Police in Ethiopia' (2022) 6(2) Journal of Autonomy and Security Studies 96–130

Friedrich C., *Trends of Federalism in Theory and Practice* (Praeger 1968)

Gabisa H., Wodajo K., and Gobana I., 'Commentary: The Constitution Should Be Interpreted, if at all, to Re-constitute, Co-govern & Co-conduct a Post-COVID-19 National Election: IOLA' (*Addis Standard*, 18 May 2020) https://addisstandard.com/commentary-the-constitution-should-be-interpreted-if-at-all-to-re-constitute-co-govern-co-conduct-a-post-covid-19-national-election-iola/ accessed 9 October 2021

Gedefaw F.M., 'For Prosperity, Ethiopia Needs Institutional Not Individual Strength' (*Ethiopia Insight*, 15 September 2020) https://www.ethiopia-insight.com/2020/09/15/for-prosperity-ethiopia-needs-institutional-not-individual-strength accessed 1 October 2023

Gemechu M., 'Ethiopia: Federalism, Party Merger and Conflicts' (2023) 42 Conflict Studies Quarterly 35

Giorgis D.W., 'Ethiopia Under Abiy is Officially a Failed State' (*BBC*, 10 April 2019) https://www.bbc.com/amharic/news-47879359 accessed 1 October 2023

Green M., 'Ukraine Understandably the Focus, but Ethiopia's Tigray Conflict is World's Largest' (*Wilson Center*, 25 October 2022) https://www.wilsoncenter.org/blog-post/ukraine-understandably-focus-ethiopias-tigray-conflict-worlds-largest accessed 1 October 2023

Gudina M., *Ethiopia: Competing Ethnic Nationalisms and the Quest for Democracy 1960–2000* (Shaker Publishing 2003)

Günerigök S., 'Ethnic Cleansing Being Committed in Tigray: Report' (*AA*, 27 February 2021) https://www.aa.com.tr/en/americas/ethnic-cleansing-being-committed-in-tigray-report/2158784 accessed 1 October 2023

Gutema G., 'An "Alien" Star in Ethiopia's Skewed Media Universe is "Cancelled"' (*OMN*, 12 August 2020) https://www.ethiopia-insight.com/2020/08/12/omn-an-alien-star-in-ethiopias-skewed-media-universe-is-cancelled/ accessed 12 August 2020

Habib J., 'Ethiopia Set a World Record for Displacement in a Single Year: 5.1 million in 2021' (*NPR*, 28 May 2022) https://www.npr.org/sections/goatsandsoda/2022/05/28/1100469734/ethiopia-set-a-world-record-for-displacements-in-a-single-year-5-1-million-in-20 accessed 1 October 2023.

Hagmann T., 'Fast Politics, Slow Justice: Ethiopia's Somali Region Two Years after Abdi Iley', LSE Conflict Research Programme Briefing Paper, 11 September 2020 https://www.lse.ac.uk/ideas/Assets/Documents/Conflict-Research-Programme/crp-memos/Hagmann-Two-years-after-Iley-final.pdf accessed 1 October 2023

Jaleta A., 'Oromo Nationalism and Ethiopian Ethnocratic Politics' (2002) 20 Horn of Africa 11–45

Jelan B. and Mekonnen S., 'Analysis: Amid Renewed Violence and Conflicting Accounts Army Places Oromo Special, South Wollo and North Shewa Zones of Amhara Region under Command Post' (*Addis Standard*, 19 April 2021) https://addisstandard.com/analysis-amid-renewed-violence-and-conflicting-accounts-army-places-oromo-special-south-wollo-north-shewa-zones-of-amhara-region-under-command-post/ accessed 1 October 2023

Kibret D., 'Meskerem Abera' (*Abay News*, 25 March 2020) https://www.youtube.com/watch?v=WZzcxrHngV4&t=1759s accessed 19 April 2021

Kiruga M., 'The Sidama Crisis and Escalating Demands for Statehood Challenge Ethiopian Constitution' (*The Africa Report*, 2 August 2019) https://www.theafricareport.com/15883/the-sidama-crisis-and-escalating-demands-for-statehood-challenge-ethiopian-constitution/ accessed 1 October 2023

Kommers D. and Miller R., *The Constitutional Jurisprudence of the Federal Republic of Germany* (3rd edn, Duke University Press 2012)

Kriek D.J., 'The Rigidity of the Constitution' in Kriek D.J. (ed.), *Federalism: The Solution*? (HSRC Publishers 1992) 57–58

Lefort R., 'Unrest in Ethiopia: The Ultimate Warning Shot?' (*Open Democracy*, 2 February 2016) https://www.opendemocracy.net/ren-lefort/unrest-in-ethiopia-ultimate-warning-shot accessed 18 April 2016

Lefort R. and Davison W., 'Federalist Façade for Centralist Front' (*Ethiopia Insight*, 18 September 2018) https://www.ethiopia-insight.com/2019/08/18/federalist-facade-for-centralist-front/ accessed 1 October 2023

Lemma T., 'After the Postponed Elections: Ethiopia's Fragile Transition Hangs in the Balance' (*BTI Transformation Index*, 24 August 2020) https://blog.bti-project.org/2020/08/24/ethiopias-fragile-transition-hangs-in-the-balance/ accessed 1 October 2023

Levine D., *Greater Ethiopia: The Evolution of a Multiethnic Society* (2nd edn, University of Chicago Press 2000)

Lutz D., 'Toward a Theory of Constitutional Amendment' (1994) 88(2) American Political Science Review 355

Mekonnen S., 'Deputy PM Recommends Arming Civilians in Metekel, Benishangul Gumuz Region as Spate of Attacks by Armed Men Leaves Dozens Killed' (*Addis Standard*, 14 October 2020) https://addisstandard.com/news-deputy-pm-recommends-arming-civilians-in-metekel-benishangul-gumuz-region-as-spate-of-attacks-by-armed-men-leaves-dozens-killed/ accessed 14 October 2020

Meseret E., 'Ethiopia Charges Prominent Opposition Figure with Terrorism' *Washington Post* (Washington DC, 9 September 2020) https://www.washingtonpost.com/world/africa/ethiopia-charges-prominent-opposition-figure-with-terrorism/2020/09/19/52249eb0-fa6c-11ea-85f7-5941188a98cd_story.html accessed 1 October 2023

'Metekel Zone Command Post Takes Measures against 23 Anti-Peace Elements' (*Fana Broadcasting Corporate*, 8 December 2020) https://www.fanabc.com/english/metekel-zone-command-post-takes-measures-against-23-anti-peace-elements/ accessed 1 October 2023

Muleta S., 'Chronicles of Sidama People's Struggle for Self-rule' (*Addis Standard*, Special Issue, 30 May 2019) http://addisstandard.com/special-edition-chronicles-of-sidama-peoples-struggle-for-self-rule/ accessed 30 May 2019

Ottaway M., 'The Ethiopian Transition: Democratization or New Authoritarianism? (2005) 2(3) Northeast African Studies 67, 73

'Overwhelming Majority of Ethiopians Support Democracy, Seek Accountable Governance' (*Afrobarometer*, 30 October 2020) https://www.afrobarometer.org/articles/overwhelming-majority-ethiopians-support-democracy-seek-accountable-governance/ accessed 1 October 2023

'Restore Law and Order, Not at the Expense of Constitutionalism' (*Addis Fortune*, 19 November 2017) https://addisfortune.net/columns/restore-law-and-order-not-at-the-expense-of-constitutionalism accessed 1 October 2023

Roznai Y., *Unconstitutional Constitutional Amendments: The Limits of Amendment Powers* (OUP 2017)

Scalia A., *A Matter of Interpretation: Federal Courts and the Law* (Princeton University Press 1998)

Schmitt C., *Constitutional Theory* (Duke University Press 2008)

Tadesse M., 'It's Time to Respect the Wolayta People's Constitutional Rights' (*Ethiopia Insight*, 28 August 2020) https://www.ethiopia-insight.com/2020/08/28/its-time-to-respect-the-wolayta-peoples-constitutional-rights/ accessed 1 October 2023

Trueman T., 'An Imperial Narrative Gets Recycled' (*Ethiopia Insight*, 24 August 2020) https://www.ethiopia-insight.com/2020/08/24/an-imperial-narrative-gets-recycled/ accessed 1 October 2023

'Update: Details of Ethiopia's State of Emergency Proclamation' (*Addis Standard*, 2 November 2021) https://addisstandard.com/update-details-of-ethiopias-state-of-emergency-proclamation/ accessed 1 October 2023

Vaughan S., *The Addis Ababa Transitional Conference of July 1991: Its Origins, History and Significance* (Centre of African Studies, University of Edinburgh 1994)

Vaughan S., 'Ethnicity and Power in Ethiopia' (PhD thesis, University of Edinburgh 2003)

Walsh D., 'Ethiopia's War Leads to Ethnic Cleansing in Tigray Region, U.S. Report Says' *New York Times* (New York, 26 February 2021) https://www.nytimes.com/2021/02/26/world/middleeast/ethiopia-tigray-ethnic-cleansing.html accessed 1 October 2023

Waluchow W.J., *A Common Law Theory of Judicial Review: The Living Tree* (CUP 2007)

Woldegiorgis D., 'Ethiopia: A Country on the Brinks' (*Borkena*, 10 April 2019) https://borkena.com/2019/04/10/ethiopia-a-country-on-the-brinks-by-dawit-woldegiorgis/ accessed 10 April 2019

Woubshet A., 'Our "Protectors" in Blue: Police Brutality and Misconduct in Ethiopia' (*Ethiopia Insight*, 14 August 2020) https://www.ethiopia-insight.com/2020/08/14/our-protectors-in-blue-police-brutality-and-misconduct-in-ethiopia/ accessed 1 October 2023

Yibeltal K., 'Ethiopia Has World's Biggest Displaced Population' (*BBC News*, 19 May 2022) https://www.bbc.com/news/topics/cwlw3xz047jt/ethiopia accessed 1 October 2023

Zewde B., *The Quest for Socialist Utopia: The Ethiopian Student Movement 1960–1974* (James Currey 2014)

12

Citizens' Collective Action, Constitutional Changes, and Constitutionalism: Lessons from the Building Bridges Initiative in Kenya

Marystella Simiyu and Trésor Muhindo Makunya

1. Introduction

A country may be confronted with the option to amend or revise its constitution in the course of its democratic trajectory. Like any 'contract', the constitution can become ill-equipped to address contemporaneous issues faced by the people, thus necessitating the adjustment of constitutional norms and institutions to better reflect the current public zeitgeist and needs.[1] The constituent power is alive to this reality, given that every modern African constitution sets some procedural and substantive rules on its amendment or revision. Some constitutions determine a set of constitutional provisions, values, and principles which cannot be the subject of constitutional amendment.[2] Among the generally problematic aspects of constitutional amendments or revisions in Africa are the motives of political actors who initiate them, the moments when they are initiated, and the degree of consultation conducted to ensure that citizens are aware of and acquiesce to proposed changes to the 'social contract'. The procedural safeguards on constitutional amendments enshrined in the constitution suggest that constitutional drafters wanted to minimize the likelihood of amendments that undermine basic constitutional principles. However rigid some of these mechanisms may be, the experience with African political leaders tends to show that those safeguards can easily be thwarted or manipulated. For example, this can be seen when a parliamentary majority chooses to pass a constitutional amendment that advances party interests or manipulates constitutional referendums.[3] Democratic collective action should thus be undertaken to exert pressure on those who misuse constitutional change, so that the amendment or revision does not undermine constitutional progress.

This chapter reviews a crucial safeguard against unconstitutional constitutional amendment in Africa, namely the role that civil society groups, citizens, and social movements can

[1] Xenophon Contiades, 'Constitutional Change Engineering' in Xenophon Contiades (ed), *Engineering Constitutional Change: A Comparative Perspective on Europe, Canada and the USA* (Routledge 2013) 2; Xenophon Contiades and Alkmene Fotiadou, 'Introduction: Comparative Constitutional Change: A New Academic Field' in Xenophon Contiades and Alkmene Fotiadou (eds.), *Routledge Handbook of Comparative Constitutional Change* (Taylor & Francis 2020) 4.

[2] Silvia Suteu, *Eternity Clauses in Democratic Constitutionalism* (OUP 2021) 1–3.

[3] Charles Manga Fombad, 'Some Perspectives on Durability and Change under Modern African Constitutions' (2013) 11(2) International Journal of Constitutional Law 382, 404–09.

Marystella Simiyu and Trésor Muhindo Makunya, *Citizens' Collective Action, Constitutional Changes, and Constitutionalism: Lessons from the Building Bridges Initiative in Kenya* In: *Constitutional Change and Constitutionalism in Africa*. Edited by: Charles M. Fombad and Nico Steytler, Oxford University Press. © Marystella Simiyu and Trésor Muhindo Makunya 2025.
DOI: 10.1093/9780198957034.003.0014

play to positively or negatively counter what they perceive as constitutional amendments that violate the tenets of constitutionalism. It looks at attempts to amend one of Africa's most progressive and transformative constitutions, the Constitution of Kenya (2010), and the discontent that the so-called Building Bridges Initiative (BBI) caused.[4] As the making of the current constitution of Kenya was participatory, one would expect that changes to it are effected through a participatory process. The preamble of the Kenyan Constitution duly reads:

> We, the people of Kenya . . . exercising our sovereign and inalienable right to determine the form of governance of our country and having participated fully in the making of this Constitution: adopt, enact and give this Constitution to ourselves and to our future generations.

The inclusion of this preambular clause was not accidental. While the description 'fully' in relation to the level of participation in the constitution-making process has been debated,[5] it is largely accepted that the Kenyan constitution-making process was a model of participatory constitutional building in Africa.[6] The 2010 Constitution was the product of a nearly two-decades-long pro-democracy and constitutional reform movement: one spearheaded by civil society, including non-governmental organizations (NGOs), lawyers, religious groups, and various politicians.[7] The tension between the demands of the people and those of political and other elites consistently beset and threatened to defeat the constitutional reform process.[8] This was a well-founded fear in view of previous instances where such processes succumbed to capture by political elites.[9] However, citizen activism dovetailed with other factors to deliver the transformative 2010 Constitution, which has been hailed for its strong Bill of Rights, devolution of power, and system of checks and balances.[10]

The adoption of the 2010 Constitution raised hopes that the country was poised for transformation, for nurturing a culture of limited government, and for exercising political power within the strictures of the Constitution.[11] It signalled the dawn of an era of

[4] 'The Building Bridges Initiative (BBI): Is There Anything New for Kenyan Youth?' (*The Youth Café*, 12 November 2020) https://www.theyouthcafe.com/perspectives/the-building-bridges-initiativebbi-is-there-anything-new-for-kenyan-youth accessed 30 May 2022.

[5] Jill Cottrell and Yash Ghai, 'Constitution Making and Democratization in Kenya (2000–2005)' (2007) 14(1) Democratisation 1.

[6] Erin Houlihan and Sumit Bisarya, *Practical Considerations for Public Participation in Constitution-Building*, International IDEA Policy Paper no 24 (2021) 45–47; Jason Gluck and Michele Brandt, *Participatory and Inclusive Constitution-Making* (Peaceworks 2015).

[7] Stephen Ndegwa, 'The Incomplete Transition: The Constitutional and Electoral Context in Kenya' (1998) 45(2) Africa Today 193, 195–97; Willy Mutunga, *Constitution-Making from the Middle: Civil Society and Transition Politics in Kenya, 1992–1997* (Mwengo 1999); Lawrence Juma, 'Ethnic Politics and the Constitutional Review Process in Kenya' (2002) 9 Tulsa Journal of Comparative and International Law 471; Peter Agweli Onalo, *Constitution-Making in Kenya* (Transfrica Press 2004).

[8] Alice Bannon, 'Designing a Constitution-drafting Process' (2007) 116(8) Yale Law Journal 1841, 1849–50.

[9] Cottrell and Ghai (n 5) 12–17; Bannon (n 8) 1849–50.

[10] Willy Mutunga, 'The 2010 Constitution of Kenya and Its Interpretation: Reflections from the Supreme Court's Decisions' 1 http://www.saflii.org/za/journals/SPECJU/2015/6.pdf accessed 14 May 2022. See also *In the Matter of the Speaker of the Senate and another*, Advisory Opinion Reference 2 of 2013 [2013] eKLR paras 51 and 52; *In the Matter of the Kenya National Commission on Human Rights*, Supreme Court Advisory Opinion Reference no 1 of 2012; [2014] eKLR para 26(b).

[11] Nkatha Kabira and Robert Kibugi, 'Saving the Soul of an African Constitution: Learning from Kenya's Experience with Constitutionalism during COVID-19' (2020) 20(2) African Human Rights Law Journal 439–40.

transformative constitutionalism in Kenya. Transformative constitutionalism 'connotes an enterprise of inducing large-scale social change and through non-violent political processes grounded in law',[12] while a transformative constitution is one which transforms the existing pre-constitutional order. As such, 'these constitutions are aspirational and are meant to empower the newly democratized state to make significant changes to the existing social and economic order'.[13]

An examination of the history, text, and structure of the Kenyan Constitution reveals why it can rightfully be defined as transformative.[14] Therefore, when confronted with the divisive question of the validity of the constitutional amendments proposed by the BBI, the courts were categorical in analysing the role of the people in the making of the Constitution of Kenya (Amendment) Bill of 2020 (CKAB, 2020).[15] Public participation is a constitutionally recognized national value and principle of good governance.[16] It also represents a core legitimizing factor in constitution-making and reform processes.[17] The role of the people in constitution-making and constitutional change was situated not only in the immediate context of the BBI but also historically. The picture that emerges is of a relentless struggle for the placement of citizens at the centre of constitution-making and reform processes in Kenya.

In the next section, this chapter examines the meaning and forms of collective citizen action against constitutional change by looking at how citizen and private groups have mobilized in some African countries in the context of attempts by presidents to unconstitutionally overstay their welcome in power.[18] The third section examines the different ways in which political leaders have consolidated their powers in Kenya through unconstitutional constitutional amendments, and the popular resistance, or lack thereof, that these attempts have encountered. The section draws on Kenya's post-1990 constitution-making process to locate the origin of a culture of resistance to unconstitutional amendments: a culture which explains how private groups came to mobilize against the BBI project. The fourth section shows that institutional mobilization through the judiciary reinforced the legitimacy of collective action against the BBI project: a situation that points to several lessons about African constitutionalism. The chapter concludes by noting that, while amending or revising a constitution is a natural democratic process, stakeholders should primarily consider the will of the people and ensure that they do not undermine the underlying principles of constitutionalism.

[12] Karl Klare, 'Legal Culture and Transformative Constitutionalism' (1998) 14(1) South African Journal on Human Rights 146, 150.

[13] Heinz Klug, 'Transformative Constitutions and the Role of Integrity Institutions in Tempering Power: The Case of Resistance to State Capture in Post-Apartheid South Africa' (2019) 67(3) Buffalo Law Review 701.

[14] Eric Kibet and Charles Fombad, 'Transformative Constitutionalism and the Adjudication of Constitutional Rights in Africa' (2017) 17(2) African Human Rights Law Journal 340, 352.

[15] Constitution of Kenya (Amendment) Bill of 2020.

[16] Constitution of Kenya, art 10.

[17] Ruth Gordon, 'Growing Constitutions' (1999) 1(3) Journal of Constitutional Law 528; John Hatchard, Muna Ndulo, and Peter Slinn, *Comparative Constitutionalism and Good Governance in the Commonwealth: An Eastern and Southern African Perspective* (CUP 2004) 57–98, 184–207; Joel Colon-Rios, 'Notes on Democracy and Constitution-Making' (2011) 9(1) New Zealand Journal of Public International Law 17.

[18] Bruce Baker, 'Outstaying One's Welcome: The Presidential Third-Term Debate in Africa' (2002) 8(4) Contemporary Politics 285.

2. The meaning and form of citizens' collective action against constitutional changes

An accurate account of constitutional revolution and reform in Africa must begin by acknowledging the significant contribution of civil society and grass-roots organizations, along with international organizations and other actors, to defining the structure and nature of the political regimes of modern African states.[19] The winds of change that blew on African shores began with domestic pressure on authoritarian governments by citizens and civil society groups seeking to establish political regimes and systems based on some form of limitation on the exercise of powers. Civil society groups are rightly seen as bulwarks against 'abusive constitutionalism'.[20] This stems from their power to stand by minority groups whose constitutional rights are disregarded by the state,[21] to foster accountable government and governance, and to stop attempts to alter the transformative 'social contract' the people entered into with their governors. Post-1990 constitutions largely established a culture of constitutionalism, respect for the rule of law, and fundamental rights and freedoms, and placed citizens at the centre stage of constitution-making and reform.[22] This meant that constitutional changes must obtain the buy-in of citizens through their participation in the process, and must not contradict the gains made during the constitutional transformation. In turn, citizens, civil society organizations, and other social movements sustain the ability to mobilize against constitutional changes that undermine the core values of constitutionalism.

2.1 The meaning of citizens' collective action

According to Steven Friedman, democratic collective action 'is the process in which people combine with others to use the rules and rights of democracy to influence power regardless of the method'.[23] The action may pertain to any subject of interest to the group, for example the recognition of Afrikaans as the medium of instruction in the South African context.[24] It could also relate to an interest of the community at large, such as in free health care for persons infected with HIV/AIDS, housing facilities for the most vulnerable, or water provision to rural communities.[25]

[19] Steven Friedman, *Power in Action: Democracy, Citizenship and Social Justice* (NYU Press 2019) 61; Boniface Dulani, 'Democracy Movements as Bulwarks against Presidential Usurpation of Power: Lessons from the Third-Term Bids in Malawi, Namibia, Uganda and Zambia' (2011) 20(11) Stichproben – Vienna Journal of African Studies 189, 117.

[20] David Landau and Rosalind Dixon, 'Constraining Constitutional Change' (2015) 4 Wake Forest Law Review 859, 862.

[21] James Fowkes, *Building the Constitution: The Practice of Constitutional Interpretation in Post-Apartheid South Africa* (CUP 2016) 81.

[22] Abrak Saati, 'Participation – to Unveil a Myth' in Tania Abbiate, Markus Böckenförde, and Veronica Federico (eds), *Public Participation in African Constitutionalism* (Routledge 2018) 15–16.

[23] Friedman (n 19) 122. Reference is made only to methods that are democratically lawful.

[24] *AfriForum and Another v University of the Free State* [2017] ZACC 48.

[25] Tshepo Madlingozi, 'Social Movements and the Constitutional Court of South Africa' in Oscar Vilhena, Upendra Baxi, and Frans Viljoen (eds.), *Transformative Constitutionalism: Comparing the Apex Courts of Brazil, India and South Africa* (Pretoria University Law Press 2013) 540.

This chapter focuses on collective action by individuals or groups of individuals that are outside the political sphere and not seeking profit.[26] They are to be distinguished from the state. Following Nick Barber, the distinction between the former and the latter should be made in at least three respects.[27] First, the scope of private groups' authority and power is normally different from that of the state and its organs. Civil society organizations (CSOs) do not control their members in the way the state claims to exercise control over its citizens. Second, those who come together in collective action do so voluntarily because consent is the common denominator of membership of private groups. This differs sharply from belongingness to a state, which largely does not depend on individual choice.

Finally, private groups aim primarily to advance the interests of their individual members and do not claim to pursue the general interest as the state does. While this does not preclude actions for the greater good of citizens—for example, constitutional mobilization and literacy, public interest litigation, and provision of basic services to marginalized communities—the role of realizing the general interest lies with the state rather than with them.[28] Citizen mobilization may correct the internal deficits of representative democracy that come to light where elected officials are beholden to party positions and cannot vote against retrogressive constitutional amendments when they are submitted before Parliament.[29]

Different kinds of private groups may conduct collective action. Such groups include registered and unregistered CSOs, social movements, trade unions, pro-democracy movements, professional associations, religious groups, or concerned citizens.[30] They do not use the state's resources to mobilize. Some of them are registered in accordance with relevant domestic laws, while others may mobilize without being formally recognized by the state.[31] The latter is explained by the fact that collective action led by CSOs may at times be hindered by their non-recognition by the state, which is frequent in illiberal democracies. For these reasons, human rights bodies, including the United Nations Human Rights Council and the African Commission on Human and Peoples' Rights, have made efforts through standard-setting to ensure that unregistered groups enjoy democratic rights.[32]

Furthermore, citizens may participate in collective action 'without engaging directly in any action besides joining an organization'.[33] However, they engage with the government on a regular basis, irrespective of the selected medium. To quote Friedman, '[c]ollective action is intrinsic to all democracies—the issue is not whether citizens engage in it but which citizens do and in what way'.[34] The next subsection reviews the forms that citizens' collective action may take with respect to the issue of constitutional change.

[26] 'What Is a Civil Society? – Definition & Examples – Video & Lesson Transcript' (*Study.com*, undated) https://study.com/academy/lesson/what-is-a-civil-society-definition-examples.html accessed 31 May 2022.

[27] NW Barber, *The Principles of Constitutionalism* (OUP 2018) 123.

[28] Ibid. 124.

[29] Stephen Tierney, *Constitutional Referendums: The Theory and Practice of Republican Deliberation* (OUP 2012) 26.

[30] Dulani (n 19) 116.

[31] Case of La Lutte pour le Changement (LUCHA) in the DRC.

[32] Human Rights Council, 'Rights to Freedom of Peaceful Assembly and of Association: Report of the Special Rapporteur on the Rights to Freedom of Peaceful Assembly and of Association' (2019) A/HRC/41/41 para 13.

[33] Friedman (n 19) 123.

[34] Ibid. 145.

2.2 Forms of citizens' collective action against constitutional changes

The post-1990 wave of constitutional revival in Africa paved the way for different forms of collective action by citizens, social movements, and civil society groups, of which two are peculiar. In the first place, collective action can be conducted outside of any institutional mechanisms (extra-institutional mobilization), so as to exert concerted pressure on those who hold political power; and, in the second place, collective actors can use established institutions, for example Parliament and the judiciary, to uphold constitutional supremacy (institutional mobilization). These two forms—institutional and extra-institutional mobilization—are not mutually exclusive. Section 2.2.1 examines the first form of collective action, while section 2.2.2 examines collective action through judicial mechanisms. In section 3, we relate these models to the type of citizen- and civil-society-mobilization strategies that were used in Kenya.

2.2.1 Rights-based extra-institutional mobilization

The rights enshrined in modern African constitutions create entitlements that can be mobilized to uphold respect for the constitutional order when it is threatened with change. Constitutional rights are, on the one hand, objective norms against which the behaviour of states and non-state organs can be assessed and challenged, and, on the other, subjective privileges accruing to individuals that enable them, actively or passively, to participate in the conduct of government affairs.[35] Governments have the positive obligation to foster an environment of citizen participation, including when they are considering constitutional change.

It is thus no surprise that rights such as the right to freedom of association, assembly, demonstration, and petition are invoked by civil society movements in order to organize, either online or offline, against constitutional changes they believe are a disruption to the hard-won constitutional order.[36] Some constitutions impose a fundamental duty on citizens to mobilize against any attempts to circumvent the constitutional order, be these formal or informal unconstitutional changes.[37] Other vehicles to preserve the gains of the constitutional revolution against unconstitutional changes are steadily emerging and taking shape, chief of which is mobilization through digital technologies.[38] The latter have gone a long way to enabling citizens to mobilize freely despite the threat that digital surveillance poses to the privacy of constitutional mobilizers and members of pro-democracy movements.[39] Modern African constitutions have thus established democratic space that can be utilized by social movements to mobilize.[40]

[35] Louis Favoreu and others, *Droit Constitutionnel* (21st edn, Dalloz 2019) 936–37.

[36] Douglas NeJaime, 'Constitutional Change, Courts, and Social Movements' (2012) 111 Michigan Law Review 877, 893.

[37] For example, art 64(1) of the 2006 DRC Constitution reads as follows: 'All Congolese have the duty to oppose any individual or group of individuals who seize power by force or who exercise it in violation of the provisions of this Constitution.'

[38] Zeynep Tufekci and Christopher Wilson, 'Social Media and the Decision to Participate in Political Protest: Observations from Tahrir Square' (2012) 62(2) Journal of Communication 363; Brian D Loader and Dan Mercea, 'Networking Democracy? Social Media Innovations and Participatory Politics' (2011) 14(6) Information, Communication & Society 757.

[39] Carissa Veliz, *Privacy Is Power: Why and How You Should Take Back Control of Your Data* (Melville House 2022).

[40] Madlingozi (n 25) 532.

The phenomenon of altering or removing presidential term limits to allow an incumbent president to seek a third term or an unlimited number of terms of office (third-termism) in Africa has generated collective action in the form of mass mobilization and protests.[41] These actions were led by classic CSOs and newly formed pro-democracy movements.[42] Third-termism can be effected through formal and informal constitutional change: the former occurs when a formal constitutional amendment changes the number of terms, alters the duration of terms, repeals the age limit, or removes term limits altogether; the latter is undertaken through constitutional interpretation.

Citizens, civil society, and social movements mobilize against informal constitutional changes as well. In this context, they protest against constitutional interpretations by constitutional courts that pave the way for the president to run for additional terms.[43] Decisions by constitutional courts suggesting that the entry into force of a new constitution resets the counter of term limits to zero[44] have been met with robust civil society and citizen mobilization. Similarly, citizens have mobilized against judgments which have ruled that, pending the inauguration of a new president, the incumbent president remains in office,[45] whether elections have been organized or not.

The 'reset of the counter' tactic was witnessed in Kenya during its return to multiparty politics. The 1991 constitutional amendment that reintroduced multipartyism also set a presidential two-term limit. The government conveniently interpreted the clause to commence with the upcoming 1992 elections, paving the way for the incumbent President Moi to vie for office.[46] He also unsuccessfully attempted to prolong his term in office in the lead-up to the 2002 elections, under the guise of allowing elections to take place under a new constitution scheduled to be promulgated in 2003.[47] This decision, however, drew public ire and citizen mobilization and was quickly shelved. Then, to fast-forward to 2022, Kenyans were treated to another Machiavellian scenario under the BBI.[48] There was wide speculation that the proposed constitutional amendments were a ploy at power consolidation.[49] Collective action against the BBI aimed to stop such a consolidation of power but took an institutional route through the courts.

[41] Trésor Muhindo Makunya and Kwadwo Appiageyi-Atua, 'Soldiers in Civilian Uniforms: The Role of the Military in the Pursuit of Third-Termism' in Aderomola Adeola and Makau W Mutua (eds.), *The Palgrave Handbook of Democracy, Governance and Justice in Africa* (1st edn, Palgrave Macmillan 2022).

[42] Phidias Ahadi Senge Milemba, *Mouvements citoyens africains: creuset de l'éveil civique et briseurs de l'ordre néolibéral?* (L'Harmattan 2021).

[43] Julien Adayé, 'Manifestation contre un Troisième Mandat en Côte d'Ivoire' (*dw.com*, 19 October 2020) https://www.dw.com/fr/manifestation-contre-un-troisi%C3%A8me-mandat-en-c%C3%B4te-divoire/a-55328440 accessed 31 May 2022.

[44] Decision no CI-2020-EP-009/14-09/CC/SG 14 September 2020, paras 39–40; Constitutional Court of Guinea, Decision AC 014 of 11 June 2020; Adem K Abebe, 'Côte d'Ivoire: Ouattara's Bid for 3rd Term Opens up a Can of Worms' (*The Africa Report*, 23 July 2020) https://www.theafricareport.com/34674/cote-divoire-ouattaras-bid-for-3rd-term-opens-up-a-can-of-worms/ accessed 31 May 2022.

[45] Nelson Alusala, 'Why Kabila's Bid to Remain in Power Is Bad News for the Democratic Republic of the Congo' (*The Conversation*, 31 July 2017) http://theconversation.com/why-kabilas-bid-to-remain-in-power-is-bad-news-for-the-democratic-republic-of-the-congo-81414 accessed 31 May 2022.

[46] Jeffrey Steeves, 'Presidential Succession in Kenya: The Transition from Moi to Kibaki' (2006) 44(2) Commonwealth & Comparative Politics 211, 213–14.

[47] 'Kenya's Moi Seeks to Prolong Rule' (*CNN*, 29 June 2002) http://edition.cnn.com/2002/WORLD/africa/06/29/kenya.moi/ accessed 31 May 2022.

[48] See section 3 below for an in-depth analysis of the BBI project.

[49] Justus Wanga and Onyango K'Onyango, 'What is President Uhuru Kenyatta's Power Plan after Leaving Office in August?' *The Nation* (Nairobi, 7 March 2022) https://nation.africa/kenya/news/politics/uhuru-game-plan-after-august-polls-3738726 accessed 30 May 2022.

2.2.2 Institutional mobilization against constitutional changes through the judiciary

The constitutional review processes established to guarantee the supremacy of the constitutions in many African countries can be (and have been) utilized to counter and sometimes legitimize unconstitutional constitutional changes. This strategic use of constitutional litigation and the mobilization of legal arguments in courts to protect the constitutional order—also known as 'constitutional lawfare'[50]—can lead to successful outcomes. For example, in Benin, the 'Do Not Touch My Constitution' campaign, led by social movements against the opportunistic amendment to what was then considered the most progressive francophone constitutional dispensation in Africa, resulted in the Constitutional Court's nullifying proposed amendments that would have granted additional presidential terms to the president.[51]

The success of constitutional lawfare hinges on several variables, however. These include whether the legal framework establishing courts enables direct citizen access; whether judges are independent enough to resist arbitrary removal should they decide against the policy preference of powerful political actors; whether citizens are prepared to mobilize through the judiciary; whether the judiciary is seen, by other actors, as an important player or arbitrator of the political game; and whether the judiciary's decisions will be respected by all the parties involved, irrespective of the outcome.

Another thing that varies from country to country is the constitutional tradition; the nature of these traditions affects the ability to mobilize against constitutional changes.[52] The two main legal traditions, common law and civil law, have influenced the culture of constitutional mobilization. Under common law, collective action through the courts is possible and often successful.[53] By contrast, under civil law, individuals increasingly resort to the street, perhaps because mobilizing through formal channels (whether parliamentary or judicial) does not always yield the desired outcomes. It is generally assumed that, in contradistinction to their civil law counterparts, citizens living in most African common law countries have a more accommodative constitutional culture. This tradition enables them to advocate for constitutional transformation through legal mobilization without fear of reprisal.[54] This is hardly the case in African civil law countries. For example, the number of public interest litigation cases against Covid-19 regulations in Kenya, South Africa, and Uganda[55] were much higher than in the many francophone African countries which similarly experienced retrogressive Covid-19 measures.

[50] Michelle Le Roux and Dennis Davis, *Lawfare: Judging Politics in South Africa* (Jonathan Ball 2019).

[51] Segnonna Horace Adjolohoun, 'Centralized Model of Constitutional Adjudication: The Constitutional Court of Benin' in Charles Manga Fombad (ed.), *Constitutional Adjudication in Africa* (OUP 2017) 67.

[52] Serges Djoyou Kamga, 'An Assessment of the Possibilities for Impact Litigation in Francophone African Countries' (2014) 14(2) African Human Rights Law Journal 449, 463–69.

[53] J Oloka-Onyango, 'Human Rights and Public Interest Litigation in East Africa: A Bird's Eye View' (2015) 47 George Washington International Law Review 763.

[54] Hugh Corder and Cora Hoexter, '"Lawfare" in South Africa and Its Effects on the Judiciary' (2017) 10(2-3) African Journal of Legal Studies 105, 111–16.

[55] Ebenezer Durojaye and Robert Doya Nanima, 'From Muhammed and Others to De Beer and Others: Striking the Balance between Public Health Measures and Human Rights during Covid-19 Era in South Africa' (2021) 47(1) Commonwealth Law Bulletin 175; Daniël Eloff, 'The Rationality Test in Lockdown Litigation in South Africa' (2021) 21(2) African Human Rights Law Journal 1157, 1157–80; Martin van Staden, 'Constitutional Rights and Their Limitations: A Critical Appraisal of the COVID-19 Lockdown in South Africa' (2020) 20(2) African Human Rights Law Journal 484; Ian Freckelton, 'COVID-19 Curfews: Kenyan and Australian Litigation and Pandemic Protection' (2020) 28(1) Journal of Law and Medicine 117.

The decentralized constitutional review system applicable in Kenya also strengthens the ability of private groups to engage meaningfully with other actors on matters of constitutional change. Public interest litigation paved the way for robust intra- and extrajudicial dialogue on the validity of constitutional changes.[56] The dialogue not only involved many actors but also enabled them to understand the motivations of the contending sides of the argument, regardless of whether they were persuaded or not. In addition, it improved the quality of the actors' argumentation and allowed their case to be heard on appeal by higher judicial organs. This process is fundamental to building a culture promotive of constitutionalism based on popular participation and, correlatively, reducing the likelihood of contestation escalating into violence.

The discussion above highlights the existence of several avenues that private groups can take in order to harness collective action as a means of countering the resurgence of a culture of abusive constitutional amendments in Africa. It is relevant to see how these avenues work in the concrete situation of attempts at curbing the gains of transformative constitutionalism. The next section reviews what has been a controversial amendment proposal in Kenya by looking at its origins and manifestations, as well as the mobilization to which it led.

3. Collective action against Kenya's BBI

3.1 The origin of the BBI

It is hard to miss the irony that, right from its conceptualization, a project called 'Building Bridges' was the cause of so much acrimony and litigation. The BBI was the brainchild of President Uhuru Kenyatta and his long-time political rival Raila Odinga, following their rapprochement after the contentious 2017 general elections.[57] This settlement of political differences is referred to as 'the handshake', in reference to the symbolic gesture that served to seal their memorandum of understanding (MoU).[58] The MoU identified nine areas of challenge to national unity: ethnic antagonism and competition; lack of a national ethos; inclusivity; devolution; divisive elections; safety and security; corruption; shared prosperity; and responsibility and rights.[59] The president then appointed the Building Bridges to Unity Advisory Taskforce (BBI Taskforce) to evaluate the identified challenges facing lasting unity in Kenya and to develop practical recommendations and reform proposals.[60]

In undertaking its mandate, the BBI Taskforce was required to consult 'citizens, the faith-based sector, cultural leaders, the private sector and experts at both the county and national levels'.[61] The BBI Taskforce reported that it undertook consultations in all 47 counties, where it engaged with more than 7,000 citizens of diverse ethnicity, gender, religion, culture, and socio-economic status. The consultations included more than 400 current and

[56] Discussed in section 4 below.
[57] Onyango K'Onyango, 'From BBI to Azimio, the Handshake Continues to Divide Political Opinion' *The Nation* (Nairobi, 9 March 2022) https://nation.africa/kenya/news/politics/handshake-continues-to-divide-political-opinion-3741678 accessed 14 May 2022.
[58] Ibid.
[59] Kenya Gazette no 55 of 3 May 2019, vol CXXI 1708.
[60] Ibid.
[61] TORs of Kenya Gazette Notice no 5154 of 31 May 2018, vol CXX no 64, s 1.

former elected leaders, prominent local voices from the community and youth, and engaged with 123 individuals representing major institutions, including constitutional bodies and stakeholders in the civil and private sector spaces. The Taskforce received 261 emailed responses from organizations and individuals, along with 755 handwritten submissions after public forums at the county level.[62]

Following the submission of the interim report by the BBI Taskforce, President Kenyatta appointed the Steering Committee on the Implementation of the Building Bridges to a United Kenya Taskforce Report (BBI Steering Committee), also via gazette notice.[63] The BBI Steering Committee was tasked with validating the report submitted by the BBI Taskforce through stakeholder consultations. It was further mandated to 'propose administrative, policy, statutory or constitutional changes' towards the implementation of the BBI Taskforce report, taking into consideration the stakeholder input.[64] It was this report submitted by the BBI Steering Committee which became the CKAB, 2020.

Arguably, with the Constitution then almost clocking a decade, it was ripe for review to assess whether it was working for the Kenyan people. Constitutional experts who argued for this constitutional review envisioned a people-centred process.[65] The contention behind the derivation and substance of the CKAB, 2020 played out through both institutional and extra-institutional avenues. The familiar tension between the desires of the people and those of the political elite featured prominently in analysing the legitimacy of the CKAB, 2020 and whether it upheld the core tenets of constitutionalism under the 2010 Constitution.

While there was provision for public participation in the making of the CKAB, 2020, it fell short of a meaningful and comprehensive engagement, given the critical changes the bill meant to introduce to the 2010 Constitution. The next subsection brings out this difference by examining how citizen participation and activism defined the constitutional review process that culminated in the 2010 Constitution. This is juxtaposed with the case of the CKAB, 2020, in order to highlight the strong citizen mobilization that developed in response to the BBI project and the effect this mobilization had on the culture of constitutional protection in Kenya.

3.2 Popular participation in Kenya's constitutional reform processes

3.2.1 The consolidation of power through (un)constitutional amendments in post-independence Kenya

The 2010 Constitution was the upshot of the constitutional reform movement that spanned almost twenty years.[66] It was part of the push for democratic governance that marked the 1980s and 1990s and came to be known as the third wave of democratization

[62] BBI Taskforce, *Building Bridges to a United Kenya: From a Nation of Blood Ties to a Nation of Ideals* (October 2019) 135.

[63] Kenya Gazette Notice no 264 of 10 January 2020 vol CXXII no 7.

[64] Ibid. s 1.

[65] Kitavi Mutua, 'Experts Support Push to Amend Constitution' *The Nation* (Nairobi, 28 June 2020) https://nation.africa/kenya/news/experts-support-push-to-amend-constitution-67302 accessed 15 May 2022.

[66] Christina Murray, 'Kenya's 2010 Constitution' (2013) 61 Neue Folge Band Jahrbuch des offentlichen Rechts 747.

in Africa.[67] As in many African countries, the impetus for the democratization movement in Kenya arose against the backdrop of breakdowns in the rule of law, rampant corruption, imperial presidentialism, patrimonialism, gross human rights violations, and a culture of non-constitutionalism fomented by post-independence governments.[68]

Africa's Independence Constitutions were generally democratic, with guarantees for human rights, provisions for checks and balances, and a central focus on limiting state power.[69] However, these documents were often negotiated in foreign lands and lacked an autochthonous quality reflective of the African context; as such, they were arguably unfit for the nascent governments of the independence era.[70] Okoth-Ogendo writes:

> As the minimum and necessary adaptation, the colonial powers imposed upon the new African regimes constitutions which were inherently fragile and which depended for their stability largely upon the maintenance of good public relations in politics—the one thing which most ruling elites were not prepared to guarantee.[71]

This shortfall of political goodwill from post-independence African leaders enabled the practice of unconstitutional amendments to constitutions by African governments for political expediency as opposed to the public interest. These processes failed both on the procedural and substantive front, with leaders using constitutional amendments as vehicles for increased centralization of power.[72] The situation was no different in Kenya.

A culture of constitutional amendments that were substantively or procedurally flawed, or both, started a year after Kenya's independence. In 1964, the Kenyan government passed the first constitutional amendment to convert the parliamentary system into a presidential one and so consolidate power in the presidency.[73] Between 1964 and 1991, the Kenyan Constitution underwent 26 amendments that were substantively wanting, and which served to increase the powers of the president to those of an imperial president, to limit the system of checks and balances, and to weaken the rule of law.[74] There was little pretence that these government-initiated amendments were meant to do anything more than fortify personal rule.[75] This culture of flawed constitutional amendment processes and

[67] Charles Manga Fombad, 'Constitutional Reforms and Constitutionalism in Africa: Reflections on Some Current Challenges and Future Prospects' (2011) 59(4) Buffalo Law Review 1007, 1007–08.

[68] Hastings Okoth-Ogendo, 'The Politics of Constitutional Change in Kenya Since Independence, 1963–69' (1972) 71(282) African Affairs 9; Hastings Okoth-Ogendo, 'Constitutions without Constitutionalism: Reflections on an African Political Phenomenon' in Issa Shivji (ed), *State and Constitutionalism: An African Debate on Democracy* (SAPES 1991).

[69] Yash Ghai and Patrick McAuslan, *Public Law and Political Change in Kenya: A Study of the Legal Framework of Government from Colonial Times to the Present* (OUP 1970) 180.

[70] Okoth-Ogendo, 'The Politics of Constitutional Change in Kenya Since Independence, 1963–69' (n 68) 9–10; CoE, *Final Report of The Committee of Experts on Constitutional Review* (2010) 18.

[71] Okoth-Ogendo, 'The Politics of Constitutional Change in Kenya Since Independence, 1963–69' (n 68) 10.

[72] Ibid.; Duncan Okubasu, 'The Implication of Conflation of Normal and "Constitutional Politics" on Constitutional Change in Africa' in Richard Albert, Xenophon Contiades, and Alkmene Fotiadou (eds), *The Foundations and Traditions of Constitutional Amendment* (Hart Publishing 2017) 327, 331.

[73] Makau Mutua, *Kenya's Quest for Democracy: Taming Leviathan* (L Rienner Publishers 2008) 64.

[74] Ibid.; CKRC, *Final Report of the Constitution of Kenya Review Commission* (2005) 30–34; *Council of Governors and 47 Others v Attorney General and 3 Others; Katiba Institute and 2 Others (Amicus Curiae)*, Reference 3 of 2019 [2020].

[75] Robert Jackson and Carl Rosberg, 'Personal Rule: Theory and Practice in Africa' (1984) 16(4) Comparative Politics 421, 428.

hyper-amendment gravely altered the Constitution's values and principles.[76] Notably, the 1982 amendment to section 2A made Kenya a *de jure* one-party state and dealt a major blow to pluralistic politics.[77]

Strong citizen activism—led by religious groups, NGOs, lawyers, academics, and some politicians—against this dismembering of the Constitution and the resultant human rights violations dates back to the post-independence period. It persisted despite the imposition of an 'ideology of order' that vilified people who questioned the excesses of the state or challenged single-party politics as instigators of public disorder and enemies of national unity.[78] It also weathered a harsh state response, with activists being harassed, assaulted, arrested, detained, and assassinated by the regime.[79] Combined with external pressure, a sustained pro-democracy movement led by these internal actors ultimately forced the government to reintroduce multiparty rule a decade later.[80] This, however, did not translate into a return to democratic governance. The regime remained intact following the flawed 1992 and 1997 elections, and reports of human rights violations persisted. This fuelled demands for constitutional reform.[81]

3.2.2 Constitution of Kenya Review: 1997–2005

Baby steps towards constitutional reform began in 1997 with the enactment of the Constitution of Kenya Review Act (CKRA) and a few reforms prior to the 1997 elections. These reforms were developed under the stewardship of the Inter-Parties Parliamentary Group (IPPG) and saw the increased independence of the electoral commission and the repeal of various laws that restricted civil and political rights.[82] Prior to the IPPG reforms, the National Convention Executive Council (NCEC), made up of civil society groups and certain opposition politicians, mobilized citizens for more comprehensive constitutional reforms with the rallying call 'no reforms, no elections'. In typical governmental fashion, state forces descended on these rallies, resulting in loss of lives and severe injuries.[83] The IPPG had emerged from a government bowing to the pressure for constitutional reforms but seeking to steer the process. While some opposition candidates were enticed into joining the IPPG, the NCEC condemned the proposed reforms as inadequate in comparison to what it itself had proposed.[84]

The CKRA was further amended in 1998 following consultations between the government and opposition parties. However, the government still maintained a stranglehold on the constitutional reform process, with there being little participation by opposition parties and civil society.[85] This sidelining of civil society inspired a parallel constitutional review

[76] *David Ndii and others v Attorney General and others*, Petitions E282, 397, E400, E401, E402, E416, and E426 of 2020 and Petition 2 of 2021 (Consolidated) [2021] para 406; Okubasu (n 72) 327, 331.

[77] CoE (n 70) 18–19.

[78] Eisha Atieno-Odhiambo, 'Democracy and the Ideology of Order' in Michael Schatzberg (ed), *The Political Economy of Kenya* (Praeger 1988) 177.

[79] Korwa Adar and Isaac Munyae, 'Human Rights Abuse in Kenya under Daniel Arap Moi, 1978–2001' (2001) 5(1) African Studies Quarterly 1, 7.

[80] Mutunga (n 7).

[81] 'Kenya: Old Habits Die Hard: Rights Abuses Follow Renewed Foreign Aid Commitments' (*Human Rights Watch*, July 1995) http://www.hrw.org/legacy/reports/1995/Kenya.htm accessed 17 May 2021.

[82] CKRC (n 74) 41–42; Cottrell and Ghai (n 5) 5.

[83] Roger Southall, 'Moi's Flawed Mandate: The Crisis Continues in Kenya' (1998) 25(75) Review of African Political Economy 101, 103.

[84] Ibid. 104.

[85] Cottrell and Ghai (n 5) 5–6.

process, led by CSOs and religious groups and dubbed the Ufungamano Initiative, which sought to organize a people-driven constitutional review process.[86] It was only in 2001, under the leadership of Yash Pal Ghai, that the Constitution of Kenya Review Commission (CKRC) found common ground among the government, opposition parties, and CSOs on the conduct of the constitutional review under a unified process.[87]

The central objective of the CKRC was to ensure a comprehensive review of the Constitution 'by the people of Kenya'.[88] The will of the Kenyan people therefore featured prominently in the development of the constitutional review road map. In fulfilling this mandate, the CKRC faced a daunting challenge in facilitating public participation. This was done by way of civic education, collecting and collating the views of Kenyans on constitutional proposals, and conducting studies, research, and evaluations.[89] In addition, the views of vulnerable and disadvantaged groups, such as minority and marginalized communities, women, and persons with disabilities (PWDs), were given special consideration.[90]

The CKRC prepared civic education materials that were widely distributed in hard copy as well as available online. Together with CSOs, the Commission embarked on nationwide civic education entailing public meetings and workshops on the Constitution.[91] The constitutional review process was comprehensively covered by print and broadcast media in both English and Kiswahili, as well as, in some cases, local languages.[92] The process was also inclusive, with provision made for sign language and subtitles during television programmes so as to cater for PWDs. This public engagement culminated in the receipt of more than 37,000 submissions to the Commission.[93] The engagement by government in the submission process was wanting, however, with President Moi eventually withdrawing his submission, and the ruling party, the Kenya African National Union (KANU), submitting a document regarded as paltry.[94]

In their totality, the groups and individuals involved in the constitutional review process were highly diverse and representative of the Kenyan people. Other than the CKRA, which was an independent body of experts, there was a National Constitutional Conference (NCC), tasked with discussing and adopting the draft constitution submitted by the CKRC.[95] It had 629 members, including among them the CKRC commissioners, all Members of Parliament, three representatives of each district, a delegate from each registered political party, and representatives of 'religious organizations, professional bodies, women's organizations, trade unions and non-governmental organizations'.[96] The National Assembly would thereafter enact the amendments to the Constitution.[97]

However, citizen activism through institutional mechanisms intercepted the National Assembly's enaction of the amendments to ensure that citizens' voices featured strongly in the reform process. The landmark case brought by Reverend Timothy Njoya (a clergy

86 CKRC (n 74) 4.
87 Cottrell and Ghai (n 5) 5–6.
88 Constitution of Kenya Review Act (CKRA) 2001, ss 3, 5, and 17.
89 Ibid. s 17.
90 Cottrell and Ghai (n 5) 11–12.
91 Ibid. 9–10.
92 Ibid. 10–11.
93 Ibid. 9.
94 Ibid. 10.
95 CKRA 2001, s 27(1).
96 Ibid. s 27(2); CKRC (n 74) 362–66.
97 CKRA 2001, s 28(4).

member and activist) and private citizens, *Timothy Njoya and Others v CKRC and the NCC Conference*, was a game-changer: the court held that the prerogative to replace the Constitution was of the Kenyan people, rather than Parliament, and that the people should be allowed to exercise this prerogative through a referendum.[98]

The 1997–2005 constitutional review process continued to mould the capabilities of Kenyan citizens to serve as champions for reform, opponents of state capture of reform processes, and vital participants in constitutional review. But the momentum of the constitutional review process was ultimately stalled and distorted by the government—in this case by both the departing government of Moi and the incoming one under the presidency of Mwai Kibaki, albeit in different ways. On Moi's part, the move to dissolve Parliament and call for the scheduled 2002 elections effectively halted the process before the work of the NCC had begun.[99]

3.2.2.1 Bomas and Wako Drafts

The promise by the Mwai Kibaki administration to deliver a new constitution within 100 days did not come to pass.[100] While the 2002 elections were a momentous event for Kenyan democracy that upended a 24-year dictatorship by way of the ballot box, it soon emerged that the incumbent administration was not committed to constitutional reform, especially if such reform limited its powers.[101] The NCC process that was to follow was delayed until 28 April 2003.[102] When it finally took off, it degenerated into an acrimonious affair in which contentious issues relating to devolution and the system of government took centre stage.[103] Orchestrated delays, disagreements between delegates, and boycotts by politicians and government officials frustrated the process even more.[104] Nevertheless, a final charter, known as the Bomas Draft, was developed: one that adopted devolution and a parliamentary system of government. It was, furthermore, seen as reflective of the will of the people, and civil society was supportive of it.[105]

However, these very same aspects were not welcomed by the incumbent government.[106] In 2004, Parliament amended the CKRA to empower it to amend contentious issues of the draft constitution by a simple majority.[107] The draft was further amended by the Attorney General, Amos Wako, to the extent that it acquired a new moniker ('the Wako Draft') as well as changing in form. Especially significant were its amendments reinforcing presidential powers and setting limits on devolution.[108] This was the draft submitted to the Kenyan

[98] *Reverend Dr Timothy M Njoya and 6 Others v Honourable Attorney General and Another*, High Court Misc Application no 82 of 2004 [2004].

[99] Bannon (n 8) 1834; T Gathii, 'Popular Authorship and Constitution Making: Comparing and Contrasting the DRC and Kenya' (2008) 49(4) William & Mary Law Review 1109, 1118.

[100] Denis Kadima and Felix Owuor, 'The National Rainbow Coalition: Achievements and Challenges of Building and Sustaining a Broad-Based Political Party Coalition in Kenya' in Denis Kadima (ed), *Politics of Party Coalitions in Africa* (EISA 2006) 179, 196.

[101] Carter Centre, 'Observing the 2002 Kenya Elections Final Report' (2003); European Parliament, 'Report on the Mission to Observe the Elections of 27 December 2002 in Kenya' (2003); Freedom House, *Freedom in the World 2003* (Freedom House 2004) 299 https://freedomhouse.org/sites/default/files/2020-02/Freedom_in_the_World_2003_complete_book.pdf accessed 19 May 2022.

[102] Cottrell and Ghai (n 5) 11–12.

[103] CoE (n 70) 20–21.

[104] Ibid.

[105] Cottrell and Ghai (n 5) 12.

[106] Ibid. 16.

[107] Bannon (n 8) 1840.

[108] Ibid.

public for a referendum. Citizen mobilization for popular participation in the referendum led to a relatively fair turnout of 52 per cent.[109] Of these voters, an overwhelming 57 per cent rejected the Wako Draft.[110]

The 2005 referendum has been widely debated, and while there were a number of reasons that the proposed constitution was rejected, the one most relevant to this chapter is the government and political elite's usurpation of the role of the people. The referendum was certainly a triumph for the people, but also an indictment of the government.[111] While it resulted in the rejection of the proposed constitution, it did not mean that Kenyans wished to retain the extant Constitution. Rather, it was a reflection of Kenyans' rejection of a document that shunned their input in favour of political expediency.

A conclusion that the defeat was solely a result of public discontentment with the substance of the document is also inaccurate. Admittedly, the hijacking of the process by the government and the subsequent mutilation of the Bomas Draft sowed the seeds of public resentment and inspired citizen mobilization against the Wako Draft. However, citizen mobilization for and against the constitution was highly concentrated along ethnic and party lines.[112] For example, the Kikuyu community—from which President Mwai Kibaki hailed—and its ethnic cousins, the Embu and Meru communities, generally voted for the proposed constitution.[113] Indirect voter-buying by the government also aimed at influencing the voting process. Furthermore, misinformation about the implications of accepting or rejecting the draft was rife and interfered with a meaningful public grasp of the substance of the document.[114] While this state of affairs may have been countered by concerted civic education by civil society groups, their presence was not as prominent as it had been in previous elections. It was suggested that civil society groups felt that they were biased since they had already publicly spoken against the proposed draft.[115]

3.2.2.2 The 2010 Constitution

The aftermath of the 2007 elections revived the constitutional reform process. Admittedly, the democratic expectations of Kenyans had been buoyed by the 2002 elections and 2005 referendum, where the will of the people had prevailed over that of government.[116] All of this dissipated with the flawed 2007 elections and the subsequent post-election violence, which led to the death of more than 1,000 people and the displacement of over 600,000 people.[117] It took the mediation of the African Union Panel of Eminent African Personalities, chaired

[109] Bård Anders Andreassen and Arne Tostensen, 'Of Oranges and Bananas: The 2005 Kenya Referendum on the Constitution', CMI Working Paper (2005) v–vi.

[110] Ibid.

[111] Cottrell and Ghai (n 5) 16.

[112] Kadima and Owuor (n 100) 220; Mwangi Kimenyi and William Shughart, 'The Political Economy of Constitutional Choice: A Study of the 2005 Kenyan Constitutional Referendum' (2008) University of Connecticut Economics Working Papers 200808 21–22 https://opencommons.uconn.edu/cgi/viewcontent.cgi?article=1166&context=econ_wpapers accessed 19 May 2022.

[113] Andreassen and Tostensen (n 109) 3–4.

[114] Ibid. v–vi; Mutua (n 73) 228; Bannon (n 8); Michael Chege, 'Weighed down by Old Ethnic Baggage, Kenya Races to Another Historic Election' (*Center for Strategic and International Studies*, 22 June 2007) https://www.csis.org/analysis/weighed-down-old-ethnic-baggage-kenya-races-another-historic-election accessed 15 May 2022; Gathii (n 99) 1120.

[115] Andreassen and Tostensen (n 109) vi.

[116] Beth Elise Whitaker and Jason Gierschb, 'Voting on a Constitution: Implications for Democracy in Kenya' (2009) 27(1) Journal of Contemporary African Studies 1, 2, 16.

[117] Phillip Waki, *Kenya: Commission of Inquiry into the Post-Election Violence (CIPEV)* (2008) 22–23.

by Kofi Annan, for peace and order to be restored,[118] after which the signing of the National Accord and Reconciliation Act on 28 February 2008, under the Kenya National Dialogue and Reconciliation (KNDR) framework, brought the unprecedented conflict to an end.[119]

Thereafter, a government of national unity was formed between Mwai Kibaki and Raila Odinga as a short-term solution, but it was recognized that long-term issues had engendered the crisis. Indeed, agenda item 4 of the KNDR called for redress of systemic challenges, including constitutional, legal, and institutional reforms.[120] A constitutional review process was also recommended in the reports of the commissions established under the framework, including the Commission of Inquiry on Post-Election Violence (CIPEV), the Independent Review Commission (IREC), and the Truth, Justice and Reconciliation Commission (TJRC).[121]

The reverberations of the 2007–08 crisis, the institutional arrangements put in place under the KNDR, and the momentum generated by the CKRA propelled the post-2007 constitutional process to success. In 2010, there was also commonality of purpose between the principals in government, namely the president (Mwai Kibaki) and prime minister (Raila Odinga)—a factor which had been missing in 2005. Although there was seldom unanimity on contentious issues, politicians were able to negotiate, compromise, and reach a consensus.[122] One such issue was the establishment of a presidential system of government while maintaining devolution.[123]

The legislative foundation of the revamped constitutional review process was the Constitution of Kenya Review Act of 2008 and the Constitution of Kenya (Amendment) Act. The purpose of the legislation was to bring the constitutional review process to fruition through the Committee of Experts (CoE), the Parliamentary Select Committee, the National Assembly, and the referendum.[124] The CoE was to be guided by the existing drafts of the constitution and, from these, identify non-contentious issues and contentious issues that were still unsettled, following which it would embark on comprehensive public consultations, studies, research and evaluation, and civic education. Ultimately, the CoE was to present a harmonized draft constitution to the National Assembly.[125] The final decision-making power fell to the CoE rather than Parliament, thereby insulating the process from political elite amendments.[126]

However, the CoE struggled to build public trust in the public participation process, given the political machinations in 2005 that led to the alteration of the Bomas Draft.[127] Nevertheless, it still embarked on civic education aimed at enhancing understanding of the

[118] Gilbert Khadiagala, 'Forty Days and Nights of Peace-Making in Kenya' (2008) 7(2) Journal of African Elections 4, 13; Monica Juma, 'African Mediation of the Kenyan Post-2007 Election Crisis' (2009) 27(3) Journal of Contemporary African Studies 407, 413.

[119] 'The Kenya National Dialogue and Reconciliation: Building a Progressive Kenya' (*Relief Web*, December 2011) 1 https://reliefweb.int/report/kenya/kenya-national-dialogue-and-reconciliation-building-progressive-kenya-background-note accessed 20 May 2022.

[120] Ibid.

[121] Kofi Annan, *The Kenya National Dialogue and Reconciliation: Building a Progressive Kenya – Our Common Vision Views of Stakeholders* (Kofi Annan Foundation 2012).

[122] Karuti Kanyinga and James Long, 'The Political Economy of Reforms in Kenya: The Post-2007 Election Violence and a New Constitution' (2012) 55(1) African Studies Review 31, 45–47.

[123] Ibid.

[124] Constitution of Kenya Review Act (CKRA) 2008, s 5.

[125] Ibid, s 23.

[126] Ibid.

[127] CoE (n 70) 26.

constitutional review process and facilitating discussion of the proposed drafts of the constitution. This was done, inter alia, through in-person public discussions, Short Message Services (SMSs), and print, broadcast, and social media, such as Facebook and blogs.[128] The CoE publicized slogans such as '*Jisomee. Jiamulie. Jichagulie.*' (Kiswahili for 'Read for yourself. Decide for yourself. Choose for yourself.'), which called for people-ownership of the document.[129] More than 10 million copies of the proposed constitution were available in diverse formats, including English and Kiswahili translations, Braille, simplified versions, soft copies, and newspaper pull-outs.[130]

The Election Management Body (EMB), civil society and international organizations played a crucial role in citizen mobilization for voter registration and conducted widespread civic education drives.[131] This process culminated in a referendum with a 72 per cent turnout, a much-improved attendance compared to the 2005 referendum. The proposed constitution passed with a 67 per cent vote and was inaugurated with much fanfare.[132] Since then, the Kenyan people have adopted both institutional and extra-institutional means to defend the 2010 Constitution.[133]

3.3 The BBI cases: The role of citizens' collective action

The determination on the constitutionality of the BBI in the *David Ndii and others v Attorney General and others* case and subsequent appeals (hereafter, BBI cases) gave due weight to the role of the people in the BBI process as juxtaposed with Kenya's constitutional reform process. The procedural defect in the BBI process featured prominently in the constitutionality discussion. On 31 March 2022, the *coup de grâce* to the BBI was dealt by the Supreme Court, which agreed with the judgments of the High Court and Court of Appeal on the unconstitutionality of the BBI.[134]

In its judgment, the High Court painstakingly reflected on the history of constitution-making in Kenya in recognizing the desire for Kenyans to deliver a constitution 'debated and designed' by the people rather than the political elite.[135] The Court considered, furthermore, the structure of the Constitution, in protecting it from arbitrary amendments

[128] Ibid. 32–34, 143, and 146.

[129] Ibid. 144.

[130] Ibid. 145–46.

[131] Brian Kennedy and Lauren Bieniek, 'Moving Forward with Constitutional Reform in Kenya: A Report of the CSIS Africa Program' (CSIS 2010) 1–2 https://csis-website-prod.s3.amazonaws.com/s3fs-public/legacy_files/files/publication/101203_Kennedy_MovingForwardKenya_Web.pdf accessed 25 May 2022.

[132] Murray (n 66) 149.

[133] For institutional protective measures through the judiciary, see cases including *Centre for Rights Education And Awareness (CREAW) & 7 others v Attorney-General* (2011) eKLR http://kenyalaw.org/caselaw/cases/view/73751 accessed 25 July 2023; *AIDS Law Project v Attorney-General & 3 Others* [2015] eKLR, http://kenyalaw.org/caselaw/cases/view/107033/ accessed 25 July 2023; *Federation of Women Lawyers Kenya (FIDA) v Attorney-General & another* [2018] eKLR http://kenyalaw.org/caselaw/cases/view/152142/ accessed 25 July 2023; *CK (A Child) through Ripples International as her guardian & next friend) & 11 others v Commissioner of Police/Inspector General of the National Police Service & 3 others* [2013] eKLR http://kenyalaw.org/caselaw/cases/view/89322/ accessed 25 July 2023.

[134] *Attorney-General & 2 others v Ndii & 79 others; Prof Rosalind Dixon & 7 others (Amicus Curiae)* (Petitions 12, 11 & 13 of 2021 (Consolidated)) [2022] KESC 8 (KLR) (31 March 2022) (Judgment) (with dissent). See also 'Supreme Court BBI Ruling' (*The Nation*, Nairobi, 31 March 2022) https://www.youtube.com/watch?v=0rFkTaoigFY accessed 18 May 2022.

[135] *Ndii and others v AG and others* (n 76) paras 469, 471.

by the political elite that may conflict with the will of the people.[136] In the Court of Appeal judgment, Justice Kiage stated:

> Kenyans were quite clear that they were not going to cede the Constitution to the vicissitudes and vagaries of political expediency. Having birthed it, they were prepared to nurture it and protect it from mutilation or dismemberment. They desired to be involved in its fate and fortune and were essentially saying that only as they made it could it be substantively altered—with their full and informed participation.[137]

Public participation is a national value and principle of good governance, as articulated under articles 10(2), 118, and 196 of the Constitution. It is, therefore, unsurprising that the legitimacy of the process behind the conception of the CKAB, 2020, in relation to whether there was meaningful public participation, was analysed by the courts.[138] The documents emerging from the BBI included the BBI Taskforce Report, the BBI Steering Committee's Final Report, and the Constitution of Kenya Amendment Bill. Unlike in the previous constitutional reform process, these documents were available only in English, with no translations or formats being accessible to PWDs. Although these documents were not distributed physically and were only available online, the promoters of the bill proceeded to collect signatures in support of it.[139] The High Court judgment and majority determination of the Court of Appeal found that there was a lack of meaningful public participation.[140] The Supreme Court specifically pointed to the lack of public participation on the second schedule of CKAB, 2020.[141]

The legality of the genesis of, and process behind, the CKAB, 2020 was also a key defect. The bill was purported to have been brought by popular initiative,[142] but the courts held that an amendment through a popular initiative was the preserve of registered voters as opposed to the president or government.[143] Given that the CKAB, 2020 emerged from an initiative by the president, it failed to meet the standard of a popular initiative.[144]

Furthermore, the High Court and the majority decision of the Court of Appeal determined that the 'basic structure doctrine' was applicable in Kenya. As such, the Constitution could be changed only through the exercise of three powers: the primary constituent power, which entails civic education, public participation, the constituent assembly, and a referendum; the secondary constituent power, which involves public participation and a referendum only; or the constituted power, which is the preserve of Parliament.[145] It was the determination that fundamental aspects of the Constitution may be changed only through the exercise of the primary constituent power. The exercise of the secondary constituent

[136] Ibid. paras 472–73.

[137] *Independent Electoral and Boundaries Commission (IEBC) and 4 others v David Ndii and 82 others; Kenya Human Rights Commission and 4 others (Amicus Curiae)* (Petition E291 of 2021 and Civil Appeals E292, E293 & E294 of 2021 (Consolidated)) [2021] eKLR para 172.

[138] Ibid. paras 15, 18, 26, 63, 104,114, 119, 133, 134, 135, 208, 222, 264, 268, 267,284, 336, 378, 385, 389, 408, and 412.

[139] *Ndii and others v AG and others* (n 76) para 562.

[140] Ibid. paras 572–76.

[141] *Attorney-General & 2 others v Ndii & 79 others* (n 134).

[142] Constitution of Kenya, art 257.

[143] *Ndii and others v AG and others* (n 76) para 481.

[144] Ibid. para 499; *IEBC and others v Ndii and others* (n 137) Orders.

[145] *Ndii and others v AG and others* (n 76) paras 472–74; *IEBC and others v Ndii and others* (n 137) Orders.

power and the constituted power are, however, limited to changes to non-fundamental aspects of the Constitution.[146] The final majority judgment of the Supreme Court differed, though, finding that the basic structure doctrine is not applicable in Kenya, and noting as follows:

> The intention of the framers of the Constitution and the people of Kenya in bestowing that charter on Kenyans and their future generations was not to implicitly prohibit amendment of its content and structure, whether identified as basic or not; it was to ensure that, through that very Constitution, any process of amendment was undertaken in the finest spirit of Kenya's democracy, fully cognizant of Kenya's historical context, present experiences and aspirations for the future. Such protection was found both expressly and implicitly in the provisions attendant to the process of amendment within the Constitution.[147]

The determination by the Supreme Court has opened a window of opportunity for the revival of a constitutional reform process, as long as its genesis and process are constitutional. The inapplicability of the basic structure doctrine in Kenya, and the Court's emphasis on the Constitution as the foundation of any change, still situates the power to amend or replace the Constitution in the sovereign will of the people. With this decision, the spirit of collective civic action in Kenya for and against constitutional changes arguably finds greater room in which to manifest itself. The Supreme Court determination provides for flexibility in regard to constitutional changes as long as they are in compliance with the Constitution, with citizens, civil society, and institutions such as the media and the judiciary remaining at the vanguard of promoting constitutionalism in changes to the Constitution.

Discourse around the reintroduction of the constitutional reform agenda featured in the build-up to Kenya's elections in 2022.[148] It is vital that, should the incumbent administration pursue constitutional reform, such reform should be substantively and procedurally sound, in sync with the transformative nature of the Kenyan Constitution, and citizen-driven.

3.4 The manifestation of civic activism in the BBI Project

Unlike many other African countries, where mobilization against constitutional changes that are substantively or procedurally defective tends to take the form of street protests, collective action in Kenya against the BBI project took two main forms: institutional mobilization through the judiciary and an extra-institutional mobilization through public rallies as well as mainstream and online media. The BBI cases were categorical about the central role of citizens in constitution-making and constitutional change in Kenya—a standard that the BBI process failed to meet. Kenyans' zeal in protecting this transformative charter is evident in the mobilization that took place in regard to the BBI issue.

[146] *Ndii and others v AG and others* (n 76) para 474

[147] *Attorney-General & 2 others v Ndii & 79 others* (n 134) 77–78.

[148] Onyango K'Onyango and Walter Menya, 'Azimio to Resume BBI Reggae after Poll Victory' *The Nation* (Nairobi, 2 April 2022) https://nation.africa/kenya/news/azimio-to-resume-bbi-reggae-after-poll-win--3768720 accessed 21 May 2022; Ibrahim Oruko and Simon Ciuri, 'Storm over Kenya Kwanza Power-sharing Deal as MPs Accuse Ruto of Hypocrisy' *The Nation* (Nairobi, 13 May 2022) https://nation.africa/kenya/news/politics/storm-over-kenya-kwanza-power-sharing-deal-as-mps-accuse-ruto-of-hypocrisy-3813902 accessed 21 May 2022.

Public interest litigation was a favoured method to challenge the BBI, given that 83 litigants supported the BBI High Court case. CSOs such as Kenya Human Rights Commission (KHRC) and Katiba Institute participated as an amicus curiae and an interested party, respectively, and made submissions that challenged the constitutionality of the BBI.[149] Academics also featured as amici in assisting the Court to interpret constitutional questions, including those in regard to the constitutional and good-governance value of public participation.[150] Critical to their submissions was the call for the courts to protect the Constitution from the culture of hyper-amendment.[151]

The BBI case was, however, no unicorn: several previous cases had challenged aspects of the BBI, including the legality of the formation of the BBI Taskforce[152] and the BBI Steering Committee,[153] Parliament's right to discuss and adopt the bill,[154] and the use of state funds in the BBI process.[155] These questions were settled conclusively with the Supreme Court decision. Also noteworthy are previous attempts at constitutional amendment through popular initiatives, such as Okoa Kenya ('Save Kenya') and Punguza Mizigo ('Reduce the Baggage'), which failed to garner enough popular support to take off.[156] These endeavours are instructive in that they reveal an underlying need to address aspects of the Constitution that might not be working for the Kenyan people. This was, arguably, the red-herring justification of the BBI project, a politically hot topic that received wide coverage in mainstream and online media as well as at political rallies, and drew considerable public interest.

Furthermore, the BBI spurred the Linda Katiba (Swahili for 'Protect the Constitution') movement, which was composed of civil society groups and politicians who were vehemently opposed to the BBI.[157] Civil society groups were vocal critics of the BBI in broadcast, print, and online media, including in blog posts analysing the BBI[158] and forums discussing the BBI and the BBI judgments.[159] This active discourse on the BBI kept the topic alive in the public sphere and prompted citizens to engage with the attempted constitutional change process. The vanguard role of the people and the judiciary in protecting the Constitution therefore comes to the fore. Indeed, the BBI cases made reference to the critical role of the judiciary in interpreting the Constitution and doing so holistically in a manner that upholds its transformative nature.[160]

Unfortunately, citizen mobilization on ethnic grounds continues to mar meaningful citizen engagement in constitutional reform processes in Kenya. This was also the case

[149] *Ndii and others v AG and others* (n 76) para 59.

[150] Ibid. paras 64–68.

[151] Ibid. para 68.

[152] *Thirdway Alliance Kenya and another v Head of the Public Service – Joseph Kinyua and 2 others; Martin Kimani and 15 others (Interested Parties)* Constitutional Petition 451 of 2018 [2020].

[153] *Okiya Omtata v Attorney General and Another*, Nairobi Constitutional Petition no 12 of 2020.

[154] *Thirdway Alliance Kenya and another v Head of the Public Service and others* (n 152); *Thirdway Alliance v the Speaker of the National Assembly and others*, Nairobi High Court Petition no E 302 of 2020.

[155] *Thirdway Alliance Kenya and another v Head of the Public Service and others* (n 152).

[156] Jill Ghai, 'Katiba: Okoa Kenya Mess Reborn as Punguza Mizigo' *The Star* (Nairobi, 9 March 2019) https://www.the-star.co.ke/siasa/2019-03-09-katiba-okoa-kenya-mess-reborn-as-punguza-mizigo/ accessed 22 May 2022.

[157] Justus Ochieng, 'Lobby Group Says There's No Legal Crisis to Warrant BBI Constitutional Reforms' *The Nation* (Nairobi, 30 November 2020) https://nation.africa/kenya/news/politics/bbi-a-mockery-of-justice-activists-say-3213718 accessed 21 May 2022; Linda Katiba, https://twitter.com/lindakatiba accessed 21 May 2022.

[158] 'Linda Katiba', *The Elephant* https://www.theelephant.info/editions/linda-katiba accessed 21 May 2022.

[159] ICJ Kenya, 'Katiba@11: Deconstructing the BBI Judgment' (27 August 2021) https://www.youtube.com/watch?v=WfNcwodDKh4&ab_channel=ICJKenya accessed 21 May 2022.

[160] *Ndii and others v AG and others* (n 76) paras 398–400.

with the BBI discussions.[161] Often, when these engagements are led by politicians, especially in the context of electoral campaigns, misrepresentation and misinformation on constitutional reform issues compromise meaningful public sensitization and education. Civil society groups were critical stakeholders in countering these narratives and ensuring the public had access to accurate and credible information through in-person and online engagements.

The BBI also generated significant online discussion, especially among the youth and urban population who make up a significant segment of Kenya's netizens. The power of the online space as a vehicle for mobilizing citizens has not escaped politicians, who are not above exploiting it. BBI discussion inspired many trending hashtags, such as '#BBIorNothing', '#RejectBBI', '#BBIPeoplesAgenda', '#RIPBBI', '#BBINonsense', '#Nobodycanstopreggae', and '#Reggaehasbeenstopped'.[162] The diversity of public opinion speaking for or against the BBI agenda was vibrant, especially in the lead-up to, and during, the determination of the BBI cases. '#BBIjudgment' trended during the respective readings of the judgments by the High Court, Court of Appeal, and Supreme Court judges. In this tumult, analyses by journalists, lawyers, political analysts, and CSOs meshed in with public discourse on the content of the judgments and their implications, revealing that Kenyans in their droves had an undeniable interest in wanting to engage with the vicissitudes of the BBI process.

However, the risk of manipulated consent was apparent given the hiring of popular social media influencers by politicians to amplify certain hashtags, a practice that skewed public debate by producing what is characterized as inauthentic coordinated behaviour.[163] A report by Mozilla revealed the vulnerability of journalists, judges, and civil society activists to coordinated online campaigns of disinformation and harassment.[164] Campaigns like these were rife during the BBI cases, with members of CSOs and the judiciary becoming the targets of online harassment for their positions on BBI. Threatening and negative hashtags—among others, '#Weshallrevisit', '#Justiceforsale', '#AnarchistJudges', '#JudiciaryRevenge', and '#JudicialPayback'—were deployed against the judiciary.[165]

Unsurprisingly, these campaigns engendered self-censorship among public voices that were crucially needed to inject credible content and rational discourse into the online information ecosystem and counter false narratives. The Mozilla report concluded that, by and large, the Kenyan people had picked up on the propaganda, but it sounded a cautionary note about the insidious effect that disinformation campaigns have in sowing public distrust and compelling self-censorship.[166]

[161] Joseph Muchiri, 'DP Ruto Vows to Stop "Ethnic-driven" BBI Rallies' *The Standard* (Nairobi, 24 February 2020) https://www.standardmedia.co.ke/central/article/2001361590/dp-ruto-vows-to-stop-ethnic-driven-bbi-rallies accessed 23 May 2022.

[162] ANCIR, 'The BBI Report: Online Trends Analysis' (December 2020) 4 https://investigate.africa/ancir/dist/assets/reports/BBI_report_online_trends.pdf accessed 23 May 2022.

[163] Ibid. 4.

[164] Mozilla, 'Inside the Shadowy World of Disinformation for Hire in Kenya' 3 https://assets.mofoprod.net/network/documents/Report_Inside_the_shadowy_world_of_disinformation_for_hire_in_Kenya_5._hcc.pdf accessed 23 May 2022.

[165] Ibid.; Emmanuel Onyango, 'Kenyan Influencers Paid to Take "Guerrilla Warfare" Online' (*BBC News*, 13 September 2021) https://www.bbc.com/news/world-africa-58474936 accessed 24 May 2022.

[166] Mozilla (n 164) 11.

Encouragingly, the BBI saga represents the ensuing Kenyan culture to mobilize against defective constitutional amendment processes through and outside available institutions. Given the strong citizen interest in the BBI, there is momentum for a powerful citizen-led movement for or against any future constitutional change or reform initiatives.

4. The effects of citizens' action on African constitutionalism

The BBI debacle in Kenya reflects the dramatic shift in African constitutionalism that was marked by the entry into force of the third generation of African constitutions.[167] This has entailed a repositioning from a constitutional law and culture centred on the wishes and desires of those who wield political power to one oriented to the ideals of people-centred limitations on amendment powers. The culture of resistance against unconstitutional amendment in Kenya may be traced to civil society efforts to establish a parallel constitution-making process via the 'Ufungamano Initiative', and to subsequent efforts to ensure that the modifications the Bomas Draft underwent were not validated by the people in tokenistic participation in a referendum.[168] Civic education and constitutional literacy are two important mechanisms that private groups have utilized to sensitize the people about the relevance of the Constitution in order to oppose abusive exercises of executive power. Civil-society-led civic education is critical given that government-supported civic education tends to be partial, to be driven by the government's political agenda, and/or to stoke ethnic divisions. Many African countries where referendums are hijacked and manipulated by politicians can draw inspiration from the failure of the BBI project and the rejection of the Wako Draft through a referendum.[169]

By contrast, constitutional changes in most francophone African countries since the return to democracy in the early 1990s tend to meet no resistance. All the referendums that have been organized hitherto in these countries have approved the proposed amendments.[170] Unlike in Kenya, the ease with which constitutional changes can be made elsewhere can be associated in part with poor constitutional culture and literacy, as well as with the failure of private groups to amalgamate their efforts in collective action against retrogressive amendments.

A few examples from francophone African jurisdictions highlight the distinctiveness of the Kenyan experience and how beneficial it could be to collective mobilization in these countries. In 2023, Gabon's National Assembly and Senate adopted constitutional amendments submitted by the government that, among other things, reduced the terms of office of the president from seven to five years, as well as those of senators, members of the National Assembly, and locally elected officials. Furthermore, a single round of voting for

[167] Dominique Rousseau, Pierre-Yves Gahdoun, and Julien Bonnet, *Droit du contentieux Constitutionnel* (LGDJ-Lextenso éditions 2016) 837.

[168] Wanjala S Nasong'o, 'Revisiting the "Two Faces of Civil Society" in Constitutional Reform in Kenya' in Godwin R Murunga, Duncan Okello, and Anders Sjögren (eds.), *Kenya: The Struggle for a New Constitutional Order* (Zed Books 2014) 106.

[169] Fombad (n 3) 382, 404–09.

[170] Charles Manga Fombad and Trésor Muhindo Makunya, 'The Struggle for Constitutional Identity in Francophone Africa' in Charles M Fombad and Nico Steytler (eds.), *Constitutional Identity and Constitutionalism in Africa* (OUP 2022).

the presidential election was instituted; the age of eligibility of presidential candidates was set at a minimum of 30 years instead of 18; and the age of eligibility of senators was reduced from 40 years to 35.[171] The proposed constitutional amendment followed consultation by the president with parties in the ruling coalition and opposition, with a view to reforming the electoral system and holding peaceful elections. However, opposition parties, although unable to block the amendment, saw it as an attempt to consolidate the president's powers, as well as an initiative which, at a procedural level, did not involve popular consultation. In sum, reforms that could have strengthened constitutionalism in Gabon—such as presidential term limits and the introduction of two rounds of voting for presidential elections—were discarded.

Moreover, unlike with the citizen mobilization and media debates that accompanied the BBI project in Kenya, the Gabonese constitutional amendment attracted much less attention from citizens and the media. What is notable is the ease with which Gabon's Constitution could be amended without significant parliamentary and extra-parliamentary debate. In fact, when the vote was taken, an overwhelming majority of congresspersons (178 of the 198 present)—most of whom were members of the Gabonese Democratic Party, the party led by the president—approved the amendment. The small number of opposition parties were unable to prevent the amendment. Given Gabon's recurrent constitutional amendments,[172] it is clear that citizen mobilization has not played any material role in taming executive authoritarianism, seeing as the government can push through constitutional amendments at will and without any challenge.

On the basis of practice, it is doubtful that institutional mobilization via the judiciary, in this case Gabon's Constitutional Court, could produce results that foster constitutionalism. In accordance with article 116(3) of the Gabonese Constitution, the Constitutional Court was consulted before the draft constitutional revision was debated in Congress. In 2018, the Constitutional Court informally amended article 13 of the Constitution, which determines the modalities of presidential vacancy, to allow the bedridden president to retain his office. Given that the president of the Constitutional Court has headed the Court since its creation in 1991,[173] having been appointed several times by the president of the republic, and given—*en passant*—that she is the stepmother of the president, it is doubtful if the Court would ever decide against the president's interests. This lack of institutional independence makes the notion of mobilizing citizens through the judiciary a futile venture.

Thus, one cannot agree more with Ondo that citizens have internalized the fact that challenging government actions in Gabon is a fruitless endeavour, given that, on the evidence available, judges decide in accordance with the regimes' policy preference.[174] The other

[171] 'Gabon: la révision de la Constitution actée par le Parlement réuni en Congrès' (*RFI*, 6 April 2023) https://www.rfi.fr/fr/afrique/20230406-gabon-la-r%C3%A9vision-de-la-constitution-act%C3%A9e-par-le-parlement-r%C3%A9uni-en-congr%C3%A8s accessed 18 April 2023.

[172] There were amendments in 2017, 2018, 2020, and 2023. See, among others, 'La révision constitutionnelle adoptée par l'Assemblée nationale au Gabon' (*VOA*, 15 December 2017) https://www.voaafrique.com/a/la-revision-constitutionnelle-adoptee-par-l-assemblee-nationale-au-gabon/4165060.html accessed 18 April 2023.

[173] She has ruled the Court for 33 years. In 2019, she was sworn in for another nine-year term. Based on the 2018 constitutional amendment, this would be her final term. Other judges have been, or were, at the Court for many years: Louise Angue (1991 to date), Harvé Moutsinga (1998–2021), and Marc Aurélien Tonjokoué, Dominique Bongouéré, and Jean-Pierre Ndong (1991–2012). See Télésphore Ondo, 'Le contentieux constitutionnel au Gabon' (2022) 2 Revue de la Recherche Juridique 1189, 1252.

[174] Ibid. 1189, 1259–60.

obstacle is purely constitutional, in that the Constitutional Court is not empowered to review constitutional amendment laws—a further consideration that makes citizen mobilization through the judiciary (unlike in Kenya) well-nigh impossible.[175]

Another example of the lack of mobilization is the 2011 constitutional amendment process in the Democratic Republic of the Congo (DRC). Eight provisions were amended, resulting in the elimination of two rounds for the presidential election; in allowing parliamentarians who had lost their mandate because they held an incompatible office, for example as a member of the government, to regain their parliamentary function; and in empowering the president to dissolve provincial legislatures and dismiss provincial governors in the case of serious and persistent political crises.[176] As in Gabon, the constitutional amendment was passed by Parliament, but did not result in popular consultation or mobilization by citizens to try to stop what was seen as a mechanism for the incumbent president to win the election in the first round.

A Member of Parliament petitioned the Supreme Court of Justice, which at the time acted as the constitutional court, to rule on the constitutional validity of the amendment, but the petition was never heard, for reasons unknown to the authors.[177] The DRC example shows that attempts to mobilize the judiciary against constitutional amendments require judges to be aware of their role in consolidating democracy and protecting constitutionalism, as in Kenya, rather than to remain silent on petitions before them.[178] They also require an entrenched culture of independence of the judiciary, given that francophone judges who adopt judgments that do not align with the policy preferences of the dominant political party or the president, including in matters of constitutional amendments, often face arbitrary removals. This was a reality that Kenyan judges faced in the bygone Moi era—a reality which has since been corrected by judicial reform measures underpinned by the values and principles of the 2010 Constitution.[179]

Another case in point is the removal, in October 2022, of the president of the Central African Republic's Constitutional Court. A month earlier, the Court had annulled presidential decrees that established constitutional review committees on the grounds that they were unconstitutional.[180] Similarly, Benin was for many years the exception to this authoritarian trend, given that private groups and opposition political parties have relied on the Constitutional Court to tame what was excessive presidentialism. However, a jurisprudential turn in which the Court has refrained from reviewing the validity of constitutional amendments[181] has meant that undertaking collective action against constitutional changes

[175] Constitution of Gabon, art 84.

[176] arts 71, 110, 149, 197, 198, 218, and 226. See Loi 11/002 du 20 janvier 2011 portant révision de certains articles de la Constitution de la République démocratique du Congo du 18 février 2006.

[177] 'Révision de la Constitution: Lisanga Bonganga saisit la Cour suprême' (*Radio Okapi*, 18 March 2011) https://www.radiookapi.net/emissions-2/linvite-du-jour/2011/03/18/revision-de-la-constitution-lisanga-bonganga-saisit-la-cour-supreme accessed 18 April 2023.

[178] Babacar Kanté, 'L'étrange Alchimie de La Vie et de La Loi Du Juge Albie Sachs: Commentaire' (*AfricLaw*, 5 January 2022) https://africlaw.com/2022/01/05/letrange-alchimie-de-la-vie-et-de-la-loi-du-juge-albie-sachs-commentaire/> accessed 18 April 2023.

[179] Mutunga (n 10) 2–3.

[180] 'Nouvelle Constitution: la Justice Centrafricaine Annule les Décrets du Président Touadera' (*VOA*, 23 September 2022) https://www.voaafrique.com/a/centrafrique-un-comité-de-rédaction-d-une-nouvelle-constitution-invalidé/6760129.html accessed 18 April 2023.

[181] Trésor Muhindo Makunya, 'The Application of the African Charter on Human and Peoples' Rights in Constitutional Litigation in Benin' in Frans Viljoen and others (eds.), *A Life Interrupted: Essays in Honour of the Lives and Legacies of Christof Heyns* (Pretoria University Law Press 2022) 482–83.

through the judiciary has become, as is the case in many other francophone African countries, an illusion.

The Kenyan case provides other significant lessons on how collective action via institutional mechanisms can nurture constitutional dialogue. Collective action in Kenya was a dialogical process pitting together several actors—in particular, CSOs, lawyers, independent institutions, academics, and state officials—who variously countered or supported the BBI project. The first aspect of this dialogue to note is the horizontal and vertical intra-judicial dialogue. Horizontal intra-judicial dialogue entails a process in which judges, within a lower or superior court, contest each other's resolutions until they reach the best acceptable solution for the problem submitted to them, while at the same time leaving the possibility open for judges who dissent or concur to append their opinions to the majority decision.[182] By contrast, vertical intra-judicial dialogue takes place in a complementary framework between lower- and higher-court judges, with the latter drawing on the findings and arguments of the former to develop new positions on the rationality of constitutional amendments.

Both aspects of these dialogues serve to enhance the quality and transparency of constitutional reasoning, and may be seen as internal accountability mechanisms in regard to judges. To connect this observation to the Kenyan context, it may be remarked that the BBI petition provided the judiciary—from the High Court to the Supreme Court via the Court of Appeal—with an opportunity to debate how best to protect the Kenyan Constitution from self-serving amendments. The aim thereof was to ensure that, in making changes to the much-vaunted transformative Constitution, the baby was not thrown out with the bathwater. Both forms of dialogue enhance the quality of debate and the understanding that social and political actors have of the Constitution's supreme relevance in society. Collective action has served to enrich and sustain this vital dialogue, and, in the process, cement the protection of the Constitution against future unconstitutional amendments. The second dialogue involves, on the one hand, private groups made up of individual citizens, academics, and non-Kenyan constitutional law experts, and, on the other, state representatives, around matters of constitutional amendment.

Efforts to revise or amend a constitution always raise suspicions about the motives of those who initiate them.[183] Thus, as Evariste Boshab points out, one needs to find a fair balance between ensuring that the constitution, as a living document, is revised to consider new issues and ensuring that the process is conducted within the strictures of the constitution.[184] Collective action through judicial mobilization is one significant mode which, in the case of Kenya, has allowed those institutions established to protect the constitutional order to persuasively show whether or not the amendment has undermined constitutionalism.

In a constitutional democracy, everyone's voices and arguments should be heard and confronted in regard to what the constitution provides. This approach can reduce tension and violence, not least in Kenya, where there is no shortage of violence fuelled by political contestation. Not every Kenyan opposed the BBI, and in some milieux, the proposed constitutional reforms were welcomed. For example, the *Kieleweke* wing of the ruling Jubilee coalition supported constitutional reforms for the unity that they would foster, as well as

[182] Edwin Cameron, 'Foreword' in Dikgang Moseneke (ed.), *All Rise: A Judicial Memoir* (Picador Africa 2020) ix.
[183] Evariste Boshab, *Entre la Révision de la Constitution et l'inanition de la Nation* (Éditions Larcier 2013) 72–73.
[184] Ibid.

the positive impact they would have on the socio-economic empowerment of marginalized groups, and on the reduction of the ethnic rivalries that tend to characterize elections in Kenya.[185] The judicial scrutiny that originated from collective action did, nevertheless, help to diffuse tensions and conclude the contention within an institutionalized process.

5. Conclusion

The 2010 Constitution of Kenya was adopted against the backdrop of a growing awareness among citizens of the importance of the Constitution as a power map. Adopted after a failed attempt to impose on the people a constitution that consolidated presidential power, citizens quickly learnt that, for the 2010 Constitution to stand the test of time, they had to be prepared to stand up and protect the promises of the constitutional text against opportunistic amendments designed by those seeking to perpetuate their hold on power. This Constitution is a 'bridge' between a past of ethnic tensions and violence, and unaccountable political leadership, and a present—and future—based on limited government.

It is not surprising, therefore, that collective action has been taken to stymie attempts to weaken the 2010 Constitution through the BBI. For citizens and other private groups to take the defence of the Constitution seriously, there has had to be a strengthened constitutional culture, one which in turn is facilitated by an enabling constitutional framework in the form of fundamental rights and institutional mechanisms where people can lay their grievances. Resistance to the BBI project took, in essence, the form of institutional mobilization through the judiciary. This is due to the Kenyan culture of seeking sociopolitical transformation through judicial institutions: a culture which has judicialized many matters, ranging from electoral,[186] political, and socio-economic matters to private ones.

Mobilization through mainstream and social media also raised awareness of the constitutional amendments among those who could not join the constitutional petition. These forms of mobilization by private groups were essential in ensuring that the proposed constitutional amendments respect procedural and substantive guarantees against regressive amendments that undermine the will of the people. Any constitution, as the manifestation of a social contract rather than an imposed arrangement, remains the 'soul' of the nation,[187] one that must be protected by all—all the more so by private groups, which historically have proven their ability to resist opportunistic amendments that serve no other interests than those of power-holders.

The legitimacy of collective action against constitutional amendments does not depend on whether or not every citizen participates in it. Nor does it matter that, when a few members of society mobilize in the courts or through digital technologies to oppose amendments, they may be seen as imposing their will on the entire population. What matters is the noble purpose of collective action in itself, namely the endeavour to protect a Constitution

[185] Philip Onguny, 'The Politics behind Kenya's Building Bridges Initiative (BBI): Vindu Vichenjanga or Sound and Fury, Signifying Nothing?' (2020) 54(3) Canadian Journal of African Studies 557, 566–67.

[186] Marystella Simiyu, 'Kenyan Supreme Court Approach to Handling Election Related Digital Threats: Lessons from the 2013 and 2017 Kenyan Elections' in Christopher Mbazira (ed.), *Budding Democracy or Judicialisation: Lessons from Africa's Emerging Electoral Jurisprudence* (AJJF 2021) 141.

[187] Hassen Ebrahim, *The Soul of a Nation: Constitution-Making in South Africa* (1st edn, OUP 1999).

that the people prior to these actants have approved in their overwhelming numbers. In Kenya, collective actions also ended up in courts which helped mediate conflicts and diffuse tensions. By virtue of the Constitution, courts have the 'constitutional mandate to arbitrate political, social and economic disputes amongst the people or among the three arms of the government'.[188]

Bibliography

Abebe A.K., 'Côte d'Ivoire: Ouattara's Bid for 3rd Term Opens up a Can of Worms' (*The Africa Report*, 23 July 2020) https://www.theafricareport.com/34674/cote-divoire-ouattaras-bid-for-3rd-term-opens-up-a-can-of-worms/ accessed 31 May 2022

Adar K. and Munyae I., 'Human Rights Abuse in Kenya under Daniel Arap Moi, 1978–2001' (2001) 5 African Studies Quarterly 1

Adayé J., 'Manifestation contre un Troisième Mandat en Côte d'Ivoire' (*dw.com*, 19 October 2020) https://www.dw.com/fr/manifestation-contre-un-troisi%C3%A8me-mandat-en-c%C3%B4te-divoire/a-55328440 accessed 31 May 2022

Adjolohoun S.H., 'Centralized Model of Constitutional Adjudication: The Constitutional Court of Benin' in Fombad C.M. (ed.), *Constitutional Adjudication in Africa* (OUP 2017)

Alusala N., 'Why Kabila's Bid to Remain in Power Is Bad News for the Democratic Republic of the Congo' (*The Conversation*, 31 July 2017) http://theconversation.com/why-kabilas-bid-to-remain-in-power-is-bad-news-for-the-democratic-republic-of-the-congo-81414 accessed 31 May 2022

ANCIR, *The BBI Report: Online Trends Analysis* (December 2020) https://investigate.africa/ancir/dist/assets/reports/BBI_report_online_trends.pdf accessed 23 May 2022

Andreassen B.A. and Tostensen A., 'Of Oranges and Bananas: The 2005 Kenya Referendum on the Constitution', CMI Working Paper (2005) v–vi

Annan K., *The Kenya National Dialogue and Reconciliation: Building a Progressive Kenya – Our Common Vision Views of Stakeholders* (Kofi Annan Foundation 2012)

Atieno-Odhiambo E., 'Democracy and the Ideology of Order' in Schatzberg M. (ed.), *The Political Economy of Kenya* (Praeger 1988) 177

Baker B., 'Outstaying One's Welcome: The Presidential Third-Term Debate in Africa' (2002) 8(4) Contemporary Politics 285–301

Barber N.W., *The Principles of Constitutionalism* (OUP 2018)

BBI Taskforce, *Building Bridges to a United Kenya: From a Nation of Blood Ties to a Nation of Ideals* (October 2019)

Boshab E., *Entre la Révision de la Constitution et l'inanition de la Nation* (Éditions Larcier 2013)

Cameron E., 'Foreword' in Moseneke D. (ed.), *All Rise: A Judicial Memoir* (Picador Africa 2020)

Carter Centre, 'Observing the 2002 Kenya Elections Final Report' (2003)

Chege M., 'Weighed down by Old Ethnic Baggage, Kenya Races to Another Historic Election' (*Center for Strategic and International Studies*, 22 June 2007) https://www.csis.org/analysis/weighed-down-old-ethnic-baggage-kenya-races-another-historic-election accessed 15 May 2022

Constitution of Kenya Review Commission (CKRC), *Final Report of the Constitution of Kenya Review Commission* (2005)

Committee of Experts (CoE), *Final Report of The Committee of Experts on Constitutional Review* (2010)

Contiades X., 'Constitutional Change Engineering' in Contiades X. (ed.), *Engineering Constitutional Change: A Comparative Perspective on Europe, Canada and the USA* (Routledge 2013)

Contiades X. and Fotiadou A., 'Introduction: Comparative Constitutional Change: A New Academic Field' in Contiades X. and Fotiadou A. (eds.), *Routledge Handbook of Comparative Constitutional Change* (Taylor & Francis 2020)

Corder H. and Hoexter C., '"Lawfare" in South Africa and Its Effects on the Judiciary' (2017) 10 African Journal of Legal Studies 105

Dulani B., 'Democracy Movements as Bulwarks against Presidential Usurpation of Power: Lessons from the Third-Term Bids in Malawi, Namibia, Uganda and Zambia' (2011) 11 Stichproben – Vienna Journal of African Studies 189

[188] *IEBC and others v Ndii and others* (n 137) para 4.

Durojaye E. and Nanima R.D., 'From Muhammed and Others to De Beer and Others: Striking the Balance between Public Health Measures and Human Rights during Covid-19 Era in South Africa' (2021) 47 Commonwealth Law Bulletin 175

Ebrahim H., *The Soul of a Nation: Constitution-Making in South Africa* (1st edn, OUP 1999)

Eloff D., 'The Rationality Test in Lockdown Litigation in South Africa' (2021) 21 African Human Rights Law Journal 1157

European Parliament, 'Report on the Mission to Observe the Elections of 27 December 2002 in Kenya' (2003)

Favoreu L. and others, *Droit Constitutionnel* (21st edn, Dalloz 2019)

Fombad C.M., 'Constitutional Reforms and Constitutionalism in Africa: Reflections on Some Current Challenges and Future Prospects' (2011) 59 Buffalo Law Review 1007, 1007–08

Fombad C.M., 'Some Perspectives on Durability and Change under Modern African Constitutions' (2013) 11 International Journal of Constitutional Law 382

Fombad C.M. and Makunya T.M., 'The Struggle for Constitutional Identity in Francophone Africa' in Fombad C.M. and Steytler N. (eds.), *Constitutional Identity and Constitutionalism in Africa* (OUP 2022)

Fowkes J., *Building the Constitution: The Practice of Constitutional Interpretation in Post-Apartheid South Africa* (CUP 2016)

Freckelton I., 'COVID-19 Curfews: Kenyan and Australian Litigation and Pandemic Protection' (2020) 28 Journal of Law and Medicine 117

Freedom House, *Freedom in the World 2003* (Freedom House 2004) 299 https://freedomhouse.org/sites/default/files/2020-02/Freedom_in_the_World_2003_complete_book.pdf accessed 19 May 2022

Friedman S., *Power in Action: Democracy, Citizenship and Social Justice* (NYU Press 2019)

'Gabon: la révision de la Constitution actée par le Parlement réuni en Congrès' (*RFI*, 6 April 2023) https://www.rfi.fr/fr/afrique/20230406-gabon-la-r%C3%A9vision-de-la-constitution-act%C3%A9e-par-le-parlement-r%C3%A9uni-en-congr%C3%A8s accessed 18 April 2023

Gathii T., 'Popular Authorship and Constitution Making: Comparing and Contrasting the DRC and Kenya' (2008) 49 William & Mary Law Review 1109

Ghai J., 'Katiba: Okoa Kenya Mess Reborn as Punguza Mizigo' *The Star* (Nairobi, 9 March 2019) https://www.the-star.co.ke/siasa/2019-03-09-katiba-okoa-kenya-mess-reborn-as-punguza-mizigo/ accessed 22 May 2022

Ghai Y. and McAuslan P., *Public Law and Political Change in Kenya: A Study of the Legal Framework of Government from Colonial Times to the Present* (OUP 1970)

Gordon G., 'Growing Constitutions' (1999) 1(3) Journal of Constitutional Law 528–83

Human Rights Council, 'Rights to Freedom of Peaceful Assembly and of Association: Report of the Special Rapporteur on the Rights to Freedom of Peaceful Assembly and of Association' (2019) A/HRC/41/41

ICJ Kenya, 'Katiba@11: Deconstructing the BBI Judgment' https://www.youtube.com/watch?v=WfNcwodDKh4&ab_channel=ICJKenya (27 August 2021) accessed 21 May 2022

Jackson R. and Rosberg C., 'Personal Rule: Theory and Practice in Africa' (1984) 16 Comparative Politics 421

Juma L., 'Ethnic Politics and the Constitutional Review Process in Kenya' (2002) 9 Tulsa Journal of Comparative and International Law 471

Juma M., 'African Mediation of the Kenyan Post-2007 Election Crisis' (2009) 27 Journal of Contemporary African Studies 407

K'Onyango O., 'From BBI to Azimio, the Handshake Continues to Divide Political Opinion' *The Nation* (Nairobi, 9 March 2022) https://nation.africa/kenya/news/politics/handshake-continues-to-divide-political-opinion-3741678 accessed 14 May 2022

K'Onyango O. and Menya W., 'Azimio to Resume BBI Reggae after Poll Victory' *The Nation* (Nairobi, 2 April 2022) https://nation.africa/kenya/news/azimio-to-resume-bbi-reggae-after-poll-win--3768720 accessed 21 May 2022

Kabira N. and Kibugi R., 'Saving the Soul of an African Constitution: Learning from Kenya's Experience with Constitutionalism during COVID-19' (2020) 20 African Human Rights Law Journal 439–40

Kadima D. and Owuor F., 'The National Rainbow Coalition: Achievements and Challenges of Building and Sustaining a Broad-Based Political Party Coalition in Kenya' in Kadima D. (ed.), *Politics of Party Coalitions in Africa* (EISA 2006) 179

Kamga S.D., 'An Assessment of the Possibilities for Impact Litigation in Francophone African Countries' (2014) 14 African Human Rights Law Journal 449

Kanté B., 'L'étrange Alchimie de La Vie et de La Loi Du Juge Albie Sachs : Commentaire' (*AfricLaw*, 5 January 2022) https://africlaw.com/2022/01/05/letrange-alchimie-de-la-vie-et-de-la-loi-du-juge-albie-sachs-commentaire/ accessed 18 April 2023

Kanyinga K. and Long J., 'The Political Economy of Reforms in Kenya: The Post-2007 Election Violence and a New Constitution' (2012) 55 African Studies Review 31

Katiba L., https://twitter.com/lindakatiba accessed 21 May 2022

Kennedy B. and Bieniek L., 'Moving Forward with Constitutional Reform in Kenya: A Report of the CSIS Africa Program' (CSIS 2010) https://csis-website-prod.s3.amazonaws.com/s3fs-public/legacy_files/files/publication/101203_Kennedy_MovingForwardKenya_Web.pdf accessed 25 May 2022

Kenya Gazette no. 55 of 3 May 2019, vol CXXI 1708

Kenya Gazette Notice no. 264 of 10 January 2020, vol CXXII no. 7

Kenya Gazette Notice no. 5154 of 31 May 2018, vol CXX no. 64

'Kenya: Old Habits Die Hard: Rights Abuses Follow Renewed Foreign Aid Commitments' (*Human Rights Watch*, July 1995) http://www.hrw.org/legacy/reports/1995/Kenya.htm accessed 17 May 2021

'Kenya's Moi Seeks to Prolong Rule' (*CNN*, 29 June 2002) http://edition.cnn.com/2002/WORLD/africa/06/29/kenya.moi/ accessed 31 May 2022

Khadiagala G., 'Forty Days and Nights of Peace-Making in Kenya' (2008) 7 Journal of African Elections 4

Kibet E. and Fombad C.M., 'Transformative Constitutionalism and the Adjudication of Constitutional Rights in Africa' (2017) 17 African Human Rights Law Journal 340

Kimenyi M. and Shughart W., 'The Political Economy of Constitutional Choice: A Study of the 2005 Kenyan Constitutional Referendum' (2008) University of Connecticut Economics Working Papers 200808 https://opencommons.uconn.edu/cgi/viewcontent.cgi?article=1166&context=econ_wpapers accessed 19 May 2022

Klare K., 'Legal Culture and Transformative Constitutionalism' (1998) 14(1) South African Journal on Human Rights 146

'La révision constitutionnelle adoptée par l'Assemblée nationale au Gabon' (*VOA*, 15 December 2017) https://www.voaafrique.com/a/la-revision-constitutionnelle-adoptee-par-l-assemblee-nationale-au-gabon/4165060.html accessed 18 April 2023

Landau D. and Dixon R., 'Constraining Constitutional Change' (2015) 4 Wake Forest Law Review 859

Le Roux M. and Davis D., *Lawfare: Judging Politics in South Africa* (Jonathan Ball 2019)

Loader B.D. and Mercea D., 'Networking Democracy? Social Media Innovations and Participatory Politics' (2011) 14 Information, Communication & Society 757

Madlingozi T., 'Social Movements and the Constitutional Court of South Africa' in Vilhena O., Baxi U., and Viljoen F. (eds.), *Transformative Constitutionalism: Comparing the Apex Courts of Brazil, India and South Africa* (Pretoria University Law Press 2013)

Makunya T.M., 'The Application of the African Charter on Human and Peoples' Rights in Constitutional Litigation in Benin' in Viljoen F. and others (eds.), *A Life Interrupted: Essays in Honour of the Lives and Legacies of Christof Heyns* (Pretoria University Law Press 2022)

Makunya T.M. and Appiageyi-Atua K., 'Soldiers in Civilian Uniforms: The Role of the Military in the Pursuit of Third-Termism' in Adeola A. and Mutua M.W. (eds.), *The Palgrave Handbook of Democracy, Governance and Justice in Africa* (1st edn, Palgrave Macmillan 2022)

Milemba P.A.S., *Mouvements citoyens Africains: Creuset de l'éveil Civique et Briseurs de l'ordre Néolibéral?* (L'Harmattan 2021)

Mozilla, 'Inside the Shadowy World of Disinformation for Hire in Kenya' https://assets.mofoprod.net/network/documents/Report_Inside_the_shadowy_world_of_disinformation_for_hire_in_Kenya_5._hcc.pdf accessed 23 May 2022

Muchiri J., 'DP Ruto Vows to Stop "Ethnic-Driven" BBI Rallies' *The Standard* (Nairobi, 24 February 2020) https://www.standardmedia.co.ke/central/article/2001361590/dp-ruto-vows-to-stop-ethnic-driven-bbi-rallies accessed 23 May 2022

Murray C., 'Kenya's 2010 Constitution' (2013) 61 Neue Folge Band Jahrbuch des offentlichen Rechts 747

Mutua K., *Kenya's Quest for Democracy: Taming Leviathan* (L Rienner Publishers 2008)

Mutua K., 'Experts Support Push to Amend Constitution' *The Nation* (Nairobi, 28 June 2020) https://nation.africa/kenya/news/experts-support-push-to-amend-constitution-67302 accessed 15 May 2022

Mutunga W., *Constitution-Making from the Middle: Civil Society and Transition Politics in Kenya, 1992–1997* (Mwengo 1999)

Mutunga W., 'The 2010 Constitution of Kenya and its Interpretation: Reflections from the Supreme Court's Decisions' http://www.saflii.org/za/journals/SPECJU/2015/6.pdf accessed 14 May 2022

Nasong'o W.S., 'Revisiting the "Two Faces of Civil Society" in Constitutional Reform in Kenya' in Murunga G.R., Okello D., and Sjögren A. (eds.), *Kenya: The Struggle for a New Constitutional Order* (Zed Books 2014) 106

NeJaime D., 'Constitutional Change, Courts, and Social Movements' (2012) 111 Michigan Law Review 877

'Nouvelle Constitution: la Justice Centrafricaine Annule les Décrets du Président Touadera' (*VOA*, 23 September 2022) https://www.voaafrique.com/a/centrafrique-un-comité-de-rédaction-d-une-nouvelle-constitution-invalidé/6760129.html accessed 18 April 2023

Ochieng J., 'Lobby Group Says There's No Legal Crisis to Warrant BBI Constitutional Reforms' *The Nation* (Nairobi, 30 November 2020) https://nation.africa/kenya/news/politics/bbi-a-mockery-of-justice-activists-say-3213718 accessed 21 May 2022

Okubasu D., 'The Implication of Conflation of Normal and "Constitutional Politics" on Constitutional Change in Africa' in Albert R., Contiades X., and Fotiadou A. (eds.), *The Foundations and Traditions of Constitutional Amendment* (Hart Publishing 2017)

Okoth-Ogendo H., 'The Politics of Constitutional Change in Kenya Since Independence, 1963–69' (1972) 71 African Affairs 9

Okoth-Ogendo H., 'Constitutions without Constitutionalism: Reflections on an African Political Phenomenon' in Shivji I. (ed.), *State and Constitutionalism: An African Debate on Democracy* (SAPES 1991)

Oloka-Onyango J., 'Human Rights and Public Interest Litigation in East Africa: A Bird's Eye View' (2015) 47 George Washington International Law Review 763

Ondo T., 'Le contentieux constitutionnel au Gabon' (2022) 2 Revue de la Recherche Juridique 1189

Onguny P., 'The Politics behind Kenya's Building Bridges Initiative (BBI): Vindu Vichenjanga or Sound and Fury, Signifying Nothing?' (2020) 54 Canadian Journal of African Studies 557

Onyango E., 'Kenyan Influencers Paid to Take "Guerrilla Warfare" Online' (*BBC News*, 13 September 2021) https://www.bbc.com/news/world-africa-58474936 accessed 24 May 2022

Oruko I. and Ciuri S., 'Storm over Kenya Kwanza Power-sharing Deal as MPs Accuse Ruto of Hypocrisy' *The Nation* (Nairobi, 13 May 2022) https://nation.africa/kenya/news/politics/storm-over-kenya-kwanza-power-sharing-deal-as-mps-accuse-ruto-of-hypocrisy-3813902 accessed 21 May 2022

'Révision de la Constitution: Lisanga Bonganga saisit la Cour suprême' (*Radio Okapi*, 18 March 2011) https://www.radiookapi.net/emissions-2/linvite-du-jour/2011/03/18/revision-de-la-constitution-lisanga-bonganga-saisit-la-cour-supreme accessed 18 April 2023

Rousseau D., Gahdoun P.Y., and Bonnet J., *Droit du contentieux Constitutionnel* (LGDJ-Lextenso éditions 2016)

Saati A., 'Participation – to Unveil a Myth' in Abbiate T., Böckenförde M., and Federico V. (eds.), *Public Participation in African Constitutionalism* (Routledge 2018)

Simiyu M., 'Kenyan Supreme Court Approach to Handling Election Related Digital Threats: Lessons From The 2013 And 2017 Kenyan Elections' in Mbazira C. (ed.), *Budding Democracy or Judicialisation Lessons From Africa's Emerging Electoral Jurisprudence* (AJJF 2021) 141

Southall R., 'Moi's Flawed Mandate: The Crisis Continues in Kenya' (1998) 25 Review of African Political Economy 101

Suteu S., *Eternity Clauses in Democratic Constitutionalism* (OUP 2021)

'The Building Bridges Initiative (BBI): Is There Anything New For Kenyan Youth?' (*The Youth Cafe*, 12 November 2020) https://www.theyouthcafe.com/perspectives/the-building-bridges-initiativebbi-is-there-anything-new-for-kenyan-youth accessed 30 May 2022

'The Kenya National Dialogue and Reconciliation: Building a Progressive Kenya' (*ReliefWeb*, December 2011) https://reliefweb.int/report/kenya/kenya-national-dialogue-and-reconciliation-building-progressive-kenya-background-note accessed 20 May 2022

Tierney S., *Constitutional Referendums: The Theory and Practice of Republican Deliberation* (OUP 2012)

Tufekci Z. and Wilson C., 'Social Media and the Decision to Participate in Political Protest: Observations From Tahrir Square' (2012) 62 Journal of Communication 363

Van Staden M., 'Constitutional Rights and Their Limitations: A Critical Appraisal of the COVID-19 Lockdown in South Africa' (2020) 20 African Human Rights Law Journal 484

Veliz C., *Privacy Is Power: Why and How You Should Take Back Control of Your Data* (Melville House 2022)

Waki P., *Kenya: Commission of Inquiry into the Post-Election Violence (CIPEV)* (2008)

Wanga J. and K'Onyango O., 'What is President Uhuru Kenyatta's Power Plan after Leaving Office in August?' *The Nation* (Nairobi, 7 March 2022) https://nation.africa/kenya/news/politics/uhuru-game-plan-after-august-polls-3738726 accessed 30 May 2022.

'What Is a Civil Society? – Definition & Examples – Video & Lesson Transcript' (*Study.com*, undated) https://study.com/academy/lesson/what-is-a-civil-society-definition-examples.html accessed 31 May 2022

Whitaker B.E. and Gierschb J., 'Voting on a Constitution: Implications for Democracy in Kenya' (2009) 27 Journal of Contemporary African Studies 1

13

Craving Stability, Flirting with Change: Understanding Constitutional Change in Malawi Since 1994

Mwiza Jo Nkhata

1. Introduction

Constitutions occupy a special place in the life of any nation.[1] According to Ismail Mohammed, the former Chief Justice of South Africa, a constitution is not simply a statute that mechanically defines the structures of government and the relations between the government and governed, but 'is a mirror reflecting the national soul, the identification of the ideals and aspirations of a nation; the articulation of values binding its people and disciplining its government'.[2]

Given their special status, one view holds that constitutions, once adopted, must never be tampered with;[3] a more pragmatic view—one which is in alignment with global constitutional practice—is that, while their special role and place is acknowledged, this does not mean they should never be changed. It is for this reason that many constitutions expressly prescribe the procedures that must be followed if change becomes necessary. Since constitutions are, by nature, elevated beyond all legislation, changes to them are of cardinal significance and, unsurprisingly, not without controversy.

Tales of constitutional change convey a cautionary message, since, for example, a constitution that has no inbuilt means for facilitating change to itself increases the possibility of extra-legal change;[4] however, if the means for facilitating change are within easy reach, there is a risk that the fundamental principles and institutions that a constitution establishes can 'readily be swept away by a majority momentarily enraptured with a new idea'.[5]

As a result, constitutional framers have always grappled with the difficulty of trying to strike a balance between a constitution which is not too easy to change yet at the same time amenable to change under appropriate circumstances.[6] A common solution is to include

[1] John Hatchard, Muna Ndulo, and Peter Slinn, *Comparative Constitutionalism and Good Governance in the Commonwealth: An Eastern and Southern African Perspective* (CUP 2004) 12.

[2] *State v Acheson* 1991 (2) SA 805 (Nm) 813.

[3] The suggestion, often attributed to Locke, that a constitution should 'remain the sacred and unalterable form and rule of government . . . forever' has not gained much traction over the years. See 'The Fundamental Constitutions of Carolina, 1 March 1669' (*The Avalon Project*) https://avalon.law.yale.edu/17th_century/nc05.asp accessed 3 May 2022.

[4] Peter Suber, 'Amendment' in Christopher B Gray (ed.), *Philosophy of Law: An Encyclopedia* (Garland 1999).

[5] Ibid.

[6] Markus Böckenförde, *Constitutional Amendment Procedures* (International IDEA 2017) 1–32.

Mwiza Jo Nkhata, *Craving Stability, Flirting with Change: Understanding Constitutional Change in Malawi Since 1994*
In: *Constitutional Change and Constitutionalism in Africa*. Edited by: Charles M. Fombad and Nico Steytler, Oxford University Press.
 DOI: 10.1093/9780198957034.003.0015

one or more clauses within a constitution that permit certain changes upon the fulfilment of certain conditions. Properly crafted, such clauses can bring about both stability and flexibility. Such an approach, after all, ensures the protection of 'what the enacting generation thinks wise, but [while] permitting future generations to think otherwise'.[7]

In the case of Malawi, the 1994 Constitution of the Republic of Malawi (the Constitution or the 1994 Constitution) dedicates its Chapter XXI to amendment procedures.[8] In the almost three decades that the Constitution has been in force, recourse has been had to these procedures on several occasions. The resulting amendments have dealt with a diversity of issues, ranging from the correction of innocuous typographical errors to the introduction of entirely new substantive provisions. Given the Constitution's commitment to constitutionalism, it is important to interrogate, generally, the impact that the scheme for amending the Constitution has had on democracy, constitutionalism, and the rule of law. Specifically, it is apposite to explore some key dynamics that have influenced changes to the Constitution. Such an interrogation may contribute to a better understanding of the scheme in Chapter XXI of the Constitution at the normative level, while at the same time shedding light on the practical factors that have influenced constitutional change in Malawi.

The next section reprises some principles underlying constitutional design and constitutional change, after which a brief history of the adoption of the Constitution is provided. The section thereafter discusses the provisions governing the amendment of the Constitution, while the subsequent one analyses dynamics that have influenced constitutional change in Malawi. In analysing these dynamics, the chapter scrutinizes the frequency of amendments, the means adopted for effecting them, the motivations for some of them, and the role of the judiciary and other stakeholders in the amendment process. The chapter then proceeds to discuss the impact that the framework for, and practice of, constitutional amendment have had on democracy, the rule of law, and constitutionalism, after which it presents its conclusions.

2. Of constitutional design and constitutional change

Constitutional change can occur through several avenues.[9] It can be through amendment, revision, judicial interpretation, replacement, a shift in constitutional conventions, or irregular (non-legal and unconstitutional) means.[10] However, 'not all forms of constitutional change in fact involve processes of constitutional amendment, properly so called'.[11] Even

[7] Suber (n 4).

[8] Constitution of the Republic of Malawi (1994), ch XXI.

[9] Donald Lutz, 'Toward a Theory of Constitutional Amendment' (1994) 88(2) American Political Science Review 355; Bjorn Rasch and Roger D Congleton, 'Amendment Procedures and Constitutional Stability' in Roger D Congleton and Birgitta Swedenborg (eds.), *Democratic Constitutional Design and Public Policy: Analysis and Evidence* (MIT Press 2006) 536–61; Yaniv Roznai, 'Towards a Theory of Constitutional Unamendability: On the Nature and Scope of the Constitutional Amendment Powers' (*Jus Politicum*, 2015) http://juspoliticum.com/article/Towards-A-Theory-of-Constitutional-Unamendability-On-the-Nature-and-Scope-of-the-Constitutional-Amendment-Powers-1183.html accessed 1 May 2022.

[10] Venice Commission, 'Report on Constitutional Amendment' (19 January 2010), Council of Europe Study No 469/2008 https://www.venice.coe.int/webforms/documents/default.aspx?pdffile=CDL-AD(2010)001-e accessed 1 May 2022.

[11] Rosalind Dixon, 'Constitutional Amendment Rules: A Comparative Perspective' (2011), University of Chicago: Public Law and Legal Theory Working Paper No 347 https://chicagounbound.uchicago.edu/cgi/viewcontent.cgi?article=1070&context=public_law_and_legal_theory accessed 1 May 2022.

if the distinction between amendment and other means of constitutional change is not always clear, the fact is that the latter do not require actual amendment to a constitution. Constitutional amendment, as a form of constitutional change, is distinguishable because it requires the adoption of a formal text effecting change to an existing constitution.[12]

As for the other means of achieving constitutional change, constitutional replacement involves a political decision to create a new legal order.[13] This inevitably involves the drafting and adoption of a new constitution to replace an existing one.[14] Replacement, therefore, is distinguishable from amendment, as well as judicial interpretation, since the latter are mechanisms of legal adaptation that preserve the continuity of a constitution in a changing environment. Given its disruptive nature, constitutional replacement is rare and occurs only in extraordinary times, for example during a revolution or other major political crisis.[15]

According to Rasch and Congleton, 'less than 4 per cent of the world's constitutions lack articles on formal amendment procedures'.[16] Dixon suggests that 'formal provision for constitutional amendment is now a near universal feature of national constitutions'.[17] The ubiquity of provisions dealing with constitutional change stems from the fact that, for various reasons, a constitution must change. Constitutional change may be necessary due to, among others, the need to 'correct provisions that have proven to be inadequate or unworkable, to respond to new needs or changing public demands and to reflect evolving concepts of rights'.[18]

The necessity of constitutional change raises a dilemma for constitutional designers: how to strike a balance between a constitution's flexibility and its rigidity. This balance is structured differently from one country to the other, depending on, inter alia, the political and social context, the constitutional culture, and the age, detail, and characteristics of the constitution;[19] even within the same polity, the balance is not static and may shift over time in tandem with social, political, and economic change.[20] Yet, while it is readily accepted that finding the correct balance between rigidity and flexibility involves establishing a procedure for amending a constitution which is 'neither too easy nor too difficult',[21] what this entails in practice is not easy to discern.[22] In attempting to find the correct balance, the duty of constitutional designers is to create a process for constitutional change that 'allows a constitution to be changed for the public good, when necessary, when supported by a sufficient consensus, and after careful deliberation, but that prevents it from being changed for self-interested, partisan, destructive or short-term motives'.[23]

[12] Ibid.

[13] Gabriel Negretto, 'Replacing and Amending Constitutions: The Logic of Constitutional Change in Latin America' (Paper prepared for delivery at the 2011 American Political Science Association Meeting, Seattle, Washington, 1–4 September 2011) https://biblioteca.cejamericas.org/bitstream/handle/2015/3313/Replacing-and-Amending-Constitutions-The-Logic-of-Constitutional-Change-in-Latin-America.pdf?sequence=1&isAllowed=y accessed 27 April 2022.

[14] Melbourne Forum on Constitution-Building, 'Constitutional Beginnings: Making and Amending Constitutions' (2018) 1 Constitutional Insights 2.

[15] Negretto (n 13).

[16] Rasch and Congleton (n 9).

[17] Dixon (n 11).

[18] Böckenförde (n 6) 3.

[19] Venice Commission (n 10).

[20] Ibid.

[21] Lutz (n 9) 356.

[22] Negretto (n 13) 13–14.

[23] Böckenförde (n 6).

With these general remarks in mind, and as a prelude to analysing constitutional change in Malawi, the next section provides a brief history of the adoption of the Constitution.

3. The birth of the Constitution of Malawi (1994)

The 1994 Constitution is a result of the process of constitutional replacement that took place during Malawi's transition from a one-party state to a multiparty democracy. During this transition, the 1966 Constitution of the Republic of Malawi was repealed and replaced. Malawi's transition to a multiparty democracy, inclusive of the adoption of the Constitution, has been the subject of much analysis.[24] Consequently, apart from highlighting certain major developments relevant to constitutional change, this chapter does not dwell on the transition's intricacies.

The transition from a one-party state to a multiparty democracy began in earnest in March 1992 with the release, by Catholic bishops, of a pastoral letter critical of the government.[25] The letter called for better wages, education, and health care; freedom of expression; justice and rights protection; a climate of openness; a more just distribution of wealth; and an end to corruption. Its frankness in addressing the country's sociopolitical challenges was unprecedented, given the totalitarian system established by Dr Kamuzu Banda, Malawi's first president. Against a backdrop both of Africa's third wave of democratization, and of international pressure for the opening up of political space in the country, Dr Banda called for a national referendum: one in which Malawians voted in favour of the reintroduction of multiparty politics.[26]

While the outcome of the referendum was unequivocal, it also brought the need for legal reform into relief, especially given that the legal system was premised on the fact that the country was a one-party state with a president-for-life.[27] Some of the reforms that were undertaken after the referendum included amending the 1966 Constitution to bring back the Bill of Rights,[28] abolishing the life presidency, truncating presidential powers, and repealing or amending laws deemed oppressive and controversial.[29] Although this contributed to opening up the political space, it was realized that what the country truly needed was an entirely new constitution rather than piecemeal amendments to the existing one.

[24] See Jande Banda, 'The Constitutional Change Debate of 1993–1995' in Kings Phiri and Kenneth Ross (eds.), *Democratisation in Malawi: A Stocktaking* (CLAIM 1998) 316; Dianna Cammack, 'Democratic Transition in Malawi: From Single Party-rule to a Multi-party State' in John Daniel and others (eds.), *Voting for Democracy: Watershed Elections in Contemporary Anglophone Africa* (Ashgate 1999) 183; Julius Ihonvbere, 'From Despotism to Democracy: The Rise of Multiparty Politics in Malawi' (1997) 18(2) Third World Quarterly 225.

[25] 'Living our Faith: Pastoral Letter of the Catholic Bishops of Malawi' (*Almendron*, 12 July 2017) https://www.almendron.com/tribuna/wp-content/uploads/2017/12/1992-Malawi-Pastoral-Letter.pdf accessed 30 May 2022.

[26] Fidelis Kanyongolo, *Malawi: Justice Sector and the Rule of Law* (OSISA 2006) 35; Lewis Dzimbiri, 'The Malawi Referendum of June 1993' (1994) 13(3) Electoral Studies 229–34.

[27] Mwiza Nkhata, 'Rethinking Governance and Constitutionalism in Africa: The Relevance and Viability of Social Trust-based Governance and Constitutionalism' (LLD thesis, University of Pretoria 2010) 108.

[28] Constitutional (Amendment) Act 3 of 1993.

[29] Msaiwale Chigawa, 'The Fundamental Values of the Republic of Malawi Constitution of 1994' (Concept Paper One: The Law Commission Constitutional Review Conference, March 2006) https://acjr.org.za/resource-centre/fundamental_values_constitution_full.pdf/view accessed 30 May 2022. Among the laws that were repealed were the Forfeiture Act, Cap 14:06 of the Laws of Malawi, repealed by Act 22 of 1993; and the Decency in Dress Act, Cap 7:04, repealed in 1993. The Preservation of Public Security Act, Cap 14:02 of the Laws of Malawi, was not repealed as such, but was substantially amended.

To facilitate the transition, the government established the National Consultative Council (NCC) and National Executive Committee (NEC) to ensure that the change to multipartyism was independently managed.[30] The NEC was entrusted with executive power, while the NCC was tasked with, among other things, initiating appropriate legislative measures to amend the Constitution in ways necessary for holding the impending general elections.[31] The decision to adopt a new constitution, rather than amending the 1966 Constitution, was taken in November 1993 at a workshop convened by the NCC. In February 1994, the NCC hosted a Constitution Drafting Conference attended by appointees of political parties, the result of which was the adoption of an interim constitution that provided the basis on which the elections of May 1994 were held.[32] In a bid to refine the interim constitution, a Constitution Review Conference was convened in February 1995. It reviewed this constitution and made recommendations to Parliament for improvement. The final Constitution was adopted by Parliament in May 1995.[33]

The way in which Malawi's transition was managed, especially the decision to discard the 1966 Constitution, confirms that, during a transition, the choice of replacing a constitution or amending it depends on whether it is deemed capable of effectively and legitimately accommodating the incoming regime.[34] What is also material is the balance of influence between the outgoing regime and the forces of change. In the case of Malawi, the 1966 Constitution was clearly deemed incapable of supporting the incoming democratic regime, as it would have required numerous amendments to infuse it with an acceptably democratic tenor. It is also clear that the forces of change overwhelmingly supported the adoption of a new constitution rather than the mere amendment of the 1966 Constitution. Significantly, at the time that the transitional arrangements were being put in place, the influence of Dr Banda and his Malawi Congress Party (MCP) was declining, while that of the opposition was in the ascendancy. This gave the opposition leverage in terms of influencing the direction of change.

The next section explores some general issues that underlie the amendment of constitutions before presenting and analysing the scheme for amending the Constitution.

4. Constitutional amendment and the 1994 Constitution

Amendment procedures are important as a measure of how a constitution balances entrenchment and change, but these procedures also have a bearing on how a constitution stands the test of time.[35] Formal amendment rules provide a legal and transparent framework within which changes to a constitution can be undertaken.[36]

A key preoccupation in constitutional design is framing the necessary balance between rigidity and flexibility. Here, a common solution is to set different thresholds for amending

[30] See Clement Ng'ong'ola, 'Managing the Transition to Political Pluralism in Malawi: Legal and Constitutional Arrangements' (1996) 34(2) Journal of Commonwealth and Comparative Politics 85–110.

[31] NCC Act, s 5(1).

[32] Banda (n 24) 321–22.

[33] Republic of Malawi (Constitution) Act 7 of 1995.

[34] Negretto (n 13).

[35] Roznai (n 9) 5–6.

[36] Richard Albert, 'The Expressive Function of Constitutional Amendment Rules' (2015) 2(1) Revista de Investigacoes Constitucionais 7, 13.

different provisions. This approach provides stability and certainty by guaranteeing that some parts of a constitution are inherently more rigid than others while permitting greater flexibility to other parts.[37] Taking this approach, however, invites further challenges. For example, in balancing flexibility and rigidity, how are the parts to be accorded rigidity, and those to be accorded flexibility, to be identified?[38] Even assuming that the sections to be given rigidity have been identified, the preferred form of the rigidity has to be determined. This requires identifying the threshold and procedures that would suffice to legally change the provisions of a constitution.

A possible solution to balancing flexibility and rigidity lies in creating different 'tracks' for constitutional amendments. The value of this approach lies partly in the fact that, by creating a more difficult procedure for some amendments than others, a constitution may thereby automatically draw public attention to proposed amendments and, arguably, improve deliberation about them.[39] This, in turn, might promote the role of reason in the amendment process by creating room for the 'cooling down of passions' about particular amendments.[40] While formal amendment procedures are useful for identifying the broad norms and basic commitments behind a constitution, the stringency of these procedures reflects a polity's commitment to entrenching certain rules and procedures.[41]

In the case of Malawi's Constitution, it has not made any of its provisions unamendable. It simply prescribes different procedures for amending different provisions, thereby making some difficult to amend and others easier. Moreover, the Constitution has no provisions prescribing a procedure for its replacement.[42] This suggests, arguably, that its replacement, were it to happen, would be effected through either a revolutionary act or a regime change.

The Constitution vests the power for its amendment in the National Assembly, so long as it acts in accordance with the provisions of Chapter XXI.[43] The scheme in Chapter XXI distinguishes between amendment procedures for provisions in the Schedule to the Constitution (the scheduled provisions) and those for the rest of the provisions (unscheduled provisions). As for the unscheduled provisions, section 197 of the Constitution allows the National Assembly to amend any such provisions if a 'Bill proposing the amendment is supported by at least two-thirds of the total number of members of the National Assembly entitled to vote'. In regard to scheduled provisions, two 'tracks', described below, are available for amending them.

As for the first track, under section 196(1) of the Constitution, the National Assembly may amend any of the scheduled provisions, including Chapter XXI itself, if two conditions are satisfied. First, the provision to be amended and the proposed amendment to it must have been put to a referendum of the people of Malawi and the majority of those voting must have voted for the amendment. Second, the Electoral Commission must certify to the Speaker of the National Assembly that the outcome of the referendum favours the

37 Böckenförde (n 6).
38 Ibid.
39 Dixon (n 11) 103.
40 Venice Commission (n 10).
41 Rasch and Congleton (n 9); Albert (n 36) 7, 12–17.
42 s 212(5) of the Constitution (n 8), which was part of Malawi's transitional arrangements, envisaged that if extensive changes to the Constitution were recommended, Parliament could repeal or replace the Constitution after the lapse of the period of provisional application.
43 Ibid. s 195.

amendment. Once these conditions have been satisfied, the National Assembly may pass a bill, with a simple majority, proposing the amendment(s).[44]

The second track for amending scheduled provisions is in section 196(3) of the Constitution. According to this provision, the National Assembly can pass a bill containing an amendment to scheduled provisions without a referendum where three conditions are fulfilled. First, the amendment must be such that it 'would not affect the substance or effect of the Constitution'.[45] Second, the Speaker must confirm the preceding fact with his or her certificate.[46] Third, the bill proposing the amendment(s) must be 'supported by a majority of at least two-thirds of the total number of members of the National Assembly entitled to vote'.

Thus, as the foregoing makes clear, a key determinant of the procedure for amending the Constitution lies in whether the provision to be amended is scheduled or not. Given the centrality of the Schedule, a word about it is necessary. The following are listed in the Schedule: Chapter 1 of the Constitution, which concerns the foundations of the state; Chapter II, which deals with the application and interpretation of the Constitution; Chapter III, which outlines the Constitution's fundamental principles and the principles of national policy; Chapter IV, which is on human rights; section 47, on citizenship; section 77, on the franchise; and a few provisions, in Chapter IX, relating to judicial independence.

In overall terms, then, the Schedule covers two broad areas: human rights and the fundamentals of the organization of the state. It is arguable that there is a distinct historicity underlying the scheme in the schedule. For example, the entire Chapter IV of the Constitution, plus the provisions on citizenship and the franchise, were scheduled in order to banish the widespread violation of human rights that occurred under the one-party state. In addition, the Constitution is generous in its provision for civil and political rights but not for socio-economic rights.[47] This is attributable to the fact that, while there was a clamour for civil and political rights in the transition to multipartyism, support for socio-economic rights was muted.[48]

The provisions relating to the fundamentals of the organization of the state were, arguably, scheduled to make it more difficult for the country to return to authoritarianism. Warrant for this can be discerned from the inclusion, in the Schedule, of Chapter 1, which protects, among other things, the separation of powers, checks and balances, and the supremacy of the Constitution. The historical roots of the Schedule's scheme can also be discerned from its inclusion of provisions governing judicial independence. Clearly, the preservation of judicial independence was seen as pivotal to the survival of the new legal order, hence the additional effort to protect judicial independence by scheduling certain provisions relating to it. This sought to ensure that the judiciary would never again be relegated to the peripheries of governance, as had been the case under the 1966 Constitution.[49]

44 Ibid. s 196(2).

45 Ibid. s 196(3)(a).

46 Ibid. s 196(3)(b).

47 The Constitution provides a long list of civil and political rights in ch IV, but only a few socio-economic rights are included as justiciable rights: the rest are relegated to being principles of national policy, which are merely directive. See Danwood Chirwa, 'A Full Loaf is Better than Half: The Constitutional Protection of Economic, Social and Cultural Rights in Malawi' (2005) 49(2) Journal of African Law 207–41.

48 See Harri Englund, *Prisoners of Freedom: Human Rights and the African Poor* (University of California Press 2006).

49 See Rachel Ellett, *Politics of Judicial Independence in Malawi* (Freedom House 2014) https://freedomhouse.org/sites/default/files/inline_images/Politics%20of%20Judicial%20Independence%20in%20Malawi_1.pdf accessed 31 May 2022.

Under closer analysis, however, the scheme for amending the Constitution reveals an Achilles heel in respect of the procedures for amending scheduled provisions. Of the two options permitted by the Constitution, the holding of a referendum for the purposes of amending scheduled provisions is unlikely to be utilized regularly—in fact, at the time of this writing, no referendum on a proposed constitutional amendment has ever been held in the country in the 29 years since the Constitution was adopted. Holding a referendum simply for the sake of approving or rejecting an amendment is likely to be prohibitively expensive in a resource-constrained country like Malawi. It is also likely to falter due to the absence of enabling legislation.[50] Thus, the only realistic avenue for amending scheduled provisions is through the Speaker's certification and a two-thirds majority vote in the National Assembly.

The power to amend scheduled provisions using the Speaker's certification and a two-thirds majority in the National Assembly comes with an inbuilt restriction, namely that the amendment must not affect the substance and effect of the Constitution. To begin with, there is no hard and fast delineation of provisions whose amendment may affect the substance and effect of the Constitution. Although the Constitution has left the determination of whether a purported amendment affects its substance and effect to the Speaker, this is not an easy determination, as the substance and effect could be altered by changing but a single word in a provision.[51] Additionally, neither the Standing Orders of the National Assembly nor any other law provide clarity as to how the Speaker must determine if a proposed amendment affects the substance and effect of the Constitution or not. This lack of clarity exposes the process to the risk of manipulation by political forces. To complicate matters, research for this chapter was unable to identify a transparent and established practice for issuing the Speaker's certificate.[52]

A possible solution in this regard would have been for the Constitution to be explicit about the need either for debate in Parliament or for a referral to the High Court, sitting as a constitutional court, before the Speaker issues the certificate.[53] As matters stand, though, the framers may have intended to make the scheduled provisions more difficult to amend, but the current design leaves these provisions vulnerable. Given this context, the next section explores the dynamics involved in constitutional amendment in Malawi.

5. Dicing with stability and change

Given the sheer number of constitutional provisions that have been amended, the following analysis of the dynamics of constitutional change in Malawi deals with selected examples

[50] In 2018, Parliament adopted a bill on the holding of referenda in the country—the Referendum Act 6 of 2018—but although it was assented to, it is not yet operational.

[51] Danwood Chirwa, 'Democratisation in Malawi 1994–2002: Completing the Vicious Circle' (2003) 19(2) South African Journal on Human Rights 316, 321.

[52] The author spoke to several senior officers at the Ministry of Justice and Constitutional Affairs, who confirmed that the Speaker's certificate has been used previously to facilitate amendments to the Constitution; however, none of them could point to an established practice by which the Speaker's certificate is issued. The most that was conceded was that some Speakers have, in the past, consulted the Attorney General before issuing a certificate. It is not clear whether, in such a case, the Speaker is bound by the Attorney General's advice. The author's email enquiry to the National Assembly, through the Office of the Clerk of Parliament, did not receive a response.

[53] Technically, Malawi does not have a constitutional court; instead, the High Court sits with a reconfigured quorum to hear constitutional disputes. See Mwiza Nkhata, 'The High Court of Malawi as a Constitutional Court: Constitutional Adjudication the Malawian Way' (2020) 24(1) Law, Democracy & Development 442–67.

and focuses only on the following themes: the frequency of amendments; the means (either formal or informal) adopted to effect change; the motivations for such changes, be they opportunistic or dictated by necessity; and the role of the judiciary and other stakeholders in the process.

5.1 Frequency of constitutional amendments

By 2006, the Constitution had been amended by nine amendment Acts that affected more than 90 sections.[54] At least a further six constitutional amendment Acts had been adopted by the end of 2021, with these affecting about 49 sections of the Constitution, in addition to creating a new Chapter XXA. (This count excludes any amendments being contemplated at the time of writing.) In sum, in the 29 years in which the Constitution has been in force, amendments have affected at least 139 provisions. As Chirwa notes, the current text of the Constitution is, as a result, 'considerably different from the one adopted in 1994'.[55]

Importantly, while tracking the magnitude and frequency of formal amendments to a constitution is a useful exercise, this must be undertaken with caution, especially if one wants to understand changes to a constitution in a comprehensive fashion. The danger in focusing on formal amendments is that it risks ignoring other changes that may have come about through informal means.[56]

For example, in relation to the frequency of amendments, the 1994 Constitution has been amended by, at least, fifteen amendment Acts affecting 139 provisions, whereas, by way of comparison, the Constitution of the United States of America (US), which is more than 200 years old, has been amended on only 27 occasions.[57] Nominally, this suggests that there have been too many amendments to the 1994 Constitution in a very short period. In fairness, however, and insofar as the frequency of amendment is concerned, it is erroneous to make a simple comparison between the US and Malawian constitutions. Not only do the two constitutions govern distinctly different polities, but they also contain very different amendment procedures, with the US Constitution generally having a far more rigid procedure than the Malawian Constitution. It is also worth noting that, in the case of the US Constitution, as against the 27 successful amendments, there have been at least 11,000 attempts at amending it.[58]

Although it is undesirable to make a direct comparison of the rate of constitutional amendment in Malawi and the US, the gulf between the two countries offers a useful basis for understanding the frequency with which countries amend constitutions. The nominally higher frequency of constitutional amendment in Malawi is not, of itself, an indication of the ease with which the 1994 Constitution can be amended. This is partly because, in comparative constitutional law, questions of the relationship between the frequency of constitutional amendment and the stringency of the amendment procedures remain

[54] Anthony Kamanga, 'Amendments to the Constitution Since 18 May 1994' (Paper presented at the Constitution Review Conference 28–31 March 2006, Capital Hotel, Lilongwe (copy on file with author)).
[55] Chirwa (n 51) 321.
[56] See Rasch and Congleton (n 9).
[57] See 'List of Amendments to the US Constitution' (*Britannica*) https://www.britannica.com/topic/list-of-amendments-to-the-U-S-Constitution-1787122 accessed 1 June 2022.
[58] 'The Constitution of the United States: Fast Facts' (*National Constitution Centre*, undated) https://constitutioncenter.org/education/classroom-resource-library/classroom/constitution-fast-facts accessed 1 October 2023.

inconclusive.[59] As Dixon points out, 'existing comparative constitutional scholarship is still at a relatively early stage of development in what it tells us about the actual determinants of the rate or difficulty of constitutional amendment in various jurisdictions.'[60] To understand the frequency of constitutional amendment properly, it is important to evaluate both the formal rules governing amendments and the broad sociopolitical context.

Since the formal rigidity or flexibility of a constitution is not necessarily the key determinant of the frequency of constitutional amendment, what, then, determines the frequency with which a country changes its constitution? It seems to be the case—without belittling the importance of the formal rules—that the frequency of constitutional change is a product of a country's political, economic, and social factors, as well as, generally, its 'constitutional culture'.[61] What is meant by 'constitutional culture' is the general public's attitude towards constitutionalism. This entails that, for example, where there is a dominant political party, it may be far easier to adopt changes to a constitution than in a situation where there are numerous small parties. However, even in a context without a dominant political party, but where interests among political parties converge, it is not uncommon to see parties coordinating to support constitutional changes.[62]

In assessing the situation in Malawi, it is important to note that a substantial number of constitutional amendments arose due to the need to correct textual errors and ambiguities, as well as to improve the text. Given the manner in which the Constitution was adopted—conceived at the end of 1993, drafted and adopted by early 1994[63]—it was inevitable that the document would have textual errors and ambiguities. Some amendments, therefore, were for purposes of 'cleaning' the document. It is also important to recall that the Constitution began its life with a one-year period of provisional operation. Upon the lapse of this period, a constitutional review conference was convened, the result of which was a raft of proposed amendments.[64] Although not all the recommendations of the constitutional review conference were implemented, this process contributed to an increase in the frequency of amendments in the first decade after the Constitution's adoption. In the same vein, some of the amendments have followed from recommendations made by the Malawi Law Commission (hereinafter referred to as 'the Law Commission') in its technical review of the Constitution.[65] As is demonstrated later, however, while the technical review processes have contributed to raising the frequency of amendments, political expedience has been a key mover of constitutional amendments.

Given that, since 1994, no single political party has dominated the political landscape for any sustained period, support for constitutional amendments has often involved machinations by political parties with representation in the National Assembly. For example, the National Assembly easily united to support the repeal of section 64 of the Constitution, given that the provision at issue was perceived as placing the tenure of all parliamentarians

[59] Rasch and Congleton (n 9).
[60] Dixon (n 11).
[61] Venice Commission (n 10).
[62] Negretto (n 13).
[63] Nkhata (n 27) 127.
[64] Government of Malawi, 'Report of the Constitution Committee to the National Assembly on the National Constitutional Conference on the Provisional Constitution' (1995).
[65] Malawi Law Commission, *Law Commission Report on the Technical Review of the Constitution* (1998); Malawi Law Commission, *Report of the Law Commission on the Review of the Constitution* (2007).

in jeopardy.[66] Although the first Parliament, after the 1994 general elections, was heavily polarized, in repealing section 64 a clear convergence of interests permitted parliamentarians to set aside their differences temporarily in dealing with a perceived common threat. This pattern, it is argued, persists to date. The Malawian situation lends credence to the assertion that the frequency of constitutional amendment has no direct correlation to the stringency or lack thereof of the amendment procedures—and that it is the sociopolitical context which is determinative.

5.2 Means of change: Formal and/or informal?

A strict reading of the Constitution suggests that the only permitted avenue for its change is through the procedures outlined in Chapter XXI. The Chapter XXI procedures, however, represent formal amendment procedures. Comparative constitutional practice confirms that 'formal amendment is not the only form of constitutional change, and in some systems not even the most important'.[67] Aside from the formal amendment procedures, the two most important alternative means of legitimate constitutional change are judicial interpretation and the evolution of unwritten political conventions supplementing or contradicting the written text.[68] Informal constitutional change may also come about when constitutional procedures and constraints are ignored or reconfigured without reference to the constitution's text.[69]

In practice, formal and informal means of constitutional amendment often complement each other, sometimes in ways that are quite different from what the actual text of a constitution prescribes.[70] A perfect example of the interface between formal and informal amendment to the 1994 Constitution can be seen in the amendment to section 80(2).[71] This provision, as originally framed, provided that 'the president shall be elected by a majority of the electorate through direct, universal and equal suffrage'. In 2000, the Malawi Supreme Court of Appeal (MSCA) held that section 80(2) is an embodiment of the first-past-the-post electoral system, meaning that, to be declared a winner, a presidential candidate simply has to get more votes than any of his or her competitors.[72] In 2020, however, the High Court of Malawi departed from the 2000 decision and held that section 80(2) required a presidential candidate to obtain at least 50 per cent plus one of the total votes cast to be validly elected.[73] This interpretation was subsequently confirmed by the MSCA.[74]

[66] s 64(1) provided as follows: 'The seat of a member of the National Assembly shall become vacant: (g) if a member is subject to recall by his constituency in accordance with an Act of Parliament and the provisions of this Constitution.'

[67] Venice Commission (n 10).

[68] Ibid.

[69] Rasch and Congleton (n 9).

[70] Venice Commission (n 10).

[71] Another example would be the amendment to s 50 on the quorum of the National Assembly. As originally enacted, s 50 required the presence of at least two-thirds of the members entitled to vote at the beginning of a sitting for there to be a quorum. Currently, the provision stipulates a quorum of 'one half plus one', which is a direct consequence of the litigation in *Malawi Congress Party and Others v Attorney General* [1996] MLR 244 and *Attorney General v Malawi Congress Party and Others* [1997] 2 MLR 181.

[72] *Gwanda Chakuamba and others v Attorney General and others* MSCA Civil Appeal no 20 of 2000.

[73] *Saulos Chilima and another v Peter Mutharika and another*, Constitutional Reference no 1 of 2019. The High Court's judgment confirms that it was aware it was departing from a binding precedent, but it justified its approach by distinguishing the earlier decision from the MSCA.

[74] *Peter Mutharika and another v Saulos Chilima and another*, MSCA Constitutional Appeal no 1 of 2020.

Given that, prior to the 2020 judgment, all presidents in Malawi had been elected on the basis of the first-past-the-post system, it is clear that the courts effected an amendment to the Constitution in relation to the formula for electing a president. Notably, however, although the genesis of the amendment to section 80(2) may be said to have been informal, it was subsequently formalized by Constitution (Amendment) Act 5 of 2020. The formal amendment to section 80(2) reiterates the formula for electing a president that was endorsed by both the High Court and the MSCA. The amendment also provides details about how the second ballot should be conducted should there be no candidate obtaining the required majority in the first round of voting.

Although a distinction is often drawn between formal and informal constitutional change, what seems like a formal change may, upon scrutiny, be revealed as an informal one. This is likely to be the case where a supposedly formal change flouts the formal procedures. In this regard, the repeal of sections 68 to 72 of the 1994 Constitution appears to be an example of an informal amendment. Sections 68 to 72 of the Constitution provided for a second chamber of Parliament: the Senate.[75] However, through Constitution Amendment Act 4 of 2001, the National Assembly abolished the Senate by excising all constitutional provisions relating to it. It is arguable, though, that Parliament did not follow the Constitution in abolishing the Senate, especially given that section 45(9) of the Constitution provides that 'under no circumstance shall it be possible to suspend this Constitution or any part thereof or dissolve any of its organs, save as is consistent with the provisions of this Constitution'.

At least three arguments can be made against the action taken by Parliament, and in support of the possible illegality of its conduct. First, given the role the Constitution conferred on the Senate as an instrument of governance, any amendment to the provisions establishing the Senate had a bearing on the substance and effect of the Constitution. In terms of section 196 of the Constitution, amending these provisions would have required either a referendum or a Speaker's certificate, yet there is no evidence that these procedures were followed. Second, contemporaneous evidence suggests that Parliament went ahead with the abolition of the Senate despite significant public opposition, and without adequate consultation on the matter.[76] Strikingly, litigation against the proposed amendment was still pending when Parliament moved to finalize the Senate's abolition.[77] Lastly, continuing pressure for the reintroduction of the Senate suggests that Parliament may have acted against the interests of the people of Malawi, in contradiction of the directive in section 8 of the Constitution.[78] On the whole, while the formal parliamentary processes may have been adhered to, the abolition of the Senate, it is submitted, may qualify as an informal amendment to the 1994 Constitution.

[75] See Msaiwale Chigawa, 'The Senate as the Second Chamber of Parliament in Malawi: Its Relevance, Composition and Powers' (Malawi Law Journal Launch Conference, 16–17 July 2008, Blantyre, Malawi (copy on file with author)).

[76] Chifundo Kachale, 'Judicial (In)activism in Malawi: A Critical Analysis of the Impact of Constitutional Jurisprudence on Constitutionalism and the Rule of Law' (PhD thesis, University of London 2012) 190–92.

[77] Nandini Patel, 'The Representational Challenge in Malawi' in *Towards the Consolidation of Malawi's Democracy* (Konrad Adenaeur Foundation 2008) 21, 25–26.

[78] Hopkins Nyirenda, 'MP wants Senate Recall Provision' (*All Africa*, 28 October 2005) https://allafrica.com/stories/200510280042.html accessed 14 August 2023.

5.3 Motivation for change: Opportunistic or dictated by necessity?

In Kamanga's summation:

> the amendments to the Constitution include [not only] correction of textual errors and ambiguities identified after the adoption of the Constitution, as well as improvement of the text of the Constitution, and the introduction of new substantive provisions to fill perceived gaps; but also the amendment of substantive provisions of the Constitution for reasons of political expedience or to address political realities.[79]

A 2006 discussion paper by the Law Commission endorsed this analysis of the motivations for constitutional change in Malawi.[80] The practice post-2006 would seem to involve much the same factors. Accordingly, the analysis below focuses on selected examples falling into the category either of 'necessity' or 'opportunism'.

To begin with 'necessity', several changes to the Constitution were motivated by the need to resolve ambiguities, correct textual errors, or simply improve the Constitution. The following examples suffice:

- The amendment of section 73(1) introduced the requirement that the president, in respect of bills presented to him or her for assent, must signify or withhold assent within 21 days (since no period had been prescribed before).
- Section 73(3) provides that, if any bill is again passed by the National Assembly within three months (and not the originally provided six months) of the president's withholding assent, then the bill shall again be presented to the president for assent.
- The introduction of section 213 broadened the category of individuals required to disclose their assets and liabilities fully to include members of the National Assembly, members of the Senate, public officers, and senior officers of statutory bodies (arguably as a way of entrenching broader transparency and accountability across government).[81]
- The amendment of section 67 prescribes the date on which the National Assembly is dissolved and harmonizes the dates for holding parliamentary and presidential elections (the first Parliament under the 1994 Constitution was sworn in on 29 June 1994, while the president was sworn in on 21 May 1994, with the result that the tenures of the president and Parliament expired on different dates, even though the law requires presidential and parliamentary elections to be held simultaneously).[82]
- The amendment replacing the expression 'Defence Forces of Malawi' with 'Defence Force of Malawi' across the Constitution.[83]
- The amendment of section 159 confirms that the Defence Force of Malawi is constituted under the Constitution, while the amendment of section 160 prohibits the

[79] Kamanga (n 54).
[80] Malawi Law Commission, *Amendments to the Constitution and Preservation of its Sanctity* (2006) Constitution Review Programme, Discussion Paper No 7 (copy on file with author).
[81] Act 1 of 1997.
[82] Constitution Amendment Act 38 of 1998.
[83] Constitution Amendment Act 4 of 2004.

deployment of the Defence Force outside of Malawi for more than 90 days except with the authority of Parliament, thereby guaranteeing accountability for the decision to deploy outside the country.[84]
- The bulk of the amendments introduced by Act 11 of 2010 were necessary to clarify the Constitution's language and align some of its provisions with the country's obligations under international law.[85]

While the changes above can be defended for their necessity, in other cases opportunism may have been the operative motivation.[86] Indeed, it was not long after the Constitution was adopted that caprice began driving changes—the first set of amendments to the Constitution were, in fact, made while it was still only provisionally in force.[87] Among other things, these amendments created the office of the second vice president by amending sections 79 and 80 of the Constitution.

What cannot be seen from the text of the amendments is that the need for the second vice presidency arose from a political alliance between the United Democratic Front (UDF), which was then governing, and the Alliance for Democracy (AFORD), which was in opposition.[88] The second vice presidency was created as a token to be given to AFORD for agreeing to be part of the alliance, in addition to the ministerial positions that other AFORD members took up. The amendment was made in the face of widespread public criticism and an unsuccessful attempt was made to challenge it in the High Court.[89] Although section 80(5) requires the president to appoint a second vice president only if it is in the national interest, ironically, and perhaps as confirmation of the opportunistic nature of the amendment, to date no other person apart from the then leader of AFORD has been appointed to this office.

The second set of opportunistically motivated amendments to the Constitution also related to recommendations emanating from the Constitution Review Conference that was held after the Constitution's one year of provisional operation.[90] Opportunistic tendencies clearly informed the manner in which Parliament dealt with the recommendations, especially in how most of them were disregarded.[91] It is the repeal of section 64, however, that stands out as a prime example of the opportunism that was at work. Section 64 permitted constituents to recall a Member of Parliament (MP) and the Speaker to declare his or her seat vacant where there had been a successful recall. Although the 1995 Constitution

[84] Act 13 of 2001.

[85] For example, the renumbering of s 12 was for the purposes of making it consistent with drafting practice in Malawi. Similarly, s 23 was amended to refer expressly to 'the best interests of the child', so as to align the Constitution with international law, while the amendment of s 43 was to clear up linguistic ambiguities. In turn, Act 13 of 2020 introduced many changes that became necessary as a result of litigation surrounding the 2020 presidential election.

[86] Other amendments, arguably opportunistically adopted but not analysed in this chapter, include the amendment of the quorum of the National Assembly in s 50, and the alteration of the qualifications of presidential candidates in s 80(6)(c). For a discussion, see Wapona Kita and Christopher Chiphwanya, 'Constitutional Amendment or Constitutional Disbandment' (2003) UNIMA Students Law Journal 19–33.

[87] Act 31 of 1994.

[88] Denis Kadima and Samson Lembani, 'Making, Unmaking and Remaking Political Party Coalitions in Malawi: Explaining the Prevalence of Office-Seeking Behaviour' (*Academia*, 2006) https://www.academia.edu/72578663/Making_Unmaking_and_Remaking_Political_Party_Coalitions_in_Malawi accessed 1 October 2023.

[89] *RB Kachere v The President and the Speaker of the National Assembly*, MSCA Civil Appeal no 20 of 1995. The case was dismissed on the grounds that the applicants did not have *locus standi*.

[90] See Constitution (Amendment) Act 6 of 1995.

[91] Chirwa (n 51) 318.

Review Conference recommended the retention of this provision, the National Assembly proceeded to repeal it. Calls have been made for the reintroduction of section 64, but the National Assembly has steadfastly refused to heed them.[92] Given that the recall was meant to help ensure parliamentarians' accountability to their constituents, the failure to reintroduce the provision highlights the challenges facing democracy and constitutionalism in Malawi.

The amendment of section 65 also manifests an opportunistic intervention. As originally framed, section 65 provided as follows:

1. The Speaker shall declare vacant the seat of any member of the National Assembly who was, at the time of his or her election, a member of one political party represented in the National Assembly, other than by that member alone but who has voluntarily ceased to be a member of that party and has joined another political party represented in the National Assembly.
2. Notwithstanding subsection (1), all members of all parties shall have the absolute right to exercise a free vote in any and all proceedings of the National Assembly, and a member shall not have his or her seat declared vacant solely on account of his or her voting in contradiction to the recommendations of a political party, represented in the National Assembly, of which he or she is a member.

In Act 8 of 2001, Parliament amended section 65(1) but kept section 65(2) intact. The result is that section 65(1) now provides as follows:

> The Speaker shall declare vacant the seat of any member of the National Assembly who was, at the time of his or her election, a member of one political party represented in the National Assembly, other than by that member alone but who has voluntarily ceased to be a member of that party or has joined another political party represented in the National Assembly *or has joined any other political party, or association or organization whose objectives or activities are political in nature* [the amended portion is italicized].

The original section 65 sought to proscribe floor-crossing by MPs in the classical sense; that is, as between political parties in Parliament.[93] The amended section 65 extends the proscription *outside of* Parliament and is not limited to political parties but includes associations or organizations whose objectives are political in nature.

Under scrutiny, the 'need' to amend section 65 is traceable to a fallout in the then governing UDF that prompted some leading members to form a splinter group, the National Democratic Alliance (NDA). In terms of the original section 65, MPs from the UDF could not be deemed to have crossed the floor if they had joined the NDA, since it was not, at the time, a political party that was represented in Parliament. To dissuade parliamentarians from joining the NDA, the UDF sponsored the amendment to section 65, in the process

[92] Jordan Phiri, 'Traditional Leader Dares Malawi Parliament to Re-introduce Recall Provision for MPs' (*All Africa*, 28 October 2020) https://allafrica.com/stories/202010280193.html accessed 1 June 2022.

[93] See Msaiwale Chigawa, 'The Concept of Crossing the Floor under Malawian Constitutional Law' (2008) 2(2) Malawi Law Journal 185–208; Louis Chimango, 'Section 65 of the Malawian Constitution: The Role of the Speaker, 2005–2009' (2012) 6(2) Malawi Law Journal 212–42.

broadening the meaning of 'crossing the floor'.[94] Over the years, however, the application of the amended section 65 has been selective and inconsistent:[95] recourse to the provision, as experience has demonstrated, has been dependent on the prevailing political priorities.[96] The result is that enthusiasm for enforcing the provision has been high when its application would also settle political scores.[97]

Three abortive amendments are also revealing as to the motivations for changing the Constitution. First, Constitution Amendment Bill 1 of 2002 (also known as the Open Terms Bill) sought to amend section 83(3) of the Constitution in order to remove limitations on the number of terms that a president could serve. The bill was introduced in Parliament but failed to garner the necessary majority to pass into law. Second, Constitution Amendment Bill 14 of 2004 (also known as the Third Term Bill) proposed to amend section 83(3) to allow any president to serve a maximum of three consecutive terms, as well as to entrench section 83 so that any further amendment would have to comply with section 196 of the Constitution. This bill was introduced in Parliament but subsequently withdrawn. Third, Bill 20 of 2004 was designed to extend the life of the National Compensation Tribunal by five years from 18 May 2005 or until all claims registered with the Tribunal were determined. The bill was later cancelled by a notice published in the *Gazette*.

As has been the case with many constitutional developments in Malawi, the real stories behind these three bills lie in political developments in the country. The Third Term Bill ought to be understood together with the Open Terms Bill, since both were proposals initiated with the aim of keeping the then president, Bakili Muluzi, in office beyond the constitutionally prescribed two terms. These proposals were made in the face of widespread public opposition, and with the intention of subverting the 1994 Constitution.[98] On a positive note, the failure to amend presidential term limits stands as proof of the utility of the Constitution's amendment procedures and offers hope for constitutionalism. This is because, notwithstanding massive lobbying, the required majority proved a bridge too far for the proponents of the amendment.

As for Bill 20 of 2004, the National Compensation Tribunal's lifespan was designed to expire ten years after the adoption of the Constitution. As this period approached its end, it was clear that the Tribunal had not completed its work. Seeking an extension of its lifespan, therefore, was a necessity, given that the Tribunal was still seized of unresolved claims. Unfortunately, by 2004 there was no political will to support the extension of its mandate, in part because many of the key political players who had claims before the

[94] Redson Kapindu, 'Separation of Powers and the Accountability Role of NHRIs: The Malawi Human Rights Commission through the Courts' in David Bilchitz and David Landau (eds.), *The Evolution of the Separation of Powers: Between the Global North and the Global South* (Edward Elgar 2018) 206, 221.

[95] See Ann Maganga, 'An Investigation of the Political Factors Contributing to Floor Crossing in the Malawi National Assembly: 2003–2009' (MA thesis, University of South Africa 2011) https://uir.unisa.ac.za/bitstream/handle/10500/4833/thesis_maganga_a.pdf?sequence=1&isAllowed=y accessed 30 October 2023.

[96] See 'Section 65 Issue Re-emerges' (*Economist Intelligence Unit*, 11 June 2012) http://country.eiu.com/article.aspx?articleid=989126883&Country=Malawi&topic=Politics&subtopic=Re_10 accessed 1 June 2022.

[97] For example, when Bingu wa Mutharika left the UDF to form his Democratic Progressive Party (DPP), even though he was president, he ended up with a political party that had no MPs, since the DPP had not contested the 2004 general election. Notwithstanding that many parliamentarians 'defected' to join the DPP, due to numerous legal challenges the application of s 65 was effectively put on hold until the 2009 general elections.

[98] Fidelis Kanyongolo, 'Constitutionalism and the Removal of Presidential Term Limits from the Constitution of Malawi' (2003) 7(1) UNIMA Students Law Journal 59–72.

Tribunal had already been compensated.[99] The Tribunal thus wound up without completing its work.

The two examples above demonstrate how, in the one case, political will was available to push forward changes that threatened the Constitution's core values, while, in the other, no such will could be summoned to support changes born of the necessity of finalizing the demands of transitional justice. This confirms that, when constitutional change is at stake, the logic of politics trumps everything.

5.4 The role of the judiciary and others: Active, passive, or reactive?

In Malawi, the judiciary has the responsibility of interpreting, protecting, and enforcing the Constitution and all laws in an independent and impartial manner while having regard only to 'legally relevant facts and the prescriptions of law'.[100] In discharging its responsibility, the judiciary is enjoined to use the Constitution as the yardstick. This responsibility entails that the judiciary can be a significant actor in constitutional change,[101] as when judicial intervention leads to the judiciary's development of new interpretations of the Constitution that trump existing ones.[102] Judicial interpretation, in other words, is an alternative to amendment as a mechanism of constitutional adaptation.[103] The extent to which courts consider themselves competent to develop constitutions by way of interpretation varies between jurisdictions, depending on national doctrine, tradition, and context,[104] but, generally speaking, the more difficult it is to amend a constitution, the more likely it is that adjustments will be made through judicial interpretation, as the case of the US proves.[105]

In Malawi, the judiciary has had a role to play in constitutional change, but this has been a reactive one. Notably, Malawi does not have a system of automatic review of legislation for constitutionality after it has been passed by Parliament. Given the adversarial nature of litigation, the judiciary must wait to be moved before intervening in any legal dispute. This notwithstanding, disputes about changes to the Constitution have ended up with the judiciary. For example, as noted earlier, an attempt was made to stop the abolition of the Senate, but this became futile since Parliament concluded the process before the litigation could be finalized. Another example of the judiciary playing a role in constitutional change can be seen in *Chilima and another v Mutharika and another* (discussed earlier),[106] where the High Court pronounced a fresh meaning of the term 'majority' for purposes of electing a president.

The litigation surrounding the amendment of section 65 of the Constitution also illustrates the judiciary's role in constitutional change. As mentioned, the amended section 65 proscribes floor-crossing by MPs even outside of Parliament. In 2003 a challenge was

[99] See Office of the Ombudsman, *Malawi's Unhealed Wounds: A Report on an Investigation into Allegations of Maladministration and Other Irregularities by Malawi Government over the Manner in Which the National Compensation Tribunal was Set Up, Operated and Wound Up* (Office of the Ombudsman 2017).

[100] Constitution (n 8) s 9.

[101] See Melbourne Forum on Constitution-Building (n 14) 7.

[102] Dixon (n 11).

[103] Negretto (n 13).

[104] Venice Commission (n 10).

[105] Böckenförde (n 6).

[106] *Saulos Chilima and another v Peter Mutharika and another* (n 73).

lodged against the amendment, with the High Court finding the amendment unconstitutional for unreasonably stretching the meaning of floor-crossing, in particular by prohibiting MPs from joining any association or organization whose objectives or activities are political in nature.[107] Ultimately, the High Court's decision confirmed the judiciary's role in reviewing the constitutionality of changes to the Constitution.

Section 65, however, was back before the High Court in 2005 due to a presidential referral.[108] The referral questioned, among other things, the validity of section 65(1) as read with the political rights guaranteed in the Constitution. A quirky fact in this regard is that the referral was premised on the amended section 65(1), which had been nullified by the High Court in *The Registered Trustees of the Public Affairs Committee v Attorney General and others* (the *PAC Case*).[109] The High Court nevertheless proceeded to consider the referral as framed, and upheld the validity of the amended section 65(1).[110] In its determination, the Court made only passing reference to its earlier decision in the *PAC Case*, and at no point attempted to distinguish the earlier judgment.

On 'appeal' to the MSCA, the determination of the High Court was upheld.[111] The MSCA, however, made observations that directly questioned the High Court's findings in the *PAC Case*. According to the MSCA, no court in Malawi has the power to invalidate any constitutional provision—this effectively overruled the *PAC Case*. The MSCA reasoned that 'amendments to the Constitution, once duly passed in the normal way by the National Assembly and thereby becoming part of the Constitution . . . cannot be invalidated or declared to be unconstitutional or inconsistent with the other provisions of the Constitution'.[112]

While the MSCA was correct in concurring with the High Court that courts do not have the power to invalidate any constitutional provision, the pronouncement relating to courts' power of review in relation to constitutional amendments evinces a deference to Parliament that might not be well-grounded.[113] As demonstrated earlier, the scheme for constitutional change in Malawi leaves room for potential subversion of the Constitution's fundamental values. This suggests, arguably, that the judiciary may be the only bulwark for checking any excesses by Parliament and the executive in relation to changing the Constitution. The abdication pronounced by the MSCA thus may have been misplaced.[114]

Aside from the courts, other stakeholders have a role in constitutional change. Civil society organizations have maintained a footprint in constitutional change, albeit a reactive one. For example, as noted above, there was a civil society-led attempt to challenge the abolition of the Senate, even though this did not achieve much. More sustained civil society agitation surrounded the attempted amendment to section 83 to remove presidential term

[107] *The Registered Trustees of the Public Affairs Committee v Attorney General and others*, Civil Cause no 1861 of 2003.

[108] Presidential referrals of constitutional disputes are permitted by s 89(1)(h) of the Constitution.

[109] *The Registered Trustees of the Public Affairs Committee v Attorney General and others* (n 107).

[110] *In the Matter of Section 65 of the Constitution and in the Matter of the Question of Crossing the Floor by Members of Parliament*, Presidential Referral no 2 of 2005.

[111] *In the Matter of Section 65 of the Constitution and in the Matter of the Question of Crossing the Floor by Members of Parliament*, Presidential Reference Appeal no 44 of 2006.

[112] Ibid.

[113] See Kachale (n 76) 194–96.

[114] Fundamentally, the s 65 litigation highlighted the question of whether the basic structure doctrine is relevant in Malawi. While the matter is beyond the scope of this chapter, it suffices to note that no Malawian court has pronounced itself on this issue yet.

limits, with some citizens organizing themselves into a grouping called the Forum for the Defence of the Constitution.[115] Churches also rallied to take a stand, and opposition to the amendment included public demonstrations in Malawi's major urban areas.[116] It is arguable that public agitation contributed to the failure to garner the required majority in the National Assembly.

Only the Law Commission can be said to have had an active engagement with constitutional change processes in Malawi. Nevertheless, its statutory set-up automatically limits its influence—this is because it has no control of what becomes of its recommendations for reform.[117] Recommendations from the Law Commission are submitted to the Ministry of Justice and are subject to Cabinet approval before they are taken for Parliament's consideration. Unsurprisingly, many of these recommendations either take an inordinately long time before being tabled in Parliament or never get there at all.[118] Successive regimes have also perfected the habit of cherry-picking from the Law Commission's recommendations and proceeding to Parliament only with those recommendations deemed acceptable. However, only the proposals of the Law Commission can be said to have been non-reactive and free from overt political bias.

6. Lessons for democracy, constitutionalism, and the rule of law

Constitutional change lies at the heart of constitutional theory and practice.[119] This is because such change is not simply a legal technicality but, in the words of the Venice Commission, 'a norm-set the details of which may heavily influence or determine fundamental political processes'.[120] Crucially, while not every demand for constitutional change is meant to advance broad societal interests,[121] changes to a constitution, whatever their provenance, have an impact on democracy, constitutionalism, and the rule of law—and in this regard, a key concern is that they should not undermine constitutionalism. This section thus seeks to bring to light the impact that changes to the 1994 Constitution have had on democracy, constitutionalism, and the rule of law in Malawi, and, in so doing, identify some of the lessons that may be learnt.

As may be recalled, the Constitution was born of the transition from a one-party state, with many of its provisions duly reflecting a commitment to multiparty democracy founded on the rule of law. While some changes to the Constitution were inevitable and necessary, others, such as the abolition of the Senate and the repeal of section 64, suggest a fickle commitment to constitutionalism and a dilution of the fundamentals of democracy and the rule of law. For example, the repeal of section 64 attenuated the mechanisms available to constituents for holding MPs accountable. Equally, the proposed Open Terms and Third Term

[115] Nandini Patel and others, 'Consolidating Democratic Governance in Southern Africa: Malawi' (*Academia*) https://www.academia.edu/1800003/Consolidating_Democratic_Governance_in_Southern_Africa_Malawi accessed 1 October 2023.

[116] See *Malawi Law Society and others v The State and Others*, Miscellaneous Civil Cause no 78 of 2002.

[117] Constitution (n 8) s 132.

[118] See 'Government Sits on Crucial Bills' *The Nation* (Nairobi, 16 October 2022) https://mwnation.com/govt-sits-on-crucial-bills/ accessed 20 October 2022.

[119] Venice Commission (n 10).

[120] Ibid.

[121] Rasch and Congleton (n 9).

Bills, though abortive in the end, signalled an intention to weaken accountability in the presidency. The attempt to remove term limits revealed a propensity by politicians to discard portions of the Constitution seen as inconvenient, which again points to a lack of constitutionalism.[122] Overall, while the power to change the Constitution is uncontested, it is a power that can undermine democracy, constitutionalism, and the rule of law if it is used irresponsibly.

Constitutions are generally regarded as a higher law, and thus distinguishable from ordinary legislation, due to the functions they perform in society.[123] The importance of constitutions in the organization of political life requires that their provisions should have a measure of stability. This is not to suggest that they should not be open to change but to stress that all changes to them should be approached with deliberation and circumspection. A high frequency of changes to a constitution may make it seem like an ordinary law, thereby diluting its special status[124] and consequently impairing constitutional and political stability.[125] This is so because a constitution represents a compact between the governors and the governed: for purposes of better governance, the terms of this compact should be changed only through a careful process of renegotiation. The rather large number of provisions affected by amendments to the 1994 Constitution suggests that the compact has not been stable, especially insofar as some of the amendments have dealt with substantive issues. Nevertheless, the fact that the Constitution, even with the changes, is routinely invoked as a central pillar of governance suggests that it is, generally, still accepted as a viable blueprint for governance and constitutionalism.[126]

Malawi's experience confirms that, in relation to constitutional change, political parties always play a critical role. This is because the primary site for controlling constitutional change is Parliament, and Parliament is where parties tend to exercise the most influence. Whether this influence can be harnessed to support constitutionalism or not depends on the prevailing political exigencies; at a bare minimum, however, in order to have parties that contribute ably to constitutionalism, it is important to enhance intra-party democracy. Political parties that adhere to democratic ideals in their internal arrangements are more likely to support democratic ideals at the national level than those that do not. For example, the proposed Open Terms and Third Term Bills were promoted by the UDF, but this led to a split in the party, as not all its members, especially at senior level, supported extending Bakili Muluzi's tenure.[127] In the main, the attempt to change term limits was able to emerge from the UDF and become a national issue only due to the suppression of democratic processes within the UDF. Conversely, one may surmise that more robust intra-party democracy could have dealt internally with Bakili Muluzi's ambitions for the 'illicit' extension of his term.

The Malawian experience also demonstrates that, irrespective of factionalism in Parliament, it can happen that parties work together temporarily to support constitutional changes that advance their collective interests— whether or not this promotes

[122] Fidelis Kanyongolo, 'The Constitution' in Nandini Patel and Lars Svasand (eds.), *Government and Politics in Malawi* (Kachere Books 2007) 23, 26.

[123] Elliot Bulmer, *What is a Constitution: Principles and Concepts* (International IDEA 2017).

[124] Albert (n 36) 12.

[125] Venice Commission (n 10).

[126] Nkhata (n 27).

[127] See 'Third Term Divides Ruling Party' (*The New Humanitarian*, 24 October 2002) https://www.thenewhumanitarian.org/news/2002/10/24/third-term-divides-ruling-party accessed 20 October 2022.

constitutionalism (as the abolition of the Senate and repeal of section 64 demonstrate). In addition, political parties, when in power, have also been known to solicit support from other parties in Parliament to back their legislative initiatives, including ones aimed at constitutional change.[128] The solicitation of support has included offering financial incentives to opposition politicians.[129] Given the influence that political parties will continue to exercise over constitutional change, it is important that the citizenry keep watch of transient parliamentary majorities lest these get carried away in supporting changes that undermine constitutionalism.

7. Conclusion

Constitutional change in Malawi has been a fact of life ever since the 1994 Constitution entered into force. The Constitution itself, in Chapter XXI, creates a scheme for facilitating change that attempts to balance rigidity against flexibility. While the practice of constitutional change in Malawi reveals several avenues that it could take, the bulk of the changes have followed the route of formal (legislative) amendments. A precise count of the reasons corresponding to particular constitutional changes is difficult to achieve; nevertheless it can fairly be surmised that barring the changes necessary to correct ambiguities and other textual errors, a number of substantive constitutional changes have been motivated by opportunism.

As for the large number of constitutional provisions affected by amendments, perhaps not too much should be read into this given that the Constitution needed substantial editorial work to clean up the text after its adoption. Since the Constitution permits changes, it is likely that further changes will be undertaken in the future. The challenge for the citizenry remains guarding against changes that undermine constitutionalism, while acceding to necessary changes. The rather frequent resort to the constitutional change, however, risks diluting the fundamentals of the governance compact that the Constitution stands for. The only hope is that adequate reflection will accompany further changes to the Constitution.

Bibliography

Albert R., 'The Expressive Function of Constitutional Amendment Rules' (2015) 2(1) Revista de Investigacoes Constitucionais 7

Banda J., 'The Constitutional Change Debate of 1993–1995' in Phiri K. and Ross K. (eds.), *Democratisation in Malawi: A Stocktaking* (CLAIM 1998) 316

Böckenförde M., *Constitutional Amendment Procedures* (International IDEA 2017)

Bulmer E., *What is a Constitution: Principles and Concepts* (International IDEA 2017)

Cammack D., 'Democratic Transition in Malawi: From Single Party-rule to a Multi-party State' in Daniel J. and others (eds.), *Voting for Democracy: Watershed Elections in Contemporary Anglophone Africa* (Ashgate 1999) 183

[128] Wiseman Chirwa, Nandini Patel, and Fidelis Kanyongolo, *Democracy Report for Malawi* (International IDEA 2000).

[129] South African Institute of International Affairs, 'Strengthening Parliamentary Democracy in SADC Countries: Malawi Country Report' (*Academia*, 2004) https://www.academia.edu/79158841/Strengthening_parliamentary_democracy_in_SADC_countries_Malawi_country_report accessed 1 October 2023.

Chigawa M., 'The Fundamental Values of the Republic of Malawi Constitution of 1994' (Concept Paper One: The Law Commission Constitutional Review Conference, March 2006) https://acjr.org.za/resource-centre/fundamental_values_constitution_full.pdf/view accessed 30 May 2022

Chigawa M., 'The Concept of Crossing the Floor under Malawian Constitutional Law' (2008) 2(2) Malawi Law Journal 185–208

Chigawa M., 'The Senate as the Second Chamber of Parliament in Malawi: Its Relevance, Composition and Powers' (Malawi Law Journal Launch Conference, 16–17 July 2008, Blantyre, Malawi (copy on file with author))

Chimango L., 'Section 65 of the Malawian Constitution: The Role of the Speaker, 2005–2009' (2012) 6(2) Malawi Law Journal 212–42

Chirwa D., 'Democratisation in Malawi 1994–2002: Completing the Vicious Circle' (2003) 19(2) South African Journal on Human Rights 316–38

Chirwa D., 'A Full Loaf is Better than Half: The Constitutional Protection of Economic, Social and Cultural Rights in Malawi' (2005) 49(2) Journal of African Law 207–41

Chirwa W., Patel N., and Kanyongolo F., *Democracy Report for Malawi* (International IDEA 2000)

Dixon R., 'Constitutional Amendment Rules: A Comparative Perspective' (2011) University of Chicago: Public Law and Legal Theory Working Paper No. 347 https://chicagounbound.uchicago.edu/cgi/viewcontent.cgi?article=1070&context=public_law_and_legal_theory accessed 1 May 2022

Dzimbiri L., 'The Malawi Referendum of June 1993' (1994) 13(3) Electoral Studies 229–34

Ellett R., *Politics of Judicial Independence in Malawi* (Freedom House 2014) https://freedomhouse.org/sites/default/files/inline_images/Politics%20of%20Judicial%20Independence%20in%20Malawi_1.pdf accessed 31 May 2022

Englund H., *Prisoners of Freedom: Human Rights and the African Poor* (University of California Press 2006)

'Government Sits on Crucial Bills' *The Nation* (Nairobi, 16 October 2022) https://mwnation.com/govt-sits-on-crucial-bills/ accessed 20 October 2022

Government of Malawi, 'Report of the Constitution Committee to the National Assembly on the National Constitutional Conference on the Provisional Constitution' (1995)

Hatchard J., Ndulo M., and Slinn P., *Comparative Constitutionalism and Good Governance in the Commonwealth: An Eastern and Southern African Perspective* (CUP 2004)

Ihonvbere J., 'From Despotism to Democracy: The Rise of Multiparty Politics in Malawi' (1997) 18(2) Third World Quarterly 225–47

Kachale C., 'Judicial (In)activism in Malawi: A Critical Analysis of the Impact of Constitutional Jurisprudence on Constitutionalism and the Rule of Law' (PhD thesis, University of London 2012)

Kadima D. and Lembani S., 'Making, Unmaking and Remaking Political Party Coalitions in Malawi: Explaining the Prevalence of Office-Seeking Behaviour' (*Academia*, 2006) https://www.academia.edu/72578663/Making_Unmaking_and_Remaking_Political_Party_Coalitions_in_Malawi accessed 1 October 2023

Kamanga A., 'Amendments to the Constitution since 18 May 1994' (Paper presented at the Constitution Review Conference 28–31 March 2006, Capital Hotel, Lilongwe (copy on file with author))

Kanyongolo F., 'Constitutionalism and the Removal of Presidential Term Limits from the Constitution of Malawi' (2003) 7(1) UNIMA Students Law Journal 59–72

Kanyongolo F., *Malawi: Justice Sector and the Rule of Law* (OSISA 2006)

Kanyongolo F., 'The Constitution' in Patel N. and Svasand L. (eds.), *Government and Politics in Malawi* (Kachere Books 2007) 23

Kapindu R., 'Separation of Powers and the Accountability Role of NHRIs: The Malawi Human Rights Commission through the Courts' in Bilchitz D. and Landau D. (eds.), *The Evolution of the Separation of Powers: Between the Global North and the Global South* (Edward Elgar 2018) 206

Kita W. and Chiphwanya C., 'Constitutional Amendment or Constitutional Disbandment' (2003) 7(1) UNIMA Students Law Journal 19–33

'List of Amendments to the US Constitution' (*Britannica*) https://www.britannica.com/topic/list-of-amendments-to-the-U-S-Constitution-1787122 accessed 1 June 2022

'Living our Faith: Pastoral Letter of the Catholic Bishops of Malawi' (*Almendron*, 12 July 2017) https://www.almendron.com/tribuna/wp-content/uploads/2017/12/1992-Malawi-Pastoral-Letter.pdf accessed 30 May 2022

Lutz D., 'Toward a Theory of Constitutional Amendment' (1994) 88(2) American Political Science Review 353–70

Maganga A., 'An Investigation of the Political Factors Contributing to Floor Crossing in the Malawi National Assembly: 2003–2009' (MA thesis, University of South Africa 2011) https://uir.unisa.ac.za/bitstream/handle/10500/4833/thesis_maganga_a.pdf?sequence=1&isAllowed=y accessed 30 October 2023

Malawi Law Commission, *Law Commission Report on the Technical Review of the Constitution* (1998)
Malawi Law Commission, *Amendments to the Constitution and Preservation of its Sanctity* (2006) Constitution Review Programme, Discussion Paper No. 7 (copy on file with author)
Malawi Law Commission, *Report of the Law Commission on the Review of the Constitution* (2007)
Melbourne Forum on Constitution-Building, 'Constitutional Beginnings: Making and Amending Constitutions' (2018) 1 Constitutional Insights 2
Negretto G., 'Replacing and Amending Constitutions: The Logic of Constitutional Change in Latin America' (Paper prepared for delivery at the 2011 American Political Science Association Meeting, Seattle, Washington, 1–4 September 2011) https://biblioteca.cejamericas.org/bitstream/handle/2015/3313/Replacing-and-Amending-Constitutions-The-Logic-of-Constitutional-Change-in-Latin-America.pdf?sequence=1&isAllowed=y accessed 27 April 2022
Ng'ong'ola C., 'Managing the Transition to Political Pluralism in Malawi: Legal and Constitutional Arrangements' (1996) 34(2) Journal of Commonwealth and Comparative Politics 85–110
Nkhata M., 'Rethinking Governance and Constitutionalism in Africa: The Relevance and Viability of Social Trust-based Governance and Constitutionalism' (LLD thesis, University of Pretoria 2010)
Nkhata M., 'The High Court of Malawi as a Constitutional Court: Constitutional Adjudication the Malawian Way' (2020) 24 (1) Law, Democracy & Development 442–67
Nyirenda H., 'MP wants Senate Recall Provision' (*All Africa*, 28 October 2005) https://allafrica.com/stories/200510280042.html accessed 14 August 2023
Patel N., 'The Representational Challenge in Malawi' in *Towards the Consolidation of Malawi's Democracy* (Konrad Adenauer Foundation 2008) 21
Patel N. and others, 'Consolidating Democratic Governance in Southern Africa: Malawi' (*Academia*) https://www.academia.edu/1800003/Consolidating_Democratic_Governance_in_Southern_Africa_Malawi accessed 1 October 2023
Phiri J., 'Traditional Leader Dares Malawi Parliament to Re-introduce Recall Provision for MPs' (*All Africa*, 28 October 2020) https://allafrica.com/stories/202010280193.html accessed 1 June 2022
Rasch B. and Congleton R.D., 'Amendment Procedures and Constitutional Stability' in Congleton R.D. and Swedenborg B. (eds.), *Democratic Constitutional Design and Public Policy: Analysis and Evidence* (MIT Press 2006) 536–61 http://www.rdc1.org/forthcoming/DCD%20(Chap%2012,%20Amendment%20Procedures,%20Congleton%20and%20Rausch).pdf accessed 26 April 2022
Republic of Malawi, *Malawi's Unhealed Wounds: A Report on an Investigation into Allegations of Maladministration and Other Irregularities by Malawi Government over the Manner in Which the National Compensation Tribunal was Set Up, Operated and Wound Up* (Office of the Ombudsman 2017)
Roznai Y., 'Towards a Theory of Constitutional Unamendability: On the Nature and Scope of the Constitutional Amendment Powers' (*Jus Politicum*, 2015) http://juspoliticum.com/article/Towards-A-Theory-of-Constitutional-Unamendability-On-the-Nature-and-Scope-of-the-Constitutional-Amendment-Powers-1183.html accessed 1 May 2022
'Section 65 Issue Re-emerges' (*Economist Intelligence Unit*, 11 June 2012) http://country.eiu.com/article.aspx?articleid=989126883&Country=Malawi&topic=Politics&subtopic=Re_10 accessed 1 June 2022
South African Institute of International Affairs, 'Strengthening Parliamentary Democracy in SADC Countries: Malawi Country Report' (*Academia*, 2004) https://www.academia.edu/79158841/Strengthening_parliamentary_democracy_in_SADC_countries_Malawi_country_report accessed 1 October 2023
Suber P., 'Amendment' in Gray C.B. (ed.), *Philosophy of Law: An Encyclopedia* (Garland 1999)
'The Constitution of the United States: Fast Facts' (*National Constitution Centre*) https://constitutioncenter.org/education/classroom-resource-library/classroom/constitution-fast-facts accessed 1 October 2023
'The Fundamental Constitutions of Carolina, 1 March 1669' (*The Avalon Project*) https://avalon.law.yale.edu/17th_century/nc05.asp accessed 3 May 2022
'Third Term Divides Ruling Party' (*The New Humanitarian*, 24 October 2002) https://www.thenewhumanitarian.org/news/2002/10/24/third-term-divides-ruling-party accessed 20 October 2022
Venice Commission, 'Report on Constitutional Amendment' (19 January 2010) Council of Europe Study No 469/2008 https://www.venice.coe.int/webforms/documents/default.aspx?pdffile=CDL-AD(2010)001-e accessed 1 May 2022

14

The Complex Path of Constitution-Making in Conflict-Ridden States: A Case Study of Libya

Rania Hussein Khafaga

1. Introduction

Constitution-making processes have always been associated with moments of major political transformation. In the 1960s, new constitutional arrangements emerged in Africa, Asia, and Latin America to mark the birth of independent states in the aftermath of liberation struggles. In the 1990s, with the third wave of democratization came a second generation of constitutions that abandoned the one-party state and introduced multiparty systems. Many constitutional processes, however, took place in the aftermath of violent conflict. In countries such as Iraq, Afghanistan, Sudan, South Africa, Northern Ireland, Bosnia, and Somalia, constitutional processes were an integral part of political settlements aiming to end protracted conflicts.

Thus, a new concept of 'transitional constitutionalism' or 'neo-constitutionalism' emerged to differentiate between constitution-making in conflict contexts and traditional constitution-making in more politically stable environments. This reflects a recognition of the particularity of constitution-building as a vehicle for change in conflict-ridden or post-conflict states.[1] Constitution-building in conflict-ridden countries or countries emerging from conflict is particularly important given that the resultant constitutions are expected to address issues such as the form of the state, the system of government, the basic principles and values governing the new state, wealth and power-sharing, and other issues closely related to the conflict.

Nevertheless, constitution-making in conflict contexts is confronted with numerous challenges, such as societal divisions and differences between conflict parties that are sometimes too profound to be bridged in the process.[2] Additionally, insufficient local capacity to support the complex constitution-making process makes the involvement of external actors inevitable, thus jeopardizing national ownership of this process.[3] What has proven to

[1] Kirsti Samuels, 'Post-Conflict Peace-Building and Constitution-Making' (2006) 6(2) Chicago Journal of International Law 667. See also Adem Abebe and others, *Annual Review of Constitution-Building 2018* (International IDEA 2020); Winluck Wahiu, *A Practical Guide to Constitution-Building: An Introduction* (International IDEA 2011) 7.

[2] International IDEA, *Constitution-Building after Conflict: External Support to a Sovereign Process* (International IDEA 2011) 8.

[3] Wahiu (n. 1) 6.

Rania Hussein Khafaga, *The Complex Path of Constitution-Making in Conflict-Ridden States: A Case Study of Libya*
In: *Constitutional Change and Constitutionalism in Africa*. Edited by: Charles M. Fombad and Nico Steytler, Oxford University Press.
 DOI: 10.1093/9780198957034.003.0016

be even more problematic is the relationship between constitutional arrangements, on the one hand, and peace processes, on the other.[4]

The particularity of constitution-making in conflict contexts is perhaps most evident in Libya. Since the fall of the Qaddafi regime in 2011, the country has entered one of the longest and most complex political transition arrangements in the modern age. In the absence of a constitutional framework of any sort, conflict parties failed to agree on a settlement that could end the ongoing conflict and usher in a post-conflict political dispensation.

This chapter investigates the interplay between the constitution-making process and the broader political transition process in Libya since 2011. It argues that the volatile and ambiguous relationship between the two processes resulted in the current stalemate in which the draft constitution completed by the Constituent Assembly has not been put to a referendum and the legislative and presidential elections have not been held. In order to examine the complex constitution-making process and its interplay with the wider political process, the chapter proceeds, in section 2, to provide a brief account of the Libyan constitutional experience prior to 2011. Section 3 looks at the legal framework of constitution- making since 2011, as well as the process that produced the 2017 draft constitution, while section 4 undertakes a critical examination of the constitution-making and political settlement nexus. Finally, the conclusion draws lessons from the Libyan case and considers the prospects for its future.

2. Libyan constitutional history prior to 2011

Libya had fairly limited constitutional experience before 2011. Nevertheless, since the demise of Qaddafi regime, this limited experience has influenced the ongoing constitutional processes. Prior to the military coup orchestrated by Muammar Qaddafi in 1969, Libya had known several constitutional regimes developed by the Italian-occupied Libyan territories, the oldest of which was the Constitution of May 1919 of the Tripoli Republic, followed in October 1919 by Constitution of Cyrenaica.

Although these constitutional regimes were short-lived, they were significant developments in Libya's constitutional history. This constitutional tradition was an early expression of the historical divide between the and western regions of Libya, a factor that has remained pertinent in constitutional debates to this day. The divide between Libya's regions continued under British guardianship after Italy's defeat in the Second World War. In October 1949, a constitutional commission, assisted by British advisers, drafted the Cyrenaica Constitution, which consisted of ten chapters and 70 articles and adopted constitutional monarchy as the form of government.

International dynamics have also played a role in Libya's constitutional experience. Three Libyan delegations, representing Cyrenaica, Tripoli, and Fezzan, attended the

[4] Yash Ghai and Guido Galli, *Constitution Building Processes and Democratization* (International IDEA 2006) 7. See also Vivian Hart, 'Constitution-Making and the Transformation of Conflict' (2001) 26 (2)Peace and Change 153–76; Reconstituted Joint Monitoring and Evaluation Commission (RJMEC), 'Post-Conflict Constitution-Making Processes: Lessons and Best Practices for South Sudan, Final Report 2020' https://jmecsouthsudan.org/index.php/reports/rjmec-quarterly-reports/169-post-conflict-constitution-making-processes-lessons-and-best-practices-for-south-sudan-final-report-2020/file accessed 10 May 2021; Michele Brandt and others, *Constitution-making and Reform Options for the Process* (Interpeace 2011).

United Nations (UN) General Assembly session in 1951 at which UN Resolution 289 was adopted. The resolution provided for Libyan independence by no later than January 1952. It stipulated, too, that the delegates from the three regions would meet in a national assembly to decide on Libya's constitution and form of government, with the writing of the constitution to be entrusted to a national constituent assembly.

This assembly was made up of 60 members representing the three historical regions of Cyrenaica, Tripoli, and Fezzan. After deliberations between 1950 and 1951 in Tripoli and Benghazi, the Constituent Assembly adopted the 213-article constitution, which, unlike previous regional constitutional regimes, was the first constitutional document to cherish and strengthen Libyan unity.

The most prominent provision of this 1951 Constitution was its adoption of constitutional monarchy as a system of government. As a means to prevent the division of the state, the Constitution adopted federalism despite the objections of political elites. In 1963, however, federalism was abandoned by constitutional amendment due to the state's limited resources and inability to sustain the high cost of a federal system. This short-lived constitutional experiment ended in 1969 when the monarchy was overthrown in a military coup led by Muammar Qaddafi, who issued a declaration abolishing the constitutional monarchy and instating a democratic republican system.

Under Qaddafi's rule, the central government was increasingly empowered and strengthened. Many essential public institutions, such as the Oil Authority, Libyan Airlines, and the National Insurance Company, were relocated from Benghazi to Tripoli, which led to a sense of marginalization among the two regions of Cyrenaica and Fezzan. It is against this backdrop that one may better understand these regions' efforts to restore federalism, or at least some form of expanded decentralization, in the wake of the uprising that toppled Qaddafi in 2011.

3. The post-2011 constitution-making process

In the wake of the 2011 uprising in Libya, controversy surrounded the constitutional framework that would usher in the new Libyan state. Two camps emerged: the first emphasized the importance of initiating a new constitution-making process; the second, however, argued strongly for taking the 1951 Constitution as the primary point of constitutional reference. Proponents of the latter cited three justifications for their views.

First, they argued that taking the 1951 Constitution as a point of departure would acknowledge the fact that Libya is a nation with 'constitutional roots'. Second, the process in which this Constitution was drafted enjoyed uncontested legitimacy. Finally, it was held that federalism is the most suitable form of government, given Tripoli's perceived hegemony over the other two regions. The adherents of this school of thought called for the adoption of the 1951 text except for articles on the constitutional monarchy.[5]

[5] الإتحاد الدستوري الليبي، إجابات الإتحاد الدستوري الليبي على استبيان لمقترح مبادئ ثورة 17 فبراير (Libyan Constitutional Union, 'Libyan Constitutional Union's answers to a questionnaire proposing the principles of the February 17 Revolution' (28 July 2011) https:// www.libyan cons titu tion alun ion.org/ mixed arb.htm#17feb) accessed 1 October 2023

Be that as it may, it was the first school of thought that garnered both internal and international support. The prevailing belief was that only a brand-new constitutional regime could lay down the rules of the political game and establish a socio-economic and legal system capable of meeting the demands of the masses that rose up against the Qaddafi regime.[6]

3.1 Legal framework for constitution-making

The road map for the constitutional process was outlined in the Interim Constitutional Declaration (ICD) issued by the self-proclaimed National Transitional Council (NTC) in August 2011. According to the ICD provisions, the constitutional process was to follow a precise sequence.

First, an elected interim transitional legislature, the General National Congress (GNC), would choose the constituent body. Second, in terms of article 30 of the ICD, this constituent body, no later than 60 days after its first meeting, would draft the constitution and present it before the GNC for approval. Third, the draft constitution would be put to a referendum within 30 days of GNC approval. To be enacted, the draft constitution, in terms of the ICD, needed the support of two-thirds of the voters, in which case the GNC would adopt it. If the draft constitution failed to garner the required majority, it would be returned to the constituent body for revision and put to a second referendum within no more than 30 days.[7]

However, this road map underwent a series of amendments as result of pressure by various stakeholders: amendments which eventually jeopardized the legitimacy of the constitution-making process.[8] The most important constitutional amendment concerned the way in which the constituent body was selected. Instead of this body's being appointed by the GNC, as initially stipulated by the ICD, the constitutional amendment of March 2013 provided for the election of the constituent body by direct popular vote. As a result, the constituent body would consist of 60 members divided equally between Cyrenaica (east), Tripoli (north-west) and Fezzan (south-west).

Equal representation would allow representatives from Cyrenaica and Fezzan, in particular, to negotiate issues such as federalism and minority rights. In this regard, it is worth noting that giving the three regions equal weighting favours less populous regions, namely Cyrenaica and Fezzan, compared with the populous Tripoli, which is home to some 60 per cent of the Libyan population.[9] Direct election, however, risks politicizing the whole process, as it undermines the possibility of selecting competent experts in the drafting of the

[6] عبد المجيد الجمل،"تاريخية المسألة الدستورية في ليبيا"، شئون ليبية (2016) العدد(2) (Abdel Majeed Al-Jamal, 'The History of The Constitutional Question in Libya' (*Libyan Affairs*, 2016) 2).

[7] National Transitional Council Libya, 'Text of the Constitutional Declaration issued on 3rd August 2011' https://constitutionnet.org/sites/default/files/interim_constitution-3_aug_2011_arabic_signed.pdf accessed 1 October 2023.

[8] Many parties challenged the legitimacy of the National Transitional Council and the interim constitutional declaration. The constitution-building process became an arena for competition between forces including Islamists, supporters of federalism, supporters of decentralization, minorities, and rival militias. See Youssef Sawani and Jason Pack, 'Libyan Constitutionality and Sovereignty Post-Qadafi: The Islamist, Regionalist, and Amazigh Challenges' (2013) 18 (4) Journal of North African Studies 523–25.

[9] Christine Bell and Kimana Zulueta-Fülscher, 'Sequencing Peace Agreements and Constitutions in the Political Settlement Process' (2016) IDEA Policy Paper No 13, 32.

constitution, such as experts on constitutional law, human rights, and electoral systems.[10] As far as the representation of women and ethnic minorities is concerned, six seats were reserved for women and two for each minority, namely the Tubu, Tuareg, and Amazigh.[11]

In November 2018, another constitutional amendment included two substantial changes to the constitution-making process. The first adopted a three-district voting system for the referendum, reflecting Libya's three historical regions—Tripoli, Cyrenaica, and Fezzan. The second entailed a significant change to the majority needed for approving the constitution: the amendment stipulated that, for the draft constitution to be approved, it required not only two-thirds of the total valid votes cast in the referendum but the approval of 50 per cent plus one of voters in each of the three regions.

As per the road map stipulated in the ICD and its subsequent amendments, the Constituent Assembly elections took place in February 2014. They saw low levels of popular participation (by 45 per cent of those eligible for participation) compared with the GNC elections in 2012.[12] Furthermore, ethnic minorities decided to boycott the election, as representatives of these ethnic minorities in the GNC believed that the six seats reserved for them in the constituent body were insufficient. They also objected to the two-thirds majority required to pass decisions in the Constituent Assembly, maintaining that this would hinder their demands and insisting instead that consensus would be a better decision-making mechanism. Instability and a deteriorating security situation further jeopardized the electoral process in some provinces and, in certain constituencies, prevented elections from being held.[13] As a result, thirteen seats remained vacant and supplementary rounds of elections had to be held at a later date.

Since its inception, the Constituent Assembly has issued three drafts of the Constitution: in October 2015, February 2016, and April 2016. On 29 July 2017, it formally adopted the draft constitution after securing more than the required two-thirds majority. The draft constitution was then referred to the House of Representatives to be put to a referendum. Although many had high hopes that this would be a prelude to resolving the Libyan crisis through the adoption of a new constitutional regime, the referendum, at the time of writing, has not yet taken place in the more than five years that have passed since the draft constitution's adoption by the House of Representatives.

3.2 Public participation and international involvement in constitution-making

The literature on constitution-making emphasizes the importance of broad public participation as a requirement for any successful constitutional process; public participation helps

[10] Democracy Reporting International, 'Civil Society's Sober Assessment of the Libyan Constitution-Making Process' (2016) Briefing Paper 71, 4.

[11] International IDEA, *Constitution Building: A Global Review (2013)* (International IDEA 2013) 7–8. See also Amnesty International, 'Libya: Historic Discrimination Threatens Right to Health of Minorities in the South amid COVID-19' (April 2020) https://www.amnesty.org/en/latest/news/2020/04/libya-historic-discrimination-threatens-right-to-health-of-minorities-in-the-south-amid-covid19/ accessed 1 October 2023.

[12] Africa Research Bulletin, 'Libya: Constitutional Panel' (1–28 February 2014) 20023. For comprehensive coverage of the Constituent Assembly elections for the drafting of the Constitution, see the Carter Center, 'The 2014 Constitutional Drafting Assembly Elections in Libya' https://www.cartercenter.org/ accessed 10 May 2021.

[13] Elections were not held in Derna, Sabha, Obari, Mrzik, or Kufra. See Africa Research Bulletin (n 12) 20023.

ensure its legitimacy and secure sustainable peace. To guarantee national ownership of the constitution-making process, all parties should be involved, with their priorities reflected in constitutional negotiations. By contrast, the exclusion or marginalization of certain actors tends to generate resentment and result in conflict. Public participation, which takes many forms, is thus linked to a variety of principles, such as inclusiveness, representation, transparency, and national ownership.

A survey by the International Institute for Democracy and Electoral Assistance (International IDEA) found that participatory, representative, and inclusive constitutional processes produce constitutions that reflect the values of democracy, freedom, equality, community justice, and human rights. Moreover, public participation serves to protect constitutions from being tampered with. Conversely, lack of participation in the constitution-building process produces biased constitutions that cater only to limited interests.[14]

In Libya, citizens' participation was limited despite the Constituent Assembly's attempts to promote public engagement. For instance, the Constituent Assembly set up a website, as well as social media pages, to provide information on the Constitution and its fundamental issues;[15] however, the website was not accessible most of the time, and public interaction with it was limited. Limited public participation could be attributed in part to ambiguity about the responsibility for public outreach—the constitutional declaration did not clarify whether this authority would lie in the hands of the GNC or the Constituent Assembly. Furthermore, there were no clear mechanisms to ensure the public's participation in the development of the Constitution, or mechanisms to receive its feedback on the draft text.

Such limited engagement with the public affected citizens' awareness of the draft constitution. A poll by the International Foundation for Electoral Systems (IFES) in 2018 revealed that more than a quarter of Libyans had not heard anything about the draft proposed by the Constituent Assembly; more than half (54 per cent) had heard only a little about it. Levels of awareness varied across regions: respondents from the southern region showed the most awareness (22 per cent of them), followed by the east (18 per cent), and the west (13 per cent).[16] Furthermore, when asked if they would participate in the constitutional referendum, only one-third of respondents answered in the affirmative.[17]

Libyan civil society organizations have tried to raise awareness to fill this knowledge gap and promote national ownership. One such organization is Lawyers for Justice in Libya, which carried out several activities to disseminate information. These included touring the country's three regions to provide forums for dialogue in which citizens could express their views on critical constitutional issues.[18]

As far as time frames are concerned, the Constituent Assembly exceeded those set by the ICD. Initially, it was supposed to complete the draft constitution within 120 days of

[14] Samuels (n 1) 668–69.
[15] ليبيا : انطلاق الموقع الإلكتروني لهيئة صياغة الدستور (ConstitutionNet, 'Libya: Launch of the website of the Constituent Assembly (September 2014)') https://tinyurl.com/3s6m7sx6 accessed 5 June 2023.
[16] International Foundations for Electoral Systems, 'IFES Survey on Voters' Intent: Libya' (August 2018) 19–20 https://www.ifes.org/publications/new-survey-libyan-voters-attitudes-toward-political-situation-and-future-elections accessed 10 May 2022.
[17] Ibid. 21.
[18] Lawyers for Justice in Libya, 'Constitution Guarantees My Right: Report and Recommendations' (2014) https://constitutionnet.org/sites/default/files/destoori_project_report-new_margins_low_res.pdf accessed 1 October 2023.

its first meeting in April 2014. However, in view of subsequent amendments to the ICD (as noted above), the Assembly's work was extended for fourteen months; a third extension was granted till March 2016, this against the backdrop of the signing of the Libyan Political Agreement. The failure to meet deadlines has raised concerns. While it is essential to establish specific time frames, unrealistic deadlines have undermined the Assembly's legitimacy.[19] Furthermore, tight time frames have denied actors in the process much-needed time in which to build trust, which is a crucial requirement for the success of constitution-making.[20]

In contrast to the limited local participation, international actors became involved in the process. Recent empirical evidence points to the increasing involvement of international actors in constitution-building worldwide. Constitution-building is at the heart of the sovereign jurisdiction of states but has become a process in which international actors now participate to an unprecedented extent, particularly in the case of states emerging from conflict.[21] International actors could be individual states, groups of states, regional organizations, international agencies, or even non-governmental organizations. These actors' success depends on factors such as their ability to enter the process, the acceptance of their role by local stakeholders, and their ability to exert influence.

The role of such external parties in constitutional processes can be classified according to the influence they exert. Three levels of influence can be distinguished. The first is where external actors have complete control of the constitutional process, with local stakeholders thus playing almost no role. On the other side of the continuum, external actors could play a marginal role in the process; in this case, their involvement is limited to providing advice to local stakeholders, who play the leading role. Apart from these two extreme cases, there is a middle-ground situation where external actors exert partial influence, yet without leaving the constitutional processes entirely to local parties. In this scenario, they remain influential in the process, and impact both on it and its outcomes while leaving drafting power in the hands of local parties.[22]

Regardless of the level of involvement, however, certain issues are worth discussing when it comes to the role of external actors.[23] The first is how this involvement might negatively affect national ownership of the constitution, and how international actors maintain a balance between adequately assisting national stakeholders and allowing them to make their own decisions.

Secondly, external involvement could influence both constitutional processes and constitutional content. As such, it is important for external actors to focus their interventions on technical support such as facilitating negotiation between national actors, building the

[19] The Constituent Assembly meetings were held in Cyrenaica province's Al-Bayda city, where reports indicate that the security environment has been unstable due to the deployment of militias. The Armed Conflict Location and Event Data Project (ACLED) has recorded incidents targeting the meetings' headquarters as well as Commission members, to exert pressure on them. These incidents raise concern about the impact of militias and other parties on the constitutional process, and consequently about the independence of this process. See https://acleddata.com. accessed 1 October 2023

[20] Democracy Reporting International (n 10).

[21] Philip Dann and Zaid Al-Ali, 'The Internationalized Pouvoir Constituent – Constitution-making under External Influence in Iraq, Sudan and East Timor' (2006) 10 Max Planck Yearbook of United Nations Law 423–63.

[22] Ibid. 429.

[23] International IDEA (n 2).

capacity of individuals and institutions related to the process, and supporting training, education, electoral processes, and the like. Such actors should avoid influencing the content, so that it reflects national needs.

Thirdly, international actors' support and assistance should be consistent with local parties' needs and preferences; moreover, support should be rendered to all parties without exception. It should be noted, too, that while external actors can play an essential role in advancing the constitutional process through various forms of support, they could also undermine the political settlement and its accompanying constitutional processes. Countries such as Libya, South Sudan, and Yemen have faced successive failures in reaching settlement of their conflicts due to international interventions and their impact on settlement and constitution-building processes. This failure can be attributed to the strategic interests pursued by international actors. In their quest to achieve these interests, such actors influence the nature of the settlement negotiations and the extent to which the parties are committed to the settlements emerging from them. External actors also influence conflict dynamics, which in turn subsequently impacts on constitutional legitimacy.

As for the role of international actors in Libya's constitutional process, this involvement has taken two forms: a direct role through technical support rendered to the constitutional process, and an indirect role through intervention in the Libyan conflict in a broader sense—one which, arguably, has influenced the process negatively.

In regard to technical support, most of the international support has come from the United Nations (UN) and its affiliated agencies as part of the UN Support Mission in Libya (UNSMIL). The head of the UNSMIL stressed that the Mission's support for the constitutional process was informed by the UN's respect for Libyan sovereignty, national ownership, and independence.

Thus, UN support was directed towards operations rather than the constitution's content. Remarks by different heads of the UNSMIL reiterated their appreciation of the role played by the Constituent Assembly despite the many political and security challenges. In the same vein, UNSMIL officials avoided commenting on the content of the draft constitution; they only emphasized the importance of the constitution's consistency with the principles of democracy, separation of powers, respect for human rights, equality before the law, and ensuring the rights of women and all components of Libyan society.[24] Given its focus on technical support, the UN gave priority to capacity-building. For example, before the 2014 elections, the United Nations Development Programme (UNDP) organized a series of workshops for candidates, aiming thereby to build their capacity in aspects of constitution-making.[25] Additionally, UNSMIL, in collaboration with the GNC, organized a forum on human rights in constitutions.[26]

[24] United Nations Support Mission in Libya, 'Kobler Welcomes Significant Progress Made in Latest Draft Constitution Agreed on by CDA Members' (22 April 2016) https://unsmil.unmissions.org/kobler-welcomes-significant-progress-made-latest-draft-constitution-agreed-cda-members accessed 2 May 2021.

[25] United Nations Support Mission in Libya, '"Inclusive Constitution" – Workshop for the Candidates of the Constitution Drafting Assembly' (3 February 2014) https://unsmil.unmissions.org/%E2%80%9Cinclusive-constitution%E2%80%9D-%E2%80%93-workshop-candidates-constitution-drafting-assembly accessed 2 May 2021.

[26] United Nations Support Mission in Libya, 'Libyans Have an Opportunity to Include Human Rights in Constitution' (19 December 2013) https://unsmil.unmissions.org/libyans-have-opportunity-include-human-rights-constitution accessed 2 May 2021.

In this vein, in November 2014, the UNSMIL, in collaboration with the UNDP and the UN Program on Gender Equality and Women's Empowerment, held a meeting in Cairo to discuss Libyan women's demands in regard to the Constitution. The meeting convened 60 women from different regions, comprising delegates from civil society and members of the House of Representatives and Constituent Assembly.[27] In August 2015, members of the Constituent Assembly met with experts from the UN Electoral Support Team to discuss election-related articles in the draft constitution.[28] Furthermore, UNSMIL's activities included raising awareness of electoral matters such as voter registration, media coverage of elections, and election-related security.[29]

Donors have also provided support to the constitutional process in Libya. A project co-funded by the governments of Britain and Switzerland aimed to support the Constituent Assembly through activities organized by Democracy Reporting International. Several countries offered to host the meetings away from the heated environment of Albida. In April 2016, the Sultanate of Oman, for example, hosted meetings that culminated in the adoption of the final draft constitution to be referred to the House of Representatives.[30] However, some members of the Constituent Assembly objected to holding meetings in foreign countries, duly boycotting the Assembly's work, including the session in which the Constitution's final draft was voted on.[31] As a result of the boycott, the draft's legality was challenged—unsuccessfully, as the Supreme Court upheld the validity of the Constituent Assembly's vote.[32]

However, recent years have witnessed a decline in UN support for the constitutional process, especially in the aftermath of the Libyan National Dialogue Forum. Statements from UN officials have reflected the attenuation of international support for the Constitution, as they began to speak instead about alternative constitutional frameworks.

UNSC Resolution 2570 of 2021 was indicative in this regard. It welcomed the agreement between Libyan parties to hold national presidential and parliamentary elections on 24 December 2021, as outlined in the road map of the Libyan Political Dialogue Forum held in Tunis in November 2020. Instead of emphasizing the need to have a referendum on the draft constitution submitted by the Constituent Assembly, the resolution spoke of the need for finalizing what it called 'the constitutional basis for elections and the relevant electoral law'. These statements have infuriated the Constituent Assembly, which sees them as reflecting an abandonment of its achievements and an attempt to initiate new constitutional frameworks instead of the ones that led to the draft constitution.[33]

[27] United Nations Support Mission in Libya, 'Libyan Women Articulate Demands for the Constitution' (5 November 2014) https://unsmil.unmissions.org/libyan-women-articulate-demands-constitution accessed 2 May 2021.

[28] United Nations Support Mission in Libya, 'CDA Members Discuss Elections and Constitution with UN Election Experts' (27 August 2015) https://unsmil.unmissions.org/cda-members-discuss-elections-and-constitution-un-election-experts accessed 2 May 2022.

[29] United Nations Support Mission in Libya, 'UN Welcomes the Announcement of the Start of the Constituent Assembly's Electoral Process to Draft the Constitution' (25 September 2013) https://bit.ly/3S6YspM accessed 2 May 2021.

[30] United Nations Support Mission in Libya, 'Martin Kobler Congratulates CDA Members on Building Consensus on a Constitution Draft' (7 April 2016) https://unsmil.unmissions.org/martin-kobler-congratulates-cda-members-building-consensus-constitution-draft accessed 2 May 2021.

[31] United Nations Support Mission in Libya (n 24).

[32] Bell and Zulueta-Fülscher (n 9) 33.

[33] United Nations Security Council, S/RES/2570(2021) (16 April 2021).

4. The nexus of political settlement and constitution-making

Although peace negotiations and constitutional negotiations may occur in different and distinct forums, the literature suggests that the two processes are closely interrelated, since their shared goal is to bring an end to the conflict and achieve sustainable peace. In this regard, it is important to think of the constitution-building process as a sequence of events within the broader political settlement. Parties to the conflict have to decide on various issues, such as ceasefire arrangements, interim measures, the timing of elections, confidence-building measures, and reconciliation. Empirical evidence suggests that resolving such issues at the outset leads to a successful constitutional process, whereas ignoring them, or dealing with them insufficiently, hampers it. Furthermore, lack of elite buy-in to the political settlement also adversely affects the constitution-making process.

In theory, it is assumed that there is a specific sequence of political settlement processes in conflict situations. This sequence includes negotiations that lead to a ceasefire agreement or a peaceful settlement that leads to a final constitution. In other words, it begins with a negotiation leading to a ceasefire or a peace agreement, which in turn leads to temporary arrangements and ends in some form of constitutional arrangement.[34] While this sequence seems logical, empirical evidence reveals a more complex and non-linear order of processes. Sometimes peace agreements are merely temporary and partial, while it is constitution-building that is the crucial step leading to a political settlement; in other cases, the peace agreement sets out the terms of negotiation and thus becomes the general framework to which the constitutional process adheres. By implication, the different contexts in which the peace process interacts with constitutional arrangements and the political settlement may reveal different forms of overlap between all these processes.

The Libyan case reveals an indicative case of a complex non-linear relationship between the constitution-building process, on the one hand, and the broader political process, on the other. Two key issues emerge in this context: the multiple constitutional amendments that were introduced to the ICD, and the controversy related to the sequence of the constitution and elections.

4.1 Constitutional amendments and their impact on the political process

The ICD was supposed to be the foundation for both the constitutional process and the political settlement. However, between 2011 and 2023, the ICD underwent thirteen constitutional amendments that changed its core underpinnings. Throughout the extended transitional period, the NTC introduced three amendments, the GNC initiated five amendments, and the House of Representatives the remaining five. These constitutional amendments impacted on both the transitional political and the constitutional processes at their core.

First, they contributed to a shaky and inconsistent interim constitutional framework. Second, they caused confusion in the transitional arrangements. Third, they altered the power positions of different political institutions and thus contributed to deepening

[34] Bell and Zulueta-Fülscher (n 9).

divisions in an already fragmented political landscape.[35] For example, the first three constitutional amendments introduced by the NTC aimed to marginalize the role of the GNC in constitutional design. Instead of a constituent assembly chosen by the GNC, the first two amendments stipulated that it be chosen through direct public vote. The amendments also made changes relating to the assembly's formation and decision-making procedures.[36]

In the same vein, subsequent constitutional amendments prolonged the transitional period by repeatedly extending the required time frame in which to accomplish certain milestones. For example, the second constitutional amendment extended the time frame required for electing the GNC from 240 days, in the original ICD, to 270 days.[37] Furthermore, constitutional amendments introduced new structures that complicated the political scene. For example, Constitutional Amendment No 12, issued by the House of Representatives in March 2022, established a committee of 24 members, representing the three main regions and chosen by the House of Representatives and the High State Council, to review the contested articles in the draft constitution; the committee was required to refer the revised version to the High National Electoral Commission to put it to the public for referendum.

Finally, Constitutional Amendment No 13, issued in February 2023, introduced drastic changes to the original ICD. This final amendment consisted of 33 articles that cover the transitional governance institutions, namely the legislature and the presidency. It also stipulated that legislative and presidential elections had to be held within 240 days of the adoption of electoral laws.[38]

4.2 The sequence of elections and constitution

It was evident at the outset that there was a lack of consensus about the sequencing of the elections and the making of the Constitution. Ongoing conflict since 2014 compounded uncertainty about that sequence. However, the Libyan Political Dialogue of 2020 contributed to ending fighting between competing factions and brought the issue of elections back to the negotiating table. In March 2021, a Government of National Unity was tasked with unifying fragmented political institutions and preparing for legislative and presidential elections by December 2021. In the run-up to the elections, the House of Representatives issued presidential and electoral laws in September and October, respectively.

However, in November 2021, the long-anticipated elections were postponed for a variety of reasons, among them disagreement about the final list of presidential candidates. To

[35] See خيري عمر، 'الأزمة الدستورية في ليبيا: أبعاد الصراع بين المكونات السياسية'، سياسات عربية، العدد 13، مارس 2015، ص ص 23–38 (Khairy Omar, 'Constitutional Crisis in Libya: Dimensions of the Conflict Between the Political Components' (*Arab Policies*, 2015) 13, 23–38) .

[36] Ibid.

[37] See المجلس الوطني الانتقالي، التعديل الدستوري رقم (1)، لسنة 2012، 13 مارس 2012. (National Transitional Council, Constitutional Amendment No 1 (March 2012)); المجلس الوطني الانتقالي، التعديل الدستوري رقم (2)، لسنة 2012، 10 يونيو 2012 (National Transitional Council, Constitutional Amendment No 2 (June 2012)); المجلس الوطني الانتقالي، التعديل الدستوري رقم (3) لسنة 2013، 5 يوليو 2012 (National Transitional Council, Constitutional Amendment No 3 (July 2012)).

[38] See ديوان مجلس النواب، التعديل الدستوري رقم (12) الجريدة الرسمية. العدد الثاني، السنة الأولى، 23 يناير 2023. (The House of Representatives, Constitutional Amendment No 12, *Official Gazette* (2023) 2);
ديوان مجلس النواب، لتعديل الدستوري رقم (13)، الجريدة الرسمية. العدد الرابع، السنة الأولى، 23 فبراير 2023. (The House of Representatives, Constitutional Amendment No 13, *Official Gazette* (2023) 4).

worsen the situation, in February 2022 the House of Representatives withdrew confidence from the Government of National Unity led by Abdel Hamid Debeba, instead appointing Fathi Bashaga as a new prime minister tasked with forming a new government and leading the country towards elections. The stalemate (current at the time of this writing) deepened the division regarding the elections–constitution sequence. Here, two distinct positions could be distinguished.

The first of these is that the House of Representatives and its political allies favour completing a constitutional document before the elections. According to them, the draft constitution should be put to referendum as a prerequisite for elections. In contrast, and turning to the second position, political actors in Tripoli prefer to proceed with legislative elections that are followed by a constitution-writing process and, finally, presidential elections. This camp believes that the political impasse is being caused by the House of Representatives and that a newly elected Parliament and government would be capable of solving the constitutional dilemma and paving the way to a presidential election.[39]

4.3 The Constituent Assembly: A technical or political body?

Although the NTC enjoyed moral and legal legitimacy, it did not have the power to impose its vision on the transitional process, and consequently avoided taking firm, clear-cut decisions that would risk antagonizing other political actors.[40] This tendency jeopardized the ICD, which was supposed to set the scene for the entire transitional and constitutional process. For its part, instead of detailing the way forward, the ICD was couched in very general terms, leaving the details of controversial issues to be dealt with later. Moreover, the constitutional declaration was subject to several amendments, as explained above, to please those who disputed its legitimacy.

Indeed, the biggest dilemma the Libyan constitutional process faced was its complex relationship with the broader political settlement. In conflict-ridden states, building a constitution needs to be primarily a 'political' project rather than just a technical one, and thus requires the involvement of all political actors in negotiations, compromises, and bargaining activities.[41] However, the Libyan situation entailed a separation between the constitutional process, on the one hand, and the political settlement process, on the other. The constituent body responsible for drafting the Constitution was deliberately separated from the latter process. It was created, that is to say, according to a completely different logic, and had no formal links with the rest of the political settlement. As a result, the draft constitution lacked much-needed political support, which explains why the referendum has not been held even though a draft constitution has existed since 2017.

In view of how the Constituent Assembly was elected, it became a non-political institution with no role in political processes. The original proposal to select the Constituent Assembly from within the GNC was enough to ensure the link between the two processes

[39] مجموعة الأزمات الدولية، مساعدة ليبيا على تجاوز مفترق الطرق، 18 مارس 2022 (International Crisis Group, 'Steering Libya Past Another Perilous Crossroads', 18 March 2022).

[40] Sawani and Pack (n 8) 532–36.

[41] Jason Gluck, 'Constitution-building in a Vacuum: Libya and Yemen in 2014' (2015) Annual Review of Constitution-building Processes 43–44.

of constitution-building and peace settlement. Even after the constitutional amendment, political parties were excluded from elections. Although the elections law that regulated the Constituent Assembly elections did not ban individuals from running as party candidates, political parties and the public have different interpretations of the law. The inevitable result was that the Assembly's membership included academics and lawyers, while representatives of the conflicting political forces were absent.[42]

This separation between what is constitutional and what is political proved to be problematic in the Libyan context in that it denied political actors any ownership of the Constitution.[43] Another opportunity to link the two tracks was wasted after the signing of the Libyan Political Agreement in 2015. The Agreement authorized the constituent body to consult with the House of Representatives and the State Supreme Council, but to date, this consultation has never happened.[44]

Finally, the relationship between the Constituent Assembly and other political institutions is problematic; given the fact that the Assembly is directly elected by the people, it becomes difficult to subject it to other structures produced by political bargaining.[45]

5. Conclusion

This chapter examined constitution-making in Libya as an example of constitution-making in conflict-ridden contexts. The lengthy process began with the IDC, which set the scene for the constitution-making process. At the time of writing—nine years after the election of the Constituent Assembly in 2014, and six years after the submission of a draft constitution by the Assembly—the process remains unfinished, with contention between competing political actors likely to prolong the transitional arrangements even further. A few themes worth highlighting emerged from the analysis.

Libya has a very brief constitutional experience. The 1951 Constitution was short-lived, as Qaddafi replaced it with the *Green Book*.[46] However, the post-2011 constitution-making process was influenced by this brief experience, particularly in regard to the three historical regions. The latter traditional division was reflected in the fact that the Constituent Assembly was formed by direct election that gave equal weight to the three regions regardless of their population size; furthermore, the rules governing the future constitutional referendum accentuate that division. This insistence on the relevance of the three traditional regions was rarely contested, even though it masks other lines of division such as cleavages within these regions themselves.

The legal framework for the constitution-making process was especially problematic. Successful constitution-making processes require a clear, solid foundation—something

[42] Ibid. 46.

[43] Sumit Bisarya, 'Introduction and Overview' in Sumit Bisarya and others, *Annual Review of Constitution-building Processes: 2015* (International IDEA 2016) 11.

[44] Ibid. 10.

[45] Michael Meyer-Resende and Omar Ould Hammady, 'These 56 People Have a Chance to Save Libya' (*Foreign Policy*, 21 April 2015) https://foreignpolicy.com/2015/04/21/these-56-people-have-a-chance-to-save-libya/ accessed 1 May 2021.

[46] The *Green Book*, written by Muammar Qaddafi in 1975, outlines his critique of Western democracy and institutions, including constitutions. In this book, Qaddafi presents the solution to governance, economic, and social problems, which he labels the Third Universal Theory.

that was lacking in Libya. Up to thirteen constitutional amendments have taken place. These complicated both the political process and the constitution-making process, leaving the original ICD barely recognizable and rendering it irrelevant. As a result, it becomes hard indeed to see how it serves as a point of reference, given how far the current text, with its thirteen amendments, has evolved from the original place of departure.

To add to the complexity of the situation, the interplay between the constitution-making process and the broader political process has significant implications. During the early stages of the constitution-making, the dominant NTC was seemingly determined to separate constitution-making from the wider political settlement, as is evident in the way the Constituent Assembly was formed. However, the political impasse and the failure to accomplish the constitutional project reveal in hindsight that the separation between the two processes was unrealistic, given that the draft constitution did not enjoy the support of the main political actors in Libya. In an attempt to change the situation, subsequent political negotiations between Libyan factions led to substantial amendments to the ICD, resulting in a shaky and inconsistent constitutional framework. Furthermore, the lack of agreement on the nature of transitional arrangements resulted in a political stalemate that has prolonged the current state of conflict in the country, with the parties continuing to fail to agree on the priorities of the political transition.

At the heart of the nexus of political processes and constitution-making is the sequence of elections and constitution-making. The two main political factions, namely the High State Council and House of Representatives, are yet to agree on the sequence of elections and constitution-making. In August 2023, a new president of the High State Council, Mohammed Takala, was elected, and concerns were raised about his commitment to ongoing negotiations between the two factions over election rules. The current state of affairs in Libya underlines the dire need for political consensus on contested issues, especially the question of the sequence of the Constitution and elections, and the question of whether the constitution-making process should build on the current draft constitution.

Bibliography

English-language sources

Abebe A. and others, *Annual Review of Constitution-Building 2018* (International IDEA 2020)

Africa Research Bulletin, 'Libya: Constitutional Panel' (1–28 February 2014) 2023

Amnesty International, 'Libya: Historic Discrimination Threatens Right to Health of Minorities in the South Amid COVID-19' (April 2020) https://www.amnesty.org/en/latest/news/2020/04/libya-historic-discrimination-threatens-right-to-health-of-minorities-in-the-south-amid-covid19/ accessed 1 October 2023

Bell C. and Zulueta-Fülscher K., 'Sequencing Peace Agreements and Constitutions in the Political Settlement Process' (2016) IDEA Policy Paper No. 13

Bisarya S., 'Introduction and Overview' (2015) in Bisarya S. and others, *Annual Review of Constitution-building Processes: 2015* (International IDEA 2016)

Brandt M. and others, *Constitution-making and Reform Options for the Process* (Interpeace 2011)

Dann P. and Al-Ali Z., 'The Internationalized Pouvoir Constituent – Constitution-making under External Influence in Iraq, Sudan and East Timor' (2006) 10 Max Planck Yearbook of United Nations Law 423–63

Democracy Reporting International, 'Civil Society's Sober Assessment of the Libyan Constitution-Making Process' (2016) Briefing Paper 71

Ghai Y. and Gall G., *Constitution Building Processes and Democratization* (International IDEA 2006)

Gluck J., 'Constitution-building in a Vacuum: Libya and Yemen in 2014' (2015) Annual Review of Constitution-building Process

Hart V., 'Constitution-making and the Transformation of Conflict' (2001) 26 issue 2 Peace and Change 153–76

International Foundations for Electoral Systems, 'IFES Survey on Voters' Intent: Libya' (August 2018) https://www.ifes.org/publications/new-survey-libyan-voters-attitudes-toward-political-situation-and-future-elections accessed 10 May 2022

International Institute for Democracy and Electoral Assistance (IDEA), *Constitution Building: A Global Review: 2013* (International IDEA 2013)

International Institute for Democracy and Electoral Assistance (IDEA), *Constitution-Building after Conflict: External Support to a Sovereign Process* (International IDEA 2011)

Lawyers for Justice in Libya, 'Constitution Guarantees My Right: Report and Recommendations' (2014) https://constitutionnet.org/sites/default/files/destoori_project_report-new_margins_low_res.pdf accessed 1 October 2023

Meyer-Resende M. and Hammady O.O., 'These 56 People Have a chance to Save Libya' (*Foreign Policy*, 21 April 2015) https://foreignpolicy.com/2015/04/21/these-56-people-have-a-chance-to-save-libya/ accessed May 2021

National Transitional Council Libya, 'Text of the Constitutional Declaration issued on 3 August 2011' https://constitutionnet.org/sites/default/files/interim_constitution-3_aug_2011_arabic_signed.pdf accessed 1 October 2023

Reconstituted Joint Monitoring and Evaluation Commission (RJMEC), 'Post-Conflict Constitution-Making Processes: Lessons and Best Practices for South Sudan, Final Report 2020' https://jmecsouthsudan.org/index.php/reports/rjmec-quarterly-reports/169-post-conflict-constitution-making-processes-lessons-and-best-practices-for-south-sudan-final-report-2020/file accessed 10 May 2021

Samuels K., 'Post-Conflict Peace-Building and Constitution-Making' (2006) 6 issue 2 Chicago Journal of International Law 667

Sawani Y. and Pack J., 'Libyan Constitutionality and Sovereignty Post-Qadafi: The Islamist, Regionalist, and Amazigh Challenges' (2013) 18 issue 4 Journal of North African Studies 523

The Carter Center, 'The 2014 Constitutional Drafting Assembly Elections in Libya' https://www.cartercenter.org/ accessed 10 May 2021

United Nations Security Council, Resolution 2570, S/RES/2570(2021) (16 April 2021)

United Nations Support Mission in Libya, '"Inclusive Constitution" – Workshop for the Candidates of the Constitution Drafting Assembly' (3 February 2014) https://unsmil.unmissions.org/%E2%80%9Cinclusive-constitution%E2%80%9D-%E2%80%93-workshop-candidates-constitution-drafting-assembly accessed 2 May 2021

United Nations Support Mission in Libya, 'CDA Members Discuss Elections and Constitution with UN Election Experts' (27 August 2015) https://unsmil.unmissions.org/cda-members-discuss-elections-and-constitution-un-election-experts accessed 2 May 2022

United Nations Support Mission in Libya, 'Kobler Welcomes Significant Progress Made in Latest Draft Constitution Agreed on by CDA Members' (22 April 2016) https://unsmil.unmissions.org/kobler-welcomes-significant-progress-made-latest-draft-constitution-agreed-cda-members accessed 2 May 2021

United Nations Support Mission in Libya, 'Libyan Women Articulate Demands for the Constitution' (5 November 2014) https://unsmil.unmissions.org/libyan-women-articulate-demands-constitution accessed 2 May 2021

United Nations Support Mission in Libya, 'Libyans Have an Opportunity to Include Human Rights in Constitution' (19 December 2013) https://unsmil.unmissions.org/libyans-have-opportunity-include-human-rights-constitution accessed 2 May 2021

United Nations Support Mission in Libya, 'Martin Kobler Congratulates CDA Members on Building Consensus on a Constitution Draft' (7 April 2016) https://unsmil.unmissions.org/martin-kobler-congratulates-cda-members-building-consensus-constitution-draft accessed 2 May 2021

United Nations Support Mission in Libya, 'UN Welcomes the Announcement of the Start of the Constituent Assembly's Electoral Process to Draft the Constitution' (25 September 2013) https://bit.ly/3S6YspM accessed 2 May 2021

Wahiu W., *A Practical Guide to Constitution-Building: An Introduction* (International IDEA 2011)

Arabic sources

الاتحاد الدستوري الليبي، إجابات الاتحاد الدستوري الليبي على استبيان لمقترح مباديء ثورة 17 فبراير.
(Libyan Constitutional Union's answers to a questionnaire proposing the principles of the February 17 Revolution (28 July 2011) https://www.libyanconstitutionalunion.org/mixedarb.htm#17feb) accessed 1 October 2023

ص ،خيري عمر، 'الأزمة الدستورية في ليبيا: أبعاد الصراع بين المكونات السياسية'، سياسات عربية، العدد 13. مارس 2015
ص 23-38

(Omar K., 'Constitutional Crisis in Libya: Dimensions of the Conflict Between the Political Components' (*Arab Policies*, 2015) 13).

عبد المجيد الجمل، 'تاريخية المسألة الدستوردية في ليبيا'، شئون ليبية (الرباط: المركز المغربي للأبحاث حول ليبيا) العدد
الثاني، اكتوبر 2016

(Al-Jamal, A.M., 'The History of The Constitutional Question in Libya' (*Libyan Affairs*, 2016) 2).

ليبيا: انطلاق الموقع الإلكتروني لهيئة صياغة الدستور. < ليبـيا: انطلاق الموقع الإلكتروني لهيئة صياغة الدستور
Libya: Launch of the website of the Constituent Assembly (September' ,2014 سبتمبر ConstitutionNet)
.(2014)' https://tinyurl.com/3s6m7sx6, accessed 5 June 2023

مجموعة الأزمات الدولية، مساعدة ليبيا على تجاوز مفترق الطرق، 18 مارس 2022

(International Crisis Group, 'Steering Libya Past Another Perilous Crossroads', 18 March 2022).

المجلس الوطني الانتقالي، التعديل الدستوري رقم (1)، لسنة 2012، 13 مارس 2012.

(National Transitional Council, Constitutional Amendment No. 1 (March 2012))

المجلس الوطني الانتقالي، التعديل الدستوري رقم (2)، لسنة 2012، 10 يونيو 2012

(National Transitional Council, Constitutional Amendment No. 2 (June 2012))

المجلس الوطني الانتقالي، التعديل الدستوري رقم (3) لسنة 2013، 5 يوليو 2012

(National Transitional Council, Constitutional Amendment No. 3 (July 2012))

ديوان مجلس النواب، التعديل الدستوري رقم (12) الجريدة الرسمية. العدد الثاني، السنة الأولى، 23 يناير 2023.

(The House of Representatives, Constitutional Amendment No. 12. *Official Gazette* (2023) 2)

ديوان مجلس النواب، التعديل الدستوري رقم (13)، الجريدة الرسمية. العدد الرابع، السنة الأولى، 23 فبراير 2023.

The House of Representatives, Constitutional Amendment No. 13. *Official Gazette* (2023) 4)

PART 6
GENERAL CONCLUSION

15

Three Decades of Trying to Avert Frequent and Abusive Changes to African Constitutions: Lessons for the Future

Charles M. Fombad

1. Introduction

Africa is again experiencing a wave of frequent and capricious tampering with constitutions. This phenomenon was a bane of post-independence African constitutionalism and paved the way for the repressive, autocratic regimes that emerged throughout the continent in the 1960s. As such, a crucial aspect of the new or revised constitutions of the post-1990s era was that their designers took steps to forestall this danger and ensure that they would not be vulnerable to easy, frequent, and arbitrary change by opportunistic politicians. The aim was not to block necessary and inevitable changes but to avert the twin dangers of, on the one hand, extra-legal or revolutionary methods of change, and, on the other, hasty and whimsical changes. Most importantly, the objective was to guard against abusive constitutional changes that subvert the sovereign will of the people. Consequently, entrenching provisions to prevent arbitrary change to constitutions is now regarded as one of the core elements of modern constitutionalism.[1]

After some respite in the 1990s, however, Africa has been witnessing a backlash in this regard since the 2000s, with an alarming spike in the number and regularity of constitutional changes having become evident. Most of these changes take place before elections, and they usually seek to weaken democratic principles, stifle political participation, undermine the separation of powers, and, more fundamentally, eliminate the possibility of an alternation of power. This raises doubts as to whether the measures in these constitutions were robust enough to deal with the problem of frequent constitutional changes. Addressing the threat posed by frequent tampering with constitutions is now of the utmost importance because it is one of the main causes of the decline in efforts to entrench an ethos of constitutionalism, democracy, good governance, and respect for the rule of law in the continent.

The chapters in this volume seek to provide insight, from the perspective of comparative constitutional change, into what has been happening in Africa since the introduction of provisions to regulate and prevent arbitrary constitutional changes. The chapters deal with

[1] For a discussion of the core elements of modern constitutionalism, see Charles M Fombad, 'Post-1990 Constitutional Reforms in Africa: A Preliminary Assessment of the Prospects for Constitutional Governance and Constitutionalism' in Alfred G Nhema and Paul Tiyambe Zeleza (eds.), *The Resolution of African Conflicts* (OSSREA & James Currey 2008) 179–99.

Charles M. Fombad, *Three Decades of Trying to Avert Frequent and Abusive Changes to African Constitutions: Lessons for the Future*
In: *Constitutional Change and Constitutionalism in Africa*. Edited by: Charles M. Fombad and Nico Steytler, Oxford University Press.
 DOI: 10.1093/9780198957034.003.0017

the theoretical and practical aspects of constitutional change, beginning with a broad overview of the constitutional framework for changing modern African constitutions.[2] This is followed by other chapters that examine aspects of constitution-making,[3] the significance of eternity clauses in preventing arbitrary constitutional changes,[4] and the role of the judiciary in ensuring that the provisions regulating the process of changing constitutions are respected;[5] thereafter, a number of case studies are presented.[6] Taken as a whole, the chapters provide a basis for serious reflection on the impacts that frequent and abusive changes to constitutions are having on constitutionalism, democracy, and respect for the rule of law in Africa. In considering whether the measures in these constitutions to guard against abusive constitutional amendments are weak and inadequate (and, if so, what needs to be done), a number of issues are highlighted.

The discussion continues in section 2 with an overview of mechanisms that have been put in place to check against abusive constitutional changes. Section 3 examines the practical impact of the implementation of these mechanisms, while section 4 considers what could serve to arrest the increasing trend towards tampering with constitutions. In conclusion, it is contended in section 5 that more needs to be done, both by ordinary citizens and by stakeholders such as the African Union (AU) and its regional economic communities (RECs).

2. An overview of measures to check frequent and abusive constitutional changes

It is necessary to preface this brief review with two preliminary issues highlighted by Charles Fombad in his chapter.[7] The first is that a variety of terms—such as 'amendment', 'alteration', 'change', 'revision', 'modification, 'repeal', and 'review and reform'—are used in the literature on constitutional change. Most scholars use these terms interchangeably, and even where they are used singly or in combination, this does not necessarily indicate the nature, extent, or scope of the constitutional change in question. Secondly, since very few constitutions implicitly or explicitly suggest the possibility of their wholesale revision, the validity of any constitutional change, regardless of its extent, will depend solely on formal and substantive compliance with the constitutional provisions regulating such change. It is such compliance that determines the legitimacy, in a legal, political, and moral sense, of the changes.[8]

Efforts to limit the scope for abusive constitutional changes were made slightly easier by the fact that the making of the post-1990 constitutions was entirely in the hands of Africans. As Heinz Klug points out,[9] post-independence leaders used a number of strategies to undermine the weak constitutional provisions that were in place to check against arbitrary

[2] See Chapter 1.
[3] See Chapters 2–4.
[4] See Chapters 5 and 6.
[5] See Chapters 7–9.
[6] See Chapters 10–15.
[7] See Chapter 1.
[8] Ibid.
[9] See Chapter 2.

changes to the constitution. The main strategies were to ignore such constraints, to amend them, or to suspend the constitution, usually following a military coup.

In a bid to avoid the errors of the past, post-1990 constitution-makers have tried to design constitutional provisions that balance flexibility in dealing with unavoidable changes in a timeous manner with rigidity in preventing opportunistic politicians from abusing the process to advance their selfish interests. How easy or difficult the amendment of a constitution is depends on the number of legal and practical obstacles that are built into the amendment process and the way in which these are implemented. From the perspective of comparative constitutional change, there are three main features that summarize the general pattern of the provisions for the changing of modern African constitutions. It is, however, important to point out that, in certain cases, some patterns are more pronounced in one or the other of the two main constitutional traditions on the continent.[10] The first is the explicit or implicit specification of the methods for changing the constitution; the second is the explicit or implicit limitation on the specified method; and the third relates to the different mechanisms provided to ensure that governments comply with the specified methods for changing the constitution.

First, as regards the methods for changing African constitutions, there are basically two—one formal, the other informal. Formal methods refer to procedures for changing the constitution that are explicitly or implicitly entrenched in the constitution. This usually entails one or more of four different approaches. The first of these involves the normal amendment procedures that are provided for in all constitutions. Additionally, they might be complemented by a special amendment procedure to change particular provisions. A third possibility appears in certain constitutions that contain time-specified amendment provisions. A fourth possibility is that the constitution provides for extraordinary amendment procedures in specified circumstances.[11]

Besides the formal methods, a variety of informal methods of constitutional change may be used by different political and institutional actors during the operation of the constitution. The key characteristic of informal methods is that they leave the constitutional text unchanged and still politically valid. These methods involve informal amendments that are introduced during judicial interpretation and application of the constitution; informal changes that result from unwritten understandings, practices, and conventions; informal constitutional changes due to inaction and neglect in implementing the constitution; and, finally, informal changes resulting from certain executive or legislative actions.

A second feature of modern African safeguards against abusive amendments is that limitations may be imposed on the manner and/or substance of a constitutional change. These limitations take a variety of forms. The main ones are, first, provisions that explicitly declare certain parts, sections, principles, and/or values in the constitution as unamendable or unalterable—the so-called eternity provisions. In a second form, such unamendability is stated only implicitly. A third form is a circumstantial or temporal limitation on amendability; in other words, the limitation applies to the timing or duration of a constitutional amendment. A fourth, and fairly controversial, limitation is imposed by the judiciary when applying the so-called basic structure doctrine. The last category is broad and

[10] The two main constitutional traditions in Africa are the common law tradition, which is found in anglophone countries, and the civil law tradition, found in francophone, lusophone, and hispanophone countries.

[11] For a detailed discussion, see Chapter 1.

consists of all other limitations. These relate, inter alia, to the nature of the majorities required to approve an amendment; the requirement of a referendum of a particular form; and stipulations in regard to popular participation or the role that different political actors and other stakeholders have to play in the amendment process.

The third feature of post-1990s measures to counter abusive changes consists of mechanisms for ensuring compliance with prescribed methods for amending the constitution. It is futile to entrench checks against abuse without providing measures to ensure that non-compliance with these checks is sanctioned promptly and effectively. Generally, in all jurisdictions, regardless of constitutional tradition, the primary responsibility for upholding respect for the constitution lies with the judiciary. However, in most civil law jurisdictions, the judiciary's ability to do so is severely limited by practical and theoretical constraints on its powers of review.[12] It is thus unsurprising that, in most civil law jurisdictions, the constitutional courts or councils (which usually have exclusive jurisdiction over constitutional matters) are still influenced by the practice of the French Constitutional Council under the 1958 French Constitution and, as a result, do not have the powers to review a constitutional amendment to assess its compliance with the procedure for such amendments laid out in the constitution. This may create a number of anomalies. For example, given that most francophone constitutions have eternity clauses, how could it be determined whether or not these clauses have been violated other than by means of a judicial review process?

Be that as it may, judicial review is the main instrument for ensuring that the requirements for changing the constitution are complied with. There are two key points to note about the different approaches provided for in African constitutions.

The first is that the courts that undertake the review differ from country to country. In some countries, it is carried out by ordinary courts, while in others, such as those with a civil law tradition, the review is carried out by a specialized court, usually the constitutional court or constitutional council. Moreover, the increasing internationalization of constitutional law has resulted in the enactment by the AU and RECs of a variety of international instruments setting out standards of constitutionalism, democracy, and good governance. These supranational standards have an impact on the ability of national governments to change their constitutions. This has created the possibility of supranational judicial review of changes to national constitutions. The basis of this is article 34 of the Protocol to the African Charter on Human and Peoples' Rights on the Establishment of an African Court on Human and Peoples' Rights, which allows member states to sign a declaration under article 5(3). This opens the possibility for the citizens of countries that have signed this declaration to appeal to the African Court to review the legality of a constitutional amendment in their country. A number of cases based on supranational review of legality of constitutional changes have come before the African Court; although this has provoked a backlash, with some of the ten countries that signed a declaration giving notice to withdraw their declarations, it remains an important means of putting pressure on countries to respect the sanctity of their constitutions.

The second key point in regard to judicial review concerns the scope allowed for such review. In principle, and unless explicitly or implicitly stated, the assumption is that the review covers both formal and substantive compliance with provisions regulating the process of constitutional change. However, a number of constitutions, especially in civil law

[12] For a general discussion insofar as the constitution is concerned, see Charles M Fombad (ed.), *Constitutional Adjudication in Africa* (OUP 2017).

jurisdictions, sometimes allow the courts to review either only procedural or only substantive compliance. Unless they are explicitly prohibited from doing so, it would seem that courts may still carry out a procedural review to see whether or not an amendment has violated an eternity clause, without going into the substance of the violation. In any case, it is difficult to see how a substantive review could be undertaken without assessing if the correct formalities were adhered to.

The question that arises, and which most of the chapters in this volume seek to address in different ways, is how all these measures to curb abusive changes to the constitutions in African states have been working. Has there been a notable improvement on the pre-1990 situation?

3. Impact on constitutionalism of measures to check frequent and arbitrary changes

The post-1990 constitutional dispensation tried to provide an enhanced system for managing constitutional changes: one premised on a recognition that revisions are necessary to adapt the constitution to changing economic, social, political, and societal needs. However, as we will see, the frequency and nature of the changes pose a clear threat to attempts to entrench an ethos of constitutionalism, democracy, and good governance in Africa.

3.1 The frequency of constitutional changes

A few caveats are worth noting when considering the frequency of constitutional changes in Africa over the last three decades. First, what follows refers only to formal constitutional change; it does not cover the numerous changes brought about through the informal methods mentioned above. Second, frequency of constitutional change does not necessarily reflect the extent of the changes or their actual or potential impact on constitutionalism, democracy, and respect for the rule of law. For example, the oldest constitution in the world, the Norwegian Constitution of 1814, has been amended more than 200 times, though but slightly; the second-oldest, the US Constitution of 1789, has been amended only 27 times (even though about 11,000 amendments have been proposed). As Bjorn Rasch and Roger Congleton point out, the few changes in the US have had a substantial impact on the nature of governance;[13] by contrast, the numerous changes in Norway have had only a trivial effect. Third, although it is difficult to determine accurately how frequently African constitutions have been changed in a given period, we can still get some indication of the trend from the limited sources available.[14]

Some indication of the frequency of change to constitutions is provided in Mwiza Jo Nkhata's chapter,[15] where he observes that Malawi's 1994 Constitution has been amended

[13] Bjorn Rasch and Roger Congleton, 'Amendment Procedures and Constitutional Stability' in Roger Congleton and Birgitta Swedenborg (eds.), *Democratic Constitutional Design and Public Policy: Analysis and Evidence* (MIT 2006) 537.

[14] For an indication of the frequency of constitutional changes in African constitutions, see Constitute Project, 'Countries: Africa' https://www.constituteproject.org/countries/Africa accessed 1 September 2023.

[15] See Chapter 13 in this volume.

at least ten times in 29 years—this was achieved through fifteen Acts of Parliament, which together changed 139 sections. Likewise, Babacar Kanté notes that the Senegalese Constitution of 2001 was amended fifteen times in fifteen years.[16] Frequent changes to provisions in Africa's constitutions are a permanent source of constitutional instability and uncertainty. In many countries, this has been compounded by frequent changes to the entirety of the constitution, more often than not in order to circumvent the restrictions imposed on changing certain provisions in the constitution.

Francophone Africa enjoys the dubious distinction of having what are perhaps the most volatile constitutions in the world. Since the 1990s, most of these countries have changed their constitutions more than once. The turnover of new constitutions is as follows:

- Burundi in 1992, 2005, and 2018.
- Central African Republic in 1994, 2004, and 2016.
- Chad in 1989, 1996, and 2018.[17]
- Comoros in 1992, 1996, 2001, and 2018.
- Congo Republic in 1992, 2001, and 2015.
- Côte d'Ivoire in 2000 and 2016.
- Democratic Republic of the Congo (DRC) in 1997, 2003, and 2005.
- Guinea in 1990, 2010, and 2020.
- Madagascar in 1992, 1998, and 2010.
- Niger in 1992, 1996, 1999, 2009, and 2010.
- Rwanda in 1991 and 2003.
- Senegal in 2001.
- Togo in 1992.[18]

The record for the most frequent changes of the entire constitution is held by Niger, which has had five new constitutions since 1989.[19] There is bound to be a new constitution after the military coup on 26 July 2023. But while Niger holds the record for the highest number of constitutions since 1990, with an average of a new constitution every 6.6 years, the record for the most extensive changes to the constitution may well go to Gabon. Its 1991 Constitution has been changed nine times (in 1994, 1995, 1997, 2000, 2003, 2011, 2018, 2021, and 2023). During the past 32 years in which this Constitution has been in force, 94 of its 120 articles have been changed—in fact, some of them have been changed more than once.

These extreme cases, concentrated in francophone Africa, should not be taken as a sign of a complete failure of constitutional provisions to constrain abusive changes across the continent at large. For example, since Kenya adopted a new constitution in 2010, there have been 22 failed attempts to change it. This clearly suggests that the checks are working, particularly given, as Migai Akech shows in Chapter 9,[20] the firm stance that the courts

[16] See Babacar Kanté, 'Introductory Remarks' in this volume.

[17] The Chadian situation warrants some explanation. The country adopted a new constitution in 1989, suspended it in 1990, and then adopted an interim constitution in 1993, followed by a new constitution in 1996; it replaced the latter with another constitution in 2018, which was suspended in 2021.

[18] In addition to these permanent constitutions, many francophone African countries have adopted interim constitutions during phases of transition. For a detailed chronology of (almost) all the constitutions in francophone Africa, see Constitute Project (n 14).

[19] Its 1989 Constitution was replaced by new constitutions in 1992, 1996, 1999, 2009, and 2010.

[20] See Chapter 9 in this volume.

have taken to ensure full compliance with the procedures laid down for changing the Constitution. Indeed, what is often troubling is not the number or frequency of the changes per se but the nature and scope of these changes, and their actual or potential impact on constitutionalism and democracy—an issue to which we now turn.

3.2 The nature and scope of constitutional changes and their impact on constitutionalism

Most chapters in this volume, particularly the case studies, provide clear evidence that frequent and abusive changes to the post-1990 African constitutions, both formal and informal, have not only made it difficult for a culture of constitutionalism and democracy to take root, but have also eroded the limited progress that has been made in this regard. To appreciate the nature of these changes, it is important to note that the new or revised constitutions did not necessarily enable every single African country to join the democracy and constitutionalism bandwagon. In some countries, where restraints imposed by constitutionalism are lacking, there are no constraints on the government's ability to change the constitution at its sheer convenience. An example is Eswatini: its 2005 Constitution does no more than consolidate the absolute powers of the King in a manner that places him above the Constitution.[21] Similarly, perhaps the most illiberal and retrograde constitutions on the continent, those of Eritrea and Cameroon of 1997 and 1996, respectively, merely obfuscate and reinforce pre-existing authoritarian systems within frameworks that neither provide nor promote constitutionalism or democracy.[22]

These exceptional cases aside, numerous progressive principles of modern constitutionalism were incorporated in most post-1990 constitutions by means of elaborate checks and balances—checks and balances that have been either removed or weakened in constitutional changes over the last two decades in particular. In this regard, no country in Africa better illustrates the extreme abuse of the mechanism to change the Constitution than Gabon. The 94 of the Constitution's 120 articles that have been changed in the last 32 years have not only neutralized many of the key elements of constitutionalism, such as an independent judiciary, separation of powers, and safeguards against unconstitutional changes to the Constitution, but have also reinforced the 56-year dynastic rule of the Bongo family. In fact, a series of constitutional changes in 2023 were specifically designed to ensure that, should the then president, Ali Bongo Ondimba,[23] who was in poor health after a stroke, die, his son, Noureddine, would inherit the throne.[24]

[21] See Charles M Fombad, 'The Swaziland Constitution of 2005: Can Absolutism Be Reconciled with Modern Constitutionalism?' (2007) 23(1) South African Journal on Human Rights 93–115.

[22] See Fombad (n 1).

[23] At the time of this writing, President Ali Bongo Ondimba had been toppled in a coup barely hours after having won the presidential elections. See Jessie Yeung, 'Gabon's Military Coup Has Overthrown a Powerful Political Dynasty: Here's What to Know' (*CNN*, 31 August 2023) https://edition.cnn.com/2023/08/31/africa/gabon-military-coup-explainer-intl-hnk/index.html accessed 1 September 2023.

[24] See Telesphore Ondo and Patrice Moundounga Mouity, 'The Revision of the Gabonese Constitution: Between Contestation, Modernization and Inconsistencies' (*Constitutionnet*, 28 May 2021) https://constitutionnet.org/news/revision-gabonese-constitution-between-contestation-modernization-and-inconsistencies accessed 1 September 2023; Douglas Yates, 'Gabon Elections: How the Bongo Family's 56-year Rule has Hurt the Country and Divided the Opposition' (*The Conversation*, 17 August 2023) https://theconversation.com/gabon-how-the-bongo-familys-56-year-rule-has-hurt-the-country-and-divided-the-opposition-211537 accessed 1 September 2023; Alexis Essono Ovono and Kelly Joanna Nguema Ondo, 'Constitutional Reforms in Gabon: The President's

More generally, changes to constitutions have removed many of the key elements that were introduced in the 1990s to facilitate alternation of power and reduce the scourge of life presidencies. One of the most significant innovations to end the vicious cycle of perpetual incumbency that was common in Africa pre-1990s was the introduction of presidential term limits to ensure that no one person should monopolize power. An examination of the nature of amendments made to presidential term-limit provisions since 1990 reveals five main trends:[25]

- First, some of the amendments led to the formal extension of the presidential term from five to six years (Burundi (2018) and Chad (2018)), and five to seven years (Gabon (2003) and Rwanda (2016)); in other instances, there was an informal ad hoc extension, as in the DRC (2016) and South Sudan (2015 and 2018).
- In a second group of countries, amendments increased the number of presidential terms. In the Comoros (2018), terms were increased from one to two presidential terms, while the Republic of Congo (2015) increased the number from two to three.
- Third, in a number of countries where incumbents had reached, or were about to reach, the end of their constitutionally mandated term, the effect of the constitutional amendment was to reset the presidential term-limit clock and start it anew, uninhibited by the previous constitutional term limits. While the new 2016 Constitution of Zambia, in article 106(6)(b), failed to achieve this goal for former president Edgar Lungu, given that he lost the 2021 presidential elections,[26] the effect of new constitutions, or of the constitutional amendments in Zimbabwe (2013), the Republic of Congo (2015), and Rwanda (2015), has been to reset the clock.
- The fourth category of countries are those where the presidential term limits were removed entirely from the constitution. This happened in Algeria (2008), Cameroon (2008)—which also increased each term from five to seven years—Chad (2005), Gabon (2003), Djibouti (2009), Guinea (2001), Niger (2009), Togo (2002), Tunisia (2002), and Uganda (2005). In certain of these countries, the provisions were subsequently reinstated, sometimes opportunistically.
- An important category consists of those instances where the effect of the changes was to introduce or strengthen presidential term limits. For example, after they had become the norm, presidential term limits were introduced fairly late in the day in countries such as Côte d'Ivoire (2000), Egypt (2014), Equatorial Guinea (2011), the DRC (2006), and Senegal (2001). However, it is worth noting that they were introduced in Equatorial Guinea two years after the re-election of the incumbent and were designed to apply only when he began a new mandate. This mandate took effect in 2016 and extends until 2023, enabling him to stand for a second term that would run from 2023

Strategic Tool for Political Preservation' (*Constitutionnet*, 1 August 2023) https://constitutionnet.org/news/constitutional-reforms-gabon-presidents-strategic-tool-political-preservation accessed 1 September 2023.

[25] See ANCL/NDI, 'The State of Presidential Term Limits in Africa (1990–2022)' (forthcoming, on file with the author); Micha Wiebusch and Christina Murray, 'Presidential Term Limits and the African Union' (2019) 63(S1) Journal of African Law 131–60.

[26] Drafted under the influence of President Lungu, the new Constitution was explicitly designed to change the definition of a 'presidential term' in such a way as to ensure that Lungu qualified to contest the 2021 presidential elections, notwithstanding that, at that point, he had already served two terms and was eight months into what was technically his third term.

to 2030. Presidential term limits were reintroduced in Algeria (2016), Burkina Faso (2000), Chad (2018), Niger (2010), and Uganda (2017).

- Presidential term limits were slightly enhanced when the terms were shortened from seven to five years in Burkina Faso (2000), Côte d'Ivoire (2000), the DRC (2006), Senegal (2001 and 2016), and Rwanda (2015); from six to five years in the Central African Republic (2004), Mauritania (2006), and Zimbabwe (2013); and from six to four years in the Comoros (2001) and Egypt (2014). In Madagascar (2010) and the Seychelles (2016), constitutional changes resulted in a reduction of the number of terms a person may serve from three to two.
- In a few constitutions, changes to presidential term-limit provisions tightened them and removed ambiguity, especially as to whether the restriction applies only to consecutive terms. Examples of such clear and unambiguous formulations appear in the constitutions of Algeria (2020), Benin (2019), Botswana (2016), Guinea–Bissau (1996), Niger (2017), Tanzania (2005), Tunisia (2014), and Zimbabwe (2017).

Tampering with presidential term limits has had dire consequences for the prospects of sustaining increasingly feeble efforts at promoting constitutionalism, democracy, and good governance on the continent. First, it has revived the old pre-1990 cancer of life presidencies and dynasties. For example, the ten longest-serving presidents on the continent, who have been in power for, on average, 17.5 years and counting, have seen the removal of presidential term-limit provisions from their constitutions. They are Teodoro Obiang Nguema Mbasogo of Equatorial Guinea (43 years); Paul Biya of Cameroon (40); Dennis Sassou Nguesso of the Republic of Congo (38); Yoweri Museveni of Uganda (36); Isaias Afwerki of Eritrea (31); Ismail Guelleh of Djibouti (23); Paul Kagame of Rwanda (22); Faure Gnassingbe of Togo (17); and, until recently, Ali Bongo Ondimba of Gabon (13 years) and Alassane Ouattara of Côte d'Ivoire (12). It is no surprise that Africa has six of the ten longest-serving leaders in the world.

The removal or manipulation of presidential term limits has also facilitated the growth of political dynasties, which in turn are promoted by self-serving clientelist and patronage networks determined to protect their interests. The emergent culture of father-to-son succession began in 2001 in the DRC, when former president Joseph Kabila, with the help of the military, replaced his assassinated father, Laurent Kabila.[27] In Togo, the army was instrumental in Faure Gnassingbe's replacing his deceased father, Gnassingbe Eyadema, in 2005, in disregard of the terms of the Constitution. In 2009, Gabon's Ali Bongo took over from his father, Omar Bongo, who had been in power for 42 years; Ali Bongo was, until his removal on 30 August 2023, preparing his own son, Noureddin Bongo Valentin, to take over. In 2021, the army was again instrumental in replacing the late Chadian president Idriss Déby, in power for 31 years, with his son, General Mahamat Déby. Equatorial Guinea's President Teodoro Obiang Nguema Mbasogo, in power for the last 43 years, appointed his son, Teodoro Nguema Obiang Mangue, whom he has been grooming as successor, as vice president in 2016.

Similar dynastic successions are in the making. These include Paul Biya of Cameroon, in power for 40 years, who is planning to hand over to his son, Franck Biya. In the Republic

[27] See Issa Sikiti da Silva, 'The Rise of Africa's Political Dynasties' (*News Africa*, 5 April 2022) https://www.newsafrica.net/article/the-rise-of-africa-s-political-dynasties accessed 1 September 2023.

of the Congo, Denis Christel Sassou Nguesso, the son of President Denis Sassou Nguesso, who has been in power for 37 years, is being prepared for succession. In Uganda, General Muhoozi Kainerugaba is being prepared to replace his father, Yoweri Museveni, the president for the past 36 years.

Thirdly, in most African countries, the removal—actual or attempted—of presidential term-limit provisions has led to violence, repression, and the violation of the human rights of citizens protesting against the changes. In some cases, such as in Guinea in 2022, it has provoked coups. More generally, countries that have maintained term limits and witnessed alternation of power perform, on average, better on issues of political stability and the fight against corruption.[28]

Many of the contributions in this volume provide examples of other ways in which processes for adapting constitutions to changing circumstances have been abused. In many countries, the fundamentals of constitutionalism and the checks and balances that go with them have been abused through changes that have resulted in the concentration of powers in the person of the president, the progressive undermining of judicial independence, and the stifling of free and competitive elections.[29] Even in Africa's few federal or quasi-federal states, as Nico Steytler, Zemelak Ayele, and Henry Gichana explain, constitutional changes have resulted in more and more powers being transferred to the central governments.[30] As Rotimi Suberu points out in Chapter 10, Nigeria has had nine constitutions in 24 years of democracy. At the same time, urgent and fundamental constitutional changes that the country needs in order to move forward, such as those dealing with fiscal federalism, policing, local government, and the restructuring of procedures for amending the Constitution, have been disregarded because of the country's north–south conflict, in favour of changes that serve the selfish short-term interests of politicians.[31]

The corrosive long-term impact on constitutionalism and democracy of the slow, surreptitious manner in which African constitutions have been changed went largely unnoticed until recently because changing constitutions does not attract as much national and international attention as writing them in the first place. It is only in the last decade that ominous signs of a global democratic recession have appeared, with increased evidence of democratic deconsolidation and autocratization having become manifest. While it is now an open secret that, from the perspective of democracy and constitutionalism, the world is going through a profound governance crisis—one which has been described as 'democratic erosion' or 'democratic backsliding' and the like[32]—the situation in Africa is far worse than it is elsewhere.

Governance indicators show that most of the African countries that changed their constitutions (particularly those that removed, distorted, or ignored presidential term limits) have not fared well in terms of democratic progress, respect for the rule of law, and prospects for constitutionalism, when compared with countries that retained and respected these provisions,[33] this in spite of the numerous safeguards that were built into constitutions

[28] See Charles M Fombad and Nico Steytler (eds.), *Corruption and Constitutionalism in Africa: Revisiting Control Measures and Strategies* (OUP 2020).

[29] See Chapters 3 (by Adem Abebe), 10 (by Rotimi Suberu), and 13 (by Mwiza Jo Nkhata) in this volume.

[30] See Chapter 4 in this volume.

[31] See Chapter 10 in this volume.

[32] See Charles M Fombad and Nico Steytler (eds), *Democracy, Elections, and Constitutionalism in Africa* (OUP 2021).

[33] Ibid.

to guard against frequent and abusive changes. Most of these safeguards have not worked as well as expected. For example, the courts that, under most of these constitutions, are empowered to adjudicate disputes concerning non-compliance with the constitutional requirements for changing the constitution, have in some cases, as several chapters in this volume show, not been as effective as desired.[34] What has caused this state of affairs, and how could it be corrected?

4. Explaining mixed results and identifying prospects for the future

It is necessary to see what explains the mixed results that have come from the operation of the constitutional checks that were supposed to prevent arbitrary constitutional changes, and to see what could be done to remedy the defects.

4.1 Why the mixed results?

The reasons for the mixed success of the provisions designed to counter abusive changes to African constitutions are many and varied, and in some respects are linked to the legacy of the inherited constitutional culture. For example, the limited scope for judicial independence and weak foundation for separation of powers in civil law jurisdictions has generally contributed significantly, as noted, to the prevalence of frequent and abusive constitutional changes seen in most francophone countries.[35] The main reasons for the limited success of the safeguards against abusive constitutional changes, as discussed in several chapters of this volume, can be summarized under four key points:

- Judicial adventurism or abdication of bounden duty.
- Unruly executive behaviour.
- Exploitation of defective constitutional safeguards.
- Weaknesses due to the absence of effective public participation.

4.1.1 Judicial adventurism or abdication of bounden duty

The introductory chapter to this volume provides a broad overview of the nature, scope, and limitations within which courts operate when required to review compliance with the constitutional requirements for changing the constitution. A number of cases show that the jurisdictional remit for courts to invalidate irregular and illegal changes to the constitution is generally weaker in francophone and other civil law countries than elsewhere. Perhaps the most serious problem arises when courts themselves, through judicial adventurism, indulge in judicially inspired changes to the constitution or, when required to review the constitutionality of a constitutional change, act in deference to the executive.

[34] For a discussion of several instances of judicial intervention to review the constitutionality of changes to the constitution, see Chapters 1 (Charles M Fombad), 5 (André Thomashausen), 6 (Abdou Khadre Diop), 7 (Maame Mensa-Bonsu), 8 (Lauren Kohn), and 9 (Migai Akech) in this volume.

[35] See the following two books in this series: Charles M Fombad (ed.), *Separation of Powers in African Constitutionalism* (OUP 2016); Charles M Fombad (ed.), *Constitutional Adjudication in Africa* (OUP 2017).

Three chapters discuss the wide range of judicial interventions that can have an impact on constitutionalism. Maame Mensa-Bonsu's chapter[36] highlights lessons from Ghana on the dangers of judicially inspired changes to the Constitution. Lauren Kohn, in her chapter, argues that it is time to reduce judicial adventurism in South Africa.[37] Migai Akech, in discussing the most recent and authoritative decision of the Kenyan Supreme Court in *Attorney General & 2 Others v David Ndii & others* (*BBI* case),[38] explains the reason for the Court's rejection of the applicability of the basic structure doctrine in Kenya.[39] More broadly, Charles Fombad, in the general overview, shows that, from a comparative perspective, the provisions in the different African constitutions afford no basis for importing the Indian Supreme Court-inspired basic structure doctrine as an additional method of constraining abusive constitutional changes.

Generally, the judiciary is regarded as a bulwark against the erosion of constitutionalism, and is required, in discharging its task of interpreting and applying the law and the constitution, to fiercely defend and protect the ideals of constitutionalism. The assumption is that, when all else fails, citizens can rely on the judiciary to protect and defend them against state abuse. From this perspective, the judiciary's primary role is to ensure that changes to the constitution are compliant with the procedures provided for effecting such changes. Courts do not have the powers to change constitutions. However, as some of the chapters in this volume show, in exceptional circumstances courts do interpret and apply the constitution in a manner that may be seen as informally changing it without there being any explicit change to the constitution's wording. Apart from such exceptional circumstances, there are a number of instances, discussed in some of the chapters, where courts have arguably abused their powers and indulged in irregular changes of the constitution.

As regards informal judicial changes to the constitution, this is conceivably acceptable and legitimate in at least three exceptional circumstances, provided it does not result in the creation of new rights or principles but merely helps to clarify existing ones. The first situation is that, where there are two alternative interpretations of the constitution, the courts should prefer the one which is consistent with the constitution, regardless of the implications. Secondly, given the broad formulation of human rights provisions in modern constitutions, courts have greater interpretative leeway here than when dealing with other provisions of the constitution.[40] This has provided much-needed flexibility in interpreting provisions dealing with socio-economic rights, and has given rise to what is referred to as judicial activism.[41] However, where a provision is so open-textured that it is unclear what the constitution-maker may have intended, then the duty of the court is, at worse, to leave it as it is, or, at best, to invite the lawmaker to intervene and change the constitution and not change it by itself.

Ultimately, as both Maame Mensa-Bonsu and Lauren Kohn demonstrate in their chapters, the judicial authority to interpret and apply the constitution does not equate to the authority to update, correct, or otherwise improve on the language or any aspect of the

[36] See Chapter 7.
[37] See Chapter 8.
[38] Supreme Court Petition no 12 of 2021 as Consolidated with Petitions nos 11 and 13 of 2021.
[39] See Akech, in Chapter 9 of this volume.
[40] See Fombad (Chapter 1) and Kohn (Chapter 8), in this volume.
[41] See eg Hugh Corder, 'Judicial Activism of a Special Type: South African Top Courts Since 1994' in Brice Dickson (ed.), *Judicial Activism in Common Law Supreme Courts* (OUP 2007) 323–62; Keenan Kniec, 'The Origin and Current Meanings of Judicial Activism' (2004) 92(5) California Law Review 1441–77.

constitution, or to read in or read out certain words vis-à-vis the constitution in order for the constitution to make sense. Once courts exercise their judicial powers in such an arbitrary manner, legal stability, predictability, reliability, and certainty are placed at risk. In a number of cases discussed in this volume, the courts have informally changed constitutions by their actions or inactions.

A number of terms have been used to describe the nature of the abuses courts indulge in when they stray from their duty to interpret and apply the constitution and instead change or sanction irregular changes to it. The most serious form of judicial overreach is what amounts to judicial adventurism: an extreme form of judicial activism which entails a situation where the judiciary, in the context of this discussion, takes on the role of a constitution-maker, or that of the legislature and executive, in changing the constitution. Several cases which illustrate this abuse of judicial powers are discussed by Maame Mensa-Bonsu in Chapter 7, Lauren Kohn in Chapter 8, and Mwiza Jo Nkhata in Chapter 13. Perhaps one of the most extreme examples of this was the decision of the Constitutional Court of Gabon in November 2018 to add a subparagraph to article 13 of the Gabonese Constitution to deal with the dilemma of the protracted hospitalization overseas of the then president Ali Bongo Ondimba.

In addition, a number of decisions could be said to have been influenced by judicial populism; that is, where the judges are influenced by empathy for the public. These are instances where judges disregard constitutional principles and rules in order to appeal to popular sentiments. Perhaps the best example of judicial populism is the recourse, at the level of the High Court and the Court of Appeal, to the Indian basic structure doctrine in the early stages of the Kenyan *BBI* case—a recourse probably influenced by popular opposition to Uhuru Kenyatta's suspicious attempts to change the Constitution in 2021.[42]

More common—particularly in civil law jurisdictions, where there is considerable scope for executive control of the judiciary—is the phenomenon of judicial deference. Here, the judiciary has the opportunity to intervene decisively and declare changes to the constitution as illegal and unconstitutional but chooses not to do so. Several cases in francophone Africa, discussed by Charles Fombad in Chapter 1, highlight the failure of constitutional courts or councils to recognize and invalidate illegal changes to the constitution when approached to do so.

On the whole, while the constitutional reforms of the 1990s saw an expansion of judicial powers in a manner that was expected to give judges a greater say in checking against abusive constitutional changes, the erosion of constitutionalism has seen the erosion, in turn, of judicial powers, which has limited the judiciary's ability to act decisively. This has been due largely to abuse of the enormous powers that African constitutions gave presidents or allowed them to arrogate to themselves.

4.1.2 Unruly executive behaviour

Proceeding from a historical perspective, Heinz Klug, in Chapter 2, explains how strong executives and dominant parties—usually the nationalist or revolutionary parties that led the struggle against colonialism—exploited their positions to change or adopt new constitutions in order to create one-party systems. This paved the way for the repressive and

[42] See Akech, in Chapter 9 of this volume.

authoritarian regimes that became common across Africa prior to the 1990s. In spite of the widespread incorporation of core elements of modern constitutionalism, such as separation of powers and judicial independence, the reality is that excessive concentration of powers in the executive remains a bane in Africa to this day. This is particularly so in francophone Africa, where the centralist Gaullist constitutional philosophy is deeply entrenched. The best manifestation of this is the all-pervasive ghost of the imperial president, who still reigns strong, particularly under civilian constitutions, and dominates the other two branches of government, namely the judiciary and legislature.[43] The negative impact of this with respect to checking unruly executive abuse of the framework for changing constitutions has been at least threefold.

First, because a majority of ruling parties in Africa are hegemonic, they hardly ever vote against any bills to amend the constitution, regardless of the extent of their majority.[44] Even on those rare occasions where the ruling party does not have a majority, presidents have used intimidation, blackmail, violence, and bribery to get Members of Parliament to approve bills changing critical provisions such as those dealing with presidential term limits.[45] In addition, the party whip system in most African countries has transformed parliaments from watchdogs into lapdogs that merely do the executive's bidding. In general, the ruling party's hegemonic control and the ease with which parliaments can be captured and neutralized have meant that executives usually find ways of obtaining special majorities when this is required for changing certain provisions; alternatively, ruling parties have circumvented this when the option of a referendum is provided as an alternative to a supermajority, as is the case in most francophone constitutions.[46]

Second, in spite of the considerable strides that have been taken to make African judiciaries more independent, effective, and efficient, judiciaries in francophone Africa are still largely under the control of the president.[47] This has rendered most efforts to check presidential excesses hazardous. For example, in November 2022, President Faustin Archange Toudera dismissed the president of the Constitutional Court of the Central African Republic after the Court declared unconstitutional and invalid several decrees and a law seeking to change the Constitution to remove the presidential term limits.[48] In July 2023, the more pliant Constitutional Court that he appointed had no difficulty in approving the referendum that approved the constitutional changes removing the term limits and making it possible for him to remain president for life.[49]

[43] See Charles M Fombad and Enyinna Nwauche, 'Africa's Imperial Presidents: Immunity, Impunity and Accountability' (2012) 5 African Journal of Legal Studies 91–118.

[44] See eg Anna Christina Parkin, 'Parties of Pressure: Opposition Parties in the Dominant-party Systems of Botswana and South Africa' (PhD thesis, University of Stellenbosch 2022); Matthijs Bogaards, 'Counting Parties and Identifying Dominant Party Systems in Africa' (2004) 43(2) European Journal of Political Research 173–97.

[45] In Uganda, 5 million shillings were reportedly paid in bribes to parliamentarians in 2005 to secure the lifting of term limits. See Angelo Izama and Michael Wilkerson, 'Uganda: Museveni's Triumph and Weakness' (2011) 22(3) Journal of Democracy 75.

[46] See Fombad, in Chapter 1 of this volume.

[47] See Charles M Fombad, 'The Struggle to Defend the Independence of the Judiciary in Africa' in Shimon Shetreet, Hiram Chodesh, and Eric Helland (eds.), *Challenged Justice: In Pursuit of Judicial Independence* (Brill Nijhoff 2021) 223–48.

[48] See 'CAR: Touadera Appoints New President to Constitutional Court' (*Africa News*, 21 November 2022) https://www.africanews.com/2022/11/21/car-touadera-appoints-new-president-to-constitutional-court// accessed 1 September 2023.

[49] See 'Central African Republic's Top Court Confirms Constitutional Referendum Results' (*Africa News*, 22 August 2023) https://www.africanews.com/2023/08/22/central-african-republics-top-court-confirms-constitutional-referendum-results// accessed 1 September 2023.

Finally, in many African countries, the presidents, owing to the control they have over almost everything, get away with ignoring constitutional constraints on constitutional changes and introducing any changes that suit their self-interested agendas. Such informal constitutional changes took place in Namibia in 1998 (when presidential term limits were ignored for the benefit of Sam Nujoma). They also occurred in Senegal in 2012 (for the benefit of Abdoulaye Wade), and in Burundi in 2015 (for the benefit of Pierre Nkurunziza). The term-limit provision has been consistently ignored in the Eritrean Constitution of 1997, leaving President Isias Afwerki to rule as a life president. Assefa Fiseha, in Chapter 11, provides an elaborate account of how the ruling regime in Ethiopia has successfully changed the Constitution in several ways without bothering to comply with the constitutional provisions meant to regulate such changes. The Ethiopian regime has been able to get away with it because of the weak or near-absent system of control of the constitutionality of laws in the country. In many cases, the abuse of the constitutional safeguards has also been made easy, as we will now see, by sloppy draftsmanship.

4.1.3 Exploitation of defective constitutional safeguards

Routine and opportunistic changes to constitutions have also been facilitated by the weaknesses of the constitutional safeguards that were supposed to guard against or limit the scope for abuses. Three main weaknesses have been highlighted in various chapters of this volume: the inadequate scope provided for public participation, the misuse of referendums, and self-deluding reliance on so-called eternity clauses.

Heinz Klug, in his chapter in this volume, has described the changing modes of constitution-making. The nature and importance of popular participation through citizens' activism is also underscored in the chapter by Marystella Simiyu and Tresor Makunya. Nevertheless, the emerging reality is that the new generation of 'made-in-Africa' constitutions has, in practical terms, merely replaced constitutions imposed by colonialists with constitutions largely adopted by processes, especially in francophone Africa, controlled and manipulated by self-serving elites and their cronies, sometimes with external support, especially by France.

Two aspects of popular participation in constitution-making have had a possible impact on the present travails of frequent constitutional changes in Africa. The first is that a broad public and inclusive participatory constitution-making process not only strengthens the legitimacy of the constitution but also provides an opportunity for people to become aware of the content, values, and importance of the constitution. This enables them to gain the requisite knowledge, skills, and disposition to defend it when it is threatened by arbitrary changes. Several studies have shown that, compared with anglophone Africa, public participation in constitution-making in civil law jurisdictions, especially francophone Africa, has been token at best.[50] The general constitutional instability in francophone Africa probably reflects the fact that, due to limited public engagement in the making of constitutions, there is little popular acceptance of them and even less interest in implementing or compelling the implementation of their provisions.

The second aspect of popular participation—this of a positive nature—is discussed by Charles Fombad in his introductory chapter. He notes that there have been two innovations

50 See Charles M Fombad and Johannes Socher, 'Popular Participation in Constitution-making in Francophone Africa and Constitutionalism' (forthcoming).

in certain constitutions that provide ordinary citizens with an enhanced role not only in the constitution-making process but also (and perhaps more significantly) in any subsequent changes to the constitution. For example, some constitutions now allow ordinary citizens to initiate constitutional reforms, while others go even further to entrench the right of ordinary citizens—including civil society organizations (CSOs) and non-governmental organizations—to participate in the process.[51] The entrenchment of a duty to involve ordinary citizens both in the making of new constitutions and in the revision of existing constitutions must be seen as an imperative for checking against reckless constitutional amendments.

Referendums have been provided for in many constitutions as one of the safeguards against abusive constitutional changes. This is almost the rule in francophone Africa, where this is provided as an alternative to obtaining a special parliamentary majority.[52] Referendums are potentially one of the best ways to enhance the legitimacy and credibility of any constitutional changes, with such referendums acting, as Jon Elster puts it, as 'downstream constraints' that enable the people to act as final-stage gatekeepers.[53] A mere bland requirement of a referendum, without some safeguards such as a minimum level of public participation and/or minimum percentage of approval by those qualified to vote, as is the case in many anglophone constitutions, has failed to prevent abuses. First, most referendums, like many elections in most African countries today, are easily manipulated by incumbents to obtain the outcome they desire. Second, as a result of increasing voter apathy, the turnouts are usually low, and more often than not it is mainly the supporters of the incumbent who participate.

However, perhaps the most serious design flaw is that associated with the so-called eternity or unamendable provisions that appear in almost all civil-law-jurisdiction constitutions. In this volume, André Thomashausen discusses these provisions in the constitutions of lusophone countries,[54] while Abdou Khadre Diop examines them in the constitutions of the francophone states belonging to the Central African Economic and Monetary Union (CEMAC).[55] Generally, the eternity clauses in lusophone African constitutions are much broader and vaguer than those in francophone African constitutions. From the numerous cases that have come before the courts, it is clear that eternity clauses have failed in every respect to protect the constitutions in these countries from being amended at the whims of the presidents. It is ironic that, although these eternity clauses are supposed to protect fundamental human rights and democratic values, they are found in countries not only where constitutional democracy and the rule of law are the least respected on the continent, but also where changes to constitutions have been frequent, profound, and damaging to prospects for constitutional stability and constitutionalism.[56]

Eternity clauses are circumvented in a number of ways. One way is by replacing, or purporting to replace, the entire constitution when the real objective is to replace or amend the eternity provision, as was the situation in the Republic of Congo in 2015. Another

[51] See Fombad, in Chapter 1 of this volume.
[52] Ibid.
[53] Jon Elster, 'Forces and Mechanisms in Constitution-Making Process' (1995) 45(2) Duke Law Journal 373.
[54] See Chapter 5.
[55] See Chapter 6.
[56] See Charles M Fombad, 'Strengthening Constitutional Order and Upholding the Rule of Law in Central Africa: Reversing the Descent towards Symbolic Constitutionalism' (2014) 14 African Human Rights Law Journal 412–48.

approach is simply to ignore the eternity clause, as happened in Cameroon, Gabon, and Equatorial Guinea. The absence of an effective system of judicial review of constitutionality ensures that presidents can get away with such violations of the constitution. Another approach is to suspend the constitution, especially after a coup. This is what has happened recently, in August 2023, in Gabon, following the example of the coups in Burkina Faso, Guinea, Mali, and Niger in the last two years. Finally, some countries have used the subtler process of double amendment to circumvent the eternity clause. They start by tacitly revoking the amendment limitations and thereafter amend the eternity provisions as if they were any other provision in the constitution.

It may be suggested that, even if eternity clauses have some symbolic value, inasmuch as they hold authorities *in terrorem*, their vague and obscure formulation hardly helps, and in practice constitutional unamendability is a legal charade. It is better to provide clear, strict rules that regulate the process and substance of constitutional change than to pretend that certain provisions or principles are so important that they cannot be changed, even while knowing full well that such blanket prohibitions will not work. Having examined what has not worked, or is not working any more, we will now try to see how the situation could be improved.

4.2 Looking to the future

In spite of the innovations introduced in post-1990 African constitutions, it is clear that no constitution, country, or constitutional culture has designed and implemented a perfect and irreproachable system for preventing abusive and opportunistic constitutional changes. There are weaknesses that cut across not just the two dominant constitutional cultures—the common law and civil law—but also across systems of government, whether unitary, federal, or quasi-federal. It remains a challenge to balance the imperatives of desirable constitutional changes with the equal imperatives of political stability, predictability, and certainty. In the light of the experiences of the last three decades, it is suggested that changing constitutions in a manner that promotes and sustains constitutionalism, democracy, and good governance will require at least two important measures: the first is a more consensual approach to changing constitutions, and the second is a more proactive stance by the AU and RECs.

4.2.1 Towards a more consensual approach to constitutional change

It is time to go beyond constraints on constitutional change that rely solely on checks such as supermajority approvals in parliament; referendums; the unamendability of certain provisions, concepts, or principles; and judicial oversight. Individually or in combination, they have not been entirely successful in stopping determined political opportunists from abusing them in order to adjust the constitution when this is not necessarily for the good of the country. There are two factors to consider in engendering a more consensual approach to changing constitutions. One is promoting the role of ordinary citizens in the process, and the other is what Adem Abebe, in Chapter 3 of this volume, refers to as the emerging idea of taking national consensus as a standard for changing the constitution.

Enhancing the role of ordinary citizens individually or within the framework of CSOs is crucial for the future of constitutional stability. Besides a few constitutions, such as those of

Kenya and South Africa, ordinary citizens, as the primary constituents, are almost always excluded from processes of constitutional change. The principle of popular sovereignty dictates that ordinary citizens have an inalienable right to participate not just in the making of constitutions but also when these constitutions are being amended. Confining citizens' role to approving or rejecting changes during a referendum is not good enough.

As noted above, not only are most of the referendums in Africa rigged by those who organize them, but, at that late stage, the ordinary citizen cannot meaningfully contribute any ideas to the content of the amendment. Whether or not the change is a popular initiative, as provided for in article 257 of the Kenyan 2010 Constitution,[57] the more elaborate requirements for public participation in section 74(5) and (6) of the South African Constitution of 2016 provide a solid basis for a more progressive form of citizen and CSO participation that could reduce abusive constitutional changes.[58] As Marystella Simiyu and Tresor Makunya argue in Chapter 12, the combination of a determined citizenry and CSO mobilization could correct some of the internal defects of representative democracy that limit its ability to restrain abusive constitutional changes by the executive.

A further dimension of the consensual approach is the principle of national consensus, aspects of which are discussed in Adem Abebe's chapter. The crux of this principle is that, for changes to constitutions to be valid, this should require not just an ordinary majority but approval by an inclusive majority. At the heart of this principle is the recognition that there is a need not only for broad consultation but also for broad acceptance of changes to the constitution—and not only by the ruling party and its members but by as many opposition-party members and other stakeholders as possible. As Abebe rightly points out, it is impossible to define the exact nature of such an inclusive majoritarian principle. Nevertheless, the adoption of it would certainly necessitate cross-party and cross-community approval of constitutional changes. Securing cross-community approval would, in turn, require taking into account the cultural, linguistic, religious, and ethnic dynamics of different countries.

4.2.2 Making the AU and RECs more proactive

The AU and its RECs have several instruments designed to promote constitutionalism, democracy, and good governance. The most important instrument of the AU is the African Charter on Democracy, Elections and Governance (ACDEG), 2007. As Charles Fombad in Chapter 1 and Adem Abebe in Chapter 3 point out, the AU and its RECs have not been resolute in ensuring that African countries comply with the standards provided for in these international instruments; nor have these organizations fulfilled some of the obligations imposed on them by these instruments to promote respect for the basic principles of constitutionalism when member states amend their constitutions. The lack of an AU response to such abuses amounts to condoning the continent's slippery slide towards authoritarianism. This is especially pertinent given that the ACDEG requires the organization to set guidelines on the changing of national constitutions. The Peace and Security Council of the AU, acting in accordance with the ACDEG, in August 2018 tasked the AU Commission with

[57] The Constitution goes further, in arts 10(2), 118, and 196, to make public participation a national value and principle.

[58] See HJ Moolman, 'Public Participation in the Constitutional Amendment Process' (2020) 6(5) FarmBiz https://journals.co.za/doi/abs/10.10520/EJC-1d872450d4 accessed 1 September 2023.

developing benchmarks to guide member states when amending their national constitutions. This is yet to be done.

Considering the potential that abusive changes to post-1990 African constitutions have for reviving the spectre of military coups, the AU and RECs need to intervene decisively. First, there is a need to develop AU standards for amending or writing new constitutions, as mandated by the ACDEG. Second, these need to be popularized. Third, member-state adoption and domestication of such standards need to be promoted. Finally, an effective monitoring and enforcement mechanism is critical.

In this regard, the AU needs to set up a specialized technical committee for monitoring constitutional amendments in member states. This committee should be given the powers to undertake observation and advisory missions to member states in order to ensure that any changes being undertaken are in accordance with prescribed, agreed-upon guidelines, and that the processes followed are transparent and abide by the will of the people. The AU guidelines should make it mandatory for member states to inform the AU of any planned changes to the constitution, to enable the deployment of observer and advisory missions. The scourge of tampering with constitutions not only threatens stability but could substantially undermine the entire AU project, as encapsulated in the ACDEG, of fostering constitutionalism, democracy, good governance, and respect for human rights in Africa.

5. Conclusion

This study of the use of the constitutional review powers to change African constitutions in the last three decades has turned out to be more of a study of the misuse and abuse of these powers than anything else. It is, therefore, not surprising that constitutionalism is now under siege, at a time when democratization on the continent is either stagnating or facing reverses, given the persistence of authoritarian regimes and troubling signs that military coups are on the rise. The lights are dimming even in countries, such as Botswana, Mauritius, and South Africa, which were once hailed as beacons of good governance and constitutionalism on the continent.

As was the situation before the 1990s, the major cause of the present political instability and the rollback in the limited progress made in the last three decades is the apparent ease with which African leaders today are still able to capriciously change and distort the new generation of 'made-in-Africa' constitutions to serve their selfish ends. While most of these constitutions have elaborate provisions with procedural and substantive limitations designed to check against frequent and abusive changes to their provisions, a fair assessment of the situation today, as the various chapters in this volume have shown, suggests that the results are mixed. A number of general observations may be made.

First, as Heinz Klug reminds us in Chapter 2 (and there is sufficient contemporary literature to back this up), the processes through which constitutions are made are inextricably linked to the processes through which they are updated and remade. The extent to which there is popular participation in the making and changing of constitutions contributes not only to their legitimacy but their longevity. It could be suggested, then, that the quasi-permanent state of political and constitutional instability, particularly in francophone Africa, reflects not just the limited extent to which ordinary citizens are involved in constitution-making but also their limited participation in the changing of these same constitutions. It is imperative that popular participation in the making and changing of constitutions be entrenched in constitutions.

Second, in spite of the entrenchment of rigorous procedural and substantive requirements for changing constitutions—often involving parliamentary supermajorities, multiple veto actors, referendums, and courts—many of these safeguards are, by design, weak and vulnerable to easy manipulation. For example, courts in francophone Africa are usually given a very limited supervisory role in ensuring that the safeguards are complied with. The extensive use of eternity clauses in these countries has proven to be a sham. Constitutional precautions, particularly in francophone Africa, where the weaknesses of such precautions have been particularly evident, need to be reviewed. The suggestion, then, is that a more inclusive, consensual approach to constitutional change that requires cross-party, cross-community approval would afford better protection against opportunistic majoritarian abuse. Ultimately, courts must be mandated not to rewrite or reinterpret constitutions when there is obscurity or need for change (however desirable this may be), but to ensure formal and normative compliance with requirements for constitutional change.

Finally, a major lesson of the last three decades is that supranational constitutionalism, especially through the explicit prohibition of coups in Africa, could help. However, the promoters of supranational constitutionalism—the AU and its RECs—need to do more, since over time African dictators have contrived sophisticated ways to tame the constitutionalism tiger. There is a need for the AU to fulfil the mandate given to it by ACDEG to develop supranational standards for the making or changing of African constitutions, and to back this up with comprehensive monitoring and enforcement measures. This is one of the important ways in which the AU, supported by its RECs, could contribute to arresting the slide towards the dark days of repressive, authoritarian governance on the continent.

Bibliography

Akech M., 'The Basic Structure "Doctrine" and the Politics of Constitutional Change in Kenya: A Case of Judicial Adventurism?', in this volume

ANCL/NDI, 'The State of Presidential Term Limits in Africa (1990–2022) (forthcoming)

Bogaards M., 'Counting Parties and Identifying Dominant Party Systems in Africa' (2004) 43(2) European Journal of Political Research 173–97

'CAR: Touadera Appoints New President to Constitutional Court' (*Africa News*, 21 November 2022) https://www.africanews.com/2022/11/21/car-touadera-appoints-new-president-to-constitutional-court// accessed 1 September 2023

'Central African Republic's Top Court Confirms Constitutional Referendum Results' (*Africa News*, 22 August 2023) https://www.africanews.com/2023/08/22/central-african-republics-top-court-confirms-constitutional-referendum-results// accessed 1 September 2023

Constitute Project, 'Countries: Africa' https://www.constituteproject.org/countries/africa accessed 1 September 2023

Corder H., 'Judicial Activism of a Special Type: South African Top Courts Since 1994' in Dickson B. (ed.), *Judicial Activism in Common Law Supreme Courts* (OUP 2007) 323–62

Da Silva I.S., 'The Rise of Africa's Political Dynasties' (*News Africa*, 5 April 2022) https://www.newsafrica.net/article/the-rise-of-africa-s-political-dynasties accessed 1 September 2023

Elster J., 'Forces and Mechanisms in the Constitution-Making Process' (1995) 45(2) Duke Law Journal 364–96

Fombad C.M., 'The Swaziland Constitution of 2005: Can Absolutism Be Reconciled with Modern Constitutionalism? (2007) 23(1) South African Journal on Human Rights 93–115

Fombad C.M., 'Post-1990 Constitutional Reforms in Africa: A Preliminary Assessment of the Prospects for Constitutional Governance and Constitutionalism' in Nhema A.G. and Zeleza P.T. (eds.), *The Resolution of African conflicts* (OSSREA & James Currey 2008) 179–99

Fombad C.M., 'Strengthening Constitutional Order and Upholding the Rule of Law in Central Africa: Reversing the Descent towards Symbolic Constitutionalism' (2014) 14 African Human Rights Law Journal 412–48

Fombad C.M. (ed.), *Separation of Powers in African Constitutionalism* (OUP 2016)

Fombad C.M. (ed.), *Constitutional Adjudication in Africa* (OUP 2017)

Fombad C.M., 'The Struggle to Defend the Independence of the Judiciary in Africa' in Shetreet S., Chodesh H., and Helland E. (eds.), *Challenged Justice: In Pursuit of Judicial Independence* (Brill Nijhoff 2021) 223–48

Fombad C.M., 'An Overview of the Legal Framework for Amending Modern African Constitutions', in this volume

Fombad C.M. and Nwauche E., 'Africa's Imperial Presidents: Immunity, Impunity and Accountability' (2012) 5 African Journal of Legal Studies 91–118

Fombad C.M. and Socher J., 'Popular Participation in Constitution-making in Francophone Africa and Constitutionalism' (forthcoming)

Fombad C.M. and Steytler N. (eds.), *Corruption and Constitutionalism in Africa: Revisiting Control Measures and Strategies* (OUP 2020)

Izama A. and Wilkerson M., 'Uganda: Museveni's Triumph and Weakness' (2011) 22(3) Journal of Democracy 75

Klug H., 'Changing Modes of Constitution-Making in Africa: Do the Means Guarantee the Ends?', in this volume

Kniec K., 'The Origin and Current Meanings of Judicial Activism' (2004) 92(5) California Law Review 1441–77

Kohn L., 'Time to Reduce Judicial Adventurism: Reflections on *Glenister II* and *Sonke Gender Justice* through the Lens of the Separation of Powers and Proposals for Reform', in this volume

Mensa-Bonsu M., 'The Trouble with Judicial Amendments: Lessons from Ghana', in this volume

Moolman H.J., 'Public Participation in the Constitutional Amendment Process' (2020) 6(5) FarmBiz https://journals.co.za/doi/abs/10.10520/EJC-1d872450d4 accessed 1 September 2023

Ondo T. and Mouity P.M., 'The Revision of the Gabonese Constitution: Between Contestation, Modernization and Inconsistencies' (*Constitutionnet*, 28 May 2021) https://constitutionnet.org/news/revision-gabonese-constitution-between-contestation-modernization-and-inconsistencies accessed 1 September 2022

Ovono A.E. and Ondo K.J.N., 'Constitutional Reforms in Gabon: The President's Strategic Tool for Political Preservation' (*Constitutionnet*, 1 August 2023) https://constitutionnet.org/news/constitutional-reforms-gabon-presidents-strategic-tool-political-preservation accessed 1 September 2023

Parkin A.C., 'Parties of Pressure: Opposition Parties in the Dominant-party Systems of Botswana and South Africa' (PhD thesis, University of Stellenbosch 2022)

Rasch B. and Congleton R., 'Amendment Procedures and Constitutional Stability' in Congleton R. and Swedenborg B. (eds.), *Democratic Constitutional Design and Public Policy: Analysis and Evidence* (MIT 2006) 537

Wiebusch M. and Murray C., 'Presidential Term Limits and the African Union' (2019) 63(S1) Journal of African Law 131–60

Yates D, 'Gabon Elections: How the Bongo Family's 56-year Rule has Hurt the Country and Divided the Opposition' (*The Conversation*, 17 August 2023) https://theconversation.com/gabon-how-the-bongo-familys-56-year-rule-has-hurt-the-country-and-divided-the-opposition-211537 accessed 1 September 2023

Yeung J., 'Gabon's Military Coup has Overthrown a Powerful Political Dynasty: Here's What to Know' (*CNN*, 31 August 2023) https://edition.cnn.com/2023/08/31/africa/gabon-military-coup-explainer-intl-hnk/index.html accessed 1 September 2023

Index

For the benefit of digital users, indexed terms that span two pages (e.g., 52–53) may, on occasion, appear on only one of those pages.

Tables are indicated by an italic *t* following the page number.